THE LAW AND ECONOMICS OF CREDITOR PROTECTION

A Transatlantic Perspective

The Law and Economics of Creditor Protection

A Transatlantic Perspective

Edited by

Horst Eidenmüller

and

Wolfgang Schön

T·M·C·Asser Press
The Hague

Published by T·M·C·ASSER PRESS
P.O.Box 16163, 2500 BD The Hague, The Netherlands

<www.asserpress.nl>

T·M·C·ASSER PRESS English language books are distributed exclusively by:

Cambridge University Press, The Edinburgh Building, Shaftesbury Road,
Cambridge CB2 2RU, UK,
or
for customers in the USA, Canada and Mexico:
Cambridge University Press, 100 Brook Hill Drive, West Nyack, NY 10994-2133, USA

<www.cambridge.org>

The contributions in the main part of this book first appeared in
European Business Organization Law Review (EBOR)
ISSN 1566-7529 – Volume 7 (2006), Issue 1

ISBN 978-90-6704-263-5

Foreword

The main topic of corporate finance today is the interaction of shareholders, managers and creditors and the incentives provided for these actors in the framework of company law, accounting law and insolvency law. While in the past economists have tended to analyse the efficiency gains and losses of different institutional settings from a theoretical perspective and lawyers have tended to stick to their doctrinal skills when applying the law as it stands, recent developments have moved both professions to take a more policy-oriented approach towards this subject matter. In the United States, the demise of legal capital as a means of creditor protection, which started in the 1980s, has been fuelled by regulatory competition between the individual states and has produced alternative legal concepts like the fiduciary duties of managers towards a corporation's creditors in the vicinity of insolvency and tailor-made loan covenants in financial contracts. In Europe, the more recent recognition of the freedom of establishment for companies by the European Court of Justice in its *Centros* case law and the ensuing regulatory competition in the field of company law have triggered a debate on the future of company law harmonisation: While some scholars deplore the lack of harmonisation in relation to privately held companies, others plead for a further deregulation of EC directives for public limited companies, which would, it is hoped, stimulate individual and innovative solutions to the basic conflicts between creditors, shareholders and company directors.

This book contains the edited papers of a symposium on 'Efficient Creditor Protection in European Company Law', which took place in December 2005 as a joint venture of Munich's Ludwig Maximilians University and the Max Planck Institute for Intellectual Property, Competition and Tax Law at the premises of the Max Planck Institute in Munich. The aim of this conference was to bring to the fore all relevant academic perspectives. It assembled renowned scholars and officials who are currently working on reform projects in different Member States of the European Union, other experts on company law, insolvency law and accounting law, as well as experts on economics, in order to tackle some of the most intensely debated topics and reach a common understanding of the substantive questions lying at the heart of the current debate. The first part of this book reviews the 'case for regulation', bearing in mind that no legislation should be proposed if market solutions seem available and 'soft' legislation (enabling rules and disclosure obligations) suffices to make this market work. Part II then examines the question which rules on distributions to shareholders should be preferred, comparing the traditional 'balance sheet' approach with alternative instruments: a 'solvency test' in the framework of company law reform or a shift to insolvency law where 'fraudulent transfer' rules play a major role, as in the United States. Part III covers rules and standards for directors' behaviour 'in the vicinity of insolvency', including a 'timely trigger' for insolvency proceedings and the merits of 'wrongful trading' legislation. The case for a subordination and/or recharacterisation of shareholder loans is also discussed. Part IV, finally, embarks on the ambitious quest for a coherent overall framework for creditor protection and the best allocation of legislative competences in a multi-tier jurisdiction in the context of regulatory competition.

In many respects, this book follows the traditional line of comparative law as an academic discipline and attempts to demonstrate the fruitfulness of this discipline with respect to core issues of company law reform. As is well known, Ernst Rabel founded the world's first comparative law institute, the Institute for Comparative Law at Munich University, in 1916. Ten years later, Rabel moved to Berlin and founded a similar institute at the Humboldt University, which later was integrated into what is now the Max Planck Society for the Advancement of Sciences. Rabel emigrated from Germany in 1939 and later taught at Ann Arbor and Harvard. Hence, the authors from Germany (including Munich University and the Max Planck Society), the United States (including Harvard) and the United Kingdom were not only united by a common research theme but also by a research methodology that dates back to Ernst Rabel and the idea of comparative law as an academic discipline.

The conference programme and the approach of the authors fully reflect this tradition. Comparative law has always been functional in its approach, looking at the problem that certain rules are meant to solve rather than at the doctrinal peculiarities of a particular jurisdiction and caring less about whether certain rules formally belong to a specific branch of law (such as company law or insolvency law). For example, comparativists increasingly resort to economic theory as a fruitful instrument for assessing the merits of legal rules. The editors believe that the chapters published in this volume demonstrate the fruitfulness of the comparative method as applied to issues of company law reform. They are confident that this book will not fail to inform and influence the current policy debate.

The proceedings of this conference were published in the *European Business Organization Law Review* in 2006. They spurred considerable interest, leading the publisher of this journal, T.M.C. Asser Press, to suggest republishing them in a stand-alone book. We have accepted this invitation with pleasure. The editors hope that the manifold thoughts presented by these outstanding scholars will reach a wider audience through this volume. Moreover, as the debate on these topics rages on, we trust that new readers will find important insights while they make up their minds on the 'law and economics of creditor protection in Europe'.

Horst Eidenmüller and Wolfgang Schön

Summary Table of Contents

Detailed Table of Contents

Part II: Legal Approaches to Restricting Distributions to Shareholders

Part III: The Role of Insolvency Law

Part IV: Towards a General Framework

Abbreviations

2d Cir.	Second Circuit
6th Cir.	Sixth Circuit
13 Eliz.	Statute of Elizabeth
ABA	American Bar Association
Abacus	Journal of Accounting, Finance and Business Studies
ABF	American Bar Foundation
AC	Law Reports Appeal Cases
Academy Management Rev.	Academy of Management Review
Accounting Rev.	The Accounting Review
ACSR	Australian Corporations and Securities Reports
ADHGB	Allgemeines Deutsches Handelsgesetzbuch
AEG	Allgemeine Elektrizitäts-Gesellschaft
AEI	American Enterprise Institute for Public Policy Research
AG	Die Aktiengesellschaft
AktG	Aktiengesetz
All ER	All England Law Reports
ALR	Australian Law Reports
Am. Bankr. L.J.	American Bankruptcy Law Journal
Am. J. Comp. L.	American Journal of Comparative Law
AnfG	Anfechtungsgesetz
App. Div.	Appellate Division
APR	absolute priority rule
ASB	Accounting Standards Board
Bankr. D. Ark.	Bankruptcy Court for the District of Arkansas
BAP	Bankruptcy Appellate Panel
BB	Betriebs-Berater
BC	Bankruptcy Code
BCC	British Company Law Cases
BCLC	Butterworths Company Law Cases
Bell J. Econ.	Bell Journal of Economics
BFuP	Betriebswirtschaftliche Forschung und Praxis
BGB	Bürgerliches Gesetzbuch
BGBl	Bundesgesetzblatt
BGH	(German) Bundesgerichtshof
BGHZ	Entscheidungen des Bundesgerichtshofes in Zivilsachen
BIICL	British Institute of International and Comparative Law
BPIR	Bankruptcy and Personal Insolvency Reports
B.R.	Bankruptcy Reporter

Brook. L. Rev.	Brooklyn Law Review
Bus. Law.	Business Lawyer
CA	Court of Appeal
CBCA	Canada Business Corporations Act
CEO	Chief Executive Officer
CESR	Committee of European Securities Regulators
CFO	Chief Financial Officer
CFR	Code of Federal Regulations
Ch	English Law Reports, Chancery Divison
CLR	Commonwealth Law Reports
Cm	Command
CMLR	Common Market Law Reports
CML Rev.	Common Market Law Review
Cmnd.	Command
Co	company
Coke	Coke's King's Bench Reports
Colum. L. Rev.	Columbia Law Review
COM	European Commission document
COMI	Centre of Main Interests
Cong.	Congress
Coreper	Comité des Représentants Permanents (EU)
Cornell L. Rev.	Cornell Law Review
DB	Der Betrieb
Del. Ch.	Delaware Court of Chancery
Del. L. Rev.	Delaware Law Review
DG MARKT	Directorate General Internal Market and Services
DIP	debtor-in-possession
DM	Deutsche Mark
D. N.H.	District of New Hampshire
Doc.	Document
DStR	Deutsches Steuerrecht
DTI	Department of Trade and Industry
Duke L.J.	Duke Law Journal
EBLR	European Business Law Review
EBOR	European Business Organization Law Review
EC	European Community
ECFR	European Company and Financial Law Review
ECGI	European Corporate Governance Institute
ECJ	European Court of Justice
ECR	European Court Reports
E.D. Va.	Eastern District of Virginia
EEA	European Economic Area

EEC	European Economic Community
EFRAG	European Financial Reporting Advisory Group
EIR	European Insolvency Regulation
ELJ	European Law Journal
Emory L.J.	Emory Law Journal
Eng. Rep.	English Reports
ESRC	Economic and Social Research Council
ETH Zürich	Eidgenössische Technische Hochschule Zürich
EU	European Union
EuGH	Europäischer Gerichtshof
EuInsVO	Europäische Insolvenzverordnung
EWCA Civ	England and Wales Court of Appeal (Civil Division) Decisions
F.2d	Federal Reporter, 2nd Series
FASB	Financial Accounting Standards Board
FD	fair disclosure
Fin. Mgt.	Financial Management
FRRP	Financial Reporting Review Panel
FRS	Financial Reporting Standard
FSA	Financial Services Authority
F.Supp., F.Supp.2d	Federal Supplement, 1st and 2nd series
FT	Financial Times
GAAP	Generally Accepted Accounting Principles
GDP	gross domestic product
Geo. L.J.	Georgetown Law Journal
German LJ	German Law Journal
GeS	Zeitschrift für Gesellschafts- und Steuerrecht
GesRZ	Der Gesellschafter
GIRÄG	Gesellschafts- und Insolvenzrechtsänderungsgesetz
GM	General Motors
GmbH	Gesellschaft mit beschränkter Haftung
GmbHG	Gesetz betreffend die Gesellschaften mit beschränkter Haftung
GmbHR	GmBH-Rundschau
Harv. Int'l L.J.	Harvard International Law Journal
Harv. L. Rev.	Harvard Law Review
HGB	Handelsgesetzbuch
HL	House of Lords
HLG	High Level Group
HMSO	Her Majesty's Stationery Office
HM Treasury	Her Majesty's Treasury
HR	House of Representatives

IA	Insolvency Act
IAS	International Accounting Standards
ICAEW	Institute of Chartered Accountants in England and Wales
ICAS	Institute of Chartered Accountants of Scotland
ICCLR	International Company and Commercial Law Review
IDW	Institut der Wirtschaftsprüfer in Deutschland
IFRS	International Financial Reporting Standards
ILRM	Irish Law Reports Monthly
Inc.	Incorporated
InsO	Insolvenzordnung
Int. Rev. Law Econ.	International Review of Law and Economics
IOSCO	International Organization of Securities Commissions
IPRax	Praxis des Internationalen Privat- und Verfahrensrechts
IRB	Internal Ratings-Based Approach
IRC	Internal Revenue Code
ISAB	International Accounting Standards Board
ISBN	International Standard Book Number
J. Accounting Research	Journal of Accounting Research
J. Bus.	Journal of Business
JCLS	Journal of Corporate Law Studies
J. Corp. Fin.	Journal of Corporate Finance
J. Corp. L.	Journal of Corporation Law
J. Econ. Lit.	Journal of Economic Literature
J. Econ. Perspectives	Journal of Economic Perspectives
J. Fin.	Journal of Finance
J. Fin. Econ.	Journal of Financial Economics
JITE	Journal of Institutional and Theoretical Economics
J.L. Econ. & Org.	Journal of Law, Economics & Organization
J. Leg. Stud.	Journal of Legal Studies
J. Pol. Econ.	Journal of Political Economy
JW	Juristische Wochenschrift
JZ	Juristenzeitung
Kan.	Kansas Supreme Court
KB	King's Bench
LBO	leveraged buy-out
LIBOR	London Interbank Offered Rate
liq.	liquidation
LL.M.	Legum Magister [master of laws]
Ltd	limited

MBCA	Model Business Corporation Act
Mich. J. Int'l L.	Michigan Journal of International Law
Mich. L. Rev.	Michigan Law Review
MindestkapG	Gesetz zur Neuregelung des Mindestkapitals der GmbH
MIT	Massachusetts Institute of Technology
MJ	Maastricht Journal of European and Comparative Law
MLR	Modern Law Review
NBER	National Bureau of Economic Research
N.D. Ill.	Northern District of Illinois
N.E.	Northeastern Reporter
New L.J.	New Law Journal
NJW	Neue Juristische Wochenschrift
Norton Ann. Surv. Bankr. L.	Norton Annual Survey of Bankruptcy Law
NPV	net present value
Nw. U.L. Rev.	Northwestern University Law Review
N.Y.	New York Court of Appeals
nyr	not yet reported
NYSE	New York Stock Exchange
N.Y.S.2d	West's New York Reporter
NYU	New York University
N.Y.U. L. Rev.	New York University Law Review
NZCLC	New Zealand Company Law Cases
NZG	Neue Zeitschrift für Gesellschaftsrecht
NZI	Neue Zeitschrift für das Recht der Insolvenz und Sanierung
NZLR	New Zealand Law Reports
OECD	Organisation for Economic Co-operation and Development
OGH	Oberster Gerichtshof
OJ	Official Journal of the European Communities/Union
plc	public limited company
QC	Queen's Counsel
Q. J. Econ.	Quarterly Journal of Economics
Q. Rev. Econ. & Fin.	Quarterly Review of Economics and Finance
Rev. Econ. Stat.	Review of Economics and Statistics
Rev. Fin. Studies	Review of Financial Studies
RG	Reichsgericht
RIW	Recht der Internationalen Wirtschaft
RMBCA	Revised Model Business Corporation Act

Rutgers L. Rev.	Rutgers Law Review
Scandinavian J. Econ.	Scandinavian Journal of Economics
Sched.	Schedule
SCR	Supreme Court Reports
S.D.N.Y.	Southern District of New York
SE	Societas Europaea
SEC	European Commission documents which cannot be classified in any of the other series
SEC	Securities and Exchange Commission
Sess.	session
SFB-TR	Sonderforschungsbereich-Transregio
SI	statutory instrument
SLIM	Simpler Legislation for the Internal Market
SLT	Scots Law Times
SME	small and medium sized enterprises
SSRN	Social Science Research Network
Stan. J.L. Bus. & Fin.	Stanford Journal of Law, Business and Finance
Stan. L. Rev.	Stanford Law Review
StuW	Steuer und Wirtschaft
SZ	Entscheidungen des österreichischen Obersten Gerichtshofs in Zivilsachen
T&FV	true and fair view
TEC	Treaty establishing the European Community
TECH	Technical Release
Tenn. L. Rev.	Tennessee Law Review
Tex. Ct. App.	Texas Court of Appeals
Tex. L. Rev.	Texas Law Review
UCC	Uniform Commercial Code
U. Chi. L. Rev.	University of Chicago Law Review
UCLA	University of California, Los Angeles
UCLA L. Rev.	UCLA Law Review
UFTA	Uniform Fraudulent Transfers Act
U. Ill. L. Rev.	University of Illinois Law Review
UK	United Kingdom
UMAG	Gesetz zur Unternehmensintegrität und Modernisierung des Anfechtungsrechts
U. Pa. L. Rev.	University of Pennsylvania Law Review
URN	Unique Reference Number
US	United States
US	United States Reports
USA	United States of America
USC	United States Code

Va. L. Rev.	Virginia Law Review
Vand. L. Rev.	Vanderbilt Law Review
Wall St. J.	Wall Street Journal
Wis. L. Rev.	Wisconsin Law Review
WL	Westlaw
WLR	Weekly Law Reports
WM	Wertpapier-Mitteilungen
WODC	Wetenschappelijk Onderzoek- en Documentatiecentrum
WPg	Die Wirtschaftsprüfung
Yale L.J.	Yale Law Journal
ZGR	Zeitschrift für Unternehmens- und Gesellschaftsrecht
ZHR	Zeitschrift für das gesammte Handelsrecht und Wirtschaftsrecht
ZInsO	Zeitschrift für das gesamte Insolvenzrecht
ZIP	Zeitschrift für Wirtschaftsrecht
ZvglRWiss	Zeitschrift für vergleichende Rechtswissenschaft

Part I

The Case for Regulation

H. Eidenmüller and W. Schön (eds.), The Law and Economics of Creditor Protection 3

Legal Capital: An Outdated Concept?

John Armour*

Abstract

This paper reviews the case for and against mandatory legal capital rules. It is argued that legal capital is no longer an appropriate means of safeguarding creditors' interests. This is most clearly the case as regards mandatory rules. Moreover, it is suggested that even an 'opt in' (or default) legal capital regime is unlikely to be a useful mechanism. However, the advent of regulatory arbitrage in European corporate law will provide a way of gathering information regarding investors' preferences in relation to such rules. Those creditor protection rules that do not further the interests of adjusting creditors will become subject to competitive pressures. Legislatures will be faced with the task of designing

---

* Faculty of Law and Centre for Business Research, University of Cambridge. I am most grateful for helpful comments received from participants in the conference on 'Efficient Creditor Protection in European Company Law' in Munich, December 2005.

mandatory rules to deal with the issues raised by 'non-adjusting' creditors in a proportionate and effective manner, consistent with the Gebhard *formula.*

Keywords: corporate law, creditor protection, legal capital, regulatory competition.

Some seven men form an Association
(If possible, all Peers and Baronets)
They start off with a public declaration
To what extent they mean to pay their debts.
That's called their capital: if they are wary
They will not quote it at a sum immense
The figure's immaterial – it may vary
From eighteen million down to eighteen pence.

I should put it rather low;
The good sense of doing so
Will be evident to any debtor.
When it's left to you to say
What amount you mean to pay,
Why the lower you can put it at, the better.[1]

1. Introduction

Rules relating to 'legal capital' have received much attention in recent European company law debates.[2] The core concept is that legal restrictions are imposed on corporate activity by reference to the shareholders' capital investment, as shown on the balance sheet. This is instantiated in various ways in different company law systems, which typically harness the concept to perform one or both of the following functions: (i) prescribing a minimum level of equity capital which must be invested in a trading company, and (ii) restricting transfers of assets to

---

1 W.S. Gilbert and A. Sullivan, *Utopia Ltd* (1893).

2 Recent contributions include J. Armour, 'Share Capital and Creditor Protection: Efficient Rules for a Modern Company Law?', 63 *MLR* (2000) p. 355; L. Enriques and J. Macey, 'Creditors Versus Capital Formation: The Case against the European Legal Capital Rules', 86 *Cornell LR* (2001) p. 1165; P.O. Mülbert and M. Birke, 'Legal Capital – Is There a Case against the European Legal Capital Rules?', 3 *EBOR* (2002) p. 696; J. Rickford, ed., 'Reforming Capital: Report of the Interdisciplinary Group on Capital Maintenance', 15 *EBLR* (2004) p. 919; W. Schön, 'The Future of Legal Capital', 5 *EBOR* (2004) p. 429; E. Ferran, *The Place for Creditor Protection on the Agenda for Modernisation of Company Law in the European Union*, ECGI Law Working Paper No. 51 (2005).

shareholders where the net assets fall below the value of the equity capital invested.

Whilst legal capital rules have fallen out of favour as a means of protecting creditors in common law jurisdictions,[3] the principles for which they stand continue to be taken seriously in continental European countries. Until very recently, it was possible to dismiss these differences as simply matters of domestic legal preference, with the rider that in any event divergences were likely to be ironed out in time, a significant step in this direction having been made with the Second Company Law Directive.[4] Although not universally admired, it was not doubted that, in contrast to its obsolescence in North America, legal capital had a future in (continental) Europe.

However, the past few years have seen a seismic shift in the European debate. This was triggered by two things. On the one hand, the ECJ's decision in *Centros* and its progeny opened up the possibility of real regulatory choice in European company law – at least for private companies.[5] Many continental entrepreneurs have responded by choosing to incorporate their businesses in the United Kingdom, where legal capital rules for private companies are relatively permissive.[6] This controversial development pushed into the spotlight the question whether legal capital rules are useful or desirable. Consequently, various Member State legislatures have started question their attachment to them.

At the same time, the European Commission has been seeking to reform the Second Directive. This idea was first raised as part of the 'SLIM' (Simpler Legislation for the Single Market) initiative,[7] and was subsequently added to the agenda for the Commission's High-Level Expert Group on Company Law.[8] A

---

[3] For example, in most US States, legal capital rules have either been abolished outright or simply withered into marcesence: see, e.g., B. Manning, *Legal Capital*, 2nd edn. (Mineola, NY, Foundation Press 1982). In the United Kingdom, pending reforms will considerably relax the application of legal capital rules to private companies: see *infra*, text to nn. 17-19.

[4] Second Council Directive 77/91/EEC of 13 December 1976, *OJ* 1977 L 26/1 (formation of public companies and maintenance and alteration of capital).

[5] ECJ, Case C-212/97 *Centros Ltd* v. *Erhvervs-og Selskabssyrelsen* [1999] *ECR* I-1459, [2000] Ch 446; ECJ, Case C-208/00 *Überseering BV* v. *Nordic Construction Company Baumanagement GmbH (NCC)* [2002] *ECR* I-9919; ECJ, Case C-167/01 *Kamer van Koophandel en Fabrieken voor Amsterdam* v. *Inspire Art Ltd* [2003] *ECR* I-10155.

[6] J. Armour, 'Who Should Make Corporate Law: EC Legislation versus Regulatory Competition', 48 *Current Legal Problems* (2005) p. 369 at pp. 385-386; M. Becht, C. Mayer and H.F. Wagner, *Corporate Mobility Comes to Europe: The Evidence*, Working Paper, Université Libre de Bruxelles/Saïd Business School, Oxford University (October 2005).

[7] European Commission, Simpler Legislation for the Single Market (SLIM): Extension to a Fourth Phase, SEC (1998) 1944, Brussels, 16 November 1998, p. 3.

[8] High Level Group of Company Law Experts, *Report on a Modern Regulatory Framework for Company Law in Europe*, Brussels, 4 November 2002, pp. 86-93.

Commission proposal to simplify the Second Directive is now well advanced,[9] and debate continues about the possibility of further, more wide-ranging reforms in the future.[10]

In light of these developments, this paper reviews the case for and against mandatory legal capital rules. It is argued that legal capital is no longer an appropriate concept to employ in safeguarding the interests of creditors. This is most clearly the case as regards mandatory rules, which impose a 'one size fits all' approach that is likely to be over-regulatory. Moreover, it is suggested that even an 'opt in' (or default) legal capital regime is likely to be of doubtful utility. In any event, the advent of regulatory arbitrage in European company law means that these sorts of debates will in future come to be resolved with an eye on the preferences of firms. The future of legal capital may therefore be determined by investors rather than legislatures.

The rest of this paper is structured as follows. Section two gives a brief description of two different 'ideal types' of legal capital rule, and indicates some of the combinations in which they exist in Member States' company laws. Section three explains how these rule-types may be rationalised as creditor protection mechanisms. Section four then critiques these rationales. Section five turns to the impact of new-found opportunities for regulatory arbitrage, and section six concludes.

2. TYPES OF LEGAL CAPITAL RULE

In this section, we will describe two 'ideal types' of rule that restrict corporate behaviour based on legal capital. As will be seen, different combinations of these rules are applied in different legal capital regimes.

2.1 Distribution rules

A rule prohibiting return of capital seeks to prevent a company from making distributions to its shareholders at any point at which the company's net assets do not exceed the stated value of its capital accounts.[11] In the United Kingdom, the key statutory provision embodying this 'capital maintenance' rule is section 263

---

[9] European Commission, Proposal for a Directive of the European Parliament and the Council amending Council Directive 77/91/EEC, as regards the formation of public limited liability companies and the maintenance and alteration of their capital, COM (2004) 730 final, Brussels, 21 September 2004.

[10] European Commission, Modernising Company Law and Enhancing Corporate Governance in the European Union – A Plan to Move Forward, COM (2003) 284 final, Brussels 21 May 2003, pp. 17-18. See generally, Rickford, loc. cit. n. 2; Ferran, op. cit. n. 2.

[11] For public companies, see, e.g., Second Council Directive, Art. 15(1).

of the Companies Act 1985.[12] This prohibits any form of distribution of corporate assets to shareholders except where the value of the distribution is less than that of the profits available for distribution. Distributable profits are defined as the company's cumulated net realised profits, minus dividends paid and losses written off to capital.[13] As profits are necessarily defined in contradistinction to capital, this means that capital may not be returned to shareholders.

For such rules to impose a genuine restriction on companies' ability to make payments to shareholders, the ban on distributions must be truly watertight. Hence, the rules must also cover other forms of transaction whereby assets are directly or indirectly transferred to shareholders for less than market value – including share repurchases,[14] the giving of financial assistance by a company for the acquisition of its own shares,[15] and undervalue transactions between a company and its members.[16]

It follows that reforms which permit capital to be returned to shareholders by any route will tend to relax the system's constraints generally: rather than being a restriction on corporate action, they become a means for channelling actions into particular forms. In the United Kingdom, for example, it is already permissible for private companies to return capital to shareholders by means of a share repurchase, contingent on the directors' ability to declare that the company will remain solvent for twelve months.[17] Pending reforms will permit any form of reduction of capital through such a declaration of solvency.[18] As a result, whilst the formal framework of legal capital will remain in place, the effective constraint on private companies' ability to distribute to shareholders will come to be based upon solvency, as opposed to the capital 'yardstick'.[19]

---

[12] The notion of 'maintenance of capital' refers not to the assets contributed to the company, but the subordinated status of the shareholders' capital claim. See Armour, loc. cit. n. 2, pp. 365-366.

[13] A public company must also demonstrate that its net assets exceed the sum of its capital accounts plus its cumulated net *un*realised profits by at least the amount of the proposed distribution: Companies Act 1985, s. 264.

[14] Second Council Directive, Arts. 19(1)(c), 39; Companies Act 1985, ss. 159-170, 263(2)(b).

[15] Second Council Directive, Art. 23; Companies Act 1985, ss. 151-158.

[16] *Re Halt Garage (1964) Ltd* [1982] 3 *All ER* 1016; *Aveling Barford Ltd* v. *Perion Ltd* (1989) 5 BCC 677; *Clydebank Football Club Ltd* v. *Steedman* (2002) SLT 109 at 124. See generally E. Ferran, *Company Law and Corporate Finance* (Oxford, Oxford University Press 1999) pp. 426-429; J. Armour, 'Avoidance of Transactions as a "Fraud on Creditors" at Common Law', in J. Armour and H.N. Bennett, eds., *Vulnerable Transactions in Corporate Insolvency* (Oxford, Hart Publishing 2003) p. 281 at pp. 295-300.

[17] Companies Act 1985, ss. 171-177.

[18] Company Law Reform Bill 2005, cl. 562.

[19] The law regarding fraudulent conveyances – in English law, now known as 'transactions as an undervalue' and 'transactions defrauding creditors' (Insolvency Act 1986, ss. 238 and

2.2 Minimum capital rules

A minimum capital rule requires that those incorporating a business place assets of at least the specified minimum value into the corporate asset pool. For public companies, a harmonised rule is imposed by the Second Company Law Directive, mandating a minimum share capital of at least €25,000.[20] On the other hand, the existence and scope of any minimum capital requirement for *private* companies is left to Member States, and widely differing stances are taken. In contrast to the position in many continental European jurisdictions, English company law imposes no minimum capital requirement for private companies.[21]

Minimum capital rules can be of little real significance unless coupled with anti-avoidance provisions designed to ensure that assets to the required minimum value are *in fact* contributed. That is, some sort of independent report on the value of non-cash consideration is required,[22] lest those conducting initial transactions on the company's behalf be minded to value such assets optimistically. It also may be thought desirable to include rules subordinating shareholder 'loans', particularly of a secured variety, which when coupled with non-cash consideration can be used to place any capital contributed beyond the reach of the creditors.[23]

3. The economic case(s) for legal capital rules

By virtue of the Second Directive, both distribution restrictions and a minimum capital requirement apply to public companies throughout Europe. However, in respect of private companies, some jurisdictions – such as the United Kingdom –

423, respectively) – would strike down a transaction under which the company receives significantly less consideration than it gives and which takes place within two years of its entering corporate insolvency proceedings, provided that it was unable to pay its debts at the time of the transaction, or became so as a result. A distribution to shareholders is viewed in English law as a gratuitous transaction (*Associated British Engineering Ltd* v. *IRC* [1941] 1 KB 15; *Wigan Coal and Iron Co Ltd* v. *IRC* [1945] 1 *All ER* 392). Hence, if the distribution were such as to cause the company to become unable to pay its debts, it would be open to avoidance by a liquidator, in the same way as a return of capital failing the solvency test.

[20] Second Council Directive, Art. 6(1). That said, only 25 per cent of this need actually be paid up on formation: Art. 9(1).

[21] Companies Act 1985, ss. 11, 118 (minimum capital requirement stated to apply only to public companies).

[22] See, e.g., Second Council Directive, Art. 10.

[23] See M. Gelter, *The Subordination of Shareholder Loans in Bankruptcy*, Working Paper (2005). English law has never restricted this practice: see, e.g., *Salomon* v. *A Salomon & Co Ltd* [1897] AC 22.

apply distribution restrictions but do not impose a minimum capital requirement. It seems likely that in the future some jurisdictions will abolish these rules entirely. Unsurprisingly, given this diversity, the appropriate degree to which creditors should be protected by legal capital rules is a contentious matter. Just as it is undesirable to offer creditors *too little* protection, it may be equally undesirable to mandate *too much* protection: that is, to emphasise creditors' interests at the expense of other constituencies. This section considers the economic rationale(s) for various combinations of legal capital rules. How persuasive these rationales are will be considered in the next section.

In understanding the way in which the legal capital rules operate, it is helpful, analytically, to distinguish between those creditors who are able to change the terms on which they lend to reflect the associated risks of default, and those who are not so able – sometimes termed 'adjusting' and 'non-adjusting' creditors respectively.[24] Adjusting creditors are those voluntarily advancing a sufficiently large sum of money to be willing to incur the transaction costs – gathering information, negotiation and the like – necessary to adjust the terms upon which credit is extended so as to compensate them appropriately for the risk they are bearing. A paradigm adjusting creditor might be a bank, which would be able to capture economies of scale in gathering information and setting terms for debtors. Non-adjusting creditors are those who do not alter the terms on which they extend credit in response to a debtor's riskiness. Tort victims are the most intuitive example of a non-adjusting creditor, but the category is often also said to include others, such as the State in right of tax and environmental claims, and voluntary creditors – e.g., consumers, employees and trade creditors – who may lack the economies of scale to be able to adjust their terms easily to respond to the individual characteristics of each borrower.

3.1 Distribution rules

A restriction on the return of capital to shareholders can be understood as protecting creditors against the risk of opportunistic behaviour by the shareholders. Distributions to shareholders reduce a company's net assets, making it more exposed to the risk of default. Creditors' interests can be harmed even if the company does not actually become insolvent.[25] Such a transfer will still decrease

[24] The terminology is derived from L.A. Bebchuk and J.M. Freid, 'The Uneasy Case for the Priority of Secured Claims in Bankruptcy', 105 *Yale LJ* (1996) p. 857 at pp. 881-890.

[25] If such a transfer renders the company insolvent, then other legal provisions protect creditors. A liquidator or administrator could seek to recover the payments as a transaction at an undervalue (Insolvency Act 1986, s. 238). Alternatively, the distribution may constitute a transaction defrauding creditors (ss. 423-425).

the *expected* value of their claims,[26] whilst commensurately enhancing the combined value of shareholders' private wealth and their stake in the firm. A restriction on distributions can prevent this from happening.

However, for non-adjusting creditors, a restriction on the return of capital to shareholders is by itself of little assistance. This is because, if creditors do not adjust, the optimal level of capitalisation by shareholders is zero.[27] Thus it is a truism that those carrying on hazardous enterprises – which are likely to result in tort claims – have a tendency to structure their affairs using thinly-capitalised subsidiaries.[28]

A distribution restriction can, however, be understood as protecting *adjusting* creditors against the risk of opportunistic behaviour by the shareholders. If lenders' loans were priced on the basis of pre-existing levels of net assets, then a transfer of assets to shareholders will decrease the expected value of creditors' claims,[29] whilst commensurately enhancing the combined value of shareholders' private wealth and their stake in the firm. Creditors' interests will be harmed even if the company does not actually become insolvent,[30] because by reducing a company's net assets, distributions make it more exposed to the risk of default. A restriction on distributions can prevent this sort of wealth transfer from happening.

It might initially be thought odd that such restrictions should benefit adjusting creditors: surely, if they are able to adjust, then they have no need of such protection? The answer is that such restrictions can deter *ex post* actions by

---

[26] In other words, the 'best current market estimate' of their worth. This will be their face value, discounted for the time value of money and discounted further for the risk of default. Even if the debtor does not become insolvent, creditors are still prejudiced if the *risk* of default increases above that at which they had priced it, and if the value of their debt claim matters to them as an *asset*. This would be the case if they wished to realise the value of the loan before maturity, as with bonds, secondary markets for syndicated loans, factoring of book debts, etc.

[27] See, e.g., the quotation from Gilbert and Sullivan's *Utopia Ltd*, *supra* text to n. 1.

[28] For an instance well known to English lawyers, see *Adams* v. *Cape Industries Ltd* [1990] Ch 433. For empirical evidence that this is a general phenomenon, see A.H. Ringleb and S.N. Wiggins, 'Liability and Large-Scale, Long-term Hazards', 98 *Journal of Political Economy* (1990) p. 574 (increases in liability risk in US industries during 1967-1980 correlated with decrease in capitalisation of firms in that industry).

[29] In other words, the 'best current market estimate' of their worth. This will be their face value, discounted for the time value of money and discounted further for the risk of default. Even if the debtor does not become insolvent, creditors are still prejudiced if the *risk* of default increases above that at which they had priced it, and if the value of their debt claim matters to them as an *asset*. This would be the case if they wished to realise the value of the loan before maturity, as with bonds, secondary markets for syndicated loans, factoring of book debts, etc.

[30] If such a transfer does in fact render the company insolvent, then other provisions protect creditors in any event. See *supra* n. 19.

shareholders (or, more accurately, directors acting on their behalf),[31] which will be *inefficient*, in the sense of failing to maximise the expected value of the corporate assets, and which are taken with the view of transferring wealth, in an expected value sense, from creditors to shareholders.[32] This sort of action will result in social losses *ex post* if assets are withdrawn from valuable projects in order to fund such distributions. This would be priced into the interest rate by adjusting creditors; hence it is in shareholders' interests to commit not to do it *ex ante*.[33] Moreover, because there are limits to the interest rates it is feasible to charge,[34] the possibility of such distributions being paid may deter creditors from lending at all *ex ante*. The result either way would be underinvestment in good projects.[35] Moreover, either way, shareholders too would prefer such restrictions to be imposed *ex ante*.

It might be thought that a straightforward solution would simply be to ban all asset transfers to shareholders. However, there may be circumstances in which such transfers are efficient. Where a firm has surplus cash and no good projects in which to invest, it is efficient for the money to be returned to shareholders for investment elsewhere, rather than be poured into an underperforming project. The problem in this case is the flipside of that where no restriction obtains.[36]

One technique for balancing these concerns is to use a conditional restriction. The maintenance of capital doctrine can be understood as providing restriction of this sort: a company is only permitted to make payments to its shareholders at a time when its net assets exceed its capital accounts.[37] Adjusting creditors, in

---

31 For the purposes of this discussion, it will be assumed for the sake of simplicity that directors act in the interests of shareholders. The key point for present purposes is simply that directors' interests are more closely aligned with those of shareholders (who appoint and remove them) than with creditors.

32 M.C. Jensen and W.H. Meckling, 'Theory of the Firm: Managerial Behaviour, Agency Costs and Ownership Structure', 3 *Journal of Financial Economics* (1976) p. 305 at pp. 333-343.

33 See M. Bradley and M.R. Roberts, *The Structure and Pricing of Corporate Debt Covenants*, Working Paper, Fuqua School of Business, Duke University (March 2004) (debt covenants, designed to restrict perverse investment incentives, are associated with riskier borrowers, and affect pricing).

34 Such constraints may arise (i) from legal restrictions on high interest rates (e.g., Insolvency Act 1986, s. 244, rendering 'extortionate' credit transactions unenforceable in the debtor's insolvency); (ii) from 'adverse selection' problems in markets for corporate credit: very high interest rates tend to be least unattractive to those who do not intend to repay (J. Stiglitz and A. Weiss, 'Credit Rationing in Markets with Imperfect Information', 71 *American Economic Review* (1981) p. 393).

35 S.C. Myers, 'Determinants of Corporate Borrowing', 5 *Journal of Financial Economics* (1977) p. 147.

36 See, e.g., W.L. Megginson, *Corporate Finance Theory* (Reading, MA, Addison-Wesley 1997) pp. 377-380.

37 Armour, loc. cit. n. 2, pp. 367-368.

advancing funds to the company, can take into account the figure at which the constraint will become binding, and price their loans on that basis.

Many creditors in fact contract for protection – in the form of loan covenants – from the perverse investment incentives which limited liability can, under certain circumstances, give to shareholders and those acting on their behalf.[38] Distribution restrictions based on earnings are a commonly used covenant in US loan agreements drafted by sophisticated creditors, in an institutional environment in which there are few mandatory restrictions on distributions in company law.[39] Making a dividend restriction conditional on cumulative net profits, as opposed simply to a given financial ratio or cash flow target, encourages shareholders to take into account the expected impact of liabilities generated by the firm's operations, as well as simply financial creditors, in making investment decisions.[40] A cumulative profits test requires provisions made for expected future liabilities to be taken into account today.[41]

A prohibition on return of capital can thus be understood as saving creditors the cost of writing such a term into their loan contracts – a sort of implied

[38] C.W. Smith and J.B. Warner, 'On Financial Contracting: An Analysis of Bond Covenants', 7 *Journal of Financial Economics* (1979) p. 117; W.W. Bratton, 'Bond Covenants and Creditor Protection: Economics and Law, Theory and Practice, Substance and Process', in this volume.

[39] US studies from the early 1980s found a high incidence of dividend restrictions in covenants granted by randomly selected samples of firms. See, e.g., A. Kalay, 'Stockholder-Bondholder Conflict and Dividend Constraints', 10 *Journal of Financial Economics* (1982) p. 211 at pp. 214-216 (100 per cent of sample of bond indentures). More recent studies find that dividend restrictions (and covenants generally) are less commonly found, and less restrictive, in bonds than in bank debt: cf., R.C. Nash, J.M. Netter and A.B. Poulsen, 'Determinants of Contractual Relations Between Shareholders and Bondholders: Investment Opportunities and Restrictive Covenants', 9 *Journal of Corporate Finance* (2003) p. 201 at p. 218 (39.7 per cent of 1989 sample and 20.8 per cent of 1998 sample of bond indentures), with Bradley and Roberts, op. cit. n. 33, Table V (87 per cent of sample of bank loans over 1993-2001).

[40] C. Leuz, 'The Role of Accrual Accounting in Restricting Dividends to Shareholders', 7 *European Accounting Review* (1998) p. 579. See also F. Gjesdal and R. Antle, 'Dividend Covenants and Income Measurement', 6 *Review of Accounting Studies* (2001) p. 53.

[41] In an oblique sense, this 'protects' the involuntary creditors: see Schön, loc. cit. n. 2, at p. 441; D. Kershaw, *Between Function and Effect: Why Capital Maintenance Regulation is Not Trivial for Involuntary Creditors*, Working Paper, Warwick Law School (2005). However, the extent of such protection depends on adjusting creditors permitting non-adjusting creditors to free ride. If there are significant levels of non-adjusting creditors (e.g., because of a hazardous line of business), then both shareholders and adjusting creditors will be better off by arranging for the hazardous business to be carried on by a thinly capitalised subsidiary, or (the inverse) for non-adjusting creditors to be structurally subordinated by transferring 'safe' assets to a finance subsidiary, to which entity adjusting creditors then lend. See also *supra* text to nn. 27-28.

covenant.[42] Whilst incorporators lack the freedom to say whether or not they want this framework to apply to their firm, they do have considerable flexibility in setting the conditions under which the maintenance of capital rules will restrict distributions.[43] Their application will be determined by the size of a company's share capital and share premium account, which – in the absence of a minimum capital requirement – the shareholders are free to set.

3.2 Minimum capital rules

Minimum capital rules, coupled with anti-avoidance requirements, can be understood as providing a sort of guarantee to creditors that those using the corporate form will at the very least have a certain amount of their own money at stake. As such, they are sometimes described as 'the entry price for limited liability'.[44] Clearly, it is unnecessary for adjusting creditors to have such a mandatory guarantee. Should it be efficient for such protection to be taken, they can contract for it. Provided that distribution restrictions are in place, this can be achieved simply by requiring the desired level of capitalisation. Thus, the justification for these rules must be sought in relation to non-adjusting creditors.[45] Provided that a minimum capital rule is coupled with a restriction on distributions, it makes it more difficult to carry on hazardous business through a thinly-capitalised subsidiary. Such a rule can thereby serve to ameliorate the perverse incentives which might otherwise accompany undercapitalised companies in relation to non-adjusting creditors.

4. ARE THESE RATIONALES PERSUASIVE?

We now consider whether the rationales considered in the previous section are persuasive. The enquiry is structured by considering the size of the likely benefits

---

[42] G.P. Miller, *Das Kapital: Solvency Regulation of the American Business Enterprise*, University of Chicago Working Paper in Law & Economics (2d) No. 32 (April 1995) p. 5; B.R. Cheffins, *Company Law: Theory, Structure and Operation* (Oxford, Oxford University Press 1997) pp. 521-524.

[43] This does not, however, render the application of the distribution rules anything other than mandatory, because companies are unable to choose to raise equity capital without their operation (Ferran, op. cit. n. 2, at pp. 10-13; cf. Schön, loc. cit. n. 2, at pp. 438-439).

[44] See D.D. Prentice, 'Corporate Personality, Limited Liability and the Protection of Creditors', in R. Grantham and C. Ricketts, eds., *Corporate Personality in the Twentieth Century* (Oxford, Hart Publishing 1998) p. 99.

[45] See ECJ, Case 212/97 *Centros Ltd* v. *Erhvervs-og Selskabsstyrelsen* [1999] 2 *CMLR* 551, 586-587, in which the Danish Government sought to justify their country's minimum capital laws on the basis, *inter alia*, that they protected involuntary claimants.

yielded by these forms of creditor protection, and comparing these in each case with the likely costs of mandatory rules. Where appropriate, consideration will also be paid to alternative regulatory strategies.

4.1 Distribution rules

It was noted that rules prohibiting returns of capital impose restrictions on transactions which might harm creditors' interests. However, restrictions of the sort these rules create might alternatively be generated through loan covenants. Thus the 'benefits' of the legislation are not the costs which the prohibited transactions would impose on creditors, but rather savings in contracting costs which might otherwise be incurred.

Sophisticated (i.e., 'adjusting') creditors do in fact frequently include loan covenants that restrict debtors' ability to engage in transactions harmful to lenders' interests.[46] Thus there are potentially significant savings to be made through company law providing 'creditor terms' which restrict such transactions. Commercial parties could thereby be spared the costs of writing such terms themselves.

Nevertheless, it seems most unlikely that a distribution restriction that conditioned on legal capital would succeed in capturing these benefits.[47] Whilst there may clearly be benefits to imposing dividend constraints based on net asset values, it is hard to understand why it would make sense to calibrate those restrictions by reference to historic contributions by shareholders, as opposed to the state of the balance sheet at the time the loan is advanced.[48] The utility of capital as a yardstick will diminish over time, as the value of the company's assets bears less and less resemblance to the amount of the shareholders' capital claims. If this is the case, then any 'savings' in terms of drafting costs will tend to diminish as the age of the debtor company increases.

Moreover, it should be appreciated that the appropriateness of distribution restrictions – and hence the preferences of commercial parties – will differ depending on the debtor company. This point is relevant for consideration of both the benefits and costs of a mandatory rule: where a distribution rule is appropriate, it creates a benefit, and where inappropriate, a cost. In theory, a distribution restriction is likely to be particularly useful for companies which have a large proportion of their value tied up in growth opportunities.[49] Where the exploitation of such opportunities must be financed with equity (as, for example, if they are

[46] See sources cited *supra* in nn. 33, 38 and 39.

[47] Manning, op. cit. n. 3, at pp. 33-34.

[48] Armour, loc. cit. n. 2, at pp. 373-374.

[49] Myers, loc. cit. n. 35.

based on 'soft' assets upon which security cannot be taken) then there is likely to be an underinvestment problem: advances of further funds to exploit the opportunities will transfer wealth from shareholders to existing creditors. Thus shareholders will be deterred from making such investments. A distribution restriction can, for such firms, force shareholders to retain equity in the firm and therefore reduce this problem. This theory predicts that the appropriateness of distribution restrictions will vary with the degree of growth opportunities. Empirical evidence suggests that, in the United States, where these matters are left to contract, there is a significant difference in the use of contractual distribution restrictions depending on the level of growth opportunities.[50] This tends to confirm our intuition that one size probably does not fit all, and that a mandatory set of rules implied into all contracts with creditors may generate mismatch costs in many cases.

4.2 Minimum capital rules

As we have seen, a minimum capital requirement imposes an 'entry price' for limited liability. The effect of such a restriction is most likely to be felt on small firms. For such firms, which are typically owner-managed,[51] limited liability is not used to reduce risk-bearing costs by permitting shareholders to diversify, as it is for listed companies.[52] Rather, the principal benefit brought by limited liability

---

50 See Bradley and Roberts, op. cit. n. 33, at p. 27 (high-growth firms significantly *more* likely to use dividend restriction in *private* debt agreements); Nash et al., loc. cit. n. 39, at p. 218 (high investment-opportunity firms significantly *less* likely to include dividend restriction in *public* debt agreements). This disparity probably reflects the fact that high-growth firms face particular uncertainty. In these circumstances, a covenant that might be readily triggered would be a useful lever of control for creditors who can renegotiate easily (see I.D. Dichev and D.J. Skinner, 'Large-Sample Evidence on the Debt Covenant Hypothesis', 40 *Journal of Accounting Research* (2002) p. 1091: private lenders set covenants tightly to use them as 'trip wires'). However, such a covenant would be a hostage to fortune for dispersed creditors (public debt) who cannot renegotiate easily.

51 See A. Cosh and A. Hughes, 'Size, Age, Growth, Business Constraints and Management Characteristics', in A. Cosh and A. Hughes, eds., *Enterprise Challenged: Policy and Performance in the British SME sector 1999-2002* (Cambridge, ESRC Centre for Business Research 2003) p. 3 at p. 10.

52 The benefits of limited liability for the financing of listed firms are well known, namely that they: (i) permit share prices to be independent of the purchaser's wealth and thereby to reflect information about the value of the firm; (ii) allow for diversification by shareholders, reducing the cost of risk-bearing; (iii) make passive investment a rational strategy, allowing for specialisation in the management and risk-bearing functions; and (iv) lower monitoring costs, both for creditors and shareholders, who no longer need to check on shareholders' wealth levels. See, e.g., F.H. Easterbrook and D.R. Fischel, *The Economic Structure of Corporate Law* (Cambridge, MA, Harvard University Press 1991) pp. 40-62.

is probably the reduction in risk it offers to entrepreneurs. The willingness of marginal individuals to engage in entrepreneurial activity does appear to be affected by the actual or perceived riskiness of such endeavour. For example, more lenient personal insolvency laws are associated with higher levels of self-employment,[53] plausibly because by reducing the harshness of the consequences of failure, they make entrepreneurial activity more appealing to risk-averse individuals. A similar effect could be expected to be associated with the ease of obtaining limited liability.[54] That is, inability to gain access to limited liability (because of lack of sufficient resources to meet a minimum capital requirement) might deter individuals from engaging in entrepreneurial activity.[55] Consistently with this, one study finds a negative correlation between size of minimum capital requirements (scaled for GDP) and self-employment – a common proxy for entrepreneurship – in European countries during the 1990s.[56]

To be sure, facilitating access to limited liability may be expected to result in would-be entrepreneurs coming forward with more marginal projects, in terms of quality. Whether or not these will be funded (in the absence of a minimum capital requirement) depends on the ability of private creditors to discriminate in terms of project quality. A greater demand for credit (associated with no minimum capital requirement) can be expected to spur the development of information intermediaries in private credit markets, who can assist financial creditors in distinguishing good projects from bad.[57] Moreover, there is nothing to stop an entrepreneur credibly signalling the quality of his or her project in the absence of a minimum capital requirement, either by committing personal funds to the corporate enterprise

---

[53] W. Fan and M.J. White, 'Personal Bankruptcy and the Level of Entrepreneurial Activity', 46 *Journal of Law and Economics* (2003) p. 543; J. Armour and D.J. Cumming, *Bankruptcy Law and Entrepreneurship*, University of Cambridge ESRC Centre for Business Research Working Paper No. 300 (March 2005).

[54] Of course, the true extent of its impact will depend on a combination of factors, including the severity of the consequences of personal insolvency, and the extent to which corporate creditors demand personal guarantees from those setting up private companies.

[55] It is worth noting that an individual's endowment of wealth has been shown to affect propensity to entrepreneurship (see, e.g., D. Blanchflower and A. Oswald, 'What Makes an Entrepreneur? Evidence on Inheritance and Capital Constraints', 16 *Journal of Labour Economics* (1997) p. 26). The most plausible interpretation of this result turns on risk aversion. Because of the declining marginal utility of money, a wealthier individual will suffer a lower decrease in utility for any given loss than will a poorer individual. Thus a wealthier individual will exhibit less aversion to bearing a risk of losing a sum of money.

[56] Armour and Cumming, op. cit. n. 53, at p. 20 (Table 3). This result, using data on minimum capital requirements from the World Bank's 'Doing Business' survey (available at: <http:// www.doingbusiness.org>) is however only for a univariate correlation.

[57] See S. Djankov, C. McLeish and A. Shleifer, *Private Credit in 129 Countries*, NBER Working Paper No. 11078 (January 2005) pp. 18, 31 (incidence of private credit rating agencies positively correlated with level of private credit).

or by agreeing to stand guarantor for its debts. Thus, provided adjusting creditors are able to distinguish project quality, or require shareholders to give a personal guarantee (by way of signal), then a minimum capital requirement will impose a social cost, by preventing some entrepreneurial projects from being undertaken.[58]

We have on the other hand hypothesised that a minimum capital regime may yield social benefits, through the amelioration of the position of non-adjusting creditors. Whilst adjusting creditors may be able to screen out the more marginal projects associated with ready access to limited liability, non-adjusting creditors cannot. The existence and extent of any benefits for such creditors through the imposition of a minimum capital regime therefore merits careful scrutiny.

The analysis is complicated by the fact that the social welfare implications of the treatment of non-adjusting creditors depend not on the fact that they are unable to adjust, but rather on the reasons for which they become creditors. Consider first tort victims. In economic terms, tortious liability is imposed on those conducting hazardous activity in order to encourage them to internalise the social costs of their actions.[59] Yet the amount necessary to capitalise a business adequately so as to internalise the risks of hazardous activities will depend on the nature of the business, and a unitary minimum capital requirement is likely to be a very haphazard means of achieving this. Moreover, there are more precise means of achieving the same goal. One is to regulate hazardous activity and to require that firms carry insurance commensurate with their potential risk.[60] The pricing of insurance premia would be a more precise internalisation mechanism than a 'fixed-rate' minimum capital requirement, not least because the insurance company would act as an ongoing monitor for the firm's activities.[61]

---

[58] The grant of a personal guarantee does of course undermine the benefit of risk-reduction for the entrepreneur. In the United Kingdom, such guarantees, whilst common, are not ubiquitous: see J. Freedman and M. Godwin, 'Incorporating the Micro Business: Perceptions and Misperceptions', in A. Hughes and D.J. Storey, *Finance and the Small Firm* (London, Routledge 1994) p. 232 at p. 246 (53.6 per cent of sample of owner-managers had given personal guarantees). And for those entrepreneurs that do not give personal guarantees, limited liability brings meaningful risk reduction.

[59] See generally, G. Calabresi, *The Costs of Accidents* (New Haven, Yale University Press 1971); S. Shavell, *Foundations of Economic Analysis of Law* (Cambridge, MA, Belknap Press 2004) pp. 177-206.

[60] The strategy is indeed adopted in Germany: see Schön, loc. cit. n. 2, at p. 438. In the United Kingdom, the Third Parties (Rights against Insurers) Act 1930 transfers liability insurance claims against an insurer of an insolvent firm from the firm to the party to whom it has incurred the liability, ensuring that tort victims need not share their recoveries with the debtor's other creditors.

[61] Other strategies include imposing *pro rata* unlimited liability on shareholders for corporate torts (H.B. Hansmann and R. Kraakman, 'Towards Unlimited Shareholder Liability for Corporate Torts', 100 *Yale LJ* (1991) p. 1879) and granting priority in insolvency to tort

A second category of creditor commonly classified as 'non-adjusting' is the State, in right of tax claims. However, a minimum capital rule is also inapposite in this context. Consider that no company is able to finance its commencement of operations solely on unpaid tax claims. This is because tax claims do not arise until taxable events take place in the course of operating a business. The initial finance for such business will need to come from adjusting creditors. Thus at the outset, the State may free-ride on the screening activity of others. The point in time at which tax claims are used to 'finance' a business is not on start-up, but if and when financial difficulties subsequently emerge. At that stage, adjusting creditors tend to press for payment. What commonly happens is that unpaid tax monies are then used to finance the continuation of the business beyond the point at which it should have been closed. A minimum capital requirement on formation is therefore irrelevant to the State as tax creditor: by definition, equity capital will have been lost by this stage. Moreover, although the State cannot typically levy differential interest on tax claims, it does have considerable economies of scale in both gathering information and organising enforcement. By varying the alacrity of enforcement with the creditworthiness of the debtor, it is able to some extent to adjust its position.

Trade creditors are a third category of supposedly 'non-adjusting' claimant. It is argued by some that trade creditors' adjustment may only be partial, because of information and transaction costs relative to the amount at stake. Indeed, empirical studies confirm that trade creditors tend to offer the same terms to all 'borrowers' (that is, customers who purchase on credit).[62] Some suggest that the use of such a 'blended' term in the face of asymmetric information about borrower quality may result in good-quality borrowers being overcharged and poor-quality borrowers being undercharged, implying an inefficient 'subsidy'.[63] Yet empirical studies also report that the *amount* of trade credit granted is a function of the borrower's creditworthiness and of the scope for misbehaviour by the debtor.[64] This implies that trade creditors do in fact adjust across the margin of amount of credit extended as opposed to variations in terms.

---

creditors (D.W. Leebron, 'Limited Liability, Tort Victims, and Creditors', 91 *Colum LR* (1991) p. 1565).

[62] Trade credit is typically offered on very similar terms within an industry: C.K. Ng, J.K. Smith and R.L. Smith, 'Evidence on the Determinants of Trade Credit Terms in Interfirm Trade', 54 *Journal of Finance* (1999) p. 1109.

[63] See Bebchuk and Fried, loc. cit. n. 24, at pp. 885-886.

[64] See, e.g., M.A. Petersen and R.J. Rajan, 'Trade Credit: Theories and Evidence', 10 *Review of Financial Studies* (1997) p. 661 at pp. 678-679 (borrowers with observably higher credit quality obtain more trade credit); M. Burkart, T. Ellingsen and M. Giannetti, *What You Sell is What You Lend? Explaining Trade Credit Contracts*, ECGI Finance Working Paper No. 71 (November 2004) (more trade credit is granted where buyer is less able to divert inputs supplied to another use).

It appears, therefore, that it is hard to find a category of non-adjusting creditors for whom minimum capital rules offer useful protection.

4.3 A future for 'creditor terms'?

The foregoing points imply that the costs of mandatory rules based on legal capital are likely to outweigh their benefits. One issue arising consequently is whether a case may nevertheless be made out for *default* rules.[65] Whilst such a reformulation is obviously not available as regards minimum capital rules on formation, distribution rules could be recast as frameworks to which companies opt in or opt out on formation. On this analysis, these rules are viewed as equivalent to collective terms in loan contracts, and are enforceable by a liquidator on behalf of creditors, should the company go into insolvency.[66]

As opposed to leaving the matter solely to individual contracting between companies and their creditors, default creditor terms might be thought to yield potential benefits. By reducing the need for creditors to bargain for individual protection, they could economise on negotiation costs. By permitting a company's obligations to be centrally specified, it would at the same time render them more transparent and more tractable. Default terms might also assist in reducing 'free-rider' problems in the provision of creditor protection. These arise because adjusting creditors do not capture the whole benefit of their expenditure in negotiating loan covenants – as some of it is conferred on non-adjusting creditors – and consequently may be expected to invest suboptimally in negotiating loan covenants and monitoring the same for breach.

Yet there are two serious difficulties with this justification for default rules as 'collective creditor terms'. The first is the well-aired point that there is likely to be considerable heterogeneity of demand amongst creditors, implying that the range of terms for which it might be possible for the State to capture economies of scale are very limited.[67] The second is less straightforward. As we have seen, the utility of loan covenants depends crucially upon the level at which they are set. Too lax, and they permit the debtor to harm creditors' interests; too strict, and they stifle valuable projects. Over time, what is optimal may change. Thus, in negotiating loan covenants, private parties face a trade-off between the costs of

---

[65] See Armour, loc. cit. n. 2, at pp. 375-377; Schön, loc. cit. n. 2, at pp. 438-442.

[66] Alternatively enforcement could be effected by a regulatory agency.

[67] This could occur both within firms – creditors having differing time horizons, priorities, and repayment schedules – and between firms – creditors' requirements varying with the debtor's business and size – and means that a single term is unlikely to suit all. See H. Kanda, 'Debtholders and Equityholders', 21 *Journal of Legal Studies* (1992) p. 431 at p. 440; M. Kahan, 'The Qualified Case against Mandatory Terms in Bonds', 89 *Northwestern University Law Review* (1995) p. 565 at pp. 609-610.

debtor misbehaviour and the costs of renegotiating the covenants should they cease to be appropriately set. Loan covenants tend on average to be less stringent where the costs of renegotiation are expected to be higher. That is, public debt contains less covenants than private debt.[68] A 'collective covenant' included in the corporate constitution would in principle be with all a company's creditors – adjusting and non-adjusting. It follows that there would need to be some input from non-adjusting creditors in order to vary its terms, should circumstances change.[69] Hence, it would be appropriate to set the level of constraint it imposed at one *lower* than that which would be desired by most adjusting creditors, were they contracting privately. In turn, many adjusting creditors would therefore find themselves dissatisfied with such a term, and seek to include more stringent provisions in their loan agreements. This could easily result in a net *increase* in contracting costs as compared with a regime relying solely on private contracting.[70]

These theoretical difficulties may be substantiated by reference to English law. It is technically possible for an English company to insert a collective term into its constitution which would restrict distributions on the basis of a condition that is more effective than legal capital rules. Such a 'creditor term' could be made unalterable by inserting it into the memorandum of association.[71] However, such provisions are not encountered in practice, presumably because it is considered too risky to include an unalterable provision lest changed circumstances render it a hindrance.

5. THE IMPACT OF REGULATORY COMPETITION

5.1 The ECJ's case law

Until recently, it was thought that there were insuperable legal obstacles to regulatory arbitrage in company law within the European Union.[72] The conflicts of law

---

[68] See *supra* nn. 39 and 50.

[69] Most jurisdictions provide a general mechanism for renegotiating creditor contracts external to the constitution by means of a composition, whereby a majority of creditors can bind a dissenting minority. Nevertheless, it is usually the case that all creditors must at least be notified.

[70] These problems may be illustrated obliquely by reference to the difficulties caused by an earlier form of 'collective term', that is, the corporate objects clause. Originally conceived as a means of protecting investors, the mechanism was abandoned in the twentieth century, essentially because its costs exceeded its benefits: see Cheffins, op. cit. n. 42, at pp. 527-531.

[71] Companies Act 1985, s. 17. The better view is that breach of such a restriction would render the distribution void: see *EIC Services Ltd* v. *Phipps* [2004] EWCA Civ 1069 (protection for third parties for acts in excess of company's powers provided by First Directive does not extend to shareholders in their capacity as such).

[72] See, e.g., Cheffins, op. cit. n. 42, at pp. 426-431.

rules of most Member States made use of the 'real seat' theory in determining the existence and proper law of a company. In contrast to the 'incorporation theory' used in the United Kingdom and the United States, the 'real seat' theory applies the law of the place where the company has its main place of business. When combined with rules on the recognition of the existence of corporate persons, it effectively prevented any regulatory arbitrage in company law.[73]

However, matters have changed dramatically following the ECJ's decisions in *Centros*, *Überseering* and *Inspire Art*.[74] These cases relate to company law arbitrage at the point of formation.[75] Each of the decisions concerned the treatment by Member State B (the 'host State') of a company doing business exclusively in – and thereby having its 'real seat' in – that Member State, but being incorporated under the laws of, and having its registered office in, Member State A (the 'home State'). The ECJ considered that the application of the real seat theory so as to deny recognition of the existence of the company in Member State B because it was not validly incorporated there amounted to an interference with the company's freedom of establishment. Essentially, the Court ruled that as a matter of EC law, a company, once validly formed under the laws of *any* Member State, becomes a 'person' and is consequently entitled to exercise the Treaty freedoms.[76] As a consequence, any laws of Member State B which have the effect of making the exercise of that freedom less attractive to companies incorporated in Member State A may be struck down by the Court unless they satisfy the four-stage criteria set out in *Gebhard*:[77] that is, they (i) are applied in a

---

[73] For example, if a company incorporated in Member State A (which applied the incorporation theory) then carried on business in Member State B (which applied the real seat theory), the courts of Member State B would reason that the company's proper law would be that of Member State B, and consequently, because it was not incorporated under that law, it was not validly formed at all.

[74] See *supra* n. 5.

[75] See generally E. Wymeersch, '*Centros*: A Landmark Decision in European Company Law', in T. Baums, et al., eds., *Corporations, Capital Markets and Business in the Law* (London, Kluwer Law International 2000) p. 629; M. Siems, 'Convergence, Competition, *Centros* and Conflicts of Law: European Company Law in the 21st Century', 27 *European Law Review* (2002) p. 47; C. Kersting and C.P. Schindler, 'The ECJ's *Inspire Art* Decision of 30 September 2003 and its Effects on Practice', 4 *German LJ* (2003) p. 1277; S. Rammeloo, 'At Long Last: Freedom of Establishment for Legal Persons in Europe Accomplished', 11 *MJ* (2004) p. 379; J. Lowry, 'Eliminating Obstacles to Freedom of Establishment: The Competitive Edge of UK Company Law', 63 *Cambridge Law Journal* (2004) p. 331.

[76] Moreover, the mere fact that the company was incorporated in Member State A solely to avoid laws which would otherwise apply were it incorporated in Member State B does not constitute an 'abuse' of that freedom: *Centros*, *supra* n. 5, at paras. 27-29; *Inspire Art*, *supra* n. 5, at para. 96.

[77] ECJ, Case C-55/94 *Gebhard* v. *Colsiglio dell'Ordine degli Avvocati e Procuratori di Milano* [1995] *ECR* I-4165.

non-discriminatory manner; (ii) are justified by imperative requirements of the public interest; (iii) secure the attainment of their objective; and (iv) are not disproportionate in their effect.

5.2 Do legal capital rules pass the *Gebhard* test?

The rule in question in the *Centros* decision was of course the Danish minimum capital provision, which Mr and Mrs Bryde, both Danish nationals resident in Denmark, had sought to avoid by incorporating their company in the United Kingdom. In response to the Danish Government's argument that the minimum capital requirements were justified in the overriding public interest for the protection of non-adjusting creditors, the Court ruled that they were neither necessary nor proportionate to achieve that goal.[78] Similarly, in *Inspire Art*, the Court concluded that, for adjusting creditors, a minimum capital was simply unnecessary, as they would be put on notice, by the fact that the company was incorporated in the United Kingdom, that English company law's protections were applicable.[79]

It remains to be seen whether a requirement that 'formally foreign' companies be subjected to domestic distribution restrictions would similarly fall foul of the Treaty. The case is rather less clear-cut than minimum capital rules, as it is not beyond argument that distribution rules would even constitute a hindrance to the exercise of corporate free movement. The better view, however, is that they do. Consider a company, incorporated under the law of Member State A, which has under that law considerable distributable profits. Assume that the company moves the entirety of its business operation to Member State B. If Member State B imposes stringent restrictions on distributions, both by domestically incorporated companies and by 'formally foreign' companies, then it is possible that such a stringent restriction would constitute a hindrance to the company's exercise of its freedom of establishment in Member State B. If so, then the arguments put in the previous section would imply that it would be appropriate for the Court to find such restrictions to be unnecessary and disproportionate.

5.3 Is the boundary between company and insolvency law significant?

It has been argued by some that the impact of the ECJ's case law is limited to the appropriate rules for choice of company law. Hence, the argument goes, if a rule is properly characterised as one of insolvency law, as opposed to company law,

78 *Centros*, *supra* n. 5, at paras. 35-37.
79 *Inspire Art*, *supra* n. 5, at para. 135.

then the *Centros* line of authorities is not relevant.[80] This argument is said to draw support from fact that jurisdiction and choice of law in European insolvency proceedings is governed by *sui generis* legislation, the European Insolvency Regulation ('EIR').[81] The EIR is widely thought to be based upon connecting factors that bear more in common with the 'real seat' theory than the incorporation theory.

If correct, this argument would imply that were legal capital rules to be framed by lawmakers so that they could plausibly be characterised as part of corporate insolvency law, as opposed to company law, then they would be outwith the ambit of the ECJ's case law. However, the ECJ's judgment in *Inspire Art* is framed not in terms of connecting factors in company law, but of legal provisions that impede corporate freedom of establishment. Why should this apply any differently to rules formally characterised as 'corporate insolvency law' than to rules of 'company law'? The existence of the EIR, which does not purport to govern the content of insolvency laws, but merely the connecting factor for choice of jurisdiction and choice of law, provides no justification for saying that the rules selected by its procedures should not be compatible with Treaty freedoms.[82]

5.4 Regulatory competition and creditor protection

The ECJ's recent case law is having two related effects on legal capital rules in Member States' company laws. First, for practical purposes, it resolves the issue whether legal capital rules are a meaningful way of responding to the policy problems concerning non-adjusting creditors. By ruling that they are not, the ECJ has, in essence, unleashed a process of 'negative harmonisation'. This is because, following the three recent cases, there has been large-scale regulatory arbitrage over company formation.[83] This is most clearly evidenced in a recent study by Becht, Mayer and Wagner,[84] who show that since 2003 approximately 6,000

---

[80] See, e.g., C. Kersting and C.P. Schindler, loc. cit. n. 75, at p. 1290; T. Koller, 'The English Limited Company – Ready to Invade Germany', 15 *ICCLR* (2004) p. 334 at pp. 341-343; Rammeloo, loc. cit. n. 75, at pp. 403-406.

[81] Council Regulation (EC) No. 1346/2000 of 29 May 2000 on insolvency proceedings, *OJ* 2000 L 160/1. Jurisdiction over insolvency proceedings was specifically excluded from the Brussels Convention (now consolidated as Council Regulation (EC) No. 44/2001 of 22 December 2001 on jurisdiction and the recognition and enforcement of judgments in civil and commercial matters, *OJ* 2001 L 12/1: see Art. 1(2)(b)).

[82] Armour, loc. cit. n. 6, at pp. 405-406.

[83] In addition, the adoption on 25 October 2005 of the Tenth Company Law Directive on Cross-Border Mergers (2005/56/EC, *OJ* 2005 L 310/1) will now facilitate regulatory arbitrage for established companies.

[84] See *supra* n. 6. See also Armour, loc. cit. n. 6, at p. 386.

private companies per annum have been formed under English law by entrepreneurs living and trading in Germany. Similar results are expected for other European countries. Anecdotal evidence from the websites of company formation agents is strongly suggestive that the driver of regulatory arbitrage by entrepreneurs is clearly the restrictive capital adequacy and maintenance requirements of many continental jurisdictions.[85] The result of this arbitrage has been to provoke a spate of 'defensive' regulatory competition, as continental European lawmakers respond to the threat of large-scale arbitrage. Some, such as France and Spain, have already relaxed their capital maintenance regimes;[86] others, such as Germany, are planning to do so shortly.[87]

Although these developments are being driven by a desire to avoid regulatory compliance, this is not a 'race to the bottom'. Concomitantly with this relaxation of minimum capital requirements, policymakers must reconsider the treatment of non-adjusting creditors, to see whether the issues to which they give rise can be addressed using more proportionate measures which will satisfy the *Gebhard* formula. To the extent that such measures – several of which have been canvassed in this paper – are able to achieve effective and targeted solutions to the problems, their succession to the minimum capital regimes is to be warmly welcomed.

The second effect of *Centros* is that, insofar as adjusting creditors are concerned, regulatory arbitrage will result in a 'race to the top'. The impact of choice of company law will be priced by such creditors into their lending agreements, making it worth entrepreneurs' while to select laws which are efficient. The previous section considered whether distribution rules could usefully play a role as default rules, rather than mandatory rules. The advent of regulatory competition will, it seems, have the effect of rendering their status closer to default rules in any event. Moreover, Member States wishing to attract incorporations will have incentives to offer such creditor protection mechanisms (if any) as adjusting creditors will find value in reducing their costs of contracting.

---

85 A typical example of many such agents found by a Google search is Coddan CPM UK, which offers, via the internet, same-day incorporation of a UK private company for a fee of £42. The website has versions, explaining arbitrage opportunities, in Spanish and German. See <http://www.ukincorp.co.uk>.

86 See J. Simon, 'A Comparative Approach to Capital Maintenance: France', 15 *European Business Law Review* (2004) p. 1037; E.-M. Kieninger, 'The Legal Framework of Regulatory Competition Based on Company Mobility: EU and US Compared', 6 *German Law Journal* (2005) p. 740 at p. 768.

87 Rammeloo, loc. cit. n. 75, at p. 409.

6. CONCLUSIONS

It has been argued that legal capital has no future as a body of mandatory rules of European private company law. Legal capital rules are a form of primitive regulatory technology which, as a matter of theory, is likely to generate more costs than benefits. This is particularly the case for minimum capital rules, which impede entrepreneurs' ability to gain access to limited liability. However this paper has argued that other mandatory rules based on legal capital are also likely to be over-regulatory. On the one hand, the restrictions imposed by such rules are unlikely to be appropriate for all companies; on the other hand, it is hard to see how rules that condition distributions on historic capital contributions could be useful constraints even for companies for which such restrictions are appropriate. Moreover, it is arguable that even in relation to those companies for which distribution restrictions would be appropriate, their inclusion as 'collective creditor terms' in corporate constitutions are likely to be less effective than having them written into loan covenants. In any event, the advent of regulatory competition in European corporate law means that those creditor protection rules that do not further the interests of adjusting creditors will become subject to competitive pressures. Legislatures will be faced with the task of designing mandatory rules to deal with the issues raised by non-adjusting creditors in a proportionate and effective manner, consistent with the *Gebhard* formula. At the same time, regulatory arbitrage will provide a way of gathering information regarding adjusting investors' preferences in relation to such rules.

H. Eidenmüller and W. Schön (eds.), The Law and Economics of Creditor Protection 27

Legal Capital: A Navigation System for Corporate Law Scholarship

Holger Fleischer*

Keywords: legal capital, creditor protection, rules and standards, mandatory and default provisions, legal transplants.

---

* Professor of Law, Director of the Institute for Commercial and Economic Law, University of Bonn.

1. CREDITOR PROTECTION LAW AND LEGAL CAPITAL

I would like to use (or abuse) my comment on John Armour's thoughtful paper to sketch out a conceptual approach towards legal capital with an emphasis on *structure* rather than on *substantive regulation*.

1.1 Morphology of creditor protection law

1.1.1 *Creditor protection law as a cross-section subject*

At the outset, one should accentuate that creditor protection is dealt with in different areas of law. It touches *company law* as well as *insolvency law*, and it is also deeply rooted in *accounting law* and *contract law* – to mention just the most important fields.[1] To put it differently, creditor protection law is a *cross-section subject* with all the challenges, pitfalls and misunderstandings of legal frontier regions this entails.

1.1.2 *Creditor protection law as a 'movable system'*

Moreover, creditor protection law offers fertile ground for a methodological approach associated with the Austrian legal scholar Walter Wilburg: the idea of a *movable system* according to which an area of law is often structured and shaped by different and frequently competing principles which set more or less realisable standards.[2] I might add that Wilburg received the inspiration for his conceptual approach from comparative law studies.[3] In the area of creditor protection law, the underlying principles might be (1) transparency of creditors' risks; (2) self-responsibility of creditors; (3) equal treatment of creditors; and (4) barriers to *ex post* risk shifting. Within this framework, legislators and courts are confronted with the Herculean task[4] of harmonising these principles, finding consistent

---

[1] Similarly G. Hertig and H. Kanda, 'Creditor Protection', in R. Kraakman, et al., *The Anatomy of Corporate Law* (Oxford, Oxford University Press 2004) p. 71: 'The need to protect corporate creditors, however, does not necessarily imply that *corporate* law must do the protecting: the job could be left entirely to contracting between the parties or to the general law of debtor-creditor relations.'

[2] See W. Wilburg, *Entwicklung eines beweglichen Systems im geltenden Recht* (Graz, Verlag Jos. A. Kienreich 1950).

[3] See W. Posch, 'Die Bedeutung des Beweglichen Systems für die Rechtsvergleichung und das Einheitsprivatrecht', in F. Bydlinski, H. Krejci, B. Schilcher and V. Steininger, eds., *Das Bewegliche System im geltenden und künftigen Recht* (Vienna/New York, Springer 1986) p. 253 at p. 254 et seq.

[4] The metaphor is taken from R.M. Dworkin, *Law's Empire* (Cambridge, Harvard University Press 1986) p. 239.

compromises between them and restricting none of them more than necessary by the furtherance of counter-principles. This *optimising task* has, by its nature, *several* possible solutions.

1.2 Competing designs of creditor protection

Analysed through the lens of a movable system,[5] it is thus not surprising that we find competing institutional designs of creditor protection: legal capital on the continent and alternative approaches in the United States and – more and more – in the United Kingdom. An additional insight to be gained from viewing creditor protection law via Wilburg's way of thinking is this: a movable system in his sense consists of *various* elements that can *substitute* each other to a certain degree.[6] To give two examples in our context: a *minus* of directors' personal liability may be compensated by a *plus* of shareholder liability via veil piercing, and *vice versa*,[7] while a reduction of *initial* capital requirements can be balanced out by *late-stage* equitable subordination of shareholders' loans.

2. ANATOMY OF LEGAL CAPITAL

This leads me to some *less abstract* remarks on the anatomy of legal capital.

2.1 Protective dimensions of legal capital

2.1.1 *Shareholder protection*

The anatomy lessons should begin with a basic insight. The Second Company Law Directive[8] reminds us in the second recital of its preamble that rules on legal capital are designed to ensure protection for both creditors *and* shareholders of

[5] This approach is suggested by H. Fleischer, 'Kapitalschutz und Durchgriffshaftung bei Auslandsgesellschaften', in M. Lutter, ed., *Europäische Auslandsgesellschaften in Deutschland* (Cologne, Otto Schmidt 2005) p. 49 at p. 107 et seq.

[6] See F. Bydlinski, 'Die "Elemente" des Beweglichen Systems: Beschaffenheit, Verwendung und Ermittlung', in B. Schilcher, P. Koller and B.-C. Funk, eds., *Regeln, Prinzipien und Elemente im System des Rechts* (Vienna, Verlag Österreich 2000) p. 9 et seq.

[7] See L.C.B. Gower and P.L. Davies, *Principles of Modern Company Law*, 7th edn. (London, Sweet & Maxwell 2003) p. 190: 'British law has approached that problem [i.e., inadequate capitalisation] through the statutory doctrine of wrongful trading rather than through lifting the veil.'

[8] Second Council Directive of 13 December 1976, *OJ* 1977 L 26/1.

public companies.[9] Scholarly analysis focusing only on the creditor dimension thus does not fully appreciate the range and ratio of legal capital rules.[10] An alternative system which abolishes legal capital altogether has to resort to functional substitutes in order to maintain the appropriate amount of shareholder protection, the most plausible candidate being the principle of equal treatment for all shareholders.[11] Having said this, I will leave aside the issue of shareholder protection through legal capital, since our conference is entitled 'Efficient *Creditor* Protection in European Company Law'.

2.1.2 *Creditor protection: voluntary and involuntary creditors*

As far as creditor protection is concerned, law and economics orthodoxy tells us to differentiate between sophisticated and unsophisticated, voluntary and involuntary, and adjusting and non-adjusting creditors.[12] While voluntary creditors can fend for themselves,[13] involuntary creditors cannot, and the discussion soon centres around alternative venues of protection for this second group of creditors. In my view, two aspects should be considered more closely.

First, involuntary creditors are far from being a homogenous group. Unlike John Armour, I would not exaggerate the protective need of the State as a tax creditor. Comparative law shows how the State interferes in its own interest by introducing liability provisions for directors into tax laws, for example, section 69 of the German General Tax Code (*Abgabenordnung*) or Article 266 of the French *Livre des procedures fiscales.*[14] More troubling is the legal protection of consumer creditors in cases where small claim problems arise and non-financial

---

[9] The second recital states: 'Whereas in order to ensure minimum equivalent protection *for both shareholders and creditors* of public limited liability companies, the coordination of national provisions relating to their formation and to the maintenance, increase or reduction of their capital is particularly important.'

[10] See H. Fleischer, 'Systematische Darstellung 6: Die Finanzierung der GmbH', in L. Michalski, *GmbH-Gesetz* (Munich, C.H. Beck 2002) n. 7.

[11] See Art. 42 of the Second Council Directive: 'For the purposes of the implementation of this Directive, the laws of the Member States shall ensure equal treatment to all shareholders who are in the same position.'

[12] See F.H. Easterbrook and D.R. Fischel, *The Economic Structure of Corporate Law* (Cambridge, Harvard University Press 1991) p. 50 et seq.; H. Fleischer, 'Grundfragen der ökonomischen Theorie im Gesellschafts- und Kapitalmarktrecht', 30 *Zeitschrift für Unternehmens- und Gesellschaftsrecht* (2001) p. 1 at p. 19.

[13] In analogy to the famous formulation aimed at investors in *SEC* v. *Ralston Purina Co.*, 346 US 119 at 125 (1953).

[14] See H. Fleischer, 'Erweiterte Außenhaftung der Organmitglieder im Europäischen Gesellschafts- und Kapitalmarktrecht', 33 *Zeitschrift für Unternehmens- und Gesellschaftsrecht* (2004) p. 437 at p. 445 et seq.

creditors, for instance trade creditors and small subcontractors, that may lack bargaining and informational resources.[15]

Second, critics of legal capital rules usually point to alternative means of protection for involuntary creditors: piercing the corporate veil for tort victims,[16] mandatory insurance for hazardous activities[17] and personal tort liability for directors.[18] I would like to add a supplementary proposal that has almost fallen into oblivion but was recently reanimated by scholars on both sides of the Atlantic: *preferential* treatment for tort creditors in the case of insolvency of the company.[19] I do not want to take a firm position here as to whether this is the cure for involuntary creditors or whether it leads to the outbreak of just another illness, but I think it is worth discussing.

2.2 Types of companies

2.2.1 *Private and public companies*

A second dividing line in our discussion should separate private and public companies – for a variety of reasons. First of all, as John Armour mentions in passing, the principle of limited liability is much easier to justify for publicly traded companies.[20] Moreover, some instruments from the creditor protection toolbox are well suited to *private* companies and ill suited to *public* companies: veil piercing is one example,[21] the doctrine of equitable subordination another. Conversely, the protective power of mandatory disclosure and market forces is – for obvious reasons – the domain of publicly held and listed companies. Finally, it should not escape notice that some arguments for and against legal capital have force only in a particular setting. By way of illustration, the advantage that a

---

[15] See P. Mankowski, 'Does Contract Suffice to Protect the Interests of the Creditors of a Company Properly?', in M. Lutter, ed., *Legal Capital* (Berlin, De Gruyter 2006, forthcoming).

[16] Most prominently, H. Hansmann and R. Kraakman, 'Toward Unlimited Shareholder Liability for Corporate Torts', 100 *Yale L.J.* (1991) p. 1879.

[17] See Easterbrook and Fischel, op. cit. n. 12, at p. 47 et seq.

[18] See Hertig and Kanda, loc. cit. n. 1, at p. 88 et seq.

[19] See L.M. LoPucki, 'The Unsecured Creditor's Bargain', 80 *Va. L. Rev.* (1994) p. 1987; G. Wagner, 'Deliktshaftung und Insolvenzrecht', in E. Schilken, et al., eds., *Festschrift für Walter Gerhardt* (Cologne, RWS Verlag 2004) p. 1043 at p. 1067 et seq.

[20] See S.M. Bainbridge, *Corporation Law and Economics* (New York, Foundation Press 2002) p. 132 et seq.; Fleischer, loc. cit. n. 12, at p. 16 et seq.

[21] See R.B. Thompson, 'Piercing the Corporate Veil: An Empirical Study', 76 *Cornell L. Rev.* (1991) p. 1036, showing that veil piercing almost always takes place in close corporations; for a similar result, see C. Mitchell, 'Lifting the Corporate Veil in the English Courts: An Empirical Study', 3 *Company, Financial and Insolvency Law Review* (1999) p. 15 at p. 21: 'No case was found in which the English courts have even been asked to fix the shareholders of a public company with liability for its obligations.'

balance-sheet-oriented distribution rule makes it easier for managers to withstand pressure from shareholders in times of crisis is convincing in a *Berle/Means*-type of public company but looses its thrust in a manager-owned private company.

2.2.2 *Groups of companies*

I can only mention in passing the complex legal capital world of corporate groups, which gives rise to special problems. The most intriguing question is whether Article 15(1) of the Second Company Law Directive[22] also covers so-called *hidden distributions*,[23] which would have a major impact on the judicial review of *intra-group transactions*.

3. ANALYTICAL FRAMEWORK FOR LEGAL CAPITAL

3.1 **Levels of reasoning: theoretical arguments and empirical evidence**

The first wave of scholarship on legal capital began by *collecting* arguments for and against the established regime of the Second Company Law Directive.[24] The arguments are largely derived from and couched in terms of traditional or neo-institutional law and economics. We identify asymmetrical information between the participants in the corporate contract, we point to transaction costs and possible cost savings by interpreting legal capital as a collective offer to creditors[25] and we sometimes view legal capital as a signalling device.[26] This is all extremely valuable, but only at an intermediate stage of our discussion. The next step must be to *test* our arguments and theories against the empirical evidence. In this respect, German *legal scholars* – or should we blame our colleagues from the *business school?* – are lagging behind, and John Armour's paper is particularly

[22] Article 15(1)(a) states: 'Except for cases of reductions of subscribed capital, no distribution to shareholders may be made when on the closing date of the last financial year the net assets as set out in the company's annual accounts are, or following such a distribution would become, lower than the amount of the subscribed capital plus those reserves which may not be distributed under the law or the statutes.'

[23] See P.O. Mülbert and M. Birke, 'Legal Capital – Is There a Case against the European Legal Capital Rules?', 3 *EBOR* (2002) p. 695 at p. 705 et seq.; H. Fleischer, 'Hidden Distributions and the Capital Directive', in Lutter, op. cit. n. 15.

[24] Beginning with J.R. Macey and L. Enriques, 'Creditors Versus Capital Formation: The Case Against the European Legal Capital Rules', 86 *Cornell L. Rev.* (2001) p. 1165.

[25] See W. Schön, 'The Future of Legal Capital', 5 *EBOR* (2004) p. 429 at p. 438 et seq.

[26] See K. Heine and K. Röpke, 'Die Rolle von Qualitätssignalen – eine ökonomische und juristische Analyse am Beispiel der deutschen Kapitalschutzregeln', 70 *Rabels Zeitschrift* (2006) p. 138.

promising. Some authors conjecture that information costs might be an insurmountable barrier for the self-help of small trade creditors; John Armour provides us with statistics.[27] Some authors theorise that trade creditors are unable to discriminate between borrowers on the basis of creditworthiness; John Armour cites studies which test and contest the validity of this claim.[28]

Several of these studies, however, are disputed. A recently published bankruptcy business study documents the presence of substantial numbers of creditors who have little meaningful opportunity to negotiate with their debtors or adjust their prices to reflect risk.[29] Despite this contradictory evidence, it remains true in creditor protection law that the *practical* often informs the *theoretical*, and that efficiency gains by a particular rule must be demonstrated, not merely presumed or asserted.

3.2 Underlying assumptions: rational corporate actors and cognitive deficiencies

A further and oft-neglected aspect of the legal capital debate concerns the underlying assumptions of our reasoning. Conventional economic wisdom teaches us to model the different actors in the corporate setting as fully *rational* players.[30] As a starting point and working hypothesis, this was and still is indispensable. On the other hand, we are increasingly confronted with experimental evidence of cognitive deficiencies.[31] A well-known example in our context is the over-optimism of top management throughout a company's lifespan and especially in times of crisis.[32] English company law has coined the phrase 'sunshine doctrine', referring to directors who in stormy weathers still hope that the clouds will go away and the sun will shine again.[33] If corroborated by further evidence,

---

27 See M.A. Petersen and R.G. Rajan, 'Does Distance Still Matter? The Information Revolution in Small Business Lending', 57 *Journal of Finance* (2002) p. 533.

28 See M.A. Petersen and R.G. Rajan, 'Trade Credit: Theories and Evidence', 10 *Review of Financial Studies* (1997) p. 661.

29 See E. Warren and J.L. Westbrook, 'Contracting out of Bankruptcy: An Empirical Intervention', 118 *Harv. L. Rev.* (2005) p. 1197.

30 See Bainbridge, op. cit. n. 20, at p. 23 et seq.

31 See C.R. Sunstein, ed., *Behavioral Law and Economics* (Cambridge, Cambridge University Press 2000); H. Fleischer, 'Behavioral Law and Economics im Gesellschafts- und Kapitalmarktrecht – ein Werkstattbericht', in A. Fuchs, et al., *Festschrift für Ulrich Immenga* (Munich, C.H. Beck 2004) p. 575.

32 See D.C. Langevoort, 'Organized Illusions: A Behavioral Theory of Why Corporations Mislead Stock Market Investors (and Cause Other Social Harm)', 146 *U. Pa. L. Rev.* (1996) p. 101 at p. 161; Fleischer, loc. cit. n. 14, at p. 459 et seq.

33 See *Re White & Osmond (Parkstone) Ltd.*, unpublished but cited in *R.* v. *Grantham* [1984] 2 *All ER* 166 at 170.

these and other anomalies must be taken into account when designing legal rules in the vicinity of insolvency and when shaping a timely trigger for company insolvency. This is not to say that creditor protection law has to be completely rewritten from a behavioural law and economics perspective. Often, we can explain a certain pattern of behaviour from different perspectives. The seemingly irrational over-optimism of company directors, for example, may turn out to be a fully rational gamble for resurrection in the vicinity of insolvency.[34]

3.3 Categories of legal norms

We reach the next intellectual junction when we try to mould our results into legal norms. Here, attention should be paid to different techniques that have long been underexposed in the manuals of good corporate law-making.

3.3.1 *Mandatory and default provisions*

A key point in John Armour's paper and in the whole debate on legal capital is the respective place we assign to mandatory and default provisions.[35] John Armour favours default provisions with respect to distribution rules. I would like to ask whether the logic behind that also applies to insolvency law, which is generally understood as a mandatory system, and whether a bankruptcy regime negotiated in the marketplace will be more efficient than the standardised contract provided by our insolvency codes.[36]

3.3.2 *Rules and standards*

A second differentiation recently rediscovered in accounting and corporate law is the rules-standards distinction.[37] It plays an important role in designing distribution provisions. A rules-based regime coupled with the company's commercial

---

[34] See R.A. Brealey and S.C. Myers, 'How Much Should a Firm Borrow', *Principles of Corporate Finance*, 7th edn. (New York, McGraw 2003) p. 489.

[35] For a recent survey of the rich literature, see H. Fleischer, 'Gesetz und Vertrags als alternative Problemlösungsmodelle im Gesellschaftsrecht', 168 *Zeitschrift für das gesamte Handels- und Wirtschaftsrecht* (2004) p. 673 at p. 886 et seq.

[36] See B.A. Adler, 'Financial and Political Theories of American Corporate Bankruptcy', 45 *Stan L. Rev.* (1993) p. 311; R.K. Rasmussen, 'Debtor's Choice: A Menu Approach to Corporate Bankruptcy', 71 *Tex. L. Rev.* (1992) p. 51; A. Schwartz, 'A Contract Theory Approach to Business Bankruptcy', 107 *Yale L.J.* (1998) p. 1807; contra: S. Block-Lieb, 'The Logic and Limits of Contract Bankruptcy', *U. Ill. L. Rev.* (2001) p. 503; L.M. LoPucki, 'Contract Bankruptcy: A Reply to Alan Schwartz', 109 *Yale L.J.* (1999) p. 317.

[37] For a key contribution, see L. Kaplow, 'Rules Versus Standards: An Economic Analysis', 42 *Duke L.J.* (1992) p. 557.

balance sheet promises to be less vulnerable *vis-à-vis* manipulative manoeuvres and overly optimistic projections by managers than an open-ended standard. This higher degree of objectivity, though, comes at a price: the loss of flexibility in corporate finance. One issue in this respect is whether legal uncertainty created by *vague* standards can nevertheless induce a *cautious* distribution policy by management on the grounds that there is always a certain probability that courts will regard specific projections or forward-looking statements as unacceptable. This depends largely on the willingness of courts to qualify solvency statements as decisions based on business judgment.

3.4 Legal and social environment

3.4.1 *National preferences and legal culture*

In an overall picture of creditor protection, we must finally not forget that different jurisdictions have different preferences and different attitudes towards entrepreneurship and management control. English *contract law*, for example, is largely based on the tenets of self-responsibility and *caveat emptor*,[38] whereas German *contract law* stresses the virtues of cooperation and good faith.[39] *Similar* value judgments may explain *some* of the divergences of *creditor protection* law in both countries.[40]

Moreover, when deciding which creditor protection instruments are suitable in a particular legal environment, much can be learned from the rich literature on *legal transplants*.[41] The key concepts are micro-fit and macro-fit. *Micro-fit* is how well a new rule complements the pre-existing legal infrastructure in a certain country; *macro-fit* is how well a new rule complements the pre-existing institutions of the political economy in that country.[42] It may well turn out that some

---

38 Most prominently *Walford* v. *Miles* [1992] 2 A.C. 128 at 138.

39 See H. Fleischer, *Informationsasymmetrie im Vertragsrecht* (Munich, C.H. Beck 2001) p. 567 et seq.

40 On this point with respect to German and US law, see H. Fleischer, 'Der Gläubigerschutz im Recht der Delaware Corporation', 51 *Recht der Internationalen Wirtschaft* (2004) p. 92; see also Gower and Davies, op. cit. n. 7, at p. 190: 'Indeed, at a more general level, the approach of British law to regulation of the abuse of limited liability is a combination of facilitating self-help and statutory constraints.'

41 See generally A. Watson, *Legal transplants. An Approach in Comparative Law*, 2nd edn. (Athens/London, The University of Georgia Press 1993); with a view to company law, see H. Fleischer, 'Legal Transplants im deutschen Aktienrecht', *Neue Zeitschrift für Gesellschaftsrecht* (2004) p. 1129 with further references.

42 See H. Kanda and C.J. Milhaupt, *Re-examining Legal Transplants: The Director's Fiduciary Duty in Japanese Corporate Law*, Columbia Law and Economics Working Paper No. 219 (2003) p. 9, available at: <http://ssrn.com/abstract=391821>.

instruments which are highly efficient in their home country will not succeed at all in their new environment and suffer from a 'transplant shock'.[43]

3.4.2 *Switching costs and path dependence*

A last point to be considered in an economic calculus when comparing different creditor protection systems has emerged in the ongoing corporate governance discussion. It is the phenomenon of *switching costs* and path *dependence*.[44] Jurists, after all, prefer *incremental* rather than *radical* reform steps,[45] and a malicious tongue has argued that this also mirrors the legal academy's reward structure.[46]

---

43 D. Berkowitz, K. Pistor and J.F. Richard, 'The Transplant Effect', 51 *Am. J. Comp. L.* (2003) p. 163.

44 See M.J. Roe, 'Path Dependence, Political Options, and Governance Systems', in K.J. Hopt and E. Wymeersch, eds., *Comparative Corporate Governance – Essays and Materials* (Berlin, de Gruyter 1997) p. 165.

45 See H. Fleischer, 'Legal Transplants in European Company Law – The Case of Fiduciary Duties', *European Company and Financial Law Review* (2005) p. 378 at p. 393; see also M. Bors, 'Recht und Autorität', in P. Tercier, ed., *Festschrift für Peter Gauch* (Zürich, Schulthess 2004) p. 37 at p. 42 et seq.

46 See M. Tushnet, '"Everything Old is New Again": Early Reflections on the "New Chicago School"', *Wis. L. Rev.* (1998) p. 579 at p. 581: 'Ambitious younger scholars, of whom there is rarely an undersupply, have obvious incentives to discover some novel approach. In general, however, the legal academy's reward structure requires that novel approaches be one that the younger scholars' elders can appreciate as continuing a tradition with which the elders are associated.'

H. Eidenmüller and W. Schön (eds.), The Law and Economics of Creditor Protection

Bond Covenants and Creditor Protection: Economics and Law, Theory and Practice, Substance and Process

William W. Bratton*

* Professor of Law, Georgetown University Law Center.

Abstract
This article examines contractual protection of unsecured financial creditors in US credit markets. Borrowers and lenders in the United States contract against a minimal legal background that imposes the burden of protection on the lender. A working, constantly updated, set of contractual protections has emerged in response. But actual use of available contractual technology varies widely, depending on the level of risk and the institutional context. The credit markets sort borrowers according to the degree of the risk of financial distress, imposing substantial constraints only on the borrowers with the most dangerous incentives. At the same time, the contracting practice is sticky and lumpy, never quite managing to conform to the predictions of first generation agency theory. Levels of protection vary with institutional contexts. Exhaustive contracts providing something approaching complete protection against agency costs prove feasible only in relational contexts conducive to ongoing renegotiation over time due to small numbers of lenders operating under reputational constraints. The public bond markets do not hold out such a process context, and accordingly shut out the riskiest borrowers. The larger, less risky firms that do gain access to the bond markets borrow under contracts offering incomplete protection, with the level of protection roughly correlating to the borrower's risk level. This leaves bondholders confronting a residuum of agency costs and relying on secondary protections like monitoring, exit, diversification, and hedging. This has worked reasonably well in practice, subject to an historical exception concerning the risk of high-leverage restructuring. The bond markets searched for two decades for a stable solution to this problem, finally settling on across-the-board contractual protection only in recent years.

Keywords: agency costs, bank loans, bonds and bondholders, bond covenants, creditors' rights, legal capital, private placements, trust indentures.

1. Introduction

Creditor protection came into corporate law in the United States with the enactment of the first general corporation laws in the mid-nineteenth century. These extended limited liability to the shareholders as a usual consequence of incorporation,[1] simultaneously imposing creditor protective provisions now known as the

---

[1] During the time of the special charter incorporation, corporate status did not inevitably imply limited liability, and charters did not contain creditor-protective provisions. See J.W. Hurst, *The Legitimacy of the Business Corporation in the Law of the United States, 1780-1970* (Charlottesville, University Press of Virginia 1970) p. 51.

legal capital rules. The original legal capital rules mandated minimum capital, requiring that shareholders pay in full for stock issued and constraining their receipt of dividends and other distributions of capital. The rules made creditor protection as intrinsic an aspect of incorporation as limited liability.[2] The judicial doctrine of disregarding the corporate fiction appeared during the same period,[3] stemming from the related notion that the benefits of limited liability should apply only so long as a corporation conducted its business according to the legal model's basic requirements. The corporation, in short, had to maintain both formal integrity and fiscal responsibility. If it did not, the law reverted to the rule of individual responsibility and held the corporation's shareholders responsible for its debts.

Large corporations performing multiple tasks of production and marketing appeared around 1890. They rapidly came to dominate the American economy. Corporate law supported the new corporations, and changed in so doing. Charter competition appeared in 1888 when New Jersey created and marketed the first management-friendly corporate code. Diluted legal capital rules were a central part of the competitive package, and the other states quickly followed New Jersey's lead. As a practical matter, corporate creditors no longer received legal protection outside of insolvency.[4]

Financial creditors of large corporations took the changes in stride. The new firms' managers proved less likely to act against their creditors' interests than did entrepreneurial owner-managers of smaller corporations. They took a long-term, institutional view, investing with an eye to continuity and eschewing short-term gambles.[5] The zone of common interests had limits, however. Lenders, rather than relying on it exclusively, developed new contractual protections. Mortgage indentures, in use since the 1830s, already facilitated secured debt financing for large capital projects, railroads most importantly, solving problems of enforcement

---

[2] Ibid., at pp. 27-28, 51-52.

[3] See *Central Trust Co.* v. *Bridges*, 57 F. 753, 766 (6th Cir. 1893), modified sub. nom. *Central Trust Co.* v. *Condon*, 67 F. 84 (6th Cir. 1895); *Atchison, T. & S.F.R.R.* v. *Davis*, 34 Kan. 209, 210, 8 P. 530, 531 (1885); P. Blumberg, 'Limited Liability and Corporate Groups', 11 *J. Corp. L.* (1986) p. 573 at pp. 594, 609-611.

[4] The incorporation statutes authorized low-par and no-par common stock, permitted minimal paid-in capital and later reductions of capital, and dropped requirements for minimum debt-equity ratios. See Hurst, op. cit. n. 1, at p. 53. Legal capital rules persist in US corporate codes, in many cases retaining the same form taken in the nineteenth century. But the forms can be satisfied by a nominal fixed capital. As a practical result, the rules bar only against transfers made to shareholders of insolvent firms, tracking protection independently provided under fraudulent conveyance statutes. For a complete description of the field, see B. Manning, *Legal Capital*, 2nd edn. (Mineola, Foundation Press 1982).

[5] Hurst, op. cit. n. 1, at pp. 54-55.

and monitoring by widely dispersed bondholders.[6] The debenture indenture appeared around 1900, just after the states diluted the legal capital rules, extending the indenture form to facilitate public sales of unsecured debt by large firms. The new indentures introduced the business covenant as a more flexible security device than the real property mortgage.[7] With this innovation, long-term unsecured lending made sense for the first time in financial history.

The debenture indenture, used for public bond issues, continues to perform its original function in tandem with two close cousins developed later in the twentieth century, the note purchase agreement used in private placements of long-term debt securities[8] and the term loan agreement used in long-term bank lending. Standard forms for these contracts have changed over time, developing reactively – as bond issuers have devised ways to evade covenants, bond lawyers have responded by filling in the gaps in the next generation of contracts.[9] The mature 'full set' of covenants drawn on today appeared after World War II,[10] more as product of contracting in the private placement and bank loan markets than in the bond market. The settled practice has been disrupted only once. During the 1970s, significant covenant protection disappeared from the debenture indentures of investment-grade issuers. Holders of those bonds later suffered a negative shock due to the high-leverage restructurings of the 1980s. The debt markets thereafter regained an equilibrium footing, even as contracting practice continued to evolve.

The European Union now repeats the American experience of more than a century ago. *Centros*,[11] *Überseering*,[12] and *Inspire Art*[13] usher in mobile incorporation for small firms seeking to escape national legal capital requirements. At the same time, critical questions[14] arise respecting national legal capital rules

---

[6] See T. Banks, 'Indenture Securities and the Barkley Bill', 48 *Yale L.J.* (1939) p. 533 at p. 534. The indenture solved the enforcement problem by channeling performance rights through a trustee for the benefit of the holders of the bonds issued thereunder.

[7] R. Garrett, 'A Borrower's View of the Model Corporate Debenture Indenture Provisions', 21 *Bus. Law.* (1966) p. 675 at pp. 678-680.

[8] The modern private placement market developed in the wake of the federal securities laws and their requirement of issuer registration. See C. Rodgers, 'The Corporate Trust Indenture Project', 20 *Bus. Law.* (1965) p. 551 at p. 563.

[9] A. Dewing, *The Financial Policy of Corporations*, Vol. 1, 5th edn. (New York, Ronald 1953) pp. 228-230 and (describing the development of the standard debt covenant after 1920 in response to evasions of negative pledge clauses).

[10] See American Bar Foundation, *Commentaries on the Model Debenture Indenture Provisions* (Chicago, ABF 1971) [hereafter cited as *ABF Commentaries*]; B Graham, D. Dodd and S. Cottle, *Security Analysis*, 4th edn. (New York, McGraw-Hill 1962) pp. 332-335.

[11] ECJ, Case C-212/97 *Centros* [1999] *ECR* I-1459.

[12] ECJ, Case C-208/00 *Überseering* [2002] *ECR* I-9919.

[13] ECJ, Case C-167/01 *Inspire Art* [2003] *ECR* I-10155.

[14] See F. Kübler, 'The Rules of Capital under Pressure of the Securities Markets', in K. Hopt and E. Wymeersch, eds., *Capital Markets and Company Law* (Oxford, Oxford University

governing publicly traded firms, along with the EC directive[15] that embeds them in minimum form. Law reformers, looking to the US approach, envision a retreat to the insolvency standard.[16]

Business covenants figure in this debate.[17] For legal capital's opponents they amount to a negotiated reproach to statutory mandate. No hard-wired code can duplicate their protective reach while simultaneously holding out comparable situation sensitivity. For legal capital's defenders, business covenants are beside the point. Nothing in a protective statutory regime prevents a financial creditor from negotiating for stricter protection. The statute's beneficiaries instead are trade creditors, for whom complex financial negotiations are not cost beneficial, and involuntary creditors, who get no chance to contract at all.

No efficiency template holds out a definitive resolution to these debates. The contractarians certainly make valid points: hard-wired equity capital mandates impose costs that deter entrepreneurship; lawmakers setting capital standards face an impossible task when they try to make trade-offs against an incomplete empirical background. At the same time, however, contractarianism never carries as an absolute in corporate debtor-creditor contexts. Limited liability flatly fails to pass efficiency inspection due to its allowance for externalization of risk on involuntary creditors.[18] Some form of legal intervention accordingly is justified, and legitimate policy questions respecting creditor protection never disappear. It takes more effort to state an economic case for legal protection against opportunistic

---

Press 2003) p. 95 (emphasizing that strengthened equity markets reduce the need for creditor protective rules); J. Armour, 'Share Capital and Creditor Protection: Efficient Rules for a Modern Company Law', 63 *Modern L. Rev.* (2000) p. 355 (commending reform of UK company law). See also L. Enriques and J. Macey, 'Creditors versus Capital Formation: The Case against European Legal Capital Rules', 86 *Cornell L. Rev.* (2001) p. 1165. For the case in favor of retaining the rules on a default basis, see W. Schön, 'The Future of Legal Capital', 5 *EBOR* (2004) p. 429.

15 Second Council Directive 77/91/EEC of 13 December 1976 on coordination of safeguards which, for the protection of the interests of members and others, are required by Member States of companies within the meaning of the second paragraph of Article 58 of the Treaty, in respect of the formation of public limited liability companies and the maintenance and alteration of their capital, with a view to making such safeguards equivalent, *OJ* 1997 L 26/1.

16 See J. Rickford, ed., 'Reforming Capital: Report of the Interdisciplinary Group on Capital Maintenance', 15 *European Business Law Review* (2004) p. 919. See also Proposal for a Directive of the European Parliament and of the Council amending Council Directive 77/91/EEC, as regards the formation of public limited liability companies and the maintenance and alteration of their capital of 21 September 2004, COM (2004) 730 final.

17 Compare Armour, loc. cit. n. 14, at pp. 373-375, with Schön, loc. cit. n. 14, at p. 441.

18 See H. Hansman and R. Kraakman, 'Toward Unlimited Shareholder Liability for Corporate Torts', 100 *Yale L. J.* (1991) p. 1879.

exploitation of unprotected voluntary creditors, but plausible cases have been made.[19]

This article looks at the US experience with contractual protection of financial creditors toward the end of gauging the robustness of the contractual alternative. The US experience is indeed pertinent for a Europe contemplating retreat from creditor protection in law. For more than a century, borrowers and lenders in the United States have contracted against a minimal legal background that imposes the burden of protection on the lender. A working, constantly updated, set of contractual protections has emerged in response. Actual use of available contractual technology varies widely, however. This article reviews the usage pattern.

Three points emerge. First, contracting practice correlates directly with the level of risk. A borrower's incentive to externalize at its lenders' expense increases with the prospect of financial distress. The credit markets sort borrowers according to the degree of that risk, imposing substantial constraints on the borrowers with the most dangerous incentives. So salient is the prospect of opportunism on the part of a high-risk borrower that freely contracting actors can be counted on to cut that borrower little slack, at least where the size of the loan makes complex contracting cost beneficial.

Second, the contracting practice is sticky and lumpy, never quite managing to conform to the predictions of first generation agency theory. Levels of protection vary with institutional contexts, roughly paralleling well-known patterns of shareholder governance. Numbers count. Given a small number of institutional creditors, contracting can work the way it works in close corporations, providing something approaching full protection against agency costs. With debt, such substantial protection requires an exhaustive contract, and such an *ex ante* complete contract proves feasible only in a relational context conducive to ongoing renegotiation over time due to small numbers of actors operating under reputational constraints. The public bond markets do not hold out such a process context. They accordingly shut out the riskiest borrowers. The larger, less risky firms that do gain access to the bond markets borrow under contracts offering incomplete protection, with the level of protection roughly correlating to the borrower's risk level. Bondholders, like public shareholders, are left to rely on monitoring, exit, and diversification in dealing with agency costs. This has worked reasonably well in practice, subject to the exception of event risk. Event risk is the bond market's term for leveraged restructuring and other cases where a highly rated bond issuer changes its risk profile for governance reasons unrelated

---

[19] See, e.g., L. Bebchuk and J. Fried, 'The Uneasy Case for the Priority of Secured Claims in Bankruptcy', 105 *Yale L.J.* (1996) p. 857 (contending that the US Bankruptcy Code's provision of full priority to secured claims can result in overall losses due to debtor incentives to create inefficient security interests favoring financial creditors at the expense of non-consenting tort and contract creditors).

to the fundamentals of its business. Here the bond markets have thrashed about reactively looking for a stable solution for close to two decades, finally settling on across-the-board contractual protection only in recent years.

Third, no one knows what an optimal debt contract looks like. Any good bond lawyer knows how to draft a state of the art set of protections based on the past record of opportunistic debtor behavior. Borrowers and lenders negotiate against the background of that state of the art menu of protections, trading off the borrower's interest in business flexibility against the lender's interest in financial security. The practice is efficient in the sense that the contract fixes the trade and the market prices it. The more demanding task of explaining why each variation in the practice represents a superior trade-off of risk and return remains largely unperformed. This is not surprising. The theoretical economics of optimal capital structure also have yet to yield a robust efficiency prescription.[20]

The part by part analysis proceeds as follows. Part 2 describes the agency costs of debt, the economics describing borrower incentives to act in derogation of lender interests. Part 3 sets out the contractual response to agency costs, the 'full set' of business covenants. Part 4 describes the evolution of real world contracting, focusing on variations in levels of covenant protection in different markets for long-term credit. Part 5 describes the role business covenants play in distress situations, highlighting process problems that inhibit their efficient evolution.

2. The Economic Framework: Conflicts of Interest and Costly Contracting

Economic analysis of covenants still follows from foundational studies by Michael Jensen and William Meckling,[21] Clifford Smith and Jerold Warner,[22] and Stewart Myers.[23] These describe four agency costs of debt – claim dilution, underinvestment, asset withdrawal, and asset substitution.[24]

---

20 See A. Reisz and K. John, *Temporal Resolution of Uncertainty, the Investment Policy of Levered Firms, and Corporate Debt Yields*, working paper (2002) p. 28, available at: <http://ssrn.com/abstract=303339> (questioning whether an optimal capital structure can be derived at all in the context of presenting a model of optimal debt contracting under long-term uncertainty respecting the outcome of the firm's investments).

21 M. Jensen and W. Meckling, 'Theory of the Firm: Managerial Behavior, Agency Costs, and Capital Structure', 3 *J. Fin. Econ.* (1976) p. 305.

22 C. Smith and J. Warner, 'On Financial Contracting: An Analysis of Bond Covenants', 7 *J. Fin. Econ.* (1979) p. 117.

23 S. Myers, 'Determinants of Corporate Borrowing', 5 *J. Fin. Econ.* (1977) p. 147.

24 In the literature, the concept of 'asset substitution' encompasses the concept of 'asset withdrawal' used here.

2.1 Claim dilution

Claim dilution concerns the negative impact of subsequent borrowing on the value of an earlier loan. Assume that Firm A is worth 100 and has borrowed 50 from Lender 1 pursuant to an unsecured loan. The loan was priced on the assumption of no further borrowing by Firm A but contains no explicit restrictions. Firm A then borrows 35 from Lender 2 and invests the proceeds in a project that turns out to be worthless. Firm A emerges 85 percent levered. The interest rate on the second borrowing will reflect that possibility, compensating Lender 2, while the interest rate on the first borrowing does not compensate Lender 1. Lender 1's investment declines in value, with the benefits of the decrease accruing to Firm A and Lender 2. Lender 1 is even worse off if Lender 2 makes a loan secured by assets worth 35. So long as the obligation to Lender 2 remains outstanding, the encumbered assets will not be available to satisfy Lender 1. Accordingly, Lender 1 must look for repayment to an asset base of 65 rather than the base of 100 envisaged at the time of the loan.

More generally, lenders, as fixed return claimants, can be injured by an increase in the amount of equal or prior claims in the borrower's capital structure. At the same time, borrowers have high-powered incentives to continue to borrow. Under the pecking order theory of finance, retained earnings are the cheapest source of finance, then debt, and, finally, new equity.[25] Large new projects accordingly tend to mean an increase in debt claims. An increase in the level of debt can benefit the borrower's equity holders even in the absence of a new project. The new loan's proceeds can be siphoned out as a dividend, with the added claims increasing the borrower's leverage, turning it into a higher-risk, higher-return investment. Because the fixed return lender receives no extra compensation for that higher risk, the transaction transfers wealth from the lender to the borrower's equity holders.

If we change the facts of the hypothesis and price the first loan to reflect the possibility of claim dilution, there arises a basis for trade. Assume that Firm A is content to continue to finance all projects on a 50-50 debt/equity basis. A restriction on future borrowing, tied to a 50-50 debt/equity ratio, lowers the cost of the first loan without unduly inhibiting Firm A's freedom of action. The trade illustrates the costly contracting hypothesis of Smith and Warner. This assumes that the borrower bears the entire projected agency cost of a given issue of debt when the parties set the interest rate. It follows that the borrower's interest in minimizing its borrowing cost leads it to offer covenants that restrict its ability to take actions that benefit its shareholders while injuring its lenders' interests. The parameters of the restrictions offered follow from the borrower's cost-benefit

---

[25] See S. Myers, 'Capital Structure', 15 *J. Econ. Perspectives* (2001) p. 81 at pp. 91-93.

calculation – Firm A trades off the cost of future constraints on its freedom of action against the present benefit of a lower cost of borrowing.

2.2 Asset withdrawal and underinvestment

Assume now that Firm A, with assets worth 100 and debt claims of 85, owns asset *x*, valued at 10. Firm A sells *x* to Firm B for 10 in cash, and then declares and distributes to its shareholders a dividend of 10. Because Firm A retains a net worth of 5 (and remains solvent on a going concern basis), the dividend is not a fraudulent conveyance. This asset withdrawal[26] nonetheless materially injures the interests of Lenders 1 and 2 by reducing Firm A's net worth from 15 to 5. A covenant that blocks the sale of asset *x* would enhance the positions of Lenders 1 and 2. But it would not protect them from all forms of asset withdrawal. Firm A might in the alternative liquidate an asset over time, directing the proceeds to its shareholders as received. Accordingly, Lenders 1 and 2 also need a covenant that prevents Firm A from transferring assets to its shareholders, by dividend or otherwise.

Claim dilution and asset withdrawal primarily concern wealth transfers from lenders to equity holders. Underinvestment has deeper implications for economic welfare. Assume that Firm A continues to decline in value, so that it now is worth 75 as against debt claims of 85. It has the opportunity to invest in project *k*. Project *k* is worth 10. Firm A has no other available investment opportunities. Firm A will not make the investment, assuming an identity of interests among its managers and shareholders. From the point of view of Firm A's equity, project *k* is worthless because its benefits redound entirely to Lenders 1 and 2. Given limited liability, the equity might as well walk away. Alternatively, viewing the debtor-creditor relationship as an option in the equity to repurchase the firm from the debt at maturity, the shareholders of Firm A have an out of the money option to buy Firm A back from Lenders 1 and 2 for 85. They have an incentive to invest in positive net present value (NPV) projects only to the extent the option is projected to expire in the money net of the investment. Firm A might pass up the investment even if project *k* is worth 15, depending on whether it deems the effort necessary to realize the project's value to be cost-beneficial for a return of 5.[27] The welfare cost stems from the decision to forego the investment. The lenders lose because the underinvestment heightens the risk of default, and, to the extent that no other firm is situated to pick up the opportunity, society as a whole also loses. A covenant blocking dividend payments addresses the problem indirectly,

---

[26] See D. Fischel, 'The Economics of Lender Liability', 99 *Yale L.J.* (1989) p. 131 at pp. 134-135.

[27] Myers, loc. cit. n. 23, at pp. 164-165.

by leaving Firm A no alternative other than reinvestment for its free liquid assets. Drafting a contract term that directly forces Firm A to invest in project *k* will turn out to be problematic, however.

2.3 Asset substitution and risky investment

To see the asset substitution problem, assume once again that Firm A is worth 75 as against debt claims of 85. Firm A owns asset *y*, and a potential buyer offers to buy *y* for 20 in cash. If Firm A liquidates *y* it can either pay the 20 to its lenders or invest in *z*. Asset *z* has an expected value of 20, based on the following projection: (a) a 10 percent chance that *z* turns out to be worth 200, and (b) a 90 percent chance that *z* turns out to be worthless. If the expected value of 20 is discounted to reflect the high risk of a zero return, the NPV of *z* turns out to be less than 20. It nonetheless is rational for Firm A to make the investment. If the long shot comes in, Firm A is worth 255; if the investment is worthless, Lenders 1 and 2 bear the cost of the loss. Alternatively, once again viewing the debtor-creditor relationship as an option, the shareholders of Firm A have an out of the money option to buy A back from Lenders 1 and 2 for 85. Viewed as a long holding, investment *z* is irrational due to its negative net present value. But if the equity is viewed from an option holder's point of view, *z* makes the option more valuable by increasing the volatility of the underlying asset's returns. The shareholders thus have an incentive to make an investment that decreases economic welfare, with the cost falling on the firm's lenders.

This asset substitution problem combines two actions by Firm A – the sale of asset *y* and the investment in risky asset *z*. The asset withdrawal problem already has demonstrated the value of a contract term blocking large asset sales. The underinvestment problem suggested a need for a contractual means to force Firm A to make a valuable investment for the benefit of its lenders. Now we see the need for a term that prevents Firm A from making a suboptimally risky investment.

2.4 Distress, prosperity, and the debt-equity conflict of interest

Debt-equity conflicts of interest intensify as leverage increases and, with it, the prospect of default on the debt. New borrowing need not be implicated – leverage also increases if the firm's value falls relative to its existing debt. Either way, rising leverage increases the probability that the lenders take a disproportionate share of the returns of new investment, increasing the possibility of underinvestment,[28] simultaneously magnifying the incentive to make high-risk investments at

[28] See Z. Bodie and R. Taggart, 'Future Investment and the Value of the Call Provision on a Bond', 33 *J. Fin.* (1978) p. 1187.

the lenders' expense.[29] High leverage also increases the prospect of payment default, further decreasing the debt's value. Extreme financial distress means bankruptcy, and bankruptcy entails deadweight costs[30] that independently decrease the value of the firm. The agency costs of debt, then, are the costs of financial distress.

Now consider the converse scenario: Firm A borrows from Lenders 1 and 2 and prospers. Assume that the debt contracts contain covenants that (a) restrict any future borrowing by Firm A; (b) restrict dividends and share repurchases to a small percentage of annual net earnings; and (c) block substantial asset sales. At the time of Lender 2's loan, Firm A has assets of 135 and debt of 85, leaving an 'equity cushion' of 50. The purpose of the covenants is to lock in the equity cushion as a source of value available to pay the loans. Five years later, Firm A's assets are 300 and its debt is still 85. As the equity cushion becomes larger, the loans become less risky, and, all other things being equal, increase in value. More generally, with a full set of covenants and a successful borrower, the lender's position becomes more secure over time. This reverses the wealth transfer – now the lenders gain at the shareholders' expense. Firm A can draft its debt contracts to protect its equity from this result. The covenants can be drafted so as to condition constraints on stated financial conditions, so that the restraints relax as Firm A becomes more valuable. Alternatively, Firm A can reserve a power to prepay ('call') the principal amount of the loan.

3. THE FULL SET OF COVENANTS

3.1 **Affirmative and negative**

In US practice,[31] business covenants make a formal distinction between affirmative promises and negative promises. Affirmative covenants go only to ministerial

---

29 See Jensen and Meckling, loc. cit. n. 21, at p. 342 (agency costs of debt include opportunity wealth loss caused by the effect of debt on investment decisions and bankruptcy costs).

30 See, e.g., L. Weiss, 'Bankruptcy Resolution: Direct Costs and Violation of Priority Claims', 27 *J. Fin. Econ.* (1990) p. 285 (showing direct costs as 3 to 7 percent of firm value); J. Warner, 'Bankruptcy Costs: Some Evidence', 32 *J. Fin.* (1977) p. 337 at p. 343 (studying eleven railroad bankruptcies between 1930 and 1955 and concluding that a bankruptcy costs an average of 2.5 percent of firm value during the three years preceding the bankruptcy).

31 For legal commentaries on business covenants, see *ABF Commentaries*, op. cit. n. 10; R. Nassberg, *The Lender's Handbook* (Philadelphia, ALI 1986); R. Lloyd, 'Financial Covenants in Commercial Loan Documentation: Uses and Limitations', 58 *Tenn. L. Rev.* (1991) p. 335; M. McDaniel, 'Are Negative Pledge Clauses in Public Debt Issues Obsolete?' 39 *Bus. Law.* (1983) p. 867; D. Simpson, 'The Drafting of Loan Agreements: A Borrower's Viewpoint', 28 *Bus. Law.* (1973) p. 1161.

matters. For example, the borrower in a private placement or bank term loan will affirmatively promise to make periodic informational reports. It also will make positive promises to comply with law, maintain its franchises, insure and maintain its properties, and pay all properly assessed taxes. While all of these promises imply costs,[32] none of them materially constrains management's discretion to operate the business. In contrast, covenants that protect the lender from claim dilution, asset withdrawal, underinvestment, and asset substitution can materially constrain the business judgments of the borrower's managers. These terms invariably are phrased in the negative.

Limited liability is the reason. Under US corporate law, when a creditor, acting in that capacity, exercises control power over the firm, it loses its limited liability status. If a managing creditor's business decisions work out badly, it can be held personally liable to other creditors or even to the stockholders.[33] Lenders 1 and 2, accordingly, will not reserve a contractual power to direct Firm A to invest in project *k*. If they are careful, they will not even extract affirmative promises from Firm A to invest the proceeds of their loans in the projects outlined by Firm A during negotiations. Firm A, instead of making a promise in the debt contract respecting the project, will formally represent its present intent to make the investment. Firm A, however, will not be situated so as meaningfully to represent its present intentions concerning future business decisions. At the same time, liability risk constrains the lenders from seeking direct control over Firm A's future business decisions. They accordingly seek to influence Firm A's future conduct indirectly, by specifying default events *ex ante* in negative covenants. Exercise of such indirect control presupposes contractable subject matter. Promises not to borrow, pay dividends, or sell assets all fall into this category. Advance specification respecting investment policy proves more difficult.

The longer the list of prohibited outcomes, the stronger the control. At some point the magnitude of control becomes so great as to give the lender effective

---

32 The more costly promises on the list will be negotiable accordingly. See *ABF Commentaries*, op. cit. n. 10, at pp. 312-313.

33 The classic case, *Martin* v. *Peyton*, 246 N.Y. 213, 158 N.E. 77 (1927), concerns a loan to a partnership. The liability of bank lenders to small businesses is the subject of leading cases in recent decades. See, e.g., *K.M.C. Co.* v. *Irving Trust Co.*, 757 F. 2d 752 (6th Cir. 1985); *State Nat'l Bank of El Paso* v. *Farah Mfg. Co.*, 678 Sw. 2d 661 (Tex. Ct. App. 1984). See generally M. Douglas-Hamilton, 'Creditor Liabilities Resulting from Improper Interference with the Management of a Financially Troubled Debtor', 31 *Bus. Law.* (1975) p. 343. There is a way to deflect this risk for a creditor with control power. If the creditor is a human being it forms a wholly-owned shell corporation or limited liability company to hold the debt; if the creditor is a corporation, it forms a shell wholly-owned subsidiary. Both steps are costly, and there remains a residual risk of veil piercing. A creditor simultaneously holding a controlling block of shares puts the shares into a voting trust, divesting itself of control by delegating discretion respecting the vote to an independent trustee.

control of the firm. This invites a substance over form argument by an objecting equity holder seeking to make out a case of lender liability. Courts, however, respect the formal distinction, and bond lawyers proceed with confidence in the negative framework.

3.2 Negative covenants

The following sections outline the 'full set' of negative covenants.

3.2.1 *Restrictions on debt*

Debt covenants protect against claim dilution by regulating the incurrence of new debt, allowing it when justified by the firm's financial condition. They tend to set out ratios of net tangible assets to total debt and ratios of earnings available to pay debt to debt service costs,[34] permitting new debt to be incurred to the extent that the tests are met. The targeted transactions are borrowings of money. Other transactions booked on the balance sheet's liability side, trade credit most importantly, are not customarily covered. On the other hand, debt covenants tend to restrict transactions that lenders view as the functional equivalent of borrowing, such as financial leases and the guaranties of the obligations of others. Debt covenants also can make structural distinctions between short-term borrowing and long-term debt and between subordinated and unsubordinated debt. For example, the borrowing window can be made larger for new borrowing subordinated to the loan covered by the covenant.

Debt covenants protect the lender from an increase in the number of claims on the equity cushion and the risk of insolvency. They also indirectly discourage risky investments – risky debt and risky investments tend to be concomitants. The constraints are unlikely to be absolute, however. Assuming a healthy borrower with prospects for growth, the debt covenant protects the borrower's freedom of action by restricting and regulating new debt incurrence rather than prohibiting it absolutely. The window of freedom also can hold out an incidental benefit for

---

34 Asset-based tests are variously stated. For example, the tangible net worth may substitute for net tangible assets, and funded debt may substitute for indebtedness. Borrowings for the purpose of paying down debt of the same or higher priority often are permitted explicitly. See R. Nash, J. Netter, and A. Poulsen, 'Determinants of Contractual Relations between Shareholders and Bondholders: Investment Opportunities and Restrictive Covenants', 9 *J. Corp. Fin.* (2003) p. 201 at p. 215.

These accounting-based tests will be based on results reported under US Generally Accepted Accounting Principles (GAAP), but the contract often modifies GAAP results. For example, asset-based tests may require the borrower to deduct intangible assets booked on its balance sheet's left side, producing ratios of 'hard' assets to total liabilities.

existing lenders. Additional debt can provide the borrower with additional capital for good projects the returns on which make existing lenders more secure. Put differently, flexibility respecting additional debt ameliorates the underinvestment problem.

The regime of flexibility may not, however, extend so far as to permit borrowing by subsidiary companies. To see why not, hypothesize a firm made up of two operating companies, Subsidiary 1 and Subsidiary 2, each 100 percent owned by a holding company, HC. HC is the borrower on a loan with Lender HC under a debt contract that restricts borrowing by HC but not by Subsidiaries 1 and 2. HC causes Subsidiary 1 to borrow heavily from Lender S. Because Subsidiary 1 is an entity separate from HC, HC is not a party to the debt contract with Lender S. Subsidiary 1 becomes insolvent and goes into bankruptcy reorganization. Although Subsidiary 2 remains profitable, HC goes into default on its debt and is itself forced into reorganization. When the smoke clears, Lender HC will be subordinated to Lender S so far as concerns the proceeds of Subsidiary 1's bankruptcy proceeding. Lender HC has a claim only on the assets of HC, and HC can establish a claim in Subsidiary 1's bankruptcy only in its capacity as Subsidiary 1's equity claimant. As an equity claimant, it is subordinated to Lender S. Even if Lender HC emerges from HC's bankruptcy holding HC's entire value, to the extent that Lender S's claim exceeds the value of Subsidiary 1's assets and wipes out HC's equity, Lender HC receives no proceeds from Subsidiary 1. A properly drafted debt covenant solves the problem: HC must promise not to permit its subsidiaries to borrow except from HC. HC's freedom of action is not thereby drastically constrained. If it wishes to procure debt financing for Subsidiary 1, it first borrows in its own name and then reloans the proceeds to Subsidiary 1. This way the borrowing is tested under HC's own debt covenant, and, in the event Subsidiary 1 becomes insolvent, the sole senior claimant is HC, preserving HC's senior position respecting Subsidiary 1's assets.

Extending the point, Lender HC also benefits from a covenant that prevents sales of additional equity to third parties by Subsidiaries 1 and 2. Direct equity financing by the subsidiaries makes HC, and hence its lenders, *pari passu* claimants to the subsidiaries' assets with the new shareholders. From Lender HC's point of view, new equity financing for the HC group should be accomplished directly through an equity offering by HC. As to these new equity holders, Lender HC is completely senior. If HC wants to invest the proceeds of such an equity financing in Subsidiary 1, it can siphon the capital downward either by taking additional subsidiary stock or making an intercompany loan.

3.2.2 *Restrictions on prior claims*

Covenants restricting mortgages and liens are the second principal protection against claim dilution. Unsecured creditors can look only to the borrower's unencumbered property; to the extent the property is subject to mortgages, security interests, or other liens, it is not available to pay their claims in liquidation. Secured creditors, moreover, are accorded priority in bankruptcy reorganization to the extent of the value of the property covered by their liens. Contracts governing unsecured debt accordingly tend to restrict the creation of new liens. There are two modes of drafting the restriction. The first imposes a direct and sweeping prohibition, subject to negotiated exceptions. Exceptions are most likely to be granted for purchase money mortgages and security interests. Such a rigid drafting technique is more likely to be employed in a private placement or bank term loan than in a public bond offering. The second mode of approach is the 'negative pledge' covenant. This comparatively simple provision states that no lien will be created unless the lien also equally and ratably secures the debt benefited by the provision. This version tends to show up in indentures covering public bond issues.[35]

Separate sale and leaseback prohibitions also will be found in many debt contracts. Sale and leaseback transactions take assets presently owned by the borrower and available to pay the lender and transfer title to them to a third party, with the seller-borrower emerging holding a lease on the sold premises with the buyer as lessor. Lenders view such a transaction as an extreme form of secured borrowing on the asset. The borrower sells a factory and pockets the sale price, even as the simultaneous lease back lets it leave its existing facility in place. The purchaser of the property holds a superior title to the property, which will not be available for inclusion in the estate in a borrower bankruptcy. To see the depth of a lender's aversion to such a transaction, compare a mortgage loan secured by the same factory. With a mortgage, the borrower builds up equity in the property as it pays the loan over time, further benefiting to the extent the property appreciates in value. With the sale/leaseback, the borrower starts out with a 100 percent equity interest in the property, which is transferred away. It thereafter makes lease payments over time, ending up with nothing at the lease's expiration. Furthermore, the funds generated by the sale readily can be redirected to investment in riskier assets, or, alternatively, withdrawn from the firm's asset base and distributed to its shareholders. Sale/leasebacks, in short, are just the sort of transactions

---

[35] See C. Bjerre, 'Secured Transactions Inside Out: Negative Pledge Covenants, Property, and Perfection', 84 *Cornell L. Rev.* (1999) p. 305. A negative pledge does not necessarily disable a subsequent secured loan. Suppose Firm A has assets worth 100. Debt claims of Lender 1, covered by a negative pledge clause, total 15. Firm A wishes to borrow an additional 15 from Lender 2 on a secured basis. All of its 100 of assets are unencumbered. Firm A can borrow from Lender 2 on a secured basis so long as Lender 1 also is secured by the lien. The transaction will satisfy Lender 2 so long as the lien covers property worth 30, thereby fully securing Lenders 1 and 2.

entered into by cash-strapped firms – this single transaction can implicate claim dilution, asset withdrawal, asset substitution, and risky investment.

3.2.3 *Restrictions on dividends and other payments to shareholders*

These covenants restrict transfers of corporate assets to shareholders, whether by way of a dividend or a redemption or repurchase of outstanding stock. The restriction typically operates by reference to the borrower's profitability: the covenant sets a base date, usually at or near the time of the loan, and permits dividends and redemptions only to the extent of cumulative earnings after that date, and then only up to a given percentage or amount. A fixed sum (the 'dip') may be added to the cumulative sum of earnings, increasing the total allowed sum for distributions. In addition, credit might be given for the proceeds of the sales of new equity. Bank loans can include more finally tailored variations on the theme, specifying maximum dividend amounts for given periods, limiting the frequency of dividends, and conditioning payments on stated tests such as credit ratings and financial ratios.[36] Finally, dividend covenants can be tied to other covenants in the full set – the dividend can be conditioned on the existence of room to borrow under the debt covenant and compliance with all covenants *ex post* the dividend.

The covenant serves multiple purposes. First, it prevents asset withdrawals that injure the lender's interest by locking in the firm assets at least equal in amount to those present at the time of the loan. Second, the covenant enhances the lender's position during the term of the loan. For example, if the permitted distribution amount grows as a function of 50 percent of annual earnings, then half of the incremental growth of the asset base remains contained in the borrower entity, making the loan more secure and enhancing its value. Finally, the covenant discourages underinvestment. As we have seen, as the borrower declines in value, at some point new investment redounds only to its lenders' benefit. Should such a declining business be generating free cash flow, whether from operations or as the result of disinvestment, a dividend amounts to the funds' best use from the shareholders' point of view. The covenant blocks the escape route, forcing the borrower to invest the funds for the lenders' benefit.

Such projects could hold out negative NPVs. From an equity holder's point of view, a project is suboptimal if it returns less than the cost of equity capital; under basic financial economics, funds should be paid out to the shareholders absent investments returning more than the cost of equity capital. Things look very different from a lender's point of view, however. As between a payout to shareholders and reinvestment, any investment yielding a positive cash return, no

---

[36] M. Bradley and M. Roberts, *The Structure and Pricing of Corporate Debt Covenants*, working paper (2004) p. 12, available at: <http://ssrn.com/abstract=466240>.

matter how low, is superior. Even a zero return investment enhances the asset base available to pay the debt. Despite this, the dividend covenant holds out only a minimal threat to economic welfare. So long as the loan remains outstanding, the borrower without positive investment projects can always direct its free cash flows to repayment of the loan's principal amount. In any event, as with the debt covenant, the typical dividend covenant stops well short of absolute prohibition.

Of course, only small subset of mature US firms pays regular dividends.[37] Lenders need the covenant nonetheless. Circumstances easily can change over a loan's ten or fifteen-year term so as to favor a shareholder distribution. Moreover, a distribution need not entail the implicit commitment of a regular dividend. For example, if the firm generates free cash flow in the face of a diminishing set of new investments, a program of open market stock repurchases can pump out the money so as to suit the interests of both outside shareholders and managers benefited by equity incentive plans.

3.2.4 *Restrictions on mergers and sales of assets*

A merger with another operating company can injure a lender even though the surviving corporation is a larger firm. Claim dilution can follow if the merger partner is highly levered. Alternatively, the merger partner could have a riskier business so that the merger effects a detrimental investment policy shift. A sale of all or substantially all of the borrower's assets can raise the same problems in aggravated form – such a transaction literally separates the assets supporting the loan from the corporate entity that entered into the debt contract; absent covenant protection, the lender can be left looking to a shell entity for satisfaction. In contrast, a merger into a shell acquisition subsidiary organized by a conservatively managed acquiring firm may be a matter of indifference or benefit to the lender.

Covenants dealing with prospective mergers and acquisitions range from very permissive to very strict. With public bond issues, mergers and sales of all or substantially all assets may be permitted subject to two conditions: the purchasing firm (a) must be organized within the United States, eliminating the possibility of an offshore bankruptcy proceeding, and (b) must formally assume the debt. Private placements and bank term loans likely will impose additional constraints – a transaction will be permitted only so long as the survivor or purchaser has room to borrow under the debt covenant and can demonstrate compliance with every other covenant *ex post* the closing of the merger. There are other available modes of regulating these transactions. For example, they may be permitted subject to a right of redemption in the lender.

---

37 W. Bratton, 'The New Dividend Puzzle', 93 *Geo. L. J.* (2005) p. 845 at pp. 849-852.

Piecemeal sales of assets hold out problems of asset withdrawal and risky investment policy. Any sale of producing assets raises questions respecting the adequacy of the sale price and the reinvestment of the proceeds. In an extreme case, an asset sale can imply complete redirection of the business. For example, a firm could sell off pieces of itself over a period of time and reinvest the proceeds in a riskier line of business. Covenants regulating these transactions tend to put a book value or fair value cap on the aggregate annual permissible saleable assets, along with a fair value standard to govern the terms of permitted sales.

Borrowers will likely see asset sale constraints as significant and undesirable impairments of their freedom of action. Today's managers actively trade subsidiaries and divisions in a market for going concern assets. They also enjoy increased access to liquidity. Consider a standard asset securitization – the firm sells its accounts receivable for cash to an off balance sheet special purpose entity, the equity of which is held by third parties. Such a transaction falls within the scope of a traditional covenant barring piecemeal asset sales. Whether such a transaction negatively implicates a legitimate interest of a lender depends on the case. On the one hand, liquidation of receivables could advance the borrower's investment program, benefiting the lender. In the alternative, the proceeds could be devoted to riskier investments or open market stock repurchases.

3.2.5 *Restrictions on investments*

A debt contract easily can ameliorate the problems of asset substitution and risky investment by barring sales of assets in excess of, say, 10 percent of net worth per year. It is more difficult for a debt contract to take the next step of directing the use of proceeds of particular asset sale to a particular project viewed with favor by the lender. The limited liability constraint prevents the dictation of positive instructions. Sets of negative instructions drafted in advance are ill-suited as substitutes for sound investment choices. At best, the drafter can craft an instruction keyed to positive net present value projects, or an instruction keyed to a specified hurdle rate or a hurdle rate calculation. But the factors in question present verification problems and therefore would be expensive to monitor.[38] The interests of both parties thus signal a strategy of indirect constraint of investment policy.

Debt contracts accordingly seek to constrain risky investment by blocking off definable and speculative investment alternatives. The covenants target investments in liquid and intangible assets, forcing the borrower to take its free cash flow to safe, short-term investments such as treasury securities or certificates of deposit, and prohibiting outlets like portfolios of common stocks and futures

[38] See Myers, loc. cit. n. 23, at pp. 156-158; Smith and Warner, loc. cit. n. 22, at p. 153.

contracts. In effect, the borrower is forced to devote its capital to its going concern business. A companion covenant will foreclose resort to alternative lines of business by requiring the borrower to stay in its present line of business.

These two covenants, taken together with the covenant barring asset sales, effectively prevent asset substitution and risky investment. They would, for example, prevent a borrower dissatisfied with the return on its present line of business from changing the profile of its going concern by acquiring a high-tech, high-risk subsidiary firm. They also would prevent a borrower in distress from liquidating going concern assets and putting the proceeds into high-risk, high-return financial assets. Taken together with the dividend covenant, the investment covenants also address the underinvestment problem. The investment covenant restricts the set of available investments for the borrower's free cash flow, while the dividend covenant blocks the payment of the free cash flow to the shareholders. Given spare cash and no attractive reinvestment opportunities in the going concern, the borrower's best returns on free capital may come from prepayment of the loan.

Managers are especially likely to resist restriction of discretion to make investments. Accordingly, these covenants are likely to appear only in private placements and bank loans in which the lender has substantial bargaining power.

3.2.6 *Early warning covenants*

Recall that the agency costs of debt are the costs of financial distress. When distress looms, lenders can benefit from an occasion for contract renegotiation. Toward the end of opening such a zone of freedom of action for the lender, some debt contracts contain financial maintenance tests. These tend to set a minimum level of net worth (assets minus liabilities), either as a dollar amount or a ratio. A net worth test establishes the smallest equity cushion that the lender must tolerate. Failure to meet the test functions as an early warning of distress. Such a borrower must either raise equity capital, go into default, or persuade the lender to waive the default. Toward the same end, a covenant may set a minimum ratio of cash flow to current payments of interest and principal on debt. Some contracts also include tests of working capital (current assets minus current liabilities), either as a dollar amount or as a ratio. Here, failure to meet the test gives the lender an early warning of a liquidity crisis.

The lender may profit little if it takes the occasion of a violation of one of these covenants to exercise its rights in full by declaring an event of default and accelerating the loan. Acceleration as practical matter forces the borrower to make a defensive bankruptcy filing. Bankruptcy entails not only deadweight costs but uncertainties respecting proceeds available for classes of unsecured lenders. The value of early warning covenants more likely lies in negotiation. The lender may be able to trade a waiver of the default for enhanced contract rights – stricter covenants, a higher interest rate, or an unscheduled prepayment.[39] Without the covenant, the lender does not necessarily have a basis on which to force a distressed borrower to enter into a conversation, much less to improve its standing, even as better protected interest holders may take the occasion to impose demands, perhaps extracting preferential payments.

3.2.7 *The prepayment alternative*

Shorter-term loans by banks commonly employ an alternative means to the end of protecting against claim dilution and asset substitution. Under these, a subsequent borrowing, equity offering, or asset sale triggers a duty to pay down all or part of the loan.[40] The provisions, termed 'sweeps', tie the magnitude of the triggering event to a percentage of the loan to be paid down – for example, an asset sale exceeding a stated amount or percentage of net assets triggers a duty to pay down 50 percent of the loan. Note that in the case of a sweep covering subsequent borrowing or equity issuance, the provision signals that both the bank and the borrower see the loan as an interim feature of the borrower's capital structure – the deal contemplates that the subsequent financing takes out the bank. In contrast, an asset sale sweep plays the more conventional agency cost control function. Note finally that a prepayment also can be achieved under a conventional covenant – the lender waives the covenant in exchange for a negotiated prepayment out of the proceeds of the asset sale. The difference is that under a conventional covenant the result obtains only as the outcome of a renegotiation, whereas under a sweep it follows as a matter of right.

3.3 **Event risk**

Leveraged restructuring holds out an instructive test of the efficacy of the full set of business covenants. Under the textbook 'management buyout' or 'going private' transaction, a financial promoter joins with the top managers of a publicly traded company (the 'target' firm) to borrow funds to purchase the target from its shareholders at a premium over the market price of the stock. Critically, the target's own assets provide the borrowing base. The means to the end is a merger of the target into a shell corporation organized by the promoters. The merger pays the target shareholders cash, with the loans providing the cash closing simultaneously with the merger, so that the surviving entity that serves as

---

[39] For empirical studies of negotiations in the wake of early earning default, see M. Beneish and E. Press, 'Costs of Technical Violation of Accounting-Based Debt Covenants', 68 *Accounting Rev.* (1993) p. 233; K. Chen and K. Wei, 'Creditors' Decisions to Waive Violations of Accounting-Based Debt Covenants', 68 *Accounting Rev.* (1993) p. 218.

[40] See Bradley and Roberts, op. cit. n. 36, at p. 11.

the obligor on the loans possesses the target's assets. The surviving entity emerges privately held and highly levered. The 1980s 'bust-up' hostile tender offer proceeded on the same economics. The hostile offeror, a shell entity without producing assets of its own, made a cash tender offer for the shares of the target. It financed the tender offer with debt, simultaneously closing the tender offer, the loans, and the merger of the target into the acquisition shell.

Given a full set of covenants, neither transaction can close without the occurrence of an event of default. The massive borrowing needed to take out the common stockholders violates the debt covenant. A merger covenant conditioning the existence of room to borrow under the debt covenant *ex post* the closing of the merger independently blocks the deal. Closing the deal accordingly means prepaying all covenant-protected loans. That by itself does not necessarily foreclose the transaction – new borrowing can fund the prepayment of old borrowing in addition to funding the merger consideration paid to the exiting public shareholders. At the margin, sums diverted to old debt reduce the premium paid to the shareholders.

Large US corporations experienced a wave of leveraged restructurings between 1984 and 1989. Hostile tender offers triggered the wave, with defensive management buyout transactions occurring in response and increasing the number of transactions. Both caused considerable dislocation in the bond market. Unfortunately for the bondholders, by 1984 trust indentures governing the long-term unsecured debt of investment-grade issuers[41] no longer contained full sets of covenants. Since the mid-1970s, new public, unsecured debt of large industrials had tended to contain only negative pledge and sale-leaseback covenants. Debt and dividend covenants had disappeared, surviving to restrain only smaller, non-investment-grade issuers.[42]

---

[41] Issuers pay two firms, Moody's and Standard & Poor's to rate their debt for creditworthiness. The firms assess the likelihood of default and do not cover the risk of changes in interest rates. Under Moody's rating system, 'high grade' is AAA and AA; 'medium grade' is A and BAA; 'junk' is BA and B; CAA and CA are lower still; C is in default. A 1, 2 or 3, added to a Moody's rating functions like a plus or a minus, with a 1 being a plus. Standard & Poor's rates between AAA and D (default). Junk is below BBB.

[42] Smith and Warner's survey of 87 bonds issued between 1974 and 1975 showed that 90.8 percent contained debt covenants, 23 percent contained dividend covenants, 39.1 percent restricted mergers, and 35.6 percent restricted asset sales. Smith and Warner, loc. cit. n. 22, at p. 123. McDaniel surveyed the debt contracts of Fortune's 100 largest industrials in 1984. He found that negative pledge and sale-leaseback covenants were ubiquitous. Of the 92 companies reported as having one or more senior issues, one or more subordinated issues, or both, only 28 percent of the issues contained debt covenants. Of the newer issues, only 16 percent contained a debt covenant. Dividend restrictions appeared in 35 percent of the issues, but in only 20 percent of the newer issues. See M. McDaniel, 'Bondholders and Corporate Governance', 41 *Bus. Law.* (1986) p. 413 at pp. 425-426. Malitz surveyed all long-term senior non-convertible debentures issued between 1960 and 1980 and described in Moody's Bond Survey or Moody's Industrial

unwieldy and expensive, due to the large number of dispersed holders. This implies looser constraints.[64]

Whatever the lending context, the description of pricing sensitivity and risk-return trading in a costly contracting hypothesis remains robust only in part. One does not see much evidence of the theory's prediction of borrowers trading higher levels of protection for lower yields, or trading higher yields for greater flexibility. Covenant intensity follows default risk. Accordingly, more covenants mean higher yields.

4.1 Contracting practice and market segment

A recent study by Michael Bradley and Michael Roberts describes contracting practice in the market for bank loans. Drawing on the Dealscan database, they summarize the terms of 12,425 bank loans made between 1993 and 2001, The sample, which includes 364-day facilities, revolving credit agreements, and term loans,[65] has an average maturity of 3.5 years. The mean issuer has $2.5 billion of assets and, in 2001, the average principal amount was $318 million.[66] Data are collected on six protective provisions: (1) early warning provisions grounded in accounting numbers; (2) security; (3) dividend covenants; (4) asset sweeps (requiring prepayment of the loan in the event of a sale of assets in an amount exceeding a set percentage of the principal amount); (5) debt sweeps (requiring prepayment of the loan in the event of subsequent borrowing exceeding a set percentage of the principal amount); and (6) equity sweeps (requiring prepayment of the loan in the event of a sale of new equity securities in an amount exceeding a set percentage of the principal amount). Table 1 sets out a sample of the results.

We see that substantial protection is the rule – the terms cover claim dilution, asset withdrawal, underinvestment, and asset substitution. We also see a notable shift in the practice. In 1993, sweeps were the exception; by 2001 they had become the rule. The results also imply that a small portion of the loans lacked any covenant protection, and Bradley and Roberts break out these numbers. Four percent of the loans had none of the six provisions in the set; eight percent of the loans had only one.

Shifting over to the bond market implies a reduction in the incidence and intensity of covenants, even for borrowers of the same risk class as the bank borrowers. Stuart Gilson and Jerold Warner demonstrate this, comparing the debt

---

64 See Smith and Warner, loc. cit. n. 22, at pp. 150-152.
65 Bradley and Roberts, op. cit. n. 36, at pp. 9-11.
66 Ibid., at p. 10, table 3.

contracts governing twenty-seven firms that issued junk bonds to pay down existing bank loans.[67] Table 2 sets out some of their findings.

Table 1: Covenants in bank loans, 1993-2001

Covenant	All years	1993	2001
Number of early warning covenants	2.52	2.13	2.52
Security	77%	84%	72%
Dividend	85%	82%	81%
Asset sweep	62.5%	32%	94%
Debt sweep	46%	18%	81%
Equity sweep	46%	25%	75%

Source: Bradley and Roberts (2004) from Dealscan[68]

Table 2: Same issuer junk bond and bank loan contracts compared

	Junk bond	Bank loan
Investment covenant	6%	97%
Asset sale covenant	17%	92%
Debt financing (debt covenant, negative pledge and/or sale/leaseback)	50%	98%
Early warning tests	33%	86%
Dividend covenant	69%	81%

Source: Gilson and Warner (1998)[69]

The shift from the private to the public markets clearly enhances management flexibility, most notably respecting asset management but also respecting financing.

The decrease in the number of early warning covenants reflects a particular borrower objective. Gilson and Warner show that the performance of the firms in the sample tended to decline in the period prior to the shift from the banks to the

---

[67] S. Gilson and J. Warner, *Private versus Public Debt: Evidence from Firms that Replace Bank Loans with Junk Bonds*, working paper (1998), available at: <http://ssrn.com/abstract=140093> (sample covering the period 1980-1991).

[68] Ibid., table 1.

[69] Bradley and Roberts, op. cit. n. 36, table 4.

bond market. Although not distressed, the issuers did face default on the terms of their bank loans, particularly the early warning triggers. The shift to the bond market thus averted the burden of bank loan renegotiation from a position of disadvantage, not only enhancing the issuers' flexibility, but lowering their transaction and monitoring costs.[70] The banks tend to set their warning trip wires tightly, referencing recent accounting results. Renegotiation in the wake of failure to meet the numbers is a normal event, with the banks resetting the provisions to reflect the real world outcome.[71] Default declaration and acceleration are not ordinary expedients. With junk bonds, in contrast, such seriatim renegotiations are not feasible. We accordingly can infer that the trip wires in the minority of bond contracts containing them provided a much later early warning than did the bank contracts.

Public bond contracts do indeed hold out considerable borrower flexibility. A sample of public issue bonds collected by Robert Nash, Jeffry Netter and Annette Poulsen provides an instructive comparison with the bank loan data. Nash, Netter and Poulsen went to the public filings to cull 365 bonds issued in 1989 by 259 firms and 398 bonds issued in 1996 by 241 firms. The mean duration of the bond issues is 17.4 years. In 1996, the mean issuer had $6.7 billion of assets and the mean loan principal was $177.7 million.[72] Table 3 shows some of the terms governing the issues in the sample.

Table 3: Public bond issues, 1989 and 1996

	Secured	Junk rating	Senior (not subordinated)	Dividend covenant	Debt covenant
1989	24.1%	40%	66.3%	39.7%	40%
1996	12.1%	25.4%	86.2%	20.8%	27.4%
	Negative pledge	Sale/ leaseback	Merger covenant	Poison put	Asset sales
1989	50.1%	11.2%	66.3%	31.6%	12.9%
1996	78.6%	54.8%	89.9%	28.4%	14.3%

Source: Nash, Netter and Poulsen (2003)[73]

---

[70] Ibid., at p. 4.

[71] See I. Dichev and D. Skinner, 'Large-Sample Evidence on the Debt Covenant Hypothesis', 40 *J. Accounting Research* (2002) p. 1091.

[72] Nash, Netter, and Poulsen, loc. cit. n. 34, at pp. 208-209, 211-212 and tables 1 and 2.

[73] Ibid., tables 2, 3 and 7.

The decline in the number of secured and subordinated issues reflects a wider trend in the 1990s bond market. The figures on negative pledge and sale/leaseback covenants contradict a conventional wisdom[74] that these provisions always appear, no matter how highly rated the issuer. Negative pledge and sale/leaseback clauses show up in only one-half and one-tenth of the 1989 bonds, respectively, and merger covenants appear in only two-thirds. Looking at the converse side of this, one-third of the 1989 issues apparently were entirely without covenants. The substantially increased appearance of these covenants in the 1996 bonds signals movement back toward protection. We should not make too much of this, however. The return of the negative pledge and sale/leaseback clauses protects seniority but not other claim dilution. The increased appearance of merger covenants from two-thirds to nine-tenths does not imply protection against high-leverage restructuring or other injurious mergers. As we have seen, the standard covenant only requires that the surviving firm be organized domestically and formally assume the debt, with the latter at all events occurring by operation of law. The standard covenant also covers sales of all or substantially all assets, requiring formal assumption by the purchasing firm. Here the covenant goes farther than the operation of law, but in so doing only makes an asset sale the functional equivalent of a merger. No restrictions on the successor firm's financial condition need be implied, absent debt and dividend covenants. The standard merger covenant thus holds out an important barrier against an extreme form of opportunistic stripping of the asset base from the borrower entity without otherwise significantly inhibiting management's freedom of action. The puzzle concerns not its reappearance but its omission from one-third of the 1989 bonds.

Turning now to debt and dividend covenants, note that the percentages of bonds below investment grade roughly correspond to the percentage of issues containing these covenants, inviting an association between ratings and terms. Nash, Netter, and Poulsen confirm this with a statistical showing. The more restrictive debt and dividend covenants tend to be bundled together and show up in junk issues, the less restrictive negative pledge and sale/leaseback provisions also tend to be bundled together and show up in investment-grade issues.[75] Other correlations follow suit: bonds with debt and dividend covenants tend to have higher yields, are less likely to be senior, and are more likely to be callable, convertible, and subordinated. The decrease in the appearance of debt and dividend covenants between 1989 and 1996 thus follows from shifts in the credit mix in the sample rather than from shifts in contracting practice. Note that it also follows that some, but not all, of the increase in the appearance of negative pledge

---

[74] See *supra* n. 42.

[75] Nash, Netter, and Poulsen, loc. cit. n. 34, at p. 219 and table 4.

and sale/leaseback provisions between 1989 and 1996 stems from differences in the samples.

We can take away a point about covenant protection and credit rating – relatively stronger protection obtains for riskier bonds, but not protection in full. The lower figures for asset sale covenants imply that even many junk bond contracts fall short in their coverage of predictable bondholder-stockholder conflicts, covering asset withdrawal but not asset substitution.

A larger sample of bonds has been collected by Sudheer Chava, Praveen Kumar, and Arthur Warga from the Fixed Income Security Database, which provides information on up to fifty-four different contract terms. The authors collect information on 9,149 debt securities issued between 1980 and 2003 by 3,033 different non-financial firms.[76] Table 4 presents a selection of the findings.

Table 4: Bond issues,[77] 1989-2003

	Dividend covenant	Restricted payments	Debt covenant	Investment covenant
1980-89	27.2%	12%	13.4%	5.6%
1990-94	19.7%	16.7%	19.1%	5.6%
1995-99	4.3%	23.3%	24.4%	2.6%
2000-03	1.0%	23.7%	13.9%	1.7%
	Negative pledge	Sale/ leaseback	Merger covenant	Poison put
1980-89	25.8%	15.4%	67.9%	19.7%
1990-94	51.2%	32.9%	71.2%	26.1%
1995-99	70.5%	48.0%	89.7%	46.4%
2000-03	67.4%	44.7%	91.1%	96.2%

Source: Chava, Kumar, and Warga (2004) from Fixed Income Security Database[78]

[76] S. Chava, P. Kumar and A. Warga, *Agency Costs and the Pricing of Bond Covenants*, working paper (2004) pp. 1, 11-12, available at: <http://ssrn.com/abstract=611801>.

[77] Although the database includes private placements as well as public bonds, the authors do not specifically identify the bonds as coming from one or the other market. The inference arising from the results is that the sample includes only bonds.

[78] Chava, Kumar, and Warga, op. cit. n. 76, table 2.

This data set fleshes out the evolutionary picture. The first two covenants, 'dividend' and 'restricted payments' cover the same territory – payments by the firm to shareholders whether by dividend or share repurchase. A substantial overlap between the categories safely can be assumed.[79] Given that assumption, an inference of stability arises – around one-quarter of bond contracts regulate dividends. But which contracts? The authors collect bond ratings for a large subsample, and approximately 30 percent are junk rated, a figure that roughly corresponds with the dividend protected segment.[80] But this is a tendency not a rule. Table 5 presents a rating by rating breakdown of the issues that include dividend covenants. The results are intuitively satisfying, for incidence shoots up when the bonds turn the corner to junk at 'BA' and continues to increase as creditworthiness deteriorates. But we also are left with two puzzles. Significant numbers of investment-grade issuers also give up this covenant, and the economic literature has not yet taken up the task of accounting for this phenomenon. At the same time, significant numbers of junk bond issuers do not give up the covenant. Here too one looks for an explanation.

Table 5: Dividend covenants by credit rating, 1989-2003

Rating	AAA	AA	A	BAA	BA	B	CAA
Dividend covenant	5.1%	13.1%	11.7%	9.0%	46.9%	77.7%	80.7%

Source: Chava, Kumar, and Warga (2004) from Fixed Income Security Database and Lehman Bros. Bond Database

Returning to Table 4, it becomes necessary to qualify the suggestion of a return to protection in the 1990s hypothesized in respect of Nash, Netter and Poulsen's results. While dividend covenants persist in a relatively stable proportion, debt covenants have a volatile pattern and may be in decline. Investment covenants have nearly disappeared. Growth rates in the appearance of negative pledge and sale/leaseback covenants have leveled off. But the merger covenant continues its upward trend and now is close to ubiquitous. Once again, this does not signal substantive movement in the direction of bondholder protection – the puzzle here continues to be the merger covenant's absence from one-third of the 1980s issues.

The most notable data concern poison puts. Recall that their usage peaked at the end of the era of high-leverage restructuring and then fell off.[81] Bond buyers

---

[79] One suspects unsophisticated or inconsistent coding by the database provider. Note that, depending on the drafting, a restricted payment clause also can contain a restriction on investments.

[80] Chava, Kumar, and Warga, op. cit. n. 76, table 6.

[81] The Chava, Kumar, and Warga data obscure this because the authors group the entire decade of the 1980s together and then break the time sample at 1990, the peak year.

made a clear-cut risk return decision when choosing between issues with and without this event risk protection. Around 1990, inclusion lowered the average bond yield by 24 basis points.[82] The price effect grew in magnitude as the bond rating declined – for a BAA bond the spread was 65.7 basis points.[83] But, because high-leverage restructuring almost disappeared in the early 1990s, those who bought the higher-yielding, riskier bonds appeared to have made a good deal. Conditions changed later in the decade, however.

Although high-leverage restructuring has not returned to the headlines, it has indeed returned to the markets with the resurgence of private equity transactions. Bondholders seem to have noticed. Although today's private equity financings may implicate lower leverage than did deals in the 1980s, they still combine high leverage and rating downgrades. Downgrades still trigger bond sell-offs. Indeed, increased bond market participation by foreign institutions subject to portfolio constraints aggravates the magnitude of such shocks.[84] Table 6 presents Mergerstat data on numbers of going private transactions as a percentage of total public company acquisitions.[85] The growing numbers correlate positively with the change in the bond contracting pattern.

The almost universal inclusion of poison puts in the most recent generation of bond contracts amounts to the high watermark of the incidence of protective provisions in bond contracts during the past thirty years. As such it presents a bit of a puzzle – why this sudden, pervasive resort to protection in contrast to the limited, selective response of a decade earlier? Issuer indifference seems unlikely, so the change by hypothesis has occurred on the bondholder side. Apparently, aversion to event risk has become more salient. Not only have bond buyers become concerned, they have registered their concern so emphatically with the underwriters as to prompt responsive drafting across the board. The implication is that more is at stake than the rate spread and risk premium – issue marketability seems to be at stake.

---

[82] I. Crabbe, 'Event Risk: An Analysis of Losses to Bondholders and "Super Poison Put" Bond Covenants', 46 *J. Fin.* (1991) p. 689.

[83] S. Bae and D. Klein, 'Further Evidence on Corporate Bonds with Event-Risk Covenants: Inferences from Standard and Poor's and Moody's Bond Ratings', 37 *Q. Rev. Econ. & Fin.* (1997) p. 709 at p. 720. See also K. Cremers, V. Nair, and C. Wei, *The Impact of Shareholder Control on Bondholders*, NYU Law and Economics Working Paper (2004), available at: <http://ssrn.com/abstract=516564>.

[84] See M. Whitehorse, 'LBOs May Spoil the Corporate Bond Party', *Wall St. J.* (1 August 2005) p. C1.

[85] Mergerstat defines 'going private' as an acquisition of a public company by a private investment group or individual where the buyer is not an operating business. Because going private transactions tend to involve smaller firms, the proportion of transactions measured by deal value is lower.

Table 6: Going private transactions as a percentage of public company acquisitions

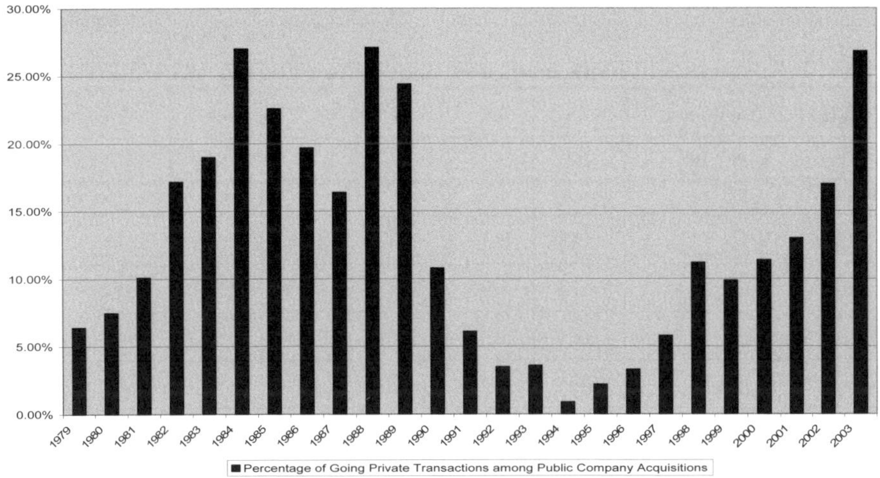

Source: Mergerstat

4.2 Covenants, risk, and return

Bradley and Roberts make a more particular showing of covenant incidence by dividing their bank loan sample based on how many of the six designated covenants appear in each contract. They sort for a range of variables, including (1) the loan spread (here the difference between the interest rate on the loan and the six-month LIBOR rate); (2) the borrower's market-to-book ratio (book liabilities plus market equity to book assets); (3) tangible assets (property plant and equipment over total assets); (4) duration (number of months to maturity); (5) the log of the market capitalization; and (6) leverage (total debt to total assets). Table 7 sets out these figures.

The numbers are intuitively satisfying. The least protected loans, those with zero or one covenant, constitute only twelve percent of the sample. These loans have notably lower interest rates, and involve borrowers with higher market capitalization, more tangible assets, and lower leverage. They also are larger firms – the log of market capitalization serves as a proxy for size, and shows that the least protected loans involve materially larger borrowers. Apparently, the large firms bargain for a zone of flexibility roughly approximating that available in the bond market.

As the number of covenants increases so do the interest rate, the time to maturity, and the borrower's leverage. At the same time, more lender protection means a lower market-to-book ratio and fewer tangible assets. More generally, covenant protection increases linearly with the risk of the loan. Nash, Netter and

Poulsen reach a similar result respecting the differential appearance in their sample of debt and dividend covenants and negative pledge and sale/leaseback covenants. The latter, lesser protection package corresponds with lower yields.[86]

Table 7: Covenants in bank loans and issuer characteristics, 1993-2001

Number of covenants	0	1	2	3	4	5	6
Percent of loans in sample	4%	8%	13%	14%	12%	19%	30%
Spread	0.43	0.77	1.82	2.10	2.18	2.41	2.69
Market-to-book	2.22	1.93	1.83	1.69	1.89	1.69	1.65
Tangible assets	36%	36%	36%	33%	33%	29%	30%
Maturity (months)	45	46	42	44	56	60	63
Log (market cap)	7.80	6.71	5.36	5.19	5.73	5.36	5.38
Leverage	24%	26%	31%	36%	40%	39%	42%

Source: Bradley and Roberts (2004) from Dealscan[87]

The strong positive correlation between covenants and yields traverses the costly contracting hypothesis. The hypothesis predicts a negative relationship between covenant intensity and yield – the issuer offers the covenants and lower agency costs in exchange for a lower cost of borrowing, much as we saw with the pricing of poison puts. The bank loan data and the hypothesis can be read together nonetheless. The parties do not make risk return trade-offs in the form of a choice between minimal and full protection across the range of borrower risk levels. The small, risky borrower is not positioned to bargain for a high interest loan under a convenantless contract. At the same time, large borrowers do not appear inclined to surrender their flexibility in exchange for a rock-bottom coupon. With a given risk class, there appears to be some trading room. Bradley and Roberts, testing for yield sensitivity to the presence or absence of a given covenant, find that the yield does decrease in the presence of four of the six covenants.[88]

4.3 Covenants, growth firms, and investment policy

Recent studies of bond covenants focus heavily on Stewart Myers' thirty-year-old hypothesis concerning underinvestment. Myers, viewing the equity as the holder

86 Nash, Netter, and Poulsen, loc. cit. n. 34, at p. 219 and table 4.
87 Bradley and Roberts, op. cit. n. 36, table 6.
88 Bradley and Roberts, op. cit. n. 36, table 8.

of an option to repurchase the firm from the debt, posited the underinvestment problem: where the option remains out of the money, net of the proceeds of a given positive NPV investment on the date the debt matures, the equity has no reason to make the investment. He suggested that the dividend covenant serves as a partial palliative, by locking capital in the firm; he noted in addition that shorter maturities also reduce the tendency.[89] Since then, economists have expanded Myers' point into a prediction that the underinvestment problem will be particularly salient in respect of growth firms. From there they go on to look for a correlation between growth firms and dividend constraints.

The option perspective gives rise to a second prediction about growth firms. Their equity, as option holders, also will want to reserve flexibility to make all feasible positive NPV investments so as to maximize the chance that the option expires in the money.[90] The prediction is that growth companies will preserve their investment flexibility by preserving concomitant financing flexibility, thus avoiding debt covenants. The two predictions coexist in tension, one predicting overinvestment and the other underinvestment. But they can be read together – the flexibility concern arises on the side of a borrower projecting good times, while the underinvestment concern arises on the side of a lender projecting bad times.

A third prediction respecting growth firms comes from Michael Barclay and Clifford Smith. Under this prediction, firms with growth opportunities can be expected to finance with secured debt and capital leases so as to reduce the likelihood that gains will be shared with existing unsecured debt claimants; incentives to underinvest thereby will be minimized. Growth firms thus can be expected to draft their contracts so as to reserve room for such high priority financing.[91] Presumably, this means that they resist negative pledge clauses and sale/leaseback constraints.

Tests of these predictions, employing the market-to-book ratio as a proxy for a growth orientation, tend to confirm the flexibility prediction and negate the dividend covenant and secured borrowing predictions. The results of Nash, Netter and Poulsen, set out in Table 8, reflect the trend.[92] They arbitrarily break their sample into a binary set of 'high growth' and 'low growth' firms; all results are statistically significant. Bradley and Roberts get the same association respecting

---

89 Myers, loc. cit. n. 23, at pp. 159-161.

90 Nash, Netter, and Poulsen, loc. cit. n. 34, at p. 205.

91 M. Barclay and C. Smith, 'The Priority Structure of Corporate Liabilities', 50 *J. Fin.* (1995) p. 899 at p. 907.

92 See also M. Kahan and D. Yermack, 'Investment Opportunities and the Design of Debt Securities', 14 *J. L. Econ. & Org.* (1998) p. 136 (showing that growth firms tend toward covenantless convertible bond contracts); Chava, Kumar, and Warga, op. cit. n. 76, at pp. 14-16.

future financing flexibility. But they also show a weaker positive correlation between growth and dividend constraints, and growth and secured status.[93]

Table 8: Growth firms

	High growth	Low growth
Dividend covenant	11.3%	28.5%
Debt covenant	15.0%	33.3%
Negative pledge	72.5%	62.6%
Sale/leaseback	44.5%	35.7%

Source: Nash, Netter and Poulsen (2003)[94]

The confirmation of the flexibility prediction is unsurprising – the borrower's interest in flexibility has driven contracting practice in the bond market for decades. The Bradley and Roberts results associating growth firms, dividend constraints, and underinvestment call for a more cautious interpretation. Credit quality determines the covenant pattern in both the public and private markets. When a dividend covenant appears, it accompanies a poor credit and more likely reflects the lender's fear of asset withdrawal than fear of underinvestment. Indeed, assuming separation of ownership and control, it is unclear whether underinvestment is particularly likely to be a problem – the managers have every reason to continue to invest in order to move the firm away from distress and hold on to their jobs whether or not the equity's option is expected to expire in the money. When negative pledge clauses show up, they serve as a minimal constraint that protects the lender's priority position in the capital structure of a good credit, a firm unlikely to be forced to borrow on a secured basis. Finally, the short maturities of the bank loans analyzed by Bradley and Roberts suggest that underinvestment is unlikely to determine contractual choices.

4.4 Summary and analysis

We noted at the outset that the agency costs of debt are the costs of financial distress. That point goes a long way toward explaining contracting practice in US credit markets. Covenants linearly follow the probability of distress. The best credits for the most part avoid their inclusion, preserving their freedom of action. Lesser credits must include them, with the intensity of lender protection increasing as creditworthiness declines.

---

93 Bradley and Roberts, op. cit. n. 36, at p. 27 and table 8.

94 Nash, Netter, and Poulsen, loc. cit. n. 34, at p. 219 and table 4.

While levels of contractual protection clearly impact the price of credit, there is relatively little of the trading of price and protection predicted by the costly contracting hypothesis. The market does not hold out a complex menu of risk-return combinations. Investment-grade credits do not offer full sets of covenants in order to minimize their cost of borrowing. Poor credits do not get the opportunity to preserve their flexibility by offering a premium price. A highly risk-averse bondholder does not get the opportunity to select a super safe portfolio of investment-grade bonds, the issuers of which all have contractually minimized possible agency costs. This bondholder instead is remitted to the ordinary expedients of portfolio diversification and hedges in the derivatives market.[95] Bond insurance, a normal recourse in the municipal bonds markets, provides an alternative recourse for a only small subset of bonds.[96]

The explanatory power of the linear link between risk, return, and contract protection is not absolute, however. Anomalies abound. We do not yet know why some investment-grade credits have had the option to issue covenantless bonds when other similarly situated firms offer minimal protection. Nor do we know why still other investment-grade issuers offer more than minimal protection. Nor do we have an explanation for the market's steadily shifting reactions to the risks of mergers, asset sales, and leveraged restructurings. Long a persistent and puzzling area of underprotection, these agency costs now prompt a protective response across the board. The costly contracting hypothesis may or may not provide cogent answers to these open questions. Where covenants are absent, free riding also holds out an explanation – perhaps the missing protections can be found in other debt contracts in the borrower's capital structure.[97] Even so, explanatory recourse to the murkier world of path dependencies, intermediary preferences, and investor behavioral shortcomings ultimately may prove necessary.

---

[95] Credit derivatives are now available for larger issuers on an intermediate term basis. See R. Blanco, S. Brennan and I. Marsh, 'An Empirical Analysis of the Dynamic Relationship of Investment Grade Bonds and Credit Default Swaps', 60 *J. Fin.* (2005) p. 2255 at pp. 2257-2262.

[96] See S. Davydenko, *The Role of Debt Insurance*, working paper (2003), available at: <http://phd.london.edu/SDavydenko/DebtInsurance.pdf>. The market concentrates on utility issues rated AA to BBB with 74 percent of the contracts covering A issues. Dealers and retail investors take out the contracts.

[97] Lenders thus relying assume significant risks. Nothing prevents the borrower from paying down the better-protected loan. In a distress situation, the better-protected lender may get an opportunity to negotiate concessions from the borrower while the unprotected lender must sit on its hands.

5. PROCESS BARRIERS

Although corporate debt contracts hold out a only a short menu of risk-return combinations and have yet to be explained fully in a number of respects, it has been many years since anyone has contended that the practice holds out significant adverse selection problems. Such a claim was voiced in the 1980s, when the contracts' failure to protect against event risk surprised many bond market participants.[98] But the point lost salience a few years later when actors in the bond markets proved willing to assume event risk in exchange for a premium ranging from 25 to 60 basis points. Today, complaints about bond contracts concern process rather than substance, in particular the mechanisms that order processes of renegotiation surrounding default.

5.1 Amendments and waivers

We have seen that covenants in public bond issues tend to be less tightly drafted than covenants in bank loans and private placements, even respecting borrowers of comparable credit standing. The stricter the covenants the more likely the need for amendment or waiver in the event the borrower's performance deteriorates. With publicly traded bonds, the amendment process is both cumbersome and expensive. Debt contracts, both public and private, typically permit covenants to be amended or waived by a majority (simple or two-thirds of principal amount) of the holders thereunder.[99] Given a large number of holders, this means a formal proxy solicitation, usually made on a take-it-or-leave-it basis without negotiation. Such dispersed bondholders, like shareholders, can suffer the classic collective action problem. The trust indenture device does nothing to alleviate the problem because it imposes no duty on the indenture trustee to represent the bondholders in connection with contract renegotiations. Institutional holding ameliorates the problem, however. Large bondholders can identify and contact one another and sometimes organize. They also have been known to reject issuer proposals.[100]

---

98 See the authorities cited *supra* at n. 52.

99 For a formal, incomplete contracts model of bond contract amendment, see N. Gareanu and J. Zwiebel, *Design and Renegotiation of Covenants*, working paper (2005), available at: <http://ssrn.com/abstract=470780>.

100 See M. Kahan and B. Tuckman, 'Do Bondholders Lose from Junk Bond Covenant Changes?', 66 *J. Bus.* (1993) p. 499. This presents the results of a study of 58 consent solicitations in which an issuer of widely held debt requested the modification of existing covenants but did not request either interest deferral or principal forgiveness. Nearly all of the issues surveyed were junk bonds. The solicitations broke down as follows: 25 were simple consent solicitations in which receipt of an offered cash payment was conditioned on consent to the amendment; 24 were accompanied by tender offers; eight were accompanied by exchange offers; one was accompanied by a tender offer and an exchange offer. A requirement of an exit

Such uncooperative behavior is unsurprising – bondholders, unlike institutional lenders, have no interest in a reputation for cooperation. It follows, at the bottom line, that issuers must induce bondholder consents with cash. All of this stiffens the borrower's *ex ante* resistance to the inclusion of covenants.

Thus do process frictions appear to impose an opportunity cost on substantive protections. This leads Yakov Amihud, Kenneth Garbade, and Marcel Kahan to propose an alternative process regime.[101] Under their proposal, bond contracts would designate a 'super trustee' empowered to negotiate covenant amendments. With a designated negotiator, they assert, covenants would not hold out dead-weight process costs on downside scenarios, permitting tighter, more effective covenants to appear in publicly traded issues. They note that this change could be accomplished on a strictly contractual basis.

The proposal assumes that, but for the process barriers, the costly contracting hypothesis would operate so that borrowers would find it in their interest to include more restrictive terms. While the assumption undoubtedly is correct at some level, the evidence presented in the preceding sections prompts questions respecting the scope of the risk-return trading zone opened thereby. Investment-grade issuers might welcome a smoother process regime, but are unlikely to follow up with substantive concessions inhibiting their freedom of action. We have seen that the best credits evade covenants even when borrowing from banks. As the authors emphasize, room for trade more likely opens in the junk bond market, where a protection differential obtains between private loans and public bonds. Borrower incentives still present a question. To the extent managers highly value the flexibility opened by relaxed covenants, they could prove willing to leave money on the table in the form of higher borrowing costs. Given separation of ownership and control, bargaining over debt contracts does not occur at the

---

consent or consent as a condition to payment was present in 44 of the 48 offers for which data could be found. The issuers sought, *inter alia*, to make leveraged acquisitions (31 percent), make dividends or other stockholder payments (13.8 percent), conduct recapitalizations (10.3 percent), sell assets (8.6 percent), and issue more debt (6.9 percent). The average payment offered in those solicitations exchanging the consent for cash was $20.51 per $1,000 face value; the median cash payment was $15 per $1,000 face value; nine of the 23 cash offers were above $20; the two largest were $60 and $95. Evidence of the result of the solicitation was found for 52 of the cases, and in 83 percent of these the solicitation succeeded. Kahan and Tuckman conclude that the issuers have not been exploiting the structural opportunity to coerce that the bond contracts create. They hypothesize that the bondholders can, in practice, coordinate their response so as to insure an adequate level of payment. As evidence, they cite the formation of bondholder groups in twelve cases; of these twelve solicitations, eleven either failed or had their terms modified before approval. Over all, in 42 percent of the cases, the issuers modified the terms after an initial failure to obtain consents.

[101] Y. Amihud, K. Garbade and M. Kahan, 'A New Governance Structure for Corporate Bonds', 51 *Stan. L. Rev.* (1999) p. 447.

financial margin, and the agency costs of equity could influence the result. Looking to the other side of the bargaining table, there is no reason to assume that, but for the process barriers, underwriters would follow the same contracting path as the agents of banks. For the underwriters, present marketability matters more than long-term performance. Meanwhile many bond buyers can be expected to continue to trade contract protection for liquidity and present yield.

5.2 Payment terms, exchange offers, and unanimous action

Now consider deeper distress situations, where default in the payment of interest or principal has become a present possibility. Here bankruptcy reorganization looms as an expensive and risky alternative for both borrowers and bondholders. Both may be better off if the borrower and its lenders can agree to a composition: the lenders agree to a scale-down of their claims to interest and principal either because the projected cost savings of avoided bankruptcy exceed the value of the rights surrendered, or, failing that, because the borrower adds a sweetener – for example, a present payment of principal from the proceeds of the sale of a piece of its business.

With bank loans and private placements, the lenders customarily coordinate and negotiate with the borrower face to face. Process problems once again prevent that with issues of bonds. Moreover, the bond contract interposes an additional process barrier. While providing for amendment of covenants by a majority assent, it requires unanimous bondholder assent to amend or waive a payment term. The unanimity rule is mandated under the Trust Indenture Act for publicly issued bonds.[102] Although the mandate does not cover private placement and bank loans, unanimous action requirements respecting payment terms remain the universal practice respecting corporate lending in the United States.[103] As a practical matter, the unanimous action requirement makes direct amendment of a bond payment term impossible outside of Chapter 11 of the Bankruptcy Code, which interposes a majoritarian voting regime.[104]

---

102 Trust Indenture Act of 1939, § 316, 15 U.S.C. § 77ppp (also providing for a delay of payment of interest of up to three years based on a 75 percent vote). M.J. Roe, 'The Voting Prohibition in Bond Workouts', 97 *Yale L. J.* (1987) p. 232 at p. 234, shows that the purpose of the section was to discourage out of court compositions so as to force the parties into the then new Chapter X bankruptcy procedure, where strong judicial supervision was provided for. Roe argues, correctly, that subsequent changes in bankruptcy law and practice remove the need for the mandate. Ibid., at p. 316.

103 H. Kashner, 'Minority Clauses and Non-Bankruptcy Corporate Reorganizations – Contractual and Statutory Alternatives', 44 *Bus. Law.* (1988) p. 123 at pp. 124-125.

104 11 U.S.C. § 1129(a).

Unanimous action provisions do not, however, present an absolute bar to debt restructuring outside of bankruptcy. A composition can be effected by indirection. Instead of being asked to vote on an amendment of their bond contracts, the bondholders are asked to exchange their bonds for substitute bonds that contain modified terms more favorable to the borrower. The borrower neither expects nor requests universal participation. But the bargaining posture is problematic. Consider the game posited in Table 9.

Table 9: Exchange offer game

		Bondholder B	
		Cooperate	Defect
Bondholder A	Cooperate	625, 625	550, 800
	Defect	800, 550	400, 400

The set-up assumes that a borrower in distress has offered its two bondholders a composition featuring substitute bonds worth 550. The bondholders cannot identify one another. The offer is stingy: if the bondholders could surmount their collective action problem and negotiate with the borrower, they can get the offer increased to 625. Under the offered terms, either or both bondholders can accept; obviously, the composition fails if both refuse. In that case, the borrower goes into bankruptcy where the projected recovery is 400, yielded after a long lapse of time.

On these facts, holding out, 'defecting' in the parlance of game theory, can mean an 800 payoff. One but not both of the bondholders can maximize on this free riding strategy. To reject an exchange offer is to hold on to your bond. The holder thereby retains the borrower's original promise to pay and all other contract rights, even as the exchanging holders make concessions in respect of the timing and amount of payments. If the offer succeeds, the holdout is 'buoyed up', benefiting from the borrowers' emergence from distress and economic recovery along with the holder who exchanges, but having made no concessions. Here, if both bondholders follow this strategy, the exchange offer fails and borrower goes into bankruptcy.

Given the set-up, it is unclear what each bondholder should do. The underlined outcomes in Table 9 show A's optimal moves given the alternatives of cooperation and defection by B. If B accepts the offer, A is better holding out and taking the 800. But if B holds out, A is better off cooperating and taking the 550, thereby avoiding the worst case payoff of 400. Since A does not know what B is going to do, it is not clear how A should play. This situation is unstable; this is a multiple equilibrium game.[105]

[105] In a standard prisoners' dilemma set-up, defection is optimal for both A and B and there is only one equilibrium.

Real world corporate exchange offers can present similarly difficult choices. They tend to be made on a take-it-or-leave-it basis, absent prior negotiation. They also tend to be structured to succeed only if the number of holdouts is small: supermajority acceptance generally is required – something more than 80 percent – to minimize the siphoning of value to holdouts. Meanwhile, specialized hedge funds, known as 'vulture funds', specialize in such strategic behavior. They purchase the bonds on the secondary market after the onset of distress at a deep discount and then play non-cooperatively.[106] This aggravates the risk of failure: if the subsidy to the holdouts is greater than the increase in value to the exchanging creditors, every one is better off refusing to exchange.[107] The failure of the offer, of course, leaves everybody worse off.

If the borrower in the above example fears the offer will fail, whether because of the holdout problem or because the bondholders will refuse to cooperate because they believe the borrower can afford a package worth 625, it can heighten the stakes and set up a coercive exchange. It now offers 550 in the form of new debt that is secured by property to which the holders of the original bonds would look for payment in bankruptcy. Nothing prevents this if the bond contract lacks a negative pledge clause. Holding out now carries additional risk. The holdout retains the original bond with its promise to pay the original amount, but the bond is junior to the new bonds issued in the exchange. The change in status reduces the value of the holdout's bonds to below 800. How low the value goes depends on the numbers. In a real world case where 90 percent of the bondholders accept the offer, the security soaks up most of the value of the firm, pushing the value of the holdout bonds well below 550. Absent coordination, the bondholders may be forced to take the bad deal. Note that here the holdout possibility arguably benefits the group as whole.[108]

The borrower can coerce the bondholders even if the bond contract contains a negative pledge. It structures an 'exit consent'. This combines the exchange offer with a proposal to amend the bond contract to remove the negative pledge, which like all terms other than payment terms is subject to majority amendment. The cooperative, exchanging bondholders vote in favor of the amendment even as they exit by sending in their old bonds for exchange. This leaves the holdouts with their original principal and interest terms intact but subject to diminution in value due to the senior status of the new bonds.[109] The courts have approved the

---

[106] J. Coffee, Jr. and W. Klein, 'Bondholder Coercion: The Problem of Constrained Choice in Debt Tender Offers and Recapitalizations', 58 *U. Chi. L. Rev.* (1991) p. 1207 at pp. 1207-1214.

[107] Roe, loc. cit. n. 102, at p. 236.

[108] Coffee and Klein, loc. cit. n. 106, at p. 1223.

[109] On the use of exit consents to engineer sovereign debt restructurings, see L. Buchheit and G. Gulati, 'Exit Consents in Sovereign Bond Exchanges', 48 *UCLA L. Rev.* (2000) p. 59.

exit consent device in the face of challenges under the contract law duty of good faith.[110]

Bond contracts easily can be drafted to block these coercive exchanges, indeed to block all exchanges. The issuer simply promises not to make any exchange offers. So long as that promise can be amended only by unanimous consent, any exchange offer is an event of default. This strategy is followed in private placement contracts[111] but not public bond indentures.[112] But revision of the bond drafting practice to follow the private placement approach is not necessarily desirable. Private placement lenders can effect compositions despite the exchange offer prohibition – small numbers make unanimous consent feasible, and relational concerns among repeat players minimize holdout problems. With public bonds, a strict unanimity regime would as a practical matter foreclose the option of out of bankruptcy composition.

5.3 Process reform in distress situations

Two routes to the amelioration of process problems inhibiting voluntary compositions by highly distressed issuers can be suggested – a greater and a lesser. The greater is a super trustee arrangement, such as that suggested by Amihud, Garbade, and Kahan. Here, as is not the case with simple covenant defaults, the Trust Indenture Act would have to be amended to permit the arrangement. The question would go to the magnitude of the delegation to the trustee – either of a full power to bind the bondholders to a payment amendment or of a power to negotiate subject to a ratifying vote. An analogy to process in Chapter 11 suggests that only the latter approach would be acceptable to the lending community. Inside the Chapter, claimants surrender negotiating power to class representatives but vote on the composition on a majoritarian basis. The lesser route is a simple amendment of the Trust Indenture Act to permit amendment of payment terms by majority (or super majority) vote.

As between the two alternatives, trustee negotiation followed by ratification holds out clear-cut advantages. Majoritarian voting opens up the possibility of side payments from the borrower to selected members of the group of lenders. A borrower, for example, can offer a preferred position in a future lending group or other business advantages in exchange for support of a composition that extracts value from a minority creditor group. Under a unanimity regime, even the suggestion of inequality across the creditor group can trigger a 'no' vote; majority

---

110 See *Katz.* v. *Oak Industries Inc.*, 508 A. 2d 873 (Del. Ch. 1986).

111 See Bratton, loc. cit. n. 54, at pp. A-54-A-55, A-70 (§§ 8.5, 17).

112 Revised Model Simplified Indenture, 55 *Bus. Law.* (2000) p. 1115 (Article 9).

rule opens up room for wheeling and dealing. The interposition of a negotiating fiduciary reduces this risk in addition to facilitating face-to-face dealing.

Reform, whether in the greater or lesser version, holds out advantages. Despite this, support from the US lending community cannot be safely assumed. Nothing has prevented the inclusion of majoritarian amendment clauses in bank loans, private placements, and sovereign debt contracts, but such innovations have been resisted. Sovereign debt contracts have shifted to a majoritarian approach in recent years, but only as a result of political pressure placed on sovereign borrowers by the US Treasury Department.[113]

Why do bondholders continue to resist the logic of collective action, which otherwise pervasively shapes corporate institutional arrangements? Myopia, path dependence, and the rest of the list of evolutionary barriers can be suggested. It also should be noted that the zone of private contractual choice for a unanimity regime overlaps the zone of institutional lending. With banks and private placement lenders, relational constraints minimize the holdout problem. But none of this satisfactorily answers the question. If the bondholder community thought that the Trust Indenture Act's unanimity mandate sacrificed substantial value, it easily could lobby to procure the Act's amendment.

It accordingly is worth considering the possibility that lenders perceive financial advantages in a unanimous consent regime. Consider a formal model of bondholding and bond voting structures articulated by Patrick Bolton and David Scharfstein.[114] This suggests that a low-quality firm would find it optimal to maximize its liquidation value: a distress default being likely, it would want contracts carrying as little cost as possible in the event of default. The smaller the number of creditors and the lower the voting barrier, the cheaper the liquidation and the greater the value of the debt.[115] A high-quality firm, in contrast, presents little risk of a distress default. Here Bolton and Scharfstein see strategic default as the dominant problem – for example, the borrower might default on a covenant because it voluntarily seeks to shift value to its equity. Factors increasing the cost of such a default – such as multiple creditors and tougher voting rules – enhance the value of the debt.[116] We emerge with a trade-off keyed to the borrower's credit quality. But Bolton and Scharfstein go on to make an additional suggestion that operates across the board: the greater the number of creditors and the higher the percentage of bondholder votes needed to approve a composition renegotiation,

---

113 See S. Choi and M. Gulati, 'Innovation in Boilerplate Contracts: An Empirical Examination of Sovereign Bonds', 53 *Emory L.J.* (2004) p. 927.

114 P. Bolton and D. Scharfstein, 'Optimal Debt Structure and the Number of Creditors', 104 *J. Pol. Econ.* (1996) p. 1.

115 Ibid., at p. 3.

116 Ibid.

the lower the borrower's surplus in the renegotiation.[117] This point says something important about lenders' preference for unanimous action: although lender dispersion disfavors enforcement when the burden to act lies on the lenders' side (due to small stakes and free-rider problems[118]), when the tables turn and the borrower must obtain the lenders' assent, a high numerical threshold can be advantageous.[119]

Of course, the holdout problem complicates the analysis. But a hard-nosed bondholder has a response: if the offer makes a generous split of a surplus, holdouts will not be so numerous as to threaten the deal. No one ever expects 100 percent participation in a composition, yet such exchange offers close all the time on the basis of supermajority acceptance. A look at the leading private case, *Katz v. Oak Industries*,[120] shows a complex exchange offer with an upset participation requirement of 85 percent. That upset calculation will change from situation to situation. Meanwhile, there is no evidence that holdouts regularly cause exchange offers to fail.[121] When offers fail, it may be that they are too low and as a result attract something much less than a supermajority of creditors.[122]

A numerical example helps explain this. Assume a distressed borrower whose bonds are trading for 650, a value that can be expected to fall further unless a composition succeeds. The borrower, already on the road to recovery, can afford to pay 950. The total bonded indebtedness is 1,000. The surplus is 950 minus 650 or 300. Let us assume that under a two-thirds majority amendment provision, the borrower can get the requisite participation by offering a bond worth 750 in exchange – a two-thirds to one-third split of the surplus in the borrower's favor. With a unanimous action provision, it will have to offer more in order to satisfy higher upset prices among the remaining bondholders. Assume that if it offers a bond worth 850, it will get 90 percent participation under a unanimous action bond contract, leaving holdouts with face value claims of 1,000. The value of the 850 exchange offer is as follows:

---

[117] Ibid., at p. 18. See also A. Bris and I. Welch, 'The Optimal Concentration of Creditors', 60 *J. Fin.* (2005) p. 2193 (summarizing the literature making this point).

[118] See B. Holmstrom, 'Moral Hazard in Teams', 13 *Bell J. Econ.* (1982) p. 324.

[119] Bris and Welch, loc. cit. n. 117, at 2193-94.

[120] 508 A.2d 873 (Del. Ch. 1986).

[121] S. Gilson, 'Transactions Costs and Capital Structure Choice: Evidence from Financially Distressed Firms', 52 *J. Fin.* (1997) p. 161, shows that the holdout problem does not seem to be so severe as to prevent the accomplishment of restructurings respecting public debt, particularly given use of coercive devices like exit consents. See also J. Helwege, 'How Long Do Junk Bonds Spend in Default?' 54 *J. Fin.* (1999) p. 341.

[122] See Kahan and Tuckman, loc. cit. n. 100.

$$\begin{array}{rcl} 850 \times .90 & = & 765 \\ 1{,}000 \times .10 & = & \underline{100} \\ & & 865 \text{ – total yield to the bondholders} \end{array}$$

This recovery reverses the percentage division of the surplus – now it is roughly two-thirds to the bondholders and one-third to the borrower. The problem lies in the possibility that too many bondholders will hold out and defeat the offer, leaving the holders with bonds worth 650. Let us assume that composition failures due to holdouts are rare – a 20 percent possibility. The question is whether that possibility makes the offer under the two-thirds majority clause more attractive. It does not:

$$\begin{array}{rcl} 865 \times .80 & = & 692 \\ 650 \times .20 & = & \underline{130} \\ & & 822 > 750 \end{array}$$

Now say the probabilities are 50-50:

$$\begin{array}{rcl} 865 \times .50 & = & 432.50 \\ 650 \times .50 & = & \underline{325\quad} \\ & & 757.50 > 750 \end{array}$$

The expected value of the offer under the unanimity clause is still greater than that of the offer under the majority amendment clause. Only at under a 50-50 chance of success does the majority amendment clause create value for the bondholders as a whole.

These numbers are posed for the sake of argument. To the extent they strike the reader as plausible, unanimity requirements are not irrational, and value creation under majority rule is not a sure thing. Process reform to improve the out of bankruptcy composition process accordingly is a low probability event.

The extension of the Chapter 11 reorganization process into the territory of pre-bankruptcy composition reinforces the presumption favoring the status quo. The Bankruptcy Code allows a distressed corporate debtor to compose a reorganization plan and solicit consents before making a formal bankruptcy filing.[123] The filing occurs after the consents have been collected, following the Bankruptcy Code's majoritarian process rule. Such a 'prepackaged' plan of reorganization then is presented to the bankruptcy court for quick confirmation.

---

123 11 U.S.C. § 1126(b).

This alternative now predominates over contractual compositions because it holds out tax advantages for the borrower. Process protections, albeit minimal, also are implicated.

5.4 Summary and analysis

The bondholder collective action problem raises two questions. The first concerns the problem's effect *ex post*: whether distressed issuers, through coercively structured, take-it-or-leave-it offers, succeed in effecting compositions more favorable than could be obtained in an arm's length negotiation with an effectively represented lender. The second question concerns the problem's effect *ex ante*: whether, but for the incremental costs of *ex post* renegotiation, public bond contracts would contain protective covenants comparable to those included in bank loans and private placements.

To answer both questions in the affirmative is to support investing the indenture trustee with the powers of a negotiating agent. To realize such a reform's full potential, the trustee-agent would need power to negotiate both amendments and waivers of payment terms as well as amendments and waivers of covenants. This could be done on an experimental basis by amending the Trust Indenture Act to include an 'opt in' permission. Specifically, the Act could provide that a qualified indenture could permit amendments and waivers presenting payment terms on a majoritarian basis, provided that the indenture also invested the trustee with negotiating power and, in the case of a payment term, also required bondholder ratification of the trustee's composition. The 'opt in' approach has the advantage of letting the market decide whether it prefers the traditional unanimous consent approach to structured negotiation and majority consent. Note that the proposal omits the requirement of bondholder ratification where the amendment or waiver concerns a covenant rather than a payment term. The reason lies in problem of *ex ante* effects. The negotiating trustee device holds out the potential *ex ante* benefit of encouraging borrowers to include tighter covenants only if the trustee's decision respecting covenant recontracting is final and the expense and uncertainty of bondholder ratification is avoided.

To answer the first question in the negative is to rely on self-protection by institutional bondholders. Such reliance is more reasonable today than at any time in bond market history. Vulture funds do not hesitate to raise their voices, to vote 'no' on consent solicitations, and even to bring lawsuits. Indeed, they are so uncooperative and obstreperous in their pursuit of maximal settlements from distressed borrowers as to suggest a negative answer to the second question. Borrowers already looking to the bond market for loans on easy terms will be disinclined toward change. The prospect of dealing with empowered trustees constrained by worries about the reactions of vulture investors will not further entice them. Underwriters who now market trust indentures containing generally-phrased terms from the contract form file will move toward more protective contracting only if the bond market registers emphatic demands. The market recently appears to have registered such demands on event risk. Whether it would take the occasion of process reform to go farther and insist on more effective protection respecting problems like claim dilution, asset withdrawal, and asset substitution is an open question.

6. CONCLUSION

This article undertook a review of corporate debt contracting practice in the United States toward the end of gauging the appropriate scope of the contractual reproach to creditor protection in positive law. It now concludes that the scope of the reproach lies in the eye of the beholder.

This article's analysis offers much to suit an observer inclined to the view that the institution of contract provides a robust and complete framework for creditor protection. The practice respecting corporate borrowing has been remarkably stable, much more so than, say, the positive law framework governing shareholder-manager relations. At the same time, the practice has proved responsive to external shocks, whether by redrafting, by repricing, or both, as occurred with event risk. Nor does the account hold out a point at which regulatory intervention clearly would push the practice in a more efficient direction. When bondholders injured by opportunistic managers and shareholders took their complaints to court in the 1980s only to be remitted back to the contracting table, the market took the matter in its stride. That it finally opted for protection against event risk after a decade's lapse bespeaks a contractual success. Finally, however provocative may be the case made for bond market process reform, nothing suggests that the market demands it – if stronger trustees add significant value to bond contracts, we would have seen them long ago.

An observer inclined to be suspicious about the robustness and completeness of contractual creditor protections can reverse this reading. Although contract law assumes that corporate debt contracts are complete, the practice shows otherwise. The market works effectively only with small numbers of lenders who have reputational incentives not to exploit borrowers who get into difficulty *ex post*. Rational borrowers enter into compete contracts *ex ante* only when the circumstances assure them of that zone for *ex post* renegotiation. Where the assurance is lacking, as with public bonds, contracts seemingly tend to be incomplete. That the contracts price out the resulting risks does not prove the optimality of the substantive allocation. Indeed, the bond markets for the most part deal with the agency cost problem not through considered contractual risk allocation but through crude appraisal based on the borrower's credit standing. Meanwhile, agency problems and transaction costs prevent the evolution of a superior contract form. The market's puzzling treatment of event risk supports these assertions. Finally, there is a favorable implication for the positive law of creditor protection: when the financial markets see a high agency cost risk, they either procure contractual protection or refuse to lend. This implies a function for positive law in contexts less suited to considered rejection of risky borrowers.

The Economics of Covenants as a Means of Efficient Creditor Protection

Klaus M. Schmidt*

Abstract

Covenants are a means to mitigate the agency problems between borrower and lender that are induced by the allocation of cash flow rights in a debt contract. This comment shows that if covenants could be renegotiated without any transaction costs they could be used to induce efficient behaviour on the part of the borrower and to fully protect lenders. Due to problems of asymmetric information, collective action and hold-up, however, covenants are imperfect. The analysis suggests several ways to improve the functioning of covenants.

Keywords: Covenants, creditor protection, agency costs of debt, renegotiation.

1. INTRODUCTION

Covenants are the prevalent and most important means of creditor protection in the United States. William Bratton[1] offers a brilliant analysis of the role of covenants that is rich in legal and historical detail and that describes and explains the evolution of real world contracting practices and the levels of various forms of covenant protection as a reaction to economic developments. The main purpose of this comment is to complement Bratton's analysis by having a closer look at the

---

* Prof. Dr Klaus M. Schmidt, Department of Economics, University of Munich, e-mail: klaus.schmidt@Lrz.uni-muenchen.de. Financial support by the Deutsche Forschungsgemeinschaft through SFB-TR 15 is gratefully acknowledged.

[1] W.W. Bratton, 'Bond Covenants and Creditor Protection: Law and Economics, Theory and Practice, Substance and Process', in this volume.

agency problems that covenants are supposed to solve. I will argue that all of these agency problems stem from a fundamental conflict of interests between creditors and debt holders that is induced by the allocation of cash flow rights through a debt contract. Then I will show how a covenant would solve this problem in an ideal world in which contracts can be renegotiated efficiently and without any transaction costs. In the real world, however, covenants will be imperfect. Nevertheless, the analysis suggests several possibilities that could be used to improve the functioning of covenants.

2. AGENCY PROBLEMS INDUCED BY A DEBT CONTRACT

Covenants are a means to protect creditors against various forms of opportunistic behaviour on the part of debt holders: claim dilution, asset withdrawal, underinvestment and asset substitution.[2] From an economic perspective, all of these agency problems stem from the same fundamental conflict of interests between borrowers and lenders. This conflict is induced by the allocation of cash flow rights in a debt contract. If the borrower is successful and can repay his debt, the lender receives a fixed return while the borrower gets all of the remaining profits. If the borrower fails and defaults on his debt, the lender can seize the assets of the borrower's firm that are not reserved for lenders of higher seniority while the borrower gets nothing. Thus, any action that increases the firm's risk by increasing its returns in case of success and reducing them in case of failure is to the benefit of the borrower at the expense of the lender. Similarly, any action that shifts assets that the lender can seize in case of default to the borrower or to new lenders is beneficial to the borrower and detrimental to the lender. This is exactly what is going on in the four agency problems mentioned above:

- Claim dilution: If the firm takes up additional credit to invest in new investment projects or to pay out dividends to shareholders, it makes default more likely and reduces the claims of the original lender in case of default.
- Asset withdrawal: If the firm sells some of its assets and transfers the proceeds to its shareholders, it again reduces the collateral of the lender.
- Underinvestment: If the firm is worth less than its outstanding debt, the borrower has no incentive to invest in profitable investment projects because all the returns would accrue to the lender. His inaction reduces the value of the debt held by his creditors.
- Asset substitution: The borrower has an incentive to invest in very risky projects even if their expected return is negative. The borrower benefits from the investment in case of success and is protected by limited liability in case of

[2] For a more detailed discussion of these problems, see Bratton, loc. cit. n. 1.

failure. Thus, most of the gains of the investment accrue to the borrower, while most of the losses are borne by the lender. If the firm is close to bankruptcy, this form of 'gambling for resurrection' is particularly attractive to the borrower.

Obviously, the higher leveraged and more risky the firm, the stronger is this conflict of interests.

It is important to note that these agency problems not only cause a redistribution of wealth from the lender to the borrower, but also give rise to substantial efficiency losses. If redistribution was the only effect, the lender could be protected by a higher interest rate as an *ex ante* compensation for the expected expropriation in the future. However, the problem is much more difficult, because the opportunistic behaviour of the borrower may destroy some or all of the surplus that could be generated. First of all, bankruptcy is (*ex post*) inefficient and leads to a substantial destruction of the firm's value. Thus, if the opportunistic actions of the borrower increase the probability of bankruptcy, they increase the expected efficiency loss due to the possibility of default. Second, if the borrower invests in a very risky project, he destroys value if the project has a negative net present value. Finally, and perhaps most importantly, it may be impossible to finance an efficient investment project if the opportunistic behaviour of the borrower cannot be prevented. Thus, from an *ex ante* perspective, it is in the *joint interest* of creditor and debtor to prevent opportunistic behaviour.

3. COVENANTS AND RENEGOTIATION

Covenants are a contractual solution to this problem. A covenant restricts the actions that the borrower can take. The desired effect is that it prevents opportunistic actions on the part of the borrower that destroy firm value at the expense of the creditor but to the benefit of the debtor. However, there may be undesired side effects. In an uncertain world, it is impossible to write a complete contingent contract that governs the borrower's behaviour in all possible states of the world. Thus, the same covenant that is intended to prevent an opportunistic action on the part of the borrower may also prevent him from taking an efficient action that would be beneficial for both debtor and creditor. Therefore, renegotiation of covenants is important.

Let us suppose for a moment that there are no transaction costs of renegotiation and that renegotiation would always lead to an *ex post* efficient agreement. In this ideal world, there would be a simple solution to the agency problems of debt. The debt contract would contain a covenant that makes any investment (and any other action) by the borrower impossible. Clearly, this prevents any opportunistic and inefficient action by the borrower. Note, however, that it does *not* prevent efficient investments. If there is an efficient investment opportunity, the borrower will approach the lender and propose to renegotiate the covenant. Because the investment is efficient, it generates a surplus that can be shared between the two parties. Because both parties have to agree, neither of them will be harmed if the covenant is renegotiated to allow for the investment. Finally, because renegotiation is costless, all efficient investment projects will be undertaken.

However, in the real world, renegotiation is imperfect and hampered by considerable transaction costs. First of all, there are often informational asymmetries between lenders and borrowers. If the borrower is better informed about the characteristics of a potential investment project than the lender, the two parties may be unable to reach an efficient agreement, no matter how the renegotiation process is structured.[3] Second, there is a collective action problem between different lenders. The more lenders there are, the more difficult it is to reach an agreement, because each lender has an incentive to free-ride on the concessions made by the other lenders. Furthermore, the provision of information about the firm's investment projects is a public good, and the smaller each creditor, the less of an incentive he has to engage in costly information provision. Thus, many creditors aggravate the problem of asymmetric information.

While asymmetric information and collective action problems may yield an *ex post* inefficient renegotiation outcome, there is also scope for two forms of *ex ante* inefficiency that may arise if the parties anticipate that the original contract will be renegotiated. First, there is a hold-up problem. If the lender has some bargaining power in the renegotiation process, he will get some of the surplus from renegotiation. But this reduces the incentives of the borrower to exert effort in order to find efficiency-enhancing investment projects. Second, there may be a soft budget constraint problem. This is the converse of the hold-up problem. If the borrower anticipates that a debt contract will be renegotiated in order to avoid inefficient bankruptcy, and if he gets a share of the surplus from this renegotiation, he has less of an incentive to work hard in order prevent default.

How important each of these transaction costs is depends not only on the investment project under consideration but also on the type of lending. For example, if the firm issues a bond, then it has to deal with many different creditors. Because of the collective action problem among bondholders, this makes renegotiation very difficult if not impossible. Thus, less restrictive covenants have to be used that give more discretion (and more room for opportunistic behaviour) to the borrower. On the other hand, bond financing imposes a hard budget constraint on the borrower (and his manager). If the firm does not meet its

---

[3] R.B. Myerson and M.A. Satterthwaite, 'Efficient Mechanisms for Bilateral Trading', 29 *Journal of Economic Theory* (1983) pp. 265-281, show that if there is asymmetric information, then there is no bargaining procedure that allows the parties to reach an efficient agreement with probability one.

financial obligations, it is impossible to renegotiate around inefficient bankruptcy. Thus, the borrower (and his manager) will work harder to avoid default.[4] Another benefit of bond financing is that bonds can be publicly traded. This allows for an efficient allocation of risk among bondholders. Furthermore, each individual bondholder feels protected because he can exit any time by selling his bond. But, of course, bondholders as a whole cannot exit.

On the other hand, if the firm takes up debt from a bank or from a private lender, it deals with only one or very few lenders. In this case, renegotiation is facilitated because collective action problems and problems of asymmetric information are less severe. Thus, covenants can be more restrictive and more effective in preventing opportunistic behaviour on the part of the borrower. On the other hand, from an *ex ante* perspective, this may be problematic if it gives rise to a hold-up or soft budget constraint problem. Furthermore, the allocation of risk among creditors will be less efficient.

4. How to Make Creditor Protection More Efficient

The economic analysis of covenants suggests several ways to improve creditor protection. First, renegotiation is burdened by informational asymmetries between debtor and creditors. Thus, any measure that reduces these asymmetries would be beneficial. For example, one could think about more informative accounting rules that are specifically designed to address the informational needs of creditors. Furthermore, there may be a role for 'informed lenders', such as venture capitalists who have detailed and specific knowledge of the industry under consideration.

A second option is to try to reduce the collective action problem among creditors in order to improve the renegotiation process. The collective action problem could be mitigated by changing the formal procedures that are required to reach an agreement among creditors. One suggestion is to have a formal renegotiation process (outside bankruptcy) that does not require unanimity to reach a binding agreement but adopts a (super-)majority rule. It has been argued that this facilitates reaching an efficient agreement among creditors. However, this need not be the case. Under a unanimity rule each creditor is pivotal, which gives a strong incentive to vote in favour of an efficiency-enhancing proposal. Furthermore, unanimity protects each creditor against potential exploitation by his fellow creditors, who cannot impose a change in the terms of the debt contract on him. A (super-)majority rule, on the other hand, may invite free-riding (because not everybody has to agree) and could also be used by a majority of creditors to

---

4 This idea is developed formally by P. Bolton and D.S. Scharfstein, 'Optimal Debt Structure and the Number of Creditors', 104 *Journal of Political Economy* (1996) pp. 1-25.

exploit a minority. Therefore, any deviation from unanimity should be considered cautiously and should require the unanimous consent of all creditors *ex ante*, i.e., at the stage of lending.

An alternative possibility would be the formal introduction of a trustee who negotiates with the borrower on behalf of all bondholders. The crucial question is whether the trustee should be allowed to take a decision on behalf of bondholders by himself (which raises obvious agency problems between the trustee and the creditors) or whether any deal with the borrower has to be unanimously agreed upon by all creditors in a final vote. Even with a final vote of all creditors a trustee could be very beneficial in coordinating creditors and preventing haggling between them.

A more radical solution to the agency problems between debtors and creditors would be to change the design of a debt contract. A debt contract allocates cash flow and control rights endogenously. If the borrower can repay, he is the full residual claimant on profits and has the residual rights of control, i.e., he is free to take any decision that does not violate the covenants of his debt contract or any other legal rules. On the other hand, if the borrower defaults, the lender is the residual claimant on profits and takes over control of the firm. This endogenous allocation of cash flow and control rights could be more sophisticated. For example, a contingent covenant could allocate specific control rights contingent on certain performance measures. If the firm is doing well, no covenants are imposed on the borrower. If, however, the firm does not reach certain milestones, the borrower is restricted by covenants that have to be renegotiated. Thus, in these states of the world, effective control is shifted to lenders.

Another example is the use of convertible securities, which are the prevalent form of financing for risky and highly leveraged start-up companies by venture capitalists. With a convertible security, the lender can choose whether he wants the debt to be repaid or whether he wants to convert his debt claim into equity of the firm. This discourages excessive risk taking by the borrower[5] and induces the lender to get more closely involved into the project.[6] Financial innovations along these lines deserve much more attention in the law and economics literature.

---

[5] See, e.g., R. Green, 'Investment Incentives, Debt, and Warrants', 13 *Journal of Financial Economics* (1984) pp. 115-136.

[6] See K.M. Schmidt, 'Convertible Securities and Venture Capital Finance', 58 *Journal of Finance* (2003) pp. 1139-1166.

Creditor Protection Through Mandatory Disclosure

Hanno Merkt*

* Professor of Law, Director of the Institute for Foreign and International Private Law, Albert Ludwigs University, Freiburg.

Abstract
Creditor protection through mandatory disclosure has long been a highly debated issue among corporate lawyers. This paper considers whether the legal system should compel corporations to disclose information publicly in order to better protect their creditors. First, the paper elaborates on the various economic rationales of mandatory disclosure advanced by proponents of that approach. Second, it reviews the theoretical framework of mandatory disclosure. Third, it gives a brief overview of the law on those mandatory disclosure requirements that primarily – or at least partially – focus on corporate creditor protection. Fourth, it outlines limitations of mandatory disclosure with respect to creditors and debtor companies. Fifth, it briefly surveys several important challenges to mandatory disclosure regulation with respect to materiality, standardization, comprehensibility and timeliness. Finally, this paper deals with various legislative options to enforce creditor-protective mandatory disclosure.

Keywords: creditor protection, mandatory disclosure, *Inspire Art*, materiality of information, soft information, Basel II, standardization, comprehensibility, timeliness, enforcement of disclosure duties.

1. INTRODUCTION

1.1 A classic debate

It is almost self-evident that those who lend money or advance credit can benefit from having reliable financial information pertaining to the corporations with whom they deal. This is true for virtually any type of creditor, be it a bank, an institutional investor, a commercial creditor in supply industries, or the proverbial small tradesman rendering services to the corporation. In dealing with the prospective debtor, all of these creditors will thus be able to carry out in a more effective fashion the process of "screening" to determine whether it is worthwhile to transact. Also, with an ongoing debt contract, a creditor can assess on a periodic basis the debtor's creditworthiness and determine whether corrective action is required.[1] It is, therefore, perfectly plausible that corporations do provide their various creditors to a very large extent with information regarding their financial status. In addition, many jurisdictions require corporations to publicly disclose certain basic information before starting business or borrowing funds. For example, virtually all important jurisdictions require corporations to file their charters with state officials or public registers, giving access to information about the incorporators, the directors, the legal capital, restrictions on director liability, and the like. Many jurisdictions have improved their public registers in recent years in order to present such information in a more user-friendly fashion. Furthermore, all jurisdictions require corporations to keep proper accounting, and many of those jurisdictions, in addition to that, require certified auditing and subsequent disclosure of accounts.[2]

And still, after almost a century of fierce legislative, judicial, and academic debate, disclosure stands right in the center of the debate over the best and most efficient ways to organize company activities *vis-à-vis* shareholders, creditors, and other market participants. Regulators literally all over the world, from New Zealand[3] and Australia[4] to the United States[5] and Europe, are in the process of addressing whether their domestic disclosure rules are rigorous enough in the light of the problems and implications thrown up by recent corporate collapses –

---

1 L.C.B. Gower and P.L. Davies, *Principles of Modern Company Law*, 7th edn. (London, Sweet & Maxwell 2003) p. 531.

2 G. Hertig and H. Kanda, 'Creditor Protection', in R. Kraakman, et al., eds., *The Anatomy of Corporate Law – A Comparative and Functional Approach* (Oxford, Oxford University Press 2005) p. 71 at p. 79.

3 See, e.g., the establishment of a Working Group for Improved Product and Investment Advisor Disclosure of the Securities Commission of New Zealand.

4 See, e.g., the recent establishment of a roundtable by the Australian SEC examining proposals for better protecting investors by reforming financial disclosure and auditor oversight.

5 See, e.g., SEC Regulation FD (Fair Disclosure) of 24 August 2000, Release No. 33-7881, analyzed by S.E. Bochner and S. Bukhari, 'The Duty to Update and Disclosure Reform: The Impact of Regulation FD and Current Disclosure Initiatives', 7 *Stan. J.L. Bus. & Fin.* (2002) p. 225; M. Steinberg and J. Myers, 'Lurking in the Shadows: The Hidden Issues of the Securities and Exchange Commission's Regulation FD', 27 *J. Corp. L.* (2002) p. 173; M. Morano, 'Reg FD: Its Effects on the Role of Analysts, Market Volatility on Wall Street, and Information Flow from Issuers', 54 *Rutgers L. Rev.* (2002) p. 535.

such as HIH and One.Tel in Australia, Enron and Worldcom in the United States, and Ahold, Comroad and Parmalat in Europe to name only few of the most spectacular ones – and the risks associated with inadequate disclosure.

1.2 The HLG approach to disclosure

Completely in line with these developments, the High Level Group of Company Law Experts in its Final Report from 2002 strongly advocated disclosure of information as a regulatory instrument.[6] According to the Report, requiring disclosure of information can be a powerful regulatory tool in company law. It enhances the accountability for and the transparency of the company's governance and its affairs. Therefore, the Group recommends that capital and control structures of listed companies should be disclosed comprehensively and that such disclosure should be updated continuously. However, the Report goes one important step further in stating: "Disclosure requirements can sometimes provide a more efficient regulatory tool than substantive regulation through more or less detailed rules. According to the Group, such disclosure creates a lighter regulatory environment and allows for greater flexibility and adaptability. Moreover, although the regulatory effect may in theory be more indirect and remote than with substantive rules, in practice enforcement of disclosure requirements as such is normally easier."[7] Hence, the Reports suggests that the European Union, in considering new – and amending existing – regulation of company law, should carefully consider whether disclosure requirements are better suited to achieve the desired effects than substantive rules.

It is that concept of superiority of mandatory disclosure over merit regulation that deserves particular attention, since it bluntly challenges firm convictions of company regulators as well as academics in many Member States of the European Union. Especially in the context of modernization of the current EU regime of creditor protection, the concept of "disclosure-over-merit-regulation" deserves attention. This paper considers whether the legal system should compel corporations to disclose information publicly in order to better protect its creditors. Part 1 of this paper elaborates on the various economic rationales of mandatory disclosure advanced by proponents of that approach. Part 2 rehearses the theoretical framework of mandatory disclosure. Part 3 gives a brief overview of the law on those mandatory disclosure requirements that primarily or at least in part aim at corporate creditor protection. Part 4 outlines limitations of mandatory disclosure

---

[6] *Report of the High Level Group of Company Law Experts on a Modern Regulatory Framework for Company Law in Europe* (hereinafter cited as 'High Level Report'), Brussels, 4 November 2002, pp. 33-35, 45-47, 95-96.

[7] High Level Report, op. cit. n. 6, at p.34.

with respect to creditors and debtor companies. Part 5 briefly surveys several important challenges to mandatory disclosure regulation with respect to materiality, standardization, comprehensibility and timeliness. Finally, part 6 deals with various legislative options to enforce creditor-protective mandatory disclosure.

2. THEORY: VIRTUES OF CREDITOR-PROTECTIVE MANDATORY DISCLOSURE

2.1 **Protective function of mandatory disclosure**

Looking somewhat closer at the economic rationale for mandatory disclosure, two basic types of justifications can be identified. First, there are various protective functions of mandatory disclosure, which in general are hardly contested today. According to one early analysis, investor confidence (in a broad sense of share and debt capital investors) in the capital market can be regarded as an overriding aim of disclosure, while investor protection, the monitoring of company law, the transparency of the market operations, and sales promotion can be regarded as subsidiary aims.[8] Other commentators have suggested that investor confidence and protection (and thereby the promotion of investor confidence) and prevention of fraud are of equal rank as functions of mandatory disclosure.[9] Still other commentators emphasize investor or individual protection and market protection (protection of the functioning of the market) as the two main protective aims of disclosure with a couple of further protective functions subordinated to each of them.[10]

2.2 **Market failure**

The second type of justification circles around market efficiency and market failure, as already mentioned, and still is far less uncontested among economists and legal academics.[11] It is well accepted that credit markets like securities markets are characterized by incomplete information, which gives rise to problems of adverse selection, moral hazard, and underproduction of information. Mandating disclosure

---

[8] E. Wymeersch, *Control of Securities Markets in the European Economic Community*, Collection Studies, Competition – Approximation of Legislation Series No. 31 (Brussels 1977) pp. 139-142; cf. also OECD Principles of Corporate Governance, SG/CG (99) 5 sub IV.

[9] N. Moloney, *EC Securities Regulation* (Oxford, Oxford University Press 2002) p. 120.

[10] K.J. Hopt, *Der Kapitalanlegerschutz im Recht der Banken* (Munich, Beck 1975); H. Merkt, *Unternehmenspublizität – Die Offenlegung von Unternehmensdaten als Korrelat der Marktteilnahme* (Tübingen, Mohr Siebeck 2001).

[11] T. Baums, 'Changing Patterns of Corporate Disclosure in Continental Europe: The Example of Germany', 30 *Giurisprudenza Commerciale* (2003) pp. 53-69.

is expected to reduce the cost of capital.[12] Therefore, it is pretty safe to say that mandatory disclosure today is not a matter of principle (disclosure does have beneficial effects),[13] but a matter of counterbalancing its positive and negative effects (is disclosure too costly in the light of its beneficial effects?). With respect to the fostering of market efficiency through promotion of price accuracy, it is argued that, where markets are efficient, in that information is reflected in prices, disclosure serves to ensure that securities or debt instruments are correctly priced, in that they reflect the intrinsic value of the issuer, and, in turn, given the role of financial markets in allocating capital, that capital is efficiently allocated. Investment or capital-allocation decisions are therefore made not on the basis of speculation or advertising but in an efficient manner, based on the value of the security. The role of disclosure in establishing a pricing mechanism has been emphasized as critical, in that behavior of securities prices has a deep effect on the efficiency of securities markets.[14] This is probably also correct for debt pricing.

At the center of the law and economics debate over disclosure as a regulatory tool stands, as already mentioned, the question whether and to what extent the mere dissemination of issuer information should be mandatory and managed by public rules or left to market forces and the incentives given to companies and other suppliers of information to provide adequate disclosure. The market-failure doctrine teaches that regulation should be imposed on the market only in order to correct a market failure. It operates on the assumption that a perfect market exists which will allocate resources efficiently and that regulation is a corrective to an imperfect market. Information may represent a market failure in this area in that, in the absence of public control, it will not be disseminated, or not sufficiently,[15] as a result of its public good nature,[16] and the efficient allocation of resources will accordingly be prejudiced.[17] Mandatory disclosure regimes can thus be viewed as

---

[12] F. Allen and D. Gale, *Comparing Financial Systems* (Cambridge, MA, The MIT Press 2000).

[13] See R. Kraakman, 'Disclosure and Corporate Governance: An Overview Essay', in G. Ferrarini, et al., eds., *Reforming Company and Takeover Law in Europe* (Oxford, Oxford University Press 2004) p. 95 at p. 96.

[14] J.C. Coffee, 'Market Failure and the Economic Case for a Mandatory Disclosure System', 70 *Va. L. Rev.* (1984) p. 717 at p. 734.

[15] On the problems of underproduction and underutilization of information, see G. Hertig, R. Kraakman, and E. Rock, 'Issuers and Investor Protection', in Kraakman, et al., op. cit. n. 2, p. 193 at pp. 204-207.

[16] On the public good nature of information, see A. Ogus, *Regulation – Legal Forms and Economic Theory* (Oxford, Clarendon Press 1994) pp. 33-35; J.P. Trachtman, 'The Applicability of Law and Economics to Law and Development: The Case of Financial Law', in J.J. Norton and M.T. Andenas, eds., *Emerging Financial Markets and the Role International Financial Organizations* (London/The Hague, Kluwer Law International 1996) p. 54.

[17] A.C. Page and R.B. Ferguson, *Investor Protection* (London, Weidenfeld and Nicholson 1992) pp. 36 et seq.

"a desirable cost reduction strategy through which society, in effect, subsidizes search costs to secure both a greater quantity of information and a better testing of its accuracy."[18] Absent mandatory disclosure, investors would also have greater private incentives to invest in the pursuit of information that gives rise to trading gains. As Coffee observes, "collectivization through mandatory disclosure minimizes the social waste that would otherwise result from misallocation of economic resources to this pursuit."[19] In addition, agency problems like opportunistic management behavior to the detriment of corporate creditors could give managers a private incentive to manipulate the disclosure of information, either by concealing bad news or exaggerating good news.[20]

Information markets are also subject to signaling problems that can make it impossible to distinguish high-quality credible information from low-quality information. These difficulties can arguably lead to a "lemons" type failure. Furthermore, even if each issuer had an incentive to provide just the right quantity and quality of information to the market, they could do so using a wide variety of different formats and reporting conventions. These variations could impose significant information-processing costs on investors seeking to compare and contrast voluntary reports. Mandatory disclosure conventions economize on these costs.[21]

Recent advances in behavioral economics provide yet another rationale for mandatory disclosure regimes. Executives and promoters are arguably subject to perceptual biases which can cause them to be honestly more optimistic than the proverbial "prudent merchant" acting under similar circumstances. A mandatory disclosure regime which requires that bad news be revealed along with an insider's honestly held optimistic assessment can arguably help correct for a range of cognitive biases and at the same time promote more accurate pricing in the markets.[22]

Alternatively, it has been argued that, left to their own devices, companies and their management will ultimately produce sufficient information for the market to provide optimum levels of protection and information for investors, because investors will discount the value of securities in respect of which less information is disclosed, as those securities represent a riskier investment when compared to

---

18 Coffee, loc. cit. n. 14, at p. 722.

19 Ibid.

20 P.G. Mahoney, 'Mandatory Disclosure as a Solution to Agency Problems', 62 *U. of Chi. L. Rev.* (1995) p. 1047.

21 M. Kahan and M. Klausner, 'Standardization and Innovation in Corporate Contracting (or "The Economics of Boilerplate")', 83 *Va. L. Rev.* (1997) p. 713.

22 D. Langevoort, 'The Epistemology of Corporate-Securities Lawyering: Beliefs, Biases and Organizational Behavior', 63 *Brook. L. Rev.* (1997) p. 629.

securities in respect of which more information is disclosed.[23] Where information would not be produced other than via a mandatory disclosure system, the benefits of the information in question are outweighed by the costs of production. As companies compete for creditors' funds, they are, one might argue, already given adequate incentives to produce information to the extent and quality required by the market. Proponents of this line of reasoning can rely on empirical research comparing the disclosure produced by US companies before and after the introduction of the mandatory federal disclosure regime in 1933 and 1934. This research found that companies typically voluntarily produced financial statements (albeit in accordance with a listing obligation) which contained, for the most part, a large proportion of the information which would be required subsequently under the mandatory federal regime.[24] In the US context, this argument has two far-reaching implications. First, voluntary disclosure is preferable over mandatory disclosure. Second, securities regulation is not a proper subject for federal jurisdiction. Hence, it should be returned to the individual state legislatures where it was before the federalization of securities legislation,[25] bringing disclosure regulation back to the realm of competition ("competitive federalism"[26]), thereby ensuring that information is disclosed in such quantity and quality as the market requires. From the perspective of pragmatism, however, it seems that public control over companies and their disclosure policies ensures that disclosure is made available in a standardized manner which facilitates investors in making comparisons. Indeed, the importance of standardization is highlighted in the reforms which have been proposed to the European Union's current disclosure regime.

3. REALITY: CURRENT STATE OF CREDITOR-PROTECTIVE MANDATORY DISCLOSURE

3.1 Harmonized EU Member State law

Today, by virtue of EU company law regulations, all EU jurisdictions share an identical minimum standard level of disclosure.[27] According to the First Company

---

[23] Cf., H.S. Scott, 'Internationalization of Primary Public Securities Markets', 63 *Law and Contemporary Problems* (2000) p. 71 at p. 75 et seq., who challenges the discounting theory.

[24] F.H. Easterbrook and D.R. Fischel, 'Mandatory Disclosure and the Protection of Investors', 70 *Va. L. Rev.* (1984) p. 669; R. Romano, 'Empowering Investors: A Market Approach to Securities Regulation', 107 *Yale L.J.* (1998) p. 2359 at p. 2373 et seq.

[25] See the thorough analysis in R. Romano, *The Advantage of Competitive Federalism for Securities Regulation* (Washington, AEI Press 2002).

[26] Romano, op. cit. n. 25, at pp. 112-146.

[27] V. Edwards, *EU Company Law* (Oxford, Oxford University Press 1999) p. 19 et seq.

Law Directive of 1968, companies have to disclose a number of documents and particulars, e.g., the instrument of constitution; the appointment, termination of office and particulars of the representatives and the directors of the company; and on an annual basis the amount of capital subscribed as well as the balance sheet and the profit and loss account.[28] The First Directive itself justifies this minimum standard with the following reasoning. The coordination of national provisions concerning disclosure is of special importance, particularly for the purpose of protecting the interests of creditors. Moreover, the basic documents of the company should be disclosed in order that creditors may be able to ascertain their contents and other information concerning the company. The duty to disclose the annual accounts is then defined more precisely in Fourth Company Law Directive of 1978, stipulating that the annual accounts shall give a true and fair view of the company's assets, liabilities, financial position, and profit or loss.[29] Finally, the Fourth Directive requires companies to submit professional audits.

However, in practice the seemingly high standard of the disclosure obligation for all companies under EU law is toned down in part for three reasons. First, European jurisdictions freely use their power to simplify accounting requirements for medium[30] and small-sized[31] companies. Second, they do not provide for satisfactory enforcement of public disclosure requirements, particularly in the case of closely held companies, which still flout EU mandatory disclosure to a remarkable extent.[32] Third, and most importantly, several jurisdictions reject EU accounting methodology and stick with traditional accounting principles. This is the case under domestic German accounting law, which still disregards the information-oriented "true and fair view" accounting standard just mentioned in favor of a more conservative so-called "precaution" approach that purports to be more protective of creditor interests by signaling that a company's assets and revenue can safely cover its liabilities or, if they might not, by ensuring that creditors know this and can file for corrective action.[33]

---

28 Art. 2(1)(a)-(f) of First Council Directive 68/151/EEC of 9 March 1968 on co-ordination of safeguards which, for the protection of the interests of members and others, are required by Member States of companies within the meaning of the second paragraph of Article 58 of the Treaty, with a view to making such safeguards equivalent throughout the Community, *OJ* 1968 L 65/8-12.

29 Art. 2(3) of Fourth Council Directive 78/660/EEC of 25 July 1978 based on Art. 54(3)(g) of the Treaty on the annual accounts of certain types of companies, *OJ* 1978 L 222/11-31.

30 Art. 47(2) of Fourth Council Directive 78/660/EEC.

31 Art. 11 Fourth Council Directive 78/660/EEC.

32 M. Habersack, *Europäisches Gesellschaftsrecht*, 2nd edn. (Munich, Beck 2003) p. 44.

33 The 'true and fair view' approach is not considered an overriding principle of accounting but is limited to the notes to the annual accounts. This is known in German accounting as the 'uncoupling' approach (*Abkopplungsthese*), see R.W. Walz, 'Der Einfluß von Globalisierung

company directors are concerned. At the same time, the Court clarified that attempts by the Member States to circumvent the incorporation principle or to introduce provisions relating to capital which discriminate against the establishment of foreign companies would be held incompatible with the principle of freedom of establishment.

In its earlier *Centros* decision,[42] the Court put a strong emphasis on mandatory disclosure as a less restrictive but suitable equivalent to a substantive minimum capital requirement. The possibilities for the company creditors and contracting parties to distinguish by way of disclosed information between a foreign branch and a domestic company, as well as supportive Community law measures (annual accounts and disclosure requirements), provide most effective protection.

According to *Überseering*,[43] the protection of domestic creditors could only under very specific circumstances and conditions justify an impairment of the freedom of establishment by substantive regulation. Obviously, the Court again favors creditor protection through disclosure over merit regulation, which is less capable of infringing upon the freedom of establishment.

In contrast to EC law, US corporate law sharply distinguishes between close and public corporations. With respect to close corporations, the law of the States only requires them to *keep* financial accounts. There is no duty to *publicly disclose* those accounts. This leaves creditors of close corporations rather unprotected by statutory law. With respect to public corporations, some protection is given to creditors through extensive financial disclosure requirements under securities regulations which originally and in the first place were designed for the protection of actual and potential shareholders, with the publication of the annual accounts lying at the center. In addition, US accounting law, like the law of the United Kingdom, seeks to protect creditors by requiring public corporations to present a true and fair view of their current financial position. In the United States, most of the information needed by creditors to evaluate the solvency of their client corporations is provided for on a private or contractual basis. Closely held US corporations have to submit detailed financial information to credit rating agencies in order to get access to financing in the ordinary course of business. Credit insurers and credit rating agencies have the power to obtain in many circumstances voluntary information on corporate accounts. Furthermore, there are additional sources they can rely upon to build up files on corporations. These include the press, privately compiled director's databases, trade references, and the payment history of corporations.[44]

---

42 ECJ, Case C-212/97 *Centros Ltd.* v. *Erhvervs-og Selskabsstyrelsen* [1999] *ECR* I-1459.

43 ECJ, Case C-208/00 *Überseering BV* v. *Nordic Construction Company Baumanagement GmbH (NCC)* [2002] *ECR* I-9919.

44 B.R. Cheffins, *Company Law, Theory, Structure and Operation* (Oxford, Clarendon Press 1997) p. 518 et seq.

4. Limitations to Creditor-Protective Mandatory Disclosure

4.1 **Creditors**

4.1.1 *Heterogeneous group*

In considering key limitations to the concept of creditor-protective mandatory disclosure, let us begin with corporate creditors. They form a pretty heterogeneous group, with banks and large institutional investors at the upper end, medium- and small-sized commercial creditors mostly in supply industries in the middle range, and the proverbial small tradesman rendering services to the corporation at the low end. Some of these creditors are very sophisticated, others are not. Most of them extend credit to several or even many corporate debtors, thereby diversifying their risk.

4.1.2 *Hybrid creditors*

Let us consider large, professional, and sophisticated creditors first. In many cases, these creditors are simultaneously shareholders of the debtor corporation, with considerable shareholdings that grant access to all internal information of the corporation. For this group of insider-creditors (or hybrid creditors), mandatory disclosure is of marginal relevance at best. It provides a first-hand or supplemental informational basis of limited value and size, while more substantial and important information is provided for by internal (and confidential) information exchange.

On the other hand, if debt is traded by securitization on large and liquid debt capital markets, the situation of creditors (mainly investment funds) is comparable to securities investors. Here, the need for extensive disclosure of debtor-related information is identical to disclosure under securities regulation.

4.1.3 *Large creditors*

What has been said about hybrid creditors is likewise true for those creditors that grant credit only on the basis of financial covenants, like public bonds, bank loans, and private placements. As we see in the US and UK credit industry (and to a growing extent in continental practice as well), creditors can find out much of what they want to know without the assistance of legislation. A party that is contemplating lending money or extending credit in most instances has the option of declining to proceed unless those running the corporation agree to provide information concerning its current financial status and submit designated material facts at relevant intervals. Those that are seeking to borrow money or obtain credit will then comply or have to look elsewhere. Creditor pressure can similarly provide a company with the incentive to arrange for an audit or similar external review.

In practice, US professional creditors do their best to install relevant safeguards into credit arrangements, typically in the form of financial covenants.[45] In these agreements, which typically are built into the loan contract, companies promise to restrict their dividend payments, maintain a certain minimum capital, and maintain a healthy relationship between proprietary and borrowed capital. This method of regulation is rounded off and effectuated by the fact that company adopts information and accountancy obligations, including, in particular, the delivery of so-called "soft" company data.[46] A comparison of these individual contracts with German capital maintenance law reveals that the two are remarkably similar.[47] Quite pointedly, it looks as though the German statutory law regarding capital maintenance is being replicated contractually.[48] On the same note, it cannot be denied that this contractual protection is less reliable.[49] Creditors must individually and contractually safeguard themselves, which leads to an increase in transaction costs. However, since financial covenants are available for many different industries as model contracts, the increase in transaction costs and the lack of reliability is limited.[50]

4.1.4 *Small creditors*

This brings us to small contractual creditors. It is obvious that the viability of the rescission of financial covenants depends on the bargaining power of the creditor in question. Small creditors, who lack sufficient bargaining power to negotiate a financial covenant in the first place, or who do not wish to negotiate a covenant because of the time, cost, and expertise required, are indirectly protected through a kind of reflex, which originates in the covenants already negotiated by the larger

---

[45] S.A. Ross, R.W. Westerfield, and J.F. Jaffe, *Corporate Finance*, 7th edn. (Boston, McGraw-Hill 2005) p. 425; B. Manning and J.J. Hanks, *Legal Capital*, 3rd edn. (Westbury, N.Y., The Foundation Press 1990) pp. 105-113; Mülbert and Birke, loc. cit. n. 37, at p. 723 et seq.

[46] For a brief discussion of soft information, see Hertig, Kraakman, and Rock, loc. cit. n. 15, at p. 199 et seq.

[47] C. Leuz, 'The Role of Accrual Accounting in Restricting Dividends to Shareholders', 7 *European Accounting Review* (1998) p. 580; R. Leftwich, 'Accounting information in private markets: evidence from private lending agreements', 58 *Accounting Review* (1983) p. 23.

[48] W. Schön, 'Gesellschafter-, Gläubiger- und Anlegerschutz im Europäischen Bilanzrecht', 29 *Zeitschrift für Unternehmens- und Gesellschaftsrecht* (2000) p. 706 at p. 727.

[49] For an overview of UK law, see A. Keay, 'Director's Duties to Creditors: Contractarian Concerns Relating to Efficiency and Over-Protection of Creditors', 66 *Modern L. Rev.* (2003) p. 665.

[50] H. Merkt, 'Der Kapitalschutz in Europa – ein rocher de bronze?', 33 *Zeitschrift für Unternehmens- und Gesellschaftsrecht* (2004) p. 305 at pp. 317-319.

creditors. Those large creditors exercise the function of a factual trustee for all small creditors. Borrowers, on the other hand, generally have longstanding relationships with one or several banks, giving the latter privileged access to firm-specific information. Hence, major banks can be expected to often have much better solvency information than other creditors.[51]

Admittedly, such protection offered to smaller creditors is not comprehensive, for they are neither able to influence the alteration nor the abolition of the contract to which they are not a party in a formal sense. Moreover, if larger creditors are able to obtain satisfactory repayment before insolvency occurs, then smaller creditors will be completely unprotected. As for the companies which are subject to the covenants, they often find themselves subject to contradictory or cumulative obligations which can restrict their trading capacity to an unreasonable extent.

Seen from the continent, however, caution is urged with regard to financial covenants, as the influence exerted by creditors can reach such an extent that, as under French or Italian law, the outside creditors could become liable under the law of bankruptcy, as a result of poor company management being attributable to the outside creditor, or, as under German law, the prohibition on the repayment of loans under the law of equity could be activated. Nonetheless, it is interesting to observe the growing significance of this individual contractual creditor protection on the continent. In particular, large banks which have advocated the statutory capital maintenance rules for decades increasingly desire to safeguard their creditors' businesses as a result of falling interest rates on loans and improved return on equity.[52]

4.1.5 *Involuntary creditors*

Let us finally consider involuntary creditors, e.g., tort victims of dangerous corporate activity. Involuntary creditors are by definition not among the addressees of disclosure. However, even involuntary creditors might benefit from disclosure since disclosure operates to the advantage of all corporate creditors, whether voluntary or not. In the case of involuntary creditors, disclosure is effective in its so-called "controlling" or "enforcement" function.[53] For example, a

---

[51] G. Hertig, *Using Basel II to Facilitate Access to Finance: The Disclosure of Internal Credit Ratings*, ECGI-Law Working Paper No. 31/2005 (March 2005) p. 9, available at: <http://ssrn.com>, advancing however this rationale in favor of mandatory disclosure of internal bank rating.

[52] K.J. Hopt, 'Gesellschaftsrecht im Wandel', in H. Hirte, K. Frey, and R. Wank, eds., *Festschrift für Herbert Wiedemann zum 70. Geburtstag* (Munich, Beck 2002) p. 1013 at p. 1019.

[53] Kraakman, loc. cit. n. 13, at p. 97.

legal requirement that the corporation has to remain solvent or may not become insolvent would be meaningless without disclosure of the annual accounts. Similarly, a limitation as to dividend payments in order to protect corporate liquidity requires extensive public disclosure to alert creditors or minority shareholders about possible violations of that limitation. However, as in the case of small contractual creditors, large creditors that negotiate for financial covenants act in their capacity as trustees for all small creditors, both voluntary and involuntary. If they insist on a conservative valuation of a company's assets, all other creditors benefit automatically. If they bargain for certain dividend payment restrictions, those restrictions are enforced to the benefit of all creditors.

4.1.6 *Preventive vs. corrective protection*

Compare this type of creditor protection to the standard creditor protection of the type still prevalent on the continent. In case of default, a senior secured creditor may have a simple interest in getting possession of collateral no matter what happens to the firm.[54] Negotiating for a pledge asset, e.g., a mortgage, a security interest, or a lien, amounts to "cherry picking" to the detriment of smaller creditors and, in most cases, accelerates insolvency instead of preventing it, because it limits the company's financial flexibility.

In sum, given the growing extent to which creditors individually contract for protection through financial covenants and the like, the market failure rationale (underproduction of information) as a justification for creditor-protective mandatory disclosure is gradually losing its persuasive power.

4.2 **Debtor companies**

4.2.1 *Trading activity vs. market participation*

In order to determine which companies are obliged to comply with mandatory disclosure, the High Level Report suggests dividing corporations into three basic types: listed companies, open companies (whose internal structure allows listing) and closed companies (whose shares are not freely transferable). According to the High Level Report, "there may be good reasons why the regulatory approach in company law for these three types of companies should be different. For listed companies, a certain level of uniform, compulsory, substantive rules may be required to sufficiently protect both shareholders (investors) and creditors. On the

---

[54] See R. La Porta, F. Lopez-de-Silanes, A. Shleifer, and R.W. Vishny, 'Law and Finance', 106 *Journal of Political Economy* (1998) p. 1113 at p. 1144.

other hand, disclosure requirements and market forces may provide powerful alternative disciplinary instruments."[55]

This appears to be a somewhat formalistic and inflexible concept of threefold disclosure for listed, open, and closed companies. First, this approach conceals rather than clarifies the true justification for disclosure. If disclosure is a suitable regulatory tool to protect creditors, then capital market trading activity is the wrong trigger for disclosure duties. Disclosure is the natural correlative not only of stock exchange or securities market trading but also, in a more general fashion, of market participation in its widest sense, be it in share capital markets, mercantile markets, markets for services, or debt capital markets. Disclosure, therefore, is determined by the market impact of the individual company.[56] This, however, calls for a much more flexible determination of both the scope and the content of disclosure. Correspondingly, creditor protection is not a one-size-fits-all function but needs to be differentiated according to the various market segments for different categories of goods traded. In that regard, it is not convincing to limit mandatory disclosure in general to limited companies, like most EU jurisdictions do, but to fine-tune the extent of disclosure within the group of limited companies according to varying criteria like size or public trading activity. If size does matter, it matters likewise in unincorporated or partnership-type firms.[57]

4.2.2 *Limited quality of small company disclosure*

A key reason why many creditors do not assign a high priority to studying the publicly filed financial statements of smaller companies is that the information submitted suffers from important limitations. At any time, the use of accounts to forecast insolvency is difficult, since a company's prospects and future plans have a much more significant bearing on its creditworthiness than does past financial performance.[58] Reliability is another problem. In a larger enterprise, controls built into the company's administrative system will provide assurance for those who study and depend on the accounts. In a smaller company, there is usually not enough staff to implement a system of controls. The accuracy of the accounts therefore ultimately depends on assertions by the directors that all of the company's transactions are reflected correctly in the records.[59]

---

55 High Level Report, op. cit. n. 6, at p. 35.

56 For a comprehensive analysis of this concept, see Merkt, op. cit. n. 10.

57 Kraakman, loc. cit. n. 13, at p. 101.

58 C. Campbell and B. Underdown, *Corporate Insolvency in Practice: An Analytical Approach* (London, Chapman 1991) p. 3 et seq.

59 J. Dunn, *Auditing: Theory and Practice* (New York, Prentice Hall 1991) p. 99.

internal rating information across jurisdictions.[64] He suggests requiring the disclosure of the internal ratings of those banks that adopt the Internal Rating of Banks Approach (IRB) under the Basel II accord for calculating capital requirements. Disclosure would occur in average form through multiple third parties, whereas borrowers would be allowed to opt out to prevent outsiders from having access to their internal ratings. This framework, he argues, would minimize the disadvantages of disclosure while preserving its advantages.

This is not the place for comprehensive discussion of mandatory internal ranking disclosure. However, five brief points might be raised. First, with internal ratings publicly disclosed, the risk of banks being held liable for their ratings is likely to jump up remarkably. This, in turn, will most likely influence rating and credit cost. Second, in most credit agreements, so-called "trigger clauses" provide for a premature termination right of the loan in case of downgrading by rating agencies.[65] If internal bank ratings are publicly disclosed, this triggering effect might activate a chain reaction with fatal consequences for debtor companies. Third, internal rating procedures and rating methods are currently regarded as business secrets of the rating banks.[66] Mandatory disclosure therefore might come close to a form of expropriation. In that context, an opt-out right in favor of banks that do not want their ratings being disclosed would not be of much help as long as opting-out is limited to hardship cases.[67] Fourth, it is debatable whether the sophisticated and demanding standards of risk analysis under IRB represent the proper standard for average creditors. Consider that IRB standards are designed to protect high-profile creditors against the risk of accumulated default, whereas average non-bank creditors do not incur comparable default risks. Even if many creditors would individually prefer a less rigorous standard, it is hard to believe that those creditors would ignore the results of a disclosed internal rating under IRB, given the very good standing of such IRB ratings in the credit community. Hence, disclosure of IBR ratings might have a "slipping" effect which in the end is detrimental to the credit market. Fifth and finally, to a certain extent the idea of requiring disclosure of internal ratings militates against what we have seen in the context of financial covenants. If information regarding solvency of single creditors is produced sufficiently on a contractual level, the case for market failure and for regulatory intervention in the form of mandatory rating disclosure is weak. And it is difficult to see why all market participants should be provided with the results of internal ratings by way of disclosure despite the fact that only a

---

64 Hertig, op. cit. n. 51.

65 See M. Habersack, 'Rechtsfragen des Emittenten-Ratings', 169 *Zeitschrift für das gesamte Handels- und Wirtschaftsrecht* (2005) p. 185 at p. 188.

66 See C. Kersting, 'Discussion Report', 169 *Zeitschrift für das gesamte Handels- und Wirtschaftsrecht* (2005) p. 242 at p. 245.

67 See Hertig, op. cit. n. 51, at p. 16.

limited number of commercial and small creditors is in need of enhanced information.

5.2 **Standardization**

5.2.1 *Standardization as cost reducing feature*

It is obvious that disclosure calls for standardization, i.e., the use of an identical format for disclosure in order to facilitate comparison of the data disclosed. Such standardization of balance sheets, income statements, and interim reporting might contribute to reducing the costs incurred by interested addressees in processing disclosed information. Standardization also presents another characteristic. Because investors are interested in comparing information gathered from various companies, it could be advisable under certain circumstances to disclose a negative piece of information that would not reach the threshold of materiality if the company were evaluated in isolation.

However, the quest for standardization finds itself to a certain degree in conflict with the call for flexible disclosure regulation that takes into account the particular needs of smaller businesses not capable of steadily publishing large amounts of information. Therefore, standardization should be limited to companies within a certain class of size.

5.2.2 *Proper regulatory level*

Closely linked to the quest for standardization is the debate over the proper regulatory level for mandatory disclosure. In the United States, economists and legal scholars have long struggled with this issue. Advocates of decentralized disclosure regulation argue that only regulatory competition might produce the regime most suitable for market participants.[68]

Apparently, the High Level Report challenges this view by advocating centralized disclosure rules at EU level in order to achieve harmonization of disclosure requirements within the Union. This conclusion can be drawn implicitly from the Report's proposition that the European Union should consider whether disclosure requirements are better suited to achieve the desired effects than substantive rules.[69] In endorsing this concept, the Commission's Action Plan[70] states: "In view

---

68 See Romano, loc. cit. n. 24.

69 High Level Report, op. cit. n. 6, at p. 34.

70 See Communication from the Commission to the Council and the European Parliament 'Modernising Company Law and Enhancing Corporate Governance in the European Union – A Plan to Move Forward', COM (2003) 284 final (hereinafter cited as 'Action Plan').

of the growing integration of European capital markets, a common approach should be adopted at EU level with respect to a few essential rules [which include mandatory disclosure] and adequate coordination of corporate governance codes should be ensured."[71] At the same time, the Action Plan leaves no doubt that "a self-regulatory market approach, based exclusively on non-binding recommendations, is clearly not always sufficient to guarantee the adoption of sound corporate governance practices."[72]

There are basically three points that need to be addressed briefly in this context. First and foremost, in light of the overriding principle of subsidiarity within the European Union, the introduction of a "common approach" to mandatory disclosure at EU level requires a sound and convincing justification. Such a justification might be derived from the simple fact that the need to comply with different disclosure requirements imposed by Member States can serve as a substantial obstacle to the credit industry. As a consequence, additional costs of gathering investor information produced under differing standards (with varying language, content, etc.) can deter the investment of funds.[73] Moreover, exposure to varying and rigorous sanctions and liability regimes can also impair the credit-raising process. Although the former have been addressed by the EU regime, the latter remain subject to Member State regulation. Today, regulators are increasingly willing to cooperate to foster the convergence of disclosure standards. The foundations for the US-Canada multi-jurisdictional disclosure system were laid in 1991. In 1998, IOSCO adopted international disclosure standards to be applied to cross-border offerings and initial listings by foreign issuers which were designed to serve as the basis for a disclosure document passport regime which would allow issuers to rely on a document prepared in accordance with the standards for multi-jurisdictional offerings and listings.[74]

In the context of supranational standardization, accounting methodology is a key element. Despite the fact that many jurisdictions have moved toward the Anglo-Saxon "fair presentation" concept, important differences remain. Accounting methodology in continental Europe still is significantly less demanding than in the United Kingdom and the United States. The effectiveness of recent reforms, such as those requiring EU firms listed on regulated markets to apply International Financial Reporting Standards beginning in 2005, remains to be seen. Today, most companies on the continent are by law permitted to submit less

---

[71] Action Plan, loc. cit. n. 70, at s. 3.1.

[72] Ibid.

[73] This point was acknowledged by the SEC in the context of the disclosure requirements applicable to foreign issuers in 1999, see SEC Release No. 33-7637 (1999).

[74] IOSCO, *International Disclosure Standards for Cross-Border Offerings and Initial Listings by Foreign Issuers* (Madrid, IOSCO 1998).

transparent accounting reports than UK and US companies, which are remarkably different from those across the Atlantic.[75]

Second, assuming that disclosure regulation interferes less with private rights than merit regulation does, a regulatory concept that combines disclosure requirements on the central level with merit regulation at Member State level appears to be preferable.

Third, mere disclosure regulation can be transferred easily from one national law to another and therefore is more in line with the concept of legal harmonization than substantive merit regulation.[76] In this context, it has recently been argued that EU directives are not the appropriate legal instruments for implementing disclosure regulation. The process from proposal (by the European Commission) to adoption to implementation, the argument goes, is too slow and reform is even slower. As in the case of merger regulation, regulations are preferable over directives.[77] The validity of this reasoning depends on the character of European disclosure regime envisaged. Certainly, a comprehensive and detailed regime of disclosure duties at European level requires direct rulemaking without burdensome and time-consuming implementation procedures. However, a basic framework leaving sufficient room for individual and competitive membership implementation, as favored by both the High Level Report and the Action Plan, is better served by the use of directives. Hence, the choice between directives and regulations is a choice between different basic regulatory concepts and requires careful analysis.

5.3 Comprehensibility

5.3.1 *What standard to chose?*

It is self-evident that disclosed information needs to be comprehensible for addressees. However, the question at what audience disclosure should be aimed is a classical yet fundamental question, even though the issue of understandability is addressed neither in the High Level Report nor in the Commission's Action Plan. In theory, three answers are possible: at the unsophisticated, at the financial expert, or at the hypothetical "reasonable" investor of average sophistication. Throughout its history, the SEC has struggled with this question. It may well be unanswerable. A balance must be struck which reflects, to the greatest extent possible, the needs of all who have a stake in the debt finance markets. The US regime's preoccupation at

[75] See La Porta, et al., loc. cit. n. 54, at p. 1144.

[76] See S. Grundmann, *Europäisches Gesellschaftsrecht* (Heidelberg, Müller 2004) p. 40 et seq.

[77] M. Becht, 'European Disclosure for the New Millennium', in K.J. Hopt and E. Wymeersch, eds., *Capital Markets and Company Law* (Oxford, Oxford University Press 2003) p. 87 at p. 89.

certain stages with making detailed disclosure fully comprehensible to a model retail investor, even though in practice such investors did not understand or even read the disclosed information, has been subjected to harsh criticism.[78]

5.3.2 *Financially literate investors*

However, the concept of disclosure for reasonably sophisticated investors becomes increasingly questionable. Despite the fact that continental Europe's financial markets traditionally are more intermediary-oriented, equity holdings and investment behavior in continental Europe are gradually shifting toward the more market-oriented patterns found in the United Kingdom and United States.[79] Most creditors lend money or extend credit to several or even many corporate debtors, thereby diversifying their risk. A diversified creditor, however, can no longer collect and evaluate all investment-relevant information on each company in his portfolio. He turns to support from various sources like rating agencies, banks, press, and intermediaries such as investment companies and pension funds. These sources process solvency-relevant information regarding the portfolio companies and, on the basis of their findings, make recommendations to, or even investment decisions for, the investor. This system certainly does not make it unnecessary to disclose material information to investors. Rather, the addressee of the disclosed information has changed from the creditor himself to the intermediary. Hence, disclosure need no longer be primarily tailored to the knowledge of the unsophisticated or average investor. Therefore, under the EC Listing and Reporting Directive, an annual financial statement, for instance, is meaningful to a "financially literate" investor.[80]

5.4 **Timeliness**

5.4.1 *Time is of the essence*

Timeliness is a pretty important feature of efficient disclosure. Channels for the dissemination of the information disclosed are as important as the information

---

[78] H. Kripke, 'The Myth of the Informed Layman', 28 *Bus. Law.* (1973) p. 631.

[79] See Hertig, op. cit. n. 51, at p. 5.

[80] See Art. 21(1) of Council Directive 2001/34/EC of 28 May 2001 on the admission of securities to official stock exchange listing and on information to be published on those securities. Some years ago, the German High Court (*Bundesgerichtshof*) held the "average investor" the relevant addressee, refusing to attribute to such average investor the ability to understand financial statements, *Wertpapiermitteilungen* (1992) p. 901 at p. 904. The decision has been subject to fierce criticism, e.g., W. Groß, *Kapitalmarktrecht*, 2nd edn. (Munich, Beck 2002) §§ 45, 46 Exchange Act No. 25; E. Schwark, *Börsengesetz*, 2nd edn. (Munich, Beck 1994) §§ 45, 46 No. 13; H. Fleischer, *Gutachten zum 64. Deutschen Juristentag* (Munich, Beck 2002) F 21.

itself. While disclosure of information is often provided for by legislation, filing and access to information can be cumbersome and costly. Within the European Union, most countries still prescribe filing with company registers and subsequent paper filing in selected local financial newspapers that are rather expensive and not necessarily circulated throughout the Union. Moreover, many Member States have a great number of local registers, as in the case of Germany, where approximately 720 local registers are simultaneously engaged in the administration of company filings.[81] In addition, documents are usually filed in a local language that investors at large or regulators do not readily understand. Another serious flaw of current disclosure results from the fact that annual reports are already outdated on the day they are published. In addition, the ultimate date currently permitted for publication of the annual accounts in most Member States is much too late, e.g., twelve months after the end of the fiscal year under the German statutory provision[82] and thirteen months under Dutch law.[83] The Dutch "Final Report on Alternative Systems for Capital Protection" of August 2005 has therefore recommended to cut down this period to six months.[84]

5.4.2 *The need for electronic filing*

These and various other obstacles to timely disclosure have led to the proposition that the company's website may be a better place for the publication of information,[85] a suggestion that has been supported by both the High Level Group[86] and the Action Plan.[87] In the meantime, the European Union has adopted two directives – on disclosure requirements[88] and transparency[89] – in order to modernize corporate disclosure and to harmonize electronic publishing via the internet.

---

[81] For a comprehensive analysis of the current German system, see U. Noack, *Infobasen für Unternehmensdaten* (Cologne, Bundesanzeiger Verlag 2003) and Noack, *Unternehmenspublizität* (Cologne, Bundesanzeiger Verlag 2002).

[82] See § 325(1) German Commercial Code.

[83] Boschma, Lennarts, and Schutte-Veenstra, op. cit. n. 36, at s. 4.2.2.

[84] Ibid.

[85] E.g., Becht, loc. cit. n. 77, at p. 89.

[86] Consultative Document of the High Level Group, Question 6(a).

[87] Action Plan, loc. cit. n. 70, at s. 3.1.2.

[88] Directive 2003/58/EC of the European Parliament and of the Council of 15 July 2003 amending Council Directive 68/151/EEC, as regards disclosure requirements in respect of certain types of companies, *OJ* 2003 L 221/13-16.

[89] Directive 2004/109/EC of the European Parliament and of the Council of 15 December 2004 on the harmonisation of transparency requirements in relation to information about issuers whose securities are admitted to trading on a regulated market and amending Directive 2001/34/EC, *OJ* 2004 L 390/38-57.

6. ENFORCEMENT OF DISCLOSURE DUTIES

6.1 Various enforcement options

Efficient creditor protection through mandatory disclosure finally depends on effective enforcement mechanisms. Enforcement of disclosure obligations is not easy, since it requires insider knowledge that usually is hard to get. Apart from extra-judicial mechanisms like reputation and warranties, relying on market intermediaries, or trusting accounting firms, the law basically offers three different ways to cope with the problem of enforcement of disclosure duties. First, it can impose liability on the debtor corporation itself for misreporting. Second, it can impose personal liability or other civil or criminal sanctions on those individuals responsible for misrepresentations. Third, it can entrust institutions with enforcement functions, like audit committees, rating agencies, intermediaries, or administrative bodies.

6.2 Liability for misreporting

Imposing liability on the debtor company itself might turn out to be counterproductive. Because misreporting would usually entitle a large number of creditors to damages, liability would impair the company's solvency and thus would indirectly harm creditors. However, imposing liability directly on those mangers or on those individuals that are responsible for misreporting is for practical reasons not as effective as one would expect. First, major misrepresentations usually occur when the company is on the verge of failure, a final period in which managers tend to make risky or even erratic and desperate attempts in order to save the company and themselves. It is a matter of experience that, under those extraordinary circumstances, managers do not tend to be overly impressed by legal rules designed to deter. Moreover, managers usually lack the personal assets to cover the damages they cause. Given the money at stake, they may not be deterred by other civil sanctions like disqualification from office. Finally, criminal sanctions impose a heavy burden of proof and in addition threaten to over-deter disclosure by risk-averse managers.

6.3 Enforcement institutions

Against this background, entrusting particular institutions, like audit committees, rating agencies, intermediaries, or administrative bodies, with enforcement functions appears to be an interesting alternative. A good example of that kind of enforcement strategy is the Sarbanes-Oxley Act of 2002, which was the principal legal answer to the preceding corporate governance scandals. The measures chosen in order to improve enforcement of disclosure duties range from requiring

CEOs and CFOs to certify financial statements and internal controls of their firms to new rules to ensure the independence and competence of audit committees, the independence of accounting firms, and the responsible advice of outside counsel. Any evaluation of these measures turns on the balance of costs and benefits. However, even three years after the adoption of Sarbanes-Oxley, a final assessment seems to be difficult.

Meanwhile, Germany has chosen a different approach by setting up a quasi-governmental institution for the audit of annual reports.[90] The so-called Auditing Agency for Financial Reporting, established under the Balance Sheet Control Act of 2004, examines whether a company's most recently approved annual accounts comply with statutory requirements. The Agency conducts an audit in one of three cases: (1) if there is reason to believe that accounting standards were violated; (2) upon request by the Federal Financial Supervisory Authority; or (3) without immediate cause (spot check).[91] It is important to note that no company is under a duty to cooperate with the Agency. However, if the company refuses to cooperate with the Agency, the latter will report it to the Federal Supervisory Authority.[92] This new and unique proceeding has still to prove its effectiveness. In addition, there are still several important legal and practical questions that have to be answered: What is the legal nature of the proceeding? What remedies are available to the company? What is the standard of review for the audit? Is it preferable to cooperate or to refuse cooperation?

However, the most fundamental questions relates to the rationale behind the administrative agency concept. Should the government interfere with the business of auditing at all? Should it take away the risk of assessing the quality of accounting and rubber-stamp annual accounts, a risk that is typically and in conformity with market mechanisms borne by market participants? This brings us back to the beginning. In the early years of US securities regulation, many states did apply merit regulation to securities offerings. Under the merit standard, the pertinent state securities administration could prevent an offering from going forward because it was not "fair, just, and equitable." Under merit regulation, therefore, adequate disclosure was not the decisive criterion. It was the substantive fairness of the offering that had to be scrutinized above all, with fatal consequences: of about 1,500 applications for admission of offerings just about 100 were admitted. The securities market was on the verge of complete collapse.[93] This example

---

90 See 69 *Federal Law Gazette I* (2004) p. 3408 et seq.; H.F. Gelhausen and H. Hönsch, 'Das Neue Enforcement – Verfahren für Jahres- und Konzernabschlüsse', 50 *Die Aktiengesellschaft* (2005) p. 511 et seq.

91 § 342b(2) German Commercial Code.

92 § 342b(6) German Commercial Code.

93 M.I. Steinberg, *Understanding Securities Law*, 2nd edn. (New York, Matthew Bender 1996) p. 90.

dramatically demonstrates that any legislator should be extremely careful with administrative merit regulation.

7. Conclusion

All in all, the case for creditor protection through mandatory disclosure is far from being unambiguous. While according to economic and legal theory mandatory disclosure is an important instrument to improve market efficiency and prevent market failure, practical experience indicates clear limitations of the concept and numerous challenges to its effectiveness. First, large professional creditors negotiating for financial covenants and thus ensuring the solvency of the company act as factual trustees of small creditors, thereby limiting the need for additional disclosure. Second, the disclosure of small firms in particular suffers from important limitations regarding solvency expectations and reliability. Third, the current mandatory disclosure regime does not sufficiently provide for soft information on the expected solvency of the company. Finally, reform with respect to comprehensibility, timeliness, and enforcement of disclosure appears to be necessary in order to protect creditors of corporations more effectively.

Codetermination as a (Partial) Substitute for Mandatory Disclosure?

Gérard Hertig*

Abstract
Employee board representation can serve information dissemination purposes. This comment argues that in Germany, which (still) has a bank-oriented financial system, transparency may be better served by using codetermination (under which up to half of the supervisory board is composed of employees) as an information channel, rather than by importing the mandatory disclosure requirements that are typical of Anglo-Saxon jurisdictions. There are two reasons for this. One is that the evidence about the efficiency of mandatory disclosure requirements is mixed. The other is that mandatory disclosure is an intrinsic component of market-oriented financial systems such as the US financial system.

Transplanting a market-oriented component into a bank-oriented financial system brings the risk of inconsistencies, as it affects the complementarities that exist among the intrinsic components of a bank-oriented system. This comment thus concludes that before suggesting ways to transplant further mandatory disclosure requirements into the German financial system, or improve existing ones, one should consider how to use or improve the use of codetermination as an information dissemination channel.

Keywords: codetermination, creditor protection, mandatory disclosure.

The debate about the benefits of corporate disclosure requirements has been going on for decades. Critics have argued that, from an information supply perspective,

---

* Professor of Law, ETH Zurich. I wish to thank Bill Bratton and Bruno Frey for their remarks.

disclosure mandates inflict excessive costs on smaller firms and are inadequate for larger firms, whereas from an information demand perspective creditors and investors alike are better served by market mechanisms.

The empirical evidence, however, remains scarce and mixed.[1] For their part, securities regulators around the world have imposed disclosure requirements upon listed firms.[2] The primary objective is to protect public shareholders, but other stakeholders obviously also benefit from securities regulation. In addition, various corporate laws, in particular in Europe, protect creditors by mandating the disclosure of legal capital or financial account information.[3]

In recent years, mandating or fostering disclosure has been on the increase in Europe. The European Commission, Member States (especially through corporate governance codes) and even the European Court of Justice have become proponents of disclosure mechanisms.[4] This evolution is related to the ongoing transformation of the bank-oriented continental European financial systems into market-oriented systems.

1. Bank-oriented and Market-oriented Financial Systems

Firms in bank-oriented systems have so-called "insider" governance regimes under which a few players (essentially lenders and controlling shareholders) have high incentives to gather information and not much data is made publicly available. Firms in market-oriented financial systems have so-called "outsider" governance regimes where large amounts of information are disseminated publicly and incentives to gather additional information are low due to free-rider problems.

---

[1] Compare recently P.G. Mahoney and J. Mei, *Mandatory vs. Contractual Disclosure in Securities Markets: Evidence form the 1930s*, Working Paper (2006), available at: <http://www.ssrn.com> (securities laws did not add measurably to the content and credibility of the NYSE's existing disclosure requirements); M. Greenstone, P. Oyer, and A. Vissing-Jørgensen, 'Mandated Disclosure, Stock Returns, and the 1964 Securities Act Amendments', 121 *Q. J. Econ.* (2006) p. 399 (results suggest that mandatory disclosure causes managers to more narrowly focus on the maximization of shareholder value); A. Ferrell, *The Case for Mandated Disclosure in Securities Regulation Around the World*, Working Paper (2005), available at: <http://www.law.harvard.edu> (mandatory disclosure enhances competition and reduces agency costs).

[2] See G. Hertig, R. Kraakman, and E. Rock, 'Issuers and Investor Protection', in R. Kraakman, et al., *The Anatomy of Corporate Law, A Comparative and Functional Approach* (Oxford, Oxford University Press 2004) p. 197.

[3] G. Hertig and H. Kanda, 'Creditor Protection', in Kraakman, et al., op. cit. n. 2, at pp. 79-83.

[4] See H. Merkt, 'Creditor Protection through Mandatory Disclosure', in this volume, at s. 3.

When capital markets start playing a more important role in jurisdictions that traditionally had a bank-oriented financial systems, trade-off issues arise.[5] In particular, one has to balance the needs of new players, such as institutional investors, for better disclosure against the private information needs of (still important) traditional players, such as controlling shareholders.

Getting the right balance is not merely a smoothening of the transition question. Two more fundamental determinants have to be taken into account. First, one cannot assume convergence towards a "pure" market-oriented system. Even in the United States, the prototypical market-oriented jurisdiction, banks do play an important role. Conversely, in the prototypical bank-oriented jurisdiction, Germany, banks will continue to play a major role for the foreseeable future. In other words, we can expect financial systems to evolve towards variable combinations of markets and intermediaries.[6] Second, financial systems comprise sets of complementary elements.[7] It follows that transplanting "capital market" components into a transitioning but still bank-oriented financial system may lead to inconsistencies that could ultimately lead to financial crisis.[8]

Thus, as pointed out by Hanno Merkt,[9] the case for creditor protection through mandatory disclosure is far from unambiguous. But this is not necessarily because the disclosure requirements that have been developed for market-oriented systems are overly costly, do not meet market needs or must be reformed with respect to comprehensibility, timeliness and enforcement. To be sure, disclosure requirements may well deserve improvements. However, it is also critical to consider the possibility of making better use of information pools and information channels that are typical of bank-oriented systems as an alternative to mandatory disclosure. For example, given the importance of lending in bank-oriented systems, it could be more efficient to give banks incentives to make their internal ratings of their borrowers available to the public. Or, to take another example, given the established governance role of employees in many bank-oriented systems, it could be more efficient to channel at least some information through the corporate

---

5 See F. Allen and D. Gale, *Comparing Financial Systems* (Cambridge, MIT Press 2000) pp. 19-21.

6 See also Allen and Gale, op. cit. n. 5, at pp. 21 and 470.

7 See already P. Milgrom and J. Roberts, 'Complementarities and Systems: Understanding Japanese Economic Organization', 1 *Estudios Economicos* (1994) p. 3 et seq.

8 See R.H. Schmidt and M. Tyrell, 'What Constitutes a Financial System in General and the German Financial System in Particular?', in J.P. Krahnen and R.H. Schmidt, eds., *The German Financial System* (Oxford, Oxford University Press 2004) pp. 19, 53-7 and 62 (emphasizing the complementary nature of a bank-dominated financial sector, stakeholder-oriented corporate governance and risk management through lending-based inter-temporal risk sharing).

9 See Merkt, loc. cit. n. 4, at s. 6.

bodies on which employees are represented, such as boards or works councils, than to disclose it directly to the public.

Whether it could prove efficient to provide information to creditors and other stakeholders by fostering the disclosure of internal ratings is an issue that will be dealt with in an article that is forthcoming in this review.[10] This comment will focus on the comparative advantages of using corporate bodies that comprise human capital representatives, in particular codetermined boards, to inform one specific class of creditors, i.e., employees.

2. Employee Directors as Information Channels

There seems to be no fundamental reason to require managers to be better informed in a market-oriented than in a bank-oriented system. In a given industry, the relative costs and benefits of information gathering and processing are likely to be similar in both systems. On the other hand, the costs and benefits of *disclosing* information held by managers are likely to vary among financial systems.

More specifically, public disclosure requirements are likely to prove less beneficial or costlier for firms in bank-oriented systems than for firms in market-oriented systems. In bank-oriented systems, information generation depends on its remaining internal to a limited number of recipients, whereas in market-oriented systems information is externalized through stock prices.[11] Hence, public disclosure is less likely to be beneficial in terms of access to external finance for firms in bank-oriented systems, as it would reduce lenders' informational advantage and make them less attractive to depositors – leading to loans becoming more expensive without certainty about corresponding decreases in the cost of bonds or equity.[12] Conversely, public disclosure is less likely to be costly for investors in market-oriented systems than for controlling shareholders in bank-oriented systems – the latter generally requiring the benefit of private information as remuneration for their more demanding monitoring role.

[10] G. Hertig, 'Using Basel II to Facilitate Access to Finance: The Disclosure of Internal Credit Ratings', *EBOR* (forthcoming).

[11] For a comparison of internal (in bank-oriented systems) and external (in market-oriented systems) information distribution, see R.H. Schmidt and M. Tyrell, 'Information Theory and the Role of Intermediaries', in K.J. Hopt, E. Wymeersch, H. Kanda, and H. Baum, eds., *Corporate Governance in Context, Corporations, States, and Markets in Europe, Japan, and the US* (Oxford, Oxford University Press 2005) p. 479 et seq.

[12] See, however, R. Elsas and J.P. Krahnen, 'Universal Banks and Relationship with Firms', in Krahnen and Schmidt, op. cit. n. 8, at pp. 197, 207 (studies on the ability of German banks to mitigate financial constraints of large listed firms yield mixed results).

There are, on the other hand, at least partial substitutes to public disclosure for firms in bank-oriented systems. In such systems, management is monitored through stakeholder voice (i.e., shareholder and employee monitoring or decision making) rather than through investor entry and exit (i.e., stock price variation and hostile takeovers). It follows that it should prove less costly or more profitable to provide at least some information through channels such as direct encounters with management, board meetings or other stakeholder gatherings than through public channels.

As a matter of fact, it is well known that in bank-oriented systems managers provide their lenders and controlling shareholders with significant private information, and there is a rich body of academic research dealing with these information channels. Corporate governance literature has paid less attention to information flows between managers and employees and their impact in terms of mandatory disclosure.[13] This could simply be because it is perceived that employees have no relevant governance function. Such a conclusion, however, would ignore the large place given to employee board participation across Europe. Employees have the right to have representatives on the board of state-owned firms in Ireland, Spain and Greece, whereas larger French firms are required to let two non-voting worker representatives attend board meetings.[14] Scandinavian countries, for their part, require boards to include three employee directors, whereas boards in Austria, Germany and Luxembourg have even larger employee representation.[15]

Another explanation for the relative lack of interest in information flows between managers and employees may be that employee board representation has no governance significance, either because employees are not interested in getting or providing information or because they are prevented from doing so by the other governance players. The informational significance of employee board participation is ultimately an empirical question that cannot be resolved here. From a theoretical perspective, however, there are reasons to believe that employee directors can play an important information role. On the one hand, their board participation may reduce information asymmetries between executives and other employees, thus reducing bargaining costs as well as the risk of strikes.[16] On the other hand, the presence of employee directors can provide the board with a

---

[13] See, however, M.M. Blair and M.J. Roe, eds., *Employees and Corporate Governance* (Washington D.C., Brookings Institution Press 1999).

[14] See H. Hansmann and R. Kraakman, 'The Basic Governance Structure', in Kraakman, et al., op. cit. n. 2, at p. 62.

[15] Ibid.

[16] See J. Kennan and R. Wilson, 'Bargaining with Incomplete Information', 31 *J. Econ. Lit.* (1993) p. 45 et seq.

well-informed source of information, which in turn makes the board less dependent on (mandated or voluntary) managerial information.[17]

There is thus both statutory and theoretical support for using employee board participation as an information channel in (still) bank-oriented continental Europe. What remains to be tackled is whether the benefits of this potential substitute to public disclosure exceed its costs. Here again, this is ultimately an empirical question.[18] However, the German codetermination experience allows for preliminary conclusions.

3. German Codetermination as an Efficient Information Channel

German law provides for the most extensive employee corporate governance participation in Europe. Employees enjoy extensive information, consultation and participation rights through works councils, which represent employees at the shop floor level (so-called *betriebliche Mitbestimmung*). In addition, the 1976 Codetermination Statute (*Gesetz über die Mitbestimmung der Arbeitnehmer*) subjects larger firms, and thus those firms that fall within the scope of securities regulation, to quasi-parity[19] employee supervisory board representation requirements (*Unternehmensmitbestimmung*).

Works councils were institutionalized by nineteenth century legislation, whereas employee participation beyond the shop floor was introduced at the beginning of the twentieth century, with board representation institutionalized in the 1950s.[20] In spite – or because – of this employee participation tradition, the 1976 Codetermination Act was strongly opposed before and after its enactment.

---

17 See M. Osterloh and B. Frey, *Shareholders Should Welcome Employees as Directors*, Working Paper (2005), available at: <http://www.ssrn.com>; A.J. Hilman and Th. Dalziel, 'Boards of Directors and Firm Performance: Integrating Agency and Resource Dependence Perspectives', 28 *Academy Management Rev.* (2003) p. 383 et seq.

18 The fact that employee board participation is rare in the absence of legal compulsion may be caused by the same factors that require disclosure to be mandated to be effective, and is therefore not necessarily evidence that such an information distribution channel has costs that exceeds its benefits. Compare Hansmann and Kraakman, loc. cit. n. 14, at p. 64; C. Windbichler, 'Cheers and Boos for Employee Involvement: Co-Determination as Corporate Governance Conundrum', 6 *EBOR* (2005) p. 507 et seq.

19 There is "quasi-parity" in the sense that while the supervisory board must comprise an equal number of shareholder and employee representatives, the chairman is elected by the shareholder bench and has the decisive vote when there is a tie.

20 For a concise description of the evolution of employee participation in Germany, see K. Pistor, 'Codetermination: A Sociopolitical Model with Governance Externalities', in Blair and Roe, op. cit. n. 13, at pp. 165-175.

The public debate lost steam after Germany's Constitutional Court upheld the law in 1979, and public controversies had practically disappeared by the 1990s.[21]

This lack of public debate could reflect the limited practical impact of codetermination. However, empirical studies on the economic effects of codetermination are rather scarce and inconclusive.[22] This is likely to mean that codetermination is either ineffective or has costs that balance its benefits.

It is quite obvious that codetermination has its disadvantages.[23] Unions may capture the employee bench and pursue policies that are detrimental to the company. Employee participation may increase transaction costs by requiring more cumbersome board preparation meetings. Employee representatives may not have the required financial and strategic knowledge. They may also have diverging interests among themselves or be prone to managerial capture. In addition, business secrets may be leaked when it is in the private interest of employee representatives. Conversely, managers may withhold information from the supervisory board under the pretense that confidentiality is critical. Finally, employee participation can increase board size to a point where group dynamics make it difficult to challenge the firm's executives.

Given these disadvantages and the inconclusive empirical evidence, codetermination must also have significant advantages. Labor peace and strike avoidance are certainly among them. But these social benefits cannot occur without codetermination also reducing information asymmetries within firms. In other words,

---

21 See also O. Riekers and G. Spindler, 'Corporate Governance: Legal Aspects', in Krahnen and Schmidt, op. cit. n. 8, at pp. 350, 361.

22 For a review, see M. Becht, P. Bolton, and A. Röell, 'Corporate Governance and Control', in G.M. Constantinides, M. Harris, and R.M. Stulz, *Handbook of the Economics of Finance, Vol. 1A: Corporate Finance* (Amsterdam, North-Holland 2002) at s. 7.6.2. See also T. Baums and B. Frick, 'The Market Value of the Codetermined Firm', in Blair and Roe, op. cit. n. 13, at p. 207 et seq. (finding that codetermination does not influence stock prices); F.A. Schmid and F. Seger, 'Arbeitnehmermitbestimmung, Allokation von Entscheidungsrechten und Shareholder Value', 5 *Zeitschrift für Betriebswirtschaft* (1998) at p. 453 et seq. (codetermination is costly for shareholders), S.N. Kaplan, 'Top Executives, Turnover, and Firm Performance in Germany', 10 *J. Law Econ. Org.* (1994) p. 142 et seq. (German firms are not comparatively slow in removing poorly performing managers); F.R. FitzRoy and K. Kraft, 'Economic Effects of Codetermination', 95 *Scandinavian J. Econ.* (1993) p. 365 et seq. (suggesting overall social gains from codetermination, but decreased firm-level profitability); G. Benelli, C. Loderer, and T. Lys, 'Labor Participation in Corporate Policy Decision Making: West Germany's Experience with Codetermination', 60 *J. Bus.* (1987) p. 533 et seq. (codetermination has no significant effect); J. Svejnar, 'Codetermination and Productivity: Evidence from the Federal Republic of Germany', 63 *Rev. Econ. Stat.* (1981) p. 188 et seq. (codetermination has no significant effect).

23 For a discussion and specific examples, see Pistor, loc. cit. n. 20, at pp. 188-191; M.J. Roe, *Political Determinants of Corporate Governance* (Oxford, Oxford University Press 2003) at pp. 73-76; K.J. Hopt, 'Labor Representation on Corporate Boards: Impacts and Problems for Corporate Governance and Economic Integration in Europe', 14 *Int. Rev. Law. Econ.* (1994) pp. 203, 205-212.

it cannot be denied that German codetermination has an information channel function.

What remains open is its role in a changing environment. The recent revival of the public debate about the value of codetermination shows that its costs and benefits may be affected by employees having more valuable firm-specific knowledge in an information society and by ongoing changes in German ownership structures, financial systems, product competition and corporate ethics.

German executives have recently expressed concerns about the rising costs of codetermination in a more market-oriented environment. Their complaints have been balanced by reports about the increasing benefits of codetermination. Hence, it is said that, these days, employee representatives sent from the works councils bring beneficial operational knowledge to the board. Moreover, employee representatives (including those designated by the unions) are allegedly more open to restructurings and less inclined to favor social benefits over the corporation's interest. In short, it is argued that "codetermination practices are becoming more micro-focused and insider-oriented."[24] Finally, and most importantly, it is argued that being a member of the supervisory board nowadays gives broad access to any relevant firm information.[25]

It thus appears that codetermination could well prove a better information channel in the current environment than in the past. The significance of this channel and the question whether its contribution could be improved by amending existing codetermination rules deserves further analysis. What cannot be disputed, however, is that codetermination has informational advantages while being an intrinsic component of the (still) predominantly bank-oriented German financial system. Conversely, it cannot be disputed that the evidence about the efficiency of mandatory disclosure requirement is mixed, and that it is an intrinsic component of market-oriented financial systems. It follows that before suggesting ways to transplant mandatory disclosure requirements into a bank-oriented system, one should consider how to use or improve information channels inherent to bank-oriented systems – including codetermination.

In sum, while Hanno Merkt makes an important point about the need to establish whether and how mandatory disclosure is beneficial to creditors, one should also consider whether and how codetermination and related mechanisms could be used as information channels between the firm and one important category of creditors: employees.

---

[24] See G. Jackson, M. Höpner, and A. Kurdelbusch, *Corporate Governance and Employees in Germany: Changing Linkages, Complementarities, and Tensions*, Working Paper (2005), available at: <http://www.ssrn.com>.

[25] See C. Leuz and J. Wüstemann, 'The Role of Accounting in the German Financial System', in Krahnen and Schmidt, op. cit. n. 8, at pp. 450, 464.

Discussion Report

Clemens Philipp Schindler*

The first afternoon session included three presentations addressing the issue of whether regulatory requirements are required or helpful to ensure efficient creditor protection. The chairman, Marcus Lutter of the University of Bonn, introduced the afternoon's topic by highlighting the positive effects a legal capital concept might have. John Armour of Cambridge University questioned this concept in his presentation by arguing that such a regime was outdated in today's economy. Holger Fleischer of the University of Bonn followed with additional critical remarks. In his comments, he referred to the distinction between voluntary and involuntary creditors, the latter having no opportunity to protect themselves by means of a contract. One example given were tort victims. John Armour focused strongly on a similar distinction; however, he referred to them as adjusting creditors and non-adjusting creditors. Most participants agreed on the major relevance of this distinction.

After the chairman opened the discussion to questions from the floor, a participant suggested that a mandatory insurance might be much more efficient to protect creditors than a concept of legal capital. Whether such an insurance should apply only to hazardous businesses was subject to a lively discussion; the majority, however, disagreed with such a notion. It was considered whether having an insurance should be a requirement for the privilege of limited liability. Another participant raised the critical issue of who should determine the relevant insurance coverage for each and every company, since different types of businesses require different coverage.

During the discussion, the problem of how to regulate distributions was brought up. In this context, one participant argued that if a system of capital maintenance was upheld, a legislator – within certain limits – implicitly agreed to a minimum legal capital. Another participant disagreed by arguing that such a concept did not require a minimum capital but rather a legal capital. This distinction was regarded by many other participants as being highly relevant. Based on this debate, someone brought up the idea that instead of requiring a minimum capital at formation, the actual capital should be disclosed in the articles and the company's commercial papers. This suggestion was held to be promising, but

---

* Dr. Clemens Philipp Schindler, LL.M., Research Fellow, Max Planck Institute for Intellectual Property, Competition and Tax Law.

again the relevance of capital maintenance was stressed in order to make such a system efficient.

Some participants favored the contractual approach, while others criticized that this would be unfair to creditors having less negotiating power. The latter argument was vigorously debated by the audience, which could not agree on how far the social responsibilities of a legislator should reach. The participants from the United States, in particular, supported the concept of a self-regulating market. On the other hand, regulatory competition between states might result in concepts relying on legal provisions. Whether the latter is desirable was subject to very different views and reminded many participants of the seemingly never-ending "race to the bottom" vs. "race to the top" discussion.

Referring to the distinction between voluntary and involuntary creditors, one participant recommended allowing tort victims to pierce the corporate veil. Personal liability of the shareholders would ensure a reasonable protection. This idea, however, did not attract a lot of sympathy from the other participants. Close to the end of the first discussion, one participant questioned whether a minimum capital deterred from entrepreneurship at all. His conclusion was that if somebody was deterred from doing business by a minimum capital then this occurred only in a loss situation. Such businesses, however, were not the focus of an efficient market system and therefore their inexistence might even prove satisfying.

The chairman closed the first round of discussion by highlighting the three most relevant issues in his view. First of all, a distinction should be made between private and public companies. Secondly, economically and financially healthy companies ensured much more efficient creditor protection than any legal concept might ever achieve. Last but not least, he argued that a legal capital concept required legal certainty for both shareholders and directors; piercing the corporate veil did not fit into this idea and thus should not be abused to reduce inefficiencies of a current regime.

The second presentation of the afternoon session was given by William Bratton of Georgetown University, who dealt with covenants as a measure of creditor (self-)protection. Comments on this presentation were given by Klaus Schmidt of the University of Munich. During the subsequent discussion, attempts were made to group the various types of covenants into certain categories. In this context, one participant suggested a distinction between cash flow rights vs. control rights. With regard to the latter, in particular, the role of the lender, as regards what he could do as well as what he should do, was vigorously debated. On the other hand, one participant found that banks in some cases might come up with better decisions than the borrower. However, no agreement could be obtained on this point.

One participant criticized that covenants were too expensive to be used on a broad scale. Especially as regards small loans, covenants do not qualify as a cost-efficient means of protection. Repayment on demand, taken as an alternative instrument to secure a loan, might achieve similar results by reducing the costs significantly. Nevertheless, it is necessary to monitor the activities of the debtor to take relevant steps accordingly. Despite this common requirement, the participants agreed that covenants did not necessarily prove suitable for medium and small-sized businesses, since in addition to the negotiation costs the actions of the borrower had to be monitored closely. Large transactions, however, by their very nature require different means of protection.

Furthermore, the problem of "free-riders" was stressed in this context, e.g., third parties that benefit from complex covenants negotiated by banks or other institutional lenders. One participant put this aspect into perspective by referring to the preferential right to ask for repayment, which only applied to the contractually protected lender but not to the "free-rider". While it was true that the latter benefited from measures taken as a result of the covenants, he nevertheless did not achieve a corresponding level of protection. Therefore, major differences remain.

Since even complex covenants do not cover all situations that might result in bad debt, the issue of renegotiation was held to be of major relevance. While some participants claimed that a renegotiation clause should be incorporated into the agreements, others argued that a change in circumstances *per se* granted the right to renegotiate. On the other hand, it was argued that the different bargaining powers of the parties involved in a transaction were often significantly more relevant than any contractual clause whatsoever.

The third presentation of the afternoon session was delivered by Hanno Merkt of the University of Freiburg, who analyzed how mandatory disclosure can improve creditor protection. Comments were given by Gérard Hertig of the University of Zurich. Although the participants agreed that information was of great relevance, major differences remained as to what kind of information was relevant in this context. Most participants stressed the problem of manipulating annual reports for purposes of disclosure that did not necessarily need to be illegal in order to present misleading results to the lender. One participant argued that annual reports had become the main source of information and that this by itself proved that they included the relevant data.

Some participants found disclosure to be a supplement rather than an independent measure of creditor protection, while others supported its function on a standalone basis. In connection with covenants, in particular, one participant argued that the disclosure requirement was inevitable and probably the major source necessary to effectively call for rights granted by covenants. A similar position was taken by another participant who felt that disclosure offered optional guidelines for an efficient creditor protection system.

Participants from the United States shared their positive experience with the Sarbanes-Oxley Act. Participants from the Europe, however, argued that such a regime did not suit the requirements of the European Union and therefore should not be adopted. One participant brought up the relationship between Sarbanes-

Oxley and the US Securities and Exchange Commission. In his opinion, the European Union should either implement a regime like Sarbanes-Oxley or install a regulatory authority like the US Securities and Exchange Commission, but not both. Another participant questioned the relevance of Sarbanes-Oxley for disclosure. In his view, the major aspects of Sarbanes-Oxley concerned issues of corporate governance and not of disclosure.

This part of the discussion proved that substantial differences exist between the US and EU approach. One participant demonstrated this by looking at the function of the respective insolvency laws. While the US provisions attempted to keep the company solvent, the European Union supported the creditor to get the last piece left. He argued that the latter approach did not take future perspectives into consideration sufficiently but tended to liquidate the business. Under the US approach, it would be more likely for a business to recover, which in the long run would allow the company concerned to fully repay the debt.

Participants from Germany raised the question how employees should be protected against insolvent companies. The ensuing discussion on this issue focused on the impact of employee codetermination in Germany and other states. Most participants agreed that the board was the wrong place to ensure the employees' participation. Major criticism was directed at the involvement of unions in the company's board. The German system was therefore considered to be outdated and unattractive to international investors. One participant argued that no correlation existed between the level of employee involvement in board activities and the economic success of a company. In his opinion, other means of integrating the employees should be therefore considered. The role of trustees and how they could represent the employee's interests was discussed in this context. Furthermore, potential effects on collective bargaining were discussed, which most participants found to be of minor relevance.

The last issue brought up during the discussion focused on how ratings could improve creditor protection. Although very different positions were taken with regard to their efficiency, most participants acknowledged the information function of ratings. One participant conceded that ratings did not suit medium and small-sized companies, at least not in Germany. A participant from the United States, however, argued that the more creditors made use of ratings, the lower were the costs involved. With regard to the US market, the latter reasoning therefore could not be upheld, since it was less expensive to receive ratings of US firms.

The chairman closed the afternoon session by stressing that he had heard many interesting arguments for alternative means of creditor protection. However, there remained strong arguments in favor of a legal capital concept. It would probably make sense to introduce additional requirements in terms of disclosure to ensure the effectiveness of the system, but information alone might not be sufficient to protect creditors. This was especially true for involuntary creditors, e.g., tort creditors.

Part II

Legal Approaches to Restricting Distributions to Shareholders

Legal Approaches to Restricting Distributions to Shareholders: Balance Sheet Tests and Solvency Tests

Jonathan Rickford*

* Professorial Fellow, British Institute of International and Comparative Law (BIICL), Visiting Professor, London School of Economics and Political Science.

Abstract

European public company law restricts most distributions by requiring maintenance of a net asset reserve ('cushion') of at least the aggregate nominal value of issued shares. This cushion is determined absolutely (without assessment of true values or ongoing solvency by directors, as is permitted in most other jurisdictions) by the latest annual statutory accounts (balance sheet test). An alternative solvency test would require directors to certify sufficiency of assets on an ongoing basis. The amount of the 'cushion' is arbitrary (with wide variations between comparable companies and Member States), unrelated to the mischief addressed and thus contrary to general European law principles. EU law establishes four possible balance sheet tests: two (with many variations) under the Fourth Directive (an historic cost and stricter revaluation based test), one (with many variations) under the Modernised Fourth Directive, which allows or requires fair value accounting, including the distribution of certain unrealised profits, and one under the International Accounting Standards (IAS) Regulation regime. These tests produce widely divergent results for distributable profits. The Fourth Directive departs markedly from reality and in practice conforms imperfectly with true and fair view principles, the implementation of which varies markedly between Member States. The Modernised Fourth Directive and the IAS regimes vary widely according to the options used, confer considerable discretion on company boards and are often very volatile, failing to provide a stable basis for prudential decisions. Prudential regulators have accordingly overridden some of these standards. The results of these tests are diverse, complex, costly, subject to regulatory arbitrage and irrational. Statements designed for financial reporting purposes are inappropriate for setting prudential decisions. The proposed solvency assurance is designed to address the mischief by a proportionate, focused assurance of solvency, with director certification before distributions of liquidity for a year and availability of sufficient assets to meet all liabilities for the foreseeable future – a stricter version of the test currently imposed in the United Kingdom for capital distributions in company reconstructions. Such a test should be adopted as an option throughout the European Union with issues of sanctions and controls being a matter for Member State discretion.

Keywords: capital maintenance, balance sheets, solvency, Second Company Law Directive, Fourth Company Law Directive, company accounts.

Introduction and Agenda

The general conference subject is the European systems for creditor protection and the scope of this paper is the European theory of capital maintenance, as it operates primarily[1] as a means of protecting company creditors from excessive distributions to shareholders. This purpose is prominent in the preamble to the Second Company Law Directive,[2] which sets up a European system of minimum standards for public companies.[3] The system is developed further by the Fourth Directive on company accounts,[4] which applies to both public and private companies.

The heart of the theory comprises of course two key rules: that share capital (or rather funds corresponding to it) is not to be distributed to shareholders, but maintained for the benefit of creditors and only eroded or reduced by trading, and that where it is so eroded or reduced it (together with an additional amount corresponding to the amount of the proposed distribution) is to be restored to cover any distribution before such distributions may again take place. This requires the familiar system of interrelated rules on restricting the raising, distribution and accounting reduction (or writing down) of the capital fund and various ancillary rules designed to ensure that the regime is not avoided. Both the amount of the share capital and the amount of the funds available for the purpose are in the European system determined by the balance sheet.

This balance sheet test, which is the particular focus of this paper, is embedded in the system and draws its purpose from all these components. The regime at

---

[1] Shareholders are also protected, primarily from dilution. This is not directly addressed in this paper.

[2] Second Council Directive 77/91/EEC of 13 December 1976 on coordination of safeguards which, for the protection of the interests of members and others, are required by Member States of companies within the meaning of the second paragraph of Article 58 of the Treaty, in respect of the formation of public limited liability companies and the maintenance and alteration of their capital, with a view to making such safeguards equivalent, *OJ* 1977 L 26/1.

[3] In European terminology, 'public' companies are those with freely transferable shares and are often widely held and have a legal right to tap the capital markets, but they are not necessarily quoted. The current proposal for a directive 'simplifying' the Second Directive now proposes maximum rules in some respects, see Council Document 12973/05 of 16 November 2005 (Council agreed approach) Art. 10b(3). This aberration is beyond the scope of this paper.

[4] Fourth Council Directive 78/660/EEC of 25 July 1978 based on Art. 54(3)(g) of the Treaty on the annual accounts of certain types of companies, *OJ* 1978 L 222/11.

European level is riddled with inconsistencies and anomalies, which would need to be covered in a comprehensive critique of the test. But such a critique, with comparative assessments of other systems, has been set out in detail elsewhere, by our BIICL interdisciplinary group[5] and it is not proposed to revisit that detail here. A general assessment of the regime and the role of the test within it will suffice. The main focus will be on the rival merits of the incumbent balance sheet test (or some variant of it), as opposed to a solvency-based test, as the basis for calculating the limits of permissible distributions.

For most of the paper it will be assumed that some variant of one or other of these tests is the appropriate approach. In the process, however, it will emerge that there are questions about the extent to which the approaches are really different and indeed whether either is needed at all.[6]

The plan of the paper is therefore as follows:

- In the first part, the general theory will briefly be revisited, the role within it of a balance sheet test (including the role of the share capital liability as the measure of a 'cushion' for creditors) will be identified and the role and implications of a rival solvency test will be examined.
- In the second part, the balance sheet test (or rather its various current versions and likely evolution) will be analysed and important recent developments in accounting, which have major implications for the evolution of the various versions of the test, will be assessed.
- The third part will set out the strengths and weaknesses of a policy which continues to rely on such a test.
- The fourth part will identify the possibilities for a rival solvency approach and consider the implications.
- Finally, an attempt will be made to sum up and reach conclusions on the best way forward for Europe and on the implications for the United Kingdom, as a Member State where the various problems are being quite acutely felt.

[5] J. Rickford, ed., 'Reforming Capital: Report of the Interdisciplinary Group on Capital Maintenance', 15 *EBLR* (2004) p. 919 (hereafter 'Reforming Capital').

[6] For a recent paper suggesting that in fact no special regime is needed or appropriate at EU level, see E. Ferran, *Creditors and Company Law: The European Debate, Papers in Honour of Klaus Hopt* (Berlin September 2005, forthcoming) (hereafter 'Ferran, Creditors'); see also E. Ferran, *The Place for Creditor Protection on the Agenda for Modernisation of Company Law in the European Union*, ECGI Law Working Paper No. 51 (2005), available on SSRN.

1. CAPITAL MAINTENANCE: ROLE OF BALANCE SHEET AND SOLVENCY TESTS

It is probably common ground that company creditors need to be protected from company insolvency and that this is their only ultimate legitimate interest relevant for our purposes,[7] that is to say, in being paid. I believe it is now also common ground that creditors cannot be protected from all risks of insolvency. Risk is an inevitable and desirable part of business activity. Distributions inevitably somewhat increase risks to creditors. But distributions are an essential reward for capital, and on this the corporate trading system depends.[8] The issue is thus one of setting a fair and proportionate balance between risks to creditors and constraints on the remuneration of shareholders. Such constraints tend to lead to increases in the cost of capital, which will affect all players. A sound capital maintenance theory must protect from insolvency brought about by 'imprudent' distributions and protect creditors from 'undue' risk in this sense.[9]

General insolvency law also protects creditors from this risk, as one of all the risks which creditors encounter. Capital maintenance therefore needs to be examined as part of the overall creditor protection system of which insolvency law also forms part. A valuable element in the developing debate on this topic has been the recognition that differing views on capital maintenance may reflect differing approaches to the activation of insolvency proceedings and their effectiveness in different jurisdictions. Indeed, capital maintenance reform may best be seen as part of insolvency reform.[10] The balance sheet test, which plays an important wider role in some insolvency systems,[11] is one object of this new perspective. However, that wider perspective also lies beyond the scope of this

---

[7] Potential creditors have an interest in assessing risk for deciding whether to lend and on what terms, and existing creditors have a similar information interest for deciding whether to invoke remedies, but these interests are not the concern of capital maintenance theory but of general transparency policy. As we shall see below there may be a conflict between the two.

[8] See 'Reforming Capital', loc. cit. n. 5, at p. 925; M. Miller, 'The Modigliani-Miller Propositions after 30 years', 2 *Journal of Economic Perspectives* (1988) p. 99.

[9] These competing interests require an appropriate accommodation or balance; this does not of course imply equal weight for each (whatever that might mean). The basis for setting the balance is discussed below. Other considerations are the capacity of creditors to protect themselves, and thus indirectly their fellow creditors, and the transaction costs. The former has been considered elsewhere, see Ferran, 'Creditors', op. cit. n. 6, at pp. 5-8, and literature there cited. Transaction costs will be dealt with incidentally below.

[10] See A. Schall, 'The UK Limited Company Abroad – How Foreign Creditors are Protected after *Inspire Art*', 16 *EBLR* (2005) p. 1534.

[11] See Schall, ibid. (Germany), J. Simon, 'A Comparative Approach to Capital Maintenance', 15 *EBLR* (2004) p. 1037 at pp. 1038-1039 (France). Cf., Insolvency Act 1986, s. 123 (UK). For an account of the latter, see R. Goode, *Principles of Corporate Insolvency Law*, 3rd edn. (London, Sweet and Maxwell 2005) ch. 4.

paper, except as providing possible models for distribution regulation and to the extent that solvency tests may be regarded as part of insolvency law because of their substantive or adjectival character.[12]

1.1 The role of the balance sheet test

Strictly limiting the discussion, then, to creditor protection from excessive distributions by capital maintenance as defined above, what is the role of the balance sheet test in this system? It provides the numbers with which the simple arithmetic of the traditional European system works. The basic equation is as follows: for a distribution to be lawful it must be less than or equal to the surplus of assets over liabilities, treating share capital as a liability. Thus, the company must maintain a 'cushion' of assets equal to its share capital when making distributions. The amount which is distributable is to be determined by the extent to which the asset surplus over other liabilities exceeds the amount of the cushion. The amounts of the cushion, the assets and the liabilities are to be determined from the balance sheet (and, as we shall see, from the profit and loss accounts which inform the balance sheet cumulatively over time[13]). It is worth emphasising at this juncture that the reference to the balance sheet is an automatic determinative process. In European law, unlike any other system of which I am aware,[14] there is no room for any intermediate managerial appreciation, appraisal or adjustment of the accounting results to take account of prudential judgement. But, of course, as long as the Second Directive remains a minimum standards one, Member States are free to add additional constraints to ensure that imprudent distributions are not made on the mere basis of a favourable balance sheet justification.[15]

---

[12] A wrongful trading test and rules about preferences and suspect periods may, for example, operate *de lege* as components of rules applicable in insolvency proceedings and/or as part of regulation of operational governance (including distribution decisions) or, because of general deterrent effects, *de facto* as both. On wrongful trading in this context, see Report of the High Level Group on Company Law ('Winter Group Report') (Brussels, European Commission 2002) pp. 86, 92; and European Commission, Modernising Company Law and Enhancing Corporate Governance in the EU – A Plan to Move Forward (Brussels, 2003) p. 16.

[13] The primacy of profit and loss accounts, or now performance statements, as informing the balance sheet (rather than *vice versa*) is, while now widely accepted, I understand a debatable issue on which fashion has changed. But this is beyond the scope of this paper.

[14] For a conspectus, see 'Reforming Capital', loc. cit. n. 5, Annex C.

[15] In the United Kingdom, such additions notably include wrongful trading, fiduciary duties and other common law rules preserved by Companies Act 1985, s. 281 (saving for other restraints on distribution). The proposals to make the Second Directive a maximum standards provision in some respects – see *supra* n. 3 – do not affect this aspect.

1.2 The cushion as a liability

The amount of the share capital cushion as a liability is to be determined from the balance sheet. But this is scarcely an important issue for the balance sheet test, as in recording the share capital liability the balance sheet records objective, historic and current legal facts. The same cannot be said for the other two variables in the equation, the assets and (other) liabilities which form the basis of the calculation of the surplus, and that is the area where the greatest debate must lie. However, since this cushion theory is one of the greatest weaknesses of the whole system it deserves proper treatment here.

The main objection to the cushion is its disproportionality: the amount generated bears no logical relationship to the policy objective. It is also, at the European level, to a significant extent at the discretion of the Member States and/or the company. The objections to the cushion approach are so fundamental that they raise questions about the lawfulness of the theory under the developing case law of the European Court of Justice.

1.3 Disproportionality

The most fundamental objection to this approach is that it depends on the assertion that the public interest in terms of prudential creditor protection is achieved by the maintenance of this cushion. But that assertion is as a matter of common experience patently not the case. The size of a company's share capital bears no relationship to the needs of the company to retain a reserve of assets or 'working capital' to ensure that the risks to creditors are reduced to an acceptable level (but no further). The share capital amount will depend on the company's experience over many years in raising such capital, whether in equity or preference form, and in generating retained earnings or reserves, which are then reflected in the premiums received on subsequent issues. Two companies with identical needs in terms of working capital may have (indeed practically always will have) quite different experience in this regard. Different companies with identical levels of share capital may have (indeed always will have) different, perhaps very different, risk profiles so far as creditors are concerned. Companies in completely different business sectors and markets, and with completely different capital structures and volatility of assets and liabilities, may have identical levels of share capital. It is almost inconceivable that their needs for working capital will be the same. Similarly, if the share capital of a particular company happens at any point in time to correspond with the needs for security of its creditors, it is most unlikely to continue to do so for long.

Thus, the European regime imposes an uneven playing field, treating like companies differently and different companies alike, in a random fashion, and fails to match the needs of creditors.[16]

This first element drawn from the balance sheet thus fails the basic test for a sound creditor protection system: it fails to maintain a fair and proportionate balance between risks to creditors and return to shareholders at the individual company level. It also fails to achieve a level playing field in economic terms between companies, even where the rules applicable to them are the same.[17]

This is not just an argument that the approach is imperfect, to which the response that we live in an imperfect world might be persuasive. The approach is simply unrelated to the mischief it claims to address.

1.4 Company and Member State discretion

This uneven outcome is exacerbated at the EU interstate level by the fact that some Member States require the whole of the consideration for the issue of shares (nominal or par value and premium) to be treated as part of the cushion,[18] while other Member States require merely that the nominal value be so treated.[19] This latter, more lax, approach is permitted by European law, which is founded on the notion of a 'minimum standards' regime. Indeed it follows that it is all that European law requires.[20] Where the nominal value is so treated, it is normally for companies to determine the par value of their shares, both on first issue and on increase of capital.[21] Thus, subject to their raising and maintaining the minimum capital[22] (a sum now widely agreed to be of little consequence in terms of creditor

[16] It has been argued that the prescriptive EU regime provides a facility enabling companies to opt into a proportionate creditor protection regime by issuing an appropriate amount of equity, see Ferran, 'Creditors', op. cit. n. 6, at pp. 10, 11 and matters there cited. There are two related reasons for rejecting this argument: companies do not issue equity for this purpose but to raise finance in accordance with a chosen capital structure. There is no reason to attach the automatic consequence, undistributability, to every such issue. Moreover, the argument justifies a facility to render capital undistributable rather than a prescriptive rule. Such a facility exists in the 'stated capital' regime in Delaware and was proposed for the United Kingdom in the BIICL report. See 'Reforming Capital', loc. cit. n. 5, at pp. 993-994. It would not be inconsistent with the adoption of a solvency test.

[17] In fact, the rules differ markedly across the European Union – see below.

[18] For example, Germany, the United Kingdom and Ireland.

[19] For example, France, Italy, the Netherlands and Spain.

[20] There is an argument that the Second Directive requires share premiums to be capitalised. See Ferran, 'Creditors', op. cit. n. 6, at p. 14; and P. Muelbert and M. Birke, 'Legal Capital – Is there a Case against the European Legal Capital Rules?', 3 *EBOR* (2002) p. 695. However, this is considered and firmly rejected in the detailed analysis below.

[21] Second Directive, Art. 9, cf., Arts. 26, 27. The point is considered further below.

[22] Second Directive, Art. 6: 50,000 euros, at least 25 per cent paid up.

protection)[23] the amount of the undistributable share capital reserve is a matter of discretion for companies so far as EU law is concerned.

The Second Directive is based on the theory that harmonisation is important in this field because of the economic significance of public companies, and in particular their cross-frontier activities, and that capital is to be maintained because it 'constitutes the creditors' security'.[24] Yet the result is a regime which produces radically different levels of protection as between different Member States, and different companies in the same Member State, and at levels which do not correspond to the needs of creditors.

1.5 European case law

It is now well established in European case law that rules in Member States requiring the application of capital maintenance regimes are to be regarded as restrictions on freedom of establishment and freedom of movement of capital. In this they are like other rules of company law which inhibit free movement of companies across frontiers and/or inhibit the freedom of Member State nationals to establish firms or invest in them.[25] The expanding scope of Community legislation in the field of company law, and in particular cross-frontier restructuring and operation, is based on the same theory.[26]

As such, these rules are not of course necessarily unlawful, but they will need to be justified by reference to the body of case law developed by the European Court of Justice. Accordingly, such rules must not be discriminatory, must be enacted to meet a legitimate policy objective in the general interest and must be proportionate, appropriate and no more restrictive than necessary for this purpose.[27] Community secondary legislation, such as the Second and Fourth Directives, must also meet these requirements.[28] It has already been argued that

---

23 Winter Group Report, op. cit. n. 12, at p. 82.

24 Second Directive, Preamble, first and fourth tirets.

25 Arts. 43 and 56 TEC. ECJ, Case C-212/97 *Centros* [1999] *ECR* I-1459 and Case C-411/03 *SEVIC* [2005] *ECR*, nyr.

26 Thus, for example, the Thirteenth Directive on takeover bids, Directive 2004/25/EC, and the Tenth Directive on cross border mergers of limited liability companies, Directive 2005/56/EC, are founded on the need to remove restrictions in freedom of establishment under Art. 44 EC. For company operation and control see the proposed directive on Shareholder Rights, European Commission Second Consultation Document on Fostering an Appropriate Regime for Shareholders' Rights, MARKT/13.05.2005, Brussels, May 2005.

27 ECJ, Case C-55/94 *Gebhard* [1995] *ECR* I-4165. For application in the company law fields, see the *Golden Shares* cases: C-367/98, C-483/99, C-503/99, C-463/00, C-98/01 and C-174/04.

28 Art. 230 TEC. See P. Craig and G. de Burca, *EU Law*, 3rd edn. (Oxford, Oxford University Press 2003) p. 534 et seq.

the result of the Community regime is disproportionate and in breach of the necessity test. It fails to respond to the needs of particular cases but rather produces random results, thus doing in some cases more, and in the others less, than is necessary to achieve the public interest objective. There is also a strong argument that it is discriminatory at Member State level, in the sense that Member States do not impose the same requirements on equivalent third-country companies trading within their territories, thus disadvantaging Community nationals on the grounds of their nationality.[29] Moreover, if it were really necessary, in order to achieve harmonised levels of creditor protection throughout the Community, that all public companies should comply with the Second Directive minimum standards, how could it be justifiable to allow equivalent third-country companies to fail to do so?

1.6 The role of a solvency test

The mathematical role described so far for the balance sheet as part of the capital maintenance regime (and the place in it of the liability for share capital) is easy enough to identify from Community law. The idea of a solvency test is not defined in this way. In 'Reforming Capital',[30] we proposed such a test as a means of focusing the law on the real mischief here addressed – the risk of default to creditors – in a way which was proportionate to the purpose. This was to be done by imposing conduct or behavioural standards and procedural hurdles at the time of distribution decisions to ensure that commitments were not entered into without appropriate assurances that they would not unduly endanger solvency.

The possible details of such a proposal and the content of the relevant solvency test are discussed in Part 4 below. But the role of such a test is so all-pervasive as to raise the question whether it is part of a capital maintenance system at all.

If such a test is adopted, many features of traditional capital maintenance fall away. Distributions remain a central concept, because the mischief addressed remains the risk to creditors from the return of assets to shareholders. But the differences drawn between different forms of distribution in capital maintenance theory are removed. Dividends, reductions of capital and share buy-backs are seen in their true light, so far as relevant at all for creditor protection, as examples of the same economic transaction, that is, the return of assets to shareholders.[31]

---

[29] The same argument applies to the real seat theory to the extent that it survives, but that is another story.

[30] 'Reforming Capital', loc. cit. n. 5, ch. 5.

[31] One of the anomalies of the European system, admittedly replicated in many others (e.g., Canada and Delaware, see 'Reforming Capital', loc. cit. n. 5, Annex C) is the far lighter

They fall to be treated with special attention by the law because the shareholders are, on the one hand, the ultimate controllers and, on the other, the ultimate deferred creditors of the company, and distribution decisions are directly or indirectly under the ultimate control of shareholders. Share capital as an undistributable reserve is redundant. The cushion, or its equivalent, is achieved by requiring an assurance of ongoing solvency. Rules about the quality of share capital raising are thus also redundant, so far as creditors are concerned, and emerge in their true shape as a matter for shareholders concerned with dilution – a point apparently now becoming recognised by Community law. Issues of shareholder dilution resulting from the issue of shares emerge in their true shape as issues of internal governance of company directors and controllers. These fall to be considered together with the relevant general issues of governance, for example about preferential treatment of shareholders and lack of business judgement by directors.[32]

Thus, the adoption of a solvency test for distributions does not imply the complete abolition of a capital maintenance regime in the broadest sense. The objective of such a test is the same as that of traditional capital maintenance: to ensure that the company remains solvent. This requires a margin of capital in the sense that the company must maintain sufficient resources to assure the necessary cash flows in the face of inevitable risks over time. This might be described as a surplus of assets. Indeed, in 'Reforming Capital', we suggested that a solvency requirement was synonymous with maintaining a surplus of assets over liabilities in the economic sense. However, as we shall see in Part 4 below, to describe this as maintenance of capital, in the sense of a surplus of assets over liabilities, is certainly stretching the language, probably beyond its breaking point.[33]

However, before we reach that debate we need to examine the content of the balance sheet test as it has developed as part of European law since the adoption

---

creditor safeguards attached to capital reductions as opposed to distributions and buy-backs. See also 'Winter Group Report', op. cit. n. 12, at p. 84.

32 Interestingly, the Tenth Directive on cross-border mergers of limited liability companies seems to recognise that valuations are not a legitimate concern of creditors, allowing waiver of expert reports by shareholders, see Directive 2005/56/EC, Art. 8(4).

33 Conventional analysis has now progressed beyond regarding assets as necessarily corresponding to physical things or legal claims. The debate in the United States and International Accounting Standards Boards (FASB and IASB) about fundamental accounting concepts is instructive. The notion of an asset as a resource which is a source of future cash flows is gaining currency. But probably, with the UK Accounting Standards Board, we would reject the notion that *every* source of cash flows is to be regarded as an asset. 'There will continue to be cases where expenditure is recognised as an expense, even where it is expected (sometimes confidently) to result in future inflows', D. Loweth and A. Lennard, 'UK Accounting Standards Board' (August 2005) p. 5, available at: <http://www.frc.org.uk/asb>, commenting on H. Bullen and K. Crook, 'Revisiting the Concepts – A New Conceptual Framework Project' (FASB and IASB, May 2005). For further discussion, see Part 4 below.

of the Second Company Law Directive in 1976, as supplemented by the Fourth Company Law Directive on the accounts of individual companies, adopted in 1978. In doing so, we shall discover that the result of changing concepts of what constitutes an asset or liability, or what their value is, has indeed led to some convergence between the notion of a balance sheet net assets test and a solvency test, or test of future cash flows. But only up to a point, and with many reservations.

2. THE BALANCE SHEET TEST IN EUROPEAN LAW: CHANGE AND VARIETY

It is now almost a quarter of a century since the adoption in European law of the fully-developed balance sheet test for dividends, with the implementation of the Second and Fourth Directives.[34] During that period, we have seen major advances in accounting theory and a progressive divergence of philosophy and techniques since the original test was adopted in the Second Directive and given content by the Fourth. There are now in fact four main versions of the balance sheet, and thus of the test (each with variants), operating in parallel.

2.1 Balance sheet tests: two 1978 versions

At the time of the adoption of the Fourth Directive, the historic cost theory of accounting was dominant in Europe, and it is the dominant model in the text. Assets are generally to be stated at their cost (purchase price or production cost) and depreciated over their economic lives. Liabilities, even long-term liabilities, are to be stated at their nominal amount. The accounting principle of prudence is given great prominence.[35] The countervailing principle of neutrality,[36] designed to ensure that accounts hold a fair balance between optimism and pessimism, does not feature, though the practice of maintaining 'secret reserves' to enable management to smooth results over time and retain resources free of the scrutiny of shareholders and others is outlawed.[37]

---

[34] The Second Directive was implemented in the United Kingdom by the Companies Act 1980. However, the distribution rules in that Act anticipated the Fourth Directive provisions on revaluation reserves, see ss. 39-45 (now Companies Act 1985, Part VIII).

[35] Fourth Directive, Art. 31(1)(c).

[36] See IASB Framework for the Preparation and Presentation of Financial Statements (April 2001) para. 36. The text of the Framework (hereafter 'IASB Framework') is usefully annexed to the European Commission's 'Comments concerning Certain Articles of Regulation (EC) No. 1606/2002', Brussels, November 2003.

[37] Fourth Directive, Art. 42. Hidden reserves flatter performance ratios, such as return on capital employed, and thus undermine accounts as an index of stewardship.

Financial information is to be presented in a limited number of detailed formats, one of two for balance sheets and one of four for profit and loss accounts.[38] The overall effect was (and still is, for as we shall see the unmodified Fourth Directive remains in force in some circumstances and may in principle apply to any company) to provide a stratified picture of the history of the business, bearing little necessary relationship to current values of assets and liabilities, in a tightly regulated format intended to generate comparable numbers. This may well have been designed to produce results favouring the dominant stakeholders in continental Community companies at the time of its original drafting. These were dominant, or block, shareholders who could expect to extract private benefits without relying on dividends, company management, which would wish to conserve company resources from the depredations of the taxman and under their own control rather than for distribution to shareholders, and powerful creditors, particularly the banks. The voice of employees was also strong. The interests of all of these stakeholders were best served by a conservative attitude to quantifying profits for distribution.[39]

At a relatively late stage in the negotiation of the Directive, the Anglo-Irish concept of the overriding principle of the 'true and fair view' (T&FV) was added, together with, after considerable resistance from some of the founding Member States, provisions for revaluation of fixed assets and inflation accounting.[40]

The T&FV principle required that, notwithstanding any contrary prescriptive provision of the Directive, if ('in exceptional cases') a particular different accounting treatment was necessary to give such a view of the assets, liabilities, financial position and profit or loss then it should be adopted. Appropriate explanation and reconciliation with the normal rules outcome was required. This is now much vaunted as a European principle. But in the form adopted in European law it is somewhat spoiled: it is open to Member States to define what the exceptional cases are to be and to prescribe the relevant special rules; such authority as there is on its meaning fails to understand the spirit of the concept.[41] Reconciling an obligation to provide a factually realistic and complete view with the conservative and formal basic approach presented considerable difficulties. The problem of giving content to 'true and fair' was solved in the United Kingdom by means of the adoption and recognition of official accounting standards.

---

38 Arts. 9, 10, 23-26.

39 This of course was not true for the recently joined Member States, at least the United Kingdom and Ireland, but on their accession both the Second and Fourth Directives were at a relatively advanced stage of development.

40 For the history, see V. Edwards, *EC Company Law* (Oxford, Oxford University Press 1999) pp. 117-121.

41 Fourth Directive, Art. 2. See Edwards, op. cit. n. 40, at pp. 128-130.

These were accepted as normally mandatory to give a T&FV.[42] In some respects, these standards came close to modifying, or even overriding, Directive requirements. For example, they required a cash flow statement as part of the annual accounts as necessary to give a T&FV.[43] In continental countries, the idea of the requirement as imposing a duty to depart from the rules to achieve a realistic picture of the financial position was not, and perhaps is still not, understood. There is still no mandatory requirement that accounts should report substance rather than form. Indeed, Member States have *an option* whether to require this or not under the 'Modernisation' Directive.[44]

The distribution rules in the Second Directive establish the balance sheet test. Although enacted before the Fourth Directive was adopted, these anticipated the Fourth Directive rules and the expected availability of a harmonised Community balance sheet and profit and loss account.

The critical provisions are in Article 15(1)(a) (the 'net assets' test) and (c) (the 'running account' profits test). These provide that:

> (a) no distribution to shareholders may be made when [at the last balance sheet date] the net assets as set out in the annual accounts are or following the distribution would become lower than the amount of subscribed capital [this means aggregate nominal capital[45]] plus those reserves which may not be distributed under the law or the statutes [sc. company articles]; and
>
> (c) The amount of the distribution to shareholders may not exceed the amount of the profits at the end of the last financial year plus any profits brought forward and sums drawn from reserves available for the purpose, less any losses brought forward and sums placed to reserve in accordance with the law or the statutes.

The effect of paragraph (a) was to put in place the formula mentioned above: distributions may not exceed the surplus of assets over liabilities plus aggregate nominal share capital as they appear in the accounts, presumably the balance sheet.

---

42 Reference is normally made to an opinion of Mary Arden QC (now Lady Justice Arden) of 21 April 1993 given to the Accounting Standards Board. This is adopted in professional and regulatory guidance, see most recently Financial Reporting Review Panel FRRP PN 85 of June 2005 on the effect of the IAS Regulation on the requirement for accounts to give a T&FV. Accounting standards were given statutory status in addition to their common law adoption in 1989, see Companies Act 1985, s. 256, and Schedule 4, para. 36A.

43 As we shall see below such a statement of changes is now mandatory under IAS.

44 Art. 4(6), discussed below.

45 For discussion of this point see 'Reforming Capital', loc. cit. n. 5, at pp. 939-941.

Member States are free to prescribe in their laws that other undistributable reserves are to be maintained, as may companies through their articles. This appears to permit, for example, the prescribing of the capitalisation of the share premium account or the accumulation of a legal reserve of a certain proportion of share capital, practices common in various Member States and in various sectors, for example in the life insurance sector.

The effect of paragraph (c) is more problematic: it is a mixed profit and loss account and balance sheet test. The amount of funds available for distribution is reached by taking the net profit for the last financial year, together with profits brought forward from prior years and other distributable reserves, and deducting accumulated losses and sums taken to undistributable reserves under the law, or perhaps so taken by company decision, for example by capitalisation of profits.

It is not entirely clear whether the amounts which make up this calculation are to be drawn from the statutory profit and loss account and balance sheet, as the amounts used under (a) explicitly are to be from the balance sheet. But the arguments that they should be are overwhelming. The balance sheet and profit and loss account are parts of a single coherent system. The former constitutes a summation and aggregation of all the profit and loss accounts over time, providing a picture of the cumulative financial position. Thus, the profit for the year is to be drawn from the profit and loss account and the other available reserves are to be identified from the balance sheet. Certainly, the UK implementation made both tests referable to the accounts.[46]

It was clear from paragraph (c) that accumulated losses must be made good before distributions could take place, thus outlawing distributions out of current profits regardless of accumulated losses ('nimble dividends'), previously probably possible in England and still allowed in many jurisdictions, including Delaware.[47]

But it was not clear what principles were to be employed in identifying profits and losses, nor what reserves could be treated as distributable under paragraph (c). Some light was arguably cast on this by Article 15(2) dealing with interim dividends. This allowed profits 'made' since the balance sheet date, together with accumulated profits net of losses and amounts transferred to reserve to be

---

46 Companies Act 1985, ss. 263, 264, 270.

47 Delaware General Corporations Law, s. 170; see B. Manning and J. Hanks, *Legal Capital*, 3rd edn. (New York, Foundation Press 1990). As I recall, the EC in negotiations invoked outlawing of nimble dividends as a justification for the addition of para. (c), but it is not evident that this was needed given the effect of (a). The German AktG relies solely on an equivalent of Art. 15(1)(c). See 'Reforming Capital', loc. cit. n. 5, at p. 1008.

distributed on the basis of interim accounts. But what was the test of whether a profit was 'made'? Could profits arising on a revaluation be regarded as made?[48]

Further light was perhaps cast on the subject by the Fourth Directive, which was under active negotiation when the Second Directive was adopted. There are two relevant articles: Article 31, which establishes the principles of accounting prudence, and Article 33, which makes special provision for an exception from historic cost principles with special safeguards.

Article 31(1)(c), the first article in section 7 (Valuation Rules), lays down that

> valuation must be made on a prudent basis and in particular: (aa) only profits made at the balance sheet date may be included, (bb) account must be taken of all liabilities arising in the course of the financial year or of the previous one, even if such liabilities become apparent only between the date of the balance sheet and the date on which it was drawn up, (cc) account must be taken of all depreciation, whether the result … is a loss or a profit.

The requirement that profits must be *'made'* to be *included in the accounts* appears to have been taken in Britain to impose a strict realisation test for recognition of profits for distribution purposes. Certainly, the overriding ('running account') test was adopted in Britain in a form requiring that both private and public companies' profits available for distribution must constitute accumulated realised profits net of realised losses and capitalisations,[49] and the enactment of Article 31(1)(c) in the British accounting rules was treated as requiring that a profit must be *'realised'* (i.e., result from a transaction rather than a valuation[50]) (as opposed to made), in order to be *included in the profit and loss account* (as opposed to being included in the accounts more generally).[51]

This of itself would prevent the distribution of unrealised profits, since the British running account test does not refer to reserves available for distribution as

---

48 However, this provision also allows sums drawn from reserves available for the purpose to be distributable, and interim accounts drawn up for the purpose will clearly include unrealised profits to date, so any additional guidance is scarcely determinative.

49 Companies Act 1985, s. 263. For an account of the old British rules (different for England and Scotland) which survive as additional requirements, see below and see L. Gower, *The Principles of Modern Company Law*, 3rd edn. (London, Stevens 1969) pp. 115-121.

50 There is also a difficulty with funds arising on a reduction of capital: are these realised profits or indeed profits at all? The UK professions finally concluded that they were both, see ICAEW, 'Technical Guidance on the Determination of Realised Profits and Losses', TECH 7/03 (London, ICAEW 2003).

51 Companies Act 1985, Schedule 4, para. 12: 'only profits *realised* at the balance sheet date shall be included *in the profit and loss account*' [emphasis added].

does Article 15(1)(c) and (2).[52] If it was done on this basis, the application of the test to private companies was a piece of over-implementation ('gold-plating') of the Directive, presumably because the current domestic law on distributable profits was regarded as unsatisfactory[53] (though it continues to apply in the United Kingdom as an additional restriction[54]). This is because the running account test does not of course apply to private companies.

Whatever the merits of the UK implementation, there were strong arguments that the rule in Article 31(1)(c) did not have the effect of prohibiting the distribution of unrealised profits. Read in context, it is about the time at which profits arise rather than their character and establishes the accounting principle of accruals, or the non-anticipation of profits. If it required profits to be realised in order to be included in the accounts then of course no unrealised profits (such as amounts arising on a revaluation) could be included.

The second relevant provision of the Directive did indeed permit revaluations to be reflected – and thus unrealised profits (or losses) arising in consequence to be 'included'[55] – in the accounts. Under Article 33(1), Member States may permit or require accounts to include revaluations of various assets on various bases, including inflation accounting for all accounting items. Article 33(2) deals with the accounting and distribution consequences and applies to all limited companies, public and private. It thus provides a distribution rule, extending beyond the scope of the Second Directive, and applying to both public and private companies.

This rule works as follows: Article 33(2) provides that the differences arising as compared with the orthodox historic cost valuation method, that is to say, the profits and losses arising on the permitted revaluations, are to be carried to a special reserve (the 'revaluation reserve'). This reserve may not be reduced except by capitalisation or because the amounts therein are no longer necessary

---

52 It has been argued that Art. 15(2) indicates by using the word 'made' that only realised profits may be distributed (because if there is a 'made' requirement for interim distributions it follows as a matter of consistency that the same view should be taken of final, or annual accounts based, distributions). However, even if 'made' in Art. 15(2) means realised in the technical accounting sense, which is to put on a simple word a technical meaning which was almost certainly not in mind at the time, the paragraph still allows the use of other distributable reserves, which at the time could have included both unrealised profits and share premium account. *Contra* Muelbert and Birke, loc. cit. n. 20, at p. 704.

53 The Jenkins Commission on Company Law Reform had proposed a ban on distributions of unrealised profits, Cmnd 1749, 1962 (London, HMSO 1962) paras. 336, 337.

54 Companies Act 1985, s. 263(3).

55 There is an argument that amounts arising on a revaluation are not 'profits' or 'losses' at all. But if they are not, there would be no need for a prohibition on their inclusion in the profit and loss account. Moreover, the argument is inconsistent with the Fair Value and Modernisation Directives, which permit such amounts arising from a fair value revaluation to be included in the profit and loss account. See below.

for the valuation purpose. In particular, 'no part of the revaluation reserve may be distributed unless it represents gains actually realised'.

This is strong evidence that Article 31 did not have the effect apparently attributed to it in the United Kingdom. If Article 31 prevented such unrealised profits from being distributed, why was it necessary to provide against this in Article 33?[56 57]

So, while Article 31(1)(c) (profits 'made') thus arguably did not require unrealised profits to be rendered undistributable, Article 33(2) (revaluation reserve) certainly did.[58] The running account surplus test, as it applies in British law (which of course permits revaluations as allowed by the Fourth Directive) not only to public but also to private companies, is therefore arguably not an over-implementation of the Second and Fourth Directives, taken together.[59] It was also necessary to complete the implementation of Article 15(1)(a) to provide in British law that any surplus in the revaluation reserve should be treated as an undistributable reserve for the purpose of the net assets test.[60]

The effect, from the European point of view, is that there is no increase in the level of distributable reserves available to a company formed under the law of a Member State which takes advantage of the option in Article 33(1) in allowing revaluations of the relevant assets, because any net increase in assets is carried to the undistributable revaluation reserve.[61] The consistency of application of the Second Directive rules was thus preserved in that respect. Unrealised profits cannot enhance distributable reserves.

However, the position was consistent for unrealised losses. In Member States which permitted revaluations, the effect of the net assets test would be to reduce the profits available for distribution for public companies suffering such losses whether or not they had a surplus in the revaluation reserve. This was because where a company engages in a revaluation, for example of its fixed tangible assets (as indeed it might feel obliged to do, in order to give a T&FV), it will almost

---

56 And why does Art. 33 use the emphatic 'actually realised' while Art. 31 uses 'made'?

57 Arguably, the United Kingdom did not need to apply Art. 15(1)(c) of the Second Directive to private companies but only to require that they set up an undistributable revaluation reserve when necessary. But at the time that requirement had the same effect as a running account test.

58 One reason why this analysis is important is that, if Art. 31 prohibits distribution of unrealised profits, then profits arising on a fair value revaluation are arguably not distributable in EU law. (The new (Fair Value) section (7a) of the Directive derogates from Art. 33, but not from Art. 31.) If it does not so prohibit then they are distributable, whether carried to profit and loss or equity. See below.

59 Until they were amended by the Fair Value Directives, see below.

60 Companies Act 1985, s. 264(3).

61 Though this reserve can be capitalised, reduced under a reduction of capital and then distributed.

certainly feel obliged, for the same reason, to engage in unfavourable valuations ('down' as well as 'up'), at least of all the assets of the same class. Both the T&FV requirement and the neutrality principle will outlaw the use of selective revaluations. The unrealised losses resulting would not at the time affect the profit and loss account (for the current position, however, see below), but they would be applied in reducing the value at which the relevant assets were stated in the balance sheet, thus reducing the net assets surplus.[62]

The result is two balance sheet tests[63] under the 1978 version of the Fourth Directive. Net assets are calculated taking account only of realised profits and losses for companies which are not permitted to engage in revaluations, or are so permitted but do not feel the need to do so. For companies which are so permitted, and feel the necessity to engage in revaluations, net assets are calculated net of unrealised losses but not enhanced by unrealised profits.

The reasonable observer may ask how, in countries where revaluations are not permitted, companies which suffer major changes in the value of their assets could give a T&FV of their financial position, and indeed how the revaluation reserve requirement can be reconciled with the accounting principle of neutrality.

The Community lawyer will probably answer that it was evident, from the fact that Member States were permitted by the Directive to outlaw revaluations in all circumstances, that accounts which failed to include them must be consistent with the T&FV requirement. As to the second point, we have already noted that neutrality is not as such a principle of Community law, at least subject to the adoption of International Accounting Standards (IAS).

The reasonable observer may also ask at this juncture, for reasons similar to those informing the first question, how this result could possibly be regarded as producing a fair measure of distributable profits having regard to the reasonable needs of creditors? This will be answered for all the balance sheet tests in Part 4 below.

It is necessary first to examine what other balance sheet tests operate in the European Union. There are two further tests:

---

62 I am not clear how German law reflects this result. If a loss arises on a revaluation or a fair value valuation which is not carried to profit and loss what reduces the amount of net assets available for distribution?

63 In fact, the Directive contains a host of other Member State and company options, mainly concerned with detailed provisions of disclosure and exemptions (forty-one Member State and thirty-five company options, see Edwards, op. cit. n. 40, at p. 117, and material there cited). But the difference between historic cost and current value accounting is by far the most important for our purposes.

- the Modernised Fourth Directive test, which results from the Fair Value and Modernisation Directives,[64] and
- the International Accounting Standards test, which results from the Regulation on International Accounting Standards (Regulation 1606).[65]

All three of these instruments are concerned with the introduction of modern accounting policies based on the need to give a realistic or 'fair value' picture of the reporting entity. The Regulation gives direct effect to International Accounting Standards (IAS) (once adopted for this purpose by the EU Commission under the Regulation[66]), which are based on this principle, making them applicable to the consolidated accounts of listed companies. Since the Second Directive distribution rules operate on the basis of the company's individual accounts, this of itself has no effect on distributions. However, the Regulation allows Member States the option, either as a permission or a requirement, in respect of all or certain classes of company,[67] of applying the same IAS regime also to the individual accounts both of such listed companies and of other companies within the Fourth and Second Directives.[68] There is a strong incentive to do so, at least for companies within the group of a listed parent, as accounts for the whole group can then be struck on a single basis without the need for special accounts to be prepared for consolidation purposes. If Member States do adopt IAS for individual accounts, the Fourth Directive regime is replaced as a matter of directly applicable Community law and the relevant accounts for distribution purposes become the IAS accounts.[69]

The resulting difference in the accounting basis on which Community companies report (as between those which adopt IAS and those which do not) is dealt

[64] Directive 2001/65/EC of 27 September 2001 amending Directives 83/349/EEC, 86/635/EEC and 91/67/EEC as regards the valuation rules for the annual and consolidated accounts of certain types of companies as well as of banks and other financial institutions, *OJ* 2001 L 283/28 ('Fair Value Directive'); and Directive 2003/51/EC of 18 June 2003 amending Directives 83/349/EEC, 86/635/EEC and 91/67/EEC on the annual accounts of certain types of companies, banks and other financial institutions and insurance undertakings *OJ* 2003 L 178/16 ('Modernisation Directive').

[65] Regulation (EC) No. 1606/2002 of 19 July 2002 on the application of international accounting standards, *OJ* 2002 L 243/1 ('IAS Regulation').

[66] By Commission Regulation under Art. 3 of Regulation 1606; for regulations in force, see below.

[67] This is implicit. Cf., the Modernisation Directive, which makes explicit provision.

[68] Regulation 1606, Art. 5.

[69] In the United Kingdom, the standards regulator has announced its intention to align domestic standards so far as possible with IAS ('the ASB's Convergence Programme'), a development welcomed by the UK Government. See DTI and HM Treasury, 'Modernisation of Accounting Directives/IAS Infrastructure – A Consultative Document' (London, DTI March 2004) p. 13.

with by the Modernisation Directive, which amends the Fourth Directive. The result, the Commission claims, is to align the position of companies which continue to report in accordance with that Directive entirely with that of companies reporting under IAS.[70] That does not appear entirely to be the case – an issue discussed below.

This paper treats the Fair Value Directive and Modernisation Directive changes together. This is done because, although the former came into operation on 1 January 2004, the Fourth Directive has operated on the basis of both since 1 January 2005. That is to say, we now have a single 'Modernised Fourth Directive' basis for the balance sheet test.

However, this modernised basis remains largely optional for Member States, which are free to decide whether or not to permit or require companies, or particular classes of companies, to apply most of the changes[71] made. These options can be exercised in different ways for different provisions. Some other changes are mandatory,[72] and some are required to be made available by Member States as company options.[73]

The overall effect is that within the European Union and within Member States the following accounting treatments are now possible and the balance sheet test will be capable of being drawn from accounts based on any of them:

(1) traditional historic cost 1978-style Fourth Directive accounts;
(2) such accounts with revaluations;[74]
(3) accounts based on some or all of the accounting changes introduced as company or Member State options under the Modernised Fourth Directive;
(4) IAS accounts, i.e., accounts which comply directly with IAS under the European Union's IAS Regulations.

We thus have four possible bases for the balance sheet test with a variety of outcomes possible under each, particularly the third. We have already examined the first two. The third and fourth are now considered.

---

[70] See European Commission, Explanatory Memorandum on the Proposal for the Modernisation Directive, COM (2002) 259/2 final, Brussels, July 2002, pp. 3, 4.

[71] These are considered separately below.

[72] These are: stricter rules on the accrual of liabilities arising before, but becoming apparent after, the balance sheet date (Art. 31(1)(bb) as amended by the Modernisation Directive) and the amendment to the meaning of provisions in Arts. 20 and 42. For the latter, see further the discussion of IAS 37, Provisions, etc., below.

[73] Fair value treatment of certain financial instruments derivatives and hedging arrangements, Art. 42a. The accounting treatment is prescribed, see below.

[74] Both (i) and (ii) now operate subject to the mandatory changes that have been made by the Modernisation and Fair Value regimes. But these are minor: see *supra* n. 72.

2.2 The Modernised Fourth Directive: new tests – modified distribution rules

The principle change introduced by the modernisation regime is to allow (but not require) fair value valuation of certain assets.

The first set of such assets are certain financial instruments and hedging arrangements. The definitions are technical. Fair value for this purpose is quite tightly defined.[75] For our purposes, the important aspect is that such valuation is not subject to the bar on distributions which arises for revaluations under the traditional approach.[76] Indeed, some of the amounts arising are obliged to be carried to profit and loss account,[77] while others are to be accounted for in equity as part of a fair value reserve. The requirement to carry certain differences to profit and loss account is said to be 'notwithstanding Article 31(1)(c)', which, as we have seen, requires that only profits 'made' at the balance sheet date should be included in the accounts. So the draftsman of the new regime believed that this provision did indeed bar transfer of valuation differences to profit and loss account. But the important point is that no bar is placed on the distribution of either kind of item. As we have seen, both the net assets and the running account test (and indeed the rules for interim distributions) allow distributions from reserves available for this purpose according to Member State law, and nothing in Article 31 prevents this. Thus, even if amounts arising on fair valuation are carried to equity (shareholders' funds in the balance sheet), the Member States are free to treat the resulting reserves as distributable so far as the Second Directive distribution rules and the amended Fourth Directive rules are concerned.

Article 33(1)(a) and (2) in its original form required differences on revaluations of financial fixed assets to be carried to the undistributable revaluation reserve. Under the new regime, the reference to financial fixed assets has been

---

[75] Essentially on the basis of market value where there is an established market (or equivalent) or otherwise of 'generally accepted models or techniques', Art. 42b.

[76] The new rules are by way of derogation from Art. 32 of the Fourth Directive, which imposes the historic cost rules. The Art. 33 revaluations were also such derogations, but the conditions which attach to revaluations under Art. 33, in particular the establishment of the undistributable revaluation reserve, do not apply to the new derogation, which is independent of Art. 33.

[77] Art 42c(1): changes in value of financial instruments except certain kinds of hedging instruments and exchange differences on monetary investments in foreign entities. These exceptions are to be accounted for in equity (fair value reserve). Member States may also permit or require changes in value in available-for-sale financial instruments ('assets?') other than derivatives to be accounted for in the fair value reserve, Art. 42c(2).

deleted, presumably reflecting the fact that Article 33 no longer applies to all financial fixed assets.[78]

The new treatment for financial assets is extended, however, by Article 42e and enables Member States to permit or require, for all or any class of companies, fair value treatment for *any assets other than financial instruments* with or without profit and loss account treatment. This was thought to be necessary to anticipate the extending range of fair valuation under IAS, which is described below.[79] The effect is to create a means for allowing any unrealised profit arising on a fair value basis to be distributable and included in profit for the year. Fair value is not defined and the accounting treatment is not prescribed for such cases.

The Commission has said that it envisages this treatment only being adopted in accordance with a recognised accounting framework. There is no such requirement in the Directive text, but the Preamble states that the purpose is to enable Member States to modify their rules 'in accordance with international developments as expressed through [IAS]'.[80]

Thus, the overall effect of the Fair Value and Modernisation Directives, taken together, is to allow any assets to be valued on a fair value basis and to prescribe what this means (both in terms of the definition of fair value and of accounting treatment) only for financial instruments and hedging assets (arrangements).

There is no requirement for an undistributable revaluation reserve where fair value is applied.[81] It is thus clear that amounts arising on such a valuation, whether or not transferred to profit and loss account, may be treated as distributable.

The other changes made by this modernisation which are important for our purposes were the following:

- Permitting Member States to permit or require additional accounting statements in the annual accounts.[82] This reflects the IAS requirement for a cash

---

[78] But this is not entirely clear: Art. 33(1) originally applied to tangible fixed assets and financial fixed assets; it continues to apply to fixed assets generally whether tangible or not. Presumably, this is subject to the special derogation for financial instruments in s. 7a.

[79] European Commission, Explanatory Memorandum on the Modernisation Directive, COM (2002) 259/2 final, Brussels, 9 July 2002, p. 3.

[80] Modernisation Directive, Preamble (7) ('balance sheet'), (8) ('application of revaluations [sic] and of fair value').

[81] Both Arts. 42a and 42e are in derogation from Art. 32, which applies the old historic cost valuation rules in Arts. 34 to 42. They are thus a separate derogation from that in Art. 33.

[82] Art. 2(1), second para. The UK Government has decided not to take advantage of this provision on the grounds that the relevant statement is already required by accounting standards. See DTI consultation document, *supra* n. 69, at pp. 18, 19. The question arises: how could such standards have been lawful if this new provision was necessary, or remain lawful without invoking it? Can a universal obligation be imposed as a T&FV requirement?

flow statement, or statement of changes, as an essential tool for assessing performance. As we have already noted, the British Accounting Standards Board made such a requirement as part of its interpretation of a T&FV many years ago (anticipating, whether lawfully or not, this EU permission). The question arises – if such additional information is necessary for assessing the prospects of the company – why is it not reflected in some way in the test of distributability? One answer is that the European Union does not regard it as essential because it is not to be mandatory. But that discussion is to anticipate the criticism reserved for Part 3 below.

- Permitting Member States to permit or require all or any classes of company to have regard to the substance of reported transactions.[83] This has already been mentioned in the context of the T&FV requirement. An example of the IAS treatments, which this is designed to allow, is the treatment of preference shares as loan liabilities[84] and dividends due thereon as debts, and the rules on accounting for financial leases as assets.[85] The true and fair requirement remains in place for Modernised Fourth Directive accounts. As we shall see below, this may well not be the case for IAS accounts.
- Permitting Member States similarly to prescribe an alternative accounting format for the balance sheet on a current/non-current basis[86] reflecting the IAS approach, which however prescribes no formats as such for balance sheets or profit and loss accounts.
- Similarly, Member States may substitute a performance statement for the profit and loss account formats as prescribed under Articles 23 to 26. This will allow the IAS approach of providing a comprehensive statement of financial performance, including a statement of recognised gains and losses.

In both cases, the Directive requires that these more flexible and comprehensive formats should provide 'information at least equivalent' to that formerly prescribed.

This should ensure that the accounting items needed for the operation of the balance sheet test are still available for these companies. (As we shall see below, there is no equivalent requirement for IAS companies.)

So there are two main developments arising from the Modernised Fourth Directive:

- The first is that the scope for the recognition of unrealised profits and losses through the fair value regime is much broadened. While the nature of such

---

83 Art. 4(6).

84 IAS 1, para. 68; IAS 32, para. 18.

85 IAS 17, paras. 20-32.

86 Art. 10a. See IAS 1.

valuation is prescribed for financial instruments (essentially in terms of a market valuation or its equivalent), there is no such definition for other assets under Articles 42e and 42f. It is clear from IAS that such valuation may be based on the directors' assessment.[87]

- The second important change is that some or all of the differences arising on a fair valuation may be treated as distributable because they do not fall into the revaluation reserve. This will be true whether or not they are carried to profit and loss account, because as we have noted above the distribution rules in Article 15(1) and (2) do not require distributions to be drawn solely from profit and loss account.

The question arises whether the effect of IAS is to weaken, or even remove, the rigid connection between accounts and the calculation of distributions, producing a system which allows for directors' overriding appraisal of the prudential position, as operates in all systems other than the European one.[88] To some extent, this is true and it seems that it is even more the case under the IAS regime, in spite of the Commission's assertions that the two are the same. To that regime we now turn.

2.3 IAS Regime and the balance sheet test

In spite of the Commission's assertion that there are no differences between Modernised Fourth Directive accounts and IAS accounts that does not appear to be the case.

2.4 Accounting philosophies: T&FV v. IAS framework

The first difference relates to the accounting philosophy on which company accounts are based. The essence of the Fourth Directive approach is the provision of the T&FV of the assets, liabilities and financial position (which will emerge from the balance sheet) and the profit or loss for the year – the two outputs of the accounting statements prescribed. This is worth stressing. The financial position and profit or loss are logically prior to the T&FV. The purpose of the T&FV is to generate these two outputs. These outputs are at the heart of the distribution regime.

The basic philosophy of IAS is rather different. It is to be found in IAS 1 (Presentation of Financial Statements).[89] Such statements are to 'present fairly the

---

[87] See, e.g., IAS 16, paras. 31-42 (revaluation model for property, plant and equipment).

[88] See 'Reforming Capital', loc. cit. n. 5, Annex C. Ferran, 'Creditors', op. cit. n. 6, at p. 22 (IFRS as effecting creeping relaxation of the legal capital regime).

[89] IAS are adopted by Commission Regulations under Regulation 1606. The texts of the relevant IAS, which are of course part of Community law, are annexed to these regulations. See Regulations (EC) Nos. 1725/2003, 707/2004, 2236-2238/2004, 1073/2005 and 1751/2005.

financial position, financial performance and cash flows of an entity'. Such presentation is to 'faithfully reflect the effects of transactions, other events and conditions in accordance with the definitions and recognition criteria set out in the IAS Accounting Framework', which describes the overall philosophical approach of IAS.[90] The Framework is thus incorporated into EU law by reference. Where the effect of compliance with an IAS requirement would produce a result which would be so misleading as to conflict with 'the objective' of the Framework, then departure is mandatory, with full disclosure of the justification for, and financial impact of, departure.[91] The objective of the Framework is *to facilitate decision making by users* of accounting statements.[92] It has been argued that this approach does not affect the T&FV requirement under the Fourth Directive, or at least that this requirement remains in place for the United Kingdom.[93] The UK Government in its implementation of the IAS regime[94] did in fact remove the T&FV requirements for the annual accounts of IAS companies. It also adjusted the requirement for audit certification of IAS companies: auditors were no longer required to certify that a T&FV had been presented, but rather that the accounts gave a fair presentation in accordance with the IAS Framework.[95] This change and the stated intention of the IASB to achieve convergence with US standards[96] prompted considerable concern in the United Kingdom that the 'principles-based' approach of the T&FV was being lost.[97] However, in its latest proposals the UK Government proposes to reinstate the T&FV.[98] Since this requirement must be regarded as subject to the IAS Regulation, it may be that we shall begin to see IAS influence on the meaning of T&FV in law as well as in practice.

---

[90] The Framework for the Preparation and Presentation of Financial Statements (hereafter 'IASB Framework') is conveniently annexed to the European Commission's 'Comments Concerning Certain Articles of Regulation 1606/2002', published in November 2003.

[91] IAS 1, paras. 13-19.

[92] IASB Framework, paras. 12-14.

[93] UK Financial Reporting Council, Press Notice 119, 9 August 2005, available at: <http://www.frc.org.uk/frrp>.

[94] Companies Act 1985 (IAS and other accounting amendments) Regulations SI 2947/2004.

[95] Companies Act 1985, ss. 235(2) and 262(2A).

[96] The agreement with the US standards organisation, FASB, to this effect is known as the Fulton Accord. For an account, see: <http://www.iasb.org.uk>.

[97] Cf., P. Schuetze, 'What are Assets and Liabilities?', 37 *Abacus* (2001) pp. 1-2; K. Jones 'True and Fair View of British Audits is in Jeopardy', *FT*, 6 July 2005; and A. Pollock, 'From Making Judgements to Following Rules', AEI, Washington, July 2005. In fact both US and IAS standards are avowedly 'principles-based', see Bullen and Crook, loc. cit. n. 33. For a detailed analysis, see D. Kershaw, 'Evading Enron: Taking Principles too Seriously in Accounting Regulation', 68 *MLR* (2005) p. 594.

[98] Companies Bill 2005, HL Bill 1 November 2005, clauses 366, 482(3).

It may be argued that the Framework cannot in practice depart from the T&FV approach because the EU Commission can only adopt an IAS if it is satisfied that it does not conflict with the T&FV requirement, as required by Article 3 of Regulation 1606. There are difficulties with this argument. It is not possible to state in advance that a standard will comply with the T&FV requirement. The question whether a T&FV has been presented has to be determined *ad hoc* by reference to the particular position of a reporting company at the time. Indeed, it is envisaged under both the EU and the IAS regime that any standard may, indeed in some circumstances will, fail on this count – that is the very *raison d'être* of the T&FV (and similar IAS Framework) override requirements. Perhaps for this reason, Article 3 of Regulation 1606 only requires the Commission, before adopting an IAS, to satisfy itself that the IAS would *not conflict* with the requirement, not that it would positively secure it.[99]

The difference in philosophy between the Fourth Directive and IAS is also reflected in a different approach to accounting statements. Instead of the two accounts of the Fourth Directive regime (balance sheet and profit and loss account,) there are three for IAS: balance sheet, performance statement and statement of changes or cash flow statement. It is envisaged that these three statements are to be taken together to enable decision makers to reach a considered view of the performance and direction of the business based on its performance so far. For this reason, the performance statement is envisaged as more comprehensive than a tradition profit and loss account (embracing all material changes in assets and liabilities so as to indicate value added or destroyed) and the cash flow statement is regarded as a vital tool for assessing performance at the cash level and in 'assessing prospective net cash inflows'.[100] Further developments in this approach are currently envisaged.[101] The result is the removal of a rigid link with financial position and profit or loss and a growing recognition that a single index of performance is neither feasible nor appropriate.[102] Financial performance is multidimensional and various indicators need to be used.[103]

While the practical importance of these philosophical and holistic changes from the Modernised Fourth Directive approach is perhaps debatable, my own judgement is that the dynamic shift is likely to be fundamental.

---

[99] But compare preamble (9), which envisages that the application of an IAS will result in a T&FV!

[100] See IAS Framework and Bullen and Crook, loc. cit. n. 33, at pp. 3, 4.

[101] Ibid.

[102] See Loweth and Lennard, loc. cit. n. 33, at p. 6.

[103] See CESR Guidance CESR/05-178b, 'Alternative Performance Measures to Ensure Best Practice by Companies in Information Prepared for Investors', Press Release, 3 November 2005. The position of the Basel II Committee on IAS, below, reflects a similar point.

We have noted that, in adapting profit and loss accounts and balance sheets to IAS under the Modernised Directive regime, companies are to ensure that equivalent information is available. There will be no necessary equivalent 'read across' from true IAS accounts.

Nor does the Modernised Directive regime capture the full force of the fair value approach of IAS. For example, IAS envisages fair valuation of liabilities and provisions as well as assets. The fair value of a long-term liability is the value of the asset required now to match it, that is to say, it should be discounted at an appropriate rate. Such discounting is clearly fundamental to an assessment of ongoing performance. There is no provision in the Modernised Fourth Directive regime for fair valuation of liabilities, except for certain financial liabilities which are within the definition of financial instruments.[104]

2.5 Contingent liabilities and provisions: Fourth Directive v. IAS; pensions

A similar likely discrepancy arises with contingent liabilities. One of the great weaknesses of the balance sheet test generated by Fourth Directive accounts (whether modernised or not), at least as the basis for a prudential standard for distributions, is their failure to reflect such liabilities on the face of the accounts. Thus, guarantees, for example warranties (e.g., for products) and other financial commitments (e.g., plant decommissioning costs) which do not fall to be treated as provisions are dealt with by disclosure in the notes.[105] This is in fact perfectly sensible insofar as the face of the financial statements is regarded as the proper place only for relatively certain financial information. The notes can be used as a place for information which requires greater evaluation by the reader and assessment for its implications. This approach is taken by the Directive to certain pension commitments also.[106]

The current treatment of such contingent liabilities in IAS is similar (though it is arguable that liabilities which are sufficiently certain to require balance sheet treatment by way of provision under the Fourth Directive are not permitted to be

---

[104] Cf., European Commission, Examination of the conformity of IAS 1 – 41 with the Accounting Directives, DG MARKT, April 2001, suggesting that this silence indicates that discounting of liabilities is permitted. This seems very unlikely and was certainly not envisaged at the time – what is the accounting treatment to be of losses or profits arising on a change in the appropriate rate? Admittedly, pension fund deficits are calculated on a discounted basis and this is currently done in Fourth Directive accounts. However, such liabilities have no fixed nominal amount and do in fact fluctuate according to contingencies of value and interest rate, see the discussion of UK FRS 17 below.

[105] Fourth Directive, Arts. 14, 20, 43.1(7).

[106] Art. 43.1(7).

so treated under IAS[107]). However, the IASB is proposing to amend IAS 37 to bring within the scope of provisions all contingent liabilities, apparently partly on the semantic grounds that a liability which is vested but in respect of which there is an unquantified obligation to pay is not a contingent liability, but a vested liability in respect of which there is uncertainty as to exposure.[108] The tendency appears to be to bring in all liabilities at their exit value.[109] It is far from clear that this makes sense for prudential purposes, even though it may be consistent with the fair valuation criterion.[110] A similar issue arises with the IASB's proposals for accounting for business combinations, which propose to treat all such combinations as acquisitions and deem fair value to be the price paid, without allowing for the fact that such a price may reflect the price which was fair to the acquirer rather than an open market price.[111]

In some respects, this attempt to bring contingencies on to the face of the accounts and to achieve an overall treatment which reflects economic realities may be an advance on the formalistic Fourth Directive approach. On the other hand, creditors habitually reflect the risk attached to lending to an entity in the rates they charge. A struggle to reflect such risk a second time in the cost of capital through restrictions on distributions may be misguided as well as an attempt to achieve the impossible.

A similar difference arises in the treatment of pensions under the Modernised Fourth Directive as compared with IAS. Under the former, if provision is made for pension liabilities, as is, for example, now required under UK standards for the actuarial deficiency or surplus, assessed annually,[112] distributable profits will be reduced accordingly. The result is very large and very volatile impacts on distributable profits in both directions.[113] Under IAS, while on initial application a full provision is required,[114] a 'corridor and spreading' approach is permitted requiring only losses, or gains, in excess of 10 per cent of the fund value to be

---

107 See discussion of IAS 37 in European Commission, 'Examination', loc. cit. n. 104.

108 IASB Exposure Draft of Proposed Amendments to IAS 37. For criticism, see European Financial Reporting Advisory Group (EFRAG) open letter to IASB of 28 November 2005 on the Exposure Draft of Proposed Amendments to IAS 36.

109 See the critical comments of the UK ASB, 28 October 2005, p. 29.

110 For example, the exit value of a product warranty may greatly exceed its economic cost to the producer.

111 IASB Exposure Draft of Amendments to IFRS 3 Business Combinations and IAS 27 Consolidated and Separate Financial Statements. See again EFRAG open letter of 28 November 2005.

112 UK standard FRS 17; for a full description, see 'Reforming Capital', loc. cit. n. 5, ch. 4.

113 Ibid. The size of the aggregate pension deficit of the FTSE 350 was assessed at £135 billion in March 2003 but had declined to £75 billion in November of that year. Deficiencies are currently rising sharply as a result of a fall in bond yields, see *FT*, 18 November 2005, p. 23.

114 See K. Olney, *Research Report, UK Equity Strategy – Are UK Dividends under Threat?* (London, Dresdner Kleinwort Wasserstein 15 September 2004) Appendix 1.

recognised and allowing these to be spread over the average fund life.[115] As the EU Commission has informally recognised, this approach is inconsistent with the requirements of the Fourth Directive that provisions should be recognised and not suppressed. It would appear therefore that companies adopting Modernised Fourth Directive accounts must recognise actuarial deficiencies in full (at least if the local Member State standard adopts this strict approach) while those adopting IAS accounts are at liberty to adopt the more relaxed spreading approach.[116] Opinions may legitimately differ about the wisdom of requiring very volatile financial differences to be reflected in accounts from year to year for reporting purposes (although there seems to me to be a strong case for this). There must be much greater doubt whether such amounts should impact on the cost of capital, often substantially impairing, or in some cases wiping out, distributable profits (e.g., British Airways this year). In my view, the argument for allowing spreading to smooth volatility is strong in this context. But on any basis it is surely indefensible that the decision whether or not to adopt IAS can produce such radical differences in the financing capacity of a company.[117] The result, as we shall see below, is to create entirely false incentives in favour of Modernised Fourth Directive reporting, as opposed to IAS reporting, or in some cases the reverse.

3. STRENGTHS AND WEAKNESSES OF BALANCE SHEET APPROACHES

The weaknesses of the balance sheet approach are, it is submitted, obvious from the above descriptions and it is not proposed to prolong matters by labouring this part of the argument.

It will suffice briefly

- to revisit the share capital cushion component;
- to recognise the wide diversity of results which the various tests produce;
- to recognise the inappropriateness of using financial statements designed for a different purpose to calibrate remuneration of capital;

---

115 IAS 19, paras. 54, 92, 93 (adopted by Commission Regulation (EC) No. 1725/2003 of 29 September 2003). See now amendments under Commission Regulation (EC) No. 1910/2005 Appendix B.

116 See European Commission, 'Examination of Conformity', loc. cit. n. 104.

117 Paradoxically, under the UK standard, if a group company has a need to make provision for a pension scheme deficiency but, because it is a group scheme, it is not possible reliably to allocate the liability to the particular company, then no provision is required, but only disclosure. This is not permitted under IAS, unless perhaps it is required by the overriding principle of reliability. The result is of course that in such cases UK companies will escape an impact on distributable profits altogether. FRS 17, Accounting Standards Board, London, November 2000, para. 9(b), Olney, op. cit. n. 114, at p. 7.

- to point out the particular problems to which each of the four versions of the test give rise; and
- finally, to recognise the complexity, cost and practical difficulties of capital maintenance systems based on balance sheet tests.

3.1 Share capital cushion

The irrationality of this component of the balance sheet tests has been sufficiently explored above. However, even if these criticisms are fully justified they are not sufficient to destroy the value of such a test. Balance sheet tests are theoretically or logically independent of any such cushion theory. A limit on distributions by reference to a net assets test is quite feasible without any requirement for a reserve for share capital (or indeed any share capital at all). British and French private companies, for example, have no significant requirement for a minimum share capital. Yet it is still possible, and indeed the law in both countries, to require them not to make distributions which produce a balance sheet, or realised profits, deficiency. Perhaps, if balance sheet tests are valid, a better measure of the cushion could be devised than share capital,[118] or it may be sufficient to rely on a balance sheet test with no cushion along these lines.

3.2 Variety and diversity of tests

It is evident from the above account that the present EU regime produces a very wide range of possible tests with very diverse results in terms of the impact on the financing capacity of companies. However, this criticism too is less than fatal to the balance sheet approach. Perhaps a uniform test could be devised (though it must be recognised that this is likely to require a special set of accounts, flying in the face of current convergence policies for financial reporting). Such a test is a core component of most systems.[119] However, none of these apply the statutory balance sheet as a rigid test without appraisal. The wisdom or unwisdom of a business decision is a matter of prudential judgement in the circumstances. We should not be surprised that all the wisdom of the accounting profession does not provide a substitute in every case. If an overriding prudential judgement is necessary, then that is where policy attention should concentrate.

---

[118] For example, in California certain accounting ratios are applied to achieve a standing net current asset surplus, see California General Corporations Law, s. 500, and the account in 'Reforming Capital', loc. cit. n. 5, at pp. 1021, 1022. However, directors appraisal of the accounts is allowed, cf., Model Business Corporations Act ABA 1999 Rev., § 6.40 (d).

[119] See the various non-EU models reviewed in 'Reforming Capital', loc. cit. n. 5, Annex C.

3.3 Inappropriateness of balance sheet as basis for prudential decision making

This is indeed the heart of the problem. Statutory accounts have never been, and are becoming increasingly less, designed to determine the amount appropriate for distributions. This is in part because accounts are simply inappropriate for this purpose and in part because they are increasingly being relied on for very different purposes.

Accounts are a single selective snapshot of a number of financial indicators. They struggle to summarise the infinite diversity of business in a set of comparable numbers. Even the most rigid and mechanical accounting approaches were always designed to generate figures to be read and appreciated in the light of information which did not appear on the face of the accounts. We have noted that contingent liabilities, which can in some circumstances be of crucial importance for solvency, are in the classic accounting approach left for assessment from the notes. Accounts have for many years been published with, and have been meant to be read with, a directors' report. In a separate initiative, the Modernisation Directive has required greater coverage of qualitative information in such reports, and some Member States now recognise that forward-looking information and strategic material is of vital importance for decision makers' assessment.[120] The cash flow statement, or statement of changes, under IAS is a vital indicator of the cash flow prospects of the business. If evidence were needed of the practical importance of such information to creditors, and thus of its relevance in making prudential decisions for creditor protection purposes, it is available from the responses to the UK Company Law Review and the Winter Review.[121] In the commercial world, the credit reference and rating agencies, on which major creditors rely, are concerned with a wide range of information of this kind. As corporate governance information is recognised as an indicator of financial stability, so such agencies are beginning also to add that to the calculus.[122]

But accounts are also designed as a snapshot of a point in time, together with a limited account of the progression to that point over the preceding year. Solvency is a function of the availability of cash to a business over time. It is matter for the future not the past. An accounting snapshot, which is history as soon as it is taken, can never be more than a very imperfect indicator of some aspects of solvency.

---

120 In the United Kingdom, the Operating and Financial Review, Companies Act 1985 ss. 234AA and 234AB.

121 Modern Company Law 3, Company Formation and Capital Maintenance (London, DTI October 1999) URN 99/1145, p. 23 et seq.; and *supra* n. 12.

122 See unpublished paper by G. Dallas on Standard and Poor's approach to corporate governance, Europaeum Symposium on Restructuring Corporate Governance, Oxford, March 2005 (forthcoming), available at: <http://europaeum.org>.

Current attempts to improve the quality of accounts by endowing them with greater economic reality and validity will only improve them as such a snapshot. That single static frame in the movie, so to speak, may be better focused and made more complete, but for the other frames in the dynamic we need to look elsewhere.

These criticisms of course apply to any version of an accounts-based balance sheet test.

3.4 Four versions of the balance sheet test: particular issues

The particular problems of the various versions of the test as they derive from different accounting approaches are already reasonably evident. A brief summary with a few added reflections is sufficient.

(1) The pure historic cost version of the Fourth Directive, with its absence of current values, failure to include contingent liabilities and inclusion of liabilities and provisions at full value, provides a clearly inadequate basis for assessing a company's true economic position or ongoing cash generating prospects.

It may be suggested that, paradoxically, this classic version of the test may be a less inadequate surrogate for evidence of future cash flows than improved, more economically realistic versions, and that this explains the increasing difficulties being felt. This may be true in some cases, but the obvious imperfections remain. Even if the argument had any force, we could hardly expect companies to continue to maintain old-style historic cost accounts, in addition to modern accounts with all their advantages, as a basis for distribution decisions in future.

(2) The second version of the Fourth Directive allows the real value of various assets to appear on the face of the accounts, but the only effect is to reduce the sums available for distribution where unrealised losses arise, in an asymmetric and biased fashion. All the other defects of the Fourth Directive approach also remain.

(3) The Modernised Fourth Directive now allows fair valuation of all kinds of assets, generating distributable profits,[123] and permits this to be done by directors' appreciation where market values are unavailable. This is a major move in the

---

123 In the United Kingdom, at least this does not dispense with the need to determine whether such profits are 'realised', since as we have noted the United Kingdom did not take advantage of the option to recognise other reserves as distributable under Art. 15(1)(c) of the Second Directive. For the attempts of the UK professions to generate guidance on when fair value profits and losses are realised, see ICAS/ICAEW, 'Distributable Profits: Implications of IFRS', TECH 21/05 (London, June 2005).

direction of the less rigid systems of balance sheet testing which obtain outside Europe. In this respect, it clearly seems to amount to a 'creeping relaxation'[124] of the Second Directive. However, the great diversity which is left to Member States and/or companies in implementation of the Directive leaves a test which is unreliable as a basis for company regulation. Moreover, with the introduction of fair value assessment comes the potential for very subjective decision making on accounting statements which may be reflected in irresponsible distribution decision making. It is also widely recognised that fair value accounting may lead to results which are highly volatile. We have seen this in the calculation of pension deficits. Similar effects are identified from the IAS rules on accounting for financial instruments and deferred tax.[125] The effects in this respect may well be to produce accounts which are an even less reliable indicator of future cash flows than traditional historic cost accounts.

The Modernised Directive still does not, in my view, make provision for fair valuation of liabilities and provisions.

(4) So far as true IAS accounts are concerned, many of the weaknesses identified for the Modernised Fourth Directive regime apply. But there are important differences. It is not evident that the 'corridor' approach to pensions is superior to the requirement that deficits are to be taken direct to the accounts. Neither approach takes account of the true issue for solvency determination purposes, namely, what are the prospects of the business to finance this staff cost over time? In that respect, the position is the same as for any other future payroll charge. The business may or may not be in a position to generate sufficient cash over time. The directors will need to take account of a number of factors if this issue is to be properly assessed. These include the prospects for variation in the size of the charge as interest rates and asset values fluctuate around a historic norm, together with a wide range of other factors, including the competitive positioning of their business and thus its security of cash generation capacity. It is very doubtful whether any accounting test will ever produce as good an answer as a properly considered and diligent judgement by directors on these lines.

Pensions also provide a good example of the delusion of comparability which even a sophisticated IAS-based approach provides. Because a pension fund deficit is treated as an existing liability (at least as a matter of substance, whether legally so or not[126]), those companies which rely on pension funds to provide defined benefits for retiring employees take a hit to their distribution capacity and thus to their cost of capital. The same burden may be incurred in entirely different ways

---

[124] I owe this graphic expression to Ferran, 'Creditors', op. cit. n. 6.

[125] IAS 39 and IAS 12, see 'Reforming Capital', loc. cit. n. 5, at p. 965. The deferred tax standard requires provision for tax which may well never need to be paid.

[126] See IAS 19, para. 6(a).

which never appear on the accounts until payment. In some Member States, a relatively generous pension arrangement is provided through mandatory state funding via high levels of payroll taxes. This inflates the future liabilities of companies for staff costs. However, these are not existing liabilities and will not appear on the balance sheet. The true economic position of such companies may well be worse than those in States with different social provision. But their cost of capital will be lower. Creditors, like other investors, have to assess these wider economic conditions without reference to the accounts.[127]

Similarly, where a company funds pensions on a defined contribution, rather than a defined benefit, future contributions will, as future and not accrued liabilities, not appear on the balance sheet.[128] They will be treated like any other future staff cost, to be brought to account at the time of payment. But the imperative to pay them may be just as strong. This provides a further incentive to adopt defined contribution schemes, rather than the socially preferable defined benefit schemes.

This discussion of pension funding illustrates the deficiencies of accounts as an indicator of prospects and the unfairness of balance sheet tests as an automatic criterion for prohibiting business decisions affecting company funding.

3.5 Views of the prudential regulators

Confirmation of the view that IAS accounts are not a sound basis for setting prudential decisions is provided by recent rulings of the Basel II Committee and the UK Financial Services Authority. As the Basel Committee has put it, 'prudential supervisors need to consider whether financial statement information is suitable for their purposes and, when it is not, to make suitable adjustments'. Accordingly 'certain IAS treatments should be excluded or overridden by supervisors' judgements [sc. in either direction]'.[129] Similarly, the UK Financial Services Authority has overruled a number of IAS, opining for example on pensions that 'we do not believe that defined benefit pension deficits should be treated as if they were current liabilities which would have to be funded over the

[127] It has been argued that the outcome criticised here is rational because the pension deficit is a liability which will arise on an insolvent liquidation, whereas onerous future payroll taxes will not. Accepting, at least for the sake of argument, that this is so, the argument still proves too much. If we are to assume an immediate liquidation for valuation purposes then most firms are technically insolvent. The issue is solvency of a going concern.

[128] For example, IAS 19, paras. 43-47.

[129] See Basel Committee, 'Supervisory Guidance on the Use of the Fair Value Option by Banks under IFRS' (July 2005) paras. 7 (general prudential override), 38 (overriding certain fair value gains and losses), 39 (excluding the own credit risk rule). See too the press release of 20 July at <http://www.bis.org/press> and the material there cited.

next 12 months'.[130] The effect in practice (though this is denied) is to require such institutions to maintain two sets of accounts for prudential purposes.

If IAS accounts are, on the highest authority, not a sound basis for regulators to assess the solvency of banks, what can justify their mandatory use to determine the prudence of company distributions, including distributions by those very banks?

3.6 Complexity and expense of the EU regime

The complexity of the legislation required to implement the balance sheet test based distribution regime has been described elsewhere.[131] In some Member States, this has attracted a large body of supplementary case law.[132] Such complexity is a significant cost in itself.

There are also substantial expenses for companies in applying the system, for example accounting advice on whether profits are to be recognised as realised. As the standards for determining this question become more abstract with the adoption of the fair value option, so this expense is likely to increase.[133]

Some companies, in order to avoid the consequences of incurring the new charges to profit and loss account resulting from the adoption of IAS, or equivalent new standards under domestic law, have had to incur the expense of capital reductions. Others have engaged in artificial transactions at subsidiary company level to generate profits, which can be paid as realised profits in dividends in the books of the distributing parent company.[134] Other groups of companies are having to maintain books in the subsidiaries in both IAS and in domestic standards terms so as to be able to consolidate in IAS terms at group level, while generating distributable profits in domestic standards terms at individual company level.[135] Thus alternative regulatory bases are being used as an opportunity for

---

[130] See FSA Policy Statement 05/05 of April 2005, and new statutory rules under ss. 138, 156 and 157 of the Financial Services and Markets Act 2000 in 'FSA Changing Accounting Framework (Prudential Capital) Instrument', FSA 2005/21. Key adjustments are removal of fair value valuations for various financial instruments and for own credit risk, and the substitution for defined benefit pension fund gains and losses of a smoothed solution over five years.

[131] Over 90 sections in the UK Act, see 'Reforming Capital', loc. cit. n. 5, ch. 2.

[132] For example, on insider subordination in Germany and financial assistance in the United Kingdom.

[133] See ICAS/ICAEW, loc. cit. n. 123. This draft guidance from the British and Scottish professional bodies on this issue extends to over fifty pages.

[134] See Olney, op. cit. n. 114, at pp. 7, 8.

[135] An open letter from Deloitte & Co. to the UK Secretary of State for Trade and Industry of 20 September 2005 explains two main difficulties: IAS 37 prevents distributions from pre-acquisition profits of subsidiaries and IAS 19 imposes a rigid rule on charging group pension fund deficits once recognised, see above.

arbitrage. A major benefit of the internationalisation of standards (convergence and the avoidance of the expense of maintaining different sets of books) is being frustrated by the European distribution rules.

3.7 Strengths of the balance sheet test?

The case against the use of company accounts as a basis for determining the legitimacy of distribution seems evident – it is very difficult to find any defence. The main objection to change may be summed up in the old English adage: 'Always keep ahold of nurse, for fear of finding something worse'. It is certainly true that we have lived with many of the weaknesses identified above for many years. But it is also true that the problems seem to be increasing as company accounts move further away from providing an approximate surrogate for a prediction of future cash flow. Nurse is looking a less secure refuge.

The critical questions are clearly whether we need special tests governing distributions at all, beyond the normal rules for disciplining company governance, and if we do whether we can devise something better. The main contender for the role of substitute is a test more closely focused on the need to provide an adequate prior assurance of solvency. The next part of the paper considers this.

4. A SOLVENCY TEST

4.1 Meaning of solvency

Solvency is a slippery concept. A company is solvent when we can predict with sufficient certainty that it has, or will be able to generate, sufficient cash to meet all its obligations and other losses of value (to the extent that they need to be made good) over time. Absolute certainty is of course not available on this. In principle, the period of consideration is infinite, although in practice we know that any company is likely to fail at some time, perhaps all are destined to do so. There is therefore a serious danger that in trying to find a solvency-based test for distributions we shall produce overkill and chill risk-taking, which is the driver of wealth creation.

4.2 Assets, liabilities and solvency

There is a temptation, or perhaps for lawyers a natural inclination, to define solvency in terms of an excess of assets over liabilities, which brings us back safely to 'nurse', in the shape of the balance sheet.

There is an element of truth here, which is in fact reflected in most solvency-based tests.[136] The definition of solvency itself offered above also has two sides: cash and potential for cash generation, on the one side, and liability to cash destruction or disbursement, on the other.

In fact, whether there is a real difference between solvency and an asset/liability surplus depends on how we define assets and liabilities. We could define assets to include all the resources available to a business, that is to say, all those conditions which operate to give it the means of actually or potentially generating value, and we could define liabilities similarly, as including all those conditions which give rise to actual or potential obligations to make expenditure and liabilities to destroy or lose value. We could then set a value on each of the benefits and detriments which will arise from those conditions, appropriately discounted to reflect the fact that they will arise at different points in time and for probability. Having done that, we would have produced a balance sheet test which was a reasonable surrogate for a predictor of solvency. In fact, the IAS Framework begins to go some distance in this direction in its definitions of assets and liabilities, which consciously avoid the classic legal definitions in favour of 'real world phenomena'.[137]

But such an exercise, if it is to be made comprehensive, is very different even from the current IAS balance sheet. It would have to include all contingent assets and liabilities. A move in this direction is proposed by IASB. But it would also have to include in some form all future assets and liabilities. (This makes some sense – we have seen above the arbitrary effect of treating differently a company which already has a commitment to fund a liability as compared with one which will as a matter of business necessity have to do so, but has as yet no such legal commitment.) Some parts of this might be covered by broadening our definition of assets and liabilities to include as intangibles those existing conditions which have the potential to generate or destroy value. Similarly, we could expand or modify our valuation theories to include the value of all future cash flows attributable to an asset or resource as part of the going concern. We might capitalise the customer base in the form of goodwill, or employees' know-how in the form of recruitment and training costs, or marketing expenditure as brands. Similarly, we might make provisions to cover a wider range of contingencies, such as future payroll taxes as part of staff costs, or even the risk of catastrophes like hurricanes. We might implement the principle that substance is to prevail over form by taking account of matters in terms of probability rather than legal commitment.

---

[136] For example, the distribution tests in MBCA s. 6.40(c)(2) and the substance of the solvency certification required by New Zealand Companies Act 1993, s. 4, see 'Reforming Capital', loc. cit. n. 5, at pp. 1017, 1025.

[137] See Loweth and Lennard, loc. cit. n. 33, at pp. 6, 7; and IASB Framework, paras. 47-68.

But at some point all this becomes artificial and indeed so speculative as to be spurious as a draft of a balance sheet. A balanced list of this kind needs to be recognised for what it is: a series of business judgements about the prospects of the business.[138] If we are going down the solvency path, we need an assurance that a business judgement of appropriate quality addressing this has been made.

4.3 Solvency assurance: precedents

In fact, in addressing solvency both company law and insolvency law have gone some distance in this direction, at least in the United Kingdom. Devising an effective solvency standard is a highly practical and empirical matter. So it is worth examining these precedents.

The key ground for the compulsory winding-up of a company is of course insolvency. While UK law prefers in practice to rely on presumptions of insolvency rather than directly on a solvency test,[139] the central grounds are either that the company is 'unable to pay its debts as they fall due' (cash flow test) or alternatively that the 'value of its assets is less than the amount of its liabilities' taking into account contingent and prospective liabilities (balance sheet test).[140]

These tests are not as strict for the company or as rigid as appears at first sight. First, the court retains a discretion whether to wind up the company, even where the grounds arise. This enables the court to consider the wider prospects. Second, the onus is on the applicant to prove the deficiency. Third, 'debts' for the purpose of the cash flow test are a narrow category of liabilities: the word means existing debts already due or liabilities under obligations, or causes of action, already accrued.[141] Finally 'prospective liabilities' does not mean future liabilities in the sense used above, but only liabilities which are vested now but due to be satisfied with or without liquidation some time in the future (*debitum in praesenti, solvendum in futuro*).[142] It should also be stressed that this is not a balance sheet test of a Second Directive kind at all. The values of assets and liabilities, or indeed their existence, are not to be determined strictly by reference to the statutory accounts. These issues, of quantum and existence, are issues of fact and law for the court, although no doubt taking the accounts into consideration.[143]

---

138 Cf., Loweth and Lennard, loc. cit. n. 33, at pp. 3-5 (not every condition generating value can sensibly be described as an asset).

139 For example, a company is presumed unable to pay its debts if a written formal demand for a sum due exceeding £750 has not been met within three weeks – Insolvency Act 1986, s. 123(1)(a).

140 Insolvency Act 1986, ss. 122, 123(1)(e) and (2).

141 See Goode, op. cit. n. 11, at pp. 4-26.

142 Ibid., at pp. 4-29.

143 Ibid.

There is probably a strong case for having a relatively strict burden to prove insolvency on an applicant for winding up (and thus an easier one for the company). Winding up is after all the *coup de grace* and in itself destroys value. A more demanding test of solvency for the company is arguably appropriate for permitting distributions. However, in English law a solvency test similar to the liquidation test is already applied for returns of capital to shareholders in private company share buy-backs.[144] A similar test is now also proposed for returns of capital by way of capital reduction.[145] Both these transactions are in economic terms indistinguishable, so far as creditors are concerned, from a distribution. The current statutory test requires of the company's directors:

> … a statutory declaration … that, having made full enquiry into the affairs and prospects of the company, they have formed the opinion that:
> (a) as regards its initial situation immediately following the payment … there will be no grounds on which the company could be found unable to pay its debts; and
> (b) as regards its prospects for the year immediately following that date … having regard to their intentions with respect to the management of the … business and the amount and character of the financial resources which will in their view be available … during that year, the company will be able to carry on its business as a going concern (and will accordingly be able to pay its debts as they fall due) throughout that year.

(The directors are required to take into account for this purpose the same liabilities (including contingent and prospective liabilities) as are brought into account for an insolvent winding-up, that is to say, on the basis of the definitions given above.)

4.4 Proposed solvency assurance: substance

This precedent is useful, at least from a UK perspective. It has worked without apparent difficulty for twenty-five years.[146] The combination of the indefinite assurance in paragraph (a) and the liquidity assurance for one year in paragraph (b) seems appropriate and practical.[147] However, it seems to provide inadequate assurance in some respects and to be too demanding in others. It seems unduly close to the insolvent winding-up test which, it has been argued above, should be

144 Companies Act 1985, s. 173(3) and (4) (own shares redeemed out of capital).

145 Companies Bill 2005, clause 562.

146 There is a very similar requirement in Companies Act 1985, s. 156(2) (private companies giving financial assistance).

147 Cf., 'Winter Group Report', at pp. 86-88.

less stringent than a distribution test. There are various ways in which it might be tightened up, but there are also reasons for taking a more relaxed view of a company which is *ex hypothesi* normally a going concern.

The enquiry obligation on directors should be less rigid. It should be to make an appropriate level of enquiry before giving the assurance; in many cases, the distribution will obviously be justified and no extensive enquiry will be necessary.

The one-year liquidity assurance in (b) seems satisfactory. On the other hand, the cash flow assurance in (a) should in principle be unlimited in duration and extent and not limited to debts in the narrow sense. It should thus extend to all the company's actual and prospective assets and liabilities (including contingent and future ones in the broadest sense), but be subject to a reasonable limitation in terms of predictability ('the reasonably foreseeable future'). On the other hand, in considering the possibility of future assets, only the prospects of the business in its ordinary course should be taken into account, and not some extraordinary or extraneous factor, such as a recapitalisation.

These considerations have led to an adapted version of the insolvent liquidation test being proposed in the United Kingdom for distribution purposes, that is to say, a requirement on the directors of the company to provide, shortly in advance of any distribution:

> a certificate that in their opinion, having made such enquiry into the affairs and prospects of the company *as is appropriate* in the circumstances, (a) *for the reasonably foreseeable future*, taking account of the company's expected prospects *in the ordinary course of business*, it can reasonably be expected to meet its [sc. all its] liabilities: and … [the liquidity requirement as in (b) above].[148]

Such solvency certification is a variant of the reform introduced in New Zealand in the early 1990s to replace the traditional British-style capital maintenance regime which operated there previously.[149] It thus has the benefit of empirical testing for a similar change to that proposed and in a similar economic environment to that of a typical medium-sized European State.

---

148 Emphasis added, see 'Reforming Capital', loc. cit. n. 5, proposal at p. 979. The certification requirement in clause 562 of the Companies Bill 2005 is significantly more lax. No enquiry is prescribed, probably because the codified duty of diligence now covers this. More significantly, the cash flow and liquidity assurances are much less exacting, though 'all liabilities' are to be taken into account.

149 See 'Reforming Capital', loc. cit. n. 5, p. 1025 for a full description.

4.5 Relevance of statutory balance sheet to solvency declaration

What should the relevance of the balance sheet be for the directors in issuing such an assurance? Clearly they would be negligent not to consider the evidence it provides. We have already noted that in many solvency-based regimes the balance sheet is treated as part of the test and presumptively permitted to resolve the issue, that is to say, a declaration founded on a balance sheet surplus should be presumed to be lawful unless the contrary is proved.

In the light of the assessment above, this seems to have dangers. A balance sheet surplus is often not sufficient to justify distributions. In the BIICL proposal under discussion, an inversion of this idea was proposed, namely that, if a distribution was proposed which led to a statutory balance sheet deficiency, a special obligation should be placed on directors to disclose the fact and explain why the distribution was nevertheless justified.[150] The value of this additional requirement is debatable. It may however have political attractions in persuading those who fear venturing too far from nurse to accept the proposal.

4.6 Proposed solvency test: process

It was also proposed that this certificate of solvency shall be published. This will add a degree of formality and discipline and raise the prospects of civil liability under general fiduciary law. Both in the New Zealand law on distributions and under the UK Companies Bill proposal for capital reductions, a criminal liability for issuing a certificate or statement without reasonable grounds also arises.

Issues of liability need to be resolved according to the culture and incentive structure which operate in any particular jurisdiction. There needs to be a sufficiently strict liability regime to ensure that directors act diligently and after proper investigation and consultation, but not so strict that legitimate distributions are deterred. This is a matter of culture, national psychology and also a function of the other incentives in the system.

Dividends received by shareholders otherwise than in good faith are also recoverable in New Zealand.[151] Under English law, dividends are also recoverable from shareholders who receive them knowing or having reasonable cause to believe that they are unlawful.[152] Such remedies should no doubt remain.

It is considered unnecessary to require such certificates to be audited. Some companies will have no auditor and it would be disproportionate to require one for every distribution. Where a company has an auditor, directors who failed to

---

150 Ibid.

151 Companies Act 1993, s. 56.

152 Companies Act 1985, s. 277.

consult him or a person of equivalent standing in a marginal case would be in breach of duty anyway. But auditors are in principle less qualified than directors to reach useful judgements on the prospects of the company.

The obvious merits of this proposal are its simplicity, the consequent elimination of the great majority of technical rules on capital maintenance as noted above, and the fact that the rule is focused on the mischief to be addressed – the risk of insolvency.

4.7 Objections to solvency certification: chilling, behavioural regulation and necessity

The most fundamental objection to this proposal is probably that it will have a 'chilling' effect, that is to say, that it will deter directors from making distributions and thus raise the cost of capital. The demand for a formal certificate or other published assurance is thought to be likely to have a particularly strong psychological effect.[153] The reality of this concern[154] is very much a question of judgement. Similar arguments were raised in the United Kingdom when the wrongful trading remedy was introduced in 1986. The best evidence is the effect of a similar change in New Zealand, which has a very similar economic and legal background to that of the United Kingdom. No difficulty has been reported there.

A second objection is in the opposite direction, namely that the test will be too lax in practice, because the proposal relies on behavioural regulation of directors, as opposed to the 'bright-line' structural rule derived from the balance sheet test. To some extent, this is a delusion. Any rational system will add a behavioural test to the balance sheet test to ensure that distributions are not made where that test fails. It is scarcely consistent for those who admit that they need to rely on an additional behavioural test to object to such a test in principle. So behavioural regulation is to some extent inevitable, and at best the balance sheet test only provides a structural floor. The answer then, at this point in the argument, is that as such the balance sheet approach is demonstrably defective. It may preclude legitimate distributions as well as justify illegitimate ones. Moreover, those many systems which no longer adopt such a rigid floor operate without difficulty.

A more fundamental objection is that no such test for distributions is necessary at all, at least in the United Kingdom. Sanctions for imprudent trading are already imposed in the United Kingdom through wrongful trading[155] and directors' duties, including a loyalty duty which shifts away from the interests of

---

153 Such certification is also argued to be impractical when *de facto* distributions are made, for example by transactions at an undervalue within groups. Such *de facto* distributions will need to be made subject to the solvency test, but certification would probably not be feasible.

154 Raised by the English Law Society in response to 'Reforming Capital', loc. cit. n. 5.

155 Insolvency Act 1986, s. 214.

shareholders and in favour of creditors as a company approaches insolvency.[156] The very strict regime for policing insolvent winding-up in the United Kingdom is probably of even greater significance. The automatic initial liquidator in every compulsory winding-up is normally a state official (the 'Official Receiver'), who has sweeping powers of investigation and examination of witnesses and the power to apply to the court for disqualification of directors guilty of wrongdoing, a sanction very frequently imposed.[157] The liquidator in a creditors' winding-up is also obliged to report wrongdoing to the Official Receiver. Disqualification is the most common and probably the most effective remedy against misfeasant directors.[158]

4.8 Difficulty of achieving coordinated approach at EU level

There are indeed strong arguments for leaving the question of assuring that distributions do not endanger solvency to the Member States to resolve in the context of local conditions. The 'fine-tuning' of such remedies is most unlikely to be capable of substantial harmonisation. But this debate encroaches on the fields of other papers to be presented to this conference.

5. Conclusion

It is submitted that the above examination convincingly demonstrates the defects of balance sheet tests as currently operative in the European Union.

Whether an insolvency test is an appropriate substitute is very much a matter of judgement: different conditions in different Member States mean different modalities will certainly be appropriate. The question then inevitably arises whether it makes sense to make provision for such a test at EU level. It has been suggested that the absence of harmonisation of the law on capitalisation of share premiums is a convincing objection to the Second Directive claims for harmonisation and that a similar failure to produce consistency of approach is inevitable here. If so, the same objection would of course arise to any attempt to harmonise in this field.[159]

---

156 *West Mercia Safety Wear* v. *Dodd* [1988] BCC 30 CA, and cases there cited.

157 Insolvency Act 1986, ss. 234-237; Company Directors Disqualification Act, ss. 6, 7.

158 Between 1,500 and 2,000 directors per year are normally disqualified in Great Britain, the vast majority as directors of insolvent companies found unfit (or admitting this by undertaking). See DTI Companies in 2004-2005, October 2005, p. 23, available at: <http://www.dti.gov.uk/cld>.

159 Ferran, 'Creditors', op. cit. n. 6, at p. 30.

But a more modest objective than the Second Directive aspiration for a harmonised equivalent minimum 'security' fund for creditors throughout the Community is in mind here. It may well be that a sufficient level of equivalence could be reached to give Community creditors reasonable assurance without intruding unduly on the necessary area of subsidiarity. A requirement could be set that company boards should publish a statement or assurance of solvency in advance of distributions in terms of reasonable expectation on the current evidence that the company is and will remain a going concern. Member States could be left to provide their detailed implementation to suit local conditions and to provide effective sanctions, subject to establishing the responsibility of the board for the statement, along the lines of board responsibility for the accounts in the proposed new Accounts Directive.[160]

But, if we cannot reach agreement on such a formula, then it seems clear that the current regime has become so defective and anomalous that we should just repeal the Second Directive. The United Kingdom will certainly at least rely on fiduciary duties (including the special duty for creditors) and wrongful trading, plus robust liquidation procedures.

But I remain convinced of the value of solvency certification, at least for the UK environment.

Perhaps as one who negotiated the Second and Fourth Directives on behalf of the United Kingdom and had a hand in their implementation, I may be allowed to end by reflecting that the history of this topic illustrates the naiveté of ambitious harmonisers (including myself) and the dangers of imposing detailed and rigid solutions which will fail to meet the test of changing times. Linking a key governance decision-making rule to the fast-moving and politically charged development of accounting philosophy has proved a grave mistake.

Perhaps at the European level, we should dispense with nurse altogether and trust the Member States to solve this problem in responsible fashion, as we appear to trust third countries.

---

160 Proposal for a Directive amending Council Directives 78/660/EEC and 83/349/EEC concerning the annual accounts of certain types of companies and consolidated accounts, see Council of the EU, 9588/05 (Coreper A item), Brussels, 2 June 2005.

Balance Sheet Tests or Solvency Tests – or Both?

Wolfgang Schön*

Abstract

One of the standard requirements of company law is the restriction of distributions to shareholders in order to protect the legitimate interests of the company's creditors. As lawful dividends do not have to be paid back when the company runs into losses at a later stage, we need a yardstick in order to decide on the availability of funds for distribution. The traditional balance sheet test is running into criticism due to the rigidity of the old rules and the conflicts between the philosophy of IAS/IFRS and the concept of creditor protection. Newly offered devices like the solvency test aim at giving a better view of the business prospects of the company, but they suffer from a limited time horizon and a wide range of discretion for directors. This makes them particularly problematic when long-term obligations have to be addressed. In the end, a combination of the balance sheet test and the solvency test seems to be a reasonable solution.

Keywords: company law reform, distributions, dividends, accounting law, creditor protection, legal capital, balance sheet, solvency test.

---

* Director, Max Planck Institute for Intellectual Property, Competition and Tax Law, Munich; Honorary Professor, Ludwig-Maximilians-Universität, Munich.

1. ENTITY SHIELDING AS A BASIC REQUIREMENT OF COMPANY AND INSOLVENCY LAW

When man created limited liability, he created legal entities which were able to act in markets, enter into contracts and commit torts without any natural person being obliged to pick up the bill in the end. Nevertheless, there are shareholders behind each (public or private) limited company who appoint its directors, control the business of the company and enjoy the proceeds of its commercial activities. They regard the company as 'their' investment and they expect dividends and other financial rewards for their funding. They will decide on the scale of their investment by estimating the future cash flow they expect to derive from the acquired shares. Any reduction in this expected cash flow – because the company withholds money in order to pay its debts or to establish reserves for this purpose – will lower the funds shareholders are willing to devote to this investment. From the perspective of the company, the cost of capital will rise. One might say that this effect distorts optimal allocation of capital within an economy.[1]

No company carries on its trade or business without relying on funds from other sources than its shareholders. The company takes out loans, enters into leasing contracts and pledges to pay its suppliers and its workforce. Moreover, obligations may arise without any contractual basis, e.g., when tort claimants or public authorities – most notably the tax authorities – come into play. All these creditors rely on the financial means of the company. If there was no collateral available, contractual creditors would either refrain from handing out money in the first place, bargain for extra risk compensation or enter into detailed covenants charging the borrower with sophisticated rules to ensure 'good behaviour'.[2] In any case, the cost of capital would rise, again damaging the optimal allocation of capital.

It is a well-known principle of company law throughout the world that neither the shareholders nor the creditors are in a position to complain if the company's funds start dwindling in the course of ordinary business. We learn from the Bible that no one is given a 'talent' in order to bury it, but in order to engage in – necessarily risky – business activities.[3] This is not our topic here. The problem we face is whether the 'talent' devoted to the company can be withdrawn by the shareholders to the detriment of the creditors or whether the creditors enjoy priority regarding access to the funds of the company.

---

1 J. Rickford, et al., 'Reforming Capital – Report of the Interdisciplinary Group on Capital Maintenance', 15 *EBLR* (2004) p. 919 at p. 947 (hereinafter, 'Reforming Capital').

2 See W.W. Bratton, 'Bond Covenants and Creditor Protection: Economics and Law, Theory and Practice, Substance and Process', in this volume.

3 St. Luke's Gospel, ch. 19 v. 11 et seq.

In his elaborate paper, Jonathan Rickford tells us that it is the task of policy-oriented legislation in company (and insolvency) law to strike a balance between the legitimate interest of the shareholders to enjoy an adequate remuneration for their funding and the legitimate interest of the creditors to get back the principal and to earn the interest of the loan (or other money owed to a third party).[4] In 'Reforming Capital', the UK group perceives a 'conflict' between the 'creditor's interest in being paid' and the 'shareholders' rights to receive a return'.[5] If we put the question like this we start with the assumption that there exists no natural or logical 'pecking order' between shareholders and creditors of a company.

I dare to contradict this. Shareholders are the true masters of the company. They control its business and its distribution arrangements and they enjoy the 'residual profit' resulting from its activities. Moreover, as a rule they are better informed about the economic prospects of the company (which is not always true, e.g., in public companies with dispersed ownership). Taken as a whole, they are in a better position to judge its prospects and they have the power to arrange for a diversion of the company's funds to themselves whenever they see fit. If they were in a position to 'externalise' their financial risk, they would tend to make inefficient investments. To make a long story short: they have both the incentives and the tools to behave in an opportunistic way towards the creditors and their claims.

It is commonly accepted today – and I have a feeling that this has always been the case – that 'entity shielding', i.e., the protection of the creditors' interest in the company's funds against withdrawals by the shareholders (and against the access of the shareholders' creditors) is a natural complement of limited liability.[6] There must be a limit to the freedom of shareholders to instruct directors to pay out monies from the company's funds. This seems to be undisputed. The real question is another one: which rules shall we implement in order to ensure the protection of the creditors' legitimate interest without preventing the company and its shareholders from behaving in an economically sensible way?

2. THE LAW OF DIVIDENDS AND OTHER DISTRIBUTIONS

In the old days, the position of the creditors was insuperable. According to the tradition of Roman law, companies were only allowed to distribute profits to their

---

4 J. Rickford, 'Legal Approaches in Restricting Distributions to Shareholders: Balance Sheet Tests and Solvency Tests', in this volume.

5 'Reforming Capital', loc. cit. n. 1, at p. 967.

6 G. Hertig and H. Kanda, 'Creditor Protection', in R. Kraakman, et al., *The Anatomy of Corporate Law* (Oxford, Oxford University Press 2004) p. 71 et seq.; H. Hansmann, R. Kraakman and R. Squire, 'Law and the Rise of the Firm', 119 *Harvard Law Review* (2006) p. 1335 at p. 1337 et seq.

shareholders after the company was liquidated and all creditors had received their funds. This was due to the theory that the 'true profit' cannot be established before the company has ceased its operations.[7] It should not go unmentioned that in the nineteenth century there were still company law experts arguing that any deviation from this principle would work to the detriment of creditors.[8] Nevertheless, when companies grew into stable entities and were not (as in the old days) restricted to one off dealings, the necessity of allowing for interim payments to shareholders became predominant. There is an efficiency argument behind this development. To wait until the final liquidation of the company would either have led to distorting 'lock-in-effects' or would have forced the shareholders to liquidate and re-establish a company just in order to get access to surplus funds, which were neither needed to finance the current business of the company nor to secure the claims of the company's creditors.[9] Therefore, the annual dividend (and interim dividend) was introduced and other related instruments (capital reduction and share buy-back) followed suit.

This was the first step taken by company law in the gradual erosion of the (perhaps too) well-established position of the company's creditors. The shareholders were entitled to dividends and other financial proceeds from the company's funds. But there is an extra benefit attached to this: once the dividend is paid to the shareholders, the recipients must not fear that the money has to be returned to the company when times get harder and expected profits do not materialise or unexpected losses occur. The shareholder may even keep an unlawful dividend if it has been received in good faith.[10] Article 16 of the Capital Directive makes this quite clear:

> Any distribution made contrary to Article 15 must be returned by shareholders who have received it if the company proves that these shareholders knew of the irregularity of the distributions made to them, or could not in view of the circumstances have been unaware of it.

---

[7] For an historical overview, see W. Schön, 'Gewinnermittlung, Gewinnverteilung und Gewinnausschüttung im Recht der Personengesellschaften und der GmbH', in P. Hommelhoff, H. Rowedder and P. Ulmer, *Max Hachenburg: Fünfte Gedächtnisvorlesung 2002* (Heidelberg, C.F. Müller 2003) p. 17 at p. 18 et seq.

[8] A. Renaud, *Recht der Actiengesellschaften* (Leipzig 1863) § 64; for an in-depth discussion in those days, see C.S. Grünhut, 'Das Recht auf die Dividende und der Dividendencoupon', *Grünhut's Zeitschrift* (1874) p. 375 at p. 384 et seq.

[9] P.O. Mülbert and M. Birke, 'Legal Capital – Is there a Case against the European Legal Capital Rules?', 3 *EBOR* (2002) p. 695 at p. 721; this effect has been described by Renaud, op. cit. n. 8, at § 64.

[10] The importance of this element has already been stressed by Grünhut, loc. cit. n. 8, at p. 387 et seq.; for an assessment of current German legal practice, see T.A. Quiel, *Rechtsfolgen unrechtmäßiger offener Gewinn-auschüttungen*, Dissertation (University of Bonn 2005).

From this we can conclude that the shareholder is entitled to keep any lawful dividend and other distribution received in good faith from the company. To be sure, any other solution would be impractical – shares are transferred extensively in an open capital market, so it would be extremely hard to raise claims against the persons who owned the shares when dividends and other distributions were made.

But it should be mentioned that there is a certain 'asymmetry' inherent in this concept. If during its lifetime a company runs into losses first and later succeeds in recovering up to its starting point, the shareholders will have no chance to withdraw assets from the company at all – at least if we do not go so far as to allow 'nimble dividends'.[11] If the company starts with high profits and later suffers heavy losses in the same amount, the shareholders may keep the dividends they received during the better half of the period. This makes clear that the measurement of funds open for distribution to the shareholders and the time horizon envisaged by this measurement seem to be extremely important when it comes to policy decisions balancing out the interests of shareholders and creditors. Any monies which have legally been paid to the shareholders will not be returned even if they were needed at a later stage to cover the debts owed to third parties.

3. The Preliminary Nature of Every Distribution Test and the Resulting Questions

If we allow funds to be paid out to the shareholders before we know for sure that all debtors will be satisfied in due course, we have to find a limit to these distributions. It is not difficult to describe this limit in a very abstract way. Funds are open to distribution if we can expect 'with sufficient certainty'[12] that they will not be needed by the company to pay its debts. I do not think that Jonathan Rickford and I are far from each other in this basic assumption. From this starting point some substantial questions become apparent:

- What do we mean by 'sufficient certainty'? Do we have an optimistic or a pessimistic picture of the future course of the company's business?
- Which factors do we include? Shall we concentrate on the economic situation of the company, its business outlook and strategies or shall we take a legal standpoint, starting with the existing assets and liabilities of the company towards third parties?

---

[11] These are accepted under Delaware Law, see s. 170 of the Delaware General Corporation Law.

[12] Rickford, loc. cit. n. 4.

- Which time frame do we apply? Shall we take into account only a limited number of years or shall we establish a rule that also tries to secure long-term obligations of the company? What importance do we ascribe to the 'liquidity' of the company in terms of net cash-flow?
- All of these 'tests' involve personal judgment. Who is going to be in charge of making these judgments in a binding way: the directors, the shareholders, the auditors or the judges?

These are the basic questions we should have in mind when discussing the choice between a balance sheet test and a solvency test, which has been laid out thoroughly in Jonathan Rickford's paper.

4. 'Optimistic' or 'pessimistic' view of the company's prospects?

The first question is whether we should start with an optimistic or a pessimistic view of the company's outlook when we consider the availability of funds for distribution to the shareholders. With respect to this sub-topic, Jonathan Rickford quite convincingly puts forward that the balance sheet test as applied under the rules of the Fourth Directive, which is strongly influenced by the 'prudence principle', leads to an asymmetric view of risks and opportunities. While profits are only recognised in the books when they are effectively 'made' (whatever that means), losses and other risks have to be shown if they are merely probable (or no more than possible). Rising market values of assets are not entered into the books, while decreasing values lead to effective write-offs in the company's accounts. Rickford prefers a more balanced view, pointing to the necessity of ensuring 'neutrality' of the picture painted in the company's books.[13] Risks and opportunities should be treated symmetrically in order to give a 'true and fair view' of the economic situation of the company.

In the accounting world of balance sheets, this concept of 'neutrality' is supported by the International Accounting Standards/International Financial Reporting Standards,[14] but it also forms the basis of the solvency test proposed by the UK group on company law reform.[15]

To be sure, even the 'conservative' balance sheets made up under the rules of the Fourth Directive include some 'optimistic' assumptions, e.g., the 'going

13 Ibid.

14 International Accounting Standards Board (IASB), *International Financial Reporting Standards* (IFRS) (London, IASCF 2005) para. 36.

15 'Reforming Capital', loc. cit. n. 1, at p. 986: 'Directors will need to consider whether the statutory balance sheet net asset balance overstates, or understates, the true commercial position.'

concern principle' under Article 31(1)(a), which enables the managers and auditors of the company to take a positive view of the ongoing existence and economic success of the business in the first place. Assets do not have to be valued at the price they would fetch if the business were to be dissolved, but at the value they represent in the context of current business operations. Nevertheless, it is true that the 'prudence principle' leads to an 'asymmetric' perspective which does not always correspond with the 'true and fair view' we have in mind when we focus on the information value of annual accounts disclosed to capital markets and the general public. It has been said that this asymmetric concept of the traditional accounting rules provides for a 'cushion' which gives an extra layer of protection to the creditors.[16] I share Rickford's view that the 'cushion theory' looks a bit 'overachieving', bearing in mind that creditors are aware of the true amount of subscribed capital under the company's statute.[17]

But before we condemn this asymmetrical view as being completely out of date, we should be aware that it corresponds to another asymmetry which has been described above. Any dividends and other distributions which have lawfully been doled out to the shareholders will never be recaptured by the company and its creditors when things turn sour and the company's fate tilts to the wrong side. Distributions made on the basis of 'symmetric' accounting will have the effect that the risk inherent in any recognition and valuation of assets and liabilities will work to the detriment of the creditors. The incentives for shareholders and directors to go for a 'neutral' perspective of the company's business outlook would be well balanced only if we were to oblige shareholders to return dividends to the company when the expected cash flow does not materialise. This is not my proposition, but if we preserve the law on dividends as it stands now, 'conservative' accounting is nothing more than a natural complement to the rule that legally paid dividends can never be forced back to the company's funds.[18]

5. Business approach or legal approach?

The second question which has to be addressed in our context concerns the alternative between a 'business-oriented' approach which takes into account the economic requirements and opportunities of the company and a 'legal' approach which focuses on its assets and liabilities towards third parties. Both approaches

---

[16] B. Pellens, D. Jödicke and M. Richard, 'Solvenztests als Alternative zur bilanziellen Kapitalerhaltung?', 58 *Der Betrieb* (2005) p. 1393 at p. 1394.

[17] Rickford, loc. cit. n. 4.

[18] W. Schön, 'Gesellschafter-, Gläubiger- und Anlegerschutz im Europäischen Bilanzrecht', 29 *ZGR* (2000) p. 706 at p. 713 et seq.

are substantiated in law and literature. A striking example concerns the recognition of future expenses. From a business perspective, future expenses ought to be taken into account before distributions are made, as the company will probably incur these expenses in the course of its operations according to the management's business plan. To identify the amount of cash open to distribution, you would have to analyse the management's investment strategy and the market situation shaping future income and expenditure. The legal perspective currently employed under the balance sheet test in European company law takes another direction. In order to account for a provision for future expenses, one requires an existing and enforceable obligation towards a third party.[19] On the other hand, 'no provision is to be recognised for costs that need to be incurred to operate in the future.'[20] A similar story can be told about the inclusion of future revenue. While from a legal point of view profits can only be distributed when they have crystallised in the form of assets forming part of the company's funds, in a business context we can also take into account future income which can reasonably be expected under a well-founded business plan of the management.

There is a certain tendency in the international discussion to do away with the legal perspective (as it is said to represent a rather 'formalistic' approach which is underachieving and overachieving at the same time) and to replace it with a more business-oriented approach which looks at the economic data of the company. Taking a closer look, one gets the impression that neither of these approaches seems to be completely satisfying. While a purely legal perspective simply does not ensure that the company is in the position to fund its future business operations (which typically requires much more than the payment of debts existing at the balance sheet date),[21] a purely business-oriented approach tends to divert our eyes from the fact that a distribution framework built on the management's 'business plans' ignores the existence and enforceability of the company's obligations towards third parties. If these obligations are 'assumed away' by painting a rosy picture of future business profits, the directors shift the true risk of future business operations from the shareholders to the creditors. This would lead to a basic distortion of current company law rules which is hard to accept. To make this point as clear as possible: distributions would not be justified by profits hitherto made but by the expectation that future income will suffice to pay the company's debts anyway.

---

[19] IASB, op. cit. n. 14, IAS 17 para. 20.
[20] Ibid., at para. 18.
[21] Rickford, loc. cit. n. 4.

6. HOW DO WE APPLY FORWARD-LOOKING DISTRIBUTION TESTS?

The choice of a 'time horizon' for the ability of a company to pay its debts can be singled out as the paramount policy question which has to be answered when discussing the future framework of shareholder distributions under company law. This is the topic where the relevant strengths of a solvency test, as strongly recommended by Jonathan Rickford,[22] and a balance sheet test, which has been the benchmark in EC legislation so far, become most evident. The merits of the two different 'tests' can best be highlighted when we ask whether the solvency test or the balance sheet test gives more leeway to the directors to hand out the funds of the company to the shareholders. The answer is neither of them, because in some cases the solvency test is stricter, while in other cases the balance sheet test seems to be less lenient in application.

The first element which has to be addressed in this context is to make sure that the company has enough liquidity at its disposal to make cash payments to its debtors. This requirement is considered when we ask for the ability of a company to pay its debts 'as they become due'. A balance sheet test does not address this question, as it does not take into account the settlement dates of a liability. Moreover, a balance sheet test does not take into account whether the company's funds are tied up in non-liquid assets and whether the course of the company's business requires the availability of additional funds for investments or current expenditure in the future. A solvency test is much better equipped to make sure that the projected cash flow of the business enables the management to meet future liabilities which it is set to incur in the course of the business.[23] Such a solvency test will not only take into account the maturity of liabilities, but will also take a look at the management's business plan and the amount of money placed in non-liquid assets. It should therefore be accepted that a solvency test has to be performed before dividends and other distributions can be handed out to the shareholders.

The second topic which has to be addressed is the question how long-term obligations are treated by the respective test. These long-term obligations do not only include loan covenants but also cover provisions for uncertain liabilities, e.g., decommissioning costs in nuclear power plants or oil refineries[24] and pension liabilities, which are discussed extensively in the Rickford report. Balance sheet tests are quite straightforward – if somewhat crude – in this respect, as they require that all liabilities which have accrued so far have to be covered by

---

[22] Ibid.; 'Reforming Capital', loc. cit. n. 1, at pp. 966.

[23] Pellens, Jödicke and Richard, loc. cit. n. 16, at p. 1395.

[24] IASB, op. cit. n. 14, IAS 17 para. 19.

existing assets on the distribution date, irrespective of the date when payment has to be performed.

In the German literature, it is generally perceived that solvency tests are more lenient than balance sheet tests as they only look at a limited time horizon for the solvency of a company.[25] Taking a closer look at existing UK legislation, i.e., the current solvency test as operated in the context of share buy-backs and the work of the Rickford group, it is at least unclear what the position of solvency tests on long-term obligations really is. The starting point should be section 173(3) of the Companies Act 1985 and clause 562 of the Companies Bill 2005, which require that a company's directors certify on the date of a distribution that 'there will be no grounds on which the company could be found unable to pay its debts'. This can be read as a requirement that 'all' debts – including long-term obligations – are expected to be covered when they have to be met. The Rickford group intends to modify this certification by extending the time frame to the 'reasonably foreseeable future' as far as this can be expected in the 'ordinary course of business'.[26] From the point of view of Jonathan Rickford, this inclusion of the 'reasonably foreseeable future' shall not be understood as a restriction on the time horizon but rather as an inclusion of all liabilities which have accrued at the time of the distributions as well as those which will accrue in the 'foreseeable future'.[27]

However, I am not convinced that this solvency test provides a reliable 'shielding' device with respect to long-term obligations. This is due to the fact that the solvency test does not ask whether 'existing' assets cover 'existing' obligations but confers upon the directors the discretion to assume that 'existing', legally accrued liabilities shall be covered by future assets and profits the accrual of which depends on future operations of the company. It may well be that directors are in the position to foresee the inflow of assets and the development of profits for some months (perhaps a bit more). But how shall this solvency test be made operative if we speak of liabilities which have to be met ten or twenty years from now? While it is true that according to current UK legislation and the proposals of the reform group a solvency test will have to take into account the existence of these long-term liabilities, I cannot see a reliable yardstick which directors could use in order to ascertain to a reasonable degree whether these long-term liabilities will find their match in future profits. In the end, the solvency test might lead to a situation where neither the benchmark of the traditional balance sheet test has to be met (accrued assets cover accrued liabilities) nor any meaningful statement can be made concerning the future solvency of the company with respect to these long-term obligations. This leads me to the conclusion

---

25 Pellens, Jödicke and Richard, loc. cit. n. 16, at p. 1395.

26 'Reforming Capital', loc. cit. n. 1, at p. 979; Rickford, loc. cit. n. 4.

27 Rickford, loc. cit. n. 4.

that the current balance sheet test has to be maintained in order to ensure a 'minimum protection' for long-term obligations.

The most relevant example is the case of pension liabilities.[28] A company's pledge of retirement payments in favour of the current and former workforce belongs to the most substantial long-term obligations of the corporate sector. Therefore, it should not go unmentioned that pension liabilities have played a major role in both business practice and academic discussion of our topic. This can be demonstrated when we look at Germany, the United States and the United Kingdom. In Germany, until 1986 there was no coherent obligation to account for pension liabilities in the balance sheet.[29] This became a prominent topic in 1982 when AEG, one of Germany's biggest electronics producers, became insolvent. When the *Pensions-Sicherungs-Verein*, a mutual insurance institution for pension liabilities, stepped in, they found that only a small fraction of retirement payments had been provided for in the company's accounts, forcing the business community to devote more than DM 1 billion to AEG's retirees.[30] Even today, German companies also tend to apply the lenient tax accounting rules on pension liabilities to financial accounts, which leads to the systematic understatement of existing obligations.[31]

Twenty-five years later, the US automotive industry faces the same problem in the case of General Motors and Delphi, its former spin-off and most important components supplier. Both have taken on huge commitments towards the workforce and retirees concerning healthcare and both have so far failed to account for these liabilities in a realistic way. Following Delphi's application for bankruptcy proceedings some time ago, GM revealed to the public that it had $7.5 billion in unfunded pension liabilities and $61 billion in unfunded retiree healthcare liabilities at the end of 2004 and that it ran the risk of being held responsible for another $11 billion in retirement costs under arrangements with Delphi.[32] Nevertheless, GM still announces to the capital market a $2 dividend per annum in order to keep shareholders happy.[33] According to the *Economist*, these 'legacy

---

[28] See 'Reforming Capital', loc. cit. n. 1, at p. 958 et seq.

[29] Following an early decision by the Federal Court of Justice (judgment of 27 February 1961, *Official Gazette* 34, p. 324 et seq.) companies had an election to recognise pension liabilities in their balance sheets.

[30] For a detailed account of the insolvency proceedings in the AEG case, see M. Hoppenrath and H.P. Wohlleben, eds., *Positionen – 25 Jahre Pensions-Sicherungs-Verein* (Cologne, RW Konzept 2000) p. 245 et seq.

[31] H.-J. Heger and T. Weppler, 'Die Pensionsverpflichtungen', in K. von Wysocki, et al., *Handbuch des Jahresabschlusses*, looseleaf, ch. III/7 (2004) para. 123 et seq.

[32] 'GM's Delphi costs make finance stake sale more likely', Bloomberg, 11 October 2005, available at: <http://www.bloomberg.com>.

[33] Forbes, General Motors Cp, 25 November 2005, available at: <http://www.forbes.com/finance>.

costs' are becoming a 'crippling burden' for a growing number of US firms.[34] Underfunding of retirement benefits in the United States is estimated at between $165 billion and $450 billion.

Referring to the United Kingdom in their extensive study 'Reforming Capital', Jonathan Rickford and his group pointed to estimates in 2003 that IAS/IFRS accounting for pension liabilities would mean an extra layer of liabilities in UK companies' balance sheets to the tune of £160-300 billion[35] (a figure which has since declined[36]). This sum would prevent UK companies from paying any dividends 'to the relevant extent'.[37] The advice is evident: 'It is in any event quite clear that to reverse this result, both UK and Community legislation will be required, and it would be desirable to put both points beyond doubt'.[38]

This case has to be taken serious by the legislator. Workers and retirees are not in a position to negotiate for sophisticated 'covenants' in order to secure their claims. So why should we allow companies to pay dividends in a situation where current assets do not cover all liabilities including long-term (pension) liabilities? The answer by Jonathan Rickford and his group is that payments for long-term liabilities have to be paid out of future profits – just like any cost incurred in the course of the business.[39] If we do not recognise future profits in our test we should also not make reserves for long-term liabilities. Yet this answer is not fully satisfactory. Pension liabilities and other long-term obligations are recognised under IAS/IFRS at a discounted value. This discount implies an assumption that the money reserved for pension payments will bear an annual return on capital (which in Germany is currently set at an optimistic rate of 6 per cent). As this discount is already a departure from 'conservative' accounting, it seems to be more than optimistic to go even further and do away with long-term obligations with reference to future profits. However, I have to concede to Rickford that adequate accounting for pensions is highly arbitrary in current accounting practice, which entails deficiencies in the application of balance sheet tests. There at least have to be transitional provisions making sure that there is a 'soft landing' for the corporate sector, as we did in Germany in 1986.

It should be made clear in this context that there are far-reaching differences in the legal and financial positions of companies which are subject to diverging 'pension schemes', i.e., those who have promised 'defined benefits', 'defined contributions' or 'payroll taxes'. Any company which has paid defined contributions or payroll taxes to a private pension fund or a public authority which takes

---

34 'Nor for the reckoning', *Economist*, 15 October 2005, p. 71 et seq.

35 'Reforming Capital', loc. cit. n. 1, at p. 960 et seq.

36 Rickford, loc. cit. n. 4.

37 'Reforming Capital', loc. cit. n. 1, at p. 964.

38 Ibid.

39 Ibid., at p. 965.

over the obligation to pay out benefits to the employees in future years has already suffered a financial loss (the payment of contributions), which is reflected in the company's profit and loss account, but there is no need to enter any additional pension liabilities into its financial accounts as there is simply no existing liability (and with respect to the services performed in the past by its employees no liability will ever accrue in the future). On the other hand, a company which has embarked on a defined benefit scheme has not yet fulfilled all its duties with respect to the services performed in the past by its employees, so it is perfectly legitimate that the financial accounts have to reflect these existing and accrued obligations (whether the technical measurement of the liabilities has to be specified in the light of the volatility of capital markets is quite another story).

Consequently, my conclusion would be that the existence of long-term obligations has to be taken seriously. Any time-limited solvency test will work to the detriment of several constituencies among long-term creditors, including the current and former workforce (in the case of pension liabilities) and even of the general public (e.g., in the case of provisions for the clean-up of nuclear waste).

One should therefore not opt for a solvency test alone, but combine this solvency test with a balance sheet test, thereby making sure that long-term obligations are adequately covered by existing assets.[40] Taking this course, we would not only be following the US example laid down in section 6.40 of the Revised Model Business Corporation Act[41] and New Zealand legislation: this path has also been supported by the recently published findings of a Dutch working group from Groningen University.[42] The argument produced by the UK reform group, namely that balance sheet tests are 'underachieving' when it comes to the true cash flow prospects of the company,[43] does not prevail if we take into account that this function has to be taken over by the additional solvency test proposed by Rickford and others.

7. RESTRICTIONS ON THE DISCRETION OF DIRECTORS

As any distribution from the company's funds to the shareholders will shift the risk of its future business operations from the shareholders to the creditors, it

[40] Group of German Experts on Corporate Law, 'Zum Report of the High Level Group of Company Law Experts on a modern Regulatory Framework for Company Law in Europe', 24 *Zeitschrift für Wirtschaftsrecht* (2003) p. 863 at p. 874.

[41] For a short overview of US law on statutory limits to distributions, see F.A. Gevurtz, *Corporation Law* (St. Paul, Minn., West Group 2000) § 2.3.2, p. 162 et seq.

[42] H.E. Boschma, M.L. Lennarts and J.N. Schulte-Veenstra, *Alternatieve systemen voor kapitaalbescherming* (Groningen, WODC, Instituut voor Ondernemingsrecht, Rijksuniversiteit Groningen 2005) English Summary.

[43] 'Reforming Capital', loc. cit. n. 1, at p. 975 et seq.

becomes clear that one of the major policy questions concerns the person making the decision – the decision being whether funds are available for distribution to the shareholders. Clearly, neither shareholders nor creditors should be in the position to have the first say in this context. Quite naturally, directors seem to be best placed to make the necessary judgment. They have the best knowledge of the business operations and prospects of the company, and they are also in charge of the accounts. From this starting point, the UK group led by Jonathan Rickford comes to the conclusion that the solvency test they recommend should be performed by the directors of the company.[44] The directors would have to provide a certificate pronouncing their view of the company's liquidity and business situation, thereby expressing the reasonable expectation that the company will be in a position to meet its liabilities, and also express a judgment as to whether the available funds will suffice to ensure payments of maturing debts. Additional examinations by auditors are characterised as superfluous and costly.[45]

I cannot suppress the feeling that the merits of this proposal will be judged quite differently, according to the concept and experience of business people and lawyers when they are confronted with the topic of independence and neutrality of directors. We all know that directors are primarily agents of the shareholders, whose funds they administrate and who appoint and dismiss them. In small and medium-sized companies, shareholders quite often act as directors themselves. Therefore, we have to find procedural and substantial provisions and sanctions which ensure that the directors will not do what seems to be most probable under behavioural aspects, i.e., to give an over-optimistic view of the company' ability to satisfy its creditors in the future. The UK and US 'instinct' seems to be to trust directors in the first place, so these countries opt for flexible standards and *ex post* sanctions, like the disqualification of directors, which is hardly practiced in continental Europe. The German tradition and other laws on the continent mistrust directors. They therefore try to establish *ex ante* mechanisms, including strict procedural and substantial rules on distributions.

In this respect, we encounter another example of the well-known game of 'rules versus standards'.[46] The advantages of both concepts have also been presented extensively. While standards are flexible, avoiding overachieving and underachieving results, hard and fast rules provide for legal certainty in advance, thus relieving actors from the necessity of taking legal risks. Under this premise, the balance sheet test employed in traditional company law works as a 'safe

---

44 Ibid., at p. 971 et seq.

45 Ibid., at p. 974.

46 L. Kaplow, 'Rules versus Standards: An Economic Analysis', 42 *Duke Law Journal* (1992) p. 557; Ch. Kuhner, 'Zur Zukunft der Kapitalerhaltung durch bilanzielle Ausschüttungssperren im Gesellschaftsrecht der Staaten Europas', 34 *Zeitschrift für Unternehmens- und Gesellschaftsrecht* (2005) p. 753 at p. 777 et seq.

haven' for directors and shareholders alike.[47] This safe haven becomes particularly important when we consider the competence of courts to control the directors' distribution policy *ex post*. Such an *ex post* assessment will most probably take place in the context of insolvency proceedings when the company's funds have been lost, and the courts will face a 'hindsight bias' as they analyse the business prospects put forward by directors when they decided on distributions in the run-up to the corporate breakdown.

Against this background, there are some elements of the judgment directors have to make which should be discussed in detail. Firstly, there is an element of 'business judgment' involved when it comes to the future prospects of the company's operations, including its business strategies and investment decisions.[48] With a liquidity test, managers are in the precarious position of judging the likely effect of their own business decisions.[49] According to the UK group's proposals, directors should start with their 'intentions'[50] when they draw up business plans and cash flow projections. How can we expect them to be impartial when we have to ascertain whether present investment decisions will bear fruit over the next years? Moreover, as the managers are in a position to change their business strategies (in particular their investment decisions), they will be able to influence the amount of free cash-flow and the availability of funds for distribution almost at will. This is likely to distort the investment decision in the first place and mislead shareholders and creditors as to the true economic position of the company.

The last point I want to make in this context refers to the change in business judgment which quite often occurs when a company enters a critical situation. When the business outlook of the company gets bleaker, shareholders have an incentive to withdraw funds from the company before creditors get their hands on them. Shareholders will ask directors to make as many funds available as possible. This might induce directors to change their accounting philosophy in these situations. This tendency will be strongly reinforced when we decide in favour of *ad hoc* tests which do not bind current valuations to former valuations and do not require directors to develop a balance sheet test on the basis of last year's accounts. This behavioural element makes it strongly advisable to opt for a balance sheet test which is linked to the annual accounts, since this will prevent

---

47 W. Schön, 'The Future of Legal Capital', 5 *EBOR* (2004) p. 429 at p. 445; Kuhner, loc. cit. n. 46, at p. 779; J. Vetter, 'Grundlinien der GmbH-Gesellschafterhaftung', 34 *Zeitschrift für Unternehmens- und Gesellschaftsrecht* (2005) p. 788 at p. 805 et seq. The value of a 'safe harbour' is also stressed in 'Reforming Capital', loc. cit. n. 1, at p. 968.

48 Pellens, Jödicke and Richard, loc. cit. n. 16, at p. 1400 et seq.

49 Kuhner, loc. cit. n. 46, at p. 778 et seq.

50 'Reforming Capital', loc. cit. n. 1, at p. 979 et seq.

managers from exaggerating assets and undervaluing liabilities in critical situations.[51] As managers will have to justify their distributions in the light of the previous accounting practice of the same firm, there is an element of 'self-commitment' when the law provides that distributions have to be in line with balance sheets drawn up for preceding periods. I presume that any dilution of this 'self-commitment', e.g., by allowing for exceptions to this rule when directors choose another 'proper commercial basis',[52] will lead to an increase in opportunistic behaviour in critical situations (even if we force directors to 'explain' at length this deviation from the accounts[53]). To dispose of the balance sheet test would – as the UK group itself argues – 'leave directors with less guidance as a matter of practice',[54] a result hardly reconcilable with their interest to establish 'safe-haven rules'.

8. What sort of balance sheet test?

From the previous comments it has become clear that we should opt for a combination of a solvency test, which covers the projected cash flow and the current business outlook for a limited period of time, and a balance sheet test, which looks at the long-term funding of liabilities by assets. Yet this leads us to the question which sort of balance sheet we should rely on: the conservative model laid down in the original Fourth Directive or the modern version which lies at the heart of IAS/IFRS and the recent amendments to the Fourth Directive?

This is not easy to answer, as annual accounts are meant to fulfil two functions at the same time: to give a 'true and fair view' of the company's financial and economic situation and to restrict distributions to shareholders. As Jonathan Rickford rightly points out in his paper, the 'true and fair view' concept requires a 'symmetrical' perspective including unrealised profits, while the 'asymmetry' between shareholders and creditors leads to a 'conservative' framework of accounting law.[55] The most systematic (but at the same time the most burdensome) approach would be to split these functions and to introduce two different accounting frameworks: one for 'information and disclosure' and one for 'dividend restrictions'. This proposal – which I advanced for the first time some eight

---

[51] As to the linkage of distributions to preceding accounts, see Federal Court of Justice, judgment of 11 December 1989, *Official Gazette* 109, p. 334 at p. 338; H.P. Westermann, in F. Scholz, ed., *Kommentar zum GmbH-Gesetz*, 9th edn. (Cologne, O. Schmidt 2000) § 30 GmbHG para. 14.

[52] 'Reforming Capital', loc. cit. n. 1, at p. 976.

[53] Ibid., at p. 980.

[54] Ibid., at p. 977.

[55] Rickford, loc. cit. n. 4; 'Reforming Capital', loc. cit. n. 1, at p. 966.

years ago[56] – has encountered fierce resistance from business practice but lies at the heart of current German reforms, under which companies are allowed to disclose annual accounts under IAS/IFRS as long as they prepare another set of accounts under the 'conservative' rules of the German Commercial Code.[57]

If we do not accept this double burden in the long run, it will be hard to find reliable ground. The obvious alternative would be to take IAS/IFRS accounts as a starting point. It belongs to the many strange features of this discussion that the linkage of distributions to IAS/IFRS is perceived in Germany as an intolerable liberalisation,[58] while the Rickford group reaches the conclusion that IAS/IFRS will restrict dividend payments more tightly than the old law,[59] although – under the Second and Fourth Directives – the law should have been the same in both jurisdictions! The two big issues are 'fair value accounting', including the revaluation of assets above the historical cost, and the recognition of self-created intangibles. Under traditional law, accounting rules referred to the historical cost of acquired or self-created assets. Although this has led to exaggerated pessimism and the creation of 'hidden reserves' distorting the 'information function' of accounting,[60] it has provided some general 'reliability', as the leeway for preparers of accounts to inflate profits or the value of assets has been greatly restricted. If we open the balance sheet test on distributions to 'fair value accounting' as they are laid down in IAS/IFRS and the recent amendments to the Fourth Directive (described by Jonathan Rickford in his paper), we enter a situation where the measurement of profits and losses becomes much more discretionary. This will entail a lot of 'hidden action' by directors. It will be hard to ascertain whether a revaluation of the company's assets is due to a true increase in the future cash flow expected to result from these assets or to machinations of the management to give an optimistic view of their own business success (a common problem in principal-agent relationships) or even to pressure from shareholders on directors to make funds available for distribution. The same holds true for the recognition and valuation of self-created intangibles which might hugely differ according to the personal views of the management preparing the accounts.

---

56 W. Schön, 'Entwicklung und Perspektiven des Bilanzrechts: Vom ADHGB zum IASC', 161 *Zeitschrift für das gesamte Handels- und Wirtschaftsrecht* (1997) p. 133 at p. 154 et seq.; Schön, loc. cit. n. 18, at p. 738 et seq.

57 § 325 HGB.

58 Arbeitskreis Bilanzrecht Hochschullehrer Rechtswissenschaft, 'Zur Fortentwicklung des deutschen Bilanzrechts', 57 *Betriebs-Berater* (2002) p. 2372 at p. 2373 et seq.

59 'Reforming Capital', loc. cit. n. 1, at p. 948 et seq. (stock options) and p. 958 et seq. (pension plans).

60 F. Kübler, 'Institutioneller Gläubigerschutz oder Kapitalmarkttransparenz', 159 *Zeitschrift für das gesamte Handels- und Wirtschaftsrecht* (1995) p. 550 at p. 552 et seq.

In the United States, section 6.40 of the Revised Model Business Corporation Act leaves it to the management to opt for such a 'fair valuation' of assets or other method of valuation 'reasonable in the circumstances'.[61] As this option tends to increase the discretion of the management, the arguments brought forward against 'opportunistic behaviour' of directors in the interest of shareholders become virulent again. Another option would be to follow California's model and to allow for dividends when the value of the company's assets under US-GAAP multiplied by a factor of 1.25 exceeds the book value of its liabilities.[62] Yet this 1.25 multiplier looks arbitrary on the face of it and has yet not found any followers in other jurisdictions. In Germany, it has been proposed to combine financial accounting under IAS/IFRS with additional undistributable reserves. The feasibility of this concept has been demonstrated by UK law in sections 263 and 264 of the Companies Act 1985, where distribution is limited to the company's profits as far as they have been 'realised'. This can be done, but since the amount of these reserves has to be followed up year by year, the company will virtually be obliged to draw up a second set of accounts, which leads us to the solution found above.

The true problem we face is the compliance burden which we unload on corporate business when we force it to draw up two parallel accounts in order to fulfil the requirements from both the 'information' side and the 'distribution' side of accounting. This problem deserves further study. It needs to be established empirically whether the current 'split' situation characterising German accounting rules can be upheld and whether the corporate sector will press for an abolition of extra accounts for creditor protection. To offer a final answer to this question is beyond the limits of this paper.

---

61 Gevurtz, op. cit. n. 41, at p. 164 et seq.

62 S. 500 of the California Corporate Code; see Gevurtz, op. cit. n. 41, at p. 162 et seq.

Legal Approaches to Restricting Distributions to Shareholders: The Role of Fraudulent Transfer Law

Douglas G. Baird*

Abstract
Fraudulent transfer law in the United States provides a safety net for corporate creditors. It prohibits insolvent debtors from making transfers or incurring obligations for less than reasonably equivalent value. Moreover, it reaches any transaction that lacks economic substance and that is designed merely to make it hard for creditors to monitor the debtor. The distinctive shape of fraudulent transfer law in the United States is not replicated in the other common law or in civil law jurisdictions. Nevertheless, the functions it performs are likely to be part of any legal regime that protects the rights of creditors and other investors.

Keywords: fraudulent transfer, fraudulent conveyance, legal capital, leveraged buyout, dividend.

Since 1571, Anglo-American law has given creditors the power to set aside any transfer a debtor makes with the intent to 'delay, hinder, or defraud' creditors. Courts in England first extended the notion of 'delay, hinder, or defraud' to transactions that, while not necessarily fraudulent, were suspect. Because such transactions bore incidents, or 'badges', of fraud, creditors were entitled to strike them down. In the United States, these badges evolved further and became

---

* Harry A. Bigelow Distinguished Service Professor of Law, University of Chicago. I am grateful to the Sarah Scaife Foundation and the Russell Baker Scholars Fund for research support.

disconnected from fraud altogether.[1] Badges of fraud are now so broadly defined that they effectively prevent the debtor from making transfers (or incurring obligations) that creditors would ordinarily prohibit if the costs of negotiating such terms explicitly were low enough.[2]

One badge has proved more important in practice than any other. Fraudulent transfer law reaches transactions in which an insolvent debtor makes transfers or incurs obligations for less than reasonably equivalent value. Regardless of intent, an individual debtor should not be able to make gifts while insolvent. It is not the debtor's money that is being given away, but rather the creditors'. Similarly, an insolvent corporation should not be able to make dividends. Other badges have become increasingly important in recent years, in particular the ones that pull into the orbit of fraudulent transfer law transactions that are concealed and have no economic purpose other than to make it hard for creditors to understand the debtor's financial affairs.

Fraudulent transfer law in the United States provides a safety net for corporate creditors. Corporate law already prevents an insolvent corporation from making a dividend to its shareholders.[3] Similarly, corporate directors owe fiduciary duties to creditors as soon as the corporation is in the zone of insolvency.[4] In addition, creditors wanting to prevent shareholders from making other kinds of distributions are free to insert covenants into their loan agreements, and they often do so.[5] Each of these mechanisms protects creditors, but to appreciate how they work, one must first understand how they operate in the shadow of fraudulent transfer law.

Part 1 of this paper sets out the basic contours of fraudulent transfer law. Part 2 focuses on how fraudulent transfer law reinforces the prohibition on dividends by insolvent corporations. Many transactions have the same economic effect as a distribution of dividends but are not 'dividends' as corporate law defines them. Part 3 shows how the problem of distributions to shareholders goes beyond preventing outright transfers and requires rules, like those in fraudulent transfer law, that deter self-dealing. Part 4 focuses on how fraudulent transfer law

---

[1] In the United Kingdom, fraudulent conveyance law evolved differently. Its legacy can still be seen in such provisions as s. 238 of the Insolvency Act 1986. See J. Armour, 'Transactions at an Undervalue', in J. Armour and H. Bennett, eds., *Vulnerable Transactions in Corporate Insolvency* (Oxford, Hart Publishing 2003) p. 37 at pp. 38-41.

[2] See D.G. Baird and T.H. Jackson, 'Fraudulent Conveyance Law and Its Proper Domain', 38 *Vanderbilt Law Review* (1986) p. 829.

[3] See, e.g., Model Business Corporation Act, s. 6.40(c).

[4] See, e.g., *Geyer* v. *Ingersoll Publications Co.*, 621 A.2d 784, 787 (Del. Ch. 1992).

[5] For an excellent discussion of the way in which covenants and creditor control alter the dynamics of modern Chapter 11 practice, see D.A. Skeel, Jr., 'Creditors' Ball: The "New" New Corporate Governance in Chapter 11', 152 *Pennsylvania Law Review* (2003) p. 917.

prevents corporate insiders from insulating themselves from monitoring by creditors.

The collapse of leveraged buyouts in the early 1990s gave rise to fraudulent transfer litigation, and fraudulent transfer law was the most important tool for unraveling many transactions in Enron. The Refco reorganization is likely to spawn many of these actions as well. The principles that animate fraudulent transfer law in the United States appear in the laws of the United Kingdom and other jurisdictions, although not exactly in the same form.[6] None of this should be surprising, as the functions it performs are likely to be part of any legal regime that protects the rights of creditors and other investors.

1. THE EVOLUTION AND PRESENT SHAPE OF FRAUDULENT TRANSFER LAW

Fraudulent transfer law evolved in three stages. In 1571, the British Parliament enacted a statute that rendered void any transfer made with intent to delay, hinder, or defraud a creditor.[7] Several decades later, Lord Coke interpreted these words expansively.[8] He held that the statute reached beyond transfers that constituted common law fraud and reached transfers that possessed 'badges of fraud'. A secret transfer, a transfer of ownership without a simultaneous transfer of possession, a transfer to an insider made while insolvent, or a transfer that served no legitimate economic purpose and simply made the creditors' lives more difficult could all be struck down. As this judicial gloss was interpreted in American courts, creditors gradually acquired a broad power to curb debtor misbehavior, a power that extended well beyond that associated with the right to bring an action for common law fraud. Badges of fraud and fraudulent transfer laws more generally began to lose all connection to fraud in the conventional sense.

Two badges of fraud proved particularly important. First was the transfer of ownership without simultaneous transfer of possession. This badge of fraud prevented most forms of secured financing from coming into being without

---

[6] In the United Kingdom, for example, the Companies Act 1985 (ss. 151-152) prohibits a company from financially assisting others in the acquisition of its own shares, much the same way that fraudulent conveyance law operates in connection with leveraged buyouts. See J. Armour, 'Share Capital and Creditor Protection: Efficient Rules for a Modern Company Law', 63 *MLR* (2000) p. 355 at pp. 368-370. As Gerhard Wagner discusses in his lucid and insightful commentary on this paper, German law protects creditors against similar abuses both through its provisions on legal capital and in its insolvency law. See G. Wagner, 'Distributions to Shareholders and Fraudulent Transfer Law', in this volume.

[7] See G. Glenn, *Fraudulent Conveyances and Preferences*, Vol. 1, rev. edn. (New York, Baker, Voorhis 1940) ss. 61-61e.

[8] *Twyne's Case*, 3 Coke 80b, 76 Eng. Rep. 809 (Star Chamber 1601).

explicit statutory blessing. Moreover, the statutes themselves typically responded to the problem that the badge of fraud identified, the problem of ostensible ownership. When a debtor possesses a machine or inventory, her creditors should be able to infer that she has not given some other creditor the right to it first. Hence, to create an effective security interest, a creditor had to solve the ostensible ownership problem by giving the world notice. The various ways in which a creditor was obliged to cure the ostensible ownership problem were eventually consolidated into Article 9 of the Uniform Commercial Code. In this sense, the US law governing security interests in personal property is a descendant of the law of fraudulent transfers.[9]

While this badge of fraud spawned the law of security interests, another increasingly became the focal point of fraudulent transfer litigation. The vast majority of transactions struck down were transfers made or obligations incurred by an insolvent debtor for less than reasonably equivalent value.[10] The intuition behind this prohibition is eminently sensible. Ordinarily debtors are free to engage in just about any transaction they please so long as their actions do not violate agreements with creditors. Thus, in the absence of some bargained-for prohibition, a corporation is free to issue dividends or engage in other transactions that remove assets from the reach of creditors. So long as the assets that remain are enough to pay the creditors in full, the debtor enjoys considerable discretion. Hence, fraudulent transfer law ordinarily does not govern transactions that a solvent debtor makes, even if the debtor does not receive reasonably equivalent value in return.

That said, it is hard to imagine that a creditor would not prohibit an insolvent corporation from issuing dividends or engaging in other transfers in which the debtor was giving up assets and getting nothing or too little in return. Such transactions would not only leave the corporation worse off but also injure the creditors, who hold the residual claims against the debtor. But although it makes sense to prohibit such transfers by insolvent debtors, it also seems clear that fraudulent conveyance law should not reach further. Even an insolvent debtor should be able to make arm's-length transactions in the marketplace. Were the law otherwise, businesses would be forced to shut down or file for bankruptcy the instant they became insolvent.

Put this way, these two characteristics (insolvency and less than reasonably equivalent value) seem to be the necessary and sufficient conditions for making a

---

[9] See G. Gilmore, *Security Interests in Personal Property*, Vol. 1 (Boston, Little, Brown 1965) pp. 24-286.

[10] See Uniform Fraudulent Transfer Act, s. 5(a) (hereafter, UFTA); Bankruptcy Code, s. 548(a)(2). In addition to reaching debtors who are formally insolvent, fraudulent transfer law reaches corporate debtors who are left with unreasonably small capital.

transfer voidable. Transfers made without both these features are seldom suspect, and those made with both almost always are. Indeed, to ensure that the doctrine works, one must count the cancellation of an antecedent debt as a form of value. A payment to one creditor reduces in equal measure the assets of and the claims against a corporation. To be sure, one creditor is preferred to another, but a preference is not a fraudulent conveyance. To be a fraudulent transfer, the transaction must make the creditors *as a group* worse off.[11]

For many years, fraudulent transfer law focused on this badge of fraud – transfers by an insolvent debtor for less than reasonably equivalent value – to the exclusion of others. It is the only badge mentioned explicitly in the Bankruptcy Code's articulation of fraudulent conveyance law. The others remain implicit in the language that generally prohibits transfers made with intent to 'delay, hinder, or defraud'.[12] But until very recently, the role that these other badges of fraud played has been quite modest. Most of the transactions that fell within the net of the other badges of fraud were also transfers made by an insolvent debtor for less than reasonably equivalent value, and it was much easier to hang a fraudulent transfer action on a statutory badge of fraud than on hoary common law precedents. Only in the wake of Enron and other financial reporting scandals did these other badges of fraud regain their significance.[13]

Fraudulent transfer law looks to substance rather than form. Courts are empowered to step different transactions together and look at their total economic effect. Transactions that appear to escape fraudulent transfer law when looked at separately fall within its net once one takes several steps back. Put differently, investment bankers and lawyers cannot play games with corporate shells and the like and insulate shareholders from liability if the transactions, when summed together, have the effect of taking assets out of corporate solution and putting them into the hands of shareholders.

---

[11] Once bankruptcy or some other collective proceeding is on the horizon, preferential payments and other forms of gun-jumping need to be regulated. See Bankruptcy Code, s. 547. But for the most part, fraudulent transfer law does not come into play in this situation. And outside a collective proceeding, fraudulent transfer law recognizes that a creditor dealing at arm's length with its debtor must rely on self-help. Loan repayments to insiders, however, do fall within the ambit of fraudulent transfer law. See UFTA, s. 5(b).

[12] These words together are a term of art. Virtually any transfer the debtor makes that transforms liquid assets into less liquid ones 'hinders' creditors, but few are fraudulent transfers. Similarly, transactions do not have to have the actual intent to 'defraud' to fall within its ambit. A transfer is made with the actual intent to 'delay, hinder, or defraud' if it possesses one or more of the 'badges of fraud' as they have evolved over time.

[13] See D.G. Baird, 'Enron and the Long Shadow of 13 Eliz.', in S. Worthington, ed., *Commercial Law and Commercial Practice* (Oxford, Hart Publishing 2003) p. 565.

Fraudulent transfer law has a broad reach,[14] and the role it plays is often apparent when one looks just beneath the surface. Courts sometimes rely on principles (such as the absence of a true sale) whose only authority derives from fraudulent transfer doctrine, although they fail to recognize this expressly.[15] Much of what happens in bankruptcy, moreover, is effected through negotiation and thus does not appear on the radar screen. In the Enron case, for example, creditors disgorged billions – in large part because of fraudulent transfer and related actions that would be brought against them – yet the vindication of these rights under fraudulent transfer law did not produce reported opinions.

From a comparative perspective, another, largely neglected characteristic of fraudulent conveyance law is especially noteworthy. A fraudulent conveyance is a species of tort against a creditor. It cannot be a feature of corporate law, for it applies equally to both individuals and corporations. While a fraudulent conveyance rule is incorporated into the Bankruptcy Code, it can also live apart from insolvency law. For this reason, conflict of laws principles play themselves out in ways that are largely unexplored.

Consider the facts of *United Feature Syndicate, Inc.* v. *Miller Features Syndicate*.[16] In that case, a Delaware corporation brought a fraudulent conveyance action in federal district court in New York against a Canadian corporation for a transfer the latter had made to two of its shareholders in Canada. Sitting in diversity, the court looked to New York conflict of laws principles and held that because the transfer took place in Canada, Canadian fraudulent conveyance law applied.[17] One can imagine any number of variations, but most striking is the possibility that a creditor domiciled in State *A* might lend to a debtor domiciled in State *B* that files a bankruptcy petition in State *C* and the fraudulent conveyance law that governs the transaction might be that of State *D*.

Ordinarily, little turns on this question in the United States. The widespread adoption of the Uniform Fraudulent Transfer Act and the broad reach of section 548, the fraudulent conveyance provision of the Bankruptcy Code, make cases such as *United Features* rare, but they nicely illustrate how rules that protect creditors from a flow of assets out of corporate solution into the hands of shareholders

---

[14] Some courts have made the reach of fraudulent transfer law seem more modest than it is by asserting (incorrectly) that in the absence of a transfer by an insolvent for less than reasonably equivalent value, a showing of outright fraud is necessary. This is wrong, as it equates 'intent to delay, hinder, or defraud' with 'intent to defraud' rather than with badges of fraud. For examples of courts using badges of fraud, see *Wall Street Associates* v. *Brodsky*, 684 N.Y.S.2d 244 (App. Div. 1999); *Citibank* v. *Benedict*, 2000 WL 322785 (S.D.N.Y. 2000).

[15] See R.C. Clark, 'The Duties of the Corporate Debtor to Its Creditors', 90 *Harv. L. Rev.* (1977) p. 505.

[16] 216 F. Supp. 2d 198 (S.D.N.Y. 2002).

[17] Ibid., at 214-216.

lack a natural home. There is no conceptual reason that the substantive principles must be embedded in either corporate or insolvency law. We should not, however, assume that the conflicts rule announced in *United Features*, one that looked to the location of the transfer of the assets out of corporate solution, is sensible. Today such transfers routinely take place in cyberspace.

The problem we face comes not from a dispute about the underlying merits. No one wants to live in a world in which corporate debtors can remove assets in a way that rational creditors would forbid if they were able. Hence, we need to ensure that the laws of different jurisdictions work in harmony with each other. Suppose State *A* prevents certain transfers through corporate law provisions that criminally punish directors who allow them. For this reason, its insolvency law neglects the matter entirely. By contrast, State *B* has a corporate law that does nothing to limit such transfers, but its insolvency law allows the receiver to recover them. Unless private covenants can completely displace the need for such background rules, we must guard against the possibility that a business could enjoy the benefits of the corporate law of State *B* and the insolvency law of State *A*. As we harness the forces of regulatory competition, we must make sure that corporate law and insolvency law work in harmony with each other.[18]

2. FORM, SUBSTANCE, AND FRAUDULENT TRANSFER LAW

State law typically prevents insolvent corporations from making dividends. At first approximation, every dollar distributed as a dividend reduces the expected recovery of the creditors by the same amount.[19] To work effectively, however, the law needs to do more than prevent transfers that are formally denominated as dividends. A prohibition on dividends prevents shareholders from taking assets out of corporate solution only if the prohibition is interpreted broadly. It must apply to all transactions that have the same economic consequences as a dividend. US corporate law, for the most part, fails to do this, and fraudulent transfer law picks up the slack.

---

[18] For an insightful discussion of this and related issues, see H. Eidenmüller, 'Free Choice in International Company Insolvency Law in Europe', 6 *European Business Organization Law Review* (2005) p. 423.

[19] It is, however, only an approximation. Suppose a corporation has only two assets, a lottery ticket with a 50-50 chance of paying \$150 and a \$10 bill. It owes its creditors \$100. Half the time the creditors expect to be paid in full and receive \$100; other times they expect to be paid only \$10. Hence, their expected recovery is \$55. After the dividend, the creditors will still be paid in full half the time, but now they will receive only \$50 otherwise. Hence, the \$10 dividend reduces their expected recovery by only \$5. The possibility that an insolvent corporation will once again become solvent drives the example.

The simplest case arises when a corporation repurchases stock from a shareholder. There is no difference between the corporation issuing a $100 dividend to a shareholder who holds 100 percent of the equity and the corporation buying back one of the shareholder's shares of stock for $100. Someone who holds all the equity of a corporation is indifferent to the number of shares she owns. Changing the number of slices does not change the size of the pie.

But one cannot stop with a simple prohibition on two-party transactions that take assets out of the corporation and put them into the hands of the shareholders. Consider the following case. An insolvent corporation guarantees a bank loan to its principal shareholder and backs the guarantee with collateral. By virtue of the guarantee, the shareholder borrows at a lower rate. The difference between the interest the shareholder pays on the loan and what he would have paid without the guarantee is the economic equivalent of a dividend. A prohibition on dividends would do nothing to prevent such a transaction. Fraudulent transfer law fills in the gap, and it picks up such a guarantee.

When the enterprise consists of a number of different corporate entities, there are additional ways to take assets out of corporate solution without making a formal dividend. Consider an enterprise that consists of an individual who owns 100 percent of the equity of ParentCo, a holding company whose only asset is the equity it holds in OperatingCo. ParentCo has no creditors. Bank and others lent money to OperatingCo, but OperatingCo is now insolvent. The equityholder can remove assets from OperatingCo without its making a dividend. To bring this about, the individual has OperatingCo make a loan to ParentCo. Once it receives the loan, ParentCo distributes the proceeds to the equityholder.

The transaction between OperatingCo and ParentCo is nominally a loan (and therefore not a dividend), but Bank is injured to exactly the same extent. Assets left OperatingCo, and it received nothing in return.[20] There has been a dividend from ParentCo to the equityholder, but a simple prohibition on dividends by an insolvent corporation is insufficient to prevent ParentCo's dividend to the equityholder. ParentCo is not insolvent.[21] Here again fraudulent transfer law reaches this transaction, as it applies to any transfer for less than reasonably equivalent value that OperatingCo makes while insolvent.

---

[20] ParentCo's promise to repay the loan is worthless since OperatingCo received nothing of value in return. ParentCo's only asset is its stock in OperatingCo and, as noted above, a corporation's financial condition is unaffected when it acquires its own stock.

[21] As noted, ParentCo has no creditors (since it is not responsible for the debts of OperatingCo) and it does have an asset (an equity interest in OperatingCo). OperatingCo is insolvent, but its equity nevertheless has value. The equity of even an insolvent firm trades at a positive price by virtue of its option value – the possibility, however remote, that the business's fortunes will turn around before the day of reckoning.

Assets can also be removed from corporate solution through a series of discrete steps, none of which is itself objectionable. Consider the following leveraged buyout.[22] TargetCo has substantial debts. Investor creates Acquiring Corp. and puts in $200,000. Acquiring Corp. buys 100 percent of the stock of TargetCo from its shareholders and promises to pay them $1 million in cash in ten days. Incurring the obligation to pay $1 million to the shareholders of TargetCo is in exchange for reasonably equivalent value since Acquiring Corp. received equity in TargetCo. TargetCo is now a wholly owned subsidiary of Acquiring Corp. The two corporations are merged to form NewCo. NewCo now borrows $800,000 from Bank. Because NewCo receives $800,000 in return for incurring the obligation, the loan by itself cannot be a fraudulent transfer. NewCo uses the loan proceeds to honor the promise Acquiring Corp. made to the old shareholders of TargetCo, an obligation that NewCo holds by virtue of being Acquiring Corp.'s successor. The payment is made on account of this antecedent debt, and as such falls within the definition of reasonably equivalent value.

No single step in this series of discrete transactions is a transfer for less than reasonably equivalent value. It takes only a moment's reflection, however, to see that when these various transactions are taken together, the consequences are the same as a transaction in which Investor bought TargetCo and then issued himself a dividend of $800,000. It is also the same as if the old shareholders awarded themselves a dividend of $800,000 and then sold their shares to Investor or if TargetCo repurchased 80 percent of its shares. No matter how one looks at it, when the discrete transactions are treated as a single transaction, there has been a transfer of ownership and a distribution of assets out of corporate solution to the detriment of TargetCo's creditors.

Modern fraudulent conveyance law permits creditors to bring a fraudulent transfer action in such situations when the corporation is insolvent at the time of the transaction or is made insolvent by it. Regardless of what it is called, any transaction that takes assets out of an insolvent corporation and puts them into the hands of the shareholders is a fraudulent transfer. Moreover, courts enjoy a broad ability to recharacterize these transactions, and each of the parties is potentially subject to a fraudulent transfer attack.[23] Assuming that TargetCo was insolvent at the time the transaction took place, all would agree that there has been a fraudulent transfer, but there is room for disagreement about the person against whom the action should lie.

---

22 For a more detailed discussion of fraudulent transfer law and leveraged buyouts, see D.G. Baird, 'Fraudulent Conveyances, Agency Costs, and Leveraged Buyouts', 20 *Journal of Legal Studies* (1991) p. 1.

23 See, e.g., *Orr* v. *Kinderhill Corp.*, 991 F.2d 31 (2d Cir. 1993).

There are a number of possibilities. A court might recharacterize the transaction as a stock repurchase and require the shareholders to turn over the proceeds of the sale, even if they did not actually receive them from TargetCo itself. Alternatively, a court could find that, in substance, Bank gave the loan proceeds directly to the old shareholders and never gave anything of value to TargetCo. Hence, when TargetCo promised to repay the loan, it incurred an obligation and received nothing of value in return.

The law does not provide clear guidance as to which recharacterization is appropriate. One could argue that knowledge of the overall transaction and the debtor's insolvency are essential to bringing a successful attack against any particular party.[24] For example, recovery against the old shareholders should be possible only if they knew about Investor's plans at the time they sold their shares to him. But such a focus has the defect associated with any test that turns on knowledge – it rewards ignorance and stupidity. And as a practical matter, shareholders, especially public shareholders, are hard to track down. Even if an action is available (and it may not be),[25] creditors usually prefer to go after someone else. Investor might seem an easy target, but she never actually received anything of value in the entire transaction – she held only equity in a limited liability corporation. Reaching Investor's own assets requires piercing the corporate veil, something typically not done in such situations.[26]

For all these reasons, the lender is usually the target of fraudulent transfer litigation when a leveraged buyout fails. This approach paves the way most effectively for other creditors, who need only persuade the court to void the lender's security interest. Allowing the action does impose on the lender a monitoring duty that is out of step with basic principles of debtor-creditor law. In practice, however, a lender that extends credit in a leveraged buyout can be confident that it is insulated from a fraudulent transfer attack only to the extent that the transaction leaves the corporation solvent and with a reasonable amount of capital. The lender must argue not that someone else should be liable but rather that *no one* should be. In the case mentioned above, NewCo's failure was caused by Investor's subsequent mismanagement of the business, not by being saddled with too much debt.[27] More precisely, to be confident that it will not be exposed to a later fraudulent transfer attack, the lender must ensure that the corporation is

---

[24] See, e.g., *United States* v. *Tabor Court Realty Corp.*, 803 F.2d 1288 (3d Cir. 1986).

[25] See Bankruptcy Code, s. 546(e).

[26] Piercing the corporate veil is rarely allowed if corporate formalities are respected. See R.B. Thompson, 'Piercing the Corporate Veil: An Empirical Study', 76 *Cornell L Rev.* (1991) p. 1036 at p. 1072. Nothing about this transaction prevents Investor from cutting square corners.

[27] See, e.g., *Moody* v. *Security Pacific Bank Business Credit Inc.*, 971 F.2d 1056 (3d Cir. 1992).

left with assets sufficient to ensure that, even if things go badly, a court will not, after the fact, find that the transaction left the corporation without sufficient capital.

Fraudulent transfer law reaches much further than this. It extends beyond transactions where there is a transfer for less than reasonably equivalent value or even where the doctrine is cited explicitly.[28] In particular, a number of bankruptcy doctrines rest on fraudulent conveyance principles. Consider the following transaction. RealtyCo's sole shareholder is Investor, and Blackacre is RealtyCo's only asset. Blackacre is a piece of real estate on the outskirts of town. RealtyCo has two creditors, Bank and Lender. Bank has made a $100 loan to RealtyCo and taken a security interest in Blackacre. Lender has made a $100 unsecured loan. Both loans require only modest interest payments for the next five years, but at the end of that period the entire principal, plus all the accumulated interest, is due and owing. Blackacre now generates barely enough to make the interest payments. There is a 50-50 chance that it will be worth $200 in five years or that development of the town will pass it by and it will be worth only $100. Bank has the right to foreclose if RealtyCo misses a loan payment.

Investor and Bank reach a deal. Investor agrees to have RealtyCo default on its interest payment to Bank. In return, Bank promises that it will bid $100 at the foreclosure sale and, if it proves to be the high bidder, give Investor a 20 percent interest in Blackacre. If the market is sufficiently liquid, Bank will not be the high bidder. The property, in expectation, is worth $150. In a liquid market, a third party will bid that amount. Bank will be repaid in full, Lender will receive $50, and Investor will be left with nothing. The deal makes sense for Bank and Investor, however, when the market is illiquid. Reflect on what happens if no one else appears. Bank will win with its $100 bid. The person conducting the sale will give title to Blackacre to Bank (as the high bidder) and give the proceeds to Bank (as the senior creditor). At this point, Bank has the same amount of cash as before, but it now owns Blackacre outright, rather than holding it as security for a debt. Lender's interest is wiped out, as is Investor's interest. At this point, Bank transfers a 20 percent interest in Blackacre to Investor as it promised.

When we again step the different transactions together, we see that Bank is better off. (It has an 80 percent interest in a piece of property that is worth, in expectation, $150. This interest is worth $120, more than Bank would have received if Investor had not defaulted.) Investor is also unambiguously better off. Before, she would have received nothing – even if she made all the interest payments and even if Blackacre turned out to be worth $200. But her deal with Bank allowed her to end up with an interest in Blackacre that is worth, in expectation, $30.

[28] See Clark, loc. cit. n. 15.

Lender is the loser. Before the transaction, it had a 50-50 chance of being paid in full. After the transaction, it receives nothing.

Fraudulent transfer principles ensure that Lender can void Investor's 20 percent interest in Blackacre, even if Lender cannot prove actual collusion. Before the foreclosure, Lender had an interest worth $50 and Investor had an equity interest that was worthless. Whatever else one says about Bank's rights, Investor should not be able to retain an interest in Blackacre while Lender's interest is wiped out. Any restructuring that has the effect of freezing out a creditor such as Lender is voidable. Although not formally denominated a fraudulent transfer, the principle is solidly entrenched in the Bankruptcy Code.[29] It derives from case law that relies on fraudulent transfer doctrine.[30] Even if one cannot precisely identify a discrete transfer from RealtyCo to Investor, it is as if RealtyCo had transferred a senior claim against Blackacre to Investor. This is enough to trigger fraudulent transfer doctrine if RealtyCo is insolvent at the time of the default.

3. FRAUDULENT TRANSFER LAW AND RELATED PARTY TRANSACTIONS

As the previous part illustrates, policing transactions in which shareholders divert value from creditors requires something more than a rule that bans dividends by insolvent corporations. The problem worsens when the shareholders wear a second hat and engage in transactions with the corporation that, if done at arm's length, would be unproblematic. This problem acquired notoriety in the nineteenth century during the construction of the great American railroads.[31] Investors from Frankfurt, Amsterdam, and other financial capitals of Europe invested hundreds of millions of dollars in railroad bonds. The insiders who owned the stock formed construction companies and exercised control over the railroad to ensure that the railroad engaged the construction companies to build the road. These construction companies proved enormously profitable, even as the railroads themselves defaulted on their bonds.

If the construction companies had entered into contracts with the railroads as third parties, they would have had nothing to fear from fraudulent transfer law. The goods and services given to a debtor necessarily constitute reasonably equivalent value when the contract itself is negotiated in the marketplace at arm's length.[32] When the supplier is an insider, however, one cannot assume that the

---

[29] See Bankruptcy Code, s. 1129(b).

[30] See *Northern Pacific Railway Co.* v. *Boyd*, 228 U.S. 482 (1913); In re *Armstrong World Industries, Inc.*, 320 Bankr. 523 (D. Del. 2005).

[31] See D.H. Bain, *Empire Express: Building the First Transcontinental Railroad* (New York, Viking 1999) p. 408.

[32] See *BFP* v. *Resolution Trust Corp.*, 511 U.S. 531 (1994).

debtor received the same kind of deal. While in form the transaction is a purchase of goods and services, in substance it might be better characterized as a combination of a third-party contract and a distribution of corporate assets to shareholders. In the case of the railroads, the great American robber barons used the construction companies to siphon off money, typically at the expense of the European creditors.

The problem repeated itself at the end of the twentieth century. Close at hand to the telecommunications companies that failed at the end of dot.com era were construction companies, controlled by related parties, that often did quite well for themselves. Today, a similar problem occurs with employment contracts. The chief executive officer of a small corporation may be one of its principal shareholders, and his salary may be in excess of his market wage. When the corporation is solvent, those most affected are the other shareholders, but when the corporation is insolvent, the costs fall principally on the creditors. Again, it is possible to disaggregate this transaction into two components, a straight salary and a dividend.

In principle, fraudulent transfer law reaches transactions involving insiders when they are overpaid for the goods or services they provide if the corporation is insolvent at the time of the transaction. Courts, however, are reluctant to extend fraudulent transfer law so far for several reasons. First, determining reasonably equivalent value is hard. Valuations by their nature are uncertain. Fischer Black famously defined an accurate valuation as one that was within 50 percent of the true value.[33] Moreover, it is hard to find the market benchmark to determine reasonably equivalent value in such transactions. There is not a liquid market for a contract to build a railroad across the Sierra Nevada in the 1860s. The appropriate wage to pay a CEO is very far from being a sum certain.

Second, spreading the net of fraudulent conveyance law too wide risks dampening perfectly acceptable transactions. When a new business is being developed, its major supplier is often a major investor as well. The other investors are completely aware of both the supplier and the terms. Such transactions should not be second-guessed. Start-up ventures are inherently risky; creditors are compensated for the risk and do not view the supplier as an insurer of the business plan. Similarly, those who run small corporations are often the principal shareholders. Indeed, making them the residual owner with respect to most decisions ensures that they have the right incentives. Given that the manager shareholders are risk averse, the optimal contract is one that pays them a fixed return and a bonus that turns on the success of the business. The optimal contract is one in which they receive a salary in addition to holding stock. One does not want a broad legal doctrine to undermine this arrangement.

---

33 See F. Black, 'Noise', 41 *Journal of Finance* (1986) p. 529 at p. 533.

In practice, fraudulent transfer law provides a backstop, albeit a weak one, for these kinds of transactions. It is weak both because of the difficulty of distinguishing objectionable from unobjectionable transactions and because of the ability of creditors to police their debtors on their own. A major investor should know whether a start-up business is using an insider as a major supplier, and prohibit it or not as she pleases in the original loan documents. Fraudulent transfer law, by its nature, is hard to opt out of. Hence, it should apply only when the transaction is one that creditors as a group would be certain to prohibit in a fully dickered loan agreement.

With respect to insider transactions, fraudulent transfer law plays an important, but largely prophylactic role. Rather than providing a substitute for creditor monitoring, it prohibits transactions that have the effect of concealing mischief from creditors. Rather than controlling distributions to shareholder directly (which it does only to some extent), fraudulent transfer law makes it harder for the shareholders and other insiders to hide transactions that have the effect of diverting value from creditors to shareholders. I turn to this issue in the next part.

4. CONTROL RIGHTS, FRAUDULENT TRANSFER LAW, AND THE TRANSPARENCY PROBLEM

Capital structures contain two crucial features: they distribute cash-flow rights and control rights. The simplest capital structure has a creditor and a shareholder. The business consists of a project run by the shareholder, and it ends at a date certain. There is a day of reckoning. The creditor receives the entire proceeds up to some fixed amount, and the shareholder is left with whatever remains. In practice, of course, cash-flow rights are considerably more complicated. It has long been a commonplace in corporate finance that no fundamental difference between debt and equity exists with respect to cash-flow rights. The cash-flow rights associated with one can be transformed into those associated with the other by acquiring the right combination of derivatives.[34] This is the basic lesson of Modigliani and Miller and a necessary consequence of put-call parity.

Control rights are equally malleable.[35] In the simplest account of debt, the creditor has no rights until the debtor fails to make a scheduled payment. So long as the debtor makes the scheduled payments, the shareholders possess all the

[34] See F. Black and M. Scholes, 'The Pricing of Options and Corporate Liabilities', 81 *Journal of Political Economy* (1973) p. 637. For a discussion of the ways in which these ideas undermine corporate taxation, see A.C. Warren, 'Financial Contract Innovation and Income Tax Policy', 107 *Harv. L Rev.* (1993) p. 460.

[35] D.G. Baird and R.K. Rasmussen, 'Control Rights, Priority Rights, and the Conceptual Foundations of Corporate Reorganizations', 87 *Virginia Law Review* (2001) p. 921.

control rights. They elect the directors and, through them, determine what projects the business undertakes. This simple account is a good approximation so long as the shareholders are, for all practical purposes, the residual claimants. If they are the ones who win or lose as a result of decisions that need to be made, they are the ones best equipped to make them.

In reality, things are much more complicated. Even when the debtor is solvent, decisions affect the creditors for better or worse. The less residual value the shareholders can claim, the more control the creditors should exercise. Covenants in private debt contracts put some control in the hands of creditors, the amount depending on the debtor's financial condition.

Loan covenants do not grant control rights explicitly. The violation of a covenant is a default under the loan that makes the entire principal due and owing. In practice, the default (or the prospect of a default) gives the creditor the opportunity to exercise control. A covenant stating that the debtor will not sell any major assets does not prevent the debtor from selling assets, but rather ensures that the debtor has to obtain the creditor's blessing. Defaults on financial covenants similarly allow the creditor to exercise control. A debtor wishing to undertake an action that violates a covenant must seek a waiver from the creditor. The creditor can use the occasion to assert control over the debtor's affairs, including, for example, replacing the chief executive officer.[36]

Private debt covenants vary with the type of loan. The more precarious the debtor's financial health, the more control the creditor is likely to exercise. Fraudulent transfer law ensures that these covenants work effectively, even when the debtor is solvent. Return again to the various distributions to shareholders that fall within the ambit of fraudulent transfer law when the debtor is insolvent, such as dividends and distributions (direct and indirect) to insiders. Creditors use covenants to police the debtor even when the debtor is not insolvent. The challenge lies in knowing how much policing to do. When the debtor's business is thriving, policing makes little sense. Hence, the financial condition of the debtor is the threshold question for creditors. For this, creditors rely in significant measure on the debtor's credit rating.[37] This reliance in turn can encourage managers to engage in transactions that inflate the credit rating. Fraudulent transfer law plays a role in limiting the managers' ability to engage in this or other actions that lull creditors into monitoring less closely than circumstances require.

Many transactions that remove assets from the reach of creditors, improve the balance sheet, and preserve a credit rating lack economic substance. Such

---

[36] See Skeel, loc. cit. n. 5.

[37] For an excellent analysis, see Yok-Nam Ng, *The Primacy of Creditors in Corporate Governance* (University of Chicago manuscript) (October 2005).

transactions, designed as they are to pull the wool over the eyes of creditors, can be struck down as fraudulent transfers regardless of the debtor's solvency. Such a transfer may take the form of a sale of a highly volatile asset (e.g., stock in a high-tech start-up) to a thinly capitalized special-purpose entity in return for cash and a promissory note.[38] (The entity raises the cash by borrowing from a third party and giving it a security interest in the asset.) The entity will be able to pay the note only if the stock keeps its value, but the debtor's books give no hint of this. From the books, it appears as if risky stock has been traded for cash and a safe note. The transaction has no purpose other than to remove an asset of uncertain value from the books. Fraudulent transfer law not only allows creditors to recover the stock, but it may allow them to avoid the security interest of the third party that lent the cash. The third party has a good faith defense, but it may know too much for such a defense to succeed. The action exists even if the debtor was solvent at the time of the transaction.

Fraudulent transfer law performs two functions in this context. First, it makes a respectable third party less likely to engage in such transactions, and hence makes it more likely for creditors to discover the debtor's financial condition and put a stop to dividends and the like. Second, if the third party is still foolish enough to participate in such transactions, it gives some recourse to creditors.

5. Conclusion

The law governing fraudulent transfers suffers from the same problem that afflicts any decision to use a flexible standard as opposed to a clear rule. The ability to go behind form to substance makes the law potent but also makes it unpredictable. The stakes for creditors, of course, are capped by the costs of putting covenants in place and then monitoring their debtors after the fact.

The future importance of fraudulent transfer law in the United States is not easy to predict, as we now find ourselves in the midst of an arms race. Transactions are far more complicated today than they were even a few decades ago, thanks to the widespread use of computers and the tools of modern finance. At the same time, creditors have become much more sophisticated in their ability to use covenants and other devices to monitor debtors.

The even greater challenge confronts jurisdictions outside the United States. Fraudulent transfer principles ought to work seamlessly with other approaches to policing distributions to shareholders even when transactions implicate multiple legal regimes. The stakes here turn on an empirical question that remains largely

38 We saw exactly this kind of transaction in Enron. See Baird, loc. cit. n. 13.

unexplored – the extent to which private covenants can police distributions to shareholders and otherwise prevent the misbehavior that fraudulent transfer law tries to keep in check.

Distributions to Shareholders and Fraudulent Transfer Law

Gerhard Wagner*

Abstract
Legal regimes of limited liability serve different functions governed by distinct normative principles. The enabling function of limited liability aims at facilitating investment in risky activities and at organising principal/agent-relationships within the firm. In this area, choice of law may readily be allowed. At the other end of the spectrum, the protective function of limited liability regimes serves the objective of protecting outsiders from externalisation of risk. In this area, choice of law is much more problematic. Fraudulent transfer law belongs in the latter group, whereas corporate law belongs in the former. However, the German version of a limited liability regime cuts across these distinctions by including the protective function in the normative scope of corporate law, thereby downgrading the law of fraudulent transfers. As will be become apparent, this structural feature explains most of the differences that emerge when comparing the German

* Gerhard Wagner, LL.M. (University of Chicago), Professor of German and European Private Law and Civil Procedure and Director of the Institute of Civil Procedure at the University of Bonn.

law of fraudulent transfers with its American counterpart. The recent case law of the ECJ poses a major challenge to the traditional approach. It seems that the best way to deal with the challenge is for German law to develop towards the American model.

Keywords: fraudulent transfer, fraudulent conveyance, legal capital, shareholder loan, distributions to shareholders, solvency test, insolvency.

1. INTRODUCTION

Starting from first principles, the role of fraudulent transfer law in restricting distributions to shareholders is straightforward to define: in bankruptcy, a priority scheme governing the distribution of the assets of the insolvent firm between the various groups of interested parties takes effect. The first group to be served are the secured creditors. They are allowed the first bite in the distribution of any proceeds earned in converting the assets encumbered with security interests into cash. To the extent that the secured creditors are paid off, they drop out of the picture. Now it is for the unsecured creditors to look to the assets for satisfaction of their claims. It is only if there is anything left after all the creditors, secured or unsecured, have received their dues that the equity holders may come to the pool of assets and take whatever remains. Of course, in the overwhelming majority of bankruptcy proceedings, nothing remains for the shareholders, so that they have to walk away empty-handed.

The function of fraudulent conveyance law is to protect this scheme of priorities from circumvention by transactions effected on the eve of bankruptcy.[1] To achieve this purpose, one must merely pose the simple question whether the transaction, made before the filing of the bankruptcy petition, works to obstruct the distributional regime that prevails in bankruptcy. For the purpose of our present inquiry, the critical point is whether the shareholders have appropriated any funds that were earmarked for the coverage of the claims of the secured or unsecured creditors. Any transfer that diverts funds away from the creditors and into the pockets of the shareholders should be subject to avoidance by the trustee in bankruptcy.

---

[1] Cf., K.-P. Kirchhof, in *Münchener Kommentar zur Insolvenzordnung*, Vol. 2, 2nd edn. (Munich, Beck 2003) § 129(2). For a detailed discussion of fraudulent transfer law in the United States, see D.G. Baird and T. H. Jackson, 'Fraudulent Conveyance Law and its Proper Domain', 38 *Vanderbilt Law Review* (1985) p. 829 at p. 829.

2. THE AMERICAN MODEL

With some exaggeration, it might be said that the American law of fraudulent conveyances is a more or less a direct application of the general principle. Under section 548(a)(1) of the Bankruptcy Code (hereinafter, BC) the trustee in bankruptcy may avoid any transfer of the debtor in property, or any obligation incurred by the debtor, that was made or incurred on or within one year before the day of the filing of the petition, if the debtor voluntarily or involuntarily made such transfer or incurred such obligation with actual intent to hinder, delay or defraud any creditor to which the debtor was or became, on or after the date that such transfer was made or such obligation was incurred, indebted.

Although there are many more heads of fraudulent transfers at both the federal and State law level, the provision cited may be thought of as a general clause of fraudulent conveyance law. As Douglas Baird has explained, the crucial prerequisite is the intention to 'hinder, delay or defraud' creditors. It is interpreted broadly, as courts place little emphasis on the subjective element of actual intent, concluding that there was such intent when a so-called badge of fraud may be identified.[2] As far as distributions to shareholders are concerned, courts implicitly relate to the priority scheme described above by asking whether the distribution of benefits to the shareholders leaves the corporation with enough assets to cover its liabilities.[3] This simple criterion is in fact highly complex when applied to individual cases. In order to establish that the corporation was left with too little funds for covering all its debts, one must take a snapshot of the assets and liabilities of the corporation at the time the transfer was made. The result obtained by such a snapshot is misleading, however, because not all the debts are due at this point in time and the assets may be worth more or less than one might think at first glance. In fact, it is necessary to determine the expectation value of the assets of the firm and then to ask whether the corporation would be able to pay off its debts as soon as they became due. Obviously, such an exercise in evaluation raises complex issues of accounting and anticipation of future developments. However, if I understand American practice correctly, courts try to do their best to paint an accurate picture of the expectation value of the firm. One popular heuristic is the one that asks whether an outside investor would have been prepared to buy the firm for more than one cent after the incriminated transfer to

---

[2] The badges of fraud originate from Twyne's case, *Attorney General* v. *Twyne*, 3 Coke 80b, 76 Eng. Rep. 809 (Star Chamber 1601). See also, e.g., *United States* v. *Gleneagles Investment Co.*, 565 F. Supp. 556, at p. 581 et seq. (equating intention to hinder and delay with debtor's knowledge of its poor financial condition).

[3] See the insolvency test in s. 101(32) BC, which states that insolvency is a financial condition such that the sum of an entity's debts is greater than all of that entity's property, at a fair valuation.

the shareholder was executed.[4] If an outside buyer attaches a positive value to the combination of assets and liabilities held by the firm, this buyer must value the assets of the firm higher than the sum of its liabilities. In this case, the creditors lose nothing to which they are entitled. The assets which are left within the control of the corporation are sufficient to cover all its debts once they become due. In short, American law follows the fair value principle in defining fraud in the context of distributions of the company's assets to shareholders.

3. THE GERMAN MODEL OF ENFORCEMENT: A COLOURFUL BUNCH OF LEGAL FLOWERS

3.1 Bankruptcy law

Under the German Insolvency Act (*Insolvenzordnung*, hereinafter InsO), the transferee is liable to return whatever was received by a fraudulent conveyance. Although section 129 InsO stipulates something like a general clause, it is not in itself enforceable in practice. Rather, the trustee may only avoid a transaction if he succeeds in showing that it satisfies the requirements of one of the categories of fraudulent conveyances or voidable preferences as defined in sections 130-136 InsO. The provision that comes closest to the principle of section 548(a)(1) BC is section 133(1) InsO. Under this rule, the trustee may avoid any transfer of an interest or debt incurred by the debtor that was made within ten years before filing of the petition in bankruptcy, provided it was made with an intention to hinder creditors. That sounds very broad indeed, but in fact it is a very narrow rule. For one thing, German courts tend to interpret the subjective element, i.e., the intention to hinder creditors, in a rather narrow way. It is not sufficient that the debtor had reason to know that the transaction would amount to an infringement of the creditor's legitimate interest in the preservation of the assets. Rather, it is necessary that the debtor somehow approved of the detrimental effect these actions would have on the interests of creditors (at least *dolus eventualis*).[5] Of course, it is very complicated to identify and prove such subjective requirements in any given case. Quite obviously, the courts enjoy some discretion when deciding upon the necessary intention of the debtor. However, it is fair to say that German courts have refrained from developing badges of fraud in cases where –

---

[4] *Covey* v. *Commercial National Bank*, 960 F. 2d 657 (7 Cir. 1992) at p. 660 et seq.; D.G. Baird, *Elements of Bankruptcy*, 3rd edn. (New York, Foundation Press 2001) p. 135 et seq.

[5] BGH 18 April 1991, *NJW* 1991 p. 2144 at p. 2145; BGH 2 April 1998, *ZIP* 1998 p. 830 at p. 835.

at root – a set of objective facts is sufficient to establish the subjective element, i.e., the intention to hinder creditors.

Even more importantly, the intention of the debtor is not sufficient in order to make a transaction subject to avoidance under German fraudulent transfer law. Rather, section 133(1) InsO requires that the other party, i.e., the transferee, had knowledge of the intention of the debtor to hinder his creditors. Although such knowledge is presumed where the transferee knew that the insolvency of the debtor was imminent and anticipated the adverse effects the transaction would have on the interests of other creditors, it is still one more hurdle to overcome for the trustee. Again, it would go too far to maintain that this hurdle is impossible to overcome in practice. The fact is, however, that the case law of German courts shows little willingness to push the subjective elements aside and focus on the objective nature of the transaction in order to allow for a broad range of application of section 133 InsO.[6]

3.2 Corporate law: capital maintenance requirements

Another set of rules which places limits on distributions of the assets of a company to its shareholders is to be found within the context of corporate law. Under sections 30 and 31 of the Limited Liability Company Act (*GmbH-Gesetz*, hereinafter GmbHG) the legal capital of the company must not be redistributed to its shareholders. Similar provisions appear in sections 57 and 62 of the Joint Stock Company Act (*Aktiengesetz*, hereinafter AktG). Where a transaction violates these provisions, the shareholders are liable to return whatever they received from the corporation.

It goes without saying that section 30 GmbHG and section 57 AktG cover direct payments from the company to the shareholders. Because the legal consequences of such transactions are so obvious, they are rare in practice. Thus, the case law developed under the said provisions deals for the most part with a variety of transactions the purpose of which is to conceal the fact that assets of the company are in fact distributed to the shareholders.[7] Pertinent examples are excessive remuneration of shareholders who serve as managers of the company, the extension of loans with an interest rate which is well below market price, the supply of assets of the company as collateral for loans taken out by the

---

[6] BGH 14 July 1969, *NJW* 1969 p. 1719; BGH 29 March 1960, *WM* 1960 pp. 546, 547; H. Hirte, in W. Uhlenbruck, ed., *Insolvenzordnung*, 12th edn. (Munich, Franz Vahlen Verlag 2003) § 133(13); Kirchhof, op. cit. n. 1, § 133(14).

[7] See M. Lutter and P. Hommelhoff, *GmbHG*, 16th edn. (Cologne, Otto Schmidt Verlag 2004) § 30(26) et seq.; H. Altmeppen, in G. Roth and H. Altmeppen, eds., *GmbHG*, 5th edn. (Munich, Beck 2005) § 30(74) et seq.; H.P. Westermann, in F. Scholz, ed., *Kommentar zum GmbH-Gesetz*, 9th edn. (Cologne, Otto Schmidt Verlag 2000) § 30(24), (28) et seq.

shareholders, and so forth. In all those cases, the shareholder is liable to return whatever he received to the company that made the transfer. Remarkably, and similarly to section 133 InsO, a rather long limitation period of no less than ten years, beginning with the date of the payment, applies.[8]

In practice, however, the managers of the company who made the fraudulent conveyance will not be prepared to enforce the liability of the shareholders, because that would undo the transaction they executed themselves. For this reason, the main field of application of sections 30 and 31 GmbHG and sections 57 and 62 AktG is in cases where the company has become insolvent. Then, the trustee in bankruptcy takes over, and one of his most important duties is to skim the commercial papers of the company in search for hidden distributions. Once such a transaction has been identified, it is for the trustee in bankruptcy to recover any benefit that amounts to an illegal distribution of assets to the shareholders. In this sense, the said provisions of corporate law serve the same function as fraudulent conveyance law.

The interesting point to note in this context is the definition of an illegal distribution that governs in German company law. Unlike the fair value standard that is used in the context of section 548 BC, the standard is a formal one. The critical threshold is not whether the transfer diminished the pool of assets of the company to which the creditors legitimately look for satisfaction of their claims but the infringement of legal capital, as stipulated in the company's charter of incorporation.[9] Sections 30 and 31 GmbHG do not require that the value of the company becomes negative under a fair valuation of all its assets and liabilities at the time the transfer is made, but focus on whether the distribution infringes upon the legal capital. In this context, a balance sheet test governs. There is no need for any independent valuation of the company's assets or the business prospects of the entity. Rather, one has to look at the balance sheet of the company as drawn up with regard to the standards of traditional German accounting rules. These follow a precautionary principle in the sense that assets will be valued according to the purchase price paid at the time of acquisition. If there is a major change of circumstances, the company and its accountants have to devalue the assets, but they must not go in the other direction, increasing the value of an asset beyond purchase price.[10] Thus, there is a built-in tendency to protect creditors by following the precautionary principle of traditional German accounting standards.

---

[8] S. 31(5) GmbHG.

[9] W. Schön, 'The Future of Legal Capital', 5 *EBOR* (2004) p. 429 at p. 445 et seq.; Lutter and Hommelhoff, op. cit. n. 7, § 30(14) et seq.; Altmeppen, op. cit. n. 7, § 30(7).

[10] For further details on valuation and accounting rules, see ss. 252-255 *Handelsgesetzbuch* (Commercial Code).

On the other hand, the fact that the capital maintenance rules work much the same way as fraudulent conveyance law is particularly apparent in light of the fact that sections 30 and 31 GmbHG even apply where the legal capital has already been dissipated anyway. According to the case law of the German Federal Supreme Court (*Bundesgerichtshof*, hereinafter BGH), if the shareholders are liable to return distributions that eat away at the legal capital, they must be even more liable where – prior to the distribution in question – there was no legal capital left.[11] The effect of such a distribution is that the value of the company, measured by traditional accounting principles, turns negative. As there is no point in protecting something which is not there, the rules on capital maintenance obviously incorporate the function of fraudulent transfer law. Distributions to shareholders which turn the company's value into the negative are void for the simple reason that they hinder creditors.

In short, the rules just described and their interrelation with accounting standards inaugurate a formal scheme of creditor protection. The idea is not to identify the true market value of the company in the form of expectation values and find out whether the distribution of assets caused this value to turn negative, but to protect the legal capital of the company as stipulated in the company's charter of incorporation and as protected by conservative accounting rules.[12]

The effects of this technique are two-fold. On the one hand, they work to the benefit of creditors in that they prohibit the distribution of assets even where the company's true value remains positive. On the other hand, they provide a rather high level of certainty for managers. They can rely on the figures in the company's balance sheet. As long as the legal capital is still there, they may be confident not to violate any standard of care and thus are not liable either to the creditors or to the company.[13]

One of the drawbacks of the protective scheme of sections 30 and 31 GmbHG is that it allows shareholders to come up with ever new strategies to avoid the scheme outlined above and defraud creditors. One such strategy is to stipulate a modest amount of legal capital only and supply other capital in the form of loans extended by the shareholders. In order to counteract this strategy, the German courts have developed a rather complicated set of rules which together serve the purpose of redefining the funds provided under a shareholder loan as legal

---

[11] BGH 5 February 1990, *ZIP* 1990 p. 451 at p. 453, *NJW* 1990 p. 1730 at p. 1731; BGH 24 March 1980, *BGHZ* 76, 326, 335; M. Fischer, 'Die Verlagerung des Gläubigerschutzes vom Gesellschafts- in das Insolvenzrecht', *ZIP* (2004) p. 1477 at p. 1479 et seq.

[12] See Schön, loc. cit. n. 9, at p. 445-447; Lutter and Hommelhoff, op. cit. n. 7, § 30(15), (26); P.O. Mülbert and M. Birke, 'Legal Capital – Is There a Case against European Legal Capital Rules?', 3 *EBOR* (2002) p. 696 at p. 720; P. Mülbert, 'Zukunft der Kapitalaufbringung/-erhaltung', *Der Konzern* (2004) p. 151 at p. 160; see also n. 9.

[13] Cf., W. Schön, 'Wer schützt den Kapitalschutz', 166 *ZHR* (2002) p. 1 at p. 5.

capital.[14] The effect is that any payment by the company on the loan is qualified as a distribution of legal capital to the shareholder. Consequently, courts have applied sections 30 and 31 GmbHG by extending their scope to shareholder loans which are being repaid while the company's legal capital has been partially dissipated.[15] The German lawmakers have tried to codify the case law which had developed over time into sections 32a and 32b GmbHG and sections 39(1)(5) and 135 InsO. In doing so, they did not go so far as to equate a shareholder loan with legal capital, but opted in favour of a solution within the context of insolvency law. Under section 32a(1) GmbHG and section 39(1)(5) InsO, in the case of bankruptcy of the firm, the claim of the shareholder for repayment of his loan is subordinated. Where the loan has been repaid by the company on the verge of bankruptcy, i.e., within one year before the filing of the petition, the trustee may avoid the transfer and force the shareholder to return whatever he received, in accordance with section 135 InsO. However, as section 135 InsO requires the company's insolvency and is limited by the one-year period, courts have been very reluctant to apply this provision and have continued to use sections 30 and 31 GmbHG instead.[16] Thus, it is once again corporate law that is said to be of more importance, as it makes it possible to hold shareholders liable even beyond the one-year period of section 135 InsO and regardless of the initiation of bankruptcy proceedings.[17] In sum, in the context of shareholder loans, the normative scope of corporate law is being extended, thereby once again downgrading the role of fraudulent transfer law and section 135 InsO in particular.

The crucial prerequisite which triggers these consequences is that the loan has been extended in a time of 'crisis', a term so vague that it is hard to pin down. It is here that German law takes resort to a very flexible and comprehensive test which comes pretty close to the fair value test governing in American law. To begin with, the balance sheet of a company is as irrelevant as the German accounting rules. It is not necessary for the purpose of assuming the existence of a crisis that the balance of the relevant year is negative. Rather, the question to ask is whether a prudent, reasonable shareholder would have provided fresh capital instead of extending a loan. In order to establish what a reasonable shareholder would have done, the critical test is the one of a reasonable outside lender. If the

---

[14] See, e.g., BGH 14 December 1959, *BGHZ* 31, 258, 269 et seq.; BGH 24 March 1980, *BGHZ* 76, 328 et seq.

[15] See BGH 26 March 1984, *BGHZ* 90, 378, 381, *NJW* 1984 p. 1891; K. Schmidt, 'Vom Eigenkapitalersatz in der Krise zur Krise des Eigenkapitalersatzrechts?', *GmbH-Rundschau* (2005) p. 797 at pp. 801-802; K. Schmidt, *Gesellschaftsrecht*, 4th edn. (Cologne, Carl Heymanns Verlag 2002) § 37(IV)(5), p. 1166 et seq.; V. Röhricht, 'Insolvenzrechtliche Aspekte im Gesellschaftsrecht', *ZIP* (2005) p. 505 at p. 512.

[16] E.g., BGH 26 March 1984, *BGHZ* 90.

[17] Schmidt, loc. cit. n. 15; ibid., op. cit. n. 15.

company would have been able to receive funds from an outside lender at market prices, the loan of the shareholder is treated like an ordinary debt.[18] However, where it seems that a reasonable outside lender would not have been prepared to extend the same loan, it is treated like legal capital.

4. EVALUATION OF THE GERMAN MODEL

The German model of protecting the interest of creditors by preserving a pool of assets sufficient to cover their claims has advantages and disadvantages.

The *advantages* are:

- German corporate law imposes rather strict rules on the maintenance of legal capital. Although they may be easily circumvented by opportunistic shareholders, the courts have gone to great lengths in order to foreclose such loopholes.
- The German capital maintenance rules are tied to the balance sheet of the company. Because German accounting rules require a conservative evaluation of the company's assets and generally follow a precautionary principle, they provide for even more creditor protection than a naked rule of legal capital maintenance would be able to provide.
- In making the balance sheet test the decisive factor for identifying fraudulent conveyances, they provide a high degree of certainty for managers.

Of course, there are also *disadvantages* to the German model:

- One obvious disadvantage is the complexity of the scheme. The foregoing analysis has supplied only the most basic outline of the relevant institutions. In reality, there are many open questions and, consequently, there is a large amount of litigation in the courts.
- The balance sheet test relevant to identifying an illegal distribution of assets to shareholders, in conjunction with conservative accounting standards, leads to overprotection of creditors.[19] The capital maintenance rules incriminate distributions even in cases where the market value of the firm remains positive.

---

[18] See, e.g., BGH 24 March 1980, *BGHZ* 76, 329 et seq., *NJW* 1980 p. 1524; BGH 28 September 1981, *BGHZ* 81, 365, 367, *NJW* 1982 p. 386.

[19] H. Merkt, 'Der Kapitalschutz in Europa – ein rocher de bronze?', *ZGR* (2004) p. 305 at p. 311 et seq.; Mülbert, loc. cit. n. 12, p. 151 at p. 160; Mülbert and Birke, loc. cit. n. 12, at p. 720 et seq.

- On the other hand, there might also be areas where creditors are underprotected for the very reason that German law tries to guarantee their protection within the context of corporate law. The general categories of fraudulent transfer law are comparatively weak and underdeveloped because they require subjective elements, on the part of both the managers and the shareholders, in order to make a transaction voidable. This may lead to underprotection in cases where the rather formal rules on maintenance of legal capital are unable to reach certain transactions which undermine the operation of the company without showing a major effect on the balance sheet.[20] Such effects are conceivable precisely because, within the context of the capital maintenance rules, rather formal accounting standards apply. These may be blind to the true economic effects of a withdrawal of crucial assets.[21]

In general, fraudulent conveyance law is much wider in scope than capital maintenance rules in corporate law and potentially covers every single business transaction that has a detrimental effect on the group of creditors. Thus, fraudulent conveyance law is more flexible and, in addition, much better able to make third parties which are not wearing the hat of a shareholder liable.

5. Key features of the German model

In comparison to American law, it seems that German law does not draw clear distinctions between different concerns within a comprehensive legal scheme for entities with limited liability.[22]

One function of such a legal framework is the *enabling function*. Limited liability is efficient because it allows investors to limit the risks associated with every single investment. In doing so, it allows them to behave in a risk-neutral way, which is in the common interest. However, the joint pursuit of business interests poses a lot of problems of collective action and of opportunistic or exploitative behaviour by other shareholders and managers which the law must address.

---

[20] V. Röhricht, 'Die GmbH im Spannungsfeld zwischen wirtschaftlicher Dispositionsfreiheit ihrer Gesellschafter und Gläubigerschutz', in K. Geiß, K. Nehm, H.E. Brandner and H. Hagen, *Festschrift 50 Jahre BGH* (Cologne, Heymanns 2000) p. 83 et seq.; W. Nassall, 'Der existenzvernichtende Eingriff in die GmbH: Einwendungen aus verfassungs- und insolvenzrechtlicher Sicht', *ZIP* (2003) p. 969 at. 972 et seq.

[21] Mülbert and Birke, loc. cit. n. 12, at p. 720; Röhricht, loc. cit. n. 15, at p. 514.

[22] Merkt, loc. cit. n. 19, at p. 311 et seq., 316.

The *protective function* aims at avoiding the externalisation of risk to the detriment of outside creditors. One important element of this function is to prohibit the distribution of such assets of the limited liability company which are necessary to cover the claims of outside creditors.

A third function is the *information function*, i.e., to provide accurate information for potential investors as to the true expectation value of the firm.

The German system of creditor protection is based on a rather complicated mixture of these functions. In particular, the concept of legal capital is primarily oriented towards creditor protection, but it is also concerned with the protection of (minority) shareholders as it determines the internal financial structure of the company with respect to shareholders' voting rights and their entitlements to distributions.[23] As set out above, rules constraining fraudulent transfers are to be found in both corporate and bankruptcy law. Furthermore, tort law and quasi veil piercing have recently been recognised as judicial responses to the abuse of limited liability and the misappropriation of a company's assets.[24]

6. CHALLENGES TO THE GERMAN MODEL

In contrast to the German system, American law tends to separate the three functions. American corporate law deals with the enabling function, the informational function is taken care of by accounting standards and capital markets regimes whereas creditor protection is the responsibility of contract, bankruptcy and tort law. European law may well develop in the same direction now that the ECJ tore down the walls which used to keep foreign companies out.[25]

---

23 Schön, loc. cit. n. 9, at p. 447; ibid., 'Gesellschafter-, Gläubiger- und Anlegerschutz im Europäischen Bilanzrecht', *ZGR* (2000) p. 706 at p. 709 et seq.; ibid., 'Playing Different Games? Regulatory Competition in Tax and Company Law Compared', 6 *EBOR* (2005) p. 331 at p. 353; cf., J. Hennrichs, 'Bilanzgestützte Kapitalerhaltung, HGB-Jahresabschluß und Maßgeblichkeitsprinzip – Dinosaurier der Rechtsgeschichte?', *Steuer und Wirtschaft* (2005) p. 256 at p. 257.

24 BGH 17 September 2001, *BGHZ* 149, 10, 16, *ZIP* 2001 p. 1874; BGH 25 February 2002, *BGHZ* 150, 61, 67 et seq., *ZIP* 2002 p. 848; BGH 24 June 2002, *BGHZ* 151, 181, 186 et seq., *ZIP* 2002 p. 1578; BGH 13 December 2004, *ZIP* 2005 p. 117; BGH 13 December 2005, *ZIP* 2005 p. 250 (developing a quasi veil-piercing concept for so-called *existenzvernichtende Eingriffe*). BGH 20 September 2004, *NJW* 2005 p. 145 (applying s. 826 BGB (tort law)).

25 Merkt, loc. cit. n. 19, at p. 306 et seq.; M. Kahan, 'Legal Capital Rules and the Structure of Corporate Law', in K.J. Hopt and E. Wymeersch, eds., *Capital Markets and Company Law* (Oxford, Oxford University Press 2003) p. 145 at p. 147; F. Kübler, 'The Rules of Capital under Pressure of the Securities Markets', in Hopt and Wymeersch, ibid., p. 95 at p. 111 et seq.; cf., Schön (2005), loc. cit. n. 23, at pp. 353-355.

Company law is designed with a primary focus on the enabling function, i.e., to allow for efficient investment in risky projects. In order to facilitate such investments, it is necessary to balance the interests of different groups of shareholders and provide for an efficient principle-agent relationship between shareholders and management. In this regard, both American law and the recent case law of the ECJ allow for choice of law, as the place of incorporation denominates the applicable corporate law.[26]

In order to provide for the necessary level of creditor protection, choice of law is obviously not an option. On the contrary, the protection of outsiders who are not parties to the corporate contract has to be guaranteed by legal regimes which are mandatory and not of a default nature. This is true for both insolvency law and – as a practical matter – tort law. Under traditional principles of conflicts of law in the area of torts, the place of injury controls. Insolvency law, for its part, reaches the same result by the principle of *lex fori concursus*. Under Article 3(1) of Council Regulation (EC) No. 1346/2000 on insolvency proceedings, the principle place of business of the debtor designates the competent bankruptcy court as well as the applicable insolvency law. The bankruptcy code in force in the debtor's main place of business also governs issues associated with fraudulent conveyance law under Articles 4(2)(m) and 13 of the Regulation. Even though determining the so-called centre of main interests (COMI) may prove difficult from time to time,[27] in most cases companies incorporated under foreign law will not be able to avoid the insolvency regime of the country in which they conduct the better part of their business and in which most of their creditors are located.

In short, the approach prevalent in the United States and increasingly followed in Europe seems to aim at a clear separation of the different functions of the limited liability regime. Whereas the enabling function of the law of limited liability is left to regulatory competition and the choice of the parties, the protective function is treated differently. Here, choice of law is not an option, as tort law and bankruptcy law impose themselves on the shareholders. Wherever the principle place of business is located, the shareholders are obliged to play by the rules of this particular jurisdiction to the extent that they aim at protecting the creditors either through tort law or by means of insolvency law. The exclusion of party autonomy from these areas is sound policy. The choice of the creditor protection regime by the parties of the corporate contract would amount to

---

[26] ECJ, Case C-167/01 *Inspire Art* [2003] *ECR* I-10155; ECJ, Case C-208/00 *Überseering* [2002] *ECR* I-9919; ECJ, Case C-212/97 *Centros* [1999] *ECR* I-1459.

[27] See B.M. Kübler, 'Der Mittelpunkt der hauptsächlichen Interessen nach Art. 3 Abs. 1 EuInsVO', in E. Schilken, G. Kreft, G. Wagner and D. Eckardt, eds., *Festschrift für Walter Gerhardt* (Cologne, RWS Verlag 2004) p. 527 at p. 541 et seq.; H. Eidenmüller, 'Free Choice in International Company Insolvency Law in Europe', 6 *EBOR* (2005) p. 423 at p. 430 et seq.

nothing less than a contract to the detriment of third parties, i.e., involuntary creditors of the firm.

The differentiation of the three functions poses a huge problem for the German system of corporate law and creditor protection. To the extent that rules on creditor protection form part and parcel of German corporate law, as is the case with the capital maintenance rules, they seem to become the subject of the choice of law made by the parties. Thus, one might argue that sections 30-32b GmbHG may easily be circumvented by incorporating the limited liability company not in Germany but in England or in one of the states of the United States. To the extent that a company with a principal place of business in Germany is incorporated in England or the United States, the corporate law provisions on capital maintenance may be avoided as they have no counterpart in American or English corporate law. On the other hand, the functional equivalents of the capital maintenance rules, i.e., a broad and effective fraudulent conveyance law, are not applicable to companies whose principal place of business is in Germany. Thus, it seems that the different approaches followed by the different systems in Europe and the world allow shareholders to avoid the system of strings attached in every single jurisdiction. Shareholders may have it both ways, i.e., they may escape the strict rules on capital maintenance enshrined in German corporate law without buying into the strict principles on fraudulent conveyances which are known in American law.

7. REMEDIES

How can German law deal with this predicament?

One solution would be the attempt to apply the principles of capital maintenance contained in German corporate law to companies incorporated under the laws of another jurisdiction which does not follow the German approach. Although the question is very controversial in the German literature,[28] it seems fair to predict that the ECJ will not be prepared to accept such an *ultra vires* application of German corporate law.[29] There cannot be any doubt that the provisions of sections 30 and 31 GmbHG were developed with specific regard to the internal organisation and financial structure of the German GmbH. Thus, they

---

[28] Cf., Fischer, loc. cit. n. 11, at p. 1480; U. Huber, 'Gesellschafterdarlehen in der Insolvenz der Auslandsgesellschaft', in M. Lutter, ed., *Europäische Auslandsgesellschaften in Deutschland* (Cologne, Otto Schmidt Verlag 2005) p. 131 at p. 144 et seq.; P. Ulmer, 'Gläubigerschutz bei Scheinauslandsgesellschaften', *NJW* (2004) p. 1201 at pp. 1207, 1209; H. Altmeppen, 'Schutz vor 'europäischen' Kapitalgesellschaften', *NJW* (2004) p. 97 at p. 102 et seq.

[29] See Fischer, loc. cit. n. 11, at p. 1480; but also Ulmer, loc. cit. n. 28, at p. 1209; Altmeppen, loc. cit. n. 28.

cannot easily be transferred to other types of legal entities in an attempt to close the gap within the system of creditor protection created by the ECJ. Furthermore, this option would cause a large number of practical problems. As capital maintenance rules are linked to the concept of legal capital, it is still an open question how and to what extent these rules could be implemented when dealing with a company that has a legal capital of €0 or whose entire financial structure is not at all familiar with this concept.[30]

The alternative would be to abandon the traditional approach and disentangle the functions of corporate law and of insolvency law. To this end, as far as creditor protection is concerned, the rules on capital maintenance would have to be given up in favour of a broad fraudulent conveyance law. This appears to be a quite radical approach. A complete abolition of capital maintenance rules would probably necessitate a complete revision of traditional positions, not only in the field of company law but in other areas such as accounting and tax law as well.[31] Under the given circumstances, however, a re-evaluation of the scope of fraudulent transfer law could well serve as a first, promising step towards an effective system of creditor protection.

The law of fraudulent conveyances would have to be reworked in order to extend its scope and make it a more efficient tool to counteract looting strategies of shareholders.[32] It has already been noted that fraudulent transfer law, in general, and the general clause of section 133(1) InsO, in particular, appear to be something like a sleeping giant. The poison that caused and maintained the long nap is easy to identify: it is the dominance of corporate law instruments which are designed to take the function of creditor protection onto themselves. In the German literature, it has been suggested that the Insolvency Act's provisions on fraudulent transfers need a revision in the form of a rather drastic expansion.[33] Whatever one may think of this, the first step would have to be a new approach towards section 133(1) InsO. If the German courts were willing to use this provision as a tool to provide the necessary degree of creditor protection, a reform might well prove to be unnecessary. In particular, the mandatory character of fraudulent conveyance law and its application under the principle of *lex fori concursus* would mitigate the negative effects that the free choice of company law might exert on creditors. In sum, what is needed is a shift of the protective

---

30 Cf., Schön, loc. cit. n. 9, at p. 444.

31 Cf., Schön (2005), loc. cit. n. 23, at p. 355.

32 Fischer, loc. cit. n. 11, at p. 1483; Röhricht, loc. cit. n. 15, at p. 514 et seq.; for a general perspective, cf. Swanson and Mason, 'Long Tail Risks and Endogenous Liabilities: Regulating Looting', 87 *The Geneva Papers on Risk and Insurance* (1998) p. 182 et seq.

33 Fischer, loc. cit. n. 11, at p. 1483; U. Wackerbarth, 'Existenzvernichtungshaftung 2005: Unternehmerische Entscheidungen auf dem Prüfstand?', *ZIP* (2005) p. 877 at p. 884; cf., W. Nassall, loc. cit. n. 20, at p. 975.

function of limited liability regimes away from corporate law and towards insolvency law. It is not too difficult to bring this change about as insolvency law already has the pertinent means as its disposal.

Such a new approach towards section 133(1) InsO would have to reinterpret key elements of this provision. Chances for a revitalisation of section 133(1) InsO are not bad, given that the time frame for avoidance of such transactions is no less than ten years, which is rather too long than too short.[34] The first step would be to mitigate the subjective elements of 'intention' and 'knowledge' in favour of objective 'badges' of fraud. This would not cause major problems. After all, both the managers and shareholders of the firm are insiders of whom it may be presumed that they know the true state of affairs. In addition, even under the current practice, it is settled law that intention may more easily be assumed where the objective features of the transaction are such as to cast its honesty into doubt.[35] The second step would have to be a special understanding of the fraudulent effect the transaction must have in order to be voidable. Again, the strategy to follow would have to involve a distinction between transactions to the benefit of third parties and others which are to the benefit of shareholders. As several provisions of the German law of fraudulent transfers already draw distinctions between related persons ('insiders') as defined in section 138 InsO and other recipients of (fraudulent) transfers, this strategy does not even require major conceptual changes.[36] Where the transferee in a substantive sense is a shareholder, fraud should be assumed automatically wherever assets earmarked for the creditors of the company are distributed to its shareholders.

---

34 Nassall, loc. cit n. 20.
35 Hirte, loc. cit. n. 6, § 133(15) et seq.
36 See ss. 131(2)(2) and 133(2) InsO.

Discussion Report

Christian Kersting*

The first round of discussion focused on the presentation by Rickford and Schön's commentary on it. It concentrated on the question of how to determine distributable profits and whether to apply a balance sheet test, a solvency test or a combination of both.

Rickford agreed with Schön's submission that, in order to determine the possibility of distributions, a balance sheet test alone did not constitute an efficient solution. He insisted, however, that a behavioural test should replace the balance sheet test and not supplement it. Rickford underscored this by referring to British Airways as an example. He explained that British Airways had no distributable profits under a balance sheet test due to a deficit in its defined benefit pension scheme. In contrast, Lufthansa and other competitors, while having similar or probably heavier future obligations to fund such payments over time could expect to do so through defined contributions or payroll taxes, which as future liabilities would not appear on the balance sheet. These inconsistencies were problematic and warranted the move towards a solvency test which would enable British Airways and its competitors to distribute profits only so long as the directors could be assured of being able to fund these obligations over time.

In response to this, Schön pointed out that the different situations of Lufthansa and British Airways regarding distributable profits were not simply due to a technical decision of how to determine distributable profits but to a substantially different legal and financial position, rightly reflected in the different possibilities of paying out dividends. Whereas Lufthansa under its defined contribution scheme had no accrued future obligation to pay out pensions itself, because it had already fulfilled its obligation by contributing to the national social security system which would pay out the pensions in the future, British Airways actually had an accrued liability to be met in a winding up. He continued that, evidently, the financial situation of a company that had already made all necessary payments regarding its past operations was different from the financial situation of a company that still had to meet its accrued liabilities in the future. Another participant added from a US perspective that it was difficult to account for pension liabilities and that under US law companies were granted a 'put-option' so that they could transfer their pension liabilities to the government. Regarding

---

* Dr. Christian Kersting, LL.M. (Yale), Research Fellow, Max Planck Institute for Intellectual Property, Competition and Tax Law.

this point, somebody else clarified that the company exercising that 'option' has to compensate the government for assuming the company's obligations. From an accounting point of view, the company therefore only substitutes one obligation for another if it exercises the 'put-option'.

A US participant supported the solvency test suggested by Rickford and considered it to be so well drafted that he would welcome its introduction in the United States. Another US participant added that under US law there were different kinds of solvency tests, some of them equivalent to the balance sheet test, which was also used by creditors in bond contracts. That participant also pointed out that neither the balance sheet test nor the solvency test could be considered too lenient or too strict, and that it all depended on the exact definition of the test. He then expressed the opinion that Schön's two-pronged test also made sense, but that once again the question of definition was crucial. Schön replied that any test had to be easy and straightforward enough to be applied not only by big corporations but also by small family-run companies. Rickford pointed out that the issue was not whether there should be provisions for the security of creditors but whether it was possible to define a solvency standard that set the proper level of precaution.

Another participant also supported Schön's suggestion of a double-pronged test that combines a balance sheet test with a solvency test and suggested that the solvency declaration should be audited despite the high costs. Schön, however, thought an audit to be superfluous in the case of a double-pronged test, and Rickford agreed that an audit did not make much sense because the issues concerned forward-looking business judgements, for which auditors were not qualified, and noted that exposing the auditors to the non-negligible risk of liability would lead to a significant increase in auditing costs. In response to this, it was pointed out that both the Prospectus Directive and the London City Code mandated an audit for such forward-looking statements. But it was also pointed out that the auditing of forward-looking statements like profit forecasts was very limited in scope, because it referred only to the underlying assumptions on which the forecast was based. This showed that the prospectus and takeover examples did not support the contention that auditors could adequately substitute their own judgements for directors' forward-looking commercial judgements.

Rickford pointed out that where countries applied a double-pronged test there was no absolute constraint by reference to the statutory accounts, leaving directors to apply their own appraisal of the financial information contained in them. He also referred to an indirect connection between the proposed solvency test and the balance sheet test by explaining that the solvency test incorporated the balance sheet test to some extent, because a director would need to have very strong arguments in order to justify a distribution under the solvency test that failed the balance sheet test. He concluded that it was nevertheless important to avoid the straightjacket of the strict balance sheet test.

From a German perspective, the question was raised how a solvency test would deal with disguised distributions that inevitably occur not only in groups, due to transfer pricing, but also in small companies, where it is not necessary to have open distributions at all, as controlling shareholders can simply pay themselves a salary. In response to this, Rickford explained that there was a body of law on transfer pricing in the United Kingdom as well. He nevertheless left aside the question whether a solvency declaration would have to be made in these cases. With regard to the payment of salaries, he replied that not every salary payment could be considered a disguised distribution. He nevertheless agreed that the question raised a problem which was not discussed in the United Kingdom and suggested that there was liability if a company became insolvent as a result of disguised distributions. Schön sided with Rickford and argued that excessive remuneration could be acceptable if everybody agreed and as long as the balance sheet test was complied with; another participant expressed the opinion that under British law it would take an extreme case for payments to be considered disguised distributions. In this context, it was also mentioned that many rules in the Second Company Law Directive were disguised rules of conduct, aimed at holding the persons making the distributions responsible.

At a different point in the discussion, Rickford pointed out that there was a school of thought according to which distribution rules were not needed at all since the rules on wrongful trading and insolvency were sufficient to protect creditors. He explained that the main criticism encountered by the solvency test proposed by the Rickford group was that it was too strict and would have a chilling effect on distributions, as directors might hesitate to sign the declaration of solvency. Schön added that there seemed to be a cultural difference between the United Kingdom and Germany. Whereas the IAS were perceived as an example of utmost lenience in Germany, they were considered to be too strict in Britain. This difference could also be shown by comparing the tendency to include provisions in the accounts. Whereas in Germany provisions accounted for 18 per cent of the balance sheet sum, they only accounted for 2 per cent in the United Kingdom. Rickford stressed that it was important under any system that future unaccrued charges, such as decommissioning charges for nuclear power stations, should be taken into account in the context of the prospective funding capacity of the company.

Finally, the question of methodology was raised. It was submitted that, since there was no generally accepted method of drafting solvency declarations, it was necessary to develop such a method. Whereas Rickford took this point and recognised the need for such a methodology, another participant pointed to the vast literature on the assessment of enterprises. He argued that the drafting of solvency declarations was possible nowadays, because one could rely on the decade-long experience of auditors calculating the net present value of enterprises. The participant conceded that these methods were controversial but insisted that they were nevertheless already used in the legal context.

The second round of discussion concentrated on Baird's presentation and Wagner's commentary. The main topic of discussion was the question of how to properly delineate the scope of the law on fraudulent conveyances and company law rules that serve the aim of creditor protection.

Following Baird's description of US law, one participant raised the question whether it made sense to apply the fraudulent conveyance law of the jurisdiction where the transaction took place and what would happen if it was also subject to regulatory competition. Baird reiterated that under US law the question of fraudulent conveyances was completely detached from State corporate laws. He thought that even if there was regulatory competition, debtors would have to make sure that they opted for a jurisdiction that offered at least some degree of protection to creditors.

A major part of the discussion then centred on the issue of conflicts law. Several participants based their comments on the fact that company law rules and fraudulent conveyance rules did not always complement each other in a meaningful way, company law rules being subject to regulatory competition as a result of ECJ judgments and the applicability of the place of incorporation doctrine, whereas the applicable rules on fraudulent conveyances depended – according to Articles 3 and 4 of the European Insolvency Regulation – on the centre of the companies' main interests. This could lead to a regulatory gap when companies from a legal system which bases creditor protection mainly on insolvency law move their centre of main interests to a system which in turn bases creditor protection chiefly on company law. From a US perspective, Baird agreed that it was difficult to promote creditor protection by dividing the relevant rules between company law and insolvency law.

Against this background, it was argued that the conflicts of law aspect should be taken into consideration when deciding on the field of law in which new rules should be introduced, the aim being to ensure that the new rules would actually be applicable to all – national and foreign – companies given the rulings of the ECJ on the freedom of establishment. Another participant held the view that, in order to ensure creditor protection, it was not enough to relabel provisions of company law as provisions of insolvency law so that they could be applied to foreign companies under the conflicts regime of the European Insolvency Directive. He argued that the ECJ would not accept simple relabelling and considered a functional approach that only looks at the function a provision performs and not at the legal text in which it is found. Wagner replied that in his commentary he did not argue in favour of a simple relabelling but that he was merely reporting an ongoing discussion. He pointed out that corporate lawyers used to be proud to designate many rules of creditor protection as corporate law, which now makes it difficult to convince the ECJ that they are in fact provisions of insolvency law that can be applied to both national and foreign companies. He then went on to emphasise the practical difficulties in applying provisions of the German law on limited liability companies (GmbHG) outside this system. This would require recourse to very abstract principles.

Another contributor to the discussion also spoke out in favour of a functional approach. However, he did not see a real gap between the applicable company law and the applicable insolvency law differing from it, as UK courts tended to find the centre of main interest in the United Kingdom despite there being in fact very little contact with the United Kingdom. This would lead to UK companies operating abroad being subject not only to UK company law but also to UK insolvency law, so that a regulatory gap could very often be avoided. He also submitted that German courts were ready to apply British insolvency law to British companies operating in Germany, even though the relevant legal rules were – as another participant noted – not used in Britain. Wagner replied that the current system seemed to be a haphazard way of combining different systems, yielding the correct result only by chance. With a view to UK practice, he added that creditor protection should be an important issue for the courts when determining the main centre of interest under the European Insolvency Regulation.

Another participant agreed with Wagner that fraudulent conveyance law can be seen as a sleeping giant. However, he saw no way of waking up the giant, because there was a *de facto* choice of insolvency law as well as a *de jure* choice of company law, since the centre of main interest was highly manipulable. He also explained that, under the European Insolvency Regulation, for a transaction to be voidable it had to be voidable both under the *lex fori concursus* and under the *lex causae*, which further reduced the effectiveness of insolvency rules. In this context, a participant also underlined the importance of legal certainty but reminded the audience that the relevant German company law rules were highly complex and therefore also lacked legal certainty. As far as creditor protection was concerned, Wagner saw no room for leaving any choice of law to the debtors, since it was them against whom the creditors needed to be protected. He therefore considered the European Insolvency Regulation to be seriously flawed, as it should be the principle place of business that determines the applicable law.

The discussion then moved on to the question whether a solution could be found by disentangling or unbundling the different functions of company law, especially by separating rules designed for creditor protection from their company law context. The suggestion was made to move a minimum capital maintenance rule from company law to insolvency law and to set it at €0. Another threshold could then be set above that, for example at €20,000, and enforced via company law. Against this suggestion the objection was raised that unbundling was already possible to some extent, since a pseudo-foreign company in Germany could be subjected to German secondary insolvency proceedings. Apart from that, it was submitted that under EU law only non-adjusting (e.g., involuntary) creditors could be protected, whereas the protection of adjusting (e.g., voluntary) creditors would be a disproportionate restriction on the freedom of establishment. Wagner disagreed with the latter argument and viewed the application of national insolvency rules to foreign companies as legitimate and non-discriminatory. In his view, a fraudulent conveyance was nothing else than a tort in the face of the creditors, which – under general principles of conflicts law – is governed by the law of the place of injury. He added the concern that even the combination of a company law designated by the seat of incorporation plus an insolvency law designated by the principal place of business might result in too little creditor protection because of a possible mismatch between the two systems of company law and insolvency law. Another participant thought that a balance between company law and insolvency law would emerge over time, since the evidence seemed to be that the cost of capital remains the same. Finally, it was submitted that unbundling was not entirely without difficulties, since German law does not allow for covenants binding the directors of the company in their business judgement, so that the possibilities of leaving creditor protection to contractual arrangements were reduced.

Part III

The Role of Insolvency Law

Trading in Times of Crisis: Formal Insolvency Proceedings, Workouts and the Incentives for Shareholders/Managers*

Horst Eidenmüller**

Abstract
Conventional economic reasoning suggests that formal insolvency proceedings should commence once the greater of the going concern value or the liquidation value of a firm falls below the value of its liabilities. Since this test is difficult to apply in practice, an additional cash flow test is needed: formal insolvency proceedings should commence if a firm is not able to pay its due debts. Two factors complicate this analysis: risk-shifting incentives of shareholders/managers in the vicinity of insolvency and the (rapid) decline of a firm's going concern value once it approaches insolvency. The former problem should be

---

* This paper originated as a comment on a main paper by another conference participant on the same subject. Since this paper was ultimately not submitted, I developed my thoughts into the present paper. Hence, there is no comment on this paper in this volume.

** Prof. Dr Horst Eidenmüller, LL.M. (Cantab.) holds the chair of Private Law, German, European and International Company Law at the University of Munich. E-mail: horst.eidenmueller@jura.uni-muenchen.de. Author's homepage: <http://www.horst-eidenmueller.de>.

addressed by a liability rule for wrongful trading. Based on a review of the current legal position in the United States, the United Kingdom and Germany, a uniform European rule is proposed that imposes liability on managers of insolvent companies for trading while they knew or should have known that insolvency was more probable than not, unless they can show that they took all reasonable steps to avoid insolvency. The decline of a firm's going concern value once it approaches insolvency provides all stakeholders with an incentive to try a workout to save as much of the going concern value as possible. However, workouts often fail in practice due to free-rider effects. Cooperation duties are proposed as a means to support workouts. Such duties should be triggered once a workout is initiated. It is suggested that bankruptcy rules, in general, and rules on the initiation of bankruptcy proceedings, in particular, should in principle be enabling rather than mandatory.

Keywords: company insolvency, trigger mechanisms, liquidation, reorganisation, formal insolvency proceedings, out-of-court restructuring, workout, cooperation duties, wrongful trading, manager liability, mandatory v. enabling nature of bankruptcy law, free choice of bankruptcy rules.

1. INTRODUCTION

The insolvency of a company is the ultimate time of reckoning for its creditors. The company's cash flow has deteriorated to an extent that not all creditors can be paid in full. If that happens, it is said that a detrimental race for the remaining assets begins.[1] The race is portrayed as being detrimental to the creditors as a group because it lowers the net value that can be distributed to it.[2] To give just a few examples: collection efforts by a large number of creditors trigger significant enforcement costs and collateral might be seized that is necessary for the continued operation of the firm. Hence, it appears that efficient creditor protection requires a collective mechanism for settling the outstanding claims.

However, setting the precise trigger for such a mechanism proves to be difficult. Backward induction by creditors might lead them to race to the assets even before the company is insolvent on a cash flow or a balance sheet basis. Moreover, it is well known that shareholders and managers have an incentive to engage in overly risky activities and even pursue projects with a negative net present value in the vicinity of insolvency. Does this mean that formal insolvency

---

[1] See T.H. Jackson, *The Logic and Limits of Bankruptcy Law* (Cambridge, Mass., Harvard University Press 1986) p. 7 et seq., especially pp. 10-13.

[2] Ibid.

proceedings should be triggered even before the company is insolvent? On the other hand, it is also well known that the going concern value of a company declines once it approaches insolvency. If formal insolvency proceedings are opened, that value declines sharply due to the negative signal communicated by this (indirect bankruptcy costs). Does this mean that instead of formal insolvency proceedings some form of out-of-court proceedings (workouts) should be initiated before the company becomes insolvent? What degree of formality should these proceedings display? Should creditors be required to participate and, if so, why?

The following paper addresses these issues. It starts in section 2 by reviewing the conventional approach towards the triggering of formal insolvency proceedings. That approach is complicated by two factors: the risk-shifting incentives of shareholders/managers in the vicinity of insolvency and the desirability of out-of-court restructurings (workouts). Section 3 then discusses how existing trigger mechanisms for formal insolvency proceedings in various jurisdictions (the United States, the United Kingdom and Germany) and liability rules in these jurisdictions contribute to containing the risk-shifting incentives of shareholders/managers. A uniform European liability rule is proposed, according to which managers of an insolvent company would be liable for trading while they knew or should have known that insolvency was more probable than not, unless they took all reasonable steps to avoid insolvency. Such a liability rule would improve the current regime for wrongful trading as embodied in section 214 of the UK Insolvency Act 1986. Triggering out-of-court restructurings and the free-rider problem associated with workouts are discussed in section 4. The latter problem could be solved by cooperation duties that would arise once workout negotiations commence. Such duties would fit in nicely with the liability rule for wrongful trading proposed in section 3. Section 5 then suggests that any trigger mechanism should in principle be enabling rather than mandatory, i.e., firms should be able to select bankruptcy rules in their charter. The main findings are summarised in section 6.

2. TRIGGER MECHANISMS – A CONCEPTUAL FRAMEWORK

Conventional economic reasoning suggests that a firm should be kept alive as a going concern as long as its going concern value (V_{gc}) is higher than its liquidation value (V_l) and that it should be liquidated if the converse holds true ($V_l > V_{gc}$).[3] Formal insolvency proceedings should be triggered if the greater of

---

[3] A going concern surplus will exist especially if and to the extent that a firm is built upon fixed and highly specialised (dedicated) assets with a low second-best value. Some believe that many 'modern' firms are not of such type. Hence, it is suggested that a going concern surplus

these two values ($V = {}_{max}(V_{gc}, V_l)$) falls below the value of the total liabilities of the firm (L), i.e., if $V < L$.[4] If that happens, the firm's assets – if put to their best use – are insufficient to satisfy all creditor claims. The creditors face a prisoners' dilemma situation (common pool problem). Incentives exist for economically inefficient efforts to seize the remaining assets. Premature liquidations might result. Note that financial failure of a firm ($V < L$) does not imply that the firm is also economically unviable ($V_{gc} < V_l$). Note also that financial distress will – *ceteris paribus* – occur earlier if the leverage of a particular firm increases.[5]

Any trigger for formal insolvency proceedings should be easily ascertainable. Otherwise, the relevant stakeholders (creditors, managers and shareholders) will not be able to adjust their behaviour, and courts would have no precise standard that could be adjudicated.[6] Here lies a difficulty with any balance sheet test. Ascertaining the value of assets and liabilities of a company depends on the applicable accounting rules, and these normally leave some margin of discretion. Moreover, the more accurately assets and liabilities are assessed in economic terms, the greater these measurement problems become. To illustrate, an accurate measure of V_{gc} would be a discounted cash flow analysis, an accurate measure of L the net present value of a firm's liabilities. Projecting future cash flows is fraught with uncertainties, as is the identification of an appropriate discount rate.

Hence, some other test that is more easily applied than a balance sheet test is needed as a trigger for formal insolvency proceedings. This other test is provided by an analysis of the firm's actual (present) cash flows. Triggering formal insolvency proceedings seems to be justified if a firm is not able to pay its due debts (company illiquidity). Note that this point in time is usually reached only after a firm is insolvent on the basis of a balance sheet test. Given information asymmetries and imperfect capital markets, even balance sheet insolvent firms are at times able to obtain credit. To be sure, such imperfections may also lead to a credit shortage for firms that are 'healthy' on an accounting basis. However, practical experience suggests that the former case is much more likely.

There are two complications that affect the conceptual framework just presented and therefore might necessitate a refinement of that framework. The first complication relates to the incentives of creditors and shareholders/managers in the vicinity of insolvency. If the performance of a particular firm declines, creditors anticipate that at some point in time (t) the firm's assets might be insufficient to satisfy all claims. Anticipating this, they have an incentive to

---

often does not exist or at least is lower than anticipated. See D.G. Baird and R.K. Rasmussen, 'The End of Bankruptcy', 55 *Stanford Law Review* (2002) p. 751 et seq.

4 See, e.g., J. Drukarczyk, *Unternehmen und Insolvenz: Zur effizienten Gestaltung des Kreditsicherungs- und Insolvenzrechts* (Wiesbaden, Gabler 1987) pp. 72-74.

5 Cf., M.H. Miller, 'Leverage', 4 *Journal of Applied Corporate Finance* (1991) p. 6 et seq.

6 See Drukarczyk, op. cit. n. 4, at p. 72.

collect on their claims before that point in time is reached (t – 1). Hence, the common pool problem might arise due to backward induction well before the firm becomes insolvent on the basis of a cash flow or balance sheet test. Furthermore, it is well known that the equity cushion of a firm and the incentives for shareholders to pursue hazardous projects with a (potentially) negative net present value are inversely related. Such incentives are maximal once equity has been wiped out economically, but they are also significant in the (immediate) vicinity of insolvency. They exist also for managers. Managers stand to loose their jobs in the event of bankruptcy and therefore have an incentive to take a gamble in order to avoid that situation. Moreover, managers will in general act in the interests of shareholders before a firm has become insolvent. Do these considerations suggest that some earlier trigger for formal insolvency proceedings is necessary? The High Level Group of Company Law Experts advising the European Commission on issues of company law reform in Europe seems inclined towards an affirmative answer: 'the general duty to file a petition for bankruptcy in the case of actual insolvency comes too late.'[7] However, it is very difficult to precisely define an earlier point in time at which a filing duty could set in. Moreover, as we shall see in a moment, there are also arguments against filing for formal proceedings too early. If therefore no filing duty before actual insolvency is proposed, at least establishing (other) effective devices to contain the risk-shifting incentives for shareholders/managers in the vicinity of insolvency seems to be a paramount necessity.

The second complication for the conceptual framework on trigger mechanisms for formal insolvency proceedings results from the fact that the going concern value (V_{gc}) of a firm tends to decline as the firm approaches insolvency. The reason for this development is straightforward: market participants tend to interpret signs of financial failure as signs of economic failure, and respond accordingly. The induced belief that the firm's economic viability is in doubt then does in fact lower the chances of the firm's future economic success. An especially strong signal of that type is associated with the opening of formal insolvency proceedings. Hence, due to high indirect bankruptcy costs, V_{gc} declines sharply once formal insolvency proceedings are opened. The company's stakeholders thus have an incentive to avoid these costs and save a greater portion of the going concern value by trying an out-of-court restructuring (workout). Formal insolvency proceedings therefore should not be triggered too early to

---

[7] High Level Group of Company Law Experts, *A Modern Regulatory Framework for Company Law in Europe* (November 2002) p. 68, available at: <http://europa.eu.int/comm/internal_market/company/modern/index_en.htm>. See also D. Baird, 'The Initiation Problem in Bankruptcy', 11 *International Review of Law and Economics* (1991) p. 223 at p. 230: 'The correct time to start bankruptcy proceedings may not be the moment before a number of creditors levy on assets, but much earlier.'

avoid an unnecessary loss of going concern value. At the same time, however, workouts often fail in practice because of free-rider effects – each creditor has an incentive to hold out and hope that the others shoulder the necessary reorganisation burdens. The question therefore arises whether some collective proceeding that reduces these free-rider effects without unduly formalising workouts would be helpful.

3. Trigger mechanisms for formal insolvency proceedings

The following section will be devoted to trigger mechanisms for formal insolvency proceedings. It will also try to answer the question how the risk-shifting incentives for shareholders/managers in the vicinity of insolvency might adequately be contained. This question can be answered with greater confidence once the principal actors with respect to triggering formal insolvency proceedings have been identified and existing trigger mechanisms in various jurisdictions have been reviewed.

3.1 Setting incentives for the principal actors

Legal rules on the triggering of formal insolvency proceedings might primarily target the shareholders/managers of a distressed firm or its creditors. Traditionally, lawmakers tend to focus on the incentives for shareholders/managers, and there is a sensible reason for this approach:[8] shareholders and managers usually enjoy an informational advantage with respect to a firm's financial and economic health, the former at least in closely held corporations. To be sure, certain creditors such as banks – especially the *'Hausbank'* – may also be well-informed in certain cases. As a general rule, however, it seems to be sound policy to single out managers and shareholders as the primary target for incentives to trigger formal insolvency proceedings.

Such incentives can either come in the form of 'sticks' or in the form of 'carrots'. Shareholders/managers can be penalised for not filing if they should (e.g., by liability for wrongful trading) or they can be rewarded if they do (e.g., by retaining an equity share in the – subsequently – reorganised firm). As a matter of principle, there is much to be said in favour of bonuses for filing as opposed to sanctions for failing to do so. Sanctions are problematic because they impose risks on shareholders/managers who are generally thought to be risk-averse (this

---

[8] On the importance of incentives for shareholders/managers, see also R.C. Picker, 'Voluntary Petitions and the Creditors' Bargain', 61 *University of Cincinnati Law Review* (1992/1993) p. 519 et seq.

general attitude is 'overcompensated' by a risk-shifting incentive in financial distress). Moreover, sanctions must be enforced, and this triggers enforcement costs. Finally, the limited wealth of shareholders/managers will at least inhibit the effectiveness of financial sanctions.[9]

Nonetheless, sanctions are probably necessary to contain the risk-shifting incentives of these actors. More specifically, rewarding shareholders with an equity share in the reorganised firm does nothing to address these incentives. On the contrary, it makes matters worse.[10] Violations of absolute priority in bankruptcy allow the beneficiaries of such violations to shift more risk to creditors: the former gain something even if the 'bad' state of the world materialises This will lead to higher interest rates which further increases the risk-shifting incentives.

Even though lawmakers traditionally quite rightly focus on shareholders/managers with respect to setting incentives for the triggering of formal insolvency proceedings, jurisdictions do of course always set such incentives for creditors, too. Depending on the relative treatment of certain creditors or creditor groups in bankruptcy, the incentives of these with respect to the filing decision differ. To give just one example, if a particular jurisdiction substantially curtailed secured creditors' rights in bankruptcy,[11] such creditors will have a strong incentive to delay the opening of formal insolvency proceedings. As these creditors tend to be better informed and are therefore better monitors than unsecured creditors, this effect appears undesirable. At the same time, however, honouring secured creditors' rights in full creates problems, too, as they do not have the best incentives to maximise the firm's value. Hence, giving full priority to secured creditors must go hand in hand with rules aimed at ensuring that decision-making power in formal insolvency proceedings is exercised in such a way that an insolvent company's assets are optimally deployed.

3.2 Existing mechanisms

If one looks at existing trigger mechanisms for formal insolvency proceedings in various jurisdictions (United States, United Kingdom and Germany), one finds striking differences as well as certain similarities. As we shall see, one similarity lies in the absence of effective devices to contain the risk-shifting incentives of shareholders/managers in the vicinity of insolvency. The UK rule on wrongful

---

9 Non-financial sanctions such as, e.g., rules on the disqualification of directors fare better in this regard.

10 See L.A. Bebchuk, 'Ex Ante Costs of Violating Absolute Priority in Bankruptcy', 57 *Journal of Finance* (2002) p. 445 et seq.

11 As suggested, e.g., by L.A. Bebchuk and J.M. Fried, 'The Uneasy Case for the Priority of Secured Claims in Bankruptcy: Further Thoughts and a Reply to Critics', 82 *Cornell Law Review* (1997) p. 1279 at p. 1321 et seq.

trading comes closest to providing a sensible solution to this problem, but even this rule has certain shortcomings.

3.2.1 *United States*

With respect to the United States, it probably still is fair to characterise the system as relatively debtor friendly, i.e., as relying heavily on bonuses for shareholders/managers to get formal insolvency proceedings started in time.[12] There are the Chapter 11 rules on the automatic stay (11 USC 362), the debtor-in-possession (11 USC 1104, 1107) and the exclusivity period for filing a reorganisation plan (11 USC 1121), and there are violations of the absolute priority rule (for the rule itself, see 11 USC 1129(b)). Such violations are an important feature of the current reorganisation practice.[13] Given the strong position of shareholders/managers in Chapter 11 proceedings, it comes as no surprise that most bankruptcy proceedings are commenced by the debtor and not by its creditors.[14]

More recently, however, the position of secured lenders in bankruptcy has been strengthened as well. As adopted by the States in the late 1990s, the new UCC 9-104 permits a creditor to take a security interest in a debtor's bank accounts. Debtors thus frequently enter bankruptcy with little if any liquid assets and require an immediate DIP (debtor-in-possession) loan. The dominant pre-bankruptcy secured lender, who already has an interest in and knowledge of the debtor, is in a unique position to provide such a loan. 'In exchange', the debtor regularly cedes control over the reorganisation process to the DIP financer.[15] Empirical evidence suggests that this development has already adversely affected

---

[12] Cf., W.T. Allen and R. Kraakman, *Commentaries and Cases on the Law of Business Organization* (New York, Aspen 2003) p. 138: 'In the United States, where management retains control when the company enters reorganisation proceedings under Chapter 11, such duties [to file for bankruptcy] are unnecessary because management often has an incentive to enter bankruptcy voluntarily in the hopes of engineering a successful recapitalization.'

[13] However, there is some controversy with respect to the dimension of these deviations. Contrast W. Beranek, R. Boehmer and B. Smith, 'Much Ado About Nothing: Absolute Priority Deviations in Chapter 11', 25 *Financial Management* (1996) p. 102 et seq. (equity is wiped out in 33.8 per cent of a sample of 68 recently reorganised firms) with A.C. Eberhart and L.A. Weiss, 'The Importance of Deviations from the Absolute Priority Rule in Chapter 11 Bankruptcy Proceedings', 27 *Financial Management* (1996) p. 106 et seq. (Beranek, Boehmer and Smith fail to measure the size of APR violations and ignore the possibility of APR violations between senior and junior creditors).

[14] See Ch.J. Tabb, *The Law of Bankruptcy* (Westbury, Foundation Press 1997) p. 92 (reporting 99 per cent voluntary petitions).

[15] Baird and Rasmussen, loc. cit. n. 3, at p. 785: '[I]t is the lender, and not the Bankruptcy Code or the bankruptcy judge, that is deciding how long the managers will have to make a go of things.'

the manager's incentives for a timely bankruptcy filing.[16] The recent changes in the Bankruptcy Code by the Bankruptcy Abuse Prevention and Consumer Protection Act of 2005[17] will probably further strengthen this trend.[18] Given that no filing duty of management exists in the United States, this should give rise to some concern. Rather than bankruptcy abuse by shareholders/managers, the real issue seems to be whether and to what extent one can expect the dominant pre-petition lender and DIP financer to exercise his control rights in an efficient manner. This is not so much an issue of a 'comparative advantage' of the DIP financer *vis-à-vis* the company's incumbent management,[19] but of a possible inter-creditor conflict. It is far from clear that the dominant secured lender who drives the reorganisation process has the incentive to maximise the firm's value in the interest of the creditors as a whole.

Another important issue relates to the risk-shifting incentives for shareholders/managers in the vicinity of insolvency. It has already been mentioned that the observable violations of the absolute priority rule in bankruptcy do not ameliorate this problem – they make it worse. Whether common law fiduciary duties of directors *vis-à-vis* a firm's creditors exist in the vicinity of insolvency must be considered as an open issue. Delaware's Chancery Court, for one, finds that view of the common law of corporations to be 'not unproblematic' and suggests that directors may select and pursue with fidelity and prudence any 'plausible [sic] strategy to maximise the firm's value.'[20] Hence, managers only seem to face common law sanctions – if at all – if they engage in obviously excessive risk taking that cannot be characterised as a 'plausible' business action. This state of the law, however, does not seem to adequately address their risk-shifting incentives in the vicinity of insolvency.

---

16 See B.E. Adler, V. Capkun and A. Weiss, *Theory and Evidence on the Bankruptcy Initiation Problem* (September 2005), available at: <http://ssrn.com/abstract=795987>.

17 The text of the Act and the legislative history are available at: <http://thomas.loc.gov/cgi-bin/bdquery/z?d109:SN00256:>.

18 The Act limits, e.g., the possible extensions of the exclusivity period (11 USC 1121) to a maximum of eighteen months after the date of the order for relief.

19 But see Baird and Rasmussen, loc. cit. n. 3, at p. 778 et seq., especially p. 785, who emphasize this point.

20 *Production Resources* v. *NCT Group*, Del. Ch., 863 A.2d 772 (2004) at p. 789 et seq. The discussion on common law fiduciary duties of directors *vis-à-vis* a firm's creditors in the vicinity of insolvency was spurred by the Court's decision in *Credit Lyonnais Bank Nederland, N.V. et al.* v. *Pathe Communications Corp. et al.*, 1991 Del. Ch. LEXIS 215 (headnote 5: 'At least where a corporation is operating in the vicinity of insolvency, a board of directors is not merely the agent of the residue risk bearers, but owes its duty to the corporate enterprise.').

3.2.2 *United Kingdom*

In the United Kingdom, secured lenders traditionally have a strong position in insolvency proceedings due to the possibility of a floating charge. This is true even after the recent legislative changes introduced by the Enterprise Act 2002.[21] The charge-holder has a very free hand to specify the events which will cause the charge to crystallise.[22] Irrespective of the financial position of the company, the charge-holder may appoint an administrator who replaces management and henceforth runs the firm (s. 248 Enterprise Act 2002, s. 8 Insolvency Act 1986 and Schedule B1, para. 14 et seq.).[23] The purpose of the administration is to rescue the company as a going concern or at least to achieve a better result for the company's creditors than would be likely if the company were wound up (Schedule B1, para. 3).[24] With respect to liquidation proceedings, a company is deemed insolvent and liable to be wound up if a written demand of a creditor to whom the company owes a sum in excess of £750 has not been honoured within three weeks (ss. 122, 123 Insolvency Act 1986).[25] Hence, it appears that 'creditor governance' plays an important role in securing the timely commencement of formal insolvency proceedings in the United Kingdom.[26] This is confirmed by recent empirical findings according to which median bank recovery rates are significantly higher in the United Kingdom than in Germany and France.[27]

---

21 For an analysis of the Act, see J. Armour and R.J. Mokal, 'Reforming the Governance of Corporate Rescue: The Enterprise Act 2002', *Lloyd's Maritime and Commercial Law Quarterly* 2005, p. 28 et seq. One of its significant features is that a certain part of the company's net property that is subject to a floating charge must be made available for the satisfaction of unsecured debts, s. 252 Enterprise Act 2002, s. 176A Insolvency Act 1986.

22 See P. Davies, *Introduction to Company Law* (Oxford, Oxford University Press 2002) p. 74.

23 However, he may not in principle appoint an administrative receiver (s. 250 Enterprise Act 2002, s. 72A et seq. Insolvency Act 1986).

24 Para. 3 in essence compels an administrator to pursue the course of action which maximises the overall net recoveries to creditors, see Armour and Mokal, loc. cit. n. 21, at p. 42 et seq., especially p. 47. Such a course would not necessarily be pursued by the secured creditors, see section 3.1 *supra*.

25 On these provisions, see A. Schall, 'The UK Limited Company Abroad – How Foreign Creditors are Protected after *Inspire Art* (Including a Comparison of UK and German Creditor Protection Rules)', 16 *European Business Law Review* (2005) p. 1534 at p. 1538.

26 See also J. Armour, B.R. Cheffins and D.A. Skeel, Jr., 'Corporate Ownership Structure and the Evolution of Bankruptcy Law: Lessons from the United Kingdom', 55 *Vanderbilt Law Review* (2002) p. 1699 at p. 1761 (concluding that even though a general appraisal of the UK system must take account of the relatively strong position of management in informal workouts, it would be 'going too far to label Britain as a manager-driven jurisdiction').

27 See S.A. Davydenko and J.R. Franks, *Do Bankruptcy Codes Matter? A Study of Defaults in France, Germany and the UK* (August 2005), available at: <http://ssrn.com/abstract=647861> (finding medians of 92 per cent in the United Kingdom, 67 per cent in Germany and 56 per cent in France). To be sure, bank recovery rates say more about the treatment of bank

In addition, the wrongful trading rule as embodied in section 214 of the Insolvency Act 1986 explicitly attempts to contain the risk-shifting incentives of managers in the vicinity of insolvency. According to this rule, a director of a company is liable 'to make such a contribution … to the company's assets as the court thinks proper' if (i) the company has gone into insolvent liquidation and (ii) at some time before the commencement of the winding up of the company, the director knew or should have concluded that there was no reasonable prospect that the company would avoid going into insolvent liquidation. However, a director will not be liable if he 'took every step with a view to minimising the potential loss to the company's creditors as … he ought to have taken.' Whereas insolvent liquidation is determined on a balance sheet basis, a cash flow test is used to assess the company's prospects with respect to avoiding that situation.[28]

The effectiveness of section 214 as a sanction for wrongful trading is debatable. One problem relates to the funding of litigating section 214 claims. Due to the common law rule against champerty, third-party financing in return for a share of the proceeds (if the claim is successful) still seems to be a closed route.[29] In addition, section 214 only sanctions wrongful trading in extreme cases. Firstly, directors are liable only if a company has gone into insolvent *liquidation:* it is not sufficient that the company has become insolvent. Secondly, there is no liability if a prudent director concluded that a *reasonable prospect* existed to avoid an insolvent liquidation of the company. For example, a 20 or 30 per cent chance is arguably such a reasonable prospect. Given these shortcomings, it does not come as a surprise that there is not much case law on section 214 and that, in the reported cases, directors apparently continued trading even though the company was already insolvent.[30] Whether and to what extent the UK courts are prepared to remedy these defects of section 214 on the basis of common law duties of directors in the vicinity of insolvency remains an open question.[31]

---

loans in bankruptcy than about the timeliness of its commencement. Moreover, the results of the study relate to a period before the Enterprise Act became effective. Since this Act has somewhat weakened the position of secured creditors in bankruptcy (see *supra* n. 21), one can expect the bank recovery rates in the United Kingdom to decline in the future.

28 See P. Davies, 'Directors' Creditor-Regarding Duties in Respect of Trading Decisions Taken in the Vicinity of Insolvency', in this volume.

29 On the funding issue and recent legislative reforms to ameliorate this problem, see H.C. Hirt, 'The Wrongful Trading Remedy in UK Law: Classification, Application and Practical Significance', 1 *European Company and Financial Law Review* (2004) p. 71 at pp. 107-113.

30 See Th. Bachner, 'Wrongful Trading – A New European Model for Creditor Protection?', 5 *European Business Organization Law Review* (2004) p. 293 at p. 301 et seq.

31 See Davies, loc. cit. n. 28. The discussion in the United Kingdom was initiated with the decision of the Court of Appeal in *West Mercia Safetywear Ltd. (in liq.)* v. *Dodd* [1988] BCLC 250, [1988] BCC 30. However, the case dealt with directors' duties regarding an insolvent company, not a company in the vicinity of insolvency.

3.2.3 *Germany*

German corporate law requires managers to file for formal insolvency proceedings within three weeks after a corporation has become insolvent on a cash flow or balance sheet basis (§ 64(1) *GmbH-Gesetz*, § 92(2) *Aktiengesetz*). They are liable in tort if they fail to meet this requirement (§ 823(2) *Bürgerliches Gesetzbuch*). Moreover, they must refrain from making payments on behalf of an insolvent company unless such payments are reasonable under the circumstances (§ 64(2) *GmbH-Gesetz*, § 92(3) *Aktiengesetz*). Compared with the United States, the position of managers/shareholders in formal insolvency proceedings can be characterised as fairly weak. Even though the German *Insolvenzordnung* (InsO) is modelled after the US Bankruptcy Code, there are significant differences. To give just two examples: (i) an insolvency administrator is usually appointed to run the failing firm – the debtor-in-possession (§ 270 et seq. InsO) is the exception, not the rule – and (ii) there is no exclusivity period with respect to the filing of an insolvency plan – both the insolvency administrator and the debtor may file such a plan at any time (§ 218 InsO).

As it stands, the present German bankruptcy law certainly does not do much in terms of setting incentives for a timely triggering of formal insolvency proceedings. A filing duty of managers upon insolvency may come too late: often, most of the going concern value will have been lost by this stage; it may also come too early, e.g., if the firm is facing a temporary liquidity crisis. Given that the bonuses for shareholders/managers upon initiation of formal insolvency proceedings are weak at best, one may safely conclude that the current regime is deficient with respect to the timely triggering of such proceedings.

It is even more deficient with respect to containing the risk-shifting incentives of shareholders/managers in the vicinity of insolvency. A filing duty of managers in the event of insolvency does not address the risk-shifting problem at all. Other provisions in the Criminal Code (§ 283(1) No. 2 *Strafgesetzbuch*) and the Civil Code (§ 826 *Bürgerliches Gesetzbuch*[32]) do address this problem. However, these provisions apply to cases of 'extreme gambling' only. They certainly do not attempt to sanction all types of unreasonably risky business actions in the vicinity of insolvency.[33] Thus, they fall short of requiring managers to take all necessary steps to minimise the losses to the firm's creditors.

---

[32] For the application of this provision to gambling in the vicinity of insolvency, see, e.g., *Bundesgerichtshof*, Judgment of 25 July 2005, *Neue Zeitschrift für das Recht der Insolvenz und Sanierung* (2006) p. 58 at p. 61.

[33] To be sure, German courts *could* develop *detailed* duties of shareholders/managers *vis-à-vis* a company's creditors in the vicinity of insolvency, including duties to abstain from risk-increasing investment projects. For a comprehensive review of the current legal position and a proposal with respect to the liability of shareholders, see especially H.Ch. Grigoleit, *Gesellschafterhaftung für interne Einflussnahme im Recht der GmbH: Dezentrale Gewinnverfolgung*

3.3 Addressing the risk-shifting problem

Given the poor performance of the current US and German legal systems, in particular, with respect to containing the risk-shifting incentives of shareholders/managers in the vicinity of insolvency, it seems worthwhile to consider alternatives. In 2002, the High Level Group of Company Law Experts suggested the introduction of a uniform wrongful trading rule in Europe,[34] and the European Commission endorsed that recommendation in its Action Plan of 2003.[35] Such a uniform wrongful trading rule could and should take section 214 of the UK Insolvency Act 1986 as its conceptual basis. However, it should aim at improving the current UK system by making the liability threat more effective. A uniform European wrongful trading rule should hold managers of an insolvent company liable for trading while they knew or should have known that insolvency – on a cash flow basis – was more probable than not, unless they can show that they have taken all reasonable steps to avoid insolvency. Note how that rule differs from section 214: liability arises once a firm becomes insolvent (as opposed to going into insolvent liquidation) and when such insolvency is more probable than not (a mere reasonable prospect of avoiding insolvency does not exclude liability). The probability test of the rule conforms to the one embodied in § 18(1) of the German *Insolvenzordnung*[36] and also to the one discussed by the UK Company Law Review Steering Group in its Final Report. The Steering Group considered the proposition that directors should take appropriate action to reduce risks once there is a substantial probability of an insolvent liquidation. Such substantial probability was believed to exist if 'a failure to meet the company's liabilities is more probable than not.'[37]

---

als Leitprinzip des dynamischen Gläubigerschutzes (Munich, C.H. Beck 2006) (suggesting that such liability should exist *vis-à-vis* the company for the benefit of its creditors). So far, however, they have not done so. The new doctrine of shareholder liability for 'destructive interference' (*existenzvernichtender Eingriff*, see, e.g., *Bundesgerichtshof*, Judgment of 13 December 2004, *Zeitschrift für Wirtschaftsrecht* (2005) p. 117 et seq.) is not directed towards risk-shifting investments by shareholders/managers in the vicinity of insolvency.

34 High Level Group of Company Law Experts, op. cit. n. 7, at pp. 68-69.

35 Commission of the European Communities, Modernising Company Law and Enhancing Corporate Governance in the European Union – A Plan to Move Forward, COM (2003) 284 final, p. 16.

36 According to this provision, formal insolvency proceedings may be commenced not only if the debtor is insolvent on the basis of a cash flow or balance sheet test, but also if insolvency on the basis of a cash flow test is more probable than not. However, the debtor's managers are not required to file a petition in this case. They simply have an option to do so. § 18(1) uses the wording *'drohende Zahlungsunfähigkeit'* (threat of insolvency). There is agreement that this criterion should be interpreted as suggested here.

37 The Company Law Review Steering Group, *Modern Company Law for a Competitive Economy – Final Report*, Vol. I (2001) p. 45.

A wrongful trading rule such as the one just described would *prima facie* set exactly the right incentives for managers/shareholders in the vicinity of insolvency. If insolvency is more probable than not, there is a high risk that managers/shareholders undertake investment projects with a (potentially) negative net present value. On the basis of the proposed rule, managers will face liability if they engage in such activities, and shareholders must of course refrain from inducing them to do so. The rule basically gives managers an option to continue trading and restructure the business (i.e., to take all reasonable steps to avoid insolvency) or to put the company into formal insolvency proceedings.[38] The firm-specific know-how of the incumbent managers is thereby utilised, and viable firms are separated from non-viable ones: managers will not take chances on a firm which in all likelihood will go into insolvency anyway. Instead of allowing them to defend themselves on the basis that all reasonable steps were taken to avoid insolvency, one could think of allowing the defence that all reasonable steps were taken to enhance firm value. Very often, these two goals will go hand in hand. However, under certain circumstances, even projects that enhance firm value will not be enough to avoid insolvency. Hence, from a creditor protection perspective, a 'financial test' seems preferable.

The main criticism that can be levied against the proposed liability rule is that firms might be liquidated prematurely. This concern was also voiced by the UK Secretary of State for Trade and Industry, who rejected the idea of tightening the grip of section 214 on the basis that such action would be inconsistent with the policy of promoting a 'rescue culture' for companies in financial difficulty.[39] However, the issue is not that rescuing companies as such would be inhibited by the proposed liability rule – quite the contrary: the rule encourages managers to take all reasonable steps to avoid insolvency, i.e., to restructure a distressed firm. The real issue is the fear that it is difficult to define such steps precisely *ex ante*. Certain managerial measures might *ex post* be considered inappropriate or even unacceptable, possibly because of a hindsight bias of the courts. If one adds risk aversion of managers, over-deterrence might result. However, risk aversion is probably counterbalanced by over-optimism,[40] a well known 'cognitive deficiency' that also affects managerial actions in times of crisis. Moreover, by the

---

38 If insolvency cannot be avoided, e.g., because the shareholders of the company block certain necessary financial measures (such as a nominal capital reduction, an infusion of new cash, etc.), managers must stop trading and file for bankruptcy. In such a situation, no *reasonable* steps (for the managers) to avoid insolvency exist.

39 Secretary of State for Trade and Industry, 'Modernising Company Law', Cm. 5553-I (2002) p. 28.

40 See D. Kahneman and A. Tversky, 'Conflict Resolution: A Cognitive Perspective', in K. Arrow, R.H. Mnookin, L. Ross, A. Tversky and R. Wilson, eds., *Barriers to Conflict Resolution* (New York, W.W. Norton 1995) p. 44 at p. 46 et seq.

time a certain 'rescue culture' in a particular jurisdiction matures and 'generally accepted rescue principles' evolve,[41] the fear of over-deterrence will be less justified. Such a development will also contribute to reducing the costs for legal advice and documentation with respect to the proper managerial actions when a firm is in financial distress.[42] In any event, the benefits of containing the risk-shifting incentives of shareholders/managers in the vicinity of insolvency should outweigh the opportunity costs of certain premature liquidations and the direct costs of compliance.

In this regard, the content of liability under the proposed rule also plays an important role. The current UK legislative regime, according to which a contribution to the company's assets can be fixed at the discretion of the insolvency court, should not be adopted by the European legislator. Such an uncertain standard would worsen the over-deterrence problem.[43] Rather, the legislative standard should in principle relate to the diminution of the company's net asset position during the objectionable trading time. That standard seems to correspond best with the concept that managers should put the company into formal insolvency proceedings if no reasonable steps can be taken to avoid such proceedings. It is clear, though, that the proposed standard has certain deficiencies, too. Firstly, it seems to overcompensate creditors if reasonable steps could have been taken to avoid insolvency, i.e., if the company was not doomed to go into insolvency anyway. However, such a defence should not be open to managers. Otherwise, the desirable incentive effects of the proposed liability rule would be diluted. Secondly, the standard does not provide an effective sanction if certain creditors are paid (in full) during the objectionable trading time. However, that problem can be adequately dealt with by the law on fraudulent transfers or preference law. Thirdly, the standard seemingly also does not adequately protect new creditors who obtain their position during the objectionable trading time. It appears justified to compensate *these* creditors in full, as they would not have traded with the firm if the managers had lived up to their duty.[44] Again, managers should not

---

[41] One should not be too pessimistic with respect to developing a set of such principles. Workouts in many European jurisdictions are already conducted according to certain generally observed routines. For the 'London approach', see section 4 *infra*.

[42] The additional costs associated with a wrongful trading rule as proposed in the text should not be overstated. Even without such a rule, (external) professional advice with respect to business actions is often obtained, board meeting minutes are taken, etc.

[43] That the uncertainty of the legislative standard *is* a problem is evidenced by the fact that the English courts, in exercising their discretion and in a quest for certainty, have settled on the diminution of the company's net asset position as the maximum quantum of liability, see, e.g., *Re Continental Assurance Company of London plc* [2001] BPIR 733, at margin number 297.

[44] See also H. Fleischer, 'Erweiterte Außenhaftung der Organmitglieder im Europäischen Gesellschafts- und Kapitalmarktrecht: Insolvenzverschleppung, fehlerhafte Kapitalmarktinformation, Tätigkeitsverbote', *Zeitschrift für Unternehmens- und Gesellschaftsrecht* 2004, p. 437

be allowed to defend themselves by asserting that reasonable steps to avoid insolvency could have been taken.[45]

4. TRIGGER MECHANISMS FOR OUT-OF-COURT RESTRUCTURINGS (WORKOUTS)

Reorganising a distressed firm within formal insolvency proceedings is costly: direct and especially indirect bankruptcy costs lower the net (reorganisation) value of the company. Hence, stakeholders have strong incentives to try an out-of-court restructuring (workout). Such workouts are associated with much lower direct and indirect bankruptcy costs than formal insolvency proceedings.[46] It is therefore safe to assume that a significant portion, if not the majority, of corporate reorganisations within formal insolvency proceedings (regardless of jurisdiction) started as workouts – and failed. Such failure can occur for various reasons. The free-rider problem probably tops the list: each creditor has an incentive to hold out in the hope that others contribute sufficiently to the financial restructuring of the distressed firm. However, if too many engage in that kind of strategic behaviour, the whole project is endangered.[47]

Jurisdictions differ with respect to the legal regime applicable to workouts. Nonetheless, it appears that there are no 'cooperation duties' of creditors and/or the debtor to ameliorate the free-rider problem in the United States, the United Kingdom or Germany. Part of the UK 'rescue culture' is the so-called 'London approach' to workouts. This approach is guided by a set of informal principles

---

at pp. 460-461 (advocating an effective compensation mechanism with respect to these creditors in particular; however, Fleischer does not specify what such a mechanism should look like).

45 Within formal insolvency proceedings, managers' liability should be vindicated by the insolvency administrator who acts for the benefit of 'old' and 'new' creditors alike. Thus, an inefficient race by the creditors for the managers' assets is avoided. However, if formal insolvency proceedings are not opened – e.g., due to a lack of sufficient funds – creditors should be entitled to go against the managers on their own.

46 See, e.g., S.C. Gilson, K. John and L.H. Lang, 'Troubled Debt Restructurings: An Empirical Study of Private Reorganisation of Firms in Default', 27 *Journal of Financial Economics* (1990) p. 315 et seq.; J.R. Franks and W.N. Torous, 'A Comparison of Financial Recontracting in Distressed Exchanges and Chapter 11 Reorganisations', 35 *Journal of Financial Economics* (1994) p. 349 et seq.

47 To be sure, the extent of the free-rider problem will depend on the facts of a particular case. If there are only few creditors or if there is one dominant (secured) creditor, collective action issues will be less of a problem. They will figure prominently, however, with respect to large (multinational) companies who typically obtain financing from a multiplicity of sources (various syndicated loans, bonds, etc.).

that were once developed with the support of the Bank of England.[48] The precise legal status of these principles is unclear. However, they certainly are not legally binding in a technical sense. In Germany, the Federal Supreme Court of Justice once held that out-of-court restructuring agreements do not bind outsiders. According to the Court, such outsiders are not required by law to participate in a workout.[49] The legal position in the United States is no different.[50]

As is well known, there are many devices to overcome free-rider effects. One such device comprises legal duties, either self-imposed by contract or imposed by law. Since high transaction costs generally make concluding an *ad hoc* 'cooperation contract' in a workout scenario impossible, only the second option is feasible.[51] The content of such cooperation duties would have to reflect what is usual and necessary in a workout. There could be duties to negotiate in good faith, but in principle there could also be duties to grant a bridging-loan or to participate in a debt restructuring or a long-term credit facility under certain circumstances. The prerequisites for such duties would have to depend on various factors. Duties to *negotiate* should exist only if a particular firm shows a restructuring need and there is a realistic chance that such restructuring can be accomplished. Duties to *agree* to certain reorganisation measures should exist only if these measures are sensible and necessary and if the firm is indeed worth more as a going concern than if liquidated. Moreover, cooperation duties should always depend on whether they are necessary in the sense that cooperation does not occur voluntarily and whether they are fair to whoever is supposed to be bound by them. Hence, fairness standards such as distributing reorganisation burdens according to the existing risk exposure of the participants should play a significant role in determining the precise content of cooperation duties.

Would such a system of cooperation duties make workouts unduly burdensome and/or costly? It cannot be denied that any legal regulation of workouts creates a potential for further disputes and thus bankruptcy costs. These are the price one has to pay for the benefit cooperation duties bring in terms of solving or at least ameliorating the free-rider problem. If the duties are formulated as

---

[48] On the 'London approach', see, e.g., J. Armour and S. Deakin, 'Norms in Private Insolvency: The "London Approach" to the Resolution of Financial Distress', 1 *Journal of Corporate Law Studies* (2001) p. 21 et seq.; H. Eidenmüller, *Unternehmenssanierung zwischen Markt und Gesetz: Mechanismen der Unternehmensreorganisation und Kooperationspflichten im Reorganisationsrecht* (Cologne, Otto Schmidt 1999) p. 236 et seq.

[49] *Bundesgerichtshof*, Judgment of 12 December 1991, *Entscheidungen des Bundesgerichtshofes in Zivilsachen* (BGHZ) 116, at p. 319 et seq.

[50] See, e.g., M.J. Roe, 'The Voting Prohibition in Bond Workouts', 97 *The Yale Law Journal* (1987) p. 232 at p. 235 et seq.

[51] For a detailed elaboration of a system of cooperation duties in workouts, see Eidenmüller, op. cit. n. 48, at p. 652 et seq.

precisely as possible and if overregulation is avoided, it should be feasible to keep the bankruptcy costs that are associated with their implementation to a minimum.

As with formal insolvency proceedings, some point in time must be specified that would trigger the operation of the system of cooperation duties, i.e., that would bring those duties into existence. Various triggers are conceivable. It certainly would be too late if cooperation duties were triggered only once the firm has become insolvent on a cash flow or balance sheet basis – restructuring efforts should commence earlier (and in practice usually do). At the same time, however, it is extremely difficult to define precisely some earlier *objective* standard that is both adjudicable and justified economically. Hence, a different approach is suggested here: cooperation duties should arise once a workout is initiated by one of the stakeholders in the company. The advantages of this criterion compared to other approaches are manifold: (i) publicity is avoided; (ii) the criterion is easy to ascertain for the participants; (iii) it is a good indicator of the restructuring needs of a particular company; (iv) it is firm-specific; and (v) it utilises the information advantage of the incumbent management. That cooperation duties in principle arise once a workout is initiated does not automatically determine the content and reach of such duties. That would need to be decided on the basis of the specific circumstances of each particular case and the considerations discussed above.

Cooperation duties such as those proposed here fit in nicely with the liability rule for wrongful trading proposed in section 3.3. If insolvency is more probable than not, managers should, if insolvency can be avoided, take all reasonable actions to attain that goal. Such actions include measures to restructure the firm according to well-established principles that are generally considered to be best practice in workout situations. This is where the system of cooperation duties kicks in.

5. Mandatory versus enabling nature of trigger mechanisms

So far, the discussion has proceeded without clarifying whether the trigger mechanisms, liability rules and cooperation duties that were analysed are mandatory or enabling in nature. Selecting bankruptcy rules in the charter of a corporation or abdicating bankruptcy altogether is currently impossible in the three jurisdictions reviewed in section 3.2. In the United States, contracting out of bankruptcy is viewed as violating the right of a debtor to file for bankruptcy.[52] In Germany, such contracting would go against the obligation of management to file

---

[52] See D.A. Skeel, Jr., *Debt's Dominion: A History of Bankruptcy Law in America* (Princeton, Princeton University Press 2001) p. 228: 'For decades, received wisdom has held that efforts to completely opt out of bankruptcy are unenforceable…'.

no later than three weeks after a corporation has become insolvent.[53] In the United Kingdom, a filing obligation follows indirectly from the wrongful trading regime under section 214 of the Insolvency Act 1986.[54]

In principle, though, much can be said in favour of allowing firms to conclude bankruptcy contracts, i.e., to specify in their charter which rules should govern in the vicinity of insolvency and insolvency.[55] All the standard efficiency arguments for the benefits of private contracting apply. With respect to trigger mechanisms for formal insolvency proceedings or workouts, in particular, allowing firms to specify these in their charter would open up the possibility of firm-specific triggers. In line with the concept of bankruptcy regimes being enabling rather than mandatory, States could provide such regimes 'off the shelf'. Such a 'menu approach' would contribute to reducing the transaction costs associated with making bankruptcy law contractable.[56]

However, free choice might and possibly should be limited in two respects. Firstly, there are creditors for whom self-help is not a viable option.[57] Tort creditors are an obvious example. We cannot expect the market mechanism to produce results that are necessarily in the interest of these creditors or creditor groups. Hence, creditors who cannot adjust should be protected by certain mandatory rules. However, such rules need not necessarily be rules on the triggering of formal insolvency proceedings or workouts. They might simply be liability rules. Secondly, allowing firms to select bankruptcy rules in their charter seems to necessitate constraining subsequent, opportunistic changes that increase the risk exposure of existing creditors. Such constraints could be imposed, e.g., by means of a time-lag requirement with respect to when such changes become effective or by stipulating that and how creditors must approve them (before they become effective). An approach that would be more congenial to the 'free choice philosophy' advocated here runs as follows: subsequent changes would be

---

53 See Eidenmüller, op. cit. n. 48, at p. 181.

54 See also the decision of the House of Lords in *British Eagle International Air Lines Ltd.* v. *Compagnie Nationale Air France* [1975] 1 *WLR* 758 (holding that the contracting-out of the provisions of s. 302 of the Companies Act 1948 was contrary to public policy, as such provisions regulate the division of the property of a company that is wound up).

55 Pioneering work in this field has been done by Robert Rasmussen and Alan Schwartz. See R.K. Rasmussen, 'Debtor's Choice: A Menu Approach to Corporate Bankruptcy', 71 *Texas Law Review* (1992/1993) p. 51; A. Schwarz, 'A Contract Approach to Business Bankruptcy', 107 *Yale Law Journal* (1998) p. 1807. For a discussion of choosing bankruptcy rules within the framework of the European Insolvency Regulation, see H. Eidenmüller, 'Free Choice in International Company Insolvency Law in Europe', 6 *European Business Organization Law Review* (2005) p. 423.

56 See Rasmussen, loc. cit. n. 55, at p. 100 et seq.

57 On 'non-adjusting' creditors, see L.A. Bebchuk and J. Fried, 'The Uneasy Case for the Priority of Secured Claims in Bankruptcy', 105 *Yale Law Journal* (1996) p. 857 at p. 882 et seq.

restricted only by the mechanisms and rules that are specified in a firm's charter itself. Thus, market participants would be able to judge and evaluate both the currently applicable bankruptcy regime and the risk that this regime might be changed later on.

6 Conclusion

The main results of this paper can be summarised as follows:

(i) Conventional economic reasoning suggests that formal insolvency proceedings should commence once the greater of the going concern value or the liquidation value of a firm falls below the value of its liabilities ($V = {}_{max} (V_{gc}, V_l) < L$).
(ii) Since this test is difficult to apply in practice, an additional cash flow test is needed: formal insolvency proceedings should commence if a firm is unable to pay its due debts (company illiquidity).
(iii) Containing the risk-shifting incentives of shareholders/managers in the vicinity of insolvency is a paramount necessity. Existing legal regimes do not address this problem at all (United States and Germany) or not adequately (United Kingdom).
(iv) A uniform European liability rule is proposed that imposes liability on managers of insolvent companies for trading while they knew or should have known that insolvency was more probable than not, unless they can show that they took all reasonable steps to avoid insolvency.
(v) If the going concern value of a firm exceeds its liquidation value, all stakeholders have an incentive to try a workout to make the net going concern value as great as possible (lower costs of financial distress than in formal insolvency proceedings). However, workouts can and do fail in practice due to free-rider effects.
(vi) An argument can be made for cooperation duties to support workouts. Such duties should be triggered once a workout is initiated.
(vii) Firms should in principle be allowed to select bankruptcy rules in their charter, i.e., bankruptcy rules should in principle be enabling rather than mandatory. This also relates to trigger mechanisms for formal insolvency proceedings and workouts.

H. Eidenmüller and W. Schön (eds.), The Law and Economics of Creditor Protection

Recharacterization and the Nonhindrance of Creditors

David A. Skeel, Jr. and Georg Krause-Vilmar*

Abstract

Using a 1977 article by Robert Clark as its starting point, this article attempts to shed new light on the question of whether and when shareholder loans to her company should be either equitably subordinated or, as courts have done in a few recent cases, recharacterized as equity. In its emphasis on the particular issue of shareholder loans, the article has a narrower compass than Clark's article, which uses a four-part typology to explore the relationship among fraudulent conveyance law, equitable subordination, veil piercing, and dividend restrictions. But the article also expands Clark's analysis in several respects. The most important adjustment involves the general Nonhindrance ideal, which we use to

* David A. Skeel, Jr., S. Samuel Arsht Professor of Corporate Law, University of Pennsylvania Law School; Georg Krause-Vilmar, LL.M 2006 (expected), University of Pennsylvania Law School. We are grateful to Bill Bratton, Andreas Cahn, Reinier Kraakman, Bob Rasmussen, and Klaus Schmidt for helpful comments on earlier drafts, and to Horst Eidenmuller and Wolfgang Schön for organizing this symposium.

identify a crucially important form of interference with the rights of creditors that Clark does not himself consider directly.

Part 2 of the article very briefly describes the 1939 Supreme Court case that served as a well-spring for equitable subordination doctrine in general, and for subordination of shareholder loans in particular. Part 3 then focuses on a series of recent decisions that have wrestled with the question whether shareholder loans should be recharacterized as equity contributions. Recharacterization doctrine is closely related to equitable subordination, but most courts view it as a separate development. Part 3 suggests that much of the confusion in the cases could be eliminated by disentangling two issues, whether the status of a loan is ambiguous (which raises issues of Truth, in terms of Clark's typology) and whether it was likely to destroy value that would otherwise go to creditors (the Nonhindrance concern); and by distinguishing bankruptcy recharacterization from the tax characterization cases that seem to have spawned the new doctrine. Part 4 then concludes by briefly considering the German and Austrian approaches to these same issues, which focus on capitalization and creditworthiness.

The most important, and initially counterintuitive, implication comes in Part 3: whereas US courts have treated security interests as a badge of legitimacy in assessing shareholder loans, secured loans are actually the most worrisome form of shareholder investment. These security interests, we argue, should be disallowed.

Keywords: corporations, corporate reorganization, fraudulent conveyance, recharacterization, bankruptcy, secured debt, shareholder loans, priority.

1. INTRODUCTION

When a company fails, the judicial autopsy that ensues often reveals that its shareholders were far more than shareholders alone. Particularly when there is a controlling shareholder or the company is enmeshed in a parent-subsidiary framework, one or more shareholders may have made loans to the company, or supplied goods on credit, or leased property. Other shareholders, creditors who are not sure they will be repaid, and the courts to whom these shareholders or creditors take their complaints have long worried that the transactions are not entirely on the up-and-up. Since the controlling shareholder stands on both sides of the transaction, there is always a risk that she will charge too much for the goods she supplies, make dubious loans, or simply siphon assets out of the corporation.

Over the years, a wide variety of doctrines have been invoked, and new doctrines created, by US courts and legislatures to address the threat of insider manipulation. Under veil-piercing doctrine, creditors can ask a court to hold shareholders personally liable for obligations of the company. Equitable subordination can be used to lower the priority status of an obligation owed to an insider or other creditor. If the company has overpaid for benefits provided by the insider, creditors can challenge the transaction under fraudulent conveyance law. And so on.

Long ago, before his illustrious career as dean of the Harvard Law School, Robert Clark wrote a seminal article arguing that many of the doctrines just mentioned can be understood as fitting a single, coherent pattern.[1] The Ur-doctrine, the doctrine from which the others flow, he argued, is fraudulent conveyance law.[2] Broadly understood, the argument continued, fraudulent conveyance law is designed to assure that a debtor honors four related moral obligations in its dealings with creditors. The first is Truth, which forbids the debtor from lying to his creditors either by filing deceptive financing statements or in other ways.[3] The second, Respect, prohibits the debtor from simply giving away money that might be used to repay creditors.[4] Evenhandedness means he cannot pay some creditors rather than others. Finally, under Nonhindrance, which Clark views as a general category that subsumes the other three, the debtor is not permitted to take actions that are designed to stymie his creditors, such as converting liquid assets to illiquid ones to make it harder for creditors to collect.

Each of these ideals, according to Clark, is embodied in traditional fraudulent conveyance law. Other, seemingly separate doctrines are best seen as adjustments made through the years to fill in the gaps of the basic fraudulent conveyance framework. The biggest gap stems from the requirement in fraudulent conveyance law that creditors must point to a particular transaction or transactions that violate the debtor's obligations to its creditors. If the debtor has engaged in numerous transactions over time, it may be difficult or impossible to prove on a transaction-by-transaction basis that the debtor has made fraudulent conveyances. Both

---

1 R.C. Clark, 'The Duties of the Corporate Debtor to Its Creditors', 90 *Harvard Law Review* (1977) p. 505. Portions of the article appear in slightly revised form in a treatise Clark published a decade later: R.C. Clark, *Corporate Law* (Boston, Little, Brown 1986) pp. 52-72.

2 Most States have adopted some form of the Uniform Fraudulent Transfer Act or the Uniform Fraudulent Conveyance Act. Although these provisions are incorporated into bankruptcy pursuant to 11 USC § 544(b) (permitting creditors to invoke nonbankruptcy causes of action), the Bankruptcy Code also includes its own, very similar fraudulent conveyance provision. 11 USC § 548. These provisions permit a debtor's creditors to challenge, among other things, transfers for which the debtor did not receive adequate consideration if the debtor was at or near insolvency when the transfer occurred (constructive fraud) and transfers that were designed to hinder, delay, or defraud creditors (actual fraud).

3 The ideal of Truth is described in Clark, loc. cit. n. 1, at p. 509. The other three ideals are described at pp. 509-513.

4 Clark later relabeled this attribute, calling it "Primacy." Clark, op. cit. n. 1, at p. 53.

equitable subordination and veil piercing plug this gap by substituting a "gestalt" approach for the transaction-specific requirements of fraudulent conveyance law.[5]

Using Clark's article as the starting point, this article attempts to shed new light on the question of whether and when shareholder loans to her company should be either equitably subordinated or, as courts have done in a few recent cases, recharacterized as equity. In its emphasis on the particular issue of shareholder loans, the article has a narrower compass than its classic predecessor. But it also expands Clark's analysis in several respects. The most important adjustment involves the Nonhindrance ideal, which we use to explore a crucially important form of interference with the rights of creditors that Clark does not himself consider directly.[6]

The article proceeds as follows. Part 2 very briefly describes the 1939 Supreme Court case that served as a well-spring for equitable subordination doctrine in general, and for subordination of shareholder loans in particular. Part 3 then focuses on a series of recent decisions that have wrestled with the question whether shareholder loans should be recharacterized as equity contributions. Recharacterization doctrine is closely related to equitable subordination, but most courts view it as a separate development. Part 3 suggests that much of the confusion in the cases could be eliminated by disentangling two issues: whether the status of a loan is ambiguous (which raises issues of Truth, in terms of Clark's typology) and whether it was likely to destroy value that would otherwise go to creditors (the Nonhindrance concern); and by distinguishing bankruptcy recharacterization from the tax characterization cases that seem to have spawned the new doctrine. Part 4 then concludes by briefly considering the German and Austrian approaches to these same issues, which focus on capitalization and creditworthiness.

The most important, and initially counterintuitive, implication comes in Part 3: whereas US courts have treated security interests as a badge of legitimacy in assessing shareholder loans, secured loans are actually the most worrisome form of shareholder investment. These security interests, we argue, should be disallowed.

---

[5] Under equitable subordination doctrine, which is now codified in 11 USC § 510, a court can subordinate the claim or interest of a creditor or shareholder who has acted inequitably. When a court pierces the corporate veil, it holds shareholders or affiliated entities liable for the obligations of a corporation. See, e.g., Clark, op. cit. n. 1, at pp. 71-85 (analyzing veil-piercing doctrine).

[6] It should go without saying that Clark himself may not agree with our appropriation of his four-part typology. Whether he would view our analysis as an adaptation or a distortion, we cannot say.

2. IN THE BEGINNING: *DEEP ROCK* AND ITS LEGACY

The subordination of shareholder loans in the United States dates back to a famous 1939 case that has long been viewed as an object lesson of the potential abuses of a parent-subsidiary framework. It is useful to describe the case in some detail in order to understand where equitable subordination came from and how far it has developed in the ensuing decades.

In *Taylor* v. *Standard Gas & Electric*,[7] generally known as the *Deep Rock* case for reasons that will soon become clear, Standard Gas & Electric Company, the parent corporation, acquired control of an oil company whose name it changed to Deep Rock Oil Corporation from its owner, C.B. Shaffer, in 1919. Shaffer initially shared voting control with Standard, but within two years Standard lost confidence in Shaffer, bought back his stock and pushed him out. Over the next decade, during which Deep Rock was invariably only "two jumps ahead of the wolf," as a Standard officer later testified, Standard ran an open account consisting of thousands of transactions between itself and Deep Rock.[8] By the time the wolf finally caught up with Deep Rock in 1933, Deep Rock's debt to Standard included $31,804,145.04 for cash contributions by Standard, $1,219,034.83 for management and supervision fees, $4,819,222.07 in interest charges, and $4,525,000 for leasing oil properties owned by another Standard subsidiary. These and other debits totaled over $52,000,000. After deducting credits of roughly $43,000,000, Standard filed a claim for $9,342,642.37 in Deep Rock's bankruptcy.

Both the bankruptcy trustee and two preferred stockholders objected to Standard's claim. "Many transactions entered in the account were attacked as fraudulent," as the Supreme Court later put it, "and it was asserted that as Standard had made Deep Rock its mere agent or instrumentality it could not transmute itself from the status of proprietor of Deep Rock's business to that of creditor."[9] The Court was persuaded that Standard's behavior over the decade it controlled Deep Rock substantiated these complaints. From the beginning, Justice Reed wrote, "Deep Rock was insufficiently capitalized, was top heavy with debt and was in parlous financial condition. Standard so managed its affairs as always to have a stranglehold upon it." Despite its precarious finances, Deep Rock paid over $3 million in dividends between 1926 and 1929, largely financed by borrowing from Standard.

[7] *Taylor* v. *Standard Gas & Electric*, 306 US 307 (1939). *Taylor* was decided the same year as another important decision subordinating a shareholder's claim, *Pepper* v. *Litton*, 308 US 295 (1939). These two cases are generally viewed as the fount of equitable subordination doctrine in the United States.

[8] Ibid., at p. 310.

[9] Ibid., at p. 312.

Under traditional fraud conveyance law, the plaintiffs would have been forced to identify each of the improper transactions they intended to challenge, and indeed it appears that they attempted to do just this. Giving the difficulty of documenting the flurry of exchanges, however, many of the transactions might have slipped through the cracks. The Supreme Court did not let this difficulty stand in the way of recovery. Based on the "equitable principle that the doctrine of the corporate entity, recognized generally and for most purposes, will not be regarded when so to do would work fraud or injustice," the Court reversed the lower courts' approval of a reorganization plan that would have fully honored much of Standard's claim. "No plan ought to be approved," the Court held, "which does not accord the preferred stockholders a right of participation in the equity in the Company's assets prior to that of Standard, and at least equal voice with Standard in the management. Anything less would be to remand them to precisely the status which has inflicted serious detriment on them in the past."[10]

Deep Rock has laid the groundwork for decades of decisions wrestling with the question whether a shareholder loan or other claim should be subordinated.[11] From time to time, courts and commentators have argued that subordination doctrine should be converted into a *per se* rule when the transactions in question involve a controlling shareholder or other insider. Judge Jerome Frank took this position in a series of cases starting in the late 1940s, arguing that the risk of manipulation by a controlling shareholder is so high that automatic subordination is justified, but he gave up this quest a few years later.[12] In 1978, Congress codified equitable subordination as part of a sweeping reform of the American bankruptcy laws, quietly dropping a provision in the original proposal that would have provided for automatic subordination of insider claims. As it turns out, this codification has helped to spawn a new set of questions about the proper treatment of shareholder loans.

3. Recharacterization: To Praise or Bury Insider Loans

In recent years, the *Deep Rock* concern with obligations to a controlling shareholder has spawned a new doctrine that is closely linked to, yet at times subtly

---

[10] Ibid., at p. 324.

[11] In determining whether to equitably subordinate a claim or interest, either of a shareholder or of an ordinary creditor, courts tend to require (1) inequitable conduct; (2) injury to creditors or an unfair benefit to the challenged claimant; and (3) that subordination not conflict with other provisions of the Bankruptcy Code. The inquiry is derived from *Matter of Mobile Steel Co.*, 563 F.2d 692 (5th Cir. 1977), which was decided shortly before equitable subordination was incorporated into the 1978 Bankruptcy Code.

[12] These cases, and Judge Frank's sympathy for a rule of automatic subordination, are described in Clark, op. cit. n. 1, at p. 537, n. 89.

different from, equitable subordination. In these cases, the bankruptcy court is asked to recharacterize debt owed to an insider-shareholder, and to treat it as equity rather than debt. Recharacterization is said to differ from ordinary subordination in two respects: it does not require a showing that the shareholder acted inequitably; and rather than simply being subordinated to other creditor claims, the shareholder's contribution is treated as equity.[13]

Courts have wrestled with recharacterization both on doctrinal grounds and as a matter of policy. Some have concluded that bankruptcy courts do not have the authority to treat debt as if it were equity. In other cases, including many of the most recent decisions, courts have concluded that they have the power to conduct this reverse alchemy, but they seem uncertain how to determine when debt should be recharacterized. A useful gauge of the uncertainty is the steady proliferation of factors courts try to take into account. After surveying the previous case law, the leading case compiled a list of eleven factors;[14] a subsequent case concluded that eleven was not enough, and added two more.[15]

This part begins by describing the recharacterization case law and arguing that much of the doctrinal uncertainty stems from the fact that several different kinds of issues are subsumed under the label "recharacterization." The doctrine has been further confused by courts' reliance on an older, superficially similar body of tax recharacterization case law. After disentangling the issues, we explore them in more detail in the second and third sections, and offer a proposed solution to the treatment of shareholder loans. The final section then revisits the multi-factor test that has emerged in the case law.

3.1 Recharacterization: disentangling the concerns

As part of a proposed bankruptcy reform that became the starting point for the Bankruptcy Act of 1978, the National Bankruptcy Review Commission proposed that equitable subordination be codified after forty years of development in the courts in the wake of the *Deep Rock* and *Pepper* v. *Litton* cases. Under the provision drafted by the Commission, the claims of insiders would have been automatically subordinated, and the bankruptcy court would have had discretion

13 See, e.g., J.H.M. Sprayregen, J.P. Friedland, J.A.J. Brighton, and S.F. Bianca, 'Recharacterization of Debt to Equity: An Overview, Update, and Practical Guide to an Evolving Doctrine', *Annual Survey of Bankruptcy Law* (2004) p. 1 at p. 4.

14 *In re Autostyle Plastics, Inc.*, 269 F.3d 726 (6th Cir. 2001). The eleven factors are listed and critiqued in section 3.4 *infra.*

15 *In re Outboard Marine Corp.*, 2003 WL 21697357 1, 5 (N.D. Ill. 2003) (adding "(12) the ratio of shareholder loans to capital and (13) the amount or degree of shareholder control").

to subordinate other claims as circumstances warranted.[16] The automatic subordination provision (a concept we will revisit below) disappeared with little fanfare, but discretionary subordination remained in the legislation that was eventually enacted. It is the terms of this codification, as it turns out, that have raised questions about bankruptcy courts' authority to recharacterize debt as equity.

The provision itself is quite simple. "[A]fter notice and a hearing," it reads, "the court may … under principles of equitable subordination, subordinate for purposes of distribution all or part of an allowed claim to all or part of another allowed claim or all or part of an allowed interest to all or part of another allowed interest."[17] The dilemma, in the view of some courts, is that this provision instructs courts to look to "principles of equitable subordination" as the basis for subordinating a claim. Yet the case law on recharacterization does not seem to rely on principles of equitable subordination at all. In most of the recharacterization cases, a shareholder or other insider supplies cash to a struggling company in the form of a loan. In some of the cases, the loan is poorly documented (or not documented at all) and the shareholder does not insist on regular payments. The question courts have often asked, as summarized by a group of prominent bankruptcy lawyers, is "whether the transaction bears the characteristics of an arm's length bargain."[18] In the equitable subordination context, by contrast, the principal issue – and thus a key principle – is whether the shareholder or creditor has engaged in inequitable conduct. In effect, then, recharacterization seems to achieve the effect of equitable subordination without requiring any showing of inequitable conduct. The cases that have questioned their own authority to recharacterize a loan have pointed to this tension between the recharacterization remedy and the language of the equitable subordination provision. "Where there is a specific provision governing these determinations," the most prominent of the cases concluded, "it is inconsistent with the Bankruptcy Code to allow such determinations to be made under different standards through the use of a court's equitable powers."[19]

Courts that conclude they have the authority to recharacterize have gently accused their more diffident peers of making a category mistake. Recharacterization and equitable subordination, they argue, are entirely different remedies. "The effect of a bankruptcy court's recharacterization of a claim from debt to equity may be similar to the court's subordination of a claim through equitable subordination," as the Sixth Circuit put it, "but there are important differences between a

---

[16] Report of the Commission on the Bankruptcy Laws of the United States, H.R. DOC. 93-137, Part II, 93d Cong., 1st Sess. 115 (1973).

[17] 11 USC § 510(c)(1).

[18] Sprayregen, et al., loc. cit. n. 13, at p. 12.

[19] *In re Pacific Express, Inc.*, 69 Bankr. 112 (9th Cir. BAP 1986) at p. 115.

court's analysis of recharacterization and equitable subordination issues. Not only do recharacterization and equitable subordination serve different *functions*, but the *extent to which a claim is subordinated* under each process may be different."[20] The question in a recharacterization case "is whether a debt actually exists."[21] With equitable subordination, by contrast, the validity of the debt obligation is not in question. The issue is "whether a legitimate creditor engaged in inequitable conduct;" if so, the principal remedy is to subordinate the creditor's claim to the claims of other creditors, not to treat the claim as equity.

There is an intuitive logic to the argument that recharacterization is simply a different creature than equitable subordination, and it seems to be prevailing in the case law. Nearly all of the most recent cases have concluded that courts do indeed have the power to recharacterize. But the line between equitable subordination and recharacterization is not quite so pristine as the cases suggest. Inequitable behavior is not a prerequisite for recharacterization – in theory, the question is simply: was the shareholder's capital infusion a loan or a contribution to capital? – yet courts' sense of the propriety of the shareholder's behavior seems to influence their decision whether to recharacterize.[22] The question whether the company was adequately capitalized at its inception also seems to figure prominently in both contexts. And courts – *Deep Rock* itself is a prime example – do not always assume that the obligations they subordinate in the equitable subordination context are legitimate claims.[23]

If this tendency to draw overly sharp distinctions between recharacterization and equitable subordination only affected courts' determination whether they have authority to recharacterize claims, it would be relatively unproblematic. Although courts have exaggerated the differences, the reasoning would go, their basic conclusion that recharacterization is not prohibited by the Bankruptcy Code is sound. But the effect is not as simple as this. The effort to identify an analytically distinct doctrinal foundation for recharacterization seems to have caused courts to confuse two different issues that arise when shareholders pump cash into a troubled enterprise. The first problem is shareholder contributions that are ambiguous in form. Although structured as loans, the contributions sometimes are

---

20 *In re AutoStyle Plastics*, 269 F.3d at p. 748 [emphasis in original].

21 In statutory terms, a "creditor" is an "entity that has a claim against the debtor," 11 USC § 101(10) and a "claim" is a "right to payment." 11 USC § 101(5). The question is whether the shareholder is a creditor who has made a loan and thus has a claim, or whether the contribution is simply an "interest."

22 In *In re Micro-Precision Technologies, Inc.*, 303 Bankr. 238 (Bankr. D. N.H. 2003) at p. 247, for instance, the Court described the recharacterization doctrine as applying to claims by corporate insiders and those who have dealt with the debtor in a potentially inequitable fashion.

23 As evidenced by the fact that the Supreme Court did not simply subordinate the controlling shareholder's claim; it also insisted that control of the reorganized company needed to be shared with the company's preferred stockholders.

not treated like ordinary loans; they may lack documentation or be repaid more erratically than other loans. Second is the question whether and on what terms loans from an insider should be encouraged when a business has encountered financial distress. Courts' reliance on tax recharacterization doctrine has further confused the analysis. Disentangling these considerations may help us to develop a new perspective on the recharacterization cases.

3.2 The ambiguous loan problem

A natural inclination of the principal shareholders of a floundering business is to look in their own pockets (and often the pockets of friends and relatives) for cash to plug the leaks. They see the problems first, and they may conclude that arranging an outside loan would be too time-consuming and uncertain. Better that those who know the business best provide the funding themselves.

The problem is that, while these cash infusions from insiders are usually described as loans, they sometimes are not treated like ordinary loans. There may not be any formal loan agreement, for instance, or the documentation that exists may omit key terms like the interest rate or repayment schedule. In one recent case, four of the five promissory notes called for in a purported secured lending transaction were never drafted, and the original loan was never properly perfected. The imaginary notes were subsequently assigned to another entity (which, like the first, was controlled by shareholders of the debtor) but no assignment document was ever executed.[24] In other, less egregious cases, no payments are made at all between the time of the capital infusion and the time the company files for bankruptcy. The absence of any payments to the shareholder is not necessarily inconsistent with the contribution being a loan – after all, demand loans have precisely this quality – but this makes it look as though the insider is trying to treat the contribution as a loan if the company performs either very well (and thus can repay it) or very poorly (winding up in bankruptcy), while treating it as a contribution to equity while the company's finances remain in a precarious state.

In Clark's terms, the key issue here is whether the ambiguous loan violates the debtor's obligation of Truth. These loans do not interfere with the expectation of Respect, since the shareholder is not giving the company's money away; and Evenhandedness is not at issue. The problem is that a shareholder's ambiguous

---

24 *Bunch* v. *J.M. Capital Fin. Ltd (In re Hoffinger Indus., Inc.)*, 327 Bankr. 389 (Bankr. D. Ark. 2005). The Court had no difficulty finding that recharacterization was appropriate on these facts. "This simply is not debt," the Court concluded. "The purpose of the JM Capital transaction was not to incur debt necessary to the debtor's operations; its purpose was to pay interest on equity and to judgment-proof the debtor." Ibid., at pp. 410-411.

loan may create a obligation that other creditors do not even know exists. A supplier who checks Dun & Bradstreet or another credit reporting service to assess the company's overall debt situation may not see any reference to the shareholder's purported loan. The misleading picture of the company's finances could, among other things, cause the supplier to provide credit it otherwise would have withheld.

Since the principal issue with an ambiguous loan is one of Truth, this objective should guide the initial decision whether it is treated as debt or equity. If there is little or no documentation, or there is other evidence that the company's creditors were or might have been misled about the existence of the claimed loan, recharacterization may be appropriate. The fact that a loan is clearly documented or shows up in the company's credit reports, by contrast, would weigh strongly in favor of treating the cash infusion as a loan.

Notice that the focus is quite different from the tax law jurisprudence on recharacterizing debt as equity.[25] The tax cases are most worried about low priority obligations that function like a class of stock but are treated like debt in order to give a shareholder the tax benefits of debt. Convertibility is worrisome from a tax perspective, since debt that can be converted into voting stock enables the company to treat the interest payments on the debt as a (deductible) business expense, while giving the security holder the option of converting to stock for the purposes of voting control. Convertibility has not been at issue in the bankruptcy recharacterization cases, and, even if it were, the existence of a right to convert would tell us little about whether the initial characterization as debt should be honored. Similarly, and more importantly, if the contribution is structured as a traditional secured loan, it poses no problems from a tax perspective. But secured shareholder loans are quite worrisome in the bankruptcy context, for reasons discussed in detail in the next section.

Where the status of a loan is ambiguous, courts would do well to focus directly on the real problem with this ambiguity – the danger that other creditors will be misled. The ideal in question is Truth, and the concern is that sloppiness or deception by the shareholder will interfere with collection by creditors of their claims.

---

25 The classic analysis of Internal Revenue Service doctrine on whether a security should be treated as debt or equity for tax purposes is W.T. Plumb, Jr., 'The Federal Income Tax Significance of Corporate Debt: A Critical Analysis and a Proposal', 26 *Tax Law Review* (1971) p. 369. For a brief overview of tax recharacterization doctrine, see D.A. Skeel, Jr., 'Markets, Courts and the Brave New World of Bankruptcy Theory', *Wisconsin Law Review* (1993) p. 465 at p. 501.

3.3 Ill-founded loans that hinder other creditors

The second, more subtle, issue is whether shareholder contributions to a faltering enterprise may interfere with creditors' collection of their claims even if there is no sloppiness or deception whatsoever.[26] The ideal in question here is not Truth so much as a more general concern, as Clark puts it, "of Nonhindrance of the enforcement of valid legal obligations against oneself, in connection with transfers of one's property."[27] Clark illustrates the ideal of Nonhindrance by imagining a debtor who sells readily marketable stock for illiquid assets in order to make it difficult for her creditors to collect the amounts they are owed. A shareholder loan seems quite different from loading up on illiquid assets – indeed our initial inclination is often to applaud the shareholder loan – but the effect may often be quite similar.

To appreciate how a shareholder loan can hinder the company's creditors, even when it is done in the light of day, consider a company that owes its creditors a total of $100, and whose assets are worth a total of $80. If the principal shareholder contributes $10 in cash to the company, the cash can be used to pursue a project that has a 50 percent probability of being worth $15 after a year's time, and a 50 percent probability of being worth $0. Because the project has a net value of negative $2.50 ($7.50 expected value minus $10 cost), pursuing it will reduce the recovery available to the company's creditors. Yet if the shareholder structures her contribution so that she is promised, say, $15 in a year's time on the principal and accrued interest for the contribution, she has a financial incentive to make the loan despite the consequences for the company's creditors.

Shift now from the artificial numerical example to the real world of financially troubled companies (particularly the small- and medium-sized businesses that figure in many of the recharacterization cases). Will troubled firms often have business projects that fit the profile of the project described above? The answer is almost certainly yes. For many troubled businesses, continuing the business for another month or year, rather than shutting down today, is, in effect, a net negative present value project. Injecting additional cash may simply prolong the inevitable demise, using up assets whose value might otherwise have gone to creditors. In theory, creditors could take matters into their own hands under these circumstances and throw the company into bankruptcy involuntarily. But the shareholder loan may itself prevent creditors from filing an involuntary bankruptcy petition. To sustain an involuntary petition, creditors must show that the

---

[26] As hopefully is clear, both concerns can be implicated by the same shareholder loan. But it is essential to keep the analysis separate.

[27] Clark, loc. cit. n. 1, at pp. 512-513.

debtor is not paying its debts as they come due.[28] If the loan enables the company to pay its current creditors for a few more months, the creditors will not be able to make this showing.

If every shareholder loan fit this pattern – good money, badly spent – a simple prohibition of shareholder loans would be in order. But sometimes shareholder loans make both creditors and the company better rather than worse off. If there is a 50 percent probability the project described above will return $15, for instance, and a 50 percent probability of $7, the $10 investment suddenly has a present value of $11 and is worth pursuing. In a world where shareholder loans may destroy value that would otherwise go to creditors, but may also fund valuable projects, how should courts respond to a request that a shareholder loan be recharacterized or subordinated?

An elegant new article that carefully explores the effects of recharacterizing shareholder loans both when a company is solvent and when it is insolvent concludes that courts should assess the quality of the project that the loan was used to finance. "A shareholder loan would fail the test," on this view, and should thus be treated as equity "when the accepted value of total assets after a rescue attempt results in a reduction" in the value of the company's assets. "If an increase in the going concern value after the rescue was to be expected, the shareholder-creditor should be treated like a third-party creditor in bankruptcy."[29] The beauty of this approach is that it neatly distinguishes between shareholder loans that benefit the company and those that impair creditors' recoveries by inappropriately postponing the company's bankruptcy. The obvious problem is that courts (and the experts whose testimony would inform a court's decision) are not well positioned to make these calculations. In addition to the complexities of the basic analysis, the scrutiny would be prone to the kinds of hindsight bias that make courts reluctant to inquire into business judgments in other contexts.

Before we can offer any conclusions about the ill-founded loan problem, we need to add one more essential variable. The analysis thus far has assumed that the shareholder is lending to the company on an unsecured basis. But a substantial proportion of shareholder loans are made on a secured basis. In these cases, the

---

28 11 USC § 303(h).

29 M. Gelter, *The Subordination of Shareholder Loans in Bankruptcy*, John M. Olin Center for Law, Economics, and Business, Harvard Law School, Fellows' Discussion Paper No. 4 (January 2005) p. 32. Gelter's analysis suggests that, if the company is insolvent, recharacterization will never preclude an efficient investment and will discourage some but not all inefficient investments. If the company is insolvent, recharacterization will have a wide variety of effects, some beneficial and some harmful, depending on the size of the difference between the expected value of the project and the liquidation value of the company's assets. The analysis considers only uncollateralized loans. As will become clear in the text below, secured loans are, in our view, the most important and worrisome form of lending by shareholders.

question is not simply whether shareholder loans should be honored and thus encouraged. There is the added issue of whether the shareholder should be permitted to claim priority for the loan.

Once again, we should begin by asking whether these loans inappropriately hinder creditors. The basic trade-off is the same: as with unsecured loans, secured lending can be used to finance projects with either a net positive or a net negative value. But the stakes are in a sense higher with secured lending. Because the promise of collateral leapfrogs the secured lender ahead of other creditors, giving her the equivalent of a seat in first class, lenders may be willing to provide credit on a secured basis even if the financing will be used for projects whose value is much less than their cost. Yet the prospect of security can also facilitate financing for a valuable project that no lender would fund on an unsecured basis, due to the fact that the lender's claim would simply be lumped together with all of the debtor's other obligations. In economic jargon, collateral sometimes leads to overinvestment, but it also can be used to solve an underinvestment or debt overhang dilemma.[30]

The implications of over- and underinvestment are initially quite counterintuitive. One might think that secured loans should always be discouraged if a company is insolvent. In reality, however, the more deeply insolvent a company is, the more serious the underinvestment problem will be; absent security, lenders will not finance even gold-plated projects if the debtor is drowning in debt.[31] The state of the company's solvency is thus a very imperfect measure of whether a secured loan should be applauded or condemned.[32]

If a shareholder's decision whether to lend money to her company were generally based on an objective assessment of the prospects for the investment, courts could simply honor both the loan and the shareholder's priority treatment. But shareholder decision making is anything but objective as a company sinks into financial distress. To be sure, shareholder-managers know the business better than anyone else. But they tend to view its prospects through the rosiest of glasses. They also have a huge human capital investment in the company. The shareholder's decision to make a loan therefore may be anything but objective.

Another set of concerns arises once the loan has been made, and applies even to loans that are not infected by the distortions we have just described. Because

---

30 The classic analysis is Stewart C. Myers, 'Determinants of Corporate Borrowing', 5 *Journal of Financial Economics* (1977) p. 147. Over- and underinvestment analysis is applied to debtor-in-possession financing in bankruptcy in G.G. Triantis, 'A Theory of the Regulation of Debtor-in-Possession Financing', 46 *Vanderbilt Law Review* (1993) p. 901.

31 See, e.g., Triantis, loc. cit. n. 30, at p. 920.

32 Indeed, to the extent one focused entirely on the company's solvency or insolvency, it would make more sense to subordinate any loan made while the company was solvent and to honor loans made after it sinks into insolvency.

the shareholder who makes the loan is also likely to be managing the business itself, there is a risk that she will take steps that increase the amount of collateral subject to her security interest to the detriment of other creditors. The shareholder can build up the company's inventory, for instance, if the security interest includes inventory. This general pattern of behavior is common enough to have a name: it is known as "feeding the lien."

One can imagine using either of two approaches to address these concerns, an *ad hoc* approach or a *per se* rule. Under a particularized, *ad hoc* approach, courts might look for evidence that the shareholder had in fact taken steps to feed her lien, and disallow the security interest only if evidence of manipulation could be found. But manipulation not only may be difficult to detect: it also is only a small part of the problem of secured shareholder loans. More serious and pervasive is the risk that the secured shareholder loan will prolong the travails of a troubled company at the expense of its creditors. Lending on a collateralized basis enables a shareholder to have her cake and eat it too: to keep the hope of a turnaround alive, while using a security interest to limit her exposure under the new loan. The risk that this will simply delay the failure of an unviable company, and that value will be destroyed in the interim, is so high, in our view, that it calls for a *per se* response: courts should automatically disallow the shareholder's security interest and treat the loan as a general, unsecured claim.

One obvious objection is that at least a few of these loans may be justified. If the company is drowning in debt, but has a valuable business opportunity, a rational shareholder might be reluctant to lend unless she were given priority, since the value of any new, unsecured loan would be diluted by the other competing claims against the debtor's assets. This is simply another way of saying that collateral may be necessary to solve an underinvestment (or debt overhang) problem. But this objection is not especially persuasive on inspection. If the company, unlike most in these circumstances, has a valuable prospect but needs to borrow on a collateralized basis to pursue it, the company still could look to an outside creditor for the loan. Moreover, if the company does find itself in bankruptcy, the generous provisions for post-petition financing make it likely that a company which truly does have good future prospects will be able to obtain financing – and the financing arrangement will be overseen by a truly objective decision maker: the bankruptcy judge.[33]

---

[33] DIP financing is authorized by 11 USC § 364. For a brief history of DIP financing, and an analysis of its use in recent cases, see D.A. Skeel, Jr., 'The Past, Present and Future of Debtor-in-Possession Financing', 25 *Cardozo Law Review* (2004) p. 1905. See also D.G. Baird and R.K. Rasmussen, 'Private Debt and the Missing Lever of Corporate Governance', 154 *University of Pennsylvania Law Review* (2006, forthcoming) (exploring lender governance both before and in bankruptcy).

A second objection arises from precisely the opposite intuition to the first. To the extent one is persuaded (as we are) that eve-of-insolvency secured loans are more likely to lead to overinvestment than to counteract underinvestment, one might go still further and subordinate even those secured loans that are made by a third party if they are made when the company is in financial trouble.[34] In our view, this view has much more to recommend it than is usually assumed, but we would be reluctant to extend the *per se* subordination this far. One reason to distinguish third-party loans from shareholder loans is that third parties are less likely to be in a position to "feed the lien" or otherwise manipulate the company's affairs to protect the new secured loan at the expense of other creditors. In addition, when a shareholder lends money to the company, she is preserving the "option value" of her equity interest in the company. The loan is in a very real sense designed to keep her interest as a shareholder of the company alive. Loans by a third-party lender are not subject to the same conflict and are somewhat less worrisome as a result.

Each of these explanations is only partial at best, however. There still remains the nagging suspicion that secured loans to financially troubled companies will often simply prolong the inevitable demise. A more compelling explanation comes from the perspective third-party lenders generally bring to their decision whether to lend to a troubled company. If these lenders simply focused on the loan in question, eve-of-bankruptcy secured loans by a third party might often lead to overinvestment. But lenders generally are not focusing simply on their initial loan. They are more likely to view the loan as the first step toward an ongoing lending relationship with the debtor. As a result, lenders are much more likely to lend to a company they expect to survive, than to make the last loan to a company that is on its way down.[35] This does not suggest there is no reason to worry about third-party secured loans to a troubled company. But it does suggest that these loans are far less troublesome than loans by a shareholder.

If secured loans by the shareholders of troubled companies are worrisome, some might be inclined to go even further than we have suggested, and disallow even unsecured shareholder loans. Under this view, every loan by a shareholder would be subordinated to all other creditors or recharacterized as equity in order to address the overinvestment concerns we have discussed. Although we believe that this position has much to recommend it, we are not inclined to go quite so far. In part, our reluctance stems from the fact that the shareholder cannot manipulate

---

34 Although he has not explicitly endorsed this view, Barry Adler has hinted at such a position. See, e.g., B.E. Adler, 'A Re-Examination of Near-Bankruptcy Investment Incentives', 62 *University of Chicago Law Review* (1995) p. 575 at p. 605.

35 See, for example, Skeel, loc. cit. n. 33, at pp. 1924-1925 (discussing the importance of ongoing lending relationships in the debtor-in-possession financing context).

an unsecured loan quite so easily as a secured loan. If the shareholder induces the company to repay her rather than other creditors on the eve of bankruptcy, for instance, the trustee may be able to invoke bankruptcy's prohibition of preferential payments as a basis for retrieving the payments.[36] In addition, shareholders may sometimes be a better source of loans than a third party, because the shareholder loan saves the transaction costs of finding and negotiating with a third-party lender. We should acknowledge that we remain less than entirely convinced by these arguments against full subordination of shareholder lending.[37] But the more pressing concern is that shareholders not be entitled to claim a secured status for loans they make to the company.

Thus far, we have assumed that the shareholder was a shareholder before she lent money to the company. In the United States, this will generally be an accurate description of the chronology. But sometimes, particularly in the European context, an existing creditor acquires equity. How should this situation be treated? In our view, the acquisition of an equity interest by an existing creditor is less problematic than a shareholder loan, because it is less likely to have a dilutive effect on the interests of current creditors. We would make one major exception, however: if the creditor acquires a controlling equity stake in the company, the risk that the creditor will use its control to favor its own interests arises, just as with a secured shareholder loan.[38] Under these circumstances, we would therefore apply the same principles as with a shareholder loan. At the very least, the secured portion should be disallowed.

Let us pause here to briefly consider an apparent tension between our starting point – a consideration of the moral obligations of debtors to their creditors – and the conclusions we have reached, which do not seem as obviously based on general moral intuitions. Indeed, the moral arguments might seem to suggest that

---

36 11 USC § 547.

37 As we discuss in more detail in section 4.2.2, another argument sometimes advanced in favor of shareholder loans is that the loans counteract shareholders' incentives to take excessive risks in order to preserve their stake in the company. This argument seems plausible to us with unsecured shareholder loans but much less so with a secured loan, since the secured loan may be protected against loss even when the shareholder gambles unsuccessfully with the company's assets. Like us, Clark is agnostic about the question whether unsecured shareholder loans should automatically be subordinated. Clark, op. cit. n. 1, at pp. 538-539. Clark does not address the issue of secured shareholder loans.

38 Interestingly, Germany provides an exception to its equity substitution rules that can be seen as addressing the issue described in the text. This provision, § 32a III 2 GmbHG, reads: "These rules [on equity substitution] do not apply to a non-managing shareholder whose equity share does not exceed 10 percent." § 32a III 3 GmbHG then adds: "If a creditor acquires equity in a crisis of the company in order to overcome this crisis, this does not lead to the application of the equity substitution laws on his existing or new loans." As the discussion in the text suggests, this second exception is more problematic in the event the creditor acquires a controlling stake.

shareholder loans, whether secured or not, should be applauded. A shareholder whose business is failing will naturally attempt to save it, the reasoning goes, and these rescue efforts should be praised rather than skeptically scrutinized. Notice, however, that this argument does not explain why shareholders should be permitted to lend on a collateralized basis. After all, security lets them have their cake and eat it too: leading a rescue effort without taking the risk of failure. Similarly but more importantly, our initial intuition that shareholders should be applauded for contributing to a rescue needs to be adjusted to consider the likelihood that the "rescue" will often destroy value and hinder creditors' ability to collect what they are owed.

UK company law is a useful comparison here. When a UK company encounters financial distress, its directors are expected to accede to insolvency proceedings rather than continuing business as usual in the hope of digging out of the company's hole. Under the United Kingdom's "wrongful trading" rules, directors who violate this expectation are subject to a wide range of sanctions, including personal liability and the possibility of a fifteen-year prohibition from serving as a director at another company.[39] The wrongful trading rule reflects an assumption that directors who carry on with ordinary trading after the company begins to hemorrhage cash are hindering their shareholders and creditors. US corporate law takes a more optimistic view of the prospects for recovery and generally does not punish directors who try to postpone the day of reckoning.[40] But with shareholder loans, a context where the risk of undermining creditor recoveries is both systematic and high, the moral assumption that secured loans will have the effect of hindering creditors is fully warranted. To put the point slightly differently, a transaction transferring a security interest to one of the company's shareholders is more like a fraudulent conveyance than an ordinary loan.

3.4 Applying the analysis: the eleven-factor *Autostyle Plastics* test

The previous two sections have argued that two different kinds of concerns may be implicated when shareholders make a loan to their own company. With ambiguous loans, courts should focus on whether the existence of the loan would be clear to an inquiring creditor. If not, and if the loan thus violates the ideal of Truth, it should be treated as a contribution to equity rather than as debt. Whether

[39] The wrongful trading rule is described in J. Armour, B. Cheffins and D. Skeel, 'Corporate Ownership Structure and the Evolution of Bankruptcy Law: Lessons from the United Kingdom', 55 *Vanderbilt Law Review* (2002) p. 1699 at pp. 1746-1747.

[40] For an argument that it should, see A.M. Dickerson, 'A Behavioral Approach to Analyzing Corporate Failures, 38 *Wake Forest Law Review* (2003) p. 101.

or not a loan is ambiguous, it also may hinder the company's creditors, dissipating value as the company's shareholders attempt to postpone liquidation. Here, the more general concern of Nonhindrance takes center stage. We have argued that this second concern should be addressed by invalidating any security interest that purports to secure the shareholder loan. As a doctrinal matter, courts would need to use equitable subordination rather than recharacterization as the basis for disallowing a shareholder's security interest on Nonhindrance grounds, since our analysis does not call for recharacterizing the secured loan as equity. Rather, it would be treated as an ordinary unsecured claim.

Recent judicial opinions addressing the recharacterization issue have conflated the Truth and Nonhindrance concerns and also have been overly influenced by the seemingly similar tax recharacterization doctrine, which, as we have seen, is aimed at a very different problem. The case law that has resulted is, to put it charitably, muddled. As a result, we will argue, courts have been too willing to honor shareholder loans according to their terms. To see this, consider the eleven-factor test laid out in the leading recharacterization case. According to the Sixth Circuit, courts should consider each of the following factors:

(1) the names given to the instruments;
(2) presence or absence of a fixed maturity date and payment schedule;
(3) presence or absence of fixed interest payments;
(4) source of repayments;
(5) adequacy or inadequacy of capitalization;
(6) identity of interest (or not) between the creditor and shareholder;
(7) security (or not) for the advances;
(8) the corporation's ability to obtain financing from outside lenders;
(9) the extent to which the advances were subordinated to other creditors;
(10) the extent to which the advances were used to acquire capital assets; and
(11) the presence or absence of a sinking fund to provide repayment.[41]

Notice the variety of different concerns that seem to be proxied by the eleven factors. The first three factors focus squarely on the ambiguous loan issue. "The absence of notes or other instruments of indebtedness," as the *Autostyle Plastics* court put it, "is a strong indication that the advances were capital contributions and not loans."[42] The fifth and eighth factors offer related but independent standards for assessing whether a cash infusion should be seen as a loan (both of which, as we shall see, are standards that are used in Germany and Austria). If a company is undercapitalized, the fifth factor implies, new cash should be viewed

41 *In re Autostyle Plastics*, 269 F.3d at p. 750.
42 Ibid.

as addressing the need for capital rather than as a loan. Under the eighth factor, the intuition is that shareholder financing should not be treated as a loan if no one else would make a similar loan on these terms. Most of the remaining factors deal with the Nonhindrance issue in one way or another, but in a fashion that is clearly influenced by tax recharacterization doctrine. Factors 7 (whether the shareholder has insisted on security), 9 (whether the obligation is subordinated) and 11 (whether the obligation has a dedicated source of repayment) can each be seen as influenced by the tax concern that shareholders will create a low priority debt security, rather than a class of stock, in order to take advantage of the deductibility of debt. Each of these factors overlaps with the Nonhindrance analysis.[43] Factor 10 then addresses Nonhindrance directly, asking whether the funds will be used to acquire capital assets or to finance operations.

There are two intactible problems with this welter of factors. The first is that many are either unhelpful or used in precisely the wrong way. Second, the overall list has tended to distort courts' analysis of what should and should not be honored as a loan.

The emphasis on undercapitalization falls into the unhelpful category. As noted earlier and discussed again in the next part, a company's financial condition is not always a good barometer of whether a loan is justified: if the project is a good one, the loan should be encouraged even if the company is heavily indebted. Moreover, the emphasis on undercapitalization conflates the recharacterization question with the analytically distinct issue of whether the corporate veil should be pierced and the company's shareholders held personally responsible for its obligations. Creditworthiness is a more defensible standard, but it too is flawed, since it may be difficult to determine whether an outside creditor would make a loan, and this willingness is itself an imperfect proxy for whether a loan would enhance or destroy value.[44]

Particularly misguided is the tenth factor (whether the advances were used to acquire capital assets). "Use of advances to meet the daily operating needs of the corporation," according to the *Autostyle Plastics* court," rather than to purchase capital assets, is indicative of *bona fide* indebtedness."[45] Although it seems sensible at first glance (at least to those who snoozed through the discussion in the last section), this distinction is very hard to defend; if anything, it gets the likely effect of a cash infusion exactly backwards. Pumping more money into the operations of a troubled firm will often simply prolong its deterioration – recall

[43] Unfortunately, however, as discussed below, tax recharacterization doctrine has led courts to apply these factors in almost exactly the wrong way in bankruptcy.

[44] See, e.g., Gelter, op. cit. n. 29, at pp. 27-30 (noting that a hypothetical lender would base her loan decision on her prospects of repayment under the terms of the loan, rather than on whether the loan is value enhancing for the debtor).

[45] *In re Autostyle Plastics*, 269 F.3d at p. 752.

that unwarranted continuation is the most frequent form of "overinvestment" – whereas the acquisition a capital asset may (though, to be sure, it also may not) be tied to a profitable new business opportunity. Similarly, the factors that seem indebted to tax law privilege secured lending. Secured loans, as we have seen, are precisely the loans that pose the greatest danger of overinvestment, particularly when the lender is a shareholder rather than a third party.

What do courts do with all of this? Faced with a welter of factors, they seem to focus heavily on whether the infusion looks like a "proper" loan. If the loan is carefully documented, courts are loath to interfere. This stance makes perfect sense for addressing the ambiguous loan issue. It also can be seen as linking the ambiguous loan factors with the factors that show a preference for secured loans, since the security interest will generally be reflected in a public filing. But the ideal of Nonhindrance seems to get lost in the enthusiasm for form and security. As a result, properly documented secured loans are almost always upheld, as in the *Autostyle Plastics* case itself. Yet these are precisely the loans that pose the greatest risk of overinvestment and of manipulation by the shareholder-manager. While clear documentation addresses the ambiguous loan problem, the Nonhindrance ideal suggests that the security interests should be subordinated and the loans treated as general unsecured obligations.

4. The German and Austrian alternatives: creditworthiness and undercapitalization

4.1 **Overview of the rules**

The German doctrine on equity substitution law (*Eigenkapitalersatzrecht*) has its roots in the same era that saw the emergence of equitable subordination in the United States. In the late 1930s, the German Imperial Court (*Reichsgericht*) decided the first German cases on equity substitution.[46] In the first case, the *Reichsgericht* viewed its decision as an individual correction of a special case of misconduct; but by the second case it had already established a more general rule regarding the subordination of shareholder loans.[47] With its *Lufttaxi* decision in 1959,[48] the German Supreme Court (*Bundesgerichtshof*, BGH) adopted this case law and developed the doctrine over the years.

---

46 RG *JW* 1938, 862; 1939, 355.

47 B. Gehde, *Eigenkapitalersetzende Gesellschafterleistungen in Deutschland und den USA* [Equity Substituting Contributions by Shareholders in Germany and the United States] (Berlin, Duncker & Humblot 1997) p. 54.

48 *BGHZ* 76, 326.

The doctrinal justifications for the equity substitution rules have both changed and accumulated in the fifty years since the original cases. Among the stated rationales are: that companies should issue equity instead of debt in times of crisis; that it is inappropriate for the company to put the financing risk solely on outside creditors; that shareholder-lenders have informational advantages that could operate to the detriment of other creditors; that the shareholders should not be permitted to speculate at the expense of other creditors; and that shareholder loans may create a misleading perception that the company is adequately capitalized.[49] In its *BuM/WestLB* decision, the BGH made it clear that it considers all of these concerns the basis for its doctrine, and the Court consolidated them into the term "responsibility for consequences of corporate finance."[50] The current doctrinal justification has been criticized,[51] but seems to be firmly established in the BGH's decisions since *BuM/WestLB*.[52] Legal scholars have added additional justifications for the doctrine, including the concern that shareholder loans circumvent the oversight of the financial markets[53] and that they create a risk of overinvestment.[54]

As in the United States, a rule calling for the subordination of all shareholder loans might seem like the best response to these concerns. Indeed, one of the *Reichsgericht's* initial decisions seemed to endorse such a *per se* rule.[55] But, even more than in the United States, shareholder loans have long been an essential source of finance for small- and medium-sized German companies.[56] It is of course possible that companies would begin to rely more on outside financing, and that outside lenders might step into the vacuum, if shareholder loans were automatically subordinated. But given the lower transaction costs of a shareholder loan, and the potential frictions that might interfere with efforts to obtain third

---

49 H. von Gerkan and P. Hommelhoff, *Handbuch des Kapitalersatzrechts* [Handbook of Equity Substitution Law], 2nd edn. (Cologne, RWS 2002) p. 30; T. Bezzenberger, 'Kapitalersetzende Gesellschafterdarlehen im Recht der GmbH' [Equity Substituting Shareholder Loans in the Law Regarding the GmbH], in H.-P. Westermann and K. Mock, eds., *Festschrift für Gerold Bezzenberger zum 70. Geburtstag* [Festschrift for Gerold Bezzenberger for his 70th Birthday] (Berlin, Walter de Gruyter 2000) p. 23 at pp. 28-29.

50 *'Finanzierungsfolgenverantwortung'*, *BGHZ* 90, 381, 388.

51 See, e.g., Bezzenberger, loc. cit. n. 49, at pp. 34-35; B. Grunewald, 'Plädoyer für eine Abschaffung der Rechtsregeln für eigenkapitalersetzende Gesellschafterdarlehen' [Plea for the Abolition of the Legal Rules Regarding Equity Substituting Shareholder Loans], 88 *GmbH Rundschau* (1997) pp. 7-10.

52 *BGHZ* 90, 381, 389; *BGHZ* 105, 168, 175; *BGHZ* 127, 336, 346.

53 Bezzenberger, loc. cit. n. 49, at p. 36.

54 E. Renger, *Gläubigerschutz durch § 32a GmbHG* [Creditor Protection by means of § 32a GmbHG] (Frankfurt, Peter Lang 2004) p. 69.

55 RG *JW* 1939, 355, 356: "The Court treats these alleged loans as what they really are: equity."

56 Von Gerkan and Hommelhoff, op. cit. n. 49, at pp. 21-22.

party loans, we are hesitant to endorse a blanket rule that would subordinate all shareholder loans. As in the United States, we need a criterion that differentiates between those shareholder loans that should be subordinated and those that should stand as loans, as we discuss in more detail in the next section.

The German rules only subordinate shareholder loans which are deemed to "substitute equity."[57] The criterion used to determine an equity substitution is whether the company's circumstances were such that a reasonable shareholder would make an equity contribution (§32a GmbHG defines such a situation as a "crisis of the company"). In order to clarify this standard, the criterion of credit-worthiness is applied. The creditworthiness test asks whether a reasonable outsider would have given the same loan under the same conditions.[58] If the answer is no, the shareholder loan is deemed an equity substitute.

The Austrian Supreme Court (*Oberster Gerichtshof*) adopted the German rules in a case decided in 1991.[59] In 2003, the Austrian Parliament codified these rules as well.[60] The main difference between the Austrian doctrine that has emerged, as compared to its German counterpart, is that the Austrian rules focus more on undercapitalization and less on creditworthiness.

4.2 Critique of the German criteria

The German creditworthiness standard has the virtue of drawing a clear, intuitively attractive line between shareholder loans that are permissible and those considered a threat to the company's other creditors. Its aim is to maintain a company's minimum capitalization and thereby to protect the company's other creditors. Although making a hypothetical, after-the-fact assessment of whether a third party would have made the loan in question may be difficult, there is now an extensive body of case law to guide the inquiry.[61] The problem with this standard

---

[57] *BGHZ* 76, 330; M. Lutter, P. Hommelhoff, et al., eds., *GmbH-Gesetz* (Cologne, Otto Schmidt 2004) at § 32a/b, Rn. 18.

[58] BGH *WM* 1972, 75; *BGHZ* 81, 262-263; BGH *ZIP* (*Zeitschrift für Wirtschaftsrecht*) 1990, 99-100.

[59] OGH 8 May 1991, 8 Ob 9/91, SZ 64/53.

[60] *Bundesgesetz über Eigenkapital ersetzende Gesellschafterleistungen, Art. I Gesellschafts- und Insolvenzrechtsänderungsgesetz* [Federal Law Regarding Equity Substituting Shareholder Contributions] 2003 – GIRÄG 2003, *BGBl. I* 2003/92.

[61] For opposing arguments on the difficulty of assessing creditworthiness, see, for example, A. Goetz, *Juristische und ökonomische Analyse des Eigenkapitalersatzrechts* [Legal and Economic Analysis of the Equity Substitution Law] (Nomos, Baden-Baden 2001) p. 43 (difficult to apply); and Gehde, op. cit. n. 47, at p. 94 (fairly simple to apply).

While creditworthiness is the key criterion, German courts also look at capitalization to determine equity substitution. Lutter and Hommelhoff, op. cit. n. 57, at § 32a/b, Rn. 33. As noted earlier, capitalization is also the main factor in Austrian equity substitution law. The

is not so much with its difficulty in application, but with the focus on creditworthiness itself. It does not identify the proper claims for subordination. As we shall see, the weakness of the test is especially evident in the case of secured shareholder loans.

4.2.1 *Inefficient results*

The most obvious problem with the creditworthiness standard is that it leads to inefficient results.[62] A hypothetical outside lender does not base her decision whether to extend a loan or not on efficiency concerns, but rather solely on the basis of her own chance of recovery.[63] Her individual benefits, however, might not coincide with the best result for society as a whole, or even for other creditors of the company. As discussed earlier, the key question for many of the companies that rely on shareholder loans is whether keeping the company afloat is cost-justified, or whether it is more likely simply to delay an inevitable failure and destroy value in the process. Ideally, the court might address this question directly and subordinate loans that have a net negative present value.[64] But, as noted earlier, courts are not well positioned to make this kind of determination.

4.2.2 *Inability to properly deal with secured shareholder loans*

The shortcomings of the creditworthiness standard are particularly evident when it comes to secured shareholder loans. As with recharacterization doctrine in the United States, the German creditworthiness standard treats secured shareholder loans as less worrisome than unsecured loans.[65] The problem with this, as we have seen, is that the risk of overinvestment – of postponing default and diverting value from creditors as a result – is particularly high if the shareholder is able to lend on a secured basis.

In addition, because the loan is made by an insider-shareholder rather than a third party, the benefits that justify secured loans in other contexts are much less

---

shortcomings of the capitalization standard are quite similar to the shortcoming of creditworthiness discussed below. Most importantly, adequacy of capitalization is a poor proxy for whether a proposed loan should be encouraged or discouraged.

62 Gelter, op. cit. n. 29, at pp. 27-30.

63 Ibid., at p. 29.

64 Ibid., at p. 28.

65 "If the company gives a security from its own assets, which an outside creditor would have required, considered sufficient in the moment of issuing the loan and actually received, it is a factor against the qualification as equity substitution, unless special circumstances require a different judgment." BGH *ZIP* 1999, 1524, 1526; BGH *ZIP* 2001, 839-840.

likely to be in evidence. Shareholder-lenders cannot be expected to monitor the debtor and its managers, for instance, if they themselves are the managers.[66]

In the German context, shareholder loans are often defended as helping to align the shareholder-managers' incentives with interests of the company's outside creditors.[67] Shareholders have incentives to engage in risks, the argument goes, since they are the ones who benefit from positive results, while being able to share the consequences of negative results with the creditors. The more highly leveraged the company is, the greater the shareholders' incentives to take risks at the expense of their creditors. The conflict in incentives is reduced, however, if the shareholder lends money to the company and thus also acts as a creditor.[68] Indeed, the shareholder may become affirmatively risk averse if her debt interest is sufficiently large.[69]

While this alignment-of-incentives defense of shareholder loans is at least plausible if the shareholder lends on an unsecured basis, it loses nearly all of its force if the loan is secured.[70] The shareholder/secured creditor does not bear the risk of default on her loan due to the security, but still receives the profits if the company succeeds. As a result, the security enables the shareholder to have her cake and eat it too. If anything, a secured loan may exacerbate the conflict between the shareholder's incentives and the interests of the outside creditors and the company as a whole. It does not remove the shareholder's incentive to take risks, and at the same time facilitates the financing that may make the risk taking possible.

In short, the creditworthiness standard is particularly difficult to defend as applied to secured shareholder loans.[71] The threat posed by secured shareholder loans is even graver in Germany than in the United States because of differences in the respective insolvency regimes. The manager-displacing quality of German insolvency law creates even stronger incentives for overinvestment, that is, investments in a company that is not worth continuing.[72] Because a managing

---

66 The role of secured credit as a mechanism for reducing agency costs is explored in detail in Renger, op. cit. n. 54, at pp. 96-98.

67 A. Engert, 'Die ökonomische Begründung der Grundsätze ordnungsgemäßer Unternehmensfinanzierung' [The Economic Grounds for the Principles of Proper Company Financing], 33 *Zeitschrift für Unternehmens- und Gesellschaftsrecht* (2004) p. 813 at p. 820 et seq.

68 Bezzenberger, loc. cit. n. 49, at p. 38.

69 Engert, loc. cit. n. 67, at p. 825, Goetz, op. cit. n. 61, at p. 167 et seq.

70 Engert, loc. cit. n. 67, at p. 831.

71 Also proposing the prohibition of secured shareholder loans in principle: A. Cahn, 'Gesellschafterfremdfinanzierung und Eigenkapitalersatz' [Outsider Financing by Shareholders and Equity Substitution], 50 *Die Aktiengesellschaft* (2005) p. 217 at p. 225.

72 The differential treatment of managers in the insolvency laws of the United States (where existing managers continue to run the company as "debtor in possession") and Germany (which provides for prompt removal of the managers) is briefly described in D.A. Skeel, Jr.,

shareholder knows that she will lose control of her company in the case of insolvency, she will try even harder to save it. A secured shareholder loan presents a relatively safe platform for a rescue attempt. This safety is gained at the expense of the unsecured creditors, however, as it creates the incentive to engage in enormous risks.[73]

Given the threats posed by secured shareholder loans and their comparative lack of benefits for anyone other than the shareholder herself, a *per se* standard of subordination seems to us the most defensible strategy. Such a standard would greatly discourage secured shareholder loans. At the same time, it would not interfere with the extension of unsecured shareholder loans and thereby would keep this measure of corporate finance relatively intact.

5. Conclusion

Both in the United States and in Germany, lawmakers and courts have long wrestled with the issue of whether to accord shareholder loans the same status as the loans made by outsiders. This article has suggested that courts have been right to worry about the potential effects of loans by shareholders to companies that later prove unable to pay their debts, but that their focus is misplaced in crucial respects. Using Robert Clark's typology of a debtor's moral obligations to its creditors as a starting point, we have considered whether and when shareholder loans should be subordinated or recharacterized as equity. Our most important conclusion is that secured shareholder loans so often and so thoroughly violate the obligation of Nonhindrance of creditors that they should always be subordinated.

One question the article has not yet addressed is why creditors do not seem to limit shareholder loans by contract. Creditors could use negative pledge clauses, for instance, to explicitly prevent some or all shareholder loans. We suspect one reason for the dearth of such clauses may be that it is difficult to distinguish good shareholder loans from bad ones – though, as we have argued, it seems likely that secured shareholder loans are rarely both good and necessary. Transaction costs may also discourage many creditors from addressing the risk of a value destroying

---

'An Evolutionary Theory of Corporate Law and Corporate Bankruptcy', 51 *Vanderbilt Law Review* (1998) p. 1325. It is also more difficult to secure post-petition financing in German insolvency proceedings. See U. Noack, 'Neues Insolvenzrecht – neues Kapitalersatzrecht?' [New Insolvency Law – New Equity Substitution Law?], in K.-P. Martens, et al., eds., *Festschrift für Carsten Peter Claussen* [Festschrift for Carsten Peter Claussen] (Cologne, Carl Heymans Verlag 1997) p. 307 at p. 316.

73 We are focusing principally on loans made by an existing shareholder. As noted earlier, we are inclined to subordinate the security interest of a creditor that later acquires equity only if the creditor acquires a large or controlling stake.

shareholder loan by contract. It may also be the case that existing general negative pledge clauses would in fact preclude shareholder loans in many instances. Whatever the explanation, our analysis suggests that, at least in the absence of an explicit agreement by creditors to give priority to a secured shareholder loan, secured shareholder loans should be subordinated.

H. Eidenmüller and W. Schön (eds.), The Law and Economics of Creditor Protection
© 2008, T.M.C.ASSER PRESS, The Hague, the Netherlands, and the authors

Equitable Subordination of Shareholder Loans?

Andreas Cahn*

Abstract
This comment concerns the financing of distressed corporations by shareholder loans. In the United States as well as in Germany, shareholder loans may be subject to subordination or even recharacterization as equity. The comment argues that the risk of an undue exploitation of a shareholder-lender's insider status can effectively be neutralized by the law of fraudulent conveyances and unlawful preferences, supplemented by a general prohibition of securing shareholder loans.

---

* Prof. Dr. Andreas Cahn, LL.M. (Berkeley), is the Director of the Institute for Law and Finance at the University of Frankfurt.

Keywords: *Eigenkapitalersatz*, shareholder loans, subordination, recharacterization.

1. INTRODUCTION

This part of the conference was originally entitled "Equitable subordination of shareholder claims," which, as will be made clear in this comment, reflected a German lawyer's idea of what equitable subordination means. Very appropriately, Skeel and Krause-Vilmar focused their paper not on subordination as the concept is understood in US law, but rather on recharacterization. In view of the different meanings attached to the term "subordination" by US and German lawyers, part 2 of this comment will briefly summarize the German rules on equitable subordination of shareholder loans, part 3 will highlight some differences between equitable subordination in US and German law, and then part 4 will focus on the merits of the subordination doctrine.

2. THE GERMAN LAW ON EQUITABLE SUBORDINATION OF SHAREHOLDER LOANS

2.1 Case law

When a company is in dire straits and requires additional funds to continue its business, it will frequently not be able to obtain loans from outside sources, as in most instances all of its valuable assets will already be encumbered with security interests. In this situation, shareholders and directors have the option either to let the corporation go out of business and file for bankruptcy or to advance the necessary funds themselves. If they choose to continue the business, they can either make additional contributions to the corporation's capital or they can advance loans to the corporation.

In either of these cases, the corporation does not raise the money by virtue of its own business operations and its own assets but by involving its shareholders. If those funds help the corporation to turn its operations into a success and thus recover from the crisis, the loans will be repaid, and additional capital contributions will yield profits. However, in a majority of cases, the shareholders' efforts at turning around the corporation's business are futile and bankruptcy is merely postponed. Shareholders are generally aware of this risk as well as of the different treatment of debt and equity in the case of the corporation being wound up. Therefore, they usually do not choose to supply additional equity, but rather provide loans in the hope of recovering at least part of this additional investment if the corporation goes bankrupt.

Since the late 1950s, however, German courts have regularly disappointed this hope by subordinating shareholder claims for repayment of loans to those of outside creditors if the shareholder loans were granted when the corporation was already in financial difficulties.[1]

The courts have applied §§ 30 and 31 of the Limited Liability Companies Act (*Gesetz betreffend die Gesellschaften mit beschränkter Haftung* – GmbHG)[2] by analogy to loans that were granted by shareholders when the corporation was in a financial crisis. "Crisis" within the meaning of this rule has been defined as a situation in which the corporation is either insolvent (i.e., unable to discharge its debts as they become due), has assets that are insufficient for the payment of its debts and other liabilities or for some other reason is unable to obtain credit from outside lenders at fair market rates. A loan granted by a shareholder in one of these scenarios will be recharacterized as additional equity and treated as if the funds had in fact been contributed to the corporation's capital. Thus, §§ 30 and 31 GmbHG apply analogously to such loans until the "crisis" (as just defined) is overcome. As long as the funds required to repay such a shareholder loan are needed to cover capital and liabilities, the loan remains recharacterized and repayment to the shareholder is prohibited by § 30 GmbHG to the extent that the funds are required to maintain the company's capital. Payments in violation of this prohibition give the company a claim pursuant to § 31(1) GmbHG to force the shareholder to disgorge these unlawful returns.

Frequently, shareholders finance their corporation with shareholder loans for legitimate reasons such as tax savings. In such cases, the corporation is usually operating successfully and could easily have obtained credit at fair market rates from outside lenders. If the corporation's financial situation subsequently deteriorates and the shareholders nevertheless fail to exercise their right to terminate the loan as the crisis becomes apparent (§ 490 BGB), the loan will be recharacterized as from that time. A failure to demand repayment will be deemed equivalent to termination of the first loan and subsequent grant of a new loan to the corporation in crisis. The only prerequisite for such recharacterization is that a conscientious and prudent shareholder must have been able to recognize the decline of the corporation's financial situation.[3]

---

1 The line of cases by the Civil Division of the German High Federal Court (*Bundesgerichtshof* – BGH) starts with the decision of 14 December 1959, *BGHZ* 31, 258.

2 The pertinent parts of these provisions read as follows:

§ 30(1) GmbHG: "Company assets required to maintain the share capital may not be distributed to shareholders. ..."

§ 31(1) GmbHG: "Payments made in violation of the provisions of § 30 shall be reimbursed to the company. ..."

3 See BGH 26 November 1979, *BGHZ* 75, 334, 337; BGH 24 March 1980, *BGHZ* 76, 326, 331; BGH 21 February 1994, *BGHZ* 125, 141, 147.

2.2 Statutory law

2.2.1 *The original concept*

In 1980, the German Parliament made an attempt to codify these rules that had been developed by the courts. The result was §§ 32a and 32b GmbHG, § 135 Insolvency Act (*Insolvenzordnung* – InsO) and § 6 of the Law Concerning the Contestability of Legal Acts of a Debtor outside of Insolvency Proceedings (*Anfechtungsgesetz* – AnfG).[4] The term "crisis of the company" as defined in § 32a(1) GmbHG refers to the definition of that term as developed in the framework of the preceding court decisions. Even though the legislative intent, as apparent from the official comments on the draft bill, was to merely cast the existing judicial precedent into statutory language, some major differences between the statute and the judicially crafted doctrine remain.

While the application of § 30 GmbHG by analogy prohibits the repayment of recharacterized shareholder loans only to the amount of the actual deficiency in the company's equity capital, § 32a GmbHG disallows repayment even of that part of a recharacterized loan that could be repaid without reducing the assets below the required, stated capital until the corporation has overcome the crisis.

---

[4] The pertinent parts of these provisions read as follows:

§ 32a(1) GmbHG: "If at a time when the shareholders acting as conscientious businessmen would have increased the company's equity capital (crisis of the company), a shareholder instead grants a loan to the company, he can claim repayment of the loan during insolvency proceedings over the assets of the company only as a subordinated creditor."

§ 32a(2) GmbHG: "If at a time when the shareholders acting as conscientious businessmen would have increased the company's equity capital, a third party instead grants a loan to the company for which the shareholder has provided security or assumed a guarantee, the third party can only file a claim in insolvency proceedings over the company's assets to the extent he has not been satisfied after calling the security or guarantee."

§ 32a(3) GmbHG: "These provisions apply as analogously to other legal acts of a shareholder or a third party which in economic terms are comparable to a shareholder loan substituting equity. …"

§ 135 InsO: "Any legal act may be contested if it provides

1. a security within ten years prior to the petition for the institution for insolvency proceedings or after the filing of such petition;
2. satisfaction during the year prior to the petition for the institution for insolvency proceedings or after the filing of such petition

for a shareholder's claim for the repayment of a loan that substitutes equity or for a similar claim."

§ 6 AnfG: "Any legal act may be contested if it provides

1. a security within ten years before this legal act has been contested;
2. satisfaction during the year before this legal act has been contested

for a shareholder's claim for the repayment of a loan that substitutes equity or for a similar claim."

On the other hand, the statute is narrower than pre-existing judicial doctrine insofar as it is only applicable when the corporation is insolvent, while cases forbid repayment of subordinated loans outside bankruptcy as well. Mainly for this reason, the rules stemming from the cases continue to be important despite the introduction of statutory provisions.

2.2.2 *Amendments to the statute*

As of April 1998, two new provisions were added to § 32a(3) GmbHG:

- Pursuant to § 32a(3)(2) GmbHG, the rules pertaining to the substitution of equity capital (i.e., the subordination rules) do not apply to non-managing shareholders with an equity interest of 10 percent or less. The rules referred to in this provision comprise both the statutory and the judicially crafted rules.
- § 32a(3)(3) GmbHG introduced an exemption from the subordination rules for creditors who acquire shares during a crisis in order to help the corporation recover from its difficulties. The rules on subordination of shareholder loans do not apply to the existing or newly extended loans of such creditors merely because the creditors have acquired equity stakes in the corporation.

2.3 Extension of the subordination rules to outside lenders and stock corporations

In a 1992 decision,[5] the High Federal Court applied these rules to a loan that was extended by a bank, even though the lender did not own any shares in the borrower corporation. The subordination was based on a combination of control and information rights that the bank had bargained for and implemented, which gave it influence similar to that of a controlling shareholder. The troublesome feature of the decision is the fact that the Court reached its decision without explaining where the line between legitimate control of the lender by means of covenants and illegitimate usurpation of shareholder rights should be drawn. The uncertainty that this decision introduced creates significant legal risks for banks and their advisors in connection with the drafting of loan contracts and covenants.

Finally, the judicially crafted rules on subordination of shareholder loans substituting equity apply to a shareholder of a stock corporation if his share of the corporation's capital is at least 25 percent.[6]

---

[5] See BGH 13 July 1992, *BGHZ* 119, 191.

[6] See BGH 26 March 1984, *BGHZ* 90, 370, 374 et seq.

3. DIFFERENCES BETWEEN US AND GERMAN RULES ON EQUITABLE SUBORDINATION

Under US law, equitable subordination is a consequence of inequitable conduct of a controlling shareholder towards his corporation. Because the shareholder has treated his corporation unfairly, usually by causing it to transfer an unjustified benefit, all of his outstanding claims against the corporation may be subordinated to the claims of other creditors, regardless of whether these claims are the result of the inequitable conduct. Thus, equitable subordination fills the gap left open by the requirement of fraudulent conveyance law that the debtor must point to a particular transaction or transactions that violate the debtor's obligations to his creditors.

In contrast, the application of the German subordination rules does not turn on unfair conduct of a shareholder towards the company. The mere fact that he has granted a loan when a third party would not have taken a similar risk is a sufficient basis for subordinating his claim. In this respect, German law resembles the US rules on recharacterization. However, subordination under German law does not apply to all shareholder claims, but only to those shareholder loans granted while the corporation was in financial distress. US law does not include this requirement. As a practical matter however, this difference is probably less significant than it might seem at first glance, since German courts consider a shareholder's failure to call a loan given prior to a company's decline to be equivalent to a loan granted while the company is in financial distress.

Since the requirements for subordination are spelled out by statute and case law, subordination is automatic once the triggering conditions are present. Unlike under US law, a German court applying these rules has no discretion with respect to subordinating loans that fall squarely within the ambit of the statutory rules or judicial doctrine.

As a matter of law, the application of the doctrine does not depend on the corporation's insolvency. The court decisions would allow such an action even if the corporation continues its business and, more importantly, even if insolvency proceedings have not been instituted because the corporation's remaining funds fail to cover its expenses.

The US rules of equitable subordination deal only with the subordination of outstanding shareholder claims in the corporation's bankruptcy. If the corporation has already settled a controlling shareholder's claim prior to bankruptcy, recovery of that benefit would be a case for fraudulent conveyance law. In contrast, under German law, payments on subordinated claims can be recovered by applying the rules on equitable subordination not only within (§ 143 InsO) but also outside of bankruptcy proceedings (§ 31 GmbHG).

Unlike under US law, control over the corporation is not a prerequisite for subordination. The subordination rules apply to any lender whose stake in a limited liability company's capital exceeds 10 percent of the total equity. With respect to stock corporations, the relevant threshold is 25 percent of the corporation's capital.

Clearly, US law on equitable subordination addresses different problems than its German counterpart. The purpose of the US rules on subordination is to provide the corporation's creditors with a remedy for damages they might suffer as a consequence of the inequitable conduct of a controlling shareholder *vis-à-vis* his corporation. Under *Deep Rock*[7] and its progeny, it is irrelevant whether or not the subordinated claims are in any way connected with the shareholder's inequitable conduct. In contrast, German law is concerned with the problems of insider loans extended when the corporation is in financial distress regardless of any inequitable conduct, and thus only these loans fall within the ambit of subordination. Therefore, as far as their rationale and their scope of application are concerned, the German subordination rules are quite similar to the US doctrine of recharacterization.

4. Do we need regulation dealing with shareholder loans and what should such regulation try to achieve?

4.1 The risks inherent in shareholder loans

In order to answer the question whether shareholder loans warrant regulation, we first have to identify the potential problems to which this type of corporate financing gives rise.

4.1.1 *Ambiguity*

Under this heading, Skeel and Krause-Vilmar address various fact patterns,[8] each of which may cause specific problems.

Lack of a written loan agreement or absence of interest payments should not *per se* give rise to sanctions as long as the loan is properly documented in the company's books, since neither is required for a valid loan.

If the loan is not recorded in the company's accounts, creditors may be misled about the corporation's financial condition. Since the responsibility for keeping the corporation's accounts lies with management, a failure to disclose shareholder loans should primarily give rise to directors' liability. If the shareholder-lender

---

7 *Taylor* v. *Standard Gas and Electric Co.*, 306 US 307 (1939).

8 See D. Skeel and G. Krause-Vilmar, 'Recharacterization and the Nonhindrance of Creditors', in this volume, at s. 3.2.

has taken part in a scheme to deceive creditors, he should also be liable for damages resulting from such conduct and this liability should not be limited to the amount he has contributed as a loan. Recharacterization is the proper remedy if the loan has been treated as equity in the company's accounts, provided that the shareholder has consented to this documentation.

Thus, the ambiguity problem is properly dealt with by disclosure requirements and liability for material misrepresentations and omissions committed with the shareholder's knowledge or consent.

4.1.2 *Change of shareholder incentives*

As the financial condition of a business declines, shareholder incentives change. As long as they have an equity stake in the company, shareholders as residual claimants are best equipped to promote the success of the corporation. Since their stake in the corporation is the first to be consumed as its fortunes decline, they have an incentive to avoid excessive risks. However, once their share in the company has effectively been eliminated and further losses will be borne by the creditors, shareholders have a significant interest to avoid the winding-up of the corporation in which they may have a large human capital investment,[9] and even to pursue projects with a negative present value.

4.2 Regulatory approaches

The objective of regulation addressing this problem is clear. Since the goal is not just creditor protection regardless of cost, but *efficient* creditor protection, the law should discourage the funding of value decreasing projects, yet not deter shareholders from investing in promising attempts to turn a failing business around.

4.2.1 *Assessment of shareholder loans on the merits of their application*

In theory, this objective would best be served by judging shareholder loans on their substantive merit, i.e., on the basis of the present value of the projects for which they are used. If the present value is positive and the loan can be expected to increase the overall value of the corporation, it passes the test. If, on the other hand, the present value is negative, the shareholder could not enforce his claim against the corporation on equal footing with the outside creditors.

I agree with Skeel and Krause-Vilmar[10] that this is not a viable approach, because judges are not well equipped to make this sort of appraisal and because the difficulties in assessing business judgments are intensified by hindsight bias.

---

[9] See ibid., at s. 3.3.

[10] See ibid.

4.2.2 *Adjustment of shareholder incentives*

Less ambitious in theory, but more workable in practice, is the idea that the law should be designed to give shareholders the right incentives to make responsible decisions. In order to do that, one has to identify the considerations underlying a potential lender's decision whether or not to supply a distressed company with additional cash.

For creditors, the potential cost of continuing the business will be an important factor when they are faced with the choice of either providing further loans or applying to wind up the business. This cost consists not only of the possible loss of new loans granted to the corporation, but also of the risk that, as the business continues, the corporation's assets could be further depleted and the value of already existing claims reduced. In contrast, shareholders (and also potential outside lenders without already existing claims against the corporation) will not care about the effect that a further decline of the corporation may have on pre-existing claims. They are likely to be concerned primarily with the repayment of their own loan.

At first glance, however, even this limited concern appears to provide a sufficient incentive to make a careful assessment of the chances for a company's recovery. In Germany, unsecured creditors receive quotas of only around 6 percent on their claims in the insolvency proceedings over the assets of a limited liability company. In almost 75 percent of company insolvencies, proceedings are not even commenced because the assets are insufficient to cover the expenses.[11] Thus, there seems to be no substantial difference between a shareholder providing additional equity or credit if a company is in distress. In both cases, shareholders put additional money at risk. One should assume that they will only do so if there is a good chance to turn the company around. If they are allowed to supply additional equity, as is clearly the case under German law, there seems to be nothing wrong with granting loans instead. In both cases the corporation is provided with funds that enable it to continue its operations, and in both cases the shareholders seem to take substantially similar risks.

However, this similarity of the risk profiles of loans and contributions to the corporation's equity would change significantly if shareholders could reduce or even eliminate the risk involved in lending to their distressed corporation. Without regulation, there would be two ways by which they could protect their loans to the corporation against the consequences of business failure. They could either seek to exploit their insider status or obtain security for their claims. Both

---

11 For statistical material for the period between 1993 and 1998, see J. Angele, *Wirtschaft und Statistik* (2001) p. 748, 752.

of these techniques could lead to overinvestment in nonviable undertakings, and thus the law should block them both.

4.2.2.1 Exploitation of shareholders' insider status

The troublesome feature of shareholder lending is the fact that shareholders of closely held corporations, in particular, are frequently privy to information not readily available to outside lenders. By virtue of their privileged access to information about the company's affairs and their influence on the directors, such shareholders will likely be the first to know if the attempts to turn the company around are failing. In this case, they will of course immediately recall their loans, seeking to influence management in order to obtain immediate satisfaction of their claims and leaving only the remaining assets for the other creditors. Regulation dealing with shareholder loans should eliminate this unfair advantage and the incentive to gamble at the expense of the outside creditors.

Arguably, however, equitable subordination as currently applied in Germany is not a coherent way to deal with this issue. On the one hand, the rules are not strict enough because their application is limited to shareholders with a significant share in the company's equity. Since the incentives for shareholders to continue the corporation's business at the expense of the creditors is shared by all shareholders, exemptions like the one carved out by § 32a(3)(2) GmbHG for non-managing shareholders whose equity share does not exceed 10 percent are an invitation for controlling shareholders to attempt evasions of the subordination rules by inducing such non-managing shareholders to extend loans to the corporation and reimbursing them for their expenses. Particularly in cases where insolvency proceedings are not commenced, it will frequently be impossible for individual creditors to prove that the loan has in substance been granted by a shareholder who would be subject to subordination.

On the other hand, the subordination rules apply to cases in which subordination of shareholder loans is not justified. Clearly, there is no abuse of inside information and no inappropriate exercise of influence on management if a shareholder leaves his loan with the company until the insolvency of the company. In such cases, he has put additional money at risk in a *bona fide* attempt to save the company. Instead of subordinating shareholder loans, the law should be designed to ensure that in their capacity as lenders shareholders receive the same treatment as other unsecured creditors. Such equal treatment requires that shareholders do not exploit their privileged access to information and their influence on management in order to obtain preferential satisfaction of their claims.

One way of implementing this concept would be to require the courts to distinguish on a case-by-case basis between undue exploitation of insider status and legitimate shareholder conduct. Obviously, such a rule would be difficult and costly to apply and introduce substantial uncertainty. Particularly in the majority of insolvencies in which formal insolvency proceedings are not commenced, so that the enforcement of claims lies with the individual creditors, the requirement to prove the pertinent facts would present an almost insurmountable obstacle. Therefore, it appears to be more appropriate, though somewhat schematic, to strike down transactions that take place during a certain period prior to bankruptcy. Under such a rule, shareholders could not recall their loans during a certain period prior to the insolvency of the corporation; if the company becomes insolvent within a certain period after a shareholder loan has been repaid, the recipient should be liable to return these funds to the company for equal distribution among all creditors (including himself). This would neutralize any advantages that shareholders may have over outside creditors while preserving as much as possible of the shareholder's discretionary freedom in choosing the instruments for financing the corporation. This is precisely the approach adopted by the rules dealing with unlawful preferences and fraudulent conveyances. Critical to the appropriate application of this concept is the definition of the relevant time period preceding the company's insolvency during which shareholder loans may not be repaid. Underinvestment might be the consequence if this period were defined too broadly, while making it too short would encourage overinvestment.

An argument in favor of subordinating shareholder claims rather than ranking them on the same level as the claims of other unsecured lenders appears to follow from fact that shareholders are entitled to participate in corporate decision-making while creditors are not. Arguably, this privilege of shareholders derives from their status as residual claimants, which gives them an incentive to maximize the value of the corporation. If shareholders continue to exercise their governance rights even though this incentive has changed because the equity has been eliminated, there seems to be a strong case for re-establishing their position as residual claimants by subordinating their claims against the corporation to those of outside creditors. However, even with a view to the correlation between shareholder governance rights and their status as residual claimants, subordination of shareholder loans would constitute an unwarranted and disproportionate interference with their freedom to decide on the means of financing the company. Frequently, creditors would be even worse off if the shareholders failed to supply additional money to the company and simply continued to operate the business until the funds supplied by the creditors are exhausted. Thus, the appropriate way to deal with the change of shareholder incentives that occurs when their residual claims are effectively eliminated does not lie in the subordination of shareholder loans but rather in granting creditors the right to apply for the opening of insolvency proceedings and the substitution of a management elected by shareholders with a trustee appointed by a court in the interest of the creditors. Under German law, the management of the corporation is under a duty to file for insolvency proceedings once the corporation is insolvent, i.e., if its assets are not sufficient to cover its liabilities.[12]

While the German experience shows that that subordination does not amount to an effective ban on shareholder loans, the law should not depart farther than necessary from the rule that shareholders are free to choose whether to finance their corporations with equity or with debt. The law's suspicion of shareholder loans is based on the concern that shareholders might abuse their insider status to secure an unfair advantage over outside creditors. However, once rules are in place to ensure that shareholder loans are in fact subject to the same risks as unsecured third-party loans, we should respect a shareholder's assessment of the chances of turning around his business and also his decision to provide the corporation with additional funds.

4.2.2.2 Secured shareholder loans

Arranging collateral for a loan is another way to shift the risk of continuing the business to the unsecured creditors. Such collateral is unnecessary as long as the company is able to meet its obligations. If the company is in difficulties, it provides security against the lending shareholder's risk and thereby becomes an incentive for him to gamble for restoration of his equity stake at the expense of the unsecured creditors. I therefore agree with Skeel and Krause-Vilmar[13] that shareholders should not be allowed to obtain collateral for their loans to the corporation.[14] When shareholders are faced with the choice of either contributing additional funds to their distressed corporation or winding it up, they should not be permitted to place themselves in a better position than an unsecured creditor.

Such a prohibition of shareholders receiving collateral for their loans would not be very effective, however, if a shareholder could simply induce an outside lender to fund projects with negative present value by having the corporation provide security for the loan.[15] If shareholders loans could thus be substituted by third-party loans, the proposed prohibition of granting shareholders collateral would either have to be abandoned or extended to outside lenders.

Creditors with existing claims against the corporation will generally not be willing to provide additional loans even if they are offered an attractive interest rate as well as collateral, unless they are convinced that the projects to be pursued

---

12 See § 92(2) Stock Corporation Act (*Aktiengesetz* – AktG) and § 64(1) GmbHG.

13 See Skeel and Krause-Vilmar, loc. cit. n. 8, at s. 3.3.

14 See also A. Engert, 'Die ökonomische Begründung der Grundsätze ordnungsgemäßer Unternehmensfinanzierung', 34 *Zeitschrift für Unternehmens- und Gesellschaftsrecht* (2005) p. 813 at p. 830 et seq.; A. Cahn, 'Gesellschafterfremdfinanzierung und Eigenkapitalersatz', 50 *Die Aktiengesellschaft* (2005) p. 217 at p. 225.

15 See Skeel and Krause-Vilmar, loc. cit. n. 8, at s. 3.3.

by the corporation have a very good chance of success. The reason for their reluctance to provide funding for a nonviable venture is the simple fact any further decline of the debtor corporation will reduce the value of their pre-existing claims.

Even outside lenders without existing claims against the corporation will not be readily disposed to lend money to a failing company merely because they are being offered security. Generally, third-party lenders tend to be cautious in their assessment of the value of collateral. Production and service facilities, intangible assets, and even real estate are usually much more valuable as parts of the lender's business as a going concern than they would be if sold at auction. In fact, there may not even be a liquid market for many of the assets that a corporation would be able to pledge as security. Potential lenders will therefore subtract very significant discounts from the value that the borrower may attribute to these assets. If, however, a corporation has sufficient unencumbered assets to pledge as security to obtain a substantial loan, this would indicate that it is hardly in financial distress.

Shareholders are likely to take a much more positive view of the value of the assets that their corporation can offer as security. One reason aside from inherent entrepreneurial optimism may be that they are familiar with the assets and do not require independent valuation. Another reason may be that, unlike an outside lender, they are able and willing to employ these assets in a new operation if the recovery of the corporation fails.

4.2.3 *Evaluation of the merits of the proposed equal treatment rule*

Rules dealing with the financing of distressed businesses should not prevent the rescue of companies that can be saved. On the other hand, they should not encourage the continuation of companies where the expected value of continuing the business is less than the proceeds from an immediate liquidation. Providing a failing company with additional funds is economically beneficial if the expected value of the company after a turnaround is higher than the cash expense of additional loans and the opportunity costs of continuing the business, i.e., the foregone proceeds that an immediate liquidation would render.

When a creditor of the company is faced with the choice of whether to liquidate the company or provide it with additional loans, he will consider both the cash expense and the opportunity costs. In contrast, a shareholder in his capacity as a member of the company would not participate in the proceeds of an immediate liquidation. He would therefore only be concerned with the likelihood of his loan being repaid and the chances of increasing the value of his share in the company, without weighing the potential decrease of the company's value as a continuing business under its immediate liquidation value.

Therefore, the equal treatment rule seems to encourage shareholder lending in cases where it might be more efficient to wind up the corporation. However, given the uncertainties inherent in calculating expected values and the fact that shareholders are not likely to put substantial amount of fresh money at stake if they do not have good reason to expect a successful turnaround, the chances in practice of fostering overinvestment are probably negligible. More importantly, shareholder loans granted under the equal treatment rule do not affect the creditors' position in a significantly different way than additional contributions to the corporation's capital, which, at least under the German model, shareholders are allowed and even expected to make. If the company is enabled to carry on its business by virtue of such shareholder contributions and eventually ends up in insolvent liquidation, creditors will also be deprived of the additional value that an immediate liquidation of the company would have rendered as compared to the postponed winding-up. The only advantage they would enjoy is that, unlike in the lending scenario, the shareholder would not compete with them for the remaining assets. Considering, however, that creditors receive only marginal payments on their claims once the debtor corporation goes into insolvent liquidation, the effect of allowing a shareholder-lender to assert claims in insolvency proceedings is likely to be negligible. On the other hand, the equal treatment rule is easier to apply than subordination rules, because it eliminates the requirement of proving that the loan has indeed been granted at a time when the company was in distress or that the shareholder failed to call in a loan even though he could have known that the company was on the decline. In the majority of cases – where formal insolvency proceedings are not commenced and creditors must fend for themselves against shareholder-lenders – the bright-line feature of the equal treatment rule outweighs potential benefits of subordination.

Directors' Creditor-Regarding Duties in Respect of Trading Decisions Taken in the Vicinity of Insolvency

Paul Davies*

---

* Cassel Professor of Commercial Law, London School of Economics and Political Science; Fellow, European Corporate Governance Institute. I am grateful to the participants at the conference held in Munich for their comments on a first draft of this paper, especially for the formal response of Gerald Spindler, who has also been most helpful in subsequent discussions, notably in relation to French law. I am also grateful for input from John Armour (both at the conference and subsequently), Vanessa Finch, Sir Roy Goode, Thomas Telfer and Peter Watts. The usual disclaimer applies.

Abstract

This paper is concerned with the risks to creditors from strategic business decisions taken by directors. It seeks to explain both why the law should impose creditor-regarding duties when the shareholders no longer have any substantial equity in the company and why such duties should not be imposed when the shareholders still have a substantial economic interest in the company. It goes on to argue that duties on directors to put the company into a formal insolvency procedure once the company has reached a state of insolvency do not adequately meet the interventionist criterion. The incidence of such duties depends in part on whether a balance sheet or a cash flow test is used for insolvency, but in any event duties to open formal insolvency procedures are too rigid unless they operate only when all hope of rescue has disappeared. However, the paper also argues that the need to promote a 'rescue culture' for companies in financial distress may lead the legislature to limit the creditor-regarding duty arising before, but in the vicinity of, insolvency to cases of liquidation and not to extend it to companies being handled through procedures whose main aim is to save the company or (parts of) its business as a going concern.

Keywords: directors' duties, creditors, trading in the vicinity of insolvency, company rescue.

1. THE SCOPE OF THE PAPER

Although this paper began life under the title of 'Directors' Liability in the Vicinity of Insolvency', its scope is rather more limited, as the current title more accurately reflects. In fact, the paper focuses not on the whole range of directors' potential liabilities in the vicinity of insolvency, but on directors' duties and liabilities in respect of their decisions to continue, terminate or restructure the company's trading or business activities in the vicinity of insolvency. Needless to say, I am interested in such duties and liabilities in their creditor-regarding or protecting aspects. Nor do I concentrate on the legitimacy of specific transactions that may occur in the course of implementing these trading decisions, but rather on the legitimacy of the strategic decision to continue trading (or not) in a particular form and to maintain that decision subsequently. Thus, I leave to one side the consideration of transactions whereby the directors, with the aim or effect of creditor avoidance, shift assets out of the company in the vicinity of insolvency, whether by way of distributions or transactions with favoured third parties.[1] On the other hand, my paper discusses what might be seen as a generalisation of the problem discussed by Professor Skeel in this volume,[2] which is the potential liability of company controllers who decide to finance the continued trading of the company by way of a loan to it.

The core question for this paper may be said to be this. Under what circumstances do directors incur liability for trading decisions taken in the vicinity of insolvency which lead to a deterioration in the company's net asset position[3] compared with what it was at the time the decision was taken? One can also ask, though this is less often done, whether there can be liability for a decision which leads to a less favourable asset position for the company compared to some other decision which was available to the directors. If one permits the second question to be asked, then a decision to cease trading is no longer a guarantee of no liability for directors.

2. Some Theory

2.1 Companies with significant shareholder funds

The focus of this paper is on liabilities to creditors. Shareholder-regarding duties, which exist at all stages of the company's existence, are not of direct concern here. Directors' creditor-regarding duties, although much discussed in recent years, are clearly of secondary significance in the overall legal regulation of the exercise of directors' discretions. Thus, one needs to explain both why creditor-regarding duties are not pervasive but also why they occur at all. Accordingly, this section advances two arguments to address these questions. With regard to the non-pervasiveness of creditor-regarding duties, it is argued that they are unnecessary so long as the company's financial statements reveal significant shareholder equity[4] or shareholders' funds, to use the accounting term. Where this

---

1 These issues are pursued by Professor Baird in this volume, at p. 199.

2 At p. 259.

3 Since the paper is concerned with creditor protection, net assets constitute the correct focus of concern because that will determine the level of creditor recovery in insolvency.

4 By 'equity', I mean the company's value after all its debts and liabilities have been allowed for, i.e., the value of the shareholders' economic interest in the company. This concept of

is the case, the rule that losses are borne by the shareholders first provides an incentive to company controllers to take on only appropriately risky projects. In such a situation, the risks of failure and the rewards of success will impact most heavily on the (ordinary) shareholders, because the value of their equity in the company will directly reflect the profits earned or losses incurred in the project. In this situation, the argument that limited liability protects shareholders against losses in excess of the amount that they have paid for their shares misses the point. Where the company has significant net assets, the failure of an excessively risky project threatens to deprive the shareholders not only of the amount they paid for their shares (which may have been negligible) but also of their interest in those assets.[5] Thus, the loss caused to the shareholders by the failure of a risky project where the company is a profitable going concern with undistributed profits may well exceed the price paid by the shareholder for the securities. In other words, if I have bought a share for 1 and its market value is now 10 but the failure of a risky project reduces its value to 0, my loss is 10, not 1.[6]

As far as strategic business decisions are concerned, therefore, creditors are *de facto* protected by the directors' shareholder-regarding duties, so long as the company has significant shareholder funds. It is true that imposing creditor-regarding duties on the directors in such a situation might give the creditors an even higher level of protection, but it is not necessarily in the public interest to do so. Rather, imposing creditor-regarding liabilities upon the shareholders where the company is a profitable going concern runs the danger of generating incentives for directors to engage only in excessively low-risk projects. As long as the company is a going concern, creditors do not benefit proportionately from the upside and downside of corporate decisions, since their returns are, normally, fixed. If there is substantial shareholder equity in the company, creditors will normally tend to favour projects which do not imperil that situation, even if a riskier project has a higher present value, because the creditors' position will not

---

'equity' involves no presumption that the shareholders have provided significant legal capital to the company. Thus, shareholders in a British private company, whose shares have been issued for a nominal consideration, nevertheless will have a substantial equity in the company if its business does in fact prosper and the resulting profits are retained within the company.

[5] The fact that those accumulated profits may be distributed does not fundamentally affect the argument. The company may be reduced to the situation where the shareholders have no equity in the company by unsuccessful trading or by distributions. The above argument in favour of imposing duties on directors in the vicinity of insolvency does not turn on how the threat of insolvency was brought about. However, the excessive distribution route to insolvency does justify legal controls over distributions, which all company laws contain. The debate in that area, which is dealt with in other papers presented to this conference, is whether legal capital or solvency-based controls do the better job in controlling excessive distributions.

[6] This explains as well why the ordinary shareholders have a continuing interest in monitoring the performance of the company's management and not just an interest which arises when the value of the shares is about to fall below what the shareholder paid for his or her holding.

be materially enhanced by the higher-value project. In short, the argument for not imposing wide-ranging creditor-regarding duties where there is substantial shareholder equity in the company is that the company is designed as a vehicle for taking entrepreneurial risks, that the creditors therefore have no *a priori* claim that corporate enterprise should be low risk (unless they contract for it)[7] and that the shareholder-regarding duties give the creditors adequate protection against excessively risky projects. Hence, no modern company law system adopts a creditor focus as its dominant principle of corporate governance.

For the avoidance of doubt, it should be made clear that the above argument is confined to the adoption by directors of strategic decisions about the company's future trading plans. It does not pretend to deal with argument that long-term lenders may be in danger of having the risk profile of the company altered unfavourably to them after they have made the advance and thus priced the loan, within the context of projects which are not overall excessively risky. Even here, however, mandatory legal protection may be inappropriate, since the lenders in question may well be able to protect themselves through covenants.[8] As for short-term creditors (notably trade creditors and tort victims), if the company is a going concern, they will be paid, by and large, through a combination of legal pressure from the creditors (applied from outside company law) and the company's concern to maintain its reputation and so obtain further credit.[9] There is still an issue where the short-term claim is such as, by itself, to put the company's continued existence in jeopardy, a situation which has arisen in relation to tort claims in the United States but, apparently, not yet in Europe.[10] In general, the European approach is to deal with such risks through mandatory insurance schemes.[11] In any event, such claims will destroy the shareholders' equity first and so these are not cases where directors' shareholder-regarding duties create incentives for them to run such risks.[12]

---

[7] Of course, if an enterprise is solely financed by debt, as with some utilities, a cautious approach to corporate projects is entirely appropriate, and large creditors in such cases will rightly contract for such an approach.

[8] This is the subject of Professor Bratton's paper in this volume.

[9] This is not to deny that short-term creditors may not suffer problems, often severe, of late payment.

[10] Though in multinational companies, the line between states is not so easy to draw. See the decision of the English High Court in *Re T&N Ltd* [2005] 2 *BCLC* 488, which represents in many ways a clash between the US tort claimants and the pension claims of the British subsidiary's workforce.

[11] Such as mandatory employer liability schemes, which, it should be noted, usually apply to non-corporate employers as well. It is a myth to think that, in the absence of limited liability, the creditor is not likely to be faced with an insufficiency of assets on the part of the defendant.

[12] Though the potential for such tort claims may create an incentive for directors, acting in the interests of both shareholders and non-tort creditors, to make opportunistic use of group structures in such cases.

2.2 Companies in the vicinity of insolvency and the generation of perverse incentives

However, once the shareholders' equity has been dissipated, or has been reduced to a very low level, and there is no prospect of its being rebuilt through the company's established business model,[13] the incentive for company controllers (if acting in the shareholder interest) is to take on excessively risky projects, for their attention can focus exclusively on the potential upside of decisions. The doctrine of limited liability provides the standard justification for the imposition of creditor-regarding liability on directors in such cases.[14] Since limited liability normally restricts the creditors to the corporate assets for the satisfaction of their claims, shareholders are relieved against the downside risk of business decisions once their equity in the company has evaporated. At this point, the creditors can no longer rely on the 'shareholders' first' rule in relation to losses to protect their interests in respect of excessively risky projects. On the contrary, the corporate law doctrine of limited liability creates an incentive structure for directors which positively favours excessively risky projects, because shareholder-regarding directors can focus solely on the upside of potential projects, no matter how remote the possibility of success may be. The position of the shareholders is now equivalent to that of the creditors when the company has significant shareholder funds, except that, where the company is a successful going concern, the creditors have only a very limited interest in the upside of corporate projects and are more focussed on the potential downside, whilst the shareholders in the vicinity of insolvency are in the reverse position, having little interest in the downside of corporate projects but standing to gain enormously from the potential upside. Thus arises the argument for creditor-regarding duties to be imposed on directors of companies in the vicinity of insolvency.

Obviously, even in this situation, company controllers are not completely indifferent to the riskiness of corporate projects. A project with a higher chance of a positive outcome is preferable to one with a lower chance of one with the same outcome. However, controllers are in a position to ignore, when comparing

---

[13] This is an important qualification to the argument. If a company is operating profitably but its profits are fully distributed at the end of each year (so that the shareholders retain little equity in the company), the incentives to take on excessively risky projects will nevertheless be weak, because the shareholders may thereby destroy the company's established profit-making potential.

[14] The argument made below is not new. For earlier statements of it, see P.L. Davies, 'Legal Capital in Private Companies in Great Britain', 43 *Die Aktiengesellschaft* (1998) pp. 346, 349; and D. Prentice, 'Creditors' Interests and Directors' Duties', 10 *Oxford Journal of Legal Studies* (1990) p. 265.

projects, the chances of a negative outcome.[15] Thus, projects with a negative present value may be undertaken as insolvency approaches and the downside risk of such projects will fall on the company's creditors. In particular, the risk will fall on the unsecured creditors, who stand next in line to bear the company's losses after the shareholders. Of course, as we have already remarked, the opportunism of corporate controllers in the vicinity of insolvency is not confined to embarking on overly risky projects in the hope of turning the company around. In fact, the greater temptation (because it demands less entrepreneurial effort) may be to spirit assets out of the company, so that creditors can no longer lay their hands on them, rather than to run the risk of increasing its liabilities by undertaking new projects. However, as stated, the focus of this paper is on the incentives to embark on overly risky projects in insolvency.

2.3 **Further points**

Four further points can be developed from the above analysis. First, whatever remedies are used to redress the perverse incentives identified above, their focus should normally be the unsecured creditor. In particular, recoveries should be in favour of unsecured rather than secured creditors. Second, if unsecured creditors are to be the focus of remedial measures, it is likely that those measures will consist of mandatory law rather than self-help measures, given the collective action problems of unsecured creditors. Third, and by way of qualification, in extreme cases unsecured creditors may have as much appetite for risk as shareholders. If the company's descent into financial difficulty is sudden and deep, the company's assets may no longer be enough to provide a substantial dividend to the unsecured creditors at the point when the controllers come to decide what steps to take. In this situation, the unsecured creditors may be as much in favour of overly risky projects as the shareholders and for the same reasons: they no longer have anything to lose if such a project fails but will be the first to gain if it is successful. So, in designing and applying legal rules, it is important not to provide recovery to creditors who have consented to or even encouraged the controllers' decision to embark on an overly risky project.[16] Fourth, even if the unsecured creditors have lost their financial interest in the company at the point

---

[15] Thus, controllers will prefer a project with, for example, a 30 per cent chance of yielding 10 over one with a 20 per cent chance of yielding 10, even if the former has a 70 per cent chance of yielding -100, whereas the latter has an 80 per cent chance of yielding -5.

[16] Thus, section 588Y of the Australian Corporations Act 2001 provides that recovery for breach of section 588G (discussed below) should not be allowed where the creditor knew at the time the debt was created that the company was insolvent. Why should a creditor advance money to an insolvent corporation? Possibly where the creditor sees this as an attractive way of enhancing the chances of the repayment of monies previously advanced.

when the company's controllers come to decide what to do, there is probably no need in that situation to make the secured creditors the focus of mandatory legal protection: they can, and do, look after themselves.[17]

2.4 Directors not accountable to shareholders

It may be argued that this analysis is plausible so long as the directors are the shareholders or are effectively accountable to the shareholders. Where the directors are independent of the shareholders, the analysis may appear less persuasive. There is certainly anecdotal evidence that in practice the problems generated by the incentive structure analysed above are to be found predominantly in close companies.[18] However, even directors without shareholdings may suffer losses if the company moves into insolvency, notably the loss of their jobs, and so the above analysis may apply in those cases as well. This is obviously a stronger argument in jurisdictions where, as is common in Europe, the initiation of an insolvency procedure leads to the immediate sidelining of the existing management of the company. In debtor-in-possession systems of corporate insolvency, loss of a job may not be an automatic consequence of triggering insolvency procedures, but it is nevertheless a real threat in these systems as well. In addition, directors may suffer reputational losses by entering into insolvency procedures, even if liquidation is ultimately avoided.

In relation to non-controlling directors of public companies, however, there is the argument that the market for executives operates so as to counteract pressure from shareholders in a particular company to embark on excessively risky projects. Executive directors will enhance their reputations with shareholders generally by dealing responsibly with corporate failure, because in future creditors will be prepared to lend at lower rates to companies run by such managers and this will be of benefit to shareholders.[19] This is a complex matter. Even where the market for executive talent is open to a particular director, it does not follow that any particular director will place a higher value on a new job (and thus act responsibly towards creditors) as against maintaining his existing post (and so support high-risk strategies to save the company). Even when one has marketable talents, changing jobs involves risks and costs which may be (or be perceived to be) higher than those associated with taking action to maintain one's existing job. In any event, even if corporate controllers who are not shareholders or shareholder-controlled are less prone to embarking on excessively risky projects as insolvency approaches, this is not a strong argument against deploying the legal

---

17 R. Mokal, *Corporate Insolvency Law* (Oxford, Oxford University Press 2005) pp. 293-295.
18 Ibid., at pp. 289-292.
19 Ibid., at pp. 285-288.

strategy suggested by the above analysis. Provided that the rules are shaped appropriately, where directors do not embark on overly risky projects, they will not be caught. This is probably a better approach than making the creditor-regarding rules dependent upon judicial assessment of whether the directors were subject to shareholder control, since that would simply increase the costs of litigation.

2.5 Perverse incentives and legal capital

It should also be noted that the issue of perverse incentives in the vicinity of insolvency arises even if in a particular legal system there are strong rules on legal capital. A high level of initial legal capital is no guarantee that assets will be maintained within the company as it trades. Equally, capital maintenance rules regulate only one form of loss of corporate assets (through distributions) and not trading losses. So, it is not irrational for a jurisdiction to have both legal capital requirements and, in addition, separate rules counteracting the incentives identified above, as the United Kingdom does in relation to public companies. It is conceivable that there might be added to a country's legal capital rules a provision to the effect that loss of legal capital requires a company to cease trading even before insolvency is reached, thus pre-empting the rules governing trading near insolvency. However, such a rule is obviously inefficient. Even Germany stops short of such a requirement, and thus has to supplement its legal capital rules with rules which focus on the duties of the directors of an insolvent company, irrespective of what the position is in regard to its legal capital. Article 92 *Aktiengesetz* 1965 (Stock Corporations Act, hereafter AktG) illustrates both points. Article 92(1) requires the *Vorstand* (managing board) to summon a meeting of the shareholders when one half of the company's legal capital is lost, but does not by itself require the company to stop trading; Article 92(2) requires the *Vorstand* to commence insolvency proceedings at the latest within three weeks of the company becoming insolvent, even if its legal capital is unimpaired.[20] This could happen, for example, if the company's assets, whilst exceeding its liabilities by the amount required by the applicable legal capital rules, were illiquid, so that the company could not pay its debts as they fell due. Thus, legal capital rules are not a substitute for rules directly addressing controllers' perverse incentives in the vicinity of insolvency.

However, is the opposite the case? Can creditor-regarding rules in the vicinity of insolvency be a substitute for legal capital requirements? Formally, the answer

---

20 For similar provisions in relation to private companies, see Arts. 49(3) and 64(1) of the *Gesetz betreffend die Gesellschaften mit beschränkter Haftung* 1892 [Limited Liability Company Act, hereafter GmbHG].

must be in the negative. Minimum capital and capital maintenance rules are designed to slow or prevent the descent into insolvency, not to deal with the perverse incentives which may arise once insolvency is reached. However, trading rules may be functional equivalents for capital rules. Tough rules on directors' duties in the vicinity of insolvency may reduce shareholders' incentives to incorporate with inadequate legal capital, even if, at that point, they are legally free to do so. Thus, effective director liability rules in the vicinity of insolvency may operate so as to reduce pressure to strengthen or introduce minimum capital rules. The difference between the two is one between *ex ante* and *ex post* controls.[21] Legal capital rules aim (probably with little success) to prevent the incorporation of inadequately capitalised companies. Rules focusing on controllers' incentives near insolvency do not procure adequate capitalisation but aim (with a degree of success which is unclear) to restrict the harm caused to creditors by undercapitalisation if undercapitalisation leads towards insolvency.

2.6 Conclusions to section 2

The theory of perverse incentives, outlined above, seeks to explain the imposition of creditor-regarding duties on corporate controllers as insolvency approaches. At least in relation to directors accountable to shareholders, such rules arguably meet the hypothetical bargaining model. Controlling shareholders might bargain *ex ante* with creditors for the imposition of constraints upon the directors' activities in the vicinity of insolvency, because the benefit of such rules is ultimately secured by them in the form of a lower cost of borrowing.[22] However, the above theory gives no warrant for imposing on corporate controllers, as a general principle of corporate governance, a creditor-centred view of corporate decision making. This is likely to lead to the opposite vice to that identified above, namely an excessively cautious approach to corporate projects.

The positive and normative predictions from the above arguments are thus that legislatures will (should) impose creditor-regarding duties on company controllers in the vicinity of insolvency but will (should) not do so outside of that zone. In order to explore these hypotheses, the paper proceeds, after having dealt with some preliminary matters (section 3) to look at directors duties when the company is in a state of insolvency (section 4), when it is in the vicinity of insolvency (section 5), and, finally, when it is in a financially healthy state (section 6).

---

[21] Davies, loc. cit. n. 14, at pp. 352-354.

[22] Mokal, op. cit. n. 17, at p. 265, denying the contrary argument by B. Cheffins, *Company Law: Theory, Structure and Operation* (Oxford, Oxford University Press 1997) pp. 537-548.

3. PRELIMINARY ISSUES

3.1 Insolvency

The above analysis depends on the identification of perverse incentives arising for corporate controllers in the vicinity of insolvency. But how do we define insolvency? It is well established that there are two main approaches. The first is an excess of liabilities over assets (the balance sheet test) and the second an inability on the part of the company to meet its debts and liabilities as they become due (the cash flow test).[23] In legal systems which do not demand any or any significant initial legal capital, the balance sheet test would appear to be an inappropriate one for the imposition of creditor-regarding duties, since many companies without significant legal capital are insolvent on a balance sheet test the minute they begin to trade.[24] To impose creditor-regarding duties at this early point would be to suggest that the company ought to have raised legal capital to some extent before it began trading. By contrast, jurisdictions which regard minimum capital rules as important would not be inhibited from using a balance sheet test for insolvency (as well as a cash flow test). Thus, Article 92(2) AktG requires the *Vorstand* to take action (by way of instituting insolvency proceedings) when or shortly after the company becomes insolvent based on either of the two tests for insolvency. By contrast, in Australia, a country which inherited the British scepticism about the value of minimum capital requirements and was not required to depart from that view by Community law, section 588G of the Corporations Act 2001, which imposes a rather similar[25] duty upon directors to that imposed by Article 92(2) AktG, applies only where the company is insolvent on a cash flow basis.[26] This point is considered further below in relation to section 214 of the British Insolvency Act 1986.

---

23 R. Goode, *Principles of Corporate Insolvency Law* (London, Sweet & Maxwell 2005) paras. 4-04 to 4.06. The distinction between the two approaches somewhat narrows if the balance sheet test is carried out on a going concern, rather than a break-up, basis.

24 This is because commencing trading usually involves exchanging cash for business-specific assets, whose open-market value may immediately fall below the cash price and whose value within the business may be uncertain.

25 Art. 92(2) requires the *Vorstand* to file for insolvency; s. 588G prohibits the board from incurring debts, but leaves the board a somewhat wider margin of discretion than the German law as to the choice of procedure for dealing with the insolvency. It also imposes liability only if the directors ought to have suspected the company was insolvent.

26 R.P. Austin, H.A.J. Ford and I.M. Ramsay, *Company Directors* (Australia, LexisNexis Butterworths 2005) para. 10.27. On minimum capital requirements in Australia, see R.P. Austin and I.M. Ramsay, *Ford's Principles of Corporations Law*, 12th edn. (Australia, LexisNexis Butterworths 2005) para. 24.360: 'there are no significant minimum capital requirements to be met by those who wish to obtain the privilege of limited liability.'

3.2 Controllers

Although the perverse incentives mentioned above operate most strongly on shareholders, the legal techniques generated in response normally identify the directors as the subjects of the duties and liabilities. This, though at first sight odd, is explicable. Shareholders as shareholders are in a weak position to cause the company to take action which responds to those incentives. They normally need to act as directors or through the directors. Imposing liabilities on directors will thus catch the shareholders who act as directors and also provide a counterincentive to directors to do what the shareholders want where the controlling shareholder sits outside the board. To the extent that directors are subject to the perverse incentives identified above, whether or not they are shareholders or subject to shareholder influence, focusing the liability rules on directors is also appropriate.

Nevertheless, there is something incomplete about imposing liability only on the directors where the shareholders act through the board (but are not directors themselves), and so many (perhaps all modern) systems extend at least some of their creditor-regarding duties to shareholders (and others) who exercise director-like influence over the company, whether they have been appointed formally to the board or not. Section 214 of the British Insolvency Act applies to both *de facto* and shadow directors,[27] as well as to those formally appointed as directors. The concept of a *de facto* director catches a person who acts as a director, whether or not he has been formally appointed to that position. A shadow director is one 'in accordance with whose directions or instructions the directors are accustomed to act', i.e., he or she is a person who dictates to the directors what decisions are to be taken without being a member of the board *de jure* or *de facto*. The French *action en comblement de passif* (discussed below) applies to the *dirigeant de fait* (*de facto* director) as well as to the *dirigeant de droit* (*de jure* director) and the notion of a *dirigeant de fait* is apparently broad enough to capture the two British notions of *de facto* and shadow directors. However, this extension is not without its problems. Too wide a definition of 'director' might discourage banks or shareholders (including parent companies) from providing further funds to companies in financial difficulty. Providers of funds to companies in distress are likely to impose greater restrictions on the management of the company than those funding healthy companies. If such restrictions are likely to lead to the funders being treated as directors of the company, such funds may become less readily available.[28]

---

27 Insolvency Act 1986, ss. 214(7) and 251. The line between the two concepts has caused some controversy but it is not normally necessary to distinguish between them.

28 British judges have shown themselves sensitive to this risk. See D. Prentice, 'Corporate Personality, Limited Liability and the Protection of Creditors', in R. Grantham and C. Rickett,

4. DIRECTORS' DUTIES ARISING UPON INSOLVENCY

An implication of the arguments made in section 2 of this paper is that directors' creditor-regarding duties which bite only when the company is in a state of insolvency are triggered too late in the process of corporate decline. The perverse incentives there identified will begin to affect the decisions of the company's controllers as soon as the shareholders' equity has been reduced to negligible proportions or even is anticipated to be so reduced, whether or not the company is at that point in a state of insolvency. A legal strategy to reset the controllers' incentives should apply at an earlier stage. Nevertheless, a number of jurisdictions contain provisions which apply only when the company is in a state of insolvency, and such provisions, whilst inadequate to deal with the whole of the problem identified in section 2, are not without purpose. Their aim appears to be to require the directors of a company which is in a state of insolvency to put it into some type of formal insolvency proceeding with reasonable promptness.[29] This is clearly expressed in Article 92(2) of the AktG,[30] where, upon the company reaching a state of insolvency, the board must within three weeks file a petition for the institution of insolvency proceedings. This requirement is bolstered by the provisions of Article 92(3), which prevents the board from making further payments out of the company's assets, except such as are 'consistent with the care of a diligent and conscientious manager'. The duty created by Article 92 is thus one which apparently applies late in the day,[31] but it is also quite specific as to what the board is required to do, i.e., it is embodied in a rule rather than a standard.

Somewhat similar is section 588G of the Australian Corporations Act 2001, which also applies only when the company is insolvent.[32] It imposes a specific duty, but in this case a negative one – to cause the company not to incur further debts – which gives the directors slightly greater freedom of manoeuvre in deciding how to deal with the company's insolvency than does the German

eds., *Corporate Personality in the 20th Century* (Oxford, Hart Publishing 1998) at pp. 114-115. On the German position, see D. Skeel in this volume.

29 R. Kraakman, et al., *The Anatomy of Corporate Law* (Oxford, Oxford University Press 2004) p. 73.

30 To like effect, Art. 64 GmbHG (and Swiss law has similar provisions). Although Art. 92 does not expressly deal with the civil liability consequences of a breach, by virtue of German tort law a violation gives rise to damages claims by creditors against directors: H. Fleischer, 'The Responsibilities of the Management and its Enforcement', in G. Ferrarini, et al., eds., *Reforming Company and Takeover Law in Europe* (Oxford, Oxford University Press 2004) p. 399.

31 Subject to the important qualification that balance sheet insolvency triggers the duty to invoke formal proceedings. See section 5 below.

32 But see the discussion above on different definitions of insolvency employed in the German and Australian provisions.

provision. It also relieves the directors from liability if there were no reasonable grounds for suspecting that the company was in fact insolvent. Nevertheless, the rationale of the provision seems close to that of Article 92 AktG, namely, that the directors' 'proper course is to relinquish control so that the company's creditors can determine its future. Any question of the company having a possibility of being rehabilitated and incurring further debts is a question for the creditors, rather than the directors.'[33]

Two criticisms can be advanced of the German and Australian provisions. The more important is that already indicated. Although the provisions deal eventually with the problem of perverse incentives by replacing the directors with an appointee accountable to the creditors, or in some other way subjecting the directors to effective third-party control, they do so only at a very late stage. Second, it can be questioned whether mandatory invocation of a formal insolvency procedure is always the correct course of action, even if the company is insolvent. Such a rule involves the compulsory exposure of the company to the costs of the insolvency procedure and a reduction of the chances of an informal work-out with the creditors. Perhaps for this reason, given the British tradition of dealing with insolvent companies out of court, that country has no provision equivalent to Article 92 or section 588. Trading whilst insolvent is not by itself either a criminal offence or a civil wrong. On the contrary, there is judicial authority that putting an insolvent company into liquidation may itself be a breach of the creditor-regarding duties created by section 214 of the British Insolvency Act 1986 and discussed further below. In *Re Continental Assurance Co of London plc*,[34] it was said that 'ceasing to trade and liquidating too soon can be stigmatised as the coward's way out.'

Nevertheless, it must be pointed out that the British provisions on wrongful and fraudulent trading (discussed below) do normally produce the result that the directors of a company which they realise or ought to have realised is in a state of insolvency have little option but to invoke a formal insolvency procedure. It is only where there is a realistic prospect of trading out of insolvency that the British provisions give the directors a freedom of action apparently denied by the German and Australian rules. In other words, the German and Australian rules seem to take as their point of departure that the company's reaching a state of insolvency is by itself a sufficient reason for transferring control to the creditors, whilst the British provisions keep the door open for the argument that the directors may appropriately in some cases continue to keep control and implement a plan to turn the company around. The aim of the British rules is to rebalance the incentives which operate on the directors when they take the

---

33 Austin, Ford and Ramsay, op. cit. n. 26, at p. 408.

34 [2001] *Bankruptcy and Personal Insolvency Reports* 733 *per* Park J at para. 281.

decision whether to trade or enter formal insolvency proceedings, but not to determine the decision for them.

It is also important to note that, whilst not requiring directors of insolvent companies to invoke formal insolvency proceedings, British law gives to any creditor, who may think he or she is suffering from directorial delay in this regard, a simple mechanism for invoking such proceedings him- or herself. If a company fails to pay an undisputed debt of at least £750 after demand for payment has been made, that will be taken as sufficient evidence that it is unable to pay its debts as they fall due, even if all other circumstance suggest that the company is solvent.[35] It has been argued that this provision is the functional equivalent of Article 92 AktG.[36]

Other countries, for example the United States and Japan, which lack any equivalent to Article 92 or section 588, achieve timely invocation of the insolvency procedures by means of a carrot rather than a stick, i.e., by permitting the incumbent management to remain in place in insolvency, which may then operate principally as a mechanism for the management unilaterally to amend the terms of unfavourable contracts (e.g., with trade unions) and introduce new finance on the basis of this readjusted cost base.[37] Although the incumbent management may remain in charge in such insolvency procedures, creditors are protected to some extent by the court scrutiny to which the directors are now exposed – though again such third-party protection comes only at a very late stage in the company's decline.

5. Directors' liabilities in the vicinity of insolvency

The theory argued for in section 2 suggests that creditor-regarding duties which are triggered only when the company is insolvent operate too late. Rather, the creditor-regarding duties should be imposed at the point at which the directors' incentives to adopt overly risky strategies become effective, i.e., when the shareholders' equity has become negligible or is anticipated to do so. We thus identify the first policy issue in designing such laws, i.e., defining in terms which courts can efficiently handle the point at which the creditor-regarding duties are to be triggered. The second policy issue is the definition of the nature of the creditor-regarding duty. Since the company typically will not be in a state of insolvency

---

[35] See Goode, op. cit. n. 23, at para. 4-23; and *Cornhill Insurance plc* v. *Improvement Services Ltd* [1986] 1 *WLR* 114.

[36] A. Schall, 'The UK Limited Company Abroad', 16 *European Business Law Review* (2005) p. 1577 at p. 1581.

[37] Kraakman et al., op. cit. n. 29, at p. 74.

(at least based on a cash flow test) at the point the duty bites, the simple solution of requiring the directors to enter into formal insolvency proceedings or to cease trading is not obviously the appropriate course of action. Nor is any alternative precise course of action obviously identifiable *ex ante* to be imposed on the directors. Consequently, legislation designed to give effect to creditor-regarding duties in advance of insolvency is likely to rely on standards rather than rules for the specification of the duty, just as the legal regulation of the duties of directors when the company is in a fully solvent state is normally based on standards rather than rules.

5.1 Section 214 of the British Insolvency Act 1986

The European Commission's High Level Group of Company Law Experts identified section 214 of the British Insolvency Act 1986 (the wrongful trading provision) as a model for creditor-regarding duties imposed in advance of insolvency.[38] The section certainly aims to meet the problem identified in section 2 of this paper.[39] It exposes to personal liability the directors (and shadow directors) of a company who, at the point that they realise or ought to have realised that the company had no reasonable prospect of avoiding insolvent liquidation, fail to take all steps which a reasonable director would have taken to minimise the potential loss to the creditors. What the directors ought to have realised and the steps they ought to have taken to minimise creditors' losses are assessed on an objective basis, i.e., according to the standard of what a reasonable director ought to have done, irrespective of the cognitive and executive talents of the particular directors in question.[40] However, no specific course of action to protect creditors is mandated by the section: the directors' actions are assessed *ex post* by a court by reference to the standard of the reasonable director. Action against the directors may be brought only if the company goes into insolvent liquidation and only by the liquidator. The principal liability of a director who has broken section 214 is to make such a contribution as the court thinks proper to the assets of the insolvent company which are then available for distribution to creditors.[41] That contribution is made available mainly to the unsecured creditors,

---

[38] Report of the High Level Group of Company Law Experts on a Modern Regulatory Framework for Company Law in Europe (Brussels, 4 November 2002) s. 4.4.

[39] P.L. Davies, *Introduction to Company Law* (Oxford, Oxford University Press 2002) p. 93 et seq.; Mokal, op. cit. n. 17, ch. 8.

[40] S 214(4). This may seem obvious, but, in the context of British company law, which has traditionally assessed directors' duties of skill and care on a subjective basis, the point is worth noting: L.C.B. Gower and P.L. Davies, *Principles of Modern Company Law*, 7th edn. (London, Thomson 2003) p. 432 et seq.

[41] S. 214(1).

because the courts have treated recoveries under section 214 as not representing the proceeds of an asset held by the company prior to insolvency, and so the recoveries are not caught by security interests granted by the company prior to insolvency.[42] Overall, the section can be seen to aim to rebalance the incentives of the directors as the shareholders' equity nears vanishing point. The directors (and shadow directors) are left in control of the company, but section 214 has the effect of exposing them to the downside of their decisions if they adopt excessively risky strategies.

Despite the apparent appropriateness of section 214 to the problem identified in section 2, it has been criticised on a number of grounds. These relate to the point at which the duty is triggered, the range of insolvency situations caught by the provision, the assessment of the contribution to be made by directors in breach, the chances of the duty being enforced in practice and the lack of guidance provided by the section to the directors subject to it.

5.1.1 *Triggering the duty*

Although the section does bite in advance of insolvency, it has been argued that it does not operate far enough in advance of insolvency. The test of 'no reasonable prospect of avoiding insolvent liquidation' has been argued not to identify accurately the point at which creditors' interests cease to be protected by the shareholders' desire to preserve their equity in the company. This argument was considered by the Company Law Review in the United Kingdom. It considered the proposition that directors should be required 'where they know or ought to recognise that there is a substantial probability[43] of an insolvent liquidation, to take such steps as they believe, in their good faith judgement, appropriate to reduce the risk, without undue caution and thus continuing also to have in mind the interests of members.'[44] The qualified way in which this proposition is put indicates the lack of agreement among the members of the Steering Group about the attractiveness of the idea. Those in favour thought the principle expressed simply what good directors ought to do; those against that fears of personal liability would lead to excessive caution on the part of directors and induce premature decisions to end or scale down trading, especially as the trigger point for the new duty might well be difficult to identify. The Steering Group simply put the idea forward for further consideration by the relevant Government

---

[42] *Re Oasis Merchandising Ltd* [1998] Ch. 170, CA. However, the now much-reduced group of preferential creditors will have a first claim on the recoveries.

[43] To be defined as meaning more probable than not.

[44] Company Law Review Steering Group, *Final Report*, Vol. 1 (London, Department of Trade and Industry 2001) para. 3.17. The section 214 duty would remain in place and bite where there was no reasonable prospect of avoiding insolvent liquidation.

Department, which later, and probably rightly, rejected it as inconsistent with its policy of promoting a 'rescue culture' for companies in financial difficulty.[45] Certainly, in the form quoted above, the court is given a very difficult balancing decision because of the lack of guidance as to how to strike the balance. The most likely result of the introduction of such a duty is that the British courts would have been highly reluctant to conclude that any particular directorial decision infringed the legal standard, so that its impact in practice would have been severely limited. In any event, the suggested duty does not appear in the Company Law Reform Bill introduced into Parliament in November 2005.

Thomas Bachner[46] has criticised section 214 from a somewhat similar standpoint, arguing that it operates too late in the company's economic decline. He argues further, and interestingly, that in fact Article 92 AktG (and the equivalent provisions for private companies) operate at an earlier point. How can the German provision, which has been criticised in the previous section as operating at too late a stage, i.e., only when the company is in a state of insolvency, be argued to come into effect at an earlier point in time than the British provision which specifically focuses on companies which have not yet reached a state of insolvency? The answer to this puzzle is to be found in a point already alluded to, namely, the different definitions of insolvency used in the two countries. The British provision operates in advance of insolvency but defines insolvency in cash flow terms; the German provision requires the company to be in a state of insolvency but defines insolvency in both balance sheet and cash flow terms. To see how this difference in the applicable definition of insolvency relates to the point at which the duties created by the provisions begin to regulate the behaviour of directors, let us look more carefully at each set of provisions in turn.

Does section 214 of the British Insolvency Act operate on a cash flow definition of insolvency? It is submitted that this is in fact the case, though the section does not appear at first sight to do so. That section imposes liability on directors who fail to take the requisite action to protect creditors when they realise or ought to have realised that the company has no reasonable prospect of avoiding insolvent liquidation and the company does in fact subsequently go into insolvent liquidation. Insolvent liquidation is defined, however, on a balance sheet basis (i.e., going into liquidation 'at a time when its assets are insufficient for the payment of its debts and other liabilities and the expenses of winding up'). Why is this? It is important to note that section 214 does not use the fact of the company going into insolvent liquidation as the trigger point for the imposition of the

---

[45] *Modernising Company Law* (London, Her Majesty's Stationery Office, July 2002, Cmnd. 5553-I) para. 3.11.

[46] T. Bachner, 'Wrongful Trading – A New European Model for Creditor Protection?', 5 *EBOR* (2004) p. 293.

creditor-regarding duties. Rather, the company going into formal liquidation proceedings is a necessary condition for the enforcement by the liquidator of duties which have arisen (and been broken) previously. (The significance of this aspect of the section is discussed further below.) Defining insolvent liquidation, as a condition for liability, in balance sheet terms makes good sense, because if the company is not insolvent at the point of liquidation on a balance sheet test (but only in cash flow terms), there is no reason to impose liability on the directors, since the creditors, *ex hypothesi*, will be fully paid in the liquidation.[47]

Going into insolvent liquidation thus does not define the point at which the creditor-regarding duties are triggered. The whole rationale of the section requires that these duties should be triggered at an earlier time. This point is in fact the point at which the directors realise, or ought to have realised, that the company has no reasonable prospect of avoiding insolvent liquidation, a point which is necessarily prior to the company's entering into formal liquidation proceedings. The crucial question is what tests the courts have developed for determining whether the company has no reasonable prospect of avoiding insolvent liquidation. For that purpose, it seems clear from the case law (the section does not deal with the point) that the courts use a cash flow test. Thus, in *Re Purpoint*,[48] the company was undoubtedly insolvent on a balance sheet test when it commenced trading in February 1998, but the court held that the director did not contravene section 214 until the end of that year, because only then was it clear that 'the company could not meet its trade debts as they fell due.' Likewise, in *Re Rod Gunner Organisation*,[49] the directors of a company, insolvent on a balance sheet basis, were held not to have breached section 214 until the point at which it became clear that the person who had come in with funds to meet the company's day-to-day needs was not going to stick by the original refinancing plan and was proposing instead an implausible flotation of the company. It is further clear that the cash flow test is applied on a 'commercial reality' basis, so that companies which have not in fact been paying their debts on time are not regarded as insolvent on a cash flow basis if they have been making payments within time-scales acceptable to their creditors.[50] In the eyes of the British courts, if the company is cash flow solvent, it will normally be safe to proceed on the basis that no creditor is likely to want or to be in a position to put the company into

---

47 Goode, op. cit. n. 23, at para. 4.06. For example, the company might have a clear excess of assets over liabilities, even when the assets are valued on a break-up basis, but be unable to pay its debts as they fall due because the assets are illiquid. In this case, the liquidation should lead to the creditors being paid in full.

48 [1991] BCLC 491.

49 [2004] 2 BCLC 110.

50 *Re Brian D Pearson (Contractors) Ltd* [1999] BCC 26.

liquidation,[51] and so the company can be said to have still a reasonable prospect of avoiding insolvent liquidation.

The above analysis of the British provisions also explains the claim that the German provision operates at an earlier stage in the company's financial decline. As the above British cases show, a company may be insolvent on a balance sheet test at some point before the section 214 duty is triggered. To the extent that the German provision would bite at this earlier stage, because it uses a balance sheet test of insolvency as well as a cash flow test, the claim to earlier operation of the German provision can be considered to be made out. Thus, Bachner rescues the German provision from one of the criticisms made of it in the previous section, i.e., that its duty is triggered too late. However, it does not rescue the German provisions from the second criticism, namely, that the content of the duty – to put the company into a formal insolvency procedure – is inappropriate. In fact, this second criticism is strengthened by Bachner's argument. If the company is solvent on a going concern test, it seems highly inapposite that the directors should be required to impose on the company the costs of a formal insolvency procedure, if there is a reasonable prospect of the company trading out of its financial difficulties. In short, early triggering of the creditor-regarding duty is not in itself a virtue. If that duty is formulated in terms of putting the company into insolvency, as the German provision is, it may in fact reduce the chances of saving viable companies. The German provision, by requiring the invocation of a formal insolvency procedure, is not apposite for operation at an early stage in the company's financial decline because it deprives the directors of all but one of the available course of action for dealing with the company's troubles.[52]

Of course, the German provision could be saved from this second criticism as well by reformulating it so as to require the directors to take reasonable steps to protect the interests of the creditors rather than, as at present, specifying a particular course of action. However, this reformulation would move Article 92 very much closer to the approach of section 214 of the British Act. Article 92 would have recourse, as does section 214, to a general standard of review of director's actions, but the duty to act would be triggered at an earlier stage than under section 214. It has already been indicated that there is a debate to be had about whether the section 214 duty is triggered too late, and so earlier triggering of a non-specific duty would not by itself be unwelcome. A more difficult

---

51 See text attached to nn. 35 and 36 above.

52 It is true that Art. 92(2) gives the directors a three-week window to find an alternative solution, but it is doubtful whether this is an adequate response to the difficulty outlined in the text. French law contained a similar provision until January 2006 in Art. L621-1 of the *Code de Commerce* [Commercial Code]. As part of the 2005 reforms (see text attached to nn. 96-98 below) the obligation was removed precisely in order to give greater scope for the operation of a rescue procedure.

question is whether a balance sheet test for insolvency defines the appropriate earlier moment at which the duty should be triggered. It is difficult to see reasons for regarding the balance sheet test as defining the appropriate moment. Its presence in the German legislation seems more a reflection of the commitment of the German system to a far-reaching system of legal capital rules than of a search for the point at which creditor-regarding standards should be triggered.

5.1.2 *The range of insolvencies caught*

This set of criticisms requires us to return to the point that it is a condition of liability under section 214 that the company goes into insolvent liquidation. This has three consequences. First, if the directors break their section 214 duty but their gamble in fact pays off, because the company recovers, they are not exposed to liability. This may be justified on the grounds that the breach of duty has not harmed the creditors; in fact, they have benefited from it. Second, and more seriously, if the company does end up insolvent but is not put into insolvent liquidation but is simply at some later date struck off the register of companies, the section 214 machinery will not operate.[53] Third, if the company reaches a state of insolvency but is not put into liquidation but rather is dealt with through the alternative mechanism of administration, again the machinery of section 214 will not operate. Let us look at the second and third points in a little more detail.

A company's dissolution without going through a formal liquidation procedure is clearly a serious potential problem for creditor-protection systems which are based on use of the formal procedure. This is so even if the dissolution of the company does not formally relieve the directors of liabilities incurred whilst the company existed or if the relevant law provides for the resurrection of dissolved companies so that they can enforce their rights.[54] This is because, without the use of a formal procedure, no independent person is likely to examine whether the company has a viable claim against the previous directors of the company. If on a cursory view the company appears not to have sufficient assets to support the costs of the formal procedure, that procedure will not be invoked, even if examination in the formal procedure might have revealed the existence of further assets in the shape of claims against the directors. On the other hand, since there will be many companies which genuinely have no assets, of any type, to support the costs of the formal procedure, some mechanism must be provided for dissolving unliquidated companies.

---

[53] I am particularly grateful to Professor Spindler for emphasising in his formal comments on my paper at the conference the significance of this point.

[54] For the relevant British law, see Gower and Davies, op. cit. n. 40, at pp. 864-870.

It is difficult to know how this situation can be handled effectively. A formal duty on the directors, as Article 92 AktG imposes, to petition for the opening of formal liquidation proceedings seems not to solve the problem. Schall has remarked that 'in about one-third of all insolvency cases in Germany the proceedings are not opened by the court due to lack of assets.'[55] The functional problem is the same in Britain and Germany: the lack of incentive to devote resources (public or private) to handle the affairs of companies which appear to have no significant assets. A bolder step would be to give the right to sue the directors for breach of the creditor-regarding duties to individual creditors, at least in those cases where the representative of the creditors collectively is not in a position to enforce it. German law already treats breaches of Article 92(2) AktG as conferring tort claims for damages on creditors individually.[56] British law could follow this lead, for example, by conferring the right to enforce section 214 on individual creditors in those cases where the company was dissolved on the grounds it was failing to carry on any business and either no liquidator had been appointed or the liquidator had ceased to act without completing the winding-up. The action would be to recover a proportionate part of the contribution which the court would have ordered the director to make to the company.[57] This would give the creditor who acted first the best chance of recovery from the director's personal assets, but this might be regarded as an appropriate reward for taking the initiative. However, it is unclear how much use would be made of such a right on the part of individual creditors. In most cases, they would still lack the information on which to judge whether such litigation was likely to be successful and the right to recover a proportionate part of the directors' contribution might not provide a strong incentive to bring litigation.

The other problem in this area is that section 214 does not apply if the insolvent company goes into administration[58] rather than liquidation. This is a major issue, since administration is clearly now the legislature's preferred way of handling insolvent companies, because that process is thought to increase the chances of (parts of) the company's business being saved. Under this procedure, as revamped by the Enterprise Act 2002, the primary objective of an administration is to 'rescue the company as a going concern'; only if that is not reasonably

---

[55] Schall, loc. cit. n. 36, at p. 1590.

[56] Fleischer, loc. cit. n. 30, at pp. 399-400. This is perhaps an example of a situation where certain assumptions follow from placing a rule in either insolvency or company law. Britain places the rule in insolvency law and so naturally adopts the collective enforcement principle of that branch of the law; Germany places the rule in company law and so does not adopt the collectivist approach.

[57] For a discussion of the different recovery rules in Britain and Germany, see below.

[58] Administration is governed largely by Schedule B1 of the Insolvency Act 1986, as amended by the Enterprise Act 2002.

practicable should the administrator pursue the secondary objective of 'achieving a better result for the creditors as a whole' than would be likely to be achieved by an immediate liquidation; and only if achieving the secondary goal is not reasonably practicable should the administrator pursue the tertiary goal of 'realising property in order to make a distribution to one or more secured or preferential creditors.'[59] Where the administrator succeeds in achieving the primary goal, then the directors escape liability under section 214, even if it was their excessively risky business decisions which brought the company to the point of needing to be rescued. Nor can the defence necessarily be used that, if the company is rescued, the creditors will have suffered no loss. An element of the rescue operation on the part of the administrator is likely to involve the agreement (partially forced, given the situation) by some or all of the creditors to scale down their claims against the company,[60] so that the creditors are likely to bear part of the costs of the rescue. In this situation, there is a major gap in the protection afforded to creditors against the perverse incentives identified in section 2 of this paper.[61]

Why should the wrongful trading provisions be limited in this way? One possible explanation is that, at the time of their adoption in the mid-1980s, the administration procedure was much less significant than it now is following the 2002 reforms. Against this is the fact that the Committee which recommended the introduction of wrongful trading in 1982 did envisage its application to the administration process.[62] This suggests a more substantial reason. Two justifications for the restriction can be advanced. The first is the desire of the legislature to encourage use of the administration procedure and especially to encourage directors of companies to initiate administration as soon as the need for it arises. As insiders, directors are better placed than external creditors to take timely action and so directors' commitment to the administration process might be thought to be worth encouraging. Removing the threat of a wrongful trading investigation by the administrator takes a way a disincentive for directors to seek an appointment. It is consonant with this argument that directors are able to appoint an administrator out of court on the basis of a simple notice filed with the court stating that the company is or is likely to become unable to pay its debts.[63]

---

59 Insolvency Act 1986, Sched. B1, para. 3.

60 As recognised in para. 49(3). And see Mokal, op. cit. n. 17, at p. 248. During the administration, there is a moratorium on creditor enforcement of their claims and, indeed, on the appointment of a liquidator: paras. 42 and 43.

61 Where the administrator pursues the second or third objectives, the problem is less pressing because there the administration is likely to be followed by a liquidation.

62 *Report of the Review Committee on Insolvency Law and Practice* (London, Her Majesty's Stationery Office 1982, Cmnd. 8558) – usually referred to after the name of its chairman as the 'Cork Committee' – at para. 1791.

63 Insolvency Act 1986, Sched. B1, para. 27(2) – note the absence of a reference to balance sheet insolvency.

By contrast, creditors, other than the holder of a floating charge,[64] are required to apply to the court for the appointment of an administrator and the court needs to satisfy itself not only that the company is or is likely to become unable to pay its debts but also that an appointment by the court is likely to achieve one of the purposes of an administration,[65] a requirement which imposes a substantial evidential burden on those seeking court appointment of an administrator.

A further argument along the same lines is that, although the administrator displaces the existing management in terms of the formal, legal allocation of authority to run the company,[66] nevertheless he or she may in practice have to rely heavily on the existing management of the company to effect the rescue plan. In fact, it can be argued that the very incentive structure which led the directors to expose the company to excessive risk can now be put to use in support of the administrator's plan to rescue the company. At least in family-controlled companies, the shareholder-directors will have made idiosyncratic investments in the company and 'given therefore that they are likely to consider themselves deeply tied up with the fortunes of the company, and given that they would often clearly be its residual claimants, shareholder-directors have every incentive to ensure that the company's value would be maximised.'[67] Given the administrator's control of the setting of the company's strategy, we need no longer fear that the incentive structure will lead to excessively risky decisions and can be more confident that the former management will work loyally to implement the rescue plan the administrator proposes and the creditors adopt. Again, it can be argued that this (perhaps optimistic) scenario would be disrupted if administrators were under a duty to investigate claims against the directors for wrongful trading. Both the arguments made above demonstrate a legislative strategy of promoting corporate rescue or turnaround over a policy of bringing home to directors a liability for the harm they have inflicted on creditors through excessively risky business decisions.

5.1.3 *Compensation*

Bachner has also pointed out[68] that the British rules on the level of compensation payable appear to be more favourable to directors than those developed under the

---

[64] Paras. 14-21. The traditional British fondness for the floating charge, although much reduced by the 2002 Act, shows itself here, but that is a topic which lies outside the scope of this paper.

[65] Para. 11.

[66] Paras. 59-64.

[67] Mokal, op. cit. n. 17, at p. 228. However, he seems later to take the view that evidence that the directors have engaged previously in wrongful trading should disqualify them from involvement in executing the rescue plan, at p. 249.

[68] Bachner, loc. cit. n. 46, at p. 310 et seq.

German rules. Although the British statute confers a discretion on the court as to the size of the contribution to be demanded from the directors who have acted in breach of section 214, the courts seem to have settled down with an approach whereby the maximum contribution is the diminution in the company's net asset position during the period of wrongful trading, with discounts being available from that theoretical maximum for directors who are not regarded as strongly blameworthy. There is no room here for taking account, as German law does, of unfavourable developments in the position of particular creditors within an overall stable net asset position for the company;[69] still less for the development of a distinction between 'old' and 'new' creditors, under which the latter (those becoming creditors after the creditor-regarding duty has been broken) are entitled to full compensation for their reliance loss.[70] The British approach reduces the chilling effect of the creditor-regarding duties on directorial decision making and thus probably demonstrates again the British tendency to promote the 'rescue culture': even if directors do embark on an excessively risky project once insolvent liquidation threatens and that project is not successful, they will not incur liability if the company is no worse off as a result. The German approach to compensation, by contrast, is consistent with the policy of requiring directors to institute formal insolvency proceedings, thus making any further trading under the directors' control illegitimate. As the BGH has memorably put it, the purpose of the provision is to keep insolvent companies out of commerce.[71]

5.1.4 *Enforcement*

The most frequent domestic criticism of section 214 concerns no so much the principle it embodies but its alleged lack of effect in practice, a conclusion drawn from the relatively few reported cases in which it has been invoked. Although the link between the level of reported cases and the impact of any particular law is complex and not by any means unilinear, there are in fact grounds for being concerned about whether financing is available for all section 214 claims which could appropriately be pursued. The *Oasis Trading* case,[72] which confirmed that

---

69 By means of the notion of *Quotenschaden*.

70 BGH 6 June 1994, *NJW* 1994 p. 2220. See also Fleischer, loc. cit. n. 30, at p. 400.

71 BGZH 126, 181 at 184: the purpose of the legislation is 'konkursreife Gesellschaften mit beschränktem Haftungsfonds von Geschäftsverkehr fernzuhalten.' (See Fleischer, loc. cit. n. 30, at p. 400.) Similar debates have arisen in Australia and New Zealand, where the current decisions seem to favour the German approach of protecting individual creditors: *Re BM and CB Jackson Ltd* (2001) 9 NZCLC 262,612 (criticised by Peter Watts, 'Company Law', *New Zealand Law Review* (2001) p. 293) and *Powell* v. *Noclex Yachts* (2001) 37 ACSR 589.

72 *Re Oasis Merchandising Ltd* [1998] Ch. 170, CA. This can be seen as an application of the long-established general principle that causes of action not created until the commencement

the proceeds of a section 214 contribution claim are not caught by security interests the company may have granted, also made it of no interest to secured creditors to fund 214 actions. The liquidator will naturally be cautious about using the company's assets available for unsecured creditors to pursue 214 claims, and is likely to pursue only the clearest cases.[73] The obvious solution is for the liquidator to transfer less-than-clear cases to a third-party financier in exchange for a share of the proceeds if the claim is successful.[74] The third-party can spread its risks over a body of 214 claims and thus pursue some risky claims which a liquidator of a particular company might be unwilling to take up. In *Oasis Trading*, however, such a course of action was held to infringe an ancient if arcane principle of civil procedure law (the rule against champerty) which was held not to have been overridden by the insolvency legislation. It seems unnecessary to pursue this domestic civil procedure debate here: it is obvious that funding for 214 claims could be made available from third parties if there was a will to adopt an appropriate mechanism.[75]

---

of the insolvency proceedings and enforceable only in the liquidator's name benefit the unsecured creditors: *Re Yagerphone Ltd* [1935] 1 Ch. 395.

[73] At one stage, it appeared that the costs of pursuing a wrongful trading claim were not to be counted as 'expenses of the insolvency' and so were not recoverable by the liquidator from the company's assets if the litigation were unsuccessful – a disastrous disincentive to enforcement by the liquidator. However, this problem has now been remedied by an amendment to the Insolvency Rules (see the Insolvency (Amendment) (No. 2) Rules 2002 (S.I. 2712) amending Rule 4.218(1)(a) of the Insolvency Rules 1986 (S.I. 1925)). However, this change does not remove the pressures on the liquidator, in discharging his duties to promote the interests of the unsecured creditors, not to take speculative cases, pressures reinforced by the requirement that the liquidator obtain court or creditors' committee approval for section 214 litigation: Insolvency Act 1986, Sched. 4, para. 3A (a linked amendment also made in 2002).

[74] The alternative of contingent fee litigation is less attractive in the UK setting, where the losing party pays the winner's legal costs, and so the British rules in this area (the so-called 'conditional fee' arrangement) require insurance against this risk to be taken out on the commencement of the litigation. Further, the 'up-lift' in costs which the lawyers achieve where the litigation is successful is less than in contingent fee litigation in the United States, so that it is less attractive to British law firms practising commercial law to fund claims (including insurance costs) where the chances of success are not great, on the basis that the costs thus incurred will be covered by recoveries in the successful cases.

[75] For an argument that the *Oasis Trading* decision has been overruled impliedly by the subsequent decision of the House of Lords in *Buchler* v. *Talbot* [2004] 2 A.C. 298, see J. Armour and A. Walters, 'Funding Liquidation: A Functional View', 122 *Law Quarterly Review* (2006) p. 295. Their argument is probably still good despite the proposed legislative repeal of the result in *Buchler*, see the Company Law Reform Bill (H L Bill 34, 1 November 2005) cl. 868.

5.1.5 *The costs of using standards*

Section 214 is also often criticised in practitioner circles for not giving directors sufficient guidance on what it is necessary to do to comply with its requirements. This is a criticism inevitably attracted by standards, in the setting of which the legislature externalises some of the costs of law-making to the courts which have to apply the standard and the persons who are subject to it. However, standards are the traditional technique for defining the duties of directors of companies in a healthy financial state, and there is no evidence as yet that the courts will apply the section 214 standard any less appropriately than the standards embodied in the common law duties of directors. The solution to the problem (perhaps easier to articulate than to apply) is for the courts to develop the legal standard so that it reflects current mores of good business practice recognised by the business community. Although difficult cases are bound to arise in the courts, it is suggested that the notion of wrongful trading is firmly grounded in the principle that companies should not trade at their (unsecured) creditors' expense and this is a recognised social principle in the business community.[76]

5.2 **Common law developments regarding directors duties 'to creditors'**

Although section 214 of the British Act provides a convenient focus for debate about the introduction of creditor-regarding duties, it is by no means the only legal development tending towards the recognition of the theory expressed in section 2 of this paper. In fact, much more widespread are judicial innovations of this type. Starting in Australia in the 1970s,[77] the notion of a duty upon directors to take account of the interests of creditors as insolvency approaches has been widely accepted throughout the common law world, including in the United States.[78] As with most significant common law developments in their early stages, there is considerable uncertainty about the conceptual boundaries of the new doctrine. For example, it is clear that creditor-regarding duties are being developed by extension of the common law duties which the law has traditionally recognised the directors as owing to the company. However, it is not always clear which of the two main strands of those traditional duties is being developed. The traditional duties may be viewed in terms of a duty to promote the interests of the

---

76 Cork Committee, op. cit. n. 62, at paras. 205-223 and 1785.

77 *Walker* v. *Wimborne* (1976) 137 CLR 1.

78 The current state of play is conveniently summarised by Andrew Keay, 'Another way of skinning a cat: enforcing directors' duties for the benefit of creditors', 17 *Insolvency Intelligence* (2004) p. 1.

protected group (fiduciary duties or duties of loyalty in common law parlance) or to avoid harm to the interests of the protected group (e.g., duties of competence). It would be conceptually possible to extend either or both of these duties to creditors. The former is a more demanding duty: in exercising their discretionary powers, directors would be required to give priority to promoting the interests of the creditors, either exclusively or, more likely, along with the interests of the shareholders. The latter would permit the directors to continue to exercise their discretion so as to promote exclusively the shareholders' interests, but impose the constraint that their action should not, as a by-product, damage creditors' interests. To the extent that the new common law duty bites in advance of insolvency, the distinction is a potentially important one.[79]

Equally unclear from the decisions is the definition of the trigger point for the creditor-regarding duty, except that there appears to be general acceptance that the duty can bite in advance of the company being in a state of insolvency. In *Credit Lyonnais Bank Nederland NV* v. *Pathe Communications Corp*,[80] Chancellor Allen suggested the test of the company 'operating in the vicinity of insolvency', whilst in *Nicholson* v. *Permakraft (NZ) Ltd*,[81] the judge conceivably was prepared to go a bit further by suggesting the duty was triggered by 'a course of action which would jeopardise solvency.' Given the difficulty, already noted, of defining in operational terms the point at which the creditor-regarding duty should be triggered, it seems likely that the courts will continue to experiment with different formulations of the trigger point for some time to come.

On the other hand, the majority view is that this duty is not in fact owed directly to creditors, but is an extension of directors' duties as traditionally understood and so is a duty owed to the company.[82] The importance of this point is that it is thus a duty which can be enforced[83] only by the company (or in a derivative action on its behalf) and not directly by creditors, so long as the

[79] If the directors must promote (not just protect) the interests of the creditors, and the creditors' claims are currently (just) covered by the company's assets, they might feel constrained to favour a project which has a 90 per cent chance of producing 5 and a 10 per cent chance of producing 0, as against one with a 50 per cent chance of producing 100 and a 50 per cent chance of producing -50. Although both projects have a positive current value, the former is less risky.

[80] Printed in 17 *Delaware Journal of Corporate Law* (1992) p. 1099. Note that in this case the duty to take account of creditor interests was invoked not by creditors but by directors in order to resist a claim by shareholders, a situation equally to be found in relation to the current statutory duty upon directors of British companies to take into account the interests of employees: *Re Saul D Harrison & Sons plc* [1995] 1 BCLC 13, CA.

[81] [1985] 1 NZLR 242.

[82] See below for a discussion of the contrary view of the Supreme Court of Canada.

[83] The duty may have legal consequences short of enforcement even before the opening of formal insolvency proceedings: see n. 86.

company has not entered into a formal insolvency procedure. Even at that point, the duty is enforceable only by the creditors collectively (e.g., by the liquidator) and not by individual creditors. As Gummow J said in the Australian High Court, 'the result is that there is a duty of imperfect obligation owed to creditors, one which the creditors cannot enforce save to the extent that the company acts on its own motion or through a liquidator.'[84]

Subject to the inevitable uncertainties involved in common law developments, especially as regards the trigger point of the creditor-regarding duty, the cases summarised above seem to fit reasonably well with the theory advanced in section 2 of this paper as to when it would be appropriate to reset the directors' incentives. The modified directors' duty exposes directors to personal liability if they embark on overly risky projects in the vicinity of insolvency, and in consequence the downside of potential projects again becomes of relevance to their decision making.

Even in the United Kingdom, where the courts have also adopted the modified common law duty, it can play a useful supplementary role to section 214. First, it may operate at an earlier stage than section 214 and thus allow the courts to impose liability in appropriate cases where section 214 does not apply. To the extent that the section 214 trigger point is too late (see the discussion above), the common law duty permits the courts to experiment with definitions which apply earlier. Second, it can be invoked in all insolvency proceedings (e.g., by an administrator) and not just in liquidation.[85] Third, the duty has legal consequences beyond the payment of compensation. In particular, breaches by directors of the creditor-regarding duty cannot be authorised or ratified by the shareholders at some time before the company enters into a formal insolvency procedure, so that the cause of action against the directors survives to be enforced by the liquidator or administrator.[86] Before the recognition of creditor-regarding duties, there was a strong risk that directors would seek authority or forgiveness from the shareholders for their actions, which the shareholders would presumably be only to happy to give since the action was aimed to promote their interests. The main disadvantage of the common law duty – and it is a significant one – is that its proceeds would appear not to go primarily to the unsecured creditors. Since the company's cause of action against the directors exists at the point the company goes into liquidation, the proceeds of its enforcement will be caught by any security interests the company has granted.

---

[84] *Sycotex Pty Ltd* v. *Baseler* (1994) 122 ALR 531, 550.

[85] Under the administrator's general management powers.

[86] See *Liquidator of West Mercia Safetywear* v. *Dodd* [1988] BCLC 250, CA and the cases mentioned in nn. 81 and 84.

6. DIRECTORS' DUTIES TO CREDITORS WHEN THE COMPANY IS NOT IN FINANCIAL DIFFICULTY

Laws imposing on directors effective creditor-facing duties even when the company is in financial good health are, usually, inconsistent with the theory developed in section 2 of this paper. If such laws are widespread, that would suggest that some alternative or additional theory would have to be developed to explain their presence.[87] As argued above, on the one hand, it appears unnecessary for the protection of the creditors, since at this stage the interests of shareholders and creditors are sufficiently aligned for the creditors not to need distinct protection, or the creditors can deal with the problem through self-help. On the other hand, if the interests of the creditors were to be taken seriously as separate from those of the shareholders, the effect might be to discourage the directors from embarking on risky projects, even if those projects have a high present value. Professor Sealy has gone so far as to remark that 'it would be contrary to all reason to burden directors with any duty towards creditors when their company is solvent: their function is to make judgements about business risks, and to take those risks…'.[88]

When looking at potential examples of general creditor-regarding duties, two questions need to be distinguished. The first is whether such duties are imposed on the directors at all and the second is whether they can be enforced by the creditors in advance of the company being put into a formal insolvency proceeding. If the general creditor-regarding duties cannot be enforced by the creditors in advance of insolvency, it is suggested that they will probably operate in practice in a way similar to duties triggered only in the vicinity of insolvency. It may be true that, formally, the court may range over the whole of the directors' conduct when the duty is enforced by the liquidator, but it is suggested that the desire to reduce the costs of litigation is likely to lead to a concentration of analysis upon the directors' conduct in the period prior to insolvency. Thus, the bigger challenge to the theory outlined in section 2 is presented by laws which both create general creditor-regarding duties and permit the creditors to enforce them short of insolvency. Such provisions are rare, but not unknown.

---

[87] Andrew Keay, 'Directors' Duties to Creditors: Contractarian Concerns Relating to Efficiency and Over-Protection of Creditors', 66 *Modern Law Review* (2003) p. 665, argues that what he terms contractarian arguments developed by the law and economics school cannot explain the adoption of creditor-regarding duties in the vicinity of insolvency and that a 'fairness' theory needs to be developed to do this job. In so far as the argument developed in section 2 of this paper is 'contractarian' or based in the law-and-economics tradition, its implication is that a broader 'fairness' theory is not needed to explain the presence of creditor-regarding duties at that stage in the company's decline. However, it does seem certain that some broader theory would be needed to explain general creditor-regarding duties, though he does not seem to argue for them.

[88] L.S. Sealy, *Cases and Materials in Company Law*, 7th edn. (London, Butterworths 2001) p. 267.

6.1 Fraud

One set of general creditor-regarding rules is explained by the fact that we are happy to accept, at all times, some restraints on directors' risk taking in favour of protecting creditors, when the risk taking is based on conduct which is outside the bounds which society has set for entrepreneurial activity. The obvious example is fraud, but others such as coercion in various forms also come to mind. In general, such provisions do not have a high profile in company law, because legal systems rely on general civil or criminal law to control such conduct.[89] However, isolated examples can be found. Thus, section 458 of the British Companies Act makes directors (and others) criminally liable for carrying on the company's business with intent to defraud its creditors (or for any other fraudulent purpose), irrespective of the company's financial position, since there is no legal policy reason for encouraging fraudulent management, even if the fraud has no adverse impact on the company's performance. There is an equivalent civil provision in section 213 of the Insolvency Act 1986, but one enforceable only when the company is in liquidation and by the liquidator. In theory, the section allows the liquidator to traverse the whole of the company's business history searching for fraud on creditors, but the requirement of intent makes the section a difficult one for liquidators to use.[90] French law has a broader concept of *'abus de biens sociaux'* (misuse of corporate assets) (not confined to insolvent companies) which provides for criminal sanctions in respect of a range of directorial conduct damaging to the company, but only where the action was in bad faith.[91]

6.2 *Action en comblement de passif* (action to restore the company's assets)

Another larger and apparently more troubling set of provisions does not confine directorial liability to fraud and operates, at least formally, at all points in the company's existence. However, although such provisions are enforceable only in the company's insolvency, they do not appear to require the court to adopt a

---

89 Indeed, the apposite question might be the opposite: given the existence of general anti-fraud laws, why are specific company or insolvency law provisions needed? In the case of section 213 of the British Insolvency Act (discussed below), the answer appears to be that it allows recovery from the directors by the liquidator on the part of creditors generally, whereas general anti-fraud law provides only for individual recovery: *Morphitis* v. *Bernasconi* [2003] 2 BCLC 53.

90 For the most recent decisions, see *Re Bank of Credit and Commerce International SA (No. 15)* [2005] 2 BCLC 328; *ditto (No. 14)* [2004] 2 BCLC 236.

91 *Code de Commerce*, Art. L242-6. In fact, the discussion of this provision in the books focuses on issues of self-dealing rather than of ignoring the interests of creditors: M. Cozian, A. Viandier and F. Deboissy, *Droit des sociétés*, 18th edn. (Paris, Litec 2005) paras. 589-595.

creditor-regarding formulation of the liability when applying it to periods when the company was in good financial health. This appears, for example, to be the case with the *action en comblement de passif* of French (and Belgian) law,[92] mentioned with approval along with the wrongful trading provisions by the High Level Group.[93] This provision applies only to companies in formal insolvency proceedings[94] and empowers the court to require the directors to make a contribution to remedy the company's deficiency of assets, where their negligence (*faute legère*) has contributed to the deficiency. To that extent, it is like section 214 of the British Insolvency Act. However, unlike section 214, the duty created by the French action is not triggered by the prospect of insolvency but applies throughout the company's life, and the fault in question is not limited to a failure to protect the interests of creditors. In fact, in the typical list of examples, found in French text books, of successful recoveries in this action what predominate are activities which would be analysed in common law jurisdictions as breaches of the duties of loyalty or competence owed by directors to shareholders.[95] As such, one can say that the *action en comblement de passif* combines the functions of sections 214 and 212 of the British Insolvency Act, since section 212 also provides for a summary procedure in winding-up for the enforcement for the benefit of the creditors of the directors' shareholder-regarding duties, which the shareholders could have enforced whilst the company was solvent, had they been aware of the breaches and able to overcome their collective action problems. For the purpose of the current analysis, however, what is important is that the *action en comblement de passif* does not require French courts to impose creditor-regarding duties on directors whilst the companies is in a healthy financial condition and there is little evidence that French courts do in fact do so.

From January 2006, the *action en comblement de passif* was replaced by the *action en obligation aux dettes sociales* (action to enforce liability for corporate debts).[96] The new action displays two contrasts with the former one. First, the grounds of liability are more explicitly stated, under five headings, the first three of which are examples of liability for self-dealing. The fifth heading is analogous to fraudulent trading under British law. The fourth heading gives the court power to make the director personally liable for some or all of the company's debts where the board has pursued a loss-making business which could not but lead to the company's inability to pay its debts as they fell due, provided such a decision was taken 'abusively' and in furtherance of a personal interest. This reformulation

92 *Code de Commerce*, Art. L624-3.
93 Report of the High Level Group, op. cit. n. 38.
94 *'Redressement'* or *'liquidation judiciaire'*.
95 Cozian, Viandier and Deboissy, op. cit. n. 91, para. 278.
96 *Code de Commerce*, Art. L652-1, the former text of Art. L624-3 being repealed.

may be thought to have brought the French provision closer to the British wrongful trading legislation than the *action en comblement de passif*, even if the verbal formulation is still very different.

Second, the range of the insolvency proceedings in which the new action can be invoked has been narrowed in a way which is very interesting from our point of view, because it produces an outcome similar to that analysed above in relation to section 214 of the British Insolvency Act. The *action en comblement de passif* was available not only in cases of liquidation (*liquidation judiciare*) but also in cases of administration (*redressement judiciare*). Under the new arrangements, not only is the *action en comblement de passif* unavailable in the newly introduced *procédure de sauvegarde* (safeguard procedure) but it is no longer to be available in *redressement judiciare*. In short, the risk of personal liability of the directors for corporate debts and liabilities will arise, as in the United Kingdom, only in the case of liquidation. The reasons given for this step in the official statement of the purposes of the legislation followed very closely the reasons suggested above for the similar outcome in the United Kingdom. The *action en comblement de passif* was 'incompatible' with the recovery plan which is to emerge from either the *procédure de sauvegarde* or from *redressement judiciare*.[97] Somewhat optimistically, it was said that, if the plan was implemented, the creditors will be paid off, a statement which ignores the fact that the rights of the creditors may be scaled down as part of the recovery plan. Consequently, the scope of the action which replaced the *action en comblement de passif* should be confined to liquidation. It is also worth noting that this whole legislative change was driven by a desire to promote a rescue culture and an analysis which suggested that the previous law led to excessively high levels of liquidation, giving rise to adverse results for both creditors and for the preservation of jobs.[98]

6.3 Section 135 of the New Zealand Companies Act 1993

A further example of a provision raising the same issues is to be found, surprisingly, in the generally deregulatory New Zealand Companies Act 1993, section 135 of which makes directors civilly liable who 'agree, cause or allow' the company's business to be carried on 'in a manner likely to create a substantial risk of serious loss to the company's creditors'. This duty applies, apparently, at all stages of a company's history, and liability under it is not dependent upon

---

[97] Assemblée Nationale, Projet de loi de sauvegarde des entreprises, Document No. 1596, 12 May 2004, Exposé des motifs, Section VIIIB. Although the text of the law changed in various ways in its passage through the legislature, this particular provision remained intact. (The document is available at: <http://www.assemblee-nationale.fr/12/projets/pl1596.asp>.)

[98] Assemblée Nationale, loc. cit. n. 97, p. 1.

proof of fraud, negligence being enough to ground liability.[99] The section thus appears to impose a general creditor-regarding duty upon a company's directors. It is arguable that in high-risk industries such a provision is potentially infringed every time the directors take a significant investment decision and the directors are thus exposed to having their judgement second-guessed by the court.[100] However, the duty appears not to be enforceable by creditors outside a formal insolvency procedure.[101] In practice, however, the section has not been heavily relied on, nor have the courts interpreted it so as to realise the worst of these fears. This may be because the side note to the section (though not conclusive for the purposes of interpretation) uses the description 'reckless trading' and because the section has its origins in the fraudulent trading provisions of the British legislation, discussed above.

6.4 The Supreme Court of Canada

The unthinking tendency of lawmakers, whether legislatures or courts, to create creditor-regarding duties operating generally, but then, in one way or another, to avoid the consequences of their actions, may finally be illustrated by a recent decision of the Supreme Court of Canada, *Peoples Department Stores* v. *Wise.*[102] In this case, Wise Stores took over Peoples Stores, but the merger proved difficult. In order to address the problems, the directors of Wise (who were also now the directors of Peoples) took various steps, including splitting procurement between the two companies, so that one company procured for both from overseas and the other for both within Canada. At the time these steps were taken, the group was apparently solvent, though not in good financial shape. Shortly thereafter, both companies became insolvent and the creditors' representative in Peoples sued the directors of Peoples and focused in particular on the steps taken to address the merger problems, which were said to be unfavourable to Peoples. The allegations were based on breaches of section 122 of the Canada Business Corporations Act (CBCA), which establishes the general duties of competence and loyalty owed by directors to their company. Thus, section 122 does not create special creditor-regarding duties in the vicinity of insolvency.[103]

---

[99] This is a disputed point in the case law.

[100] And the section is so criticised on this ground by Thomas Telfer in 'Risk and Insolvent Trading', in Grantham and Rickett, op. cit. n. 28, at pp. 140-144.

[101] Although a shareholder, it seems, can obtain an injunction to restrain a course of action proposed by the directors in breach of the section and a shareholder who was also a creditor might have an interest in so doing: s. 164.

[102] [2004] 3 SCR 461.

[103] There was a separate argument based on section 100 of the Bankruptcy and Insolvency Act, relating to transfers at an undervalue in the period before insolvency. That does not concern us here. It also failed.

The case is mainly known for its holding that the fiduciary duties created by section 122 are not owed to the creditors of the company.[104] To this extent, the decision is fully in accordance with the theory developed in section 2 of this paper. Less often noted, however, is the Court's holding that the duty of competence created by section 122 is owed to creditors (at least in Quebec) and apparently at all times during the company's existence. As such, it is apparently enforceable by the creditors (presumably individually) and not only by the corporation, even when the company is fully solvent.[105] This aspect of the case is not in accordance with the theory outlined in section 2. On the facts of the case, the court held that the directors were not liable because they had not broken their duty of competence. Thus, the impact of the decision will depend very largely on how deferential the Canadian courts continue to be to managerial decision making when applying the negligence standard (and in particular how they develop the business judgement rule), but in this respect the directors' risk of liability seems to be the same with regard to both shareholder and creditor actions.

6.5 **Article 93(5) AktG**

Finally, a hybrid approach to general creditor protection may be noted. Article 93 AktG imposes on directors a duty of competence (and perhaps loyalty) which is owed, in the traditional way, to the company and so not to creditors. However, the duty owed to the company is enforceable in certain circumstances by the creditors, and liability for damages cannot be waived by the shareholders. The circumstances in which the creditors may enforce the duty owed to the company are not confined to situations where the company is insolvent, though it appears that Article 93(5) is rarely used outside of insolvency, where only the creditors' representative may invoke its provisions.

---

[104] On the other hand, Canadian courts have held that the oppression remedy (CBCA, s. 241) is available to creditors: to secured creditors as of right and unsecured creditors at the discretion of the court. However, the practice seems to be to allow the oppression claim only in cases arising in the vicinity of insolvency. See generally D. Thomson, 'Directors, Creditors and Insolvency', 58 *University of Toronto Faculty of Law Review* (2000) p. 31. There is a contrast here with the United Kingdom, where the general oppression remedy (CA 1985, s. 459) is available only to shareholders (members) and separate provision is made in respect of unfair conduct by administrators within insolvency, which protection does extend to creditors (Insolvency Act 1986, Sched. B1, para. 74).

[105] This consequence is characterised by Stéphane Rousseau, correctly it is submitted, as a reversal of 'a fundamental principle of corporate law': 'Directors' Duty of Care after *Peoples*: Would it be Wise to Start Worrying about Liability?', 41 *Canadian Business Law Journal* (2005) at p. 225. She also indicates that the implication of the court's reasoning is that not only creditors but also other stakeholders may individually sue to enforce the duty of care.

Overall, one may conclude from this incomplete survey that, although some legal systems appear to impose creditor-regarding duties on directors of companies which are in a solvent state, this is still a minority approach except where fraud is involved. Further, there is very little evidence of such duties, where they exist, being enforced by creditors on any significant scale, outside of the vicinity of insolvency. This may well be either because such enforcement is not permitted by the laws in question or because, even where it is, effective enforcement of such duties requires a substantial monitoring input from creditors. Before insolvency threatens, unsecured creditors may regard such effort as not cost-effective, whilst secured creditors, for whom the effort may be worthwhile, will establish their own contractual control mechanisms, rather than rely on the general standards laid down in the law.

7. Conclusion

This paper has sought to justify imposing personal liability on directors for trading decisions taken in the vicinity of insolvency by reference to the incentive structure created for board decisions once the shareholders' equity in the company has become exiguous. That structure creates incentives to engage in excessively risky projects. However, the limited nature of the remedy put forward to address this situation should be noted. It has been argued that the aim of the legal strategies adopted in this area should be to restore the incentive structure which operates when the company is a going concern. It has not been argued that the legal framework for directorial decision making should be amended across the board. On the contrary, the aim is to produce a situation where the underlying principles of the legal framework for risk assessment which is in place when the company is in a steady state, giving directors an incentive to evaluate both the upside and the downside risks, continue to apply as insolvency looms, up until the point, if it is ever reached, where the directors are replaced by a creditor-appointed manager or the directors become subject to effective third-party control. It is in order to secure a continuation of a set of incentives for appropriate risk assessment that the creditors' interests have to play a bigger role in the legal formulation of directors' duties in the vicinity of insolvency.[106]

---

[106] On this analysis, the criticisms of some writers of the legal strategy here proposed seem overblown, for they have misunderstood what is at issue. As an example see D. Oesterle, 'Corporate Directors' Personal Liability for "Insolvent Trading" in Australia, "Reckless Trading" in New Zealand and "Wrongful Trading" in England (*sic*): A Recipe for Timid Directors, Hamstrung Controlling Shareholders and Skittish Lenders', in I.M. Ramsay, ed., *Company Directors' Liability for Insolvent Trading* (Melbourne, Centre for Corporate Law and Securities Regulation and CCH Australia 2000) and the response by A. Keay, 'Wrongful trading and the liability of company directors: a theoretical perspective', 25 *Legal Studies* (2005) p. 431.

The normative implications of the argument are that countries should adopt legal strategies to reset directors' incentives when the shareholders' equity in the company has been reduced to an exiguous level and there is no hope of replacing it through the company's established trading policies, so that more regard is paid to the interests of the (unsecured) creditors, who are now the residual claimants on the company. However, it is necessary to be careful not to allow the rules adopted to spill over so as to reorder the directors' incentives in a creditor-regarding manner when the shareholders are still in fact the residual claimants on the company. Perhaps the most interesting point to emerge from the analysis of incentive resetting legislation is the potential conflict between protecting creditor interests by means of compensation for past reckless business decisions and rescuing the company as a going concern for the future, which is also likely to be in the interests of the creditors. Since enforcement by the creditors' representative of wrongful trading and similar laws is likely to be incompatible with a productive working relationship between the creditors' appointee and the (former) managers of the company, both Britain and (since the beginning of 2006) France give that power and duty only to the liquidator, whose job is mainly to get in the assets and divide the proceeds among the creditors rather than to seek to rescue the company. By contrast, in those forms of insolvency procedure where rescue is the primary goal of the law, the creditors' representative is not given any enforcement role, so as not to prejudice any relationship with the former managers which that representative may seek to establish.

H. Eidenmüller and W. Schön (eds.), The Law and Economics of Creditor Protection

Trading in the Vicinity of Insolvency

Gerald Spindler*

Abstract
The paper deals with the incentive structures for directors in the vicinity of insolvency. It discusses distinctions between closely held corporations and public corporations, as well as the application of business judgement rules to decisions of directors in the vicinity of insolvency, in particular with regard to the solvency test. Finally, it stresses procedural issues, such as enforcement of director's liability without formal insolvency procedures.

Keywords: insolvency, business judgement rule, solvency test, enforcement, shadow director.

---

* Professor of Commercial Law, University of Goettingen, and member of the Academy of Sciences. I am grateful to Paul Davies for our discussions. The comments are related to the version of Davies' paper presented at the conference.

1. Introduction

It is always difficult for a commentator to present his own opinion if he more or less agrees with the analysis of the main speaker. Even though I concur with Paul Davies' analysis, I will try to focus on some salient points to which the discussion should draw more attention, namely, the relationship between corporate law and insolvency law, in general, and the relationship between the discretion of directors (corporate law) and their strict duties in the vicinity of insolvency (insolvency law), in particular. Moreover, procedural issues like the enforcement of claims against directors are grossly neglected in the current debate. Hence, the comment first discusses the liability of directors from a theoretical perspective, followed by the practical impact of an expansion of the liability of directors.

2. Theory

2.1 Incentive structures

As long as the company is prospering and directors only embark on appropriately risky projects, there is no reason for holding directors liable. Shareholders (and directors) have incentives to engage only in reasonable projects with appropriate risks as they would otherwise loose all economic benefits of their investments in the corporation (expected payment streams in the future as well as the already invested capital, both reflected in the market value). It is tautological to state that this situation of a prospering corporation does not represent any essential danger for creditors.[1] Of course, as long as a corporation is running its business successfully, there is no need to quarrel about creditor's risks.

On the other hand, it also seems to be a simple fact that directors act not in the interest of creditors but rather that of shareholders once their equity has been dissipated and they are interested in overly risky projects in order to catch any possible positive net outcome of their investment.[2] In other words, shareholders and directors become overly risk-loving.

---

[1] See also B. Cheffins, *Company Law* (Oxford, Clarendon Press 1997) p. 79.

[2] G. Hertig and H. Kanda, 'Creditor Protection', in R. Kraakman, et al., *The Anatomy of Corporate Law* (Oxford, Oxford University Press 2004) p. 73; Cheffins, op. cit. n. 1, at p. 76; S.M. Bainbridge, *Corporation Law and Economics* (New York, Foundation Press 2002) p. 431; A. Keay, 'Directors' Duties to Creditors: Contractarian Concerns Relating to Efficiency and Over-Protection of Creditors', 66 *Modern Law Review* (2003) p. 665 at p. 668; T. Bachner, 'Wrongful Trading – A New European Model for Creditor Protection?', 5 *EBOR* (2004) p. 293 at p. 297; H. Fleischer, 'Erweiterte Außenhaftung der Organmitglieder im Europäischen Gesellschafts- und Kapitalmarktrecht – Insolvenzverschleppung, fehlerhafte Kapitalmarktinformation,

Creditors for their part concentrate on safeguarding their fixed income and on the security of their invested capital; they do not share in the gains and rents from entrepreneurial risk like the shareholders. Hence, Paul Davies' analysis points out that creditor-centred corporate governance would lead to an overly risk-averse attitude of directors. However, one essential positive feature of limited liability is the general impact it has on the distribution of risk associated with business failure, whereby investors are even encouraged to take entrepreneurial risks.[3] Thus, corporate governance should be designed in a way that limits the creditor-centred duties of directors to situations when incentives are distorted, in particular when directors and shareholders favour overly risky projects. As long as the corporation is a going concern, directors' duties should reflect their entrepreneurial freedom and discretion, which are only limited by duties of loyalty to shareholders. One major emanation of these principles is the business judgement rule, widely accepted in corporate law systems and recently formally introduced in Germany.[4]

In sum, we are theoretically able to draw a clear distinction between the 'sane' corporation as a going concern and the point in time when equity is dissipated and directors have perverse incentives to invest in overly risky projects. In theory, it should also be easy to distinguish between the triggering of duties to creditors and the definition of the duties.

Nevertheless, there is a grey area between the two issues (triggering and defining the duties) which is not easy to assess. As it is generally believed that rescuing a corporation leads to better results rather than going into a formal procedure of liquidation,[5] it is not easy to draw a line between the business

---

Tätigkeitsverbote', 33 *ZGR* (2004) p. 437 at p. 446; A. Engert, 'Die ökonomische Begründung der Grundsätze ordnungsgemäßer Unternehmensfinanzierung', 33 *ZGR* (2004) p. 813 at p. 824; cf., also G. Franke and H. Hax, *Finanzwirtschaft des Unternehmens und Kapitalmarkt* (Berlin/Heidelberg, Springer 2003) p. 435; M. Adams, *Eigentum, Kontrolle und beschränkte Haftung* (Baden-Baden, Nomos 1991) p. 36 et seq.

3 Cheffins, op. cit. n. 1, at p. 499; A. Bruns, *Haftungsbeschränkung und Mindesthaftung* (Tübingen, Mohr Siebeck 2003) p. 51; H. Fleischer, 'Grundfragen der ökonomischen Theorie im Gesellschafts- und Kapitalmarktrecht', 30 *ZGR* (2001) p. 1 at p. 18; H.-B. Schäfer and C. Ott, *Lehrbuch der ökonomischen Analyse des Zivilrechts* (Berlin/Heidelberg/New York, Springer 2005) p. 661; H. Eidenmüller and A. Engert, 'Rechtsökonomie des Mindestkapitals im GmbH-Recht', 96 *GmbHR* (2005) p. 433 at p. 434.

4 S. 93(1) of the Stock Corporation Act; more details in Schneider, 'Unternehmerische Entscheidungen als Anwendungsvoraussetzung für die Business Judgment Rule', 58 *DB* (2005) p. 707; G. Spindler, 'Haftung und Aktionärsklagen nach dem neuen UMAG', 8 *NZG* (2005) p. 865 at p. 871 et seq. In this context, see also M. Ruffner, *Die ökonomischen Grundlagen eines Rechts der Publikumsgesellschaften* (Zürich, Schulthess 2000) p. 230; Fleischer, loc. cit. n. 3, at p. 24.

5 Cf., P. Davies, 'Directors' Creditor-Regarding Duties in respect of Trading Decisions Taken in the Vicinity of Insolvency', in this volume.

judgement rule for a going concern company and a company in crisis. What are reasonable rescue projects? On the one hand, they have to be distinguished from overly risky projects; on the other, they should promise a turnaround for the company. Hence, we are forced to allow for some sort of business judgement rule even in the situation of near insolvency. Certainly, the limits of this specific business judgement have to be defined more narrowly than for the corporation as a going concern. These limits remain to be structured and analysed more closely. Although most jurisdictions allow for some sort of rescuing privilege, most of them referring the issue to insolvency and administration procedures like the new French Insolvency Act,[6] the boundaries are not yet clearly shaped.

2.2 Directors of closely held and publicly held corporations

However, this basic theory tacitly assumes a concordance between the interests of shareholders and directors. But this is true only in the absence of any agency problems, hence in all (very) close corporations.[7] Regarding larger corporations or even corporations with substantial minority shares, there is no reason to suppose a strict alignment between interests (and behaviour) of directors and shareholders. A director may be more concerned with his reputation as a 'chief restructuring officer' than with shareholders' interests. In jurisdictions like the United States which accept directors as administrators during insolvency procedures, directors have little incentive to act solely in the interests of shareholders. Hence, it still remains unclear if we should distinguish between directors of closed companies and publicly held companies. Without any empirical evidence, it is not easy to assess clearly the extent of liability to be attributed to a director. Finding the exact balance would require a comprehensive analysis of empirical evidence and agency structures for directors of publicly held corporations in the vicinity of insolvency, which is not yet available. If we do not find the exact balance for these corporations, the outcome might be the over-deterrence of directors so that they tend to be overly risk-averse.[8]

Moreover, Paul Davies argues that a rule which is based on the judicial assessment of dominant shareholder control (which would exempt directors from liability) could be less efficient than an extension of director liabilities to publicly

[6] Cf., Davies, loc. cit. n. 5; more details in R. Dammann, 'Das neue französiche Insolvenzrecht', 52 *RIW* (2006) p. 16.

[7] See also F.H. Easterbrook and D.R. Fischel, *The Economic Structure of Corporate Law* (Cambridge, MA, Harvard University Press 1991) p. 56, who determine in general that managers' incentive to undertake overly risky projects is greater in close corporations. Cf., furthermore Keay, loc. cit. n. 2, at p. 669.

[8] Regarding the business judgement rule, see Ruffner, op. cit. n. 4, at p. 230; Fleischer, loc. cit. n. 3, at p. 24.

held corporations, as the litigation costs would be increased. However, the same – legal uncertainty – may also be true for liability rules for directors. As strict liability rules in the vicinity of insolvency require the distinction between 'usual' and normal business judgments, on the one hand, and insolvency-related decisions, on the other, there is enough leeway for courts in either cases. As will be shown below, the distinction, in particular, between 'good' directors who try to restructure the corporation and avoid insolvency and 'bad' ones who act in a risk-loving manner is far from being clear-cut. As a by-product, this analysis may also make a case for limiting stock options as a remuneration for directors. These kinds of payments would induce them to opt for overly risky projects in the vicinity of insolvency, as they act in the double role of shareholders and directors at the same time.[9]

In sum, due to agency asymmetries and a lower probability of overly risky projects, a distinction could be appropriate.

2.3 Mandatory rules for unsecured creditors?

Furthermore, it seems obvious that any remedy for the risks of creditors should be limited to those groups of creditors who cannot take care of themselves, mainly due to an inability to adjust to the risks of the corporation (non-adjusting creditors).[10] Mandatory law should thus help them in recovering their potential losses.[11] However, the story is more complex than that if we take into account the learning effects and incentives that market participants can use in future adjustment clauses or securities. Unsecured contractual creditors would have little incentive to improve their institutional design (contracts and securities) when contracting with corporations if they are being helped by mandatory law. Mandatory rules could thus easily lead into a trap where unsecured creditors may not try to find more efficient remedies for their risks – and become adjusted creditors. In other words, mandatory rules can be used as long as there is *prima facie* proof that all unsecured creditors are not able to demand securities *in the future*. This may be

---

[9] On the general efforts to align the interests of principal and agent via stock options, see S.G. Marks, 'The Separation of Ownership and Control', in B. Bouckaert and G. De Geest, *Encyclopedia of Law and Economics*, Vol. III (Cheltenham, Elgar 2000) p. 707; T. Sauter and Babel, 'Stock-Option-Pläne als Mittel zur Reduzierung des Principal-Agent-Konflikts', in M. Kessler and T. Sauter, *Handbuch Stock Options* (Munich, Beck 2003) marginal note 23; Ruffner, op. cit. n. 4, at p. 132.

[10] Cf., J. Armour, 'Legal Capital: An Outdated Concept?', in this volume.

[11] Cf., also Keay, loc. cit. n. 2, at p. 677, who criticises the fact that law and economics scholars often regard efficiency as either the sole value to be taken into account or as one to be weighted higher than other values, such as distributional fairness.

true for creditors such as employees,[12] but it requires a closer look at different creditor groups as well as their structures and incentives.[13]

2.4 *Ex ante* and *ex post* rules

One of the major issues discussed between the Anglo-Saxon world and continental jurisdictions is the legitimacy of legal capital requirements as an *ex ante* means to protect creditors. In contrast, the common law world makes use of an *ex post* approach by assigning duties to directors to respect creditors' interests in the vicinity of insolvency.

However, even if in theory *ex post* rules like the liability of directors may serve the same purpose of deterring engagements in overly risky projects, there are cases when shareholders and directors had been overly optimistic from the very beginning of their corporation.[14] One of famous example is the rise and fall of the Internet economy and its bubbles. It is not easy to determine whether directors should be held liable for proposing excessively risky projects. If we take a look at other areas, securities law usually provides for specific liabilities in the case of false prospects.[15] However, these liability rules are hard to apply when prospects have been excessively optimistic or, in other words, if the failure is due to a false prognosis.[16] Moreover, these liability rules are not designed to help creditors in general rather than investors. Hence, there might still be a case for *ex ante* mechanisms to deter overly risk-loving projects, in particular to protect non-adjusting creditors. In other words, if sufficient funds (equity) invested by shareholders are the only guarantee to protect creditors, because the interests of shareholders and creditors would thus be aligned,[17] then rules may be an efficient

---

12 On further creditor groups who are not able to undertake proper risk assessment or demand appropriate protection, such as employees, customers, most trade creditors and involuntary creditors, see in detail Keay, loc. cit. n. 2, at p. 693 et seq.; cf., also Hertig and Kanda, loc. cit. n. 2, at p. 72.

13 The state, for example, is one of the most important creditors which is certainly able to protect its own interests by imposing personal liability on shareholders or directors, as in the case of tax law.

14 Cf., also H. Fleischer, 'Neue Entwicklungen im englischen Konzernrecht', 44 *AG* (1999) p. 350 at p. 360.

15 Regarding the liability for false prospects in Germany, see Gerber, 'Die Haftung für unrichtige Kapitalmarktinformation', 42 *DStR* (2004) p. 1793 at p. 1794 et seq.; for a comparative law approach, see K.J. Hopt and H.-Ch. Voigt, *Prospekt- und Kapitalmarktinformationshaftung: Recht und Reform in der Europäischen Union, der Schweiz und den USA* (Tübingen, Mohr Siebeck 2005).

16 For more detail, see recently H. Fleischer, 'Prognoseberichterstattung im Kapitalmarktrecht und Haftung für fehlerhafte Prognosen', 51 *AG* (2006) p. 2 at p. 7 et seq.

17 Cf., Davies, loc. cit. n. 5.

way to induce shareholders to raise funds as soon as the corporation has been established in order to guarantee minimum consideration for creditor interests. This is the classic case for minimum legal capital requirements or liability rules that are triggered just after the corporation is established.

2.5 Who should be held liable? The extension to controlling shareholders

So far, the discussion has concentrated on directors as controllers of corporate affairs. However, the decisive factor for liability is not the formal role of being appointed as a director but rather the fact of having control over corporate affairs. Only these persons have the necessary power and information to assess the risks of new projects and investments. Hence, shareholders who engage in steering activities (shadow directors) should also be held liable for not taking action in the vicinity of insolvency.[18] The typical information asymmetry between directors and shareholders does not apply in the case of (shadow) shareholder-directors – a fact which is widely recognised in different jurisdictions such as Britain (shadow director), France (*dirigéant de fait*) and Germany (*faktischer Geschäftsführer*).[19] Moreover, we have to take into account that most of the small companies organised in the form of a limited liability company are managed by directors who are the major shareholders of these companies.

However, as Davies has pointed out, there is a dilemma, as banks or parent companies might be reluctant to invest fresh money in order to restructure companies or remedy a critical situation.[20] Nevertheless, there are good arguments to retain the extension even to these shareholders or controlling persons, as they have the same perverse incentives in the vicinity of insolvency as directors or controlling shareholders.[21] Banks, for example, which are in a controlling position and have superior knowledge, may try to secure as much as possible of their secured assets or claims.[22]

---

18 Cf., also Report of the High Level Group of Company Law Experts on a Modern Regulatory Framework for Company Law in Europe (November 2002) p. 69.

19 Cf., also Fleischer, loc. cit. n. 2, at p. 461.

20 In order to offset this impact, the German legislature adopted a corresponding privilege (*Sanierungsprivileg*) in s. 32a(3) GmbHG; see A. Hueck and L. Fastrich in A. Baumbach and A. Hueck, *GmbHG-Gesetz* (Munich, Beck 2006) s. 32a marginal note 19. In this context, see also H. Eidenmüller, *Unternehmenssanierung zwischen Markt und Gesetz* (Cologne, Schmidt 1999) p. 388 et seq.

21 Regarding parent companies, see Fleischer, loc. cit. n. 14, at p. 360.

22 However, it is not the claiming of liabilities – as a typical antagonistic creditor interest – but only the exertion of authority that causes the liability of lenders. In this context, and with specific reference to the borderline, see H. Fleischer, 'Zur aktienrechtlichen Verantwortung faktischer Organe', 49 *AG* (2004) p. 517 at p. 527.

In more general terms, the issue of the administration and restructuring of the corporation is not limited to banks or parent companies; rather, it is a general problem of balancing the duties to creditors, on the one hand, and the chances to rescue the corporation, on the other. In consequence, the dilemma described above actually depends on the definition of the vicinity of insolvency. If the duties are triggered in the case of a more than probable insolvency based on a cash flow test, then I see no reason why persons (corporations and/or banks) with major influence and persons incumbent to the same incentives as directors should be treated differently. By synchronising competence and liability, it can be ensured in general that all interests will be considered, thus achieving economically efficient results.[23] If duties are really to be restricted to the vicinity of insolvency, then banks or parent companies should not face any additional liability, as they benefit from the same privileges as directors when the company is a going concern. Moreover, if we grant liability privileges to directors if they try to rescue the company and work out a plan with creditors, then the same privileges should apply to banks and parent companies investing fresh money. Hence, liability will be triggered only in cases where banks or parent companies control the company after insolvency has become more than probable.

Consequently – and *vice versa* – the shareholders should have no influence on the decisions of the directors once the corporation is in the vicinity of insolvency. As soon as shareholders do not have incentives to adopt risk-appropriate strategies rather than preferring more risk-loving measures, they should not be allowed to act to the detriment of creditors. Therefore, directors should not be exempted from liability if even shareholders approve of their actions as long as the corporation is in crisis.[24]

2.6 **Conclusion**

To sum up, from a theoretical perspective there is a clear and sharp distinction between the corporation as a going concern and when it is in the vicinity of insolvency. The former requires a business judgement rule to give directors freedom to operate like entrepreneurs, while the latter triggers strict duties for directors as incentives are reversed to the detriment of creditors. When insolvency becomes more than probable,[25] directors should be held liable if they do not respect creditors' interests. They should abstain from overly risky projects, however, they are also called on to rescue the corporation.

---

[23] Cf., Eidenmüller, op. cit. n. 20, at p. 378.

[24] Cf., Davies, loc. cit. n. 5, at n. 62.

[25] Cf., H. Eidenmüller, 'Trading in Times of Crisis: Formal Insolvency Proceedings, Workouts and the Incentives for Shareholders/Managers', in this volume.

In practice, however, it is precisely this distinction that lies at the core of the problem, as the time of insolvency has to be fixed, particularly with regard to the business judgement rule and privileges related to efforts to rescue the company. Whereas in theory the optimal, all-informed spectator can easily identify the point in time when insolvency is more than probable, in practice things may change.

3. Practice

3.1 Solvency test, probability of insolvency and directors' discretion

As Paul Davies has clearly explained, there are in principle two ways of assessing the vicinity of insolvency: balance sheet tests and solvency tests.[26] Balance sheet tests and solvency tests do not contradict each other, as they may be combined like in German law, for example.[27] Nevertheless, solvency tests which are based on reasonable prospects of future cash flow seem to be superior to balance sheet tests, as the latter are backward looking and do not take into account future developments. Hence, balance sheet tests may step in too late, as they just reflect historic developments which might have already become dangerous for the corporation. Moreover, they do not state anything about the ability of the corporation to pay creditors in future. In fact, balance sheet tests may trigger liquidation too early if there is still a chance for the corporation to get fresh money and restructure its business.

3.2 Balance sheet tests and future developments

Thus, British courts apply cash flow tests such as in *Re Purpoint* even when corporations are insolvent on a balance sheet basis.[28] However, to believe that German law ignores all chances to rescue a company and relies solely on a balance sheet test would be somehow misleading, as German courts take future developments into account, although in a very subtle way. The 'British' cash flow test was somehow matched by correspondent German case law, which required a two-step test for assessing the date of insolvency: a balance sheet test plus a so-called prognosis of the company's future as a going concern (*Fortführungs-*

---

[26] Cf., Davies, loc. cit. n. 5.

[27] Cf., s. 92(2) of the Stock Corporation Act; more details in W. Hefermehl and G. Spindler, in *Münchener Kommentar zum Aktiengesetz* (Munich, Beck) s. 92, marginal note 19 et seq.; J. Schulze-Osterloh, in Baumbach and Hueck, op. cit. n. 20, s. 64, marginal note 5 et seq.

[28] *Re Purpoint* [1991] *BCLC* 491 at 498; cf., furthermore *Re Brian D Pierson (Contractors) Ltd.* [2000] *BCLC* 275; cf., also Bachner, loc. cit. n. 2, at p. 304.

prognose).[29] Moreover, the ninth senate of the German Federal High Court of Justice recently concentrated on the cash flow prognosis.[30] The Court elaborated on the status of inability to pay which – in addition to over-indebtedness – triggers the duty to file for an insolvency procedure. Insofar as the corporation is able to fulfil its obligations within a period of two to three weeks – the period that is required but also sufficient to raise a loan – the inability to pay is merely categorised as a stagnation of payments (*Zahlungsstockung*) and not as illiquidity (*Zahlungsunfähigkeit*); the duty to file for an insolvency procedure thus does not apply.[31] Hence, the debtor is not required to be able to pay all of his liabilities. The Court rather generally assumes stagnation up to a threshold of 10 per cent of the liabilities, unless there is no additional negative prognosis that the threshold will be exceeded within a short time.[32] The Court mentioned, *inter alia*, that a duty to file for an insolvency procedure could be disproportional in cases where the deficit is just marginal.[33] However, we have to admit that today a positive prognosis can only be applied when assessing the asset values for the balance sheet test, which are different to those of a going concern company.

3.2.1 *Vicinity of insolvency and loss of shareholder equity*

As Paul Davies has pointed out, even cash flow tests may intervene too late, as the perverse incentives already step in when shareholders have lost their equity (or the loss is to be expected).[34] However, triggering the duties of creditors subject to a loss of equity implies that we are able to assess exactly at what point in time shareholders have lost their equity. In other terms, assessing the loss requires a market test or other means to determine the value of shares, which in reality is difficult to do and ultimately returns us to some sort of balance sheet test if we do not want to depend on subjective assessments.

---

[29] See, e.g., BGH, 30 March 1998, II *ZR* 146/96, 51 *NJW* (1998) pp. 2667, 2669. The legislature meanwhile restricted this two-step test. Since then, the prognosis is only relevant for valuations in the context of the balance sheet test, see Schulze-Osterloh, loc. cit. n. 27, s. 64, marginal note 11; U. Hüffer, *Aktiengesetz* (Munich, Beck), s. 92, marginal note 10.

[30] BGH, 24 May 2005, IX *ZR* 123/04, 58 *NJW* (2005) p. 3062, *WM* (2005) p. 1468, 96 *GmbHR* (2005) p. 1117, with comment by J. Blöse; cf., also M. Neumaier, 'Wann wird eine Zahlungsstockung zur Zahlungsunfähigkeit?', 58 *NJW* (2005) p. 3041.

[31] BGH, 24 May 2005, IX *ZR* 123/04, 58 *NJW* (2005) pp. 3062, 3064 et seq.

[32] Ibid., at pp. 3062, 3065 et seq. In contrast, the court assumes illiquidity and thus a duty to file for an insolvency procedure if the debtor is not able to cover more than 10 per cent of his liabilities.

[33] Ibid. Cf., also R. Himmelsbach and H. Thonfeld, 'Gegen die Verschärfung des Begriffs der Zahlungsunfähigkeit nach § 17 II InsO', *NZI* (2001) p. 11 at p. 15.

[34] Cf., Davies, loc. cit. n. 5, at s. 4.

3.2.2 *Business judgement rule and vicinity of insolvency*

Closely related is the difficulty of determining the relevant probability of an insolvent liquidation, as proposed during the deliberations for the modernisation of British company law.[35] As we know, these proposals were more or less implicitly rejected during the course of the further discussions.[36] In practice, the relevant question concerns the standards for assessing the relevant probability. Is an objective perspective decisive or do we allow for subjective elements of directors, somehow similar to the business judgement rule? The crucial question therefore still concerns the relationship between duties (and liability) in the forefront of insolvency and the 'normal' discretion of directors to which the business judgement rule applies. The 'no reasonable prospect of avoiding insolvent liquidation' concept clearly points to a standard which is open for some sort of discretionary leeway for directors. There are good grounds to allow for such a rule. It is quite conceivable that a standard which is based on objective features and applied in a rigid manner might induce directors to adopt overly risk-averse behaviour and abstain from profitable projects. Limited liability is not pierced (with regard to shareholders or directors) only due to engagement in risky projects, as long as such projects can be qualified as appropriate *ex ante* on a reasonable basis. On the other hand, a completely objective standard of the 'reasonable director' would be somehow similar to all efforts to determine the just and appropriate amount of capital that should be invested in a corporation, which all failed,[37] since it is hard to assess this ratio of capital and risk *ex ante*. An *ex post* approach (adopted in the British model of wrongful trading) is tempting as it is hard to argue with the fact that the corporation was really already on its way to insolvency from an *ex post* perspective. However, the danger of a hindsight bias on the part of the courts is obvious.

The task for judges (and economists) is therefore to develop second-level standards regarding information procedures and risk-management systems that allow directors to recognise dangerous developments as soon as possible.[38] Recent

---

[35] Ibid., at s. 4.1. See further Company Law Review Steering Group, Modern Company Law for a Competitive Economy, Final Report, Vol. 1 (Department of Industry DTI 2001) s. 3.17, available for order at: <http://www.dti.gov.uk/publications>, Unique Reference Number (URN): 01/942.

[36] Cf., Modernising Company Law, Command Paper Cm 5553, July 2002, Vol. I para. 3.11, ISBN 0101555334, available for order at: <http://www.clicktso.com/portal.asp?DT=ADDITEM&DI=0101555326>.

[37] Cf., H. Eidenmüller and A. Engert, 'Die angemessene Höhe des Grundkapitals', 50 *AG* (2005) p. 97 at p. 100; Fleischer, loc. cit. n. 3, at p. 10.

[38] On German law, see also recently R. Veil, 'Krisenbewältigung durch Gesellschaftsrecht. Verlust des halben Kapitals, Pflicht zu ordnungsgemäßer Liquidation und Unterkapitalisierung', 35 *ZGR* (2006), forthcoming.

proposals for bank regulations which require banks to apply risk tests before lending money are going in the same direction of placing the emphasis on risk-management and rating models rather than on 'hard criteria'.[39] In fact, German law has accepted an *ex ante* business judgement rule for directors in the vicinity of insolvency,[40] and the same attitude seems to have been adopted by US courts.[41] Thus, standards on necessary information gathering and communication, as well as on internal controlling systems, will play a major role in assessing the requirements for directors to act in good faith when their corporation is in crisis.[42]

Hence, the determination of the 'reasonable' objective standard for assessing the triggering of duties is essential and not easily achieved. On the other hand, balance sheet tests (the continental European approach) offer a more formal approach, which is easier to handle (in theory but not always in practice). The problem is aggravated when we deal with common law duties to creditors, as discussed recently,[43] which shift the relevant time for the duty to act to a mere (or substantial) probability of insolvency.[44]

3.3 Enforcement without liquidation procedures?

So far, we have concentrated on 'normal' insolvency procedures. However, a substantial number of corporate bankruptcies are not dealt with via insolvency procedures as the firms in question simply lack the assets to cover even the costs and fees of an insolvency (liquidation) procedure.[45] Thus, there is no administrator or liquidator who can file actions against former directors and/or shareholders. When jurisdictions, like the British one, rely solely on liquidators to claim compensation, we are confronted with a severe enforcement problem which in effect dilutes

---

[39] In this context, see the Basle II framework which recommends an item-centred view in which every debtor is rated individually, whereas until now debtors were assigned to abstract counterparty groups in order to determine the required capital backing of banks. See H. Schulte-Mattler, in K.-H. Boos, R. Fischer and H. Schulte-Mattler, *Kreditwesengesetz* (Munich, Beck 2004) s. E (Basel II), marginal note 16.

[40] *BGHZ* 126, 181, 199; see also Fleischer, loc. cit. n. 2, at p. 459.

[41] Cf., D.J. Block, N.E. Barton and S.A. Radin, *The Business Judgment Rule*, Vol. I, 5th edn. (New York, Aspen 1998) p. 627 et seq.

[42] Cf., Veil, loc. cit. n. 38.

[43] Cf., A. Keay, 'Another Way of Skinning the Cat: Enforcing Directors' Duties to Creditors', 17 *Insolvency Intelligence* (2004) 1; Davies, loc. cit. n. 5.

[44] Fleischer, loc. cit. n. 2, at p. 457, denies a forward placement of the duties compared to the German approach, due to the difficulty of identifying the point in time at which wrongful trading occurs. Cf., also Bachner, loc. cit. n. 2, at p. 297; M. Habersack and D.A. Verse, 'Wrongful Trading – Grundlage einer europäischen Insolvenzverschleppungshaftung?', 168 *ZHR* (2004) p. 174 at p. 187.

[45] Cf., Habersack and Verse, loc. cit. n. 44, at p. 212, who describe it as common practice.

the deterrence effect and the incentives of directors' duties. Directors/shareholders may seek a 'safe harbour' by opting for strategies that really wreck the company in such a way that no assets are left to pay even the liquidator. Thus, enforcement schemes which rely only on a liquidator lead to perverse incentives and endanger the effectiveness of directors' duties in the vicinity of insolvency.[46]

However, even jurisdictions which allow creditors to sue directors (and controlling shareholders) directly, like the German one, are confronted with the serious problem of information asymmetries. Creditors are in an uneasy position to pursue their claims, as they usually lack the information necessary to sue directors effectively for having breached their duties in the vicinity of insolvency, in particular knowledge about the time of insolvency. As long as creditors have to bring evidence that a director really did not take all necessary steps to avoid insolvency at a particular time, it is hard for them to make up their mind to invest even more money in suing directors.

One may argue that *ex post* it is always clear that directors have failed to fulfil their duties in the case of insolvency. Even then, however, creditors will face problems proving the causality between their damage and the violation of the directors' duty to file for an insolvency procedure. Moreover, payments by directors are no longer distributed equally to all creditors, thus leading to a potential race between creditors.[47]

However, this problem of enforcement is a general one and is not strictly attached to the decision whether we opt for a model based on a cash flow test rather than on a balance sheet test. The enforcement of compensation claims affects both cash-flow-based models and balance-sheet-based models. An easy solution would be to turn around the burden of proof so that directors have to show evidence that they acted in good faith.

---

[46] This point is also clearly realised by Paul Davies, loc. cit. n. 5.

[47] The German Federal High Court of Justice distinguishes between old and new creditors. While the former only receive the *Quotenschaden* (the diminution after comparing the hypothetical dividend that would have been payable to the creditors at the time when the company should have filed for insolvency and the actual dividend expressed as a percentage of the nominal claims, see BGH, 30 March 1998, II *ZR* 146/96, 51 *NJW* (1998) pp. 2667, 2669; Bachner, loc. cit. n. 2, at p. 311) claimed by the liquidator (§ 92 InsO), the new creditors generally retrieve their total losses which are not to be claimed by the liquidator (BGH, 30 March 1998, II *ZR* 146/96, 51 *NJW* (1998) pp. 2667, 2669; criticised by H. Altmeppen and J. Wilhelm, 'Quotenschaden, Individualschaden und Klagebefugnis bei der Verschleppung des Insolvenzverfahrens über das Vermögen der GmbH', 52 *NJW* (1999) p. 673 et seq.). The Supreme Court recently restricted these claims to contractual creditors, excluding tort creditors, see BGH, 25 July 2005, II *ZR* 390/03, 60 *BB* (2005) pp. 2144, 2147; criticised by M. Gehrlein, 'Schadensbegrenzung bei Insolvenzverschleppung unter dem Gesichtspunkt des Schutzzweckgedankens', 58 *DB* (2005) p. 2395; see in detail H.-G. Bamberger, H. Roth and G. Spindler, *BGB* (Munich, Beck) s. 823, marginal note 211 et seq.

4. Empirical testing

Last but not least, all arguments and reasoning relies on behavioural assumptions such as distorted and perverse incentives in the vicinity of insolvency as well as an alignment of interests between shareholders and creditors in times when the company is a going concern. However, we so far have little reliable empirical evidence, as opposed to anecdotal evidence, or court cases about real behaviour. Moreover, if it is true that common law creditor protection is superior to continental balance-sheet-based approaches, we should expect *ceteris paribus* some effects on economies. For example, it would be likely that jurisdictions with optimal creditor protection would encourage more activities in risky industries, as shareholders and directors are 'effectively' shielded against risks. Certainly, we have to take path dependencies into account. Nevertheless, we need works from the likes of La Porta, Vishny, Shleifer and so forth,[48] who have tried to analyse legal impacts on economic parameters.

5. Conclusion

In sum, theory suggests that we turn to an earlier stage for triggering directors' duties in order to protect creditors more effectively, in particular when the incentives of shareholders and directors are no longer aligned with the interests of creditors. However, in practice, it is not easy to identify this point in time, as it presupposes the dissipation of equity of shareholders and their loss of positive net income in the future, thus leading to overly risk-loving attitudes. Furthermore, there are two good reasons to allow for a business judgement rule even in the vicinity of insolvency. Firstly, the chances of rescuing companies are enhanced if liability privileges are granted for such actions. Secondly, the probability of insolvency requires a prognosis of future developments which is subject to a hindsight bias on the part of the courts. Business judgement rules should be broader for directors of public companies than for directors of closed companies with a major shareholder. Finally, enforcement problems regarding compensation claims have to be addressed by easing the burden of proof for creditors in cases where there is no liquidation procedure due to a lack of assets.

---

[48] Cf., recently R. La Porta, F. Lopez-de-Silanes and A. Shleifer, 'What Works in Securities Laws?', 61 *J. Fin.* (2006) p. 1 et seq., on the effects of securities laws on stock market prices in different jurisdictions.

Discussion Report

Andreas Engert*

1. Company Insolvency: Providing for a Timely Trigger (Eidenmüller)

Many participants pointed out that management is already under a duty to attempt a turnaround, including an out-of-court workout, in most European jurisdictions. At present, it seems unclear, however, when such a duty 'in the vicinity of insolvency' would run specifically to the company's creditors. It was emphasised that the 'probability of insolvency' test proposed by Eidenmüller is not intended to trigger formal insolvency proceedings; rather, it should only give rise to the directors' duty of care to creditors in managing the company – which, as the case may be, requires directors to continue or cut back business operations, to undertake restructuring and refinancing efforts and/or to initiate formal bankruptcy proceedings. The duty should not only require directors to take action but also to abstain from 'risk-shifting,' i.e., from increasing the company's business risk to the detriment of creditors. Because bankruptcy of small and medium-sized corporations often entails individual insolvency of directors, criminal and administrative sanctions – including director disqualification – should be applied to ensure effective deterrence.

In contrast to directors' duties in the vicinity of bankruptcy, most participants were apprehensive that a specific duty to initiate formal bankruptcy proceedings ran the risk of destroying all or part of the firm's value as a going concern. While such a duty of the board of directors was needed, especially if creditors were dispersed and lacked information, most commentators urged that it be triggered no earlier than when the corporation was actually insolvent. From an American perspective, however, Baird suggested that the fear of triggering bankruptcy prematurely seemed exaggerated, because going concern values nowadays are smaller than usually assumed and could be preserved even in formal proceedings by selling the business as a whole (which now happens in 50 per cent of all Chapter 11 cases in the United States).

* Dr. Andreas Engert, LL.M. (University of Chicago), *Wissenschaftlicher Assistent* (lecturer) at the Ludwig Maximilian University of Munich. E-mail: andreas@engert.info. Author's homepage: <http://www.engert.info>.

As to possible duties owed by creditors to cooperate in an out-of-court work-out, there was concern that creditors should not be made responsible for preserving a failing business and that imposing liability on creditors would raise the costs of workout negotiations. In response to these objections, Eidenmüller pointed out that the proposed set of duties would ultimately serve the interests of creditors by addressing a free-rider problem in which each creditor hoped to benefit from concessions and contributions by others. The many cases of reorganisations in formal bankruptcy proceedings in Germany and other jurisdictions indicated that viable out-of-court workouts often failed due to opportunistic behaviour by creditors.

Some discussants were sceptical that an enabling, rather than mandatory, approach to bankruptcy law afforded creditors with sufficient protection and could be made workable. Proponents of an enabling approach invoked the general efficiency presumption in favour of contractual solutions. Information asymmetries could be overcome by information intermediaries as well as a menu approach, under which corporations could choose among a limited number of options. It was also claimed that, as a matter of fact, the European Insolvency Regulation allowed some forum shopping and thus some 'choice' of the applicable insolvency regime; an enabling approach had therefore to some degree already become a reality. Armour added that the floating charge under English company law, by effectively reserving the right to initiate insolvency proceedings to one particular creditor, amounted to a contracting device over the appropriate insolvency trigger.

2. RECHARACTERISATION AND THE NONHINDRANCE OF CREDITORS (SKEEL/CAHN)

Some participants questioned the justification for treating shareholder loans differently from those of third parties. In response, shareholders' control over the corporation was identified as the main feature distinguishing shareholders from (other) creditors. It was argued that a justification based on control explained why the recharacterisation of shareholder loans posed problems mainly for close corporations. At least to some extent, the recharacterisation of shareholder loans responded to a concern that shareholders could secure themselves preferential treatment over other creditors. Most participants did not believe that there was any other valid reason to prevent shareholders from wearing the hats of both shareholder and creditor.

Some discussants suggested that treating shareholder loans as equity might exacerbate an underinvestment problem. Especially in small businesses facing financial distress, shareholder loans were often the only available source of provisional 'bridge' financing. Cahn reported that the German recharacterisation rules (*Eigenkapitalersatzrecht*) often deterred major lenders from making an additional and badly needed equity investment and that the legislator had attempted to deal with this problem by exempting certain loans to distressed companies. On the other hand, Cahn did not see a convincing reason to permit secured lending by shareholders.

Another point raised in the discussion related to the fact that, unlike the United States and Germany, the United Kingdom does not have a recharacterisation doctrine. It was conjectured that English law relied more on avoidance of preferential treatment to address the problems that other jurisdictions dealt with by recharacterisation. According to Armour, shareholders in the United Kingdom are usually not able to lend on a secured basis.

3. DIRECTORS' CREDITOR-REGARDING DUTIES IN RESPECT OF TRADING DECISIONS TAKEN IN THE VICINITY OF INSOLVENCY (DAVIES/SPINDLER)

The discussion led to disagreement on whether it was desirable to expose directors to a significant risk of liability in the vicinity of insolvency. Many participants expressed concern that the legal uncertainty associated with such liability, together with the courts' hindsight bias, would have a chilling effect on management. It was contended that the examples cited for excessive risk taking on the brink of insolvency represented extreme cases. In addition to making risk-averse directors overly cautious, the threat of liability would produce more unneeded 'red tape' in corporate decision making in terms of costly legal advice and extensive documentation. Also, directors' interest in retaining their position as well as reputational concerns would often prevent them from incurring excessive risk on behalf of shareholders.

In this regard, Davies and Rickford reported that the Company Law Review Steering Group in the United Kingdom had contemplated, but rejected, the possibility of imposing liability for wrongful trading at an earlier point in time than under the present 'no reasonable prospect of avoiding insolvent liquidation' test of section 214 of the Insolvency Act 1986. As a justification for the existing criterion, Armour suggested that liquidity was a strong sign that creditors were still monitoring the company, so that liability was not needed. Creditors ceased disciplining management only when the company was illiquid.

Wymeersch pointed out that French law had originally taken an aggressive tack on management in the vicinity of insolvency, including criminal prosecution, under the *action du comblement de passif* which resembled wrongful trading under UK law. Yet this far-reaching liability had been considered excessive and was scaled back significantly about ten years ago. On the other hand, French law still imposed liability for *abus des biens sociaux*, which could be asserted in cases of gross mismanagement even years before the onset of insolvency.

With respect to corporation law in the United States, Baird made it clear that virtually no lawsuits were actually being brought on the theory that directors owed fiduciary duties to creditors in the vicinity of bankruptcy. It seemed that the theory served less as a basis for imposing liability than as a shield against assertions that the directors had failed to maximise shareholder value by making risky bets at the expense of creditors.

Litigation costs often impede enforcement of directors' liability in bankruptcies of small corporations. In Germany, formal bankruptcy proceedings often fail to take place because the estate does not even cover the administrative costs. Without a bankruptcy trustee, creditors are reluctant to fund expensive lawsuits if they receive only a *pro rata* share in any awards. The same or similar problems persist in other jurisdictions. One solution increasingly adopted in the United Kingdom is to sell potential claims to a third party who is prepared to litigate them. It was also suggested that enforcement might be encouraged by providing creditors with access to the corporate records and by leaving any amounts to the creditors collecting them.

Part IV

Towards a General Framework

A Synthetic View of Different Concepts of Creditor Protection, or: A High-Level Framework for Corporate Creditor Protection

Peter O. Mülbert*

* Prof. Dr Peter O. Mülbert holds the chair of Private Law, Commercial Law, and Banking Law at the University of Mainz, and serves as director of the Center for German and International Law of Financial Services at the University of Mainz. E-mail: muelbert@mail.jura.uni-mainz.de. Author's homepage: <http://www.jura.uni-mainz.de/~muelbert>.

Abstract

Protection of corporate creditors has become an important topic within the European Union. At EU level, discussion has been sparked by widespread dissatisfaction with some very rigid and cumbersome provisions, and even with the whole concept of the Second Company Law Directive. At EU Member State level, three landmark decisions by the European Court of Justice – Centros, Überseering, *and* Inspire Art *– opened the way for an all-out competition between the different company forms provided for by national company laws. At both levels, albeit for different reasons, British company law – and in particular the absence of any legal capital in the private limited company – acts as the main* *driving force putting pressure on the concept of legal capital as enshrined in the Second Directive, which in turn was modeled on German company law notions.*

The High Level Group of Company Law Experts provided the appropriate starting point for the present discussion by dealing not only with the raising and maintenance of capital, but by also taking up the wrongful trading remedy (s. 214 British Insolvency Act) and the equitable subordination remedy. This present article builds upon this broader approach, seeking to develop a conceptual framework for an efficient creditor protection regime within a purely national setting, i.e., leaving aside the additional problems created by pseudo-foreign companies and the impact of the provisions of the EU Treaty for the free movement of companies on national company laws.

Given the rich variety of creditor protection mechanisms within EU Member States, any attempt at developing even a high-level framework has to start by identifying the relevant risks against which creditors need protection and the required extent of such protection. Against this backdrop, any jurisdiction has to make a choice whether to rely mostly on creditor self-help or on mandatory protection rules. In principle, since all mechanisms for creditor self-help are inherently costly and fail to protect involuntary (tort) creditors and "weak" contractual creditors as effectively as they do "strong" contractual creditors, there is a case for mandatory protection rules. The article then goes on to review the different well-known mechanisms for mandatory creditor protection. In line with earlier findings and the criticism mostly from English scholars, the case for a German-style legal capital regime turns out to be weak, at best.

On the other hand, since shareholders' incentive to act to the detriment of creditors increases with the company becoming financially distressed, it is important to provide for mechanisms that will work to effectively control any opportunistic behavior on the shareholder's part. In this respect, equitable subordination of a shareholder's right as well as the wrongful trading remedy may serve important roles. The article concludes by taking a brief look at the resultant high-level framework for an efficient creditor protection regime.

Keywords: High Level Group, creditor protection, limited liability, financial covenants, legal capital, minimum capital requirement, capital maintenance, undercapitalization, wrongful trading, equitable subordination, recharacterization.

1. INTRODUCTION

The ultimate goal in integrating different concepts of creditor protection is to arrive at a system for efficient creditor protection. An investor protection regime based on such a system would consist of a set of well-adapted legal institutions or mechanisms – each comprising a subset of rules – that, as a whole, would ensure the required level of creditor protection, but would not accord overprotection. However, until now, such a system is not to be found anywhere.

The EU Member States' creditor protection regimes are the result of an evolutionary process rather than of any comprehensive institutional design. At EU level, the Second Company Law Directive, to a large extent, reflects the state of German law at the beginning of the 1970s,[1] while the current proposal of the EU Commission for alterations[2] responds to demands by other Member States and the EU business world to relinquish some of the more cumbersome requirements. Moreover, the Second Directive covers only parts of the various legal mechanisms dealing with the protection of creditors. Finally, Eastern European countries' rules on creditor protection are mostly the result of institutional design in the form of legal transplants.

Legal writers will often confine themselves to a partial analysis by only discussing a particular rule or mechanism for creditor protection and the problems involved therein. In contrast, scholars in the law and economics tradition employ a broader approach, but choose the opposite perspective. Their focal concern is whether limited liability is an economically beneficial institution,[3] and if they find, as has been the case with limited liability for tort claims, that the costs outweigh the benefits, they will tend to favor the abolition of limited liability as such.[4]

Only very recently, the new pan-European discussion on creditor protection brought about by the European Court of Justice with three landmark decisions – *Centros*, *Überseering*, and *Inspire Art* – has moved in the direction of a more systemic approach. In particular, the High Level Group of Company Law Experts recommended that the EU Commission should conduct a study into the feasibility of an alternative regime to the legal capital regime, doing away altogether with the concept of legal capital. Above all, the Group specified that the alternative

---

[1] For a description of the pertinent rules of the Directive, see P.O. Mülbert and M. Birke, 'Legal Capital – Is There a Case against the European Legal Capital', 3 *EBOR* (2002) p. 695 at p. 700 et seq.

[2] Proposal for a Directive of the European Parliament and of the Council amending Council Directive 77/91/EEC, as regards the formation of public limited liability companies and the maintenance and alteration of their capital, COM (2004) 730 final.

[3] See, e.g., F.H. Easterbrook and D.R. Fischel, *The Economic Structure of Corporate Law* (Cambridge, Mass., Harvard University Press 1991) p. 41 et seq.; cf., P.L. Davies, *Gower and Davies' Principles of Modern Company Law*, 7th edn. (London, Sweet & Maxwell 2003) p. 176 et seq.; B. Pettet, 'Limited liability – a principle for the 21st century?', in M.D.A. Freemann, ed., *Current Legal Problems*, Vol. 48 (Oxford, Oxford University Press 1995) p. 125 at p. 141 et seq.; H.C. Grigoleit, *Gesellschafterhaftung für interne Einflussnahme im Recht der GmbH* (Munich, C.H. Beck 2006) p. 31 et seq.

[4] See, e.g., H. Hansmann and R. Kraakman, 'Toward Unlimited Shareholder Liability for Corporate Torts', 100 *Yale Law Journal* (1991) p. 1879 et seq.

regime should provide for a solvency test to be conducted before any payment of a dividend or making any other asset distribution to shareholders, and that the directors should be held responsible for the issue of a formal solvency certificate incorporating the results of the solvency test. In addition, and this recommendation in particular reflects the "systemic approach", the Group recommended that, as an element of good corporate governance, a European framework rule should be introduced on "wrongful trading", i.e., on the responsibility of directors close to insolvency, and that the concept of the subordination of insiders' claims should be at least considered.[5] Similarly, as a contribution to the ongoing British company law reform process, the Rickford Report on "Reforming Capital" not only called for a substitution of the present capital maintenance rules by a far simpler solvency test, but supported this call for a drastic change by means of broader reflections on different mechanisms available for creditor protection.[6] Finally, the EU Commission, after having taken up the recommendations of the High Level Group in its Communication on the Company Law Action Plan,[7] very recently published a tender for a study into the feasibility of an alternative to the capital maintenance regime contained in the Second Directive requiring the contractor "to evaluate whether, under alternative regimes … creditors' and shareholders' protection can be achieved at least as effectively in a way which better supports economic growth… In particular, the study aims at establishing the degree of effectiveness of the current legal capital regime and whether there are other means to protect creditors' and shareholders' rights. … Particular reference will be needed about the role of insolvency legislation to guarantee creditors' interests."[8]

The present paper takes up the idea of a "systemic approach" by trying to identify the appropriate starting point(s) from which a discussion on how to protect corporate creditors efficiently may proceed, as well as the relevant building blocks for such a creditor protection regime, and possible interactions

---

[5] Report of the High Level Group of Company Law Experts on a Modern Regulatory Framework for Company Law in Europe, 4 November 2002, p. 14 et seq., Recommendations IV.1./10./11.

[6] J. Rickford, ed., 'Report of the Interdisciplinary Group on Capital Maintenance "Reforming Capital"', 15 *EBLR* (*European Business Law Review*) (2004) p. 919 et seq. (hereinafter, "Rickford Report").

[7] Communication of the Commission to the Council and the European Parliament – Modernising Company Law and Enhancing Corporate Governance in the European Union – A Plan to Move Forward, COM (2003) 284 final, p. 17 et seq.

[8] See Feasibility study on alternative to capital maintenance regime as established by the Second Company Law Directive 77/91/EEC of 13 December 1976 and the examination of the implications of the new EU accounting regime on profit distribution, B-Brussels: general management consultancy services 2006/S 50-051751, s. II.1.5, available at: <http://europa.eu.int/comm/dgs/internal_market/calls_en.htm>.

between these mechanisms. Admittedly, for a variety of obvious reasons, the paper must restrict itself to trying to establish a sort of high-level framework that may serve as a basis for future elaboration and refinement.

2. FOUNDATIONS

2.1 Three layers of creditor protection problems within the European Union

The basic question is how to protect corporate creditors within a purely national setting. Do the laws and court-made rules of a given jurisdiction constitute a creditor protection regime that achieves an efficient protection of the corporate creditors of a company incorporated in the said country. If not, what alterations, amendments, and sometimes even deletions are necessary to arrive at such a regime?

Additional problems arise in the case of a foreign company.[9] This is particularly true with respect to so-called pseudo-foreign corporations, i.e., if the country of a company's incorporation and the country of its main or even exclusive commercial activities differ. Then, the problems of efficient creditor protection are exacerbated by conflicts of law issues, i.e., which national laws and rules are applicable, and by enforcement issues, i.e., which State is competent to enforce the applicable national laws and rules, and whether the competent country is able and willing to enforce the applicable rules.

The third layer of problems only exists within the European Union. Companies incorporated in another Member State enjoy the freedom of establishment enshrined in Article 43 et seq. of the EC Treaty, even if they conduct business solely in their host Member States. Consequently, the freedom of the host Member State to provide for national laws and rules that aim at establishing an efficient creditor protection regime is subject to the limitations resulting from Article 43 et seq. of the EC Treaty. This restriction comes into play regardless of whether the laws and rules of the host Member State that are to be applied will be categorized as corporate law or, for example, tort law or insolvency law.

---

[9] For a comprehensive treatment from the German perspective of the problems associated with the treatment of foreign companies, in particular companies incorporated in another EU Member State, see H. Eidenmüller, ed., *Ausländische Kapitalgesellschaften im deutschen Recht* (Munich, C.H. Beck 2004); M. Lutter, ed., *Europäische Auslandsgesellschaften in Deutschland* (Cologne, Dr. Otto Schmidt 2005); cf., further O. Sandrock and C.F. Wetzler, eds., *Deutsches Gesellschaftsrecht im Wettbewerb der Rechtsordnungen* (Frankfurt am Main, Recht und Wirtschaft 2004).

2.2 The approach to designing a system for efficient creditor protection

Even in a purely national setting, it is difficult, at best, to design a coherent system for the efficient protection of corporate creditors. Apart from company law proper, other areas of law, e.g., contract law, tort law, accounting law, and insolvency law, have to be taken into account as well. Moreover, criminal law as well as administrative law may also serve a useful function.

Because of the many ways a jurisdiction may provide for creditor protection, any inter-country comparison of the respective levels of creditor protection is notoriously difficult, at best.[10] Such a comparison cannot proceed by positing a particular jurisdiction as a yardstick and by asking whether the legal order in question provides for the same or at least similar laws and rules. In particular, the comparison must not be limited to comparing the same areas of law, e.g., company law or insolvency law. Instead, such a comparison must employ a functional approach, by taking the different creditor risks and the required extent of creditor protection as its starting point and by examining a legal system as a whole with respect to its protection of corporate creditors.

The same two factors – the different types of creditor risks and the required extent of creditor protection – can also serve as the basis for designing a system of creditor protection. Regardless of a given legal system, two basic questions have to be answered at the outset: what are the relevant risks against which corporate creditors are to be protected, and what is the extent of protection to be accorded? The answers to these two questions may vary according to the legal system in question. In particular, different legal systems may opt for different approaches to determine the required extent of creditor protection.

These basic choices establish a sort of high-level framework that a given legal system has to flesh out by selecting an array of creditor protection mechanisms that cover the relevant creditor risks and provide for the appropriate extent of protection, i.e., neither leaving corporate creditors vulnerable to exploitation by the company nor according overprotection to creditors. Obviously, the selection of the creditor protection mechanisms employed varies in different legal systems. The choices are shaped by a multitude of factors,[11] for example: which particular legal remedies and actions are available in a given legal system or not; whether a legal system relies more on mandatory disclosure facilitating creditor self-help or on substantive rules according protection; whether company law or other areas of law, e.g., tort law and insolvency law will be charged with protecting creditors; and whether a legal system relies more on rules or standards for regulating the

---

10 Cf., e.g., G. Hertig and H. Kanda, 'Creditor Protection', in R. Kraakman, et al., *The Anatomy of Corporate Law* (Oxford, Oxford University Press 2004) p. 97 et seq.

11 See Hertig and Kanda, loc. cit. n. 10, at p. 97 et seq.

behavior of a corporation, its directors and its shareholders, i.e., whether a legal system relies more on rules that define admissible behavior precisely *ex ante*, or on more general standards that require *ex post* clarification by courts.[12]

2.3 The principle of non-liability of corporate decision-makers towards corporate creditors

Any framework for the protection of corporate creditors has to incorporate two additional problem dimensions as compared with the case of a natural person being the debtor. The first is the principle of limited liability or, to be more precise, the principle of non-liability of shareholders for corporate debts. As a consequence of limited liability, shareholders causing a corporation to act to the detriment of creditors are not liable for their decisions with their personal assets towards creditors. This divergence between decision-making power and personal liability fundamentally alters the incentive structure as compared with a natural person, the latter being personally liable towards the creditors. Moreover, corporations exhibit the same structural divergence between decision-making power and personal liability with respect to the directors of the company. The particular incentive structure that results from this split goes against the interests of corporate creditors, in particular, if the corporation is approaching insolvency. Hence, a framework for corporate creditor protection has to incorporate this aspect as well.

2.4 Possible reasons for protecting corporate creditors

Why a legal system would want to protect corporate creditors at all against the risks arising from limited liability is the most fundamental question. The answer has profound implications with regard, for example, to the required extent of protection.

Again, different legal systems may opt for different answers. To name but three possible responses: some German scholars (e.g., Herbert Wiedemann) perceive creditor protection by means of company law as an ethical necessity,[13] and the German Federal High Court may concur, in view of some judgments rendered in recent years.[14] The British Interdisciplinary Group on Capital Maintenance in

---

[12] As to this, see Hertig and Kanda, loc. cit. n. 10, at p. 87 et seq.

[13] H. Wiedemann, *Gesellschaftsrecht I* (Munich, C.H. Beck 1980) p. 515.

[14] See, in particular, BGH 27 September 1999, II ZR 371/98, 53 *WM* (*Wertpapiermitteilungen*) (1999) p. 2071: Commercial law starts from the principle of unlimited liability, unless statutory exceptions exist, and shareholders have to pay for the privilege of personal non-liability by compliance with the legal capital rules. Cf., BGH 16 March 1992, II ZB 17/91,

its report on "Reforming Capital" (Rickford Report) discusses desirable limits to the distribution of corporate assets to shareholders as "a question of reasonable balance, or proportionality,"[15] i.e., the Group basically invokes notions of fairness and common sense. Finally, for example, John Armour, in his inquiry into efficient creditor protection rules for a modern company law,[16] as well as Gerard Hertig and Hideki Kanda, while analyzing the "The Anatomy of Corporate Law" with respect to creditor protection,[17] advocate an economic cost-benefit analysis.

Whether the protection of corporate creditors is based on ethical considerations and notions of fairness respectively will mostly bear on the scope and contents of court-made creditor protection rules. Before the courts, issues of creditor protection will normally arise in cases where an insolvent company is unable to settle its debts. If creditor protection is rooted in notions of ethics or fairness, courts will then tend rather to favor stringent liability rules, disregarding the *ex ante* incentives which would emanate from the rule in question. Generally speaking, *ex post* court intervention will lead to a very high or even excessive level of creditor protection if courts do not base their decisions on economic welfare considerations reflecting the *ex ante* incentives.

The *Video* liability doctrine developed by the German Federal High Court (*Bundesgerichtshof*) in the mid-1990s may serve as an extreme case in point.[18] The pertinent decision virtually abolished the principle of limited liability for German one-person limited liability companies (*Ein-Personen-GmbH*). The Federal High Court only revoked this judge-made liability doctrine in its *TBB* decision after a broad public outcry by practitioners and scholars alike.[19]

2.5 Approach and organization of the paper

A combined economic and legal analysis offers the most rational approach to the problem of creditor protection. This is particularly true if – as this paper does – one seeks to develop a framework for a system of rules that ensures efficient creditor protection. Neither non-specific notions of fairness and other ethical considerations nor the more or less arbitrary set of rules that will evolve in a

---

46 *WM* (1992) p. 870; BGH 9 December 2002, II ZB 12/02, 57 *WM* (2003) p. 348 at p. 349; BGH 7 July 2003, II ZB 4/02, 57 *WM* (2003) p. 1814 at p. 1816.

15 Rickford Report, loc. cit. n. 6, at p. 967 (similarly p. 971).

16 J. Armour, 'Share Capital and Creditor Protection: Efficient Rules for a Modern Company Law', 63 *The MLR* (*Modern Law Review*) (2000) p. 355 et seq.

17 Hertig and Kanda, loc. cit. n. 10, at p. 72.

18 BGH 23 September 1991, II ZR 135/90, 45 *WM* (1991) pp. 1837-1841 (*Video*).

19 BGH 29 March 1993, II ZR 265/91, 47 *WM* (1993) pp. 687-693 (*TBB*); as to this reversal, see V. Röhricht, 'Von Rechtswissenschaft und Rechtsprechung', 28 *ZGR* (*Zeitschrift für Unternehmens- und Gesellschaftsrecht*) (1999) p. 445 at p. 464 et seq.

particular jurisdiction can serve as the starting point for designing such a system. Instead, one has to start with the different types of creditors and the respective risks they face, since the rules to be designed must correspond above all to these risks.

Reflecting this approach, the rest of the paper is thus organized as follows. Section 3 briefly describes the different types of creditors, and section 4 discusses the risks different types of creditors face from several dimensions. On the basis of this analysis, section 5 turns to one of the core questions: what are the risks against which corporate creditors need protection and to what extent do they require such protection? Section 6 discusses whether the different strategies available to creditors for protecting themselves are a more or less perfect substitute for mandatory rules designed to protect creditors. Section 7 reflects on strategies for creditor protection by means of mandatory law in general. Section 8 deals with mandatory disclosure as a means to enable creditor self-help. Section 9 discusses some of the internationally used mechanisms that aim at reducing the risk of a company approaching financial distress, and section 10 explores strategies that aim at minimizing losses that existing creditors of a company in financial distress will incur. Section 11 takes up some more technical problems the legislator and the courts face when providing for preventive or, put differently, *ex ante* creditor protection and *ex post* creditor protection by means of civil liability of directors and shareholders. Finally, section 12 offers some concluding remarks.

3. Types of corporate creditors

As is well known, voluntary and involuntary corporate creditors raise different questions with respect to creditor protection.

However, the most important involuntary creditors, namely the State (e.g., taxes) and public agencies (e.g., social insurance), can be left out of the picture. As a rule, States establish particular liability regimes that extend the liability for any taxes and social security contributions that the corporation owes to the tax authorities or other public agencies to the directors and sometimes even to the (dominant) shareholder.

As for the remaining types of involuntary creditors, "pure" tort creditors can serve as an exemplary case.

4. Types of corporate creditor risks

Whether or not corporate creditors voluntarily enter into a relationship with the corporation has a bearing on the types of risks they face. Moreover, since corporate creditors enter into a relationship with the corporation itself, an in-depth risk analysis has to take into account whether the risks result from decisions and actions, respectively, by the shareholders or by the directors.

4.1 **Voluntary corporate creditors**

The different risks that voluntary creditors face can be analyzed in three dimensions: time, cause, and originator.[20]

4.1.1 *Time*

Upon establishing a contractual relationship, creditors face the risk that the terms and conditions of the contract are (initially) inappropriate, i.e., that they do not fully reflect the risk of future non-performance by the company existing then or, in more technical parlance, that at the time of concluding the contract the initial net present value of a contractual claim is less than its nominal value. Once creditors have entered into a contract, they face the risk of a subsequent devaluation of their claim. This risk, in turn, reflects an increase in the probability that at the time the claim is due for repayment the debtor will be unable or at least unwilling to fully honor his debt, i.e., an increased probability of partial or complete non-performance by the debtor. From this perspective, default on the debtor's part simply signifies a 100 percent probability of non-performance.

4.1.2 *Cause*

Initially inappropriate contracts, i.e., if the net present value of a creditor's claims is initially less than its nominal value, are often due to inadequate or even misleading information provided by the debtor. Alternatively, the creditor may not spend enough time and energy in properly informing himself about the risks or may have miscalculated the required risk premium because of bounded rationality.

An *ex post* devaluation of a claim – be it temporary or permanent – may simply result from business misfortune due, for example, to unsuccessful management, poor business conditions, or even exogenous shocks, e.g., a steep rise in the cost of raw materials or a sharp hike in workers' wages. Alternatively, it may result from opportunistic behavior on the company's part, i.e., if the company willingly takes on additional risk. This risk increase may, in turn, be due to:[21]

---

[20] Cf., further P.O. Mülbert, 'Zukunft der Kapitalaufbringung/Kapitalerhaltung', 2 *Der Konzern* (2004) p. 151, at p. 153 et seq.

[21] For more details, see, e.g., L. Enriques and J.R. Macey, 'Creditors Versus Capital Formation: The Case Against the European Legal Capital Rules', 86 *Cornell Law Review* (2001) p. 1165 at p. 1168 et seq.; Mülbert and Birke, loc. cit. n. 1, at p. 708 et seq.

- a waste of company assets because of substandard business conduct, i.e., if the company does not conduct its business in accordance with the standards of a diligent and conscientious businessman (weak-form opportunism);
- a distribution of company assets to the shareholders, be it in the form of dividend payments or share repurchases, or in disguised form, e.g., by means of an exchange of economic goods between the corporation and a shareholder at terms that the corporation would not have agreed to if dealing with an unrelated third party (strong-form opportunism);
- a shift to a more risky business strategy (strong-form opportunism). Prime examples are strategic business decisions that cause rating agencies to downgrade a company's outstanding debt, e.g., the decision to launch a tender offer for another company or, in the case of banks, a strong expansion of the more volatile investment banking business. In addition, a shift to a riskier business strategy occurs if a company continues to do business while the probability of becoming insolvent has (sharply) increased or if it continues to do business even beyond the point where "there is no reasonable prospect that the company would avoid going into insolvent liquidation."[22] On the other hand, for a company to continue its business even after having become insolvent does not signify a shift *per se* to a riskier business strategy. This would only be the case if, because of the company's suffering further losses from continuing to do business, the dividend paid to the creditors of the insolvent company would drop even further;
- a repayment of a credit, in particular a loan, extended by a shareholder when the company is in financial distress (strong-form opportunism);
- a commingling of company and shareholder assets (strong-form opportunism).

4.1.3 *Originator*

Opportunistic behavior on the company's part may be due to actions by either its directors or its shareholders.

With regard to the directors, the most common form of opportunism is a waste of corporate assets caused by directors who, when exercising their functions, do not comply with the standard of a diligent and conscientious director, i.e., who violate their duty of care or their duty of loyalty owed to the company. In addition, if the company headed by the directors continues to do business even though it is already insolvent or, according to all reasonable expectations, will become insolvent in the future, directors may still benefit from opportunism since they continue to receive salary payments and enjoy other privileges linked with their position.

---

[22] S. 214(2)(b) British Insolvency Act 1986 (hereinafter, IA).

With respect to the shareholders, the lack of personal liability for the corporation's debts (limited liability) will serve as a powerful incentive to cause the company to act opportunistically, either in the form of a subsequent distribution of assets to its shareholders or by taking on riskier business projects, i.e., projects with more volatile earnings prospects. In practice, such kinds of opportunistic behavior will most often be initiated either by a shareholder acting in his capacity as a director or by the shareholders issuing a binding directive to the directors, or by a dominant shareholder making use of his actual influence.

4.2 Involuntary corporate creditors

The risks involuntary corporate creditors face are much the same as those run by voluntary creditors. The net present value of non-contractual claims may be less than their nominal value already at their time of coming into existence, or, alternatively, such claims may suffer a subsequent devaluation. As opposed to contractual claims, the only difference concerns possible causes for initial inappropriateness. If a claim does not adequately reflect the risk of future non-performance by the company at the time the claim comes into existence, this will be due to the company's being in financial difficulties or even being insolvent, not because of misleading information supplied by the debtor or bounded rationality on the creditor's part.

4.3 Particularities of corporate creditors' risks

Contrary to conventional wisdom, corporate creditors do not incur fundamentally different risks in comparison with creditors of natural persons. In particular, the principle of limited liability does not create unique risks but only acts to severely exacerbate the risks a creditor faces in the case of a natural person's unlimited personal liability.[23]

Neither corporations nor natural persons possess unlimited funds. Thus, the net present value of a claim when coming into existence may be less than its nominal value, regardless of the type of debtor, i.e., regardless of whether the debtor is a corporation or a natural person. This observation holds true even for non-contractual claims, e.g., tort claims, even if the probability that a small corporation will cause large or mass tort claims is far greater than in the case of a natural person.[24]

With regard to the *ex post* devaluation of claims because of opportunistic behavior, corporations as debtors and natural persons as debtors differ only in

---

23 In the same sense, see Hertig and Kanda, loc. cit. n. 10, at p. 71 et seq.

24 For a more detailed discussion, see Mülbert and Birke, loc. cit. n. 1, at p. 714 et seq.

quantitative, not in qualitative terms. Put differently, unlimited liability does not completely prevent people from acting opportunistically. Obviously, weak-form opportunism is also present among natural persons, e.g., if a person chooses a lesser paid instead of a higher paid job, thus reducing any chances of a future settlement of all of his debts. Even strong-form opportunism may be found among natural persons, for example in the case of a (nearly) insolvent debtor who transfers his assets to his spouse or children in order to prevent creditors from realizing their claims by obtaining judgment and levying execution on the debtor's goods. In this respect as well, corporations as debtors and natural persons as debtors only differ insofar as corporations are dramatically more prone to show strong-form opportunism than natural persons, since directors and shareholders, as the corporate decision-makers, are not directly liable towards the creditors.

5. THE EXTENT OF CORPORATE CREDITOR PROTECTION

5.1 Efficient corporate creditor protection and its limits

The principle of limited liability acts as a one-sided default risk-sharing rule. Notwithstanding contractual arrangements to the contrary, shareholders do not participate in any losses the creditors suffer from dealing with a corporation. Creditor protection rules and mechanisms seek to mitigate the effects of a "blind" or automatic application of the principle of non-personal liability of shareholders and directors. Developing a framework for efficient corporate creditor protection, then, begs the following question: to what extent are corporate creditors to be protected against (i) the risk of acquiring an initially overvalued claim and (ii) the risk of an *ex post* devaluation of a claim?

With respect to efficient creditor protection, the relevant criterion seems to be straightforward. Creditors are to be protected against those risks that a fully informed rational creditor would not accept voluntarily when contracting the claim in question. However, upon closer inspection, things are more complicated. On the one hand, "pure" tort creditors, for example, would not willingly accept any risks of non-performance, and even voluntary creditors will try to avoid any risk of non-performance, including the risk of simple business misfortune. If banks and other important creditors are in a position to enforce their demands, they will require the corporation to provide collateral. Additionally, they will seek personal guarantees or collateral from the shareholders and/or the directors. Generally speaking, rational corporate creditors will even try to avoid the risk of simple business misfortune, since, on the other hand, they do not participate in the residual earnings. Hence, the relevant criterion for efficient creditor protection needs a qualification. Creditors are to be protected against those risks that a fully informed rational creditor would not accept voluntarily when contracting the claim in question – except for the risk of simple business misfortune, since the essence of the principle of limited liability is to burden creditors with this risk.

Moreover, companies without a viable business and/or capable management will go bankrupt over time regardless of the amount of capital initially available to them – in the long run they are all dead. Admittedly, for individual creditors it makes an often decisive difference whether bankruptcy will occur in the near or the more distant future, since the creditor population changes over time. However, the overall result does not change along the timeline: some creditors will suffer financial losses. At first glance, this observation seems to eliminate completely the need for mandatory creditor protection, except for one case: protection against directors and/or shareholders directing the company to act opportunistically if the company would have stayed in business had this action not been taken, i.e., if the company, given its business prospects over time, would not have gone bankrupt at all. Upon closer reflection, however, this bottom line for mandatory creditor protection may be too restrictive. First, there are often long-term creditors, in particular employees holding a pension claim against the company. For them, at least, creditor protection is of major interest, even in the long-run perspective. Second, lacking any means of creditor self-help, creditors would resort to extreme short-term financing if mandatory rules would only prohibit directors and/or shareholders from taking decisions that will cause an otherwise viable company to go bankrupt. On balance, then, the "in the long term they are all dead" argument does not completely eliminate the need for mandatory protection. However, it does caution against any premature calls for raising the existing level of creditor protection simply on the grounds that introducing stricter rules serves to lower a company's probability of default. Take the case of limitations on distributions.[25] Any distribution, *ceteris paribus*, will raise a company's probability of default, albeit the increase will often be even less than tiny. On the other hand, distributions serve to attract investors. Thus, mandatory rules on limitations of distributions will have to strike a balance between the diverging interests based on economic efficiency considerations. The benefits to creditors from raising the level of creditor protection must outweigh the efficiency losses suffered by existing and future shareholders, and *vice versa*.

Finally, even given this refinement, the exact delineation of those risks corporate creditors are to be protected against does pose some problems. In particular, creditors come as a heterogeneous group.[26] They differ with respect to their appetite for risk, the size of their credit portfolio, their time horizon priorities and repayment schedules, and, last but not least, the exact point of time when entering

---

25 See also *infra* section 9.1.2.3.

26 See, e.g., Armour, loc. cit. n. 16, at p. 376 et seq.

into a (non-)contractual relationship with the company. The following discussion serves to illustrate some of the resultant problems.

5.2 Initially inappropriate contractual terms and conditions

Efficient contracts fully reflect the risk that the corporation will not be able to honor its obligation in full at the time the claim falls due for payment. At a first glance, then, a strong case does seem to exist for creditor protection against the risk of entering into a contract the conditions of which, i.e., the risk premium paid to the creditor, do not fully reflect the risk of future non-payment.[27]

However, things are more complicated than that. From the point of view of the holder of a single claim, accepting a risk premium as compensation for a given probability of future non-performance is like placing a bet on whether the corporation will honor its debt or not. Thus, depending on the individual risk preferences, risk-averse creditors will either completely refrain from entering into a contractual relationship with the corporation, or they will ask a much higher premium than those creditors holding a sufficiently diversified portfolio of claims. The latter type of creditor will demand a much lower premium, since he will calculate a risk premium for each contract to ensure that he will not suffer a financial loss with respect to the whole portfolio of claims.

An important consequence ensues from this analysis. With respect to creditor protection mechanisms targeting the formation of the contract, the appropriate level of protection depends on whether the "model creditor" to be protected is one holding a single claim or a diversified creditor. The former will need full protection against the risk of concluding a contract if the probability of default on the part of the envisaged debtor should exceed a certain threshold. The latter needs full protection against the risk of concluding a contract, the terms and conditions of which do not fully reflect the risk of non-performance by the debtor. Using the Basel II framework and terminology in order to calculate the adequate risk premium, such a creditor would need to know the probability of default by the debtor and the expected loss in the event of default, among other things.

5.3 *Ex post* devaluation of a claim

The protection of corporate creditors against the *ex post* devaluation of a claim crucially depends on whether the risk is due to opportunism on the company's part or simple business misfortune.

---

[27] By definition, this problem does not arise if the debtor provides sufficient collateral at the time of the formation of the contract, since any expected loss in the event of the debtor's default will be (practically) nil.

5.3.1 *Strong-form opportunism*

Strong-form opportunism, i.e., distribution of assets to shareholders or other forms of a deliberate increase in risk, on the corporation's part seems to be an obvious case for legal intervention in its creditors' favor. However, closer inspection reveals a more complicated picture.

To begin with, the effects of a distribution of assets to shareholders are not fundamentally different from a move by the company to a business model with more volatile earnings prospects: the probability of default increases. Nevertheless, jurisdictions all over the world pay much closer attention to the first type of behavior than to the latter and, moreover, provide for stricter limitations.[28] Virtually all industrialized countries' jurisdictions stipulate rules that limit the admissible amount of dividend payments or other forms of distributions of assets to shareholders. In this respect, jurisdictions do not differ fundamentally, regardless of whether they operate with a German-style legal capital system – involving a minimum capital requirement, rules on the raising of capital, and rules on capital maintenance – or not.

Put more generally, separating acceptable non-opportunistic from unacceptable opportunistic behavior will often be difficult. Actions by the corporation that only marginally increase the risk of default cannot be regarded as opportunistic behavior. Otherwise, dividend payments or share repurchases as well as a tiny increase in the company's leverage would constitute opportunistic behavior. However, take the recent decision by *Deutsche Börse AG* to pacify its mostly hedge-fund owners by dispensing nearly all of its cash reserves within the next two years by way of dividend payments and share buy-backs or, *inter alia*, the decision in the 1990s of *Dresdner Bank AG* to invest heavily in highly volatile investment banking which led rating agencies to downgrade the bank's outstanding corporate bonds. Do such far-reaching strategic decisions qualify as opportunistic behavior towards creditors or not?

The answer is notoriously difficult to give, since the interests of creditors as fixed claimants and the interests of shareholders as holders of residual claims diverge: creditors are more risk-averse.[29] Given a project's or a company's risk, creditors will prefer a lower debt-equity ratio, and, conversely, for a given ratio, shareholders will prefer the company to pursue more risky projects than creditors will favor. Furthermore, with a company moving more and more towards insolvency, the divergence becomes ever more pronounced.[30]

---

28 See *infra* section 9.1.2.2.

29 See, e.g., Mülbert and Birke, loc. cit. n. 1, at p. 710 et seq.

30 See, e.g., H.C. Hirt, 'The Wrongful Trading Remedy in UK Law: Classification, Application and Practice Significance', 1 *ECFR* (*European Company and Financial Law Review*)

Moreover, even if one were, for example, to qualify a huge distribution of assets to shareholders, a company's move to a much riskier business strategy or the continuation of a company's business subsequent to a major loss of working capital as being opportunistic behavior,[31] this would only hold true in relation to the creditors already existing at that time. Anybody becoming a creditor later on would not suffer from opportunistic behavior but from having accepted a riskier debtor as a party to the contract.

The upshot is, then, that only more extreme corporate decisions and actions constitute the kind of opportunistic behavior that warrants legal intervention. The bottom line is reached when, as a consequence of the company's behavior, there is no reasonable prospect that the company would avoid becoming insolvent on the ground that its liabilities exceed its assets. Creditors who feel the need for protection against less egregious behavior on the corporation's part can still impose covenants tailored to their specific needs.

5.3.2 *Weak-form opportunism*

Weak-form opportunism is different from strong-form opportunism insofar as the company itself suffers losses due to substandard business conduct on the directors' part, i.e., due to the directors violating their duty of care or their duty of loyalty. Here, too, creditors can protect themselves against this type of risk only by obtaining collateral or personal guarantees supplied by the directors and/or the shareholders.

5.3.3 *Business misfortune*

Limited liability acts as a default rule for sharing the risks between creditors and shareholders that result from business misfortune, e.g., unsuccessful management, poor business conditions, or exogenous shocks.

Obviously, the resulting partition of risks changes over time for a given company and, moreover, varies for different companies. For example, if a company becomes insolvent, all creditors belonging to one class will recover the same dividend, i.e., the same percentage of their claim, regardless of the company's risk of becoming insolvent at the time a particular claim came into existence. Moreover, the amount of time and resources spent by a creditor in informing himself about his future debtor is irrelevant. Even creditors who completely failed

---

(2004) p. 71 at p. 83 et seq.; C. Kuhner, 'Zur Zukunft der Kapitalerhaltung durch bilanzielle Ausschüttungssperren im Gesellschaftsrecht der Staaten Europas', 34 *ZGR* (2005) p. 753 at p. 769 et seq.

[31] But see *infra* section 9.2.

to collect any information will not suffer any adverse consequences, e.g., a reduction of the dividend. However, these effects result from insolvency law, not from limited liability. Hence, limited liability does not give rise to concerns with respect to any unequal treatment of creditors.

At best, one may want to take issue with the characteristics of the partition of risks established by limited liability: shareholders will take the residual profits regardless of the amount of the investment they committed themselves to up front when founding the corporation. However, this sharing arrangement constitutes the core element of the principle of limited liability, and this paper definitely does not wish to take issue with the universally recognized proposition that, at least with respect to the partition of risks between shareholders and contractual creditors, limited liability has economically beneficial effects.[32]

6. MANDATORY PROTECTION RULES V. CREDITOR SELF-HELP

Creditor self-help as an alternative to creditor protection by means of mandatory rules is not available *per se* to "pure" tort creditors but only to contractual creditors. For the latter, self-help comes in four forms: collecting information on the intended party to the contract, taking out third-party credit insurance, inserting covenants into the contract, and obtaining collateral from the corporation and/or its directors and shareholders. However, even though British law appropriately favors self-help over mandatory protective rules, at least as a starting point,[33] all four approaches to self-help do not act as a perfect substitute for creditor protection by means of mandatory law.

To begin with, any form of self-help is inherently costly. This is true for information gathering as well as for taking out third-party credit insurance, for writing[34] and contracting covenants and for supplying collateral and personal guarantees. Because of these costs, statutory limitations seem to provide a superior off-the-rack "boilerplate" solution available even to "weak" creditors with respect to those covenants, at least, that replicate the restrictions on asset distributions to shareholders mandated by the Second Company Law Directive.[35]

---

32 *Supra* n. 3 with accompanying text.

33 See Armour, loc. cit. n. 16, at p. 357 et seq.

34 However, model financial covenants are available. See, e.g., American Bar Foundation, *Commentaries on Model Debenture Indenture Provisions, 1965, Model Debenture Indenture Provisions, All Registered Issue*[*s*], *1967, and Certain Negotiable Provisions Which May Be Included in a Particular Incorporation Indenture, Buffalo* (Buffalo, NY, William S. Hein & Co. 1986) (reprint).

35 Covenants contracted in the United States, albeit with greatly declining frequency, impose restrictions similar to the limitations stipulated by the Second Directive. As to the extent

With regard to information gathering, in particular, severe adverse selection problems would arise, since directors, when providing information voluntarily, are often tempted by strong incentives to misrepresent the company's financial situation. Mandatory disclosure rules facilitating information gathering by addressing these informational asymmetries and their causes thus do not form an alternative to mandatory creditor protection but a precondition for efficient creditor self-help

Taking out third-party credit insurance is a very costly way for creditors to protect themselves. A superior alternative would be compulsory third-party insurance, since the company as debtor would be incentivized to reduce the riskiness of its business if insurance rates were designed accordingly.

Covenants as a mechanism for self-help only serve to prevent the corporation from acting opportunistically, i.e., to prevent an *ex post* devaluation of a claim.[36] Moreover, as a rule, smaller creditors are not in a position to impose covenants. The well-known argument that smaller creditors also benefit from covenants imposed by larger creditors is not wholly convincing.[37] First, some clauses, of necessity, do work to the detriment of other non-secured creditors. An obvious case in point is the event risk clause or poison put clause that gives bondholders an option to put the bonds back to the issuer, since other creditors will suffer from this drain on the company's liquidity. More generally speaking, a violation of contractual covenants entails very different consequences from those resulting from a violation of restrictions stipulated by mandatory rules. Take the case of an illegal distribution of assets. If the distribution violates contractual covenants, the creditor will either be able to renegotiate the terms of the credit, in particular to enforce an upward readjustment of the interest rate, or will obtain a claim for damages and, because of an acceleration clause or a clause that empowers him to

---

of similarity, see, e.g., E. Ferran, *The Place for Creditor Protection on the Agenda for Modernisation of Company Law in the European Union*, ECGI Law Working Paper No. 51/2005 (Brussels, European Corporate Governance Institute 2005) p. 5 et seq.; Armour, loc. cit. n. 16, at p. 373 et seq.; M.R. Alberth, 'USA: Vertraglicher Gläubigerschutz und Ausschüttungsbemessung durch Covenants als Vorbild zur Änderung des deutschen Bilanzrechts?', 50 *WPg* (*Die Wirtschaftsprüfung*) (1997) p. 744 at p. 747.

[36] For typical contents of financial covenants, see, e.g., Mülbert and Birke, loc. cit. n. 1, at p. 723.

[37] As to the following, see Mülbert and Birke, loc. cit. n. 1, at pp. 724, 730 et seq. In the same sense, H. Eidenmüller, *Unternehmenssanierung zwischen Markt und Gesetz* (Cologne, Dr. Otto Schmidt 1999) p. 146 et seq.; W. Schön, 'The Future of Legal Capital', 5 *EBOR* (2004) p. 431, at p. 443; H. Merkt, 'Der Kapitalmarktschutz in Europa – ein rocher de bronze?', 33 *ZGR* (2004) p. 305 at p. 313 et seq.; ibid., 'Creditor Protection and Capital Maintenance from a German perspective', 15 *EBLR* (2004) p. 1045 at p. 1050; Ferran, op. cit. n. 35, at p. 10; J. Hennrichs, 'Bilanzgestütze Kapitalerhaltung, HGB-Jahresabschluß und Maßgeblichkeitsprinzip – Dinosaurier der Rechtsgeschichte?', 82 *StuW* (*Steuer und Wirtschaft*) (2005) p. 256 at p. 260 et seq.; Alberth, loc. cit. n. 35, at p. 748 et seq.

terminate the contract for cause, will be entitled to recover the amount due at once. All these different consequences may lead to a further deterioration of the company's financial position, thus hurting the smaller creditors, too. Conversely, a distribution of assets in violation of statutory restrictions will entitle the company to reclaim the funds distributed to shareholders, thus strengthening its financial position. More generally speaking, mandatory rules do not suffer from the sort of collective action problems that limit the role of covenants as a mechanism for protecting even "weak" creditors.

The most effective form of creditor self-help is to obtain collateral from the corporation, its directors, and shareholders. Sufficient collateral protects the creditor against any information risks, i.e., against the risk of entering into a contract with a company that is already insolvent, or that will surely become insolvent, as well as against the risk of *ex post* opportunism on the company's part. Indeed, being personably liable acts as a powerful check on directors and/or shareholders to refrain from causing the corporation to act opportunistically. Still, this solution does suffer from some obvious drawbacks as opposed to creditor protection by means of mandatory rules. First, in practice, creditors systematically differ in their ability to obtain collateral from the corporation or personal guarantees from directors or shareholders. Large creditors and banks in particular will often be fully secured, whereas smaller creditors, in particular suppliers of services, will have no securities at all. Moreover, even personal liability towards one or more larger creditors will not prevent a shareholder or director from causing the corporation to act opportunistically if the expected benefits are large enough. In practice, a shareholder-director will often continue to do business even though he is personally liable for the company's debt and the corporation is in a crisis or even on the brink of insolvency.

7. STRATEGIES FOR MANDATORY CREDITOR PROTECTION

Prevention is the holy grail of all efforts to protect creditors by mandatory rules. Providing for mechanisms that ensure full compensation of creditors once the debtor has gone bankrupt only comes second.[38] From an economic perspective, prevention by means of mandatory rules serves to lower transaction costs, since creditor self-help as well as insolvency proceedings are costly mechanisms, and contributes to a superior allocation of resources, since adverse selection problems

[38] But see W. Zöllner, 'Konkurrenz für inländische Kapitalgesellschaften durch ausländische Rechtsträger, insbesondere durch die englische Private Limited Company', 97 *GmbHR* (*GmbH-Rundschau*) (2006) p. 1 at p. 12: the primary goal of creditor protection consists in making sure that creditors will be fully compensated when the company is bankrupt.

will be less acute, i.e., because of potential creditors withholding funds altogether or investing funds with less risky debtors. Thus, creditor protection regimes should be geared towards mechanisms and rules that block the realization of potential creditors risks, i.e., that protect creditors against concluding a contract that, from the outset, does not adequately reflect the risk of future non-performance by the debtor and against a subsequent devaluation of a creditor's claim caused by opportunistic behavior on the corporation's part. With a view to this aim, a number of different mechanisms are available, e.g., mandatory disclosure, capital requirements, the subordination of shareholder claims, and rules that sanction opportunistic behavior. However, if, despite all efforts at prevention, a risk has materialized, effective creditor protection calls for mechanisms and rules that minimize the losses incurred by existing creditors. This last line of defense requires, *inter alia*, rules that require the restructuring or winding-up of a financially distressed company; procedural rules that allow for a successful enforcement of creditors' claims against the company, its directors, and shareholders; and appropriately designed bankruptcy proceedings.

The following observations will focus on prevention. In this context, legislators and courts have two basic strategies for creditor protection at their disposal: regulating structure and regulating behavior.

Providing for structural requirements in order to protect creditors acts as a risk-preventing mechanism. The most comprehensive structural approach to creditor protection would be to disallow corporations altogether or – for a slightly less intrusive option – to disallow limited liability. Far less heavy-handed variants of this regulatory strategy are capital requirements or the mechanism of the disqualification of directors.

A particular problem common to all these pre-emptive mechanisms is overshooting. It is notoriously difficult to calibrate these structural requirements in a way that neither prevents the coming into being of "desirable" risks nor allows for the existence of an "undesirable" risk. In other words, the costs of having such structural requirements may easily exceed the benefits that may result therefrom.

Regulating behavior to protect corporate creditors boils down to providing for legal standards of behavior for directors and shareholders. The sanctions attached to these standards can either take the form of civil sanctions, most often civil liability, or criminal fines and administrative sanctions. For a particular jurisdiction, the choice between these enforcement mechanisms will depend on numerous factors, e.g., legal traditions or whether criminal fines are reserved for highly unethical behavior or are perceived as being a regular enforcement alternative.

With respect to creditor protection, at least two factors, in particular, should be kept in mind. First, contrary to criminal or administrative sanctions, civil liability provides not only for *ex ante* incentives to comply with legal standards of behavior but also for compensation for losses suffered by the creditors. Moreover, the level of deterrence of criminal and administrative sanctions depends crucially on the amount of public resources, e.g., personnel and so forth, available for this purpose. By contrast, creditors are inherently given an incentive to spend their own funds on efforts to recover at least part of the money that is due to them. However, enforcement by private litigation only provides directors and shareholders with sufficient *ex ante* incentives to comply with the legally mandated behavioral standards if creditors are in a position to effectively enforce their claims. This observation begs the question, for example, when and to what extent directors and shareholders should be liable only to the corporation and not to creditors directly and whether the directors or the shareholders should be liable for opportunistic behavior on the corporation's part.

8. REDUCING THE RISKS OF CREDITORS WHEN CONTRACTING WITH A FINANCIALLY DISTRESSED COMPANY

8.1 Mandatory disclosure unrelated to insolvency

Mandatory disclosure is universally acknowledged as an indispensable mechanism for creditor protection. More to the point, mandatory disclosure will often be a necessary prerequisite for creditor self-help, be it by way of abstaining from concluding a contract or by demanding an adequate risk premium, covenants, and/or collateral. The difficult question, then, is the extent of disclosure required. From a repeat player's point of view, e.g., a creditor holding a diversified portfolio of claims, this should ideally be all the information needed to calculate the appropriate risk premium. However, this would imply a prohibitively costly obligation to make ongoing disclosure.

On the other hand, disclosure of the amount of nominal capital, as mandated by the Second Directive, does not help much in protecting creditors, since they will not know whether the company's net assets still amount to the equivalent of the nominal capital, at least.[39]

From the creditors' point of view, the informational content of the annual accounts is much higher. Still, as experience shows, the publication of the annual accounts will not protect creditors as much as one may hope. In particular, this is true for small creditors. To name but three reasons: annual accounts are published only once a year; for lack of time and transaction cost constraints, small creditors will often not bother to obtain the annual accounts; and, even if they did, they would often lack the necessary knowledge and skills to analyze the accounts in sufficient detail.

---

[39] Mülbert, loc. cit. n. 20, at p. 157.

Conversely, effective creditor protection by means of mandatory disclosure will only be achieved if the following prerequisites are fulfilled:

- the information is easily available, e.g., via the Internet from the company's homepage or the commercial register;
- the information is renewed periodically, e.g., every three months;
- the information is standardized, i.e., all companies, *inter alia*, employ the same framework, e.g., standardized methodologies, calculations, and reporting format; and
- the information is easily understood and can easily be acted upon accordingly.

Against that backdrop, one may want to consider requiring the directors to periodically assess and publish the company's probability of default for a given timeline, e.g., within the next six months. However, assessing the risk of default is at best not an easy task. Smaller companies, in particular, will often lack the resources and ability to assess their own probability of default with any accuracy. Moreover, the higher the probability of default, the more directors would be tempted to lie, since it would be difficult to detect *ex post* whether the directors had lied about the probability of default or whether they had correctly calculated but were proven "wrong" by the subsequent developments. As a consequence, disclosure of more or less well-informed guesses on one's own probability of default would not serve any meaningful purpose, since potential creditors would not use them as a basis for their decision making.

An apparently less demanding requirement would be to disclose periodically whether the company has sufficient working capital, i.e., whether or not the company is undercapitalized. However, since broadly or even universally accepted criteria for determining the amount of working capital required for a given company are not available,[40] a simple statement that the amount of working capital is "sufficient" would not be meaningful. Instead, creditors would want to know the amount of working capital available in order to decide for themselves whether or not the working capital is sufficient. This publication could be in the form of "in excess of ...", available on the corporation's homepage (with a reference contained in the company's letterhead) and calculated four times annually.

The upshot is that the problem of creditor protection by means of efficient disclosure obligations – the benefits from having more extended disclosure obligations must still exceed the additional costs incurred by this – warrants still further exploration.

---

40 *Infra* section 9.2.

8.2 Insolvency-related mandatory disclosure

8.2.1 *German v. British law*

Insolvency-related mandatory disclosure seems to be a particularly thorny issue. In this respect, German law and British law even adopt diametrically opposed disclosure philosophies.

German law, on the one hand, requires the directors of a company to file a petition in bankruptcy without undue delay, but within three weeks at the latest if the company has become insolvent because of illiquidity, i.e., inability to pay debts as they fall due (cash flow test) or because of an excess of liabilities over assets (balance sheet test).[41] Decisions by the bankruptcy court – be it the preliminary appointment of a "weak" administrator, the decision to open insolvency proceedings and to appoint an administrator, or the decision not to open the proceedings due to a lack of sufficient funds to cover the costs of the proceedings – will be entered into the appropriate commercial register for the company,[42] thereby informing the public about its financially distressed situation and warning potential creditors against entering into any contractual relationship with it. If, due to negligence or even intent, the directors fail to comply with the requirement, they will be held liable towards all creditors. However, if the company does enter into a contract with a new creditor during the three-week grace period, the directors are not obliged to inform the other party about the company's critical situation.[43]

British law, on the other hand, does not stipulate any obligation on the directors to file a petition in bankruptcy. However, it the company does go into insolvent liquidation (net asset test) a director will be held liable according to the provision on wrongful trading contained in section 214 of the British Insolvency Act (hereinafter, IA), if he did not take "every step with a view to minimizing the potential loss to the company's creditors as … he ought to have taken." Given this risk, directors will often decide to apply for a winding-up by the court (s. 122 IA) in order to avoid personal liability. Only then will all actual and potential creditors be informed about the company's critical financial situation.

Quite in line with these differences, German law and British law also differ with respect to damages awarded to those creditors who entered into a contractual relationship with the company after the pertinent "moment of truth". According to

---

[41] S. 64(1) Limited Liability Company Act (GmbHG), s. 92(2) German Stock Corporation Act.

[42] S. 32 German Commercial Code.

[43] BGH 6 June 1994, II ZR 292/91, 48 *WM* (1994) pp. 1428-1436.

a landmark ruling by the German Federal High Court in the mid-1990s, (only) those creditors are indeed entitled to recuperate the total amount lost to the company. If they had known of the company's distressed situation, they would not have entered into a contract with the company.[44] British law, on the other hand, does not differentiate whether a person has become a creditor before or after the moment of truth.[45] This uniform treatment adequately reflects the position of British law that potential (voluntary) creditors are not in need of preventive protection by means of mandatory disclosure obligations.

8.2.2 *Timing*

Taking the position of German law as starting point, i.e., opting for the protection even of potential voluntary creditors by mandatory disclosure obligations, begs the follow-up question as to the appropriate time for the start of such additional obligations.

German law has opted for the exact point in time at which the company becomes formally insolvent, but employs a two-pronged insolvency test: assets over liabilities and inability to pay.[46] If the company fails one of the two tests, directors are under an obligation to file a petition in bankruptcy.[47] By contrast, at least according to its wording and legislative intent, the British provision on wrongful trading contained in section 214 IA has adopted a slightly earlier point in time, namely when a director knows that "there is no reasonable prospect that the company would avoid going into insolvent liquidation." One may doubt, though, whether this subtle difference between British and German law would matter much in practice.[48] Indeed, it may well be that section 214 IA, as interpreted by British courts, only kicks in at a later stage than the German provisions requiring the directors to file a petition in bankruptcy. At least some British courts have held that the "moment of truth" has not yet come with an excess of liabilities over

---

44 BGH 6 June 1994, II ZR 292/91, 48 *WM* (1994) pp. 1428-1436. As to this concept, see H. Fleischer, 'The Responsibility of the Management and of the Board and its Enforcement', in G. Ferrarini, et al., eds., *Reforming Company and Takeover Law in Europe* (Oxford, Oxford University Press 2004) p. 373 at p. 399 et seq.; T. Bachner, 'Wrongful Trading – A New European Model for Creditor Protection?', 5 *EBOR* (2004) p. 293 at p. 317 et seq.

45 See Bachner, loc. cit. n. 44, at p. 316; Fleischer, loc. cit. n. 44, at p. 398 (with further references).

46 S. 17, 19 Insolvency Act.

47 *Supra* n. 41 with accompanying text.

48 Cf., M. Habersack and D.A. Verse, 'Wrongful Trading – Grundlage einer europäischen Insolvenzverschleppungshaftung?', 168 *ZHR* (*Zeitschrift für das gesamte Handelsrecht und Wirtschaftsrecht*) (2004) p. 174 at p. 186 et seq. and at p. 213 et seq.

assets (balance sheet test) but only when the company is unable to pay its debts as they fall due (cash flow test) or have opted even for a later point in time.[49]

Apart from these considerations, the fundamental question remains, namely whether mandatory disclosure obligations should set in far earlier than provided for at present by German law, e.g., when the company is unable to obtain credit from third parties (i.e., non-shareholders), or, e.g., when it was "more likely than not" that the company would at some point become unable to pay its debts as they fell due. As has been well known for a long time, this problem amounts to an unavoidable choice between Scylla and Charybdis. A disclosure obligation that sets in early will prevent some people from becoming creditors at all, but the flipside is that financially distressed companies will stand a lower chance of a successful private workout, and *vice versa*. Given that, because of the lack of negative publicity and more flexibility, private workouts are increasingly recognized as a superior alternative to formal insolvency proceedings,[50] disclosure obligations regarding the company's financial situation should not kick in any earlier than presently mandated by German law.

9. Reducing a Company's Probability of Entering into Financial Distress

9.1 Legal capital

A comprehensive (German-style) legal capital regime comprises a whole set of statutory provisions and court-made rules.[51] They provide for a minimum capital, regulate the raising and maintenance of capital, and prohibit any circumvention of

---

[49] For an overview of relevant cases, see Hirt, loc. cit. n. 30, at p. 106 et seq.; Bachner, loc. cit. n. 44, at p. 301 et seq.; Habersack and Verse, loc. cit. n. 48, at p. 186 et seq.

[50] See, e.g., Eidenmüller, op. cit. n. 37, at p. 332 et seq.

[51] For a brief description on the basis of the pertinent articles of the Second Directive, see Mülbert and Birke, loc. cit. n. 1, at p. 700 et seq. Note, however, two qualifications: First, shareholders can dispose even of share premiums (*contra* Mülbert and Birke, loc. cit. n. 1, at p. 704; W. Schön, 'Deutsches Konzernprivileg und europäischer Kapitalschutz – ein Widerspruch?', in K.-H. Forster, et al., eds., *Festschrift für Bruno Kropff* (Düsseldorf, IDW-Verlag 1997) p. 285 at p. 294; M. Habersack, *Europäisches Gesellschaftsrecht*, 2nd edn. (Munich, C.H. Beck 2003) n. 164), since Art. 15(1)(c) of the Directive allows for distributions made from reserves available for that purpose, and share premium reserves are available in this sense, since the share premium account is not part of the "subscribed capital" (see Rickford Report, loc. cit. n. 6, at p. 939 et seq.; T. Bezzenberger, *Das Kapital der Aktiengesellschaft* (Cologne, Dr. Otto Schmidt 2005) p. 28 et seq.). Second, some EU Member States do not know (or accept?) the doctrine of disguised contributions in kind and the doctrine of disguised distributions (for the United Kingdom, see *infra* n. 65 and accompanying text). Telling in this respect is the description of the EU legal capital regime by Enriques and Macey, loc. cit. n. 21, at p. 1174 et seq.

the statutory provisions on the raising and maintenance of legal capital. These prohibitions are known in German law as the doctrine of disguised contributions in kind and the doctrine of disguised distributions.

The core element of any meaningful legal capital regime, as the authors of the Rickford Report aptly demonstrated by calling themselves the "Interdisciplinary Group on Capital Maintenance", consists in capital maintenance rules, i.e., restrictions on the distribution of company assets to shareholders. With respect to the protection of creditors, complicated rules on the raising of capital would serve no purpose if the company did not face any restrictions on the redistribution of assets received from shareholders to those shareholders.

The uncontested economic effect of any (mandatory or voluntary) capital reserve on the part of the company, i.e., a surplus of assets over liabilities, is to make the company less prone to become insolvent because of simple business misfortune or even exogenous shocks.[52] Put differently, rules restricting the distribution of assets reduce the likelihood of the insolvency of a venture by effectively binding all of the initial equity contribution to the venture. After all, it is true that, *ceteris paribus*, the lower the rate of debt to equity, the lower the chance of any insolvency of the firm. On the other hand, it is also true that capital maintenance rules, in particular, and the complex set of rules of a German-style legal capital regime, in general, do come at a cost. Most obvious are the costs of compliance for a company, perhaps most serious are the costs that the rules impose on firms by way of impeding or even blocking beneficial corporate transactions.[53]

Whether, in the name of creditor protection, the aforementioned and other economic effects do, on balance, justify a comprehensive – to the point of being hardly comprehensible any more[54] – German-style legal capital regime or whether

---

[52] See Mülbert and Birke, loc. cit. n. 1, at p. 718 et seq.; Mülbert, loc. cit. n. 20, at p. 154.

[53] For details see, e.g., Enriques and Macey, loc. cit. n. 21, at p. 1195 et seq.; Mülbert and Birke, loc. cit. n. 1, at p. 721 et seq.; Mülbert, loc. cit. n. 20, at p. 153; Ferran, op. cit. n. 35, at p. 8 et seq. In addition, because of the recent ruling by the German Federal High Court severely restricting the scope for admissible upstream loans (BGH 24 November 2003, II ZR 171/01, 58 *WM* (2004) p. 325), the setting-up of a group-wide cash pool has become noticeably more difficult. See, e.g., W. Goette, 'Aus der neueren Rechtsprechung des BGH zum GmbH-Recht', 26 *ZIP* (*Zeitschrift für Wirtschaftsrecht*) (2005) p. 1481 at p. 1484 et seq.; M. Habersack and J. Schürnbrand, 'Cash Management und Sicherheitenbestellung bei GmbH und AG im Lichte des richterrechtlichen Verbots der Kreditvergabe an Gesellschafter', 7 *NZG* (*Neue Zeitschrift für Gesellschaftsrecht*) (2004) p. 689 et seq.; A. Cahn, 'Das richterrechtliche Verbot der Kreditvergabe an Gesellschafter und seine Folgen', 2 *Der Konzern* (2004) p. 235 et seq.; W. Bayer and J. Lieder, 'Darlehen der GmbH an Gesellschafter und Sicherheiten aus dem GmbH-Vermögen für Gesellschafterverbindlichkeiten', 34 *ZGR* (2004) p. 133 et seq.

[54] For diametrically opposing views, see V. Röhricht, 'Insolvenzrechtliche Aspekte im Gesellschaftsrecht', 26 *ZIP* (2005) p. 505 at p. 515 (President of the Second Senate of the German Federal High Court, responsible for corporation law, until May 2005) and W. Goette,

a much leaner set of rules will suffice, has lately been strongly contested outside the United States, as well,[55] and even among German lawyers.[56] Here below, the salient points of the discussion will be summarized.

9.1.1 *Minimum capital*

Minimum capital requirements come in two forms: initial and ongoing minimum capital.

'Wo steht der BGH nach "Centros" und "Inspire Art"?', 43 *DStR* (*Deutsches Steuerrecht*) (2005) p. 197 at p. 198 (currently President of the Second Senate of the German Federal High Court).

[55] Enriques and Macey, loc. cit. n. 21, at p. 1165 et seq.; for the UK, see Rickford Report, loc. cit. n. 6, at p. 966 et seq.; Armour, loc. cit. n. 16, at p. 355 et seq.; Ferran, op. cit. n. 35, at p. 10; for France, see J. Simon 'A Comparative Approach to Capital Maintenance: France', 15 *EBLR* (2004) p. 1037 at p. 1040 (all parties concerned now agree that registered capital does not perform the functions assigned to it by the European Union and national legislators).

[56] Critical as to the present German legal capital regime, e.g., F. Kübler, *Aktie, Unternehmensfinanzierung und Kapitalmarkt* (Cologne, Dr. Otto Schmidt 1989); ibid., 'Kapitalmarktgerechte Aktien?', 44 *WM* (1990) p. 1853 et seq.; ibid., 'The Rules of Capital under Pressure of the Securities Markets', in K.J. Hopt and E. Wymeersch, eds., *Capital Markets and Company Law* (Oxford, Oxford University Press 2003) p. 95 et seq.; ibid., 'A Comparative Approach to Capital Maintenance', 15 *EBLR* (2004) p. 1031 et seq.; Mülbert and Birke, loc. cit. n. 1, at p. 716 et seq.; Mülbert, loc. cit. n. 20, at p. 154 et seq.; R. Kulms, 'Die US-amerikanische Limited Liability Company – Vorbild für eine deregulierte GmbH', 102 *ZVglRWiss* (*Zeitschrift für vergleichende Rechtswissenschaft*) (2003) p. 272 at p. 285; S. Grundmann, 'Wettbewerb der Regelgeber im Europäischen Gesellschaftsrecht – jedes Marktsegment hat seine Struktur', 30 *ZGR* (2001) p. 783 at p. 816 et seq.; cf., Röhricht, loc. cit. n. 54, at p. 515. In defense of the existing legal capital regime, see, in particular, Arbeitsgruppe Europäisches Gesellschaftsrecht, 'Stellungnahme zum Report of the High Level Group of Company Law Experts on a Modern Regulatory Framework for Company Law in Europe', 24 *ZIP* (2003) p. 863 at p. 871 et seq. As to individual members of the working group, see, e.g., M. Lutter, 'Gesetzliches Garantiekapital als Problem europäischer und deutscher Rechtspolitik', 43 *AG* (*Die Aktiengesellschaft*) (1998) p. 375 et seq.; Karsten Schmidt, *Gesellschaftsrecht*, 4th edn. (Cologne, Carl Heymanns 2002) p. 519, § 18(II)(2)(c); H. Fleischer, 'Grundfragen der ökonomischen Theorie im Gesellschafts- und Kapitalmarktrecht', 30 *ZGR* (2001) p. 1 at p. 13 et seq.; W. Bayer, 'Die EuGH-Entscheidung "Inspire Art" und die deutsche GmbH im Wettbewerb der europäischen Rechtsordnungen', 39 *BB* (*Betriebs-Berater*) (2003) p. 2357 at pp. 2364 and 2366. See further Schön, loc. cit. n. 37, at p. 431 et seq. (except for the minimum capital requirement); H.J. Priester, 'Die deutsche GmbH nach "Inspire Art" – brauchen wir eine neue?', 58 *DB* (*Der Betrieb*) (2005) p. 1315 et seq.; Bezzenberger, op. cit. n. 51, at p. 72 et seq.; R. Wilhelmi, 'Das Mindestkapital als Mindestschutz – eine Apologie im Hinblick auf die Diskussion um eine Reform der GmbH angesichts der englischen Limited', 97 *GmbHR* (2006) p. 13 et seq.; S. Rammert, 'Lohnt die Erhaltung der Kapitalerhaltung', 56 *BFuP* (*Betriebswirtschaftliche Forschung und Praxis*) (2004) p. 578 at p. 591 et seq.; Hennrichs, loc. cit. n. 37, at p. 256 et seq.

9.1.1.1 Initial minimum capital requirement

An initial minimum capital requirement is increasingly regarded as a preventive mechanism that does not serve a useful function,[57] even among German scholars.[58] First, if the required amount is too high, even economically beneficial projects will be deterred, whereas if the amount is too low, the requirement does not perform any screening function, since practically anybody will have access to the funds necessary. Second, a uniform minimum capital requirement lacks any economic rationale, since for a given amount of working capital companies operating in different lines of businesses will not exhibit a uniform probability of insolvency. Third, regardless of the amount chosen, a minimum capital requirement will not prevent a company from becoming insolvent as a result of ongoing poor management or ongoing poor business conditions, since in the course of time continuous losses will inevitably deplete all a company's assets. Insolvency may just be somewhat farther down the road.[59]

Proponents of a minimum capital requirement may respond by arguing as follows. An entrepreneur with a viable business project who lacks the necessary funds to comply with a minimum capital requirement will often be able to get credit financing. Since the prospective creditor will screen the business proposal relatively carefully, he will act as a gatekeeper selecting economically promising projects. Admittedly, the gatekeeper will turn down some viable prospects, and the screening process itself entails transaction costs. Still, on balance, the benefits from having excluded some non-viable projects may exceed these costs.

However, on closer inspection, this argument is flawed. In order to start doing business, the entrepreneur needs some operating capital. Hence, he has to obtain credit financing anyway, and the financier will act as a gatekeeper, regardless of whether the law requires a minimum capital or not. Moreover, informational asymmetries between the entrepreneur and the financier, e.g., regarding his abilities and the viability of the project do impair the gatekeeper function,

---

[57] Davies, op. cit. n. 3, at p. 229 et seq.; Easterbrook and Fischel, op. cit. n. 3, at p. 60; Enriques and Macey, loc. cit. n. 21, at p. 1185 et seq.

[58] Mülbert, loc. cit. n. 20, at p. 157 et seq.; Schön, loc. cit. n. 37, at p. 439 et seq.; H. Eidenmüller, 'Europäisches und deutsches Gesellschaftsrecht im europäischen Wettbewerb der Gesellschaftsrechte', in S. Lorenz, et al., eds., *Festschrift für Andreas Heldrich* (Munich, C.H. Beck 2005) p. 581 at 593; B. Grunewald and U. Noack, 'Zukunft des Kapitalerhaltungssystems der GmbH – Ein-Euro-GmbH in Deutschland', 96 *GmbHR* (2005) p. 189 et seq.; G.H. Roth, 'Gläubigerschutz bei der GmbH: Was ist unverzichtbar?', in S. Kalss, et al., eds., *Festschrift für Peter Doralt* (Vienna, Manzsche Verlags- und Universitätsbuchhandlung 2004) p. 479 at p. 482 et seq. In favor of a minimum capital requirement, e.g., Arbeitsgruppe Europäisches Gesellschaftsrecht, loc. cit. n. 56, at p. 872; ambiguous: H. Eidenmüller and A. Engert, 'Rechtsökonomie des Mindestkapitals im GmbH-Recht', 96 *GmbHR* (2005) p. 433 et seq.

[59] Mülbert and Birke, loc. cit. n. 1, at p. 719; Mülbert, loc. cit. n. 20, at p. 155.

regardless of whether the entrepreneur needs the funds in order to pay his contribution in cash or to extend credit to the company in need of working capital.

The upshot, then, is that a minimum capital requirement only deters those individuals from setting up a company who are not willing to commit enough own funds – be it as a cash contribution/contribution in kind or as collateral for bank financing – to meet the capital requirement. However, one may doubt whether, in practice, this deterrent effect will often result from a prospective founder's more careful assessment of the viability of the business project or instead from his unwillingness to put financial assets as well as human resources at risk.

9.1.1.2 Ongoing minimum capital requirement

Various EU Member States provide for an ongoing minimum capital by prescribing a recapitalization rule.[60] Typically, the shareholders will have to recapitalize the company if the net assets fall below a threshold of 50 percent of the company's nominal capital. If they fail to comply, the company will be dissolved by law.

On a theoretical level, the economic effects of such rules are rather complex. At first glance, the rules seem to clearly reduce the probability of insolvency, since, in the event of a company's suffering ongoing smaller losses due to unsuccessful management or long-lasting poor business conditions, the rule will require shareholders to react long before the company approaches insolvency. On the other hand, any recapitalization rule provides shareholders with an incentive to choose a nominal capital figure that is as low as possible, since that will facilitate any possible future recapitalization and will reduce the chances that a shareholder will not be able to partake in the recapitalization because of a lack of funds. As a consequence, companies may become more prone to insolvency because of exogenous shocks. Moreover, investors may be less willing to invest in share capital. If a recapitalization did become necessary and shareholders were unable to provide the required funds, the business venture would have to be liquidated, either by closing it down altogether or by selling it off. Both occurrences would have a negative effect on shareholders' future earnings, i.e., by lowering the expected rate of return for share investments. For this and related reasons, one Nordic country is in the process of reviewing its rules on recapitalization.

---

[60] For a comprehensive overview of the pertinent Member State rules, see J. Oelkers, 'Mindestkapital und Nennkapital – Leistungskraft für den Gläubigerschutz (Teil II)', 34 *GesRZ (Der Gesellschafter)* (2005) p. 27 et seq. For a critical assessment of this mechanism, see Enriques and Macey, loc. cit. n. 21, at p. 1201 et seq.

9.1.2 *Limitations on asset distributions to shareholders*

9.1.2.1 General observations

As noted above, limitations on the permissible distribution of assets to shareholders are a core element of any legal capital regime. However, as the rules relating to the British private limited company and US corporation law, e.g., section 6.40 of the Revised Model Business Corporate Act, demonstrate, prohibitions limiting the distribution of assets specifically to the shareholders as members of the company can also exist quite independently from the concept of legal capital. Moreover, these jurisdictions, as well as, for example, German law, provide for additional restrictions on distributions in the form of fraudulent transfer rules, either solely as part of insolvency law (England) or also as a separate statute (Germany and the United States[61]). In effect, regardless of whether or not they provide for a legal capital, virtually all industrialized countries' jurisdictions stipulate rules as part of corporation law and outside corporation law that limit the admissible amount of dividend payments or other forms of distributions of assets to shareholders.[62]

Major differences do exist, however, with respect to the minimum amount of assets that may not be distributed to the shareholders in order to prevent[63] the company from becoming financially distressed. Restrictions on "fraudulent transfers", which often complement the restrictions contained in company law proper, do not significantly alter the incoherent picture.[64] Differences exist within the United States between the corporation laws of some States, to a larger degree within EU Member States with regard to limited liability companies, at least, and are most pronounced between the United States and Member States of the European Union. Contrary to conventional wisdom, for example, the British law

---

[61] For an outline of the US fraudulent transfer laws, see M. Kahan, 'Legal Capital Rules and the Structure of Corporate Law: Some Observations on the Differences Between European and U.S. Approaches', in Hopt and Wymeersch, op. cit. n. 56, at p. 145 et seq. For a brief sketch of the interaction between the restrictions stipulated by the RMBCA and bankruptcy and fraudulent transfer law, respectively, see Mülbert, loc. cit. n. 20, at p. 160.

[62] The point is rightly stressed by the Rickford Report, loc. cit. n. 6, at p. 999 et seq.

[63] Prevention as the overriding goal of capital maintenance rules is completely missed by those (e.g., F. Rüffler, 'Gläubigerschutz durch Mindestkapital und Kapitalerhaltung in der GmbH – überholtes oder sinnvolles Konzept?', 4 *GeS* (*Zeitschrift für Gesellschafts- und Steuerrecht*) (2005) p. 140 at p. 146) who maintain that these rules provide for very efficient creditor protection if they are effectively enforced, "in particular by liquidators in case of insolvent liquidation."

[64] For an overview of statutory limitations to permissible distributions existing in major jurisdictions, see Rickford Report, loc. cit. n. 6, at p. 969 et seq. and p. 1004 et seq. See also J. Vetter, 'Grundlinien der GmbH-Gesellschafterhaftung', 34 *ZGR* (2005) p. 788 at p. 802 et seq.

on the private limited company provides for stricter limitations than the German statute on the GmbH. A private limited company's distributions to its shareholders are restricted to retained earnings, whereas distributions by a GmbH are permissible as long as the company retains assets the value of which corresponds to the nominal capital figure shown on the balance sheet, at least. On the other hand, German law is much stricter with respect to so-called disguised asset distributions, i.e., distributions by means of a contract that is unusually favorable to the shareholder, e.g., favorable intra-group transfer pricing. While German law – in line with the Second EC Directive on company law – completely prohibits disguised distributions by a stock corporation and limits such distributions by a GmbH in accordance with the balance sheet test, British law is probably much more lenient. In particular, the pending Company Law Reform Bill provides for two new sections – s. 275a and s. 280a – to be introduced in the Companies Act 1985 in order to remove the doubts to which the decision in *Aveling Barford Ltd.* v. *Perion Ltd.* [1989] BCLC 626 has given rise regarding when the transfer of an asset to a member amounts to a distribution. These new clauses preserve the position in the *Aveling Barford* case such that where a company that does not have distributable profits makes a distribution by way of a transfer of assets at undervalue, this will be an unlawful distribution. If, however, a company does have distributable profits, the amount of any distribution arising from the sale, transfer or other disposition of a non-cash asset to a member of the company should be calculated by reference to the "book value", i.e. if an asset is transferred for a consideration equal to its book value, the amount of the distribution is zero.[65]

9.1.2.2 The bottom-line test

Except for the Rickford Report, the internationally acknowledged bottom-line test for permissible distributions is a two-part distribution test. Leaving all important details aside, this adds up to the requirement that, immediately after a distribution has been made, the company's assets must still exceed its liabilities (net asset or balance sheet test) and that the company will be able, as a going concern, to meet its debts as they fall due for the foreseeable future (cash flow test). In contrast, the Rickford Report proposes having a two-part solvency test: short-term solvency and long-term solvency.[66]

Given the two-part distribution test, among the important "details" with respect to the net asset test is the valuation issue. The relevant question, phrased from the perspective of German law, is then whether the general principles and

---

65 Explanatory Notes Company Reform Law Bill [HL] as of 1 November 2005 [HL Billl 34] n. 1048 et seq.

66 Rickford Report, loc. cit. n. 6, at p. 979 et seq.; concurring: Ferran, op. cit. n. 35, at p. 29.

rules for preparing the annual accounts or, arguably, those for drawing up the balance sheet should govern whether a company has to file a petition in bankruptcy because of an excess of liabilities over assets. Another question is whether only to allow "open" distributions, i.e., in the main, dividend payments and share buy-backs, or also disguised distributions in the form, for example, of intra-group transactions based on centrally fixed transfer prices. From the perspective of the bottom-line test, the latter seems to be the case. Then, however, contrary to the recommendations of the High Level Group[67] and the Interdisciplinary Group on Capital Maintenance,[68] a lawful distribution of assets to shareholders cannot depend on the prior drawing up of a formal solvency statement. Compliance with a requirement to draw up a solvency statement for every intra-group transaction would not be possible in practice.

9.1.2.3 Providing for stricter limitations?

The economic rationale[69] for an even stricter limitation of admissible distributions is weak, at best.[70] If a company becomes insolvent for reasons other than an inadmissible distribution, the remaining assets will normally not cover its liabilities. By definition, this is true if insolvency law (also) applies a net asset test, i.e., if an excess of liabilities over assets triggers insolvency. Moreover, if a company lacks a profitable business model and/or a capable management, stricter limitations on the distribution of assets only work to the effect that it will take longer for the company to become insolvent. Creditors will still be hurt, even though that will be a different population of creditors.[71] Hence, the only relevant effect of any such stricter limitation is to lower the probability of a company's becoming insolvent because of an isolated exogenous shock. Whether this theoretical effect is also of practical importance is, however, difficult to ascertain. Statistical evidence is not available. Casual empiricism suggests that US companies are not significantly more prone to become insolvent because of exogenous shocks than their German counterparts.

---

[67] See *supra* n. 5 with accompanying text.

[68] Rickford Report, loc. cit. n. 6, at p. 972 et seq. and at p. 979 et seq.

[69] Qualifying the maintenance rules contained in the Second Directive (Art. 15) and the German Stock Corporation Act (s. 57 et seq.) as an optional collective guarantee against distributions that is provided by the shareholders (Schön, loc. cit. n. 37, at p. 440 et seq.) neither explains the underlying economic rationale nor the legal mechanism at work, since creditors will not obtain a direct (contractual?) claim against the shareholders. See also Merkt, loc. cit. n. 37, at p. 319 et seq.; ibid., loc. cit. n. 37, at p. 1055.

[70] As to the following, see Mülbert, loc. cit. n. 20, at p. 154 et seq.

[71] See also *supra* section 5.1.

Admittedly, creditors in the United States often impose financial covenants that provide for rules on the limitation of distributions by the company that are somewhat similar to the rules on distributions stipulated by the Second Company Law Directive.[72] Thus, the lack of statistical evidence could also be due to the fact that German companies and their US counterparts face similar restrictions, albeit imposed by different legal mechanisms. However, even if this explanation did hold true – which one may question anyhow, since financial covenants even in standardized form[73] were known in the US long before the Revised Model Business Corporation Act paved the way to the widespread abolition of legal capital[74] – it would not serve as an argument for mandatory limitations on the distribution of assets above the bottom-line test. Mandatory rules are only called for if private contracting would produce only less efficient solutions, e.g., because of prohibitive transaction costs or adverse selection problems. Since voluntary creditors of European companies are as free to impose financial covenants as creditors of US companies,[75] and since covenants are costly to contract and do not protect free-riding "weak" creditors as well as the party to the covenant,[76] the lack of statistical evidence on the superior welfare effects of statutory restrictions on distributions may even serve as an argument against mandatory rules providing for limitations beyond the bottom-line test just prescribed.

Involuntary creditors, such as tort creditors, on the other hand, are much better served by other approaches to creditor protection.[77] The most promising mechanism in this respect is compulsory third-party insurance,[78] offering the additional advantage of giving the company an incentive to reduce the riskiness of its business, whereas according tort creditors super-priority in bankruptcy proceedings will not offer a solution if the insolvent company is left without any assets anyway. Indeed, compulsory third-party insurance may even offer a superior solution with respect to weak creditors such as, e.g., employees or small savers. With respect to these weak creditors, even Germany did not rely on creditor protection by means of a comprehensive legal capital regime, but decided decades ago to introduce compulsory insurance for employees' pension benefit plans and deposit insurance.

---

72 See *supra* section 6.

73 Ibid.

74 Mülbert, loc. cit. n. 20, at p. 157.

75 Admittedly, in Europe, financial covenants did not see a widespread use in the domestic context, but changes may be under way even on the continent. See Kuhner, loc. cit. n. 30, at 785; Ferran, op. cit. n. 35, at p. 6, and the studies cited by them.

76 *Supra* section 6.

77 For a brief overview on possible mechanisms, see Hertig and Kanda, loc. cit. n. 10, at p. 77.

78 See in more detail, e.g., Armour, loc. cit. n. 16, at p. 372; Mülbert, loc. cit. n. 20, at p. 157.

Recently, some proponents of a German-style legal capital regime have resorted to a very different argument. Directors who are under pressure from shareholders to make a distribution will be in a much better position to withstand this pressure if they can point to a balance sheet test based on the traditional (conservative) accounting principles of the German Commercial Code (hereinafter, HGB) instead of to a solvency test, since limitations on distributions derived from German style balance sheet figures have been less prone to subjective interpretation or even manipulation,[79] and thus provide for more legal certainty.[80] However, to begin with, it still remains to be seen whether, in the future, German companies will still be allowed to draw up an individual company's balance sheet in accordance with the HGB principles, or whether the legislator will extend the use of the International Financial Reporting Standards (IFRS) from group level to that of individual companies. Moreover, very often, particularly in case of small companies which are dramatically more prone to become insolvent than large ones, the director(s) will be shareholders as well. Given such a structure, strengthening the position of directors towards shareholders is a pointless solution. Finally, above all, the argument does nothing to demonstrate that stricter limits on permissible distributions would be economically beneficial. At best, it implies that the net asset test component of a two-part distribution test should be based on the accounting rules and principles presently contained in the HGB[81] – and one may doubt even this conclusion, since less precise standards may cause shareholders to refrain from distributions in opaque situations thereby generating a higher level of creditor protection.[82]

The upshot, then, of the foregoing discussion is that mandatory restrictions for the distribution of company assets should be limited to a two-part distribution test. As a corollary, given such a simplified system of capital maintenance, any complicated rules on the raising of capital as, in particular, developed by the German Federal High Court, are dispensable, at least for the purpose of credit protection.

9.2 "Sufficient" working capital (undercapitalization)

The judge-made doctrine of piercing the corporate veil because of undercapitalization, from a functional perspective, aims at establishing a particular structure, namely a corporation having "sufficient" working capital in relation to its business

---

[79] Schön, loc. cit. n. 37, at p. 448 et seq.; cf., Rammert, loc. cit. n. 56, at p. 591.

[80] Providing for legal certainty is a paramount concern among German discussants, cf., Lutter, loc. cit. n. 56, at p. 377; Rüffler, loc. cit. n. 63, at p. 145 et seq. and at p. 148.

[81] For additional counterarguments, see Mülbert, loc. cit. n. 20, at p. 160 et seq.

[82] Kuhner, loc. cit. n. 30, at p. 778 et seq.

activities to lessen the probability of a company's becoming insolvent because of exogenous shocks. Hence, in parallel to the statutory mandated minimum capital requirement, courts may decide to lift the veil not only if, at any time after incorporation, the company's assets were manifestly insufficient with respect to its business activities, but also if the company's insufficient capital basis already existed at the time of incorporation.

Moreover, subsequent undercapitalization may not only result from losses the company incurred because of previous business activities, but also from a shift to a much riskier business strategy. Consider, for example, the case of a limited liability company that just meets the minimum capital requirement, but forms part of a well-known group, and engages in trading commodities to the extent of holding, at one (final) point in time, a bundle of commodity contracts, the volume of which exceeded €250 million. Obviously, such a shift to a far riskier business strategy may lead to undercapitalization as well. The company's working capital, even without suffering any decrease, will then be "insufficient" in relation to the company's business activities.

The pros and cons of piercing the veil because of undercapitalization have been widely discussed for a long time. To this day, the main counterargument results from the fact that there is no broad or even nearly universal consensus among economists (and lawyers) as to how to determine the working capital necessary for a given corporation. More to the point, the concept of "sufficient" working capital, prescribed by statutory law or derived from court decisions, is not workable – either in theory or in practice. Depending on the individual risk preference, shareholders who are more risk-averse will be given the incentive to inject excess capital, while those who are less risk-averse will still not inject enough capital to escape liability. In addition, even given a working capital that the courts or statutory provisions deem "sufficient", more risk-averse creditors, had they known about the true state of the company, would not have concluded a contract with the company or, at the very least, would have demanded a higher risk premium than the premium contracted. Conversely, those creditors who did know the actual amount of working capital available or who did not care to collect any pertinent information will benefit from a windfall profit if it comes to a piercing of the corporate veil.

Hence, the concept of "sufficient" working capital serves less to provide for reliable *ex ante* incentives for shareholders' behavior than to provide courts with a means for *ex post* intervention in extreme cases based on notions of fairness.[83] Up to now, the German Federal High Court has refrained from piercing the corporate

[83] Mülbert and Birke, loc. cit. n. 1, at p. 725.

veil because of a company's undercapitalization,[84] whereas British courts[85] and US courts, in particular, show somewhat less reserve in this regard. A superior alternative may be an obligation to disclose information on the working capital available on a more or less ongoing basis.[86]

9.3 Subordination of shareholder claims

Subordination of shareholder claims is a mechanism for creditor protection that has gained widespread acceptance only within the last three decades. Known as recharacterization in the United States, it is Germany that has developed the most complex set of rules and the most extensive practical experience with regard to subordination. In recent years, Austria, Italy, and Spain have followed the German example by introducing statutory provisions on subordination. On the other hand, to this day, British law provides for the possibility of subordination only as a consequence of fraudulent trading and wrongful trading, i.e., as a sanction against directors and not against shareholders as members of the company.[87]

9.3.1 *The German subordination regime*

German law on the subordination of shareholder claims comprises an intricate set of rules, or, to be more precise, two sets of rules.[88] This dualism has prevailed to this day because of the substantial differences between the two sets. Regarding the limited liability company, the German Federal High Court started to practice subordination in its present form in 1979, and the legislator, taking up judicial guidance, introduced statutory provisions on subordination already in 1980. However, since these provisions are less stringent than the court-made rules, the German Federal High Court, in a subsequent ruling, decided to apply both sets in

---

84 As to this, see W. Goette, *Die GmbH*, 2nd edn. (Munich, C.H. Beck 2002) p. 346, § 9 n. 45; M. Gehrlein, *GmbH-Recht in der Praxis* (Frankfurt am Main, Recht und Wirtschaft 2005) p. 378. However, among legal scholars, the doctrine is finding increasing acceptance. See, e.g., Habersack and Verse, loc. cit. n. 48, at p. 210 (with further references); *contra*, e.g., A. Hueck and L. Fastrich, '§ 5 n. 6', in A. Baumbach and A. Hueck, *GmbH-Gesetz*, 18th edn. (Munich, C.H. Beck 2006); H. Eidenmüller and A. Engert, 'Die angemessene Höhe des Grundkapitals', 50 *AG* (2005) p. 97 at p. 100; Vetter, loc. cit. n. 64, at p. 817 et seq.

85 See Davies, op. cit. n. 3, at p. 189.

86 See *supra* section 8.1.

87 For opposition to a subordination of shareholder claims in the British context, see Rickford Report, loc. cit. n. 6, at p. 985.

88 See, e.g., A. Hueck and L. Fastrich, 'Notes on §§ 32, 32b', in Baumbach and Hueck, op. cit. n. 84; M. Lutter and P. Hommelhoff, 'Notes on §§ 32, 32b', in ibid., *GmbH-Gesetz*, 16th edn. (Cologne, Dr. Otto Schmidt 2004).

parallel, instead of deferring to the legislator. Since then, the legislator has slightly amended the statutory provisions.[89] The resulting regime in its present form can be roughly sketched like this.

Both sets of rules apply if a shareholder of a limited liability company, as a rule, owns more than 10 percent of the membership rights, or if a shareholder of a stock corporation is not only a passive finance investor but pursues an entrepreneurial interest, i.e., if, as a rule, a shareholder owns at least 25 percent of stock. Transactions covered are a shareholder loan extended to the company but also equivalent financing techniques, i.e., if the shareholder refrains from cashing in a claim against that company that has fallen due (*Stehenlassen*), or if the shareholder supplies a security for the company's third-party credit financing. Moreover, said "transactions" must have occurred while the company was in financial distress (*Krise*), or, to be more precise, at a time when the company is not in a position to obtain credit from unrelated third parties at arm's length conditions, and subsequently, the company must not have left the zone of financial distress.

Given these facts, the consequences vary according to the exact set of rules in question. The *statutory* provisions do provide for subordination in insolvency proceedings (s. 39(1)(5) Insolvency Act) of any claims that result from said "transactions" but do no prohibit the repayment of a subordinated claim before the opening of insolvency proceedings by the court. However, they entitle the liquidator to mount a challenge to the repayment and to recover the funds on behalf of the company's assets if the repayment occurred during the time of the company being in financial distress (*Krise*); as a corollary, the fraudulent transfer act enables such a challenge to be mounted on behalf of creditors when formal insolvency proceedings do not take place.

The *court-made* provisions do not only provide for subordination (s. 39(1)(5) Insolvency Act), but also prohibit any repayment as long as the company is in financial distress. They even entitle the company to recover any paybacks on subordinated loans that occurred during the last five years. On the other hand, in contrast to the situation under the statute, the prohibition on repayments and the possibility to recover pertinent paybacks is limited. The court-made rules apply only insofar as, because of the (intended) repayment, the value of the company's remaining assets is (will be) less than the nominal capital figure shown on the balance sheet.[90]

---

[89] The relevant provisions are currently ss. 32a, 32b Limited Liability Company Act (GmbHG), ss. 39(1)(5), 135 Insolvency Act, and s. 6 Fraudulent Transfer Act (*Anfechtungsgesetz*).

[90] The limitation results from the court's approach to derive the rules on subordination from ss. 30 and 31 of the Limited Liability Act, i.e., the statutory provisions on distributions. See *infra* section 9.1.2.1 on the statutory restrictions for distributions under s. 30 of the Act.

To this day, the entrenched German Federal High Court notwithstanding, doubts as to the merits of subordination do persist. Criticism is leveled at the Court's insistence to apply the court-made rules alongside the statutory provisions[91] and at the arguments employed by the Court to justify these rules. In addition, the legal rationale,[92] as well as the economic rationale,[93] is still contested. With respect to latter, some even question whether a valid economic rationale for subordination exists at all.[94] In part, at least, even the German legislator seems to concur. In 1998, it amended section 32a of the Limited Liability Company Act (GmbHG) to the effect that claims of shareholders who own 10 percent or less of the GmbH and who do not hold the office of a director are exempt from subordination and that even a general exemption applies if the creditor acquires shares to operate a financial reorganization of the company. Finally, as a kind of collateral damage caused by the above-mentioned three decisions of the European Court of Justice – *Centros*, *Überseering* and *Inspire Art* – German lawyers are currently debating whether the two sets of rules form part of company law or insolvency law.[95] Arguably, the first is true for the court-made rules, whereas the statutory provisions contained in the Limited Liability Act should probably be qualified as insolvency law.

9.3.2 *The economic rationale*

The comprehensive German rules on subordination and, indeed, probably all of the existing subordination regimes are not to be explained by a single rationale but require a two-part explanation.

---

[91] See, e.g., L. Fastrich, 'Ketzerisches zur sogenannten Finanzierungsverantwortung', in M. Lieb, et al., eds., *Festschrift für Wolfgang Zöllner*, Vol. I (Cologne, Carl Heymanns 1999) p. 143 at p. 159; T. Bezzenberger, 'Kapitalersetzende Gesellschafterdarlehen im Recht der GmbH', in H.P. Westermann, et al., eds., *Festschrift für Gerold Bezzenberger* (Berlin, de Gruyter 2000) p. 23 at p. 45; Grunewald and Noack, loc. cit. n. 58, at p. 194.

[92] For a brief discussion of the different arguments submitted, see A. Cahn, 'Gesellschafterfremdfinanzierung und Eigenkapitalersatz', 50 *AG* (2005) p. 217 at p. 218 et seq.

[93] See, e.g., Cahn, loc. cit. n. 92, at p. 222 et seq.; A. Engert, 'Die ökonomische Begründung der Grundsätze ordnungsgemäßer Unternehmensführung', 33 *ZGR* (2004) p. 813 at p. 816 et seq., cf., Bezzenberger, loc. cit. n. 91, at p. 38 et seq.

[94] See, e.g., Eidenmüller, op. cit. n. 37, at p. 389 et seq.; Bezzenberger, loc. cit. n. 91, at p. 34 et seq.

[95] See, e.g., Röhricht, loc. cit. n. 54, at p. 505 et seq.: U. Haas, 'Der Normzweck des Eigenkapitalersatzrechts', 4 *NZI* (*Neue Zeitschrift für Insolvenzrecht*) (2001) p. 1 et seq.; J. Oechsler, 'Der Kapitalersatz als Kreditsicherheit', 169 *ZHR* (2005) p. 61 at p. 62 et seq.; K. Schmidt, 'Vom Eigenkapitalersatz in der Krise zur Krise des Eigenkapitalersatzrechts? Betrachtungen zu §§ 32a, b GmbHG, §§ 129a, 172a HGB, §§ 39, 135 InsO', 96 *GmbHR* (2005) p. 797 at p. 805 et seq.

9.3.2.1 Restrictions on repayments of shareholders loans

Restrictions on repayments of shareholders loans, be it an outright prohibition or a fraudulent transfer control, i.e., provisions that enable a challenge to be mounted in favor of the company's assets or in favor of creditors, serve to prevent opportunistic behavior by shareholders, often based on inside information. Shareholders who know or have reason to suspect, at least, that the company is approaching insolvency are prevented from realizing their claims as creditors ahead of other creditors. Moreover, when the company is in distress, any repayment will act as a further drain on its liquidity and will push it closer to insolvency. Thus, restrictions on repayments serve to eliminate shareholders' informational advantages over other creditors. In addition, if shareholders are not in a position to realize their claims ahead of other creditors, thereby aggravating the company's liquidity problems, the company's probability of insolvency will be slightly lower. To achieve these economically beneficial effects, private contracting is not readily available, since private ordering would require an agreement between shareholders and all other creditors.

Admittedly, for this mechanism to be fully effective, an *ex post* fraudulent transfer control does not suffice.[96] This would even hold true if one were to extend the possibility to mount a challenge to all repayments to shareholders that have occurred within the last year or even two to three years before insolvency or, under the German system, before the filing of a petition in bankruptcy.[97] Instead, repayment of shareholder's credit financing must be prohibited as long as the company is in financial distress. Otherwise, shareholders would be even more strongly incentivized to obtain a repayment and hope for the best, i.e., that the liquidator or the creditors will not take note of the transaction or that they will not be willing or able to enforce repayment, and so forth.

9.3.2.2 Subordination as such

Subordination as such presents a far more difficult case to justify. Obviously, other creditors will benefit, since, because of subordination, they will receive (slightly) higher dividend payouts. Given this, one may argue that the differential will compensate those shareholders, at least in part, for any losses they suffered from a reduction of the dividend due to the fact that the financially distressed company, because of shareholder credit financing, was able to continue its business activities somewhat longer before becoming insolvent.

---

[96] *Contra*, e.g., Fastrich, loc. cit. n. 91, at p. 157; Bezzenberger, loc. cit. n. 91, at p. 49 et seq.
[97] In favor of such a one-year claw-back solution, e.g., Röhricht, loc. cit. n. 54, at p. 513.

However, this line of reasoning offers, at best, an *ex post* rationalization when the company, despite a shareholder loan, goes bankrupt anyway, but does nothing to explain the economic effects in the case of a successful reorganization of the company. Indeed, any meaningful explanation must concentrate on the *ex ante* incentives of subordination for shareholders as potential creditors (and for other creditors).

To begin with, the *ex ante* incentives resulting from the threat of future subordination are often small anyway, if the company, upon insolvency, is only left with negligible assets or even no assets at all. In the case of the German GmbH, this is true for around 50 percent of all companies going bankrupt. Admittedly, some shareholders of such companies may even have been apprehensive of subordination. But still, it does seem fair to assume that, in a fair number of cases, the threat of subordination does not operate as an effective deterrent.

Apart from that, for at least two reasons, shareholders will often be willing to extend credit to the company, even though third-party creditors are no longer willing to take the risk: informational asymmetries and different incentive structures. Shareholders as insiders will sometimes be in a position to identify options for a company's successful reorganization that third parties will not. In addition, shareholders face a different incentive structure from third-party creditors. In contrast to the latter, they will not only benefit from a successful reorganization in the form of interest paid by the company, but also from their stake in the company gaining in value. Thus, their upside in a successful reorganization is much higher than that of other creditors. Conversely, they will be willing to extend credit to the company under more favorable conditions, i.e., at lower interest rates, than third parties and/or given a higher risk of insolvency.

Against this backdrop, some consider subordination as an effective mechanism for creditor protection by arguing that subordination helps to control shareholders' preference for the company to take on ever more risk in the vicinity of insolvency.[98] Because of the threat of subordination, shareholders will sometimes decide not to extend credit at all, or, at least, they will prefer the company to pursue less risky business projects than otherwise, thereby reducing the probability of default.

However, consider an alternative scenario. Shareholders are interested in maximizing the expected payoff from extending credit to the company. Now, since subordination will result in a lower (nil!) payout to shareholders if the company does become insolvent, *ex ante* they may prefer to allow the company to take on even more risk. Thus, *ex ante*, the lower payoff in insolvency will be compensated for by a higher payoff in case of a successful reorganization. If this

---

98 See, e.g., Cahn, loc. cit. n. 92, at p. 223; cf., Engert, loc. cit. n. 93, at p. 825 et seq.

scenario were true, subordination would incentivize shareholders to pursue even riskier strategies than without subordination.

The actual strategy chosen by shareholder-creditors will depend on their appetite for risk. At all events, it is submitted here that the overall *ex ante* incentives of subordination are, at best, difficult to discern and may even be harmful. Thus, subordination of shareholder claims in insolvency is dispensable and should even be discarded.[99] Highly recommendable, however, is a ban on any repayment of a shareholder loan while the company is in financial distress, regardless of the company's financial position when the shareholder extended the credit.[100]

9.4 Controlling other forms of opportunistic behavior

Distributions of a company's assets to shareholders, continuing to do business without "sufficient" working capital, be it because of previous losses or a shift to a much riskier business strategy, and the repayment of a shareholder loan while the company is in a crisis are prime examples of opportunistic behavior that, if unchecked, may result in causing a company to become financially distressed, even to the point of insolvency. However, from the point of view of creditors, other forms of opportunistic behavior do still exist, for example a commingling of assets or a transfer of assets to related parties on favorable terms, i.e., not at arm's length. Jurisdictions will often control this type of behavior either by invoking the doctrine of piercing the veil and tort law, respectively, or by means of insolvency law, i.e., provisions on fraudulent transfers.

9.5 Disqualification of directors

Disqualification of directors, although known in many EU Member States, is currently most extensively used under British law.[101] Directors are banned by a court injunction or an administrative order for a certain length of time from taking up a management position in a company with limited liability if they have violated a varying number of statutory prohibitions or requirements designed to protect corporate creditors. Hence, disqualification of directors cuts in two ways: as an *ex post* sanction for past violations and as a preemptive mechanism for creditor protection.

---

[99] In the same sense, Bezzenberger, loc. cit. n. 91, at p. 43 et seq.

[100] In addition, it follows from the analysis presented here that subordination of shareholder claims does not serve as a functional equivalent to piercing the veil because of undercapitalization. But see Goette, loc. cit. n. 54, at p. 198.

[101] See, e.g., Davies, op. cit. n. 3, at p. 211 et seq.

Precisely because of this, the costs and benefits of disqualification are particularly difficult to assess. If disqualification is geared towards an optimal level of deterrence, it may well result in a suboptimal, i.e., too far-reaching, exclusion of former directors from the future management of companies. This is a particularly thorny issue, since disqualification, in order to be effective, would have to extend to persons who, on the basis of their influence as shareholders, acted as *de facto* directors and, in addition, would have to prohibit violators from taking up a position in a company that would allow them to act as *de facto* directors. Thus, if a company form like the German GmbH allows shareholders to issue binding directives to the directors, effective disqualification would even require a violator to be barred from becoming a (dominant?) shareholder in such a company. Finally, as recent British experience has shown, whether disqualification will be an effective mechanism depends crucially on whether the State is willing to make the necessary funds available for a comprehensive enforcement effort.[102]

On balance, even from a purely economic perspective, any enthusiasm shown towards introducing more extensive provisions on disqualification seems premature, at best.[103]

10. Reducing the Risks of Existing Creditors from a Company's Being Financially Distressed

Minimizing potential losses of existing creditors is a further building block for efficient creditor protection by means of mandatory rules. In this respect, two basic intertwined questions of strategy merit closer inspection, in particular: at what point in time should mandatory rules intervene in the interest of existing creditors, and to what effect? Both questions are closely related to the above discussion of mandatory disclosure in the vicinity of insolvency.[104] Hence, in this context as well, the juxtaposition of British law and German law helps to identify the core problems. The salient features are recalled below.

British law does not stipulate a duty of the directors or the shareholders to file a petition in bankruptcy if the company is formally bankrupt. Instead, the provisions on fraudulent trading (s. 213 IA) and on wrongful trading (s. 214 IA), in particular, aim at inducing the directors to choose a future course of action with respect to the company that will minimize the losses of existing creditors. The obligation under section 214 comes into play already "when there is no reasonable prospect that the company would avoid going into insolvent liquidation," i.e.,

---

102 See Hertig and Kanda, loc. cit. n. 10, at p. 97 n. 148.
103 In the same sense, Fleischer, loc. cit. n. 44, at p. 413 et seq.
104 *Supra* section 8.2.

even before formal insolvency. Moreover, in the vicinity of insolvency, directors are under an obligation at common law to act in the interest of the creditors as a group[105] at the expense of the shareholders, the protection required varying according to the severity of the threat. This obligation does not serve as a basis for individual creditors' claims against directors[106] but opens up the possibility of challenges at common law, on creditors' behalf, to dispositions of the company's assets by the directors when insolvency is in prospect, even though the distributions have been approved by the shareholders.[107]

In contrast, German law does require the directors to file a petition in bankruptcy without undue delay, i.e., within three weeks at the latest,[108] if the company is insolvent either according to a balance sheet test (excess of liabilities over assets) or a cash flow test (permanent inability to pay). Moreover, once the company is insolvent according to one of these two tests, directors are forbidden to make any payments "except for payments which even after the occurrence of insolvency or over-indebtedness are consistent with the care of a diligent and conscientious manager."[109] On the other hand, with the exception of the tort standard established by section 826 of the *Bürgerliches Gesetzbuch* not to act intentionally *contra bones mores*, German law does not recognize any pre-insolvency duties towards the creditors as a group or even towards existing creditors as individuals. Admittedly, one seeming exception is the doctrine called *"Existenzvernichtungshaftung"* recently developed by the German Federal High Court, i.e., personal liability of shareholders towards creditors if shareholders divest the company of assets and if, as a consequence of the asset transfer caused by the shareholders, the company's liabilities exceed its assets.[110] However, upon closer inspection, this doctrine boils down to holding shareholders personally liable for a particular set of distributions prohibited anyway by capital maintenance rules:[111] distributions that (i) impose damages on the company that are not

---

105 See, e.g., Davies, op. cit. n. 3, at p. 372 et seq. This is also true for US corporations, see M.M. Sheinfeld and J.H. Pippitt, 'Fiduciary Duties of Directors of a Corporation in the Vicinity of Insolvency and after Initiation of a Bankruptcy Case', 60 *Business Lawyer* (2004) p. 79 at p. 88 et seq. (brief overview). Cf., Fleischer, loc. cit. n. 44, at p. 394 et seq.

106 See Hirt, loc. cit. n. 30, at p. 82 (with further references).

107 See, e.g., Davies, op. cit. n. 3, p. 372 et seq.

108 *Supra* n. 41 and accompanying text.

109 S. 64(2) Limited Liability Company Act (GmbHG), s. 92(3) German Stock Corporation Act.

110 BGH 17 September 2001, II ZR 178/99, 55 *WM* (2001) p. 2062 (*Bremer Vulkan*); BGH 24 June 2002, II ZR 300/00, 56 *WM* (2002) p. 1804 (*KBV*); BGH 25 February 2002, II ZR 196/00, 56 *WM* (2002) p. 960; BGH 13 December 2004, II ZR 206/02, 59 *WM* (2005) p. 176 et seq.; BGH 13 December 2004, II ZR 256, 59 *WM* (2005) p. 332 et seq.

111 Cf., Röhricht, loc. cit. n. 54, at p. 514 (the doctrine would suffice to make German capital maintenance rules completely superfluous) and at p. 515. However, some uncertainty

quantifiable and (ii) cause the company to become insolvent. Contrary to scholars' suggestions,[112] the doctrine does not extend to excessive risk taking instigated by shareholders.

Obviously, British law and German law pursue different strategies with respect to *ex post* creditor protection in the vicinity of insolvency. German law is geared towards creating legal certainty for the directors, at least as far as possible. Directors must know with as much certainty as possible when they have to act in the creditors' interest, instead of in the company's and its shareholders' interest. To this end, the law provides for insolvency as the event triggering the directors' obligation to act in the interest of creditors by prohibiting any payments except those required even despite insolvency. This holds true despite the well-known fact that creditors will (almost) invariably be hurt since, with the advent of insolvency, the valuation of a company's assets will no longer be based upon the going concern premise. Legal certainty prevails over efficient creditor protection.

British law, on the other hand, emphasizes the function of mandatory rules to minimize the losses of existing creditors at the expense of legal certainty.[113] Even before insolvency, directors are under the obligation to avoid harming existing creditors as far as possible. Seen from this perspective, suggestions for amending British law to the effect that directors have to act in the interest of creditors, when it is "more likely than not" that the company would at some point become unable to pay its debts as they fall due, were fully compatible with the philosophy of British law in this area.

A comparison of the approach chosen by British law and by German law in terms of a partial cost-benefit analysis may well lead to the conclusion that, at least in theory, the British approach may produce superior economic welfare effects.[114] In particular, the British approach may be construed to directly address the aforementioned problem that, upon approaching insolvency, companies will choose a (far) riskier business strategy, since rational shareholders will perceive such a shift as being beneficial to them. Admittedly, this interpretation crucially depends on whether a director's duty to act in the interest of creditors kicks in

---

does exist as to which transactions do fall within the ambit of the term contribution, see, e.g., Grigoleit, op. cit. n. 3, at p. 86 et seq.

112 P.O. Mülbert, 'Abschied von der TBB-Haftungsregel für den qualifiziert faktischen Konzern', 39 *DStR* (2001) p. 1937 at p. 1942; G.H. Roth, 'Gläubigerschutz durch Existenzschutz', 6 *NZG* (2003) p. 1081 at p. 1082 et seq.; cf., W. Schön, 'Zur "Existenzvernichtung" der juristischen Person', 168 *ZHR* (2004) p. 268 at p. 289 et seq. But see Vetter, loc. cit. n. 64, at p. 815 et seq. (doctrine should not be extended to serve as an all-purpose remedy).

113 With regard to the difficulties in construing the term "no reasonable prospect of avoiding insolvent liquidation", see Hirt, loc. cit. n. 30, at p. 104 et seq.

114 For a very critical assessment, see Habersack and Verse, loc. cit. n. 48, at p. 206 et seq. However, their main concern is that the wrongful trading rule is at odds with important elements and even with the whole structure of the German creditor protection regime.

even before the company becomes formally insolvent, but, as already mentioned, British case law is ambivalent, at best, with respect to this problem.[115] Moreover, building on the wrongful trading concept instead of a director's duty to file a petition in bankruptcy opens up the way to a (private) out-of-court workout even for those companies that are formally insolvent due to an excess of liabilities over assets (balance sheet test). Coupling this possibility with a very lenient petition right for creditors under section 123 IA – default with an undisputed debt of over £750 suffices to prove insolvency[116] – may indeed provide superior incentives for directors to act in the interest of creditors, as opposed to the reliance of German law on a director's duty to file a petition in bankruptcy.

On the other hand, the different approaches under British and German law can be understood as a prime example of the oft-noted standards v. rules contrast between British and German company law. Thus, the two mechanisms, established by British law and German law, respectively, are maybe more strongly path-dependent solutions than even legal capital and its absence, respectively. This observation implies first looking for complementary features within a particular jurisdiction's creditor protection regime, each reinforcing the effects of the other, before comparing different creditor protection regimes. While two such complementary mechanisms – undercapitalization[117] and subordination of shareholder claims[118] – have already been discussed above, the interrelation among the three will be considered below in some detail.[119]

11. Civil Liability of Directors and Shareholders

11.1 General observations

The most widely used mechanism for enforcing creditor protection is civil liability or, to be more precise, a variety of mandatory rules prescribing the civil liability of directors and/or shareholders.

Civil liability may serve to enforce the preventive disclosure obligations discussed above, in particular those in the vicinity of insolvency.[120] In addition, civil

---

115 *Infra* section 8.2.2, at n. 48 et seq.

116 As to the petition right under s. 123 IA, see A. Schall, 'The UK Limited Company Abroad – How Foreign Creditors are Protected after Inspire Art (Including a Comparison of UK and German Creditor Protection Rules)', 16 *EBLR* (2005) p. 1534 at. p. 1538 et seq. However, to attribute the "genius of British creditor protection law" mainly to the petition right is probably an overstatement.

117 *Supra* section 9.2.

118 *Supra* section 9.3.

119 *Infra* section 12.

120 *Supra* section 8.

liability may serve to impede directors and shareholders from causing the company to act opportunistically towards its creditors. The latter function begs the question as to whom to hold liable if the corporation acts opportunistically towards its creditors. As a rule of thumb, this will be the person(s) that caused the company's opportunistic behavior, regardless of whether that person is a director or a shareholder. *Inter alia*, this concept underlies the notions of a shadow director and a *de facto* director, respectively, which are known in many jurisdictions.

In order to protect creditors effectively, these rules on civil liability should satisfy some well-known requirements of a more general nature, e.g., the elements of the rule should be clearly specified and be easily observable in reality. In addition, creditor protection by means of liability rules also raises some specific issues. Here below, some of these are taken up briefly.

11.2 Direct liability towards creditors

11.2.1 *Direct liability as an exceptional solution*

Arguably, directors' or shareholders' direct liability towards creditors should mainly be considered if the company is insolvent, or, to be more precise, if the company's liabilities exceed its assets. Given any other situation, and that includes even an illiquid company, creditors will still be able to recover the total amount due to them. However, even in the case of insolvency, one may want to question whether direct liability is the appropriate solution. Creditors who hold direct claims against either the directors or the shareholders will be favored, since they do not have to be content with the results of a *pro rata* distribution of the debtor's assets in formal insolvency proceedings. Hence, one may want to go even further by limiting creditors' direct claims against directors and/or shareholders to either of two situations: (i) when insolvency proceedings aimed at the *pro rata* distribution of the corporation's remaining assets do not take place; (ii) when direct liability (of directors) results precisely from the fact that new creditors were not prevented from entering into a contractual relationship with a (nearly) insolvent company or from the fact that existing creditors suffered a loss because the directors, at the time when the company became (nearly) insolvent, failed to take the appropriate action, e.g., failed to file a petition in bankruptcy.

Admittedly, for different reasons, both exceptions are far from universally accepted.[121] The first exception depends on whether it is possible for the

---

[121] For an in-depth analysis under German law, see J. Meyer, *Haftungsbeschränkung im Recht der Handelsgesellschaften* (Berlin, Springer 2000) p. 1017 et seq.; G. Bitter, 'Der Anfang vom Ende des "qualifiziert faktischen Konzerns" – Ansätze einer allgemeinen Missbrauchshaftung in der Rechtsprechung des BGH', 55 *WM* (2001) p. 2133 at p. 2137 et seq.

shareholders as a whole – be it just a question of a single shareholder or all of the shareholders acting in unison – to violate the company's interests and, thus, became liable towards the company. If a jurisdiction does not recognize this concept, it will indeed be very difficult to avoid the conclusion that, from the outset, only a direct claim by a creditor against a shareholder can exist.

The second exemption, for example, is contested between German and British law. German law provides for a direct claim for compensation of damages against the directors who fail to file a petition in bankruptcy, whereas the British provision on wrongful trading (s. 214 IA) provides for the liability of directors towards the corporation for an indeterminate amount.

11.2.2 *Determining the directly liable person*

Admitting direct liability for even some exceptional situations begs the follow-up question as to the persons who are directly liable towards the creditors: the directors, the shareholders, or both? For various reasons, the creditor-friendly solution of making both groups liable will not be the preferred one. Instead, the principle will be to hold that person liable who is ultimately responsible for checking that the creditor risk in question will not materialize. Hence, at least in general, the internal distribution of competences and responsibilities between directors and shareholders will also determine who is externally liable towards creditors. The internal distribution of competences and responsibilities, in turn, will be determined by law or by the articles of association.

11.2.3 *Consequences of unlawful distributions in particular*

As a general principle, directors and shareholders will be liable towards the company only if they have violated their own duties. Against this backdrop, the unlawful open (dividend payments) or disguised distribution of assets to shareholders raises some intricate questions.

First, do shareholders have to return unlawful distributions, in particular dividend payments? Regarding dividends, the answer may very well vary according to whether or not the company's shares are publicly traded, i.e., whether or not the company is listed. Moreover, even given a non-listed company, shareholders should not be obliged to return any dividend payments if they acted in good faith, i.e., if they neither knew nor ought to have known that the distribution was unlawful. With respect to disguised distributions, one may well want to apply a stricter standard, i.e., strict liability, regardless of whether the company in question is listed or not.

Second, will shareholders be held liable for any damage caused by the unlawful open or disguised distribution of assets? In contrast to the question just mentioned, the answer should probably not depend on whether or not the company is listed, even if the problem will normally be more acute with non-listed ones. However, shareholders should only be liable if they acted negligently, at least by causing the company (through its directors) to make the distribution. If the damage caused by a shareholder-induced distribution of assets of the company cannot be assessed with any certainty, for example if the shareholder appropriated a corporate opportunity, compensation can either take the form of unlimited liability towards the company or a piercing of the corporate veil. The German Federal High Court, for example, has chosen the second solution, i.e., direct liability of a shareholder towards the company's creditors, if, as a consequence of the asset transfer caused by the shareholder, the company's liabilities exceed its assets (*Existenzvernichtungshaftung*).[122]

12. THE RESULTING FRAMEWORK

The above discussion sought to elaborate a high-level framework for the design of an efficient system of mandatory rules for creditor protection. Hence, the finer structure of European company law and, *a fortiori*, of any particular jurisdiction had to be left aside. In particular, no attempt has been made to qualify any of the rules discussed as being necessarily a part of, for example, company law, tort law, or insolvency law. Admittedly, those and other questions are important on the level of individual jurisdictions because they have far-reaching implications for the practical effectiveness of creditor protection rules. Obviously, those rules must fit the legal environment in which they are supposed to operate, i.e., in the case of EU companies operating in another Member State, first and foremost the restrictions ensuing from Article 43 et seq. of the EC Treaty to guarantee the freedom of establishment. On the other hand, precisely for this reason, the decisions as to how to implement the suggested framework and how to flesh out the details of a creditor protection regime must still be left to each jurisdiction.

The high-level framework for creditor protection ensuing from the preceding analysis is less lean than economists may care for, and much leaner than (practicing) lawyers might wish for. This can be explained by three reasons, at least:

- Corporations enjoying the benefit of limited liability operate, by and large, along similar principles in major jurisdictions, and, as a corollary, creditors face roughly the same risks when entering into a contractual or non-contractual relationship with the company: informational asymmetries and *ex post* opportunism due to directors and/or shareholders.

---

[122] *Supra* n. 110 et seq. with accompanying text.

- Since the existing variety of mechanisms for creditor protection among different jurisdictions must be understood as an answer to particular risks of creditors, the basic mechanisms for creditor protection show, by and large, similar characteristics. Obviously, this is not to negate the existence of substantial divergences among different jurisdictions, e.g., between British law and German law. However, the extent of any difference is greatest at the micro level of particular rules, i.e., whether a jurisdiction relies more on company law, tort law, or insolvency law for creditor protection, not with respect to the risks covered.
- Within a particular jurisdiction, overlapping, i.e., creditor protection by multiple mechanisms against a specific risk caused by the behavior of directors or shareholders, does exist but is less common than one might suspect. Rather, different mechanisms address different types of risks and, thus, are mostly complementary instead of redundant. As a consequence, any systemic approach to developing a creditor protection regime will have to identify (i) the relevant creditor risks and their causes; (ii) the extent to which creditors are to be protected by mandatory rules against these risks; and (iii) the mechanisms available for controlling these risks.

Following this approach, the article first identified the realm of creditor self-help, which, with respect to "weak" creditors, seems to be much smaller than often posited or suspected. This finding is of pivotal importance since, theoretically at least, large creditors are able to write and impose covenants that replicate most of the statutory provisions and judge-made rules on creditor protection. However, even large creditors refrain from such a complete contracts approach. Moreover, they do impose covenants, not with a view to enforcing the contracted behavior in the event of the debtor's non-compliance, but with a non-altruistic view to being entitled to prematurely realize their claims.

This observation opens up the way to justifying and even necessitating mandatory protective rules, even with respect to voluntary creditors. *Ex ante* protection, i.e., protection against entering into an initially disadvantageous contract, will often be far less pronounced than protection against *ex post* opportunism. In view of the paper's goal to present a "synthetic view of different concepts of creditor protection", the most important insight from the discussion of different mechanisms for controlling *ex post* opportunism, be it due to the behavior of directors or shareholders, is the problem of controlling the shareholders' preference for the company to pursue a riskier business strategy in the vicinity of insolvency. Legal capital, as well as any limitations on distributions that exist independently from legal capital, will not offer substantive protection. Instead, three mechanisms emerged as possible candidates: the piercing of the corporate veil because of undercapitalization, the subordination of shareholder claims, and the wrongful trading concept. However, upon closer inspection, neither the piercing of the veil nor subordination will achieve the desired effect of chilling shareholders' propensity to opt for a riskier business strategy.[123] Instead, at first glance, the wrongful trading remedy seems to be a promising mechanism. However, directors will benefit from the corporation's taking on more risk only if they are shareholders, as well. Otherwise, for the wrongful trading mechanism to be effective, "pure" shareholders must also be reached, e.g., either by treating influential shareholders as *de facto* directors or by explicitly extending the rule to those shareholders that take management decisions.

Whether, as a further facet of the systemic approach, the British concept of wrongful trading is compatible with a regime, e.g., German law, that, upon insolvency, requires the directors to file a petition in bankruptcy, will have to be examined elsewhere in more detail.[124] After all, the present paper has only aimed to establish a high-level framework for efficient corporate creditor protection.

---

[123] Thus, contrary to A. Schall, 'Englischer Gläubigerschutz bei der Limited in Deutschland', 26 *ZIP* (2005) p. 965 at p. 971, equitable subordination is not a functional equivalent to the wrongful trading remedy.

[124] Compatibility is contested, e.g., by Röhricht, loc. cit. n. 54, at p. 515; Habersack and Verse, loc. cit. n. 48, at pp. 174, 187, and 213. For a preliminary corroboration of this finding, see *infra* section 10, at n. 116.

Different Policies for Corporate Creditor Protection

Francesco Denozza*

Abstract
Rules on corporate creditor protection are asymmetric rules. Rules which could increase the welfare of one class of creditors could at the same time reduce the welfare of another class. Different classes of creditors often coincide with different social groups (unskilled workers, small trade creditors, etc.). As we do not have an universally accepted social welfare function, the results of the comparisons between gains and losses caused by each rule are, in terms of overall welfare (efficiency), indeterminate. In conclusion, the choice of the best system of creditor protection is not a matter of efficiency but of fairness and political judgments. From this viewpoint, many arguments can support the preference for a rule (the net system with its formal test) rather *than a more flexible standard.*

Keywords: corporate creditor protection rules, welfare, fairness, symmetric and asymmetric rules, the net system, rules versus standards.

1. First premise: not a question of efficiency but a question of fairness and political judgement

I would like to begin by fixing two premises. The first is that, in my opinion, the available theoretical and empirical knowledge with regard to the effects of

* Professore ordinario di diritto commerciale nell'Università degli Studi di Milano.

creditor protection rules does not allow us to establish whether one system of creditor protection is more, or less, efficient (efficiency meaning the ability to increase overall welfare) than another one. Consequently, such a thing as 'efficient creditor protection' (meaning a set of rules that maximises the overall welfare of all creditors or even the whole of society) does not exist or at least cannot be identified (which for all practical purposes is one and the same thing).

First and foremost, we must take into account the fact that creditor protection rules have relevant distributive effects. When a debtor becomes insolvent, we face a zero-sum game in which certain creditors gain at the expense of other creditors. This phenomenon is already made clear through the examination of even the simplest of problems that a system of creditor protection is requested to solve, namely that of defining the moment when a company's activity must be brought to a standstill in order to prevent the company's economic situation from worsening.

Let us consider two different systems, one which uses a trigger mechanism, obliging a company's managers to bring to a standstill the corporate activity at time *t*, and one in which the mechanism usually triggers later on, at time *t'*. It could easily be presumed that the distribution of the overall debt of a company at time *t'* will be different from that existing at time *t*. For example, we could speculate that in the time-period from *t* to *t'*, creditors more skilled at monitoring (e.g., certain banks) would succeed in being – partially – repaid (or at least succeed in getting rid of the debtor's bonds), while the debts towards other creditors (e.g., small trade creditors) during the same time period continue to accumulate and other debts (e.g., towards employees) that did not exist at time *t* arise.

In cases such as these (i.e., in cases where rules increase the welfare of some people while at the same time reducing the welfare of others), we need to consider whether we are confronted with symmetric or asymmetric rules. Under the first alternative, we can ignore the rules' distributive effect. Symmetric rules are the rules that govern relationships between individuals who find themselves in either one of a pair of opposite roles (e.g., injurer/victim, debtor/creditor, etc.) exactly one time each. In this reciprocal context, each individual is once a victim (a creditor, etc.) and once an injurer (a debtor, etc.). In a case such as this, we have no relevant distributive problem *ex ante*. Asymmetric rules are the rules that govern relationships between individuals who belong to completely separate social groups.

Creditors' protection rules are, in my opinion, asymmetric rules. Creditors have different attitudes, beliefs and interests. Therefore, the same rule can have different effects on the welfare of different groups of creditors. Furthermore, we are not only discussing a matter of differences among the various kinds of credit sources (the well-known distinction between voluntary and involuntary creditors) but also a matter of a difference in the ability to contract the terms of the debt and control the coming into existence of – or the exit from – the debt/credit relationship. What is more, even among creditors of the same class differences exist which influence the distributive effects of the chosen system. For example, in the case of bondholders we must take into consideration the fact that they have different capacities in perceiving the worsening of a debtor's condition in a timely manner. A phenomenon that is dramatically exemplified in Italy by the vicissitudes of the Parmalat bonds, which were palmed off for a rather long time by banks and other sophisticated investors on small unsophisticated savers before the market price could reflect the bad economic conditions of the company.

In the zero-sum game created by the insolvency of the debtor, rules that offer better protection to creditors able to contract the terms of the debt – or to creditors more skilful in monitoring – inevitably harm the less powerful and less skilful creditors. It seems to me quite evident that a legal regime compelling a debtor to stop all activity before the appearance of any external symptom of insolvency grants the most sophisticated creditors less possibilities of exploiting their monitoring ability by, for example, reducing the amount of their credit, obtaining a collateral or getting rid of a debtor's bond. Relaxing the system of directorial duties towards all creditors (a system which usually ensures an equal treatment of all creditors) inevitably has the consequence that creditors will be satisfied in proportion to their ability to protect themselves *not only against the debtor's opportunism, but also – and especially – against the other classes of creditors.*

Therefore, what might increase the welfare of a class of creditors (let us say, the most sophisticated and most powerful class) could at the same time reduce the welfare of another class of creditors. The relevant point here is that power and skill are not randomly distributed among all creditors. We cannot simply assume that every creditor always has the same probability of finding himself in the role of the most powerful or in the role of the powerless. Therefore, a rule in favour of those creditors who are able to contract the debt's terms – at the expense of other creditors – will usually increase *ex ante* the welfare of the creditors who have a higher probability of finding themselves in this category.

In contrast, a system of strict directorial duties usually increases the *ex ante* welfare of small trade creditors, unskilled workers and terminated at-will employees far more than that of the so-called adjusting creditors (banks and certain bondholders). The move from a system of mandatory directorial duties to a system of self-protection offers better chances of escaping the negative consequences of the insolvency to adjusting creditors who are able to protect themselves and less chances to non-adjusting creditors. The move would therefore have distributive effects which would not involve creditors randomly but would instead entail the increase and reduction of the welfare of different social groups.

In cases such as these, it is not a matter of choosing between aiming at efficiency or preferring fairness. Instead, the point is that the result in terms of efficiency is simply indeterminate. When we have two pies that are divided according to the same criteria, we know that by increasing the size of the pie we are increasing the overall welfare. However, when the distributive criteria change, we require a social welfare function. Lacking this function, there is no way whatsoever of establishing what is the most efficient result (as it does not necessarily coincide with the situation in which we have the biggest pie).

In conclusion, the choice of the best system of creditor protection is not a question of efficiency (i.e., a measurement of the effects of each system on overall welfare) but depends on fairness and political judgments.

2. SECOND PREMISE: THE OVERALL CONTEXT MUST BE TAKEN INTO ACCOUNT

I can be quite brief here, as the need to consider creditor protection rules as a 'system' – taking into account the whole context – is very well illustrated in Professor Mülbert's presentation.

I only wish to underline two points. The first one takes us back to the efficiency/fairness issue. We could imagine a two-step solution to the problem by separating the moment at which the size of the pie is determined from the moment at which the distribution criterion is fixed. For example, priority rules in bankruptcy could be entrusted with the task of fulfilling a fair distribution, leaving the other parts of the system free to choose the most efficient solution (that which warrants the maximisation of the resources the creditors can rely on). It is in fact quite obvious that there is less need for *ex ante* protection of creditors (e.g., employees) who enjoy strong *ex post* protection in bankruptcy.

However, we must pay careful attention to the complicated relationships that exist between the rules. A rule which warrants strong protection to some creditors in case of bankruptcy (we can once again recall the employees) may discourage other creditors, who are skilled at monitoring, from filing a petition for bankruptcy in a timely manner (they will instead be encouraged to delay the institution of insolvency procedures in the hope of succeeding in being at least partially repaid). Here, the distributive concerns clearly interfere with the efficiency considerations.

The second very obvious point concerns the importance of the accounting rules. The net system has some implications in areas where the accounting rules give stringent and precise indications with regard to the evaluation of the corporation assets and the net consists of material assets that are cautiously evaluated. The same system has very different implications in cases where the net consists entirely of goodwill (as is now definitively possible in Italy after the introduction of IAS/IFRS) or at the very least of complex assets to which it is very difficult to ascribe a meaningful economic value. In these situations, we might even wonder whether there is in fact a relevant difference between the kind of evaluations required by compliance with net system rules and those required by a generic solvency test.

3. THREE ALTERNATIVES

Coming now to the core problems of the creditors' protection, I think that the key alternatives can be summarised in the form of three fundamental questions.

The first question we face reads as follows: is a set of mandatory rules preventing managers from distributing corporation assets to shareholders and from carrying on company activity up until the moment the creditors obtain a court declaration of bankruptcy necessary?

If the answer to this question is yes, we then face a second question: do we need a regulation based on a formal test that is well defined in law (a regulation that may be qualified as a rule) or can we rely on a general directors' duty not to jeopardise creditors' interests (a kind of standard)?

If the answer is in favour of a formal test, we then face a third question: must our present system – that uses the relationship between legal capital and net amount as a test – be substituted by a different test?

With regard to the first question, I agree with Professor Mülbert. The question deserves a positive answer. I would not consider appropriate a system in which managers – lacking specific contractual commitments concerning specific creditors – are completely free to do as they please. I think that in this context the functioning of the market mechanism faces too many difficulties and that we cannot rely on its ability to produce the most efficient results.

This is a very delicate point and it may well be that a completely convincing demonstration of this thesis (as well as the opposite thesis) is very difficult to achieve. I shall limit myself to recalling a couple of causes for market failure that are present in this context and that may prevent the correct functioning of the market mechanism. The first is the collective action problem which troubles some of the potentially most important creditor protection tools. All creditors may take advantage of covenants (e.g., restrictions on dividend payment) negotiated by one or more of them.

Another possible cause for market failure is the agency problem, which receives less attention in this context, but which can have relevant effects in situations where managers may extract private benefits from their discretionary powers. Covenants, by limiting the discretionary powers of the managers, may at the same time reduce their private benefits. Managers may therefore be induced to preserve their discretion by exploiting the cheaper financing sources represented by creditors who demand appropriate commitments in a way that from the company's point of view turns out to be less than optimal.

4. Rules versus Standards

Should we decide in favour of a mandatory regulation we then face a second choice. Do we need a regulation based on a formal test described thoroughly by law (something like a rule) or can we rely on a system in which no formal test is imposed by law, although directors are still held responsible for having recklessly decided to distribute assets to shareholders or for carrying forward a hopeless activity (something like a standard)?

It is well known that the distinction between rules and standards is not a clear-cut matter but rather a matter of small movements along a continuum. Thus, it may often be difficult to classify a given regulation as a rule or a standard. This is true even in our case, where the net system at first glance appears to be a rule *par excellence* (apparently the decision depends on the results of a simple comparison of numerical data) but may appear much less rule-like if we consider the complex evaluations that are often necessary in order to establish the real and correct value of the assets that 'form' the net (especially, I believe, from the perspective of the generalised adoption of IAS/IFRS).

In any case, it seems to me that the proposed alternatives to the net system (e.g., the solvency test) are more akin to a standard. In all probability, their merit, in the eyes of many scholars, is just that of substituting a very rigid rule with more flexible criteria.

The respective costs and benefits of rules and standards are well known, and it would not be useful to recall them here. I would just like to draw attention to a couple of facts that can explain my scepticism regarding the possible improvements that could follow from the substitution of the net system with other systems that are more akin to a standard. (It could well be that this evaluation is also influenced by the traditional mistrust of civil law scholars regarding the ability of civil law courts to administer complex and vague standards. In this case, however, I think that there are many arguments to support the adoption of a rule rather than a standard.)

First of all, we have to consider that the *ex post* evaluation of the *ex ante* likelihood of a company's ability to remain – or to once again become – solvent may imply the taking into account of an innumerable series of factors. Many of these factors require hypothetical judgements, as in the case of positive events that were taken for granted at the moment at which the solvency of the company was established but in fact did not occur (new contributions, possible renewal of the terms of debts, etc.) or the predictability of other negative events which were not taken into account. In such a situation, where a well-defined legal threshold (as in the net system is the relationship between net and legal capital), is lacking, every standard inevitably becomes debatable and vague.

It seems to me that this defect is even more serious if one considers the context in which the standard should operate. It should guide the decisions of the managers, whose personal involvement in the matter may be very different from that of the driver at the crossroads, often used as an example to illustrate the difference between rules and standards. This is particularly true when managers have already perpetrated something illegal and are therefore exposed to penalty risks or – in any event – to the personal costs they hope to avoid in case of recovery.

In the context of company management, the recourse to irregular practice is seldom decided once and for all. In the beginning there is usually a venial sin – or even a simple mistake – which is then followed by wrongdoings of increasing gravity, perpetrated mainly to hide the original fault. I argue that situations such as these are better governed by rules rather than by standards. I also argue that 'bright line rules' may prevent this 'snowball' effect and may reduce managers' hopes regarding the possibility of getting away with hiding the real economic conditions of the company. In fact, rules are usually less prone to fostering illusions concerning the possibility of inventing *ex post* justifications for wrong actions.

Moreover, we must take into consideration the fact that crucial decisions (concerning the distribution of dividends or continuation of activity, etc.) are often not made by a single individual, but by complex bodies. I would argue that, in this context, a well-defined test imposed by law might facilitate the controllers' task and especially that of the non-executive directors.

To conclude on this point, I am personally very anxious about how managers of small and medium-sized Italian companies might use a power which is constrained only by the perspective of an *ex post* review before a court (based on uncertain criteria and which will occur in a – more or less – distant future) or by the intervention of experts, many of whom (not only in Italy I think) are ready and willing to 'cook' almost anything in exchange for appropriate quantities of professional appointments.

5. Conclusion

If we agree that creditors' interests are protected more effectively by rules rather than by standards, the final question is whether we can conceive another rule that is able to regulate this subject more successfully than the net system. It is well known that rules by their very nature produce false positives (companies that could recover are expelled from the market) and false negatives (the continuation of hopeless activities). In this context, therefore, we can judge a rule as better than the net system if it is able to produce less false positives without increasing the number and/or the costs of the false negatives. Does such a rule exist? In my opinion it is currently very difficult to answer such a question, and I therefore prefer to limit myself to three brief remarks.

The first is that the existence of a system of creditor protection able to produce better results than the net system is an empirical rather than theoretical issue. As such, it is an issue whose solution depends, in large measure, on the collection of all relevant empirical data. I do not know whether or not sufficient data has been collected, for example with regard to the different degrees of propensity to go to the courts in a timely manner that managers exhibit under different legal regimes, and their reasons for doing so, or with regard to the losses suffered by each class of creditors in American bankruptcies compared to European bankruptcies, and so forth.

The second remark is that even if all relevant data was available, the issue remains a political one rather than a technical one. It still entails a debatable choice about bearing the risks of too many false negatives and an even more debatable choice about which class of creditors deserves more stringent legal protection and which may instead be exposed to a major risk of losses.

The third remark is a simple *caveat* against treating as relevant data that although very important is at the same time very easy to manipulate (e.g., revenues) and against elaborating criteria so vague that the chosen rule collapses into a standard.

H. Eidenmüller and W. Schön (eds.), The Law and Economics of Creditor Protection

Regulatory Competition in European Company Law and Creditor Protection

Luca Enriques* and Martin Gelter**

* University of Bologna and European Corporate Governance Institute (ECGI). E-mail: luca.enriques@unibo.it.

** Vienna University of Economics and Business Administration. E-mail: martin.gelter@wu-wien.ac.at.

We wish to thank John Armour, Thomas Bachner, Horst Eidenmüller, Joe McCahery and Federico Mucciarelli for helpful comments on earlier drafts of this article, Niko Adensamer for helpful conversations about a number of issues of private international law and Alessandro Guccione for his valuable research assistance. The usual disclaimers apply.

States to recognize foreign EU (and EEA[7]) corporations' legal capacity and allows restrictive measures only under very limited circumstances.[8] Any such measures 'liable to hinder or make less attractive the exercise' of the freedoms need to satisfy the *Gebhard*[9] criteria, i.e., they 'must be applied in a non-discriminatory manner; they must be justified by imperative requirements in the public interest; they must be suitable for securing the attainment of the objective which they pursue, and they must not go beyond what is necessary in order to attain it.'[10] Furthermore, Member States may take measures to prevent or penalize fraud or abuse.[11]

Since those imperative requirements are apparently narrowly construed, Member States are to a large degree forced to allow for free choice among EU corporate laws. The extent of Member States' discretion is still unclear and possibly will remain so for a long time. Private international law rules largely not having been harmonized, they are still an issue of national legislation. One could conclude that only the result of the conflict of laws analysis in each particular case needs to be measured against the requirements of primary EC law.[12] However, in *Überseering*, the ECJ also held that a company validly incorporated in the Netherlands is entitled under Articles 43 and 48 of the Treaty to exercise freedom of establishment in Germany as a company incorporated in the Netherlands.[13] As a result, Member States will have to recognize not only the legal capacity of pseudo-foreign corporations but also a certain substantive core of the corporate law of the State of incorporation, although it is not clear how far this core extends.[14] Outside of it, the application of the law of the State of incorporation is

---

[7] See, e.g., BGH 19 September 2005, 51 *Recht der internationalen Wirtschaft (RIW)* (2005) p. 945 (recognizing a Liechtenstein corporation's legal capacity in Germany irrespective of its 'real seat').

[8] *Inspire Art*, *supra* n. 6.

[9] ECJ, Case C-55/94 *Reinhard Gebhard* v. *Consiglio dell'Ordine degli Avvocati e Procuratori di Milano* [1995] *ECR* 4165.

[10] Ibid., recital 37; *Centros*, *supra* n. 1, recital 34; *Inspire Art*, *supra* n. 6, recital 133.

[11] *Centros*, *supra* n. 1, recital 38; *Inspire Art*, *supra* n. 6, recital 136.

[12] See, e.g., P. Ulmer, 'Gläubigerschutz bei Scheinauslandsgesellschaften', 57 *Neue Juristische Wochenschrift (NJW)* (2004) p. 1201 at p. 1205 (pointing out that Arts. 43 and 47 of the EC Treaty do not intend to harmonize private international law).

[13] *Überseering*, *supra* n. 6, recital 80.

[14] The German *Bundesgerichtshof* recently held that it follows from the recognition of the legal personality of English companies that the liability of managers and shareholders to corporate creditors is determined by the law of incorporation. BGH 14 March 2005, 60 *Juristenzeitung (JZ)* (2005) p. 848. But see G. Rehm, 'Völker- und europarechtliche Vorgaben für die Bestimmung des Gesellschaftsstatuts', in H. Eidenmüller, ed., *Ausländische Kapitalgesellschaften im deutschen Recht* (Munich, Beck 2004) § 2, comment 70 (explaining that it would be theoretically possible to recognize foreign corporations as such, but to apply certain German law provisions to them).

not imperative, i.e., whether something is considered corporate or insolvency law is largely an issue of the national conception of these fields. Member States may even 'relabel' rules as insolvency law (if it serves the purpose of being able to apply their own law under the applicable conflict of laws rules), as long as the *Gebhard* criteria are not violated.

2.2 Positive harmonization

With positive harmonization, the European Community imposes on Member States an obligation to adopt certain rules (through directives) or directly imposes such rules through regulations. Positive harmonization can be *substantive*, whenever it defines the content of national corporate laws, or it can relate to *choice of law* itself, either by promoting or by reducing it. Substantive harmonization of creditor protection has been an important concern of European company law for a long time (most prominently in the Second Directive[15]), whereas the EIR attempts to harmonize the choice of law rules for insolvency. Member States may still deviate from the harmonized outcome, albeit in a disguised, undercover way. Member States may in fact fail to properly implement the harmonizing measure, or they may fail to enforce it or, finally, their judges and enforcers may construe the harmonized measures in line with prior, more (or less) lenient national rules.[16] In other words, Member States have various ways to cheat on the EC regulatory cartel. Whenever the EC measures are not purely optional and/or do not impose purely enabling rules on Member States, they do not only introduce EU/EEA-wide mandatory rules that are more difficult to escape from and to repeal. They also have an impact on regulatory competition, because their presence reduces the regulatory surplus businesses can gain from (re)incorporation,[17] thereby reducing the dynamism of the market for company law rules.

---

[15] Second Council Directive 77/91/EEC of 13 December 1976 on coordination of safeguards which, for the protection of the interests of members and others, are required by Member States of companies within the meaning of the second paragraph of Art. 58 of the Treaty, in respect of the formation of public limited liability companies and the maintenance and alteration of their capital, with a view to making such safeguards equivalent, as amended by Council Directive 92/101/EEC of 23 November 1992, *OJ* 1977 L 26/1 (hereinafter, Second Directive).

[16] L. Enriques, *EC Company Law Directives and Regulations: How Trivial Are They?*, ECGI Law Working Paper No. 39/2005, pp. 9-15, available at: <http://ssrn.com/abstract=730388>.

[17] See S. Lombardo, *Regulatory Competition in Company Law in the European Community* (Frankfurt am Main, Peter Lang 2002) p. 193.

2.3 Prospective harmonization

The European Community, with its positive harmonization powers, may have an impact on regulatory competition provided that the relevant actors (private parties and policymakers at State level) know that it may step in to react to any Member State's moves. Mark Roe has argued that the threat of federal intervention has shaped the development of US corporate law much more strongly than interstate competition, by creating an incentive for Delaware decision-makers not to overstep certain boundaries beyond which corporate law would become untenable to federal decision-makers.[18] It seems quite unlikely for a European State to be influenced in the way Roe describes. The European legislative process is relatively slow (compared to US Congress) and rather impervious to populist pressures due to the absence of a common European public sphere.[19] The EU legislator has rarely, if ever, been able to gain support from businesses to enact meaningful corporate law.[20] With Delaware's responsiveness to the threat of federal intervention resting on its financial dependence on franchise revenue, there is no jurisdiction upon which supranational 'competition' can exert significant pressure unless a European Delaware with similar incentives emerges. The possibility of enacting non-trivial law may even chill non-defensive regulatory competition, since one State's attempt to attract incorporations by creating significant rents by means of corporate law could just trigger a reaction by other States, which would push for harmonization in such a case.[21]

3. Regulatory competition in corporate law

3.1 Legal capital and distribution constraints as the main creditor protection mechanisms of corporate law

One of the main mechanisms of corporate law, at least in the minds of continental corporate lawyers, consists of legal capital constraints and the distribution constraints it entails. They are considered a core element of 'pre-insolvency rules', meaning those rules that apply during the company's entire lifetime. From the conflict of laws perspective, pre-insolvency rules usually follow the law of

---

[18] M.J. Roe, 'Delaware's Competition', 117 *Harv. L. Rev.* (2003) p. 588; ibid., 'Delaware's Politics', 118 *Harv. L. Rev.* (2005) p. 2491.

[19] See M. Gelter, 'The Structure of Regulatory Competition in European Corporate Law', 5 *JCLS* (2005) p. 247 at pp. 278-279.

[20] Enriques, op. cit. n. 16, at p. 44.

[21] See L. Enriques, 'EC Company Law and the Fears of a European Delaware', 15 *EBLR* (2004) p. 1259 at pp. 1269-1270.

incorporation and are hence subject to the influence of regulatory competition in corporate law. There have been substantial efforts aimed at positive harmonization of these rules. However, these efforts have borne little fruit thus far. First, many of these measures (in particular the Second Company Law Directive) apply only to public companies (such as the *Aktiengesellschaft*, the *naamloze vennootschap*, the *société anonyme* and the *società per azioni*), but not to private ones. Second, those measures have altered national corporate law less than one might expect. EC directives relating to corporate law generally leave a variety of options to Member States, where lawyers have frequently understood European law within the context of their respective national legal culture. Those provisions of secondary European law that are mandatory are typically underenforced at European level, allowing either Member States or corporations to circumvent them with relative ease.[22]

Analytically, the 'legal capital' system can be distinguished into a minimum net assets requirement and constraints on distribution.

3.1.1 *Minimum net assets*

The Second Company Law Directive requires public corporations to have a legal capital of at least €25,000,[23] which need not be entirely covered by assets at the time of incorporation. With the Second Directive not applying to private limited companies, Member States have been able to freely choose the amount for this set of corporations. This resulted in a broad variety of regulations, ranging from no such requirement[24] to €35,000.[25]

The merits of minimum capital requirements in actually protecting creditors are doubtful, for reasons that need not be reiterated here.[26] Even supporters of legal capital requirements seem to concede that their function does not lie in protecting creditors from the risk of substantial losses resulting from an unfavourable business

---

22 Enriques, op. cit. n. 16, at pp. 9-11.

23 Second Directive, Art. 6.

24 In the United Kingdom, Ireland and Cyprus, there is no minimum capital requirement for private companies.

25 The highest amount is apparently set by Austrian law. See § 6(1) of the Law on Private Limited Companies (*Gesetz über Gesellschaften mit beschränkter Haftung*). To be sure, only €17,500 needs to be paid up in cash before the company is registered (or the lower total amount of cash contributions, which is permissible if there are contributions in kind, for which the consideration has to be transferred in full (§ 10(1)).

26 See J. Armour, 'Share Capital and Creditor Protection: Efficient Rules for Modern Company Law', 63 *MLR* (2000) p. 355 at pp. 371-372; L. Enriques and J.R. Macey, 'Creditors versus Capital Formation: The Case against the European Legal Capital Rules', 86 *Cornell L. Rev.* (2001) pp. 1165-1204; P.O. Mülbert and M. Birke, 'Legal Capital – Is There a Case against the European Legal Capital Rules?', 3 *EBOR* (2002) pp. 695-732.

development but rather in signalling seriousness to the market, thus erecting a barrier against the creation of corporations with an unreasonable amount of backing by shareholders.[27] If there are any benefits to this argument, they need to be weighed against the disadvantage of preventing the formation of potentially thriving companies backed by a sound business idea but little or no assets.

The *Centros-Inspire Art* line of decisions has made it impossible for national legislators to impose minimum asset requirements on pseudo-foreign corporations. Thus, the possibilities for company law arbitrage in this field are nearly unrestricted.[28] Minimum capital has become the most important factor driving for the incorporation of continental businesses in the United Kingdom. This has arguably prompted some 'defensive regulatory competition': France effectively abolished minimum capital for private corporations,[29] and even the German Ministry of Justice proposed a reduction from €25,000 to €10,000 in early 2005.[30] The final outcome of this process may be the practical elimination of minimum capital requirements.

3.1.2 *Restrictions on distributions*

In the European Union, legal rules limiting managers' discretion over the declaration of dividends or any other way of conveying corporate assets to shareholders are intertwined with the regulation of legal capital.[31] Under Article 15(1) of the

---

[27] See, e.g., M. Lutter, 'Gesetzliches Garantiekapital als Instrument europäischer und deutscher Rechtspolitik', 43 *Die Aktiengesellschaft (AG)* (1998) p. 375 at p. 375; H. Merkt, 'Das Centros-Urteil des Europäischen Gerichtshofs', in Gesellschaftsrechtliche Vereinigung, ed., *Gesellschaftsrecht in der Diskussion 1999* (Cologne, O. Schmidt 2000) p. 110 at p. 138; R. Wilhelmi, 'Das Mindestkapital als Mindestschutz – eine Apologie im Hinblick auf die Diskussion um eine Reform der GmbH angesichts der englischen Limited', 97 *GmbH-Rundschau (GmbHR)* (2006) p. 13 at pp. 13-14.

[28] See S. Grundmann, 'Regulatory Competition in European Company Law – Some Different Genius?', in G. Ferrarini, K.J. Hopt and E. Wymeersch, eds., *Capital Markets in the Age of the Euro* (The Hague, Kluwer Law International 2002) p. 561 at pp. 583-584.

[29] Art. 1, *Loi n° 2003-721 du 1er août 2003 pour l'initiative économique* [Law for Economic Initative], *Journal officiel* n° 179 du 5 août 2003, p. 13449.

[30] *Entwurf eines Gesetzes zur Neuregelung des Mindestkapitals der GmbH (MindestkapG)* [Draft Law for a New Regulation of the Minimum Capital of Private Limited Companies], available at: <http://www.bmj.de/media/archive/908.pdf>, last accessed 28 May 2005. The proposal was rejected by the Federal Council (*Bundesrat*) with a view to the early 2005 elections, but new plans to facilitate the formation of start-up firms are currently emerging. See M. Miola, 'Legal Capital and Limited Liability Companies: The European Perspective', 2 *ECFR* (2005) p. 413 at p. 445.

[31] Of course, this does not necessarily have to be the case, since restrictions on distributions may also be related to balance sheets in the absence of legal capital rules or not be related at all to balance sheet data, as when a solvency test is required. See, e.g., § 6.40(c) of the Revised Model Bus. Corp. Act (1984). Even the prohibition of concealed distributions (described below

Second Directive, no distributions to shareholders may be made when net assets are lower or would become lower than subscribed capital plus certain reserves which may not be distributed, except in the case of a reduction of subscribed capital. Even if this does not protect creditors against regular business risk, a public company will in theory be unable to convey funds to shareholders if net assets fall below the subscribed capital, unless shareholders vote to go through a capital reduction procedure which includes certain safeguards for creditors (Arts. 30-39).

Two important caveats need to be made. First, the actual computation of net assets within the meaning of the Directive is basically a balance sheet test on the basis of the last financial year's annual accounts. Thus, the extent of 'capital maintenance' depends on the applicable accounting rules. In spite of the Fourth Directive,[32] which, on its face, harmonizes accounting law in great detail, a considerable amount of elective provisions has allowed EU Member States to uphold their national accounting cultures,[33] while the recent IAS Regulation[34] gives Member States the choice between an accounting system based on the Fourth Directive and one on IAS/IFRS for individual accounts (Art. 5(a)).[35]

Second, as a practical matter, it is not entirely clear what kind of transactions the prohibition applies to. While the Second Directive explicitly speaks only of 'distributions', German commentators generally agree that so-called concealed distributions (*verdeckte Ausschüttungen* or *verdeckte Einlagenrückgewähr*)[36] are

---

in the text accompanying nn. 36-41) could conceivably apply in the absence of minimum capital.

32 Fourth Council Directive 78/660/EEC of 25 July 1978 based on Article 54(3)(g) of the Treaty on the annual accounts of certain types of companies, *OJ* 1978 L 222/11 (hereinafter, Fourth Directive).

33 E.g., W.F. Ebke, 'Accounting, Auditing and Global Capital Markets', in T. Baums, et al., eds., *Corporations, Capital Markets and the Business in the Law: Liber Amicorum Richard M. Buxbaum* (London, Kluwer Law International 2000) p. 113 at p. 119; M. Gelter and M.M. Siems, 'Judicial Federalism in the ECJ's Berlusconi Case: Toward More Credible Corporate Governance and Financial Reporting?', 46 *Harv. Int'l LJ* (2005) p. 487 at p. 505.

34 Regulation (EC) No. 1606/2002 of the European Parliament and of the Council of 19 July 2002 on the application of international accounting standards.

35 Member States are also allowed to delegate this choice to firms. See E. Ferran, *The Place for Creditor Protection on the Agenda for Modernisation of Company Law in the European Union*, ECGI Law Working Paper No. 51/2005, pp. 21-24, available at: <http://ssrn.com/abstract=841884> (discussing the question of compatibility between the Second Directive and IFRS accounting); W. Schön, 'Internationalisierung der Rechnungslegung und Gläubigerschutz', 54 *Die Wirtschaftsprüfung* – Special Issue (2001) p. 74 at p. 76 (arguing that IAS accounting shifts risk from shareholders to creditors).

36 See W. Bayer, '§ 57', in B. Kropff and J. Semler, eds., *Münchener Kommentar zum Aktiengesetz*, Vol. 2, 2nd edn. (Munich, Beck 2003); U. Hüffer, *Aktiengesetz*, 6th edn. (Munich, Beck 2004) § 57.

also prohibited.[37] This term refers to transactions by which corporate funds are conveyed to shareholders indirectly, typically through contracts entered into on unfair terms, such as loans to shareholders with unusually low (or no) interest rates or purchases from shareholders at excessive prices. If the prohibition is to be effective, it cannot matter whether a distribution is made through the official declaration of dividends or in any other way.[38] Naturally, the German understanding of the Directive is shaped by the extensive German case law on concealed distributions to shareholders.[39] Since the Second Directive only applies to public corporations, German law totally prohibits concealed distributions only in *Aktiengesellschaften*,[40] while in *Gesellschaften mit beschränkter Haftung* they are permitted as long as they do not reduce net assets below statutory capital.[41]

By contrast, under English law, a distribution is normally defined as a transfer of assets without consideration.[42] Still, in a vein similar to the German doctrine, English courts have held excessive remuneration of directors,[43] the transfer at undervalue of real property to another company owned by the same parent[44] and providing a guarantee for another firm within the same group[45] to be unauthorized

---

[37] M. Habersack, *Europäisches Gesellschaftsrecht*, 2nd edn. (Munich, Beck 2003) comment 167.

[38] See W. Schön, 'Deutsches Konzernprivileg und europäischer Kapitalschutz – ein Widerspruch?', in K.H. Forster, et al., eds., *Aktien- und Bilanzrecht. Festschrift für Bruno Kropff* (Düsseldorf, IDW-Verlag 1997) p. 285 at p. 294; Mülbert and Birke, loc. cit. n. 26, at pp. 546-547 (both arguing that the purpose of Arts. 15 and 16 implies a general prohibition of concealed distributions).

[39] See generally *supra* n. 36.

[40] German commentators typically argue that, since Art. 15(1)(c) of the Second Directive limits distributions to profits, distributions other than through dividends are prohibited. See, e.g., Habersack, op. cit. n. 37, comment 164.

[41] § 57 *Aktiengesetz* [Law on Stock Corporations] (Germany); § 30 *Gesetz über Gesellschaften mit beschränkter Haftung* [Law on Private Limited Companies] (Germany). Cf., M. Lutter and P. Hommehoff, *GmbH-Gesetz*, 16th edn. (Cologne, Otto Schmidt 2004) § 30, comment 3. By contrast, under Austrian corporate law, which usually strongly resembles German law, concealed distributions are generally illegal in both types of corporations. See § 52 *Aktiengesetz* [Law on Stock Corporations] (Austria); § 82 *Gesetz über Gesellschaften mit beschränkter Haftung* [Law on Private Limited Companies] (Austria).

[42] *Clydebank Football Club Ltd.* v. *Steedman* [2002] *S.L.T.* 109; *Palmer's Company Law* (London, Sweet & Maxwell, looseleaf since 1992) para. 9.705; J. Armour, 'Avoidance of Transactions as a "Fraud on Creditors" at Common Law', in J. Armour and H. Bennett, eds., *Vulnerable Transactions in Corporate Insolvency* (Oxford, Hart Publishing 2003) p. 281, para. 7.38.

[43] *In Re Halt Garage* [1982] 3 *All ER* 1016.

[44] *Aveling Barford Ltd.* v. *Perion Ltd.* [1989] *BCLC* 626, 5 *BCC* 677; see M.J. Burke, 'Shareholder ratification of directors' actions', 140 *New LJ* (1990) p. 240.

[45] *Barclay's Bank plc.* v. *British and Commonwealth Holdings plc.* [1996] 1 *BCLC* 1.

returns of capital.[46] However, transactions that are not a complete sham will not be considered a 'distribution' at all,[47] meaning that, other than under German law, a subjective element is required to void a transaction.[48] The recent Company Law Reform Bill will allow distributions in kind as long as there are sufficient profits available for distribution to cover the difference between the asset's book value and the consideration received,[49] which would not be acceptable under German law. Given that the English case law on this subject is sparse, and, even more importantly, commentators appear not to see a connection with the Second Directive,[50] it is obvious that the English understanding of constraints on distributions imposed by EC law differs considerably from the German one. On top of that, concealed distributions do not appear to be much of an issue in some other countries as well.[51]

---

46 Cf., P.L. Davies, *Gower and Davies' Principles of Modern Company Law*, 7th edn. (London, Sweet & Maxwell 2003) pp. 279-280; M. Forde, *Company Law*, 3rd edn. (Dublin, Round Hall Sweet & Maxwell 1999) nn. 7-31.

47 Armour, loc. cit. n. 42, at para. 7.38.

48 For a detailed comparison, see the chapter on 'Capital Maintenance and Unlawful Distributions' in T. Bachner, *Creditor Protection in Private Companies – Anglo-German Perspectives after Centros*, Ph.D. dissertation (University of Cambridge Faculty of Law 2006).

49 Company Law Reform Bill, HL Bill 34 (November 2005), proposed section 275A.

50 For example, Vanessa Edwards discusses neither the English nor the German cases in her treatise. See V. Edwards, *EC Company Law* (Oxford, Clarendon Press 1999) p. 69. The Rickford report discusses the issue only briefly within the context of German law. See J. Rickford, 'Reforming Capital. Report on the Interdisciplinary Group on Capital Maintenance', 15 *EBLR* (2004) p. 919 at p. 1008.

51 For France, see M. Germain, *1/2 Traité de Droit Commercial G. Ripert/R. Roblot*, 18th edn. (Paris, Librairie générale de droit et de jurisprudence 2002) pp. 607-609 (discussing the issue of *'dividends fictifs'* under French Law and ignoring the issue of concealed distributions). For Spain, see J. Massaguer Fuentes, 'Spagna', in G.F. Campobasso, ed., *Armonie e disarmonie nel diritto comunitario delle società di capitali* [Harmonies and Disharmonies in EC Company Law], Vol. 2 (Milano, Giuffrè 2003) p. 1115 at pp. 1129-1132 (same for Spanish law). For Italy, a distinction has to be made between concealed distributions and concealed restitutions of contributions. The former do not appear to be an issue: see, e.g., G.E. Colombo, 'Il bilancio d'esercizio', in G.E. Colombo and G.B. Portale, eds., *Trattato delle società per azioni* [Treatise on Stock Corporations], Vol. 7/1 (Torino, UTET 1994) p. 23 at pp. 535-544 (providing a thorough analysis of the Italian provision – Art. 2433 *Codice Civile* [Civil Code] – corresponding to Art. 16 of the Second Directive and the relationships between the two, but totally ignoring the problem of concealed distributions). To be sure, until 2002, it was a crime to distribute 'in any form' fictitious profits (Art. 2621, No. 2 *Codice Civile*) and the relevant provision was construed as including the case of concealed distributions. After the 2002 reform, however, the criminal provision was reformulated without the 'in any form' clause and, in the absence of case law so far, it is widely construed as not including concealed distributions any more. See, e.g., V. Napoleoni, 'Le disposizioni penali in materia di società e di consorzi', in G. Bonfante, et al., eds., *Codice commentato delle nuove società* [Commented Code on New Companies] (Milano, IPSOA 2004) p. 1690 at p. 1773.

Restrictions on distributions may result in significant cost[52] (e.g., when planning intra-group transactions to avoid violations of such rules) and in considerable risk to shareholders if the company goes bankrupt. Differences in the law may affect company arbitrage decisions to some degree, since there appears to be widespread agreement that capital maintenance rules of the State of incorporation apply[53] and that choice of law with respect to distributions will therefore be possible.

3.2 Company law arbitrage and regulatory competition

Pre-insolvency rules are mostly the domain of corporate law, much more so than in the United States, where creditor protection is not really an issue for corporate legislators, except for restrictions on dividends that can be put down as mostly meaningless and prone to circumvention.[54] Hence, it comes as no big surprise that the American discussion on regulatory competition has little to offer concerning creditor protection. We now proceed to assess how intense regulatory competition is today within the European Union and how it is to be interpreted, and then analyze how *ex ante* and *ex post* choice of law decisions affect creditors. By *ex ante* and *ex post* decisions we mean the decision to incorporate or to reincorporate before or after credit has been extended to the firm, respectively.

3.2.1 *Company law arbitrage and regulatory competition so far*

We have seen that some regulatory arbitrage with respect to pre-insolvency rules is already happening, driven mostly by minimum capital requirements, which possibly can, at least partly, be credited for a trend toward the abolition of minimum capital requirements in some countries.[55] Still, it would probably be premature to infer any long-term trends from this. Of course, legal capital

---

[52] Cf., Mülbert and Birke, loc. cit. n. 26, at pp. 720-721 (conceding that creditors may look favourably at rules against concealed distributions, which, however, come at a significant cost).

[53] E.g., U. Forsthoff and M. Schulz, 'Gläubigerschutz bei EU-Auslandsgesellschaften', in H. Hirte and T. Bücker, eds., *Grenzüberschreitende Gesellschaften* [Cross-border Corporations] (Cologne, Heymann 2005) § 15, comment 32.

[54] See R.C. Clark, *Corporate Law* (Boston, Little, Brown and Company 1986) p. 618; B. Manning and J.J. Hanks, *Legal Capital*, 3rd edn. (New York, Foundation Press 1990) p. 93 ('Whether one views it as a blessing or a deficiency of the existing statutory systems, it is at least a fact that the corporation acts do not pursue the implementation of their own scheme with any real seriousness'). The elimination or vestigialization of legal capital rules has arguably been the outcome of regulatory competition. See also R.A. Booth, *Capital Requirements in United States Corporation Law*, University of Maryland School of Law Legal Studies Research Paper No. 2005-64 (2005) p. 64, [available at: <http://ssrn.com/abstract=864685>.

[55] See Miola, loc. cit. n. 30, at p. 437 et seq.

requirements are usually seen as an instrument of creditor protection. However, if minimum capital requirements do not actually help creditors and rational creditors should not care about them, then the changes in the law induced by company law arbitrage so far are not really an issue of creditor protection, but only a removal of administrative slack that affected the interests of the founders of new companies only. If it is true that only one interest group is affected, and in a positive way, it seems hard to doubt that the effect of regulatory competition is beneficial as well. Given the minor relevance of this issue in the perspective of creditors, however, this recent development should not be construed as evidence for either a 'race to the top' or 'race to the bottom' with respect to creditor protection.

3.2.2 *Ex ante* choice of law

Even in light of the doubts as to whether each of the current creditor protection mechanisms implemented by the Member States actually serves the interests of creditors, it is hard to rule out entirely that some of them do. Conceivably, Member States could also devise new ones that do. Hence, we ask whether regulatory competition is likely to lead to the retention and development of mechanisms creditors actually care about, i.e., whether company law arbitrage will be beneficial.

Corporate debtors, especially when the company approaches insolvency, have powerful incentives to act in ways that are detrimental to creditors, because shareholders capture most of the potential gains of increased risk, whereas creditors, whose entire benefits are limited to the amount of principal plus interest stipulated *ex ante*, have to bear most of the risk of failure.[56] However, to counter this danger, creditors frequently request contractual clauses limiting the opportunism of debtors[57] or they will charge a risk-adjusted interest rate.[58]

Hence, in line with the standard corporate law and economics literature, which considers corporate law to be a standard-form contract,[59] the applicable regime of corporate law also needs to be seen as part of the contract of lending. At least some corporate law creditor protection tools will affect the creditor's assessment of shareholder and manager opportunism. To the extent that corporate law reduces this risk, the creditor will charge a lower interest rate or find it unnecessary to add protective covenants to the lending agreement. For example, a rational creditor will take the possibility of veil piercing or equitable subordination into account and adjust the interest rate accordingly, considering the reduced risk, if

---

56 See S.C. Myers, 'Determinants of Corporate Borrowing', 5 *J. Fin. Econ.* (1977) p. 147.

57 C.W. Smith and J.B. Warner, 'On Financial Contracting', 7 *J. Fin. Econ.* (1979) p. 117.

58 See generally Lombardo, op. cit. n. 17, at p. 166.

59 F.H. Easterbrook and D.R. Fischel, *The Economic Structure of Corporate Law* (Cambridge, Harvard University Press 1991) p. 1 et seq.

only marginally. Similarly, creditors should make some adjustment depending on whether or not managers and/or shareholders have the opportunity to remove assets from the company, thus increasing the likelihood of insolvency and reducing the chances of recovery (asset diversion). It follows that rules impeding such transactions, including 'concealed distributions' doctrines or mandatory disclosure rules, should also affect their decision on the margin. Thus, assuming the ability to accurately assess risk of default and to adjust prices and conditions accordingly, creditors should be getting precisely what they bargained for in terms of *ex ante* expectations. A creditor may want a corporate debtor to observe a specific Member State's creditor protection regime. A powerful institutional lender could theoretically even have the bargaining power to induce a firm to submit itself to a particular regime. It follows from this discussion that, considering firms' *ex ante* incorporation choice, both debtors and lenders should have an incentive to lobby States to implement creditor protection rules which are beneficial to lenders (and borrowers).

However, the analysis so far ignores non-adjusting and only partially adjusting creditors. Most of all, tort claimants will not be able to adjust their claims. Small, less sophisticated creditors (e.g., suppliers) will be unable to exactly determine the risk involved and will find it too costly to draft an agreement exactly reflecting the risk of the borrower.[60] It is for these creditors that a 'boilerplate contract' corporate law will be insufficient. Hence, in the presence of non-adjusting creditors, a 'race to the bottom' is theoretically possible, as those creditors will not adequately react to the choice of a suboptimal corporate law.[61]

An obvious objection is that non-adjusting creditors may free-ride on the bargaining power of large lenders. Within certain limits, this is absolutely likely to happen, namely in those cases where the law of a specific jurisdiction is beneficial to creditors as a group. However, free-riding will not work where the choice of law involves a conflict of interests between different groups of lenders, e.g., where bank loans are collateralized while trade creditors do not possess such protection. Choice of law opportunities may therefore be detrimental to non-adjusting creditors (in particular tort creditors) *vis-à-vis* adjusting creditors.[62]

3.2.3 Ex post *reincorporation*

So far, only newly founded companies have taken advantage of company law arbitrage within the European Union. Once a specific regime has been chosen,

---

[60] See generally L.A. Bebchuk and J.M. Fried, 'The Uneasy Case for the Priority of Secured Claims in Bankruptcy', 105 *Yale LJ* (1996) p. 857 at pp. 864-865.

[61] L.A. Bebchuk, 'Federalism and the Corporation: The Desirable Limits on State Competition in Corporate Law', 106 *Harv. L. Rev.* (1992) p. 1435 at pp. 1489-1490.

[62] Gelter, loc. cit. n. 19, at p. 276.

firms are locked into a particular system of creditor protection. This is due mostly to the costs of moving: firms have needed to resort to complicated constructions in order to switch to a new regime,[63] and they face severe obstacles resulting from taxation. The first problem has been alleviated at least to some degree by the recently enacted Directive on Cross-Border Mergers and the ECJ's recent opinion in *SEVIC Systems AG*, where it found that that the German law on mergers' failure to allow for cross-border mergers violates Articles 43 and 48 of the EC Treaty.[64] The second issue should have been resolved largely by the Directive on the Taxation of Mergers, which prohibits the taxation of hidden reserves in cross-border mergers,[65] and the *Lasteyrie du Saillant* case, in which the ECJ found that the taxation of unrealized gains, where a natural person moved to another Member State, was not permissible under the freedom of establishment.[66] Since arguably this should also apply where a company reincorporates or moves to another Member State,[67] future ECJ decisions will further reduce these costs.

'Midstream' or *'ex post'* company law arbitrage – i.e., during the later life of the company – adds another dimension to the analysis. Once firms are no longer locked into a particular legal regime, it may be in the interest of both parties to commit *ex ante* to stay in a particular legal system that creditors have adjusted to. In this case, contractual creditors need to deal only with the law of one jurisdiction and should be able to adjust and penalize bad law with relative ease (assuming there are no information asymmetries about the content of the particular law). The possibility of implicitly altering the terms of the lending agreement by reincorporating compares to the US debate on mandatory rules in corporate

---

63 Consider, e.g., the Daimler-Chrysler merger (which, however, involved a German and an American company). See T. Baums, 'Corporate contracting around defective regulations: The Daimler-Chrysler case', 115 *JITE* (1999) p. 119.

64 ECJ, Case C-411/03 *SEVIC Systems AG* v. *Amtsgericht Neuwied* [2006] *ECR* nyr (hereinafter, *SEVIC*).

65 Art. 4(1) of Council Directive 90/434/EEC of 23 July 1990 on the common system of taxation applicable to mergers, divisions, transfers of assets and exchanges of shares concerning companies of different Member States, *OJ* 1990 L 225/1, at p. 20. But see International Bureau of Fiscal Documentation, *Survey on the Societas Europeaea* 78 (September 2003) (reporting on the basis of a questionnaire conducted in the then fifteen Member States that Directive 90/434 EEC 'still needs (partial) implementation in several Member States'). In the United States, reincorporation into another State is normally considered a 'reorganization' (IRC § 368(a) (2004)) not giving rise to taxation. Cf., G. Subramanian, 'The Influence of Antitakeover Statutes on Incorporation Choice: Evidence on the "Race Debate" and Antitakeover Overreaching', 150 *U. Pa. L. Rev.* (2002) p. 1795 at p. 1802. On tax impediments in Europe, see T.H. Tröger, 'Choice of Jurisdiction in European Corporate Law – Perspectives of European Corporate Governance', 6 *EBOR* (2005) p. 3 at pp. 16-18.

66 ECJ, Case C-09/02 *Hughes de Lasteyrie du Saillant* v. *Ministère de l'Economie* [2004] *ECR* I-2409.

67 E.g., Tröger, loc. cit. n. 65, at p. 17.

law, which focuses on the relation between shareholders and managers. The usual justification given for making some rules mandatory in the midstream stage is managerial opportunism. Even if the charter terms were fair when the company first went public, the argument goes, management can push through charter amendments which are not necessarily in the shareholders' interest because shareholders are rationally ignorant and subject to collective action problems, and because charter amendments need to be proposed by the board of directors in the United States. This precludes charter amendments that will be to the benefit of shareholders, but to the detriment of management.[68] It might therefore be beneficial if a company's managers or promoters were able to tie their hands with respect to charter amendments.[69]

Similarly, it may be beneficial if a firm is committed to the terms of a lending agreement, as implied by the corporate law regime of its State of incorporation. However, if the debtor is not committed to a particular system (or if such a commitment is impossible or prohibitively costly), the opportunity to move to a less creditor-friendly jurisdiction creates a new moral hazard problem *vis-à-vis* creditors.[70] Under the (default) regime created by the recent ECJ case law, shareholders may unilaterally decide to change the firm's charter or to reincorporate in another jurisdiction without creditors' approval.[71] This moral hazard opportunity raises information costs for creditors who need to deal with the laws of the multiple States in which a company might reincorporate.

With time, sophisticated creditors would probably learn how to deal with this and, at the very least, adjust interest rates accordingly. Conceivably, a lending contract or a bond covenant could require the debtor to stay within one particular legal system. In most cases, creditors will be (theoretically) in the position to protect themselves against this particular type of moral hazard. Even today, loan agreements with banks often stipulate the acceleration of the loan in the case of significant transactions such as mergers. Similarly, contracts might penalize reincorporations by raising interest rates in such a case. Such clauses may be sufficiently deterrent in many cases, at least as long as bankruptcy is not immediately impending.

---

[68] L.A. Bebchuk, 'Limiting Contractual Freedom in Corporate Law: The Desirable Constraints on Charter Amendments', 102 *Harv. L. Rev.* (1989) p. 1820 at p. 1835 et seq.

[69] J.N. Gordon, 'The Mandatory Structure of Corporate Law', 89 *Colum. L. Rev.* (1989) p. 1549 at pp. 1573-1585.

[70] See also Lombardo, op. cit. n. 17, at pp. 181-212.

[71] To be sure, the ECJ's *Daily Mail* opinion (ECJ, Case 81/87 *The Queen* v. *Treasury and Commissioners of Inland Revenue, ex parte Daily Mail and General Trust* [1988] *ECR* I-5483), which allows Member States to impose an 'export ban' on the firms incorporated under their respective law, is frequently still considered good law. See, e.g., *Bayerisches Oberstes Landgericht*, 11 February 2004, 95 *GmbHR* 490 (2004); F. Woolridge, 'Überseering: Freedom of Establishment of Companies Affirmed', 14 *EBLR* (2003) p. 227 at pp. 231-232.

Even when a 'commitment' clause is in place, it is shareholders who need to initiate a reincorporation, even though creditors need to approve. The ensuing distribution of powers between shareholders and creditors is analogous to the one between managers and shareholders in the United States.[72] One could argue that, in the (theoretical) case where a move will increase the total value of the firm by improving the position of creditors, but take away some value from shareholders, a reincorporation will not be implemented.[73]

As before, the crucial question is how well creditors are able to deal with the issue on their own, in particular by contracting for a 'commitment clause' *ex ante*. Tort creditors are of course unable to adjust, although a reincorporation to escape tort claims will not be possible, given that the private international law of torts typically follows the *lex commissi delicti*.[74] With respect to claims against the company, tort creditors will in most cases be primarily interested in post-insolvency rules. However, reincorporation may sometimes be a way to escape veil piercing.[75]

Furthermore, 'commitment clauses' or 'acceleration clauses' will typically be stipulated only to the benefit of large adjusting creditors. Again, sophisticated creditors may cooperate with shareholders and managers to the detriment of less sophisticated ones, namely by agreeing to a reincorporation in a jurisdiction

---

[72] Cf., Bebchuk, loc. cit. n. 61, at p. 1470 (explaining that, with managerial veto power over reincorporations, moves enhancing shareholder value will not ensue if they hurt managers).

[73] Of course, if lending is concentrated and negotiations can take place between creditors and managers or controlling shareholders, leaving aside the possibility of bargaining breakdowns, such a reincorporation may take place. Typically, sophisticated, adjusting creditors (such as the firm's main bank) will be able to stimulate the other groups to initiate one. However, the benefits of Coasian bargaining are limited, as it will probably be used only to the benefit of adjusting creditors. On the other side of the bargaining table, it also seems likely that only large shareholders and managers, but not the minority, will be primary beneficiaries of the negotiations.

[74] A theoretical case where corporate law could become relevant would be the implementation of unlimited shareholder liability for corporate torts in at least one country, as famously proposed by H. Hansmann and R. Kraakman, 'Toward Unlimited Liability for Corporate Torts', 100 *Yale LJ* (1991) p. 1879. Shareholders would have an incentive to reincorporate if the firm is facing a mass tort claim.

[75] Cf., G. Spindler and O. Berner, 'Gläubigerschutz im Gesellschaftsrecht nach Inspire Art', 50 *RIW* (2004) p. 7 at p. 11 (arguing that the German doctrine of *Existenzvernichtungshaftung* [liability to creditors for endangering the company's existence] follows corporate law); S. Leible, 'Rechts- und Geschäftsfähigkeit. Kaufmannseigenschaft', in Hirte and Bücker, op. cit. n. 53, § 10, comment 25 (stating that veil piercing claims for undercapitalization or commingling of assets are qualified as corporate law by German courts and authors); *Amtsgericht Bad Segeberg*, 24 March 2005, 95 *GmbHR* (2005) p. 884 (rejecting veil piercing claim for undercapitalization against an English private limited company for the reason that English law does not require private companies to have any capital).

incentives to change their laws to *attract*, as Delaware does, (re)incorporations. About this, we remain sceptical.[84]

4. Insolvency law, the EIR, and bankruptcy forum shopping

4.1 Post-insolvency rules and the EIR

There are strong complementarities between company law and insolvency law.[85] In order to analyze the interactions, we first sketch out the private international law framework for insolvencies within the European Union. The central piece of legislation in this area is now the EIR, but attention will be given more specifically to another tool, namely fraudulent conveyance laws, which has the most potential to act as a substitute for the legal capital doctrine. Hence, to the extent that legal capital becomes less central in the European Union as well, this tool may come to the foreground.

4.1.1 *Harmonization of conflict of laws rules in insolvency law: the EIR in a nutshell*

In sharp contrast to the US experience, where bankruptcy law is federal, insolvency law is still a matter of national law within the European Union: no relevant substantive harmonization of EU insolvency rules has ever been adopted (or attempted) at EC level.[86] In 2000, however, the EIR was passed in order to enhance cooperation among jurisdictions in insolvency proceedings by harmonizing conflict of laws issues relating to insolvencies.

The EIR identifies the Member State(s) having jurisdiction to open insolvency proceedings by introducing a distinction between main proceedings, which have a

---

[84] See Enriques, loc. cit. n. 21, at pp. 1266-1273, and Gelter, loc. cit. n. 19, at pp. 259-264 (both providing arguments for the implausibility of a Delaware-like scenario within the European Union). Admittedly, the best piece of evidence for active regulatory competion is the fact that the UK Companies House accepts financial statements drawn up under non-UK law for purposes of the legal filing requirement (see A.O. Westhoff, 'Rechnungslegung bei ausländischen Kapitalgesellschaften mit Sitz im Inland', in Hirte and Bücker, op. cit. n. 53, § 17, comment 111. However, other actors such as legislators and courts have a more important role in shaping future law, and it remains to be seen whether they will actively seek to attract incorporations.

[85] See W. Schön, 'Playing Different Games? Regulatory Competition in Tax and Company Law Compared', 42 *CML Rev.* (2005) p. 331 at pp. 353-354.

[86] For an account of the few substantive harmonization measures in the insolvency law field, see M. Virgós and F. Garcimartín, *The European Insolvency Regulation: Law and Practice* (The Hague, Kluwer Law International 2004) p. 9.

universal effect (at least within the European Union), and secondary proceedings, which can be opened where the debtor has an establishment[87] and only extend their effects to assets situated in the territory of the establishment's Member State (Art. 3); it identifies the law applicable to insolvency proceedings as the law of the State of the court opening the proceedings (Art. 4) with a number of exceptions (Arts. 5-15); it introduces the principle of mutual recognition of insolvency proceedings (Arts. 16-26) and provides rules for the coordination of main and secondary proceedings (Arts. 27-38); finally, it contains rules on information for creditors and on the lodgement of their claims (Arts. 39-42). What is of relevance here are rules determining the competent court(s) and, hence, the applicable insolvency law(s) and their scope.

In general, it can be said that, at least according to the drafters' intention, the EIR displays a strong disfavour towards regulatory competition in insolvency law. As recital 4 puts it, 'it is necessary for the proper functioning of the internal market to avoid incentives for the parties to transfer assets or judicial proceedings from one Member State to another, seeking to obtain a more favourable legal position (forum shopping).' As we shall see, the regulatory framework is only partly consistent with such an objective. However, it is apparent that in case of doubt in the interpretation of the EIR, recital 4 provides an important guideline against any interpretation favouring parties' free choice of the insolvency regime.

The core provisions of the EIR are Articles 3 and 4, on international jurisdiction and applicable law, respectively. According to Article 3, jurisdiction for main proceedings is identified according to the 'centre of a debtor's main interests' (COMI) criterion (para. 1), while secondary proceedings can be opened where the debtor has an establishment (para. 2). Under Article 4, 'the law applicable to insolvency proceedings and their effects shall be that of the Member State within the territory of which such proceedings are opened' (*lex fori concursus*). Article 4(2) provides a non-exhaustive list of matters included in the *lex fori concursus*, ranging from the conditions for the opening of the proceedings to the rules relating to the 'voidness, voidability or unenforceability of legal acts detrimental to all the creditors.'[88] Articles 5 to 15 contain a number of exceptions to the *lex fori concursus*, such as those concerning third parties' rights *in rem* and contracts of employment, including an important qualification with regard to detrimental acts.[89]

Despite COMI's key role in determining jurisdiction and solving conflict of laws issues in insolvency, there is, surprisingly, no definition of COMI in the text

---

[87] Art. 2(h) defines an establishment as 'any place of operations where the debtor carries out a non-transitory economic activity with human means and goods.' On this notion, see, e.g., Virgós and Garcimartín, op. cit. n. 86, at pp. 158-162.

[88] On the latter, see *infra* section 4.1.2.

[89] See *infra* section 4.1.2.

of the Regulation. What we do have is a rebuttable presumption that for companies and legal persons 'the place of the registered office shall be presumed to be the centre of its main interests in the absence of proof to the contrary.' The rationale for this presumption is that a company's head office is usually situated where the company has its registered office.[90] It is by no means evidence of the lawmakers' willingness to favour debtor's choice in insolvency matters.[91]

A definition of COMI can, however, be found in the preamble to the Regulation, where it is stated that '[t]he "centre of main interests" should correspond to the place where the debtor conducts the administration of his interests on a regular basis and is therefore ascertainable by third parties' (Recital 13),[92] whereby legal scholars and courts across the European Union agree that what counts is where the 'head office functions are carried out' on a regular basis rather than where the head office is located.[93]

A thorough investigation into the meaning of COMI is unnecessary here. Suffice it to say that, despite the emphasis in the preamble and in commentaries to the EIR on the fact that 'transparency and objective ascertainability are dominant factors' in determining COMI,[94] it is beyond question that COMI is a highly ambiguous and manipulative concept, which requires subjective and fact-intensive evaluations by judges.[95] As a consequence, not only insolvent companies with international operations, but also their creditors, are able, to some degree, to select the forum (and hence the law) of their choice. This is especially

---

[90] See, e.g., M. Virgós and E. Schmit, 'Report on the Convention on Insolvency Proceedings', para. 75 (reprinted in G. Moss, I.F. Fletcher and S. Isaacs, eds., *The EC Regulation on Insolvency Proceedings: A Commentary and Annotated Guide* (Oxford, Oxford University Press 2002) p. 263) (hereinafter, *Commentary*); Virgós and Garcimartín, op. cit. n. 86, at p. 44.

[91] But see Armour, op. cit. n. 2, at pp. 45-46 (arguing that the presumption created by Art. 3(1) should be 'a strong one').

[92] According to Virgós and Garcimartín, op. cit. n. 86, at pp. 39-40 (for various reasons this definition has 'the same value as the definitions contained in Article 2').

[93] See *Commentary*, op. cit. n. 90, at p. 169. See also *Daisytek I.S.A. Ltd.* [2003] *BCC* 562; *MG Rover Ireland Ltd. et al.* [2005] *BWHC* 874 (CHAN); *Tribunale di Roma*, 26 November 2003 (*Cirio Holding Luxembourg S.A.*), *Rivista di diritto internazionale privato e processuale* (2004) p. 691; ECJ, Case C-341/04 *Eurofood IFSC Ltd*, Opinion of Advocate General Jacobs of 27 September 2005, paras. 111-112.

[94] *Commentary*, op. cit. n. 90, at p. 39; cf., *Amtsgericht München*, 4 May 2004, 1501 IE 1276/04, 25 *Zeitschrift für Wirtschaftsrecht (ZIP)* (2004) 962.

[95] See, e.g., S.M. Franken, 'Three Principles of Transnational Corporate Bankruptcy Law: A Review', 11 *ELJ* (2005) p. 232 at pp. 249-253 (COMI is 'a highly manipulative concept, especially by debtors', that leaves 'ample discretion for creative judicial interpretation'); Eidenmüller, loc. cit. n. 5, at p. 428 (highlighting 'the fuzziness of the COMI standard'); B. Wessels, 'The European Union Insolvency Regulation: An Overview With Trans-Atlantic Elaborations', *Norton Ann. Surv. Bankr. L.* (2003) p. 481, (highlighting that decisions on COMI are 'fact intensive'); *MG Rover Ireland Ltd. et al., supra* n. 93 (citing an unreported opinion by Judge Langan, Q.C. where the decision on COMI is called 'a fact sensitive' one).

true with regard to subsidiaries within a group of companies: as a number of precedents already show, it is easy both for the court of the place where the subsidiary has its administration (and registered seat) and for the court of the place where the parent has its COMI to claim jurisdiction over the subsidiary's insolvency.[96]

Since it is with regard to the filing time that COMI has to be determined, debtors may also shop for a friendlier insolvency law by switching COMI in the proximity of insolvency. Of course, the switch of COMI immediately prior to the filing will not pass the test of continuity that is implied in the term 'on a regular basis'.[97] However, for switches taking place with some anticipation, it might be difficult not to recognize the new COMI, provided that the longer the time lag between the switch and the filing, the more difficult to resort to general abuse or fraud exceptions[98] to disregard it.

Incentives for forum shopping also derive from the EIR's solution to the problem of conflicting decisions on the opening of main proceedings: based on the idea of mutual trust between EU courts, the criterion is purely temporal. Once a main proceeding has been opened by a court, other courts have to defer to that decision,[99] with the only limit being the public policy exception (Art. 26).[100] Since courts have a tendency to recognize their own jurisdiction on insolvency proceedings, if only to protect local creditors' interests,[101] this temporal criterion implies that debtors and creditors may engage in a race to file in order to place the case

---

96 For a survey of the relevant cases, see, e.g., B. Wessels, *International Jurisdiction to Open Insolvency Proceedings in Europe, in Particular Against (Groups of) Companies*, Institute for Law and Finance – Working Paper Series No. 17 (Frankfurt, Johann Wolfgang Goethe University 2003), ss. 5 and 12-14, available at: <http://publikationen.ub.uni-frankfurt.de/volltexte/2005/862>.

97 See Virgós and Garcimartín, op. cit. n. 86, at pp. 41 and 50. See also ECJ, Case C-1/04 *Susanne Staubitz-Schreiber* [2006] *ECR* nyr.

98 Cf., Virgós and Garcimartín, op. cit. n. 86, at p. 51; M.V. Benedettelli, '"Centro degli interessi principali" del debitore e *forum shopping* nella disciplina comunitaria delle procedure di insolvenza transfrontaliera', *Rivista di diritto internazionale privato e processuale* (2004) p. 498 at p. 529.

99 See, e.g., Wessels, loc. cit. n. 95, at p. 503, n. 39.

100 See Irish Supreme Court, *Re Eurofood IFSC Ltd.* [2004] *IESC* 45 (27 July 2004) (referring to the ECJ, among other issues, the question whether Irish courts may refuse recognition to a Parma Court's decision taken after failure to grant the temporary administrator of an Irish company the right of fair hearing before it).

101 See, e.g., F. Tung, 'Is International Bankruptcy Possible?', 23 *Mich. JIL* (2001) p. 31 at pp. 82-83; see also L.M. LoPucki, 'Universalism Unravels', 79 *Am. Bankr. LJ* (2005) p. 143 at pp. 148 and 150 (in the European Union, courts tend to claim to have jurisdiction even when they clearly do not). See, however, *Tribunale di Rimini*, 6 April 2004 (*Giacomelli Sport Group SpA in amministrazione straordinaria and Giacomelli Sport España S.A.), Giurisprudenza Italiana* (2005) p. 1199 (denying it had jurisdiction over a Spanish subsidiary of a failed Italian company).

before a given (and supposedly friendlier) court and hence to obtain the most convenient applicable law.[102]

To the extent that the EIR leaves some scope for regulatory arbitrage in insolvency law, it is worth dealing briefly with the scope of the *lex fori concursus* as a useful introduction to the discussion in section 4.2 on whether 'relabelling' corporate law rules as insolvency law rules can be a viable strategy for Member States. Without going into the details of the matters mentioned in Article 4 and of the carve-outs mentioned in Articles 5 to 15, it is again in the preamble that we find a general criterion to determine what issues are covered by the *lex fori concursus*. Recital 6 provides that '[i]n accordance with the principle of proportionality this Regulation should be confined to provisions governing jurisdiction for opening insolvency proceedings and *judgments which are delivered directly on the basis of the insolvency proceedings and are closely connected with such proceedings*.'[103] This criterion (judgments directly based on insolvency proceedings and closely connected to them) is clearly reminiscent of the ECJ case law regarding the Brussels Convention (now Regulation) on civil jurisdiction[104] and more precisely on the scope of its Article 1(2)(b), which declares the Convention (and now the Regulation) not applicable to bankruptcy. The case law on the Convention had in fact clarified that this provision extends to all actions deriving directly from the bankruptcy proceeding (i.e., whose outcome depends upon insolvency law)[105] *and* closely connected to it (from a procedural point of view).[106] In *Gourdain* v. *Nadler*,[107] the ECJ concluded that the French *action en comblement du passif* is part of bankruptcy law,[108] after conducting an autonomous characterization of the relevant French provisions and of course giving no weight to the 'label' of the relevant provisions, i.e., whether they were located in French insolvency statutes or elsewhere.[109] The Court instead gave weight to the following facts: (1) the only competent court was the insolvency court; (2) only the liquidator could bring suit; (3) the rules on the burden of proof derogated from the general ones under the law of liability; (4) the statute of limitation was linked

[102] Even more so, if the ECJ follows Advocate General Jacobs' Opinion in the *Eurofood* case. According to AG Jacobs, a proceeding may be held to be opened, if the relevant national legislation so provides, at the date of filing (see Opinion of Advocate General Jacobs, *supra* n. 93, paras. 89-94).

[103] Emphasis added.

[104] Council Regulation (EC) No. 44/2001 of 22 December 2000 on jurisdiction and the recognition and enforcement of judgments in civil and commercial matters, *OJ* 2001 L 11/50.

[105] See Virgós and Garcimartín, op. cit. n. 86, at p. 61.

[106] See ibid.

[107] The legal basis for this type of lawsuit is Art. L.624-3 *Code de commerce* [Commercial Code].

[108] See ECJ, Case 133/78 *Gourdain* v. *Nadler* [1979] *ECR* I-733.

[109] Ibid., at para. 3. Cf., Virgós and Garcimartín, op. cit. n. 86, at p. 61.

to a certain stage of the insolvency proceeding; (5) if the action succeeded, it would be the general body of creditors that would benefit; and (6) managers could be declared insolvent in case they did not discharge their liabilities toward the creditors without inquiring into whether the relevant requisites for their declaration of insolvency existed.[110]

4.1.2 *Fraudulent conveyance*

All EU jurisdictions have rules against fraudulent conveyance (or fraudulent transfers) and 'preferences' for certain creditors permitting recovery of funds from the recipients of such conveyances.[111] Similarly, all US States have statutes against fraudulent transfers on their books,[112] and the federal Bankruptcy Code includes an equivalent statute on transfers[113] and another one on preferences.[114] Those statutes cover transactions in which the debtor did not receive 'reasonably equivalent value of exchange' and 'for which the remaining assets of the debtor were unreasonably small in relation to the business or transaction.'[115] The provision is interpreted widely to include also dividends and share repurchases.[116] Since the applicable fraudulent transfer law does not depend on the company's State of incorporation,[117] fraudulent transfers are not subject to regulatory competition.[118] In theory, fraudulent transfer laws would be in a position to take over the function of provisions on legal capital limiting dividends in Europe[119] and of the 'concealed distributions' doctrines used in some countries.

Under the EIR, as a general rule, the law of the State opening insolvency proceedings determines 'the rules relating to the voidness, voidability or unenforceability of legal acts detrimental to all the creditors.'[120] The EIR, however, also

---

[110] See *Gourdain* v. *Nadler*, *supra* n. 108, recital 5.

[111] Virgós and Garcimartín, op. cit. n. 86, at p. 134.

[112] The relevant uniform laws are the older Uniform Fraudulent Conveyances Act and the more recent Uniform Fraudulent Transfers Act.

[113] 11 USC 548.

[114] 11 USC 547.

[115] Uniform Fraudulent Transfer Act, s. 4(a)(2)(i).

[116] M. Kahan, 'Legal Capital Rules and the Structure of Corporate Law: Some Observations on the Differences Between European and U.S. Approaches', in K.J. Hopt and E. Wymeersch, eds., *Capital Markets and Company Law* (Oxford, Oxford University Press 2003) p. 145 at p. 146 (discussing both dividends and share repurchases). See, e.g., *Wells Fargo Bank* v. *Desert View Building Supplies*, 475 F. Supp. 693 (D. Nev. 1978).

[117] Kahan, loc. cit. n. 116, at p. 148.

[118] Ibid.; Gelter, loc. cit. n. 19, at p. 281.

[119] See, e.g., *LBO Mellon Bank* v. *Metro Communications, Inc.*, 945 F.2d 635 (3d Cir. 1991) (discussing the 'reasonable equivalent value' requirement in the context of an LBO).

[120] Art. 4(2)(m) EIR. The German and French versions of the text lend themselves to the conclusion that it need not be shown that each individual creditor was harmed, but that the

problem resulting from COMI and point out some important differences in relation to forum shopping for bankruptcy law in the United States (4.2.1). We analyze who may act as 'case placers', and what consequences this may entail (4.2.2). Finally we speculate whether States will have any incentive to attract insolvencies (4.2.3).

4.2.1 *Basic structure*

There are of course a number of notable differences between insolvency and corporate law arbitrage. To begin with, the decision about the applicable legal regime is not taken at the stage of incorporation, but when insolvency proceedings are to be initiated. This compares to the situation described in section 3.2, with the crucial difference that the borrower is unable to commit to a particular legal system. In fact, other than by avoiding transnational activity that may result in an 'unexpected' COMI altogether, firms cannot commit to insolvency proceedings in a particular jurisdiction to their creditors. The possibility of *ex post* forum shopping obviously reduces *ex ante* predictability for creditors and therefore increases the agency cost of debt.[131] However, only a limited number of jurisdictions will be within the set of available options; even though an outsider may not be able to determine COMI *ex ante* and managers have some opportunity to manipulate it,[132] sophisticated creditors may be able to narrow down the available options. To be sure, predictability may not be perfect, as the approach taken by English courts to COMI highlights: their decisions on COMI have been criticized as being hard to predict by outsiders.[133]

Second, the choice of law decision is not necessarily taken by the insolvent company. A striking difference in relation to the United States, where involuntary bankruptcies are rare, lies in the identity of the persons who petition for bankruptcy proceedings (the 'case placers'). Bankruptcy systems can been characterized as either' 'manager-driven' or 'manager-displacing'. The United States is the paradigmatic example of a manager-driven system, with executives having powerful incentives to file for Chapter 11, which allows them to attempt a

[131] Franken, loc. cit. n. 95, at p. 236.

[132] Eidenmüller, loc. cit. n. 5, at pp. 427-428.

[133] See, e.g., Franken, loc. cit. n. 95, at pp. 248-254. This lack of predictability is the reason why several authors have suggested that *ex ante* free choice should be adopted, which would allow firms both to choose the regime most appropriate to their governance structure and to commit to a particular regime that can be ascertained by creditors (see R.K. Rasmussen, 'A New Approach to Transnational Insolvencies', 19 *Mich. JIL* (1997) p. 1; R.K. Rasmussen and R.S. Thomas, 'Timing Matters: Promoting Forum Shopping by Insolvent Corporations', 94 *Nw. UL Rev.* (2000) p. 1357) or that the bankruptcy forum should be 'bundled' with company law (see Eidenmüller, loc. cit. n. 5, at pp. 438-440; Armour, op. cit. n. 2, at pp. 45-46).

turnaround of the company while staying in charge. By contrast, European bankruptcy proceedings, including the British ones, are manager-displacing, as the company is typically liquidated or sold piecemeal by an administrator.[134] Directors are not rewarded with the 'carrot' of prolonged control over the company, but threatened with the 'stick' of liability in the case of a late filing. However, it appears that this stick does not work effectively, as the case placers are usually creditors.[135]

4.2.2 *Conflicts of interest on the demand side*

Let us consider what happens when a company approaching insolvency could make a case for COMI in jurisdictions A and B. Assume both systems are manager-displacing. Managers will fear displacement and usually delay bankruptcy filings as long as possible. If creditors are a homogeneous group, they will submit a petition for bankruptcy in the jurisdiction maximizing the expected value accruing to creditors, which is not necessarily the jurisdiction maximizing total value (which might be a Member State offering a particularly effective reorganization proceeding).

If creditors are heterogeneous, and the law of jurisdiction A is favourable to group 1 (e.g., secured lenders), while jurisdiction B is favourable to group 2 (e.g., unsecured lenders or employees),[136] a race to file between creditors may develop.[137] Its outcome may depend on pure chance, but also on different prerequisites for bankruptcy in different jurisdictions[138] or even on the procedural

---

[134] See J. Armour, B.R. Cheffins and D.A. Skeel, 'Corporate Ownership Structure and the Evolution of Bankruptcy Law: Lessons from the United Kingdom', 55 *Vand. L. Rev.* (2002) p. 1699 at pp. 1723-1730.

[135] The reason may be that managers overestimate their chances to accomplish a turnaround and avoid bankruptcy or that they fear a 'hindsight bias' on the part of courts, which will find them liable to creditors even if they filed for bankruptcy when they were legally obliged to.

[136] *In Re MG Rover Espana S.A. et al.*, High Court of Birmingham, 11 May 2005, para. 8 (noting that 'in striking the balance between the interests of employees on the one hand and the interests of finance and trade creditors on the other, English insolvency law treats the claims of employees less favourably than the law of other Member States').

[137] The difference between the two groups may stem from securitization, but also from a preference for a specific location, as involvement in insolvency proceedings in a faraway country may be costly.

[138] In some jurisdictions, bankruptcy can only be declared after finding that the company is unable to pay debts as they become due. See Art. L.621-1 *Code de commerce* [Commercial Code] (France); Art. 5(2) Royal Decree No. 267 of 16 March 1942 (Italy); Art. 1 *Faillissementswet* [Insolvency Act] (Netherlands); Art. 21(1) KRR (Poland); Art. 2 *Ley Concursal* [Insolvency Act] *(Ley 22/2003 de 9 julio)* (Spain); § 2 *Konkurslag* [Insolvency Act] (Sweden). By contrast, the insolvency laws of other countries include overindebtedness as an additional, alternative criterion for limited liability associations only. In its most basic form, it is fulfilled

segment among creditors, could seize the opportunity to initiate filings. The supply of a bankruptcy law favourable to any particular group should thus be made more attractive by allowing that group to file early before another interest group launches a petition in another State.

As in regulatory competition for corporate law, any influence on the development of the law as such hinges on whether its suppliers have an incentive to cater to the interests of decision-makers. Only if there is such an incentive will the development of the law itself be influenced, turning mere forum shopping into actual regulatory competition. The biggest problems for regulatory competition are incentives on the supply side, which are often idiosyncratic and hard to predict. According to Lynn LoPucki, judges are motivated by the glamour of handling 'celebrity' bankruptcies and their increased standing in the community resulting from it.[143] While this may have been the original incentive for the individual judges who started attracting cases to New York and Delaware, pressure from the local bankruptcy bar, which wanted to avoid losing business to Delaware, seems to have become an important factor later.[144] Still, even this has not become a universal incentive for courts to adapt their procedures everywhere.[145]

Although there is little doubt that the potential rents to be gained from forum shopping are bigger if what is at issue are not just minor differences in the interpretation of a single bankruptcy code (as in the United States), but a variety of bankruptcy laws,[146] it is too early to conclude that legislators will enter regulatory competition under the EIR regime. First, the gains to be made are probably limited to a considerable degree by secondary insolvency proceedings. Second, the number of firms where gains are possible is relatively small. To be sure, this may also be true in the United States, where forum shopping for Chapter 11 'pre-packs' seems to be an option mainly for large borrowers. Similarly, the COMI standard grants forum shopping opportunities only to firms with a considerable international scope of activities, and, by means of the presumption of COMI in the State of incorporation, to pseudo-foreign companies. However, COMI allows case placers to choose from a limited selection of venues, while in the United States, 'large public companies' are 'free to file their bankruptcies pretty much everywhere they [choose].'[147]

These two factors combined make it rather unlikely that local bankruptcy lawyers in Europe will have to fear for large portions of their business. It is hard to see why Member States should allow themselves to be pressurized to change

143 LoPucki, op. cit. n. 141, at pp. 19-20.
144 Ibid., at p. 124 et seq.
145 Ibid., at p. 21 et seq. (discussing Boston judges' refusal to enter competition).
146 Ibid., at p. 207.
147 Ibid., at p. 15.

their bankruptcy laws in ways that give managers or other groups rent-seeking opportunities. Given that Member States themselves can hardly gain financially from handling bankruptcy proceedings, the crucial issue is probably to what extent particular groups, bankruptcy lawyers in particular, will be able to (and have an incentive to) influence legislators, or possibly judges, to change the law or its interpretation to generate revenue for the bar.

4.2.4 *Conclusion*

The EIR offers *ex post* forum shopping opportunities that European bankruptcy systems will have to deal with. Although an *ex ante* commitment to a particular bankruptcy system would likely be beneficial, COMI and its ambiguities for multinational groups and companies are here to stay. Consequently, at least some creditors are likely to be hurt by forum shopping. That said, we can reasonably predict that States will not actively compete to attract bankruptcies.

5. 'RELABELLING' CORPORATE LAW AS INSOLVENCY LAW AS A PANACEA FOR CREDITOR PROTECTION?

This leaves us with the question of what options policymakers have in order to protect creditors before the backdrop of free choice. As a matter of fact, various commentators do consider insolvency law (and tort law) to be a sort of safe haven protecting domestic provisions from review by the ECJ.[148] States (and legal scholars before them) may be tempted to requalify corporate law rules as insolvency law rules so as to apply their domestic law to foreign entities, as though *Centros* did not exist. However, several caveats need to be made. First, *secondary* EC law (like the EIR) can hardly mend a violation of *primary* law by a Member State. Second, it is not evident why the ECJ should take a formalistic perspective and bother to consider into which field of national law a creditor protection mechanism falls if its effects are identical.[149] In fact, as we have seen in section 4.1, the ECJ's criteria for the qualification of rules as insolvency law rules are autonomous from national laws and are strictly related to substantive and procedural features of bankruptcy law.

---

148 See, e.g., Ulmer, loc. cit. n. 12, at p. 1207; cf., also C. Kersting and C.P. Schindler, 'The ECJ's Inspire Art Decision of 30 September 2003 and its Effects on Practice', 4 *German LJ* (2003) p. 1277 at p. 1290; H. Merkt, 'Creditor Protection and Capital Maintenance from a German Perspective', 15 *EBLR* (2004) p. 1045 at p. 1057.

149 See, e.g., E.M. Kieninger, 'The Legal Framework of Regulatory Competition Based on Company Mobility: EU and US Compared', 6 *German LJ* (2004) p. 741 at p. 753; H. Eidenmüller, 'Beschränkungen der Niederlassungsfreiheit und ihre Rechtfertigung', in Eidenmüller, op. cit. n. 14, § 3, comment 9; Armour, op. cit. n. 2, at p. 43.

In light of *Gourdain* v. *Nadler*,[150] for instance, commentators tend to exclude that claims that can be brought irrespective of whether a company goes bankrupt, like claims against directors for breaches of their ongoing duties, are among those covered by the *lex fori concursus*.[151] Of course, actions based on the English provisions on wrongful trading would certainly be included among those covered by the English *lex concursus* should a proceeding be opened in England. Similarly, claims against directors arising from breach of the duty to file for insolvency are also held to be covered by the *lex fori concursus*.[152] However, this view is not uniformly held; it is sometimes thought that issues of liability for late filing should be decided according to the law of incorporation.[153]

Hence, the relabelling of company law provisions as insolvency law may only work provided that these provisions are properly 'insolvencified', i.e., so long as a (sufficient) number of features linking them to the insolvency proceeding and its objectives are introduced. As a consequence, in most cases, 'insolvencification' cannot be the product of scholarly or judicial interpretation. Instead, an intervention by national lawmakers and a profound revision of existing legal doctrines will be needed for relabelling to be successful.

In addition, 'insolvencification' may prove to be useless to extend the scope of domestic laws to entities incorporated in other Member States. Whenever insolvency law rules may be held to have a more than indirect and uncertain impact upon the exercise of freedom of establishment, they must also be consistent with the *Gebhard* criteria.[154] Admittedly, insolvency law or tort law rules will typically apply without regard to the particular legal form, meaning that one of the *Gebhard* criteria (application in a non-discriminatory manner) will be met more or less automatically,[155] in stark contrast to pseudo-foreign corporation statutes. But no automatism will work with regard to the other criteria.

Two examples come to mind where 'insolvencification', i.e., the introduction of rules that are functionally equivalent or similar to rules previously found in corporate law, may work out within the European Union. First, as previously

---

[150] See *supra* n. 108 and accompanying text.

[151] See *Commentary*, op. cit. n. 90, at p. 172.

[152] See Virgós and Garcimartín, op. cit. n. 86, at p. 82; H. Eidenmüller, 'Insolvenzrecht', in Eidenmüller, op. cit. n. 14, § 9, comments 25 et seq., 31; see also P. Ungan, 'Gläubigerschutz nach dem EuGH-Urteil "Inspire Art" – Möglichkeit einer Sonderanknüpfung für die Durchgriffshaftung in der Insolvenz?', 104 *Zeitschrift für Vergleichende Rechtswissenschaft (ZVglRWiss)* (2005) p. 355 at p. 368.

[153] See, e.g., Spindler and Berner, loc. cit. n. 75, at p. 12. See also *Amtsgericht Bad Segeberg*, 24 March 2005, 95 *GmbHR* 884 (2005) (finding, among other things, that liability for late filing cannot be applied to English companies by analogy).

[154] See Armour, op. cit. n. 2, at p. 44.

[155] E. Schanze and A. Jüttner, 'Die Entscheidung für Pluralität: Kollisionsrecht und Gesellschaftsrecht nach der EuGH-Entscheidung "Inspire Art"', 48 *AG* (2003) p. 661 at p. 668.

hinted, fraudulent conveyance could at least in theory be one of the areas. Fraudulent conveyance rules can in fact tackle opportunistic behaviour in the form of asset diversion in a similar way to company law's limits on distributions. As described above in section 4.1.2, fraudulent conveyance appears to do something functionally similar to what distributions constraints do in some EU Member States. The problem is that the EIR's Article 13 opens the door to regulatory arbitrage with regard to this kind of rules. Since insolvencification could of course not take place on a discriminatory basis, it would mean opening the door for regulatory arbitrage to domestic as well as foreign companies. If companies started to engage in concealed distributions through contracts for which parties choose the law of a Member State not allowing for any means of challenging them, the relabelling of rules on limits to distributions as fraudulent transfer might hinder the effectiveness of rules aimed at preventing asset diversion in jurisdictions where concealed distributions are now covered by company law.

The second example is subordination of loans given by shareholders to the company. Several European jurisdictions have statutes or doctrines under which such loans may be subordinated to other debt in bankruptcy, reflecting the possibility of risk enhancement detrimental to third-party creditors.[156] The best-known example is the German *Kapitalersatzrecht*, which covers not only loans given in times of crisis (i.e., not necessarily insolvency, but under circumstances where only shareholders would have extended a loan), but also loans not withdrawn at the onset of a crisis.[157] At least in Germany, it is disputed whether the doctrine is to be qualified as corporate law or insolvency law for purposes of conflict of law rules.[158] Interestingly, US courts developed the doctrine of

---

[156] For a discussion of the economic rationale of subordination, see A. Engert, 'Die ökonomische Begründung der Grundsätze ordnungsgemäßer Unternehmensfinanzierung', 33 *Zeitschrift für Unternehmens- und Gesellschaftsrecht (ZGR)* (2004) p. 813; M. Gelter, *The Subordination of Shareholder Loans in Bankruptcy*, Harvard Olin Fellows' Discussion Paper No. 4/2005, available at: <http://ssrn.com/abstract=654222>.

[157] *Kapitalersatzrecht*, which is only a borderline post-insolvency rule, was originally developed by the courts. For a historical overview, see H.G. Koppensteiner, 'Kritik des "Eigenkapitalersatzrechts"', 43 *AG* (1998) p. 308 at pp. 308-309. For Austria, see *Bundesgesetz über Eigenkapital ersetzende Gesellschafterleistungen* [Law on equity-substuting shareholder constributions], BGBl I 2003/92; for Italy, see Arts. 2467 and 2497 *quinquies Codice Civile* [Civil Code], as introduced by Legislative Decree No. 6 of 17 January 2003, *Gazz. Uff.* No. 17, *Supplemento Ordinario*.

[158] See Eidenmüller, 'loc. cit. n. 152, § 9, comment 42 et seq. (qualifying the rules as corporate law); Forsthoff and Schulz, loc. cit. n. 53, comments 40, 41 et seq. But see Weller, loc. cit. n. 128, at p. 414; Ulmer, loc. cit. n. 12, at p. 1207; U. Huber, 'Gesellschafterdarlehen in der Inlandsinsolvenz von Auslandsgesellschaften', in M. Lutter, ed., *Europäische Auslandsgesellschaften in Deutschland* (Cologne, O. Schmidt 2005) p. 131 (all arguing that only the statutory rules (*Novellen-Regeln*), but not the independent case law (*BGH-Regeln*) should apply to foreign corporations).

equitable subordination[159] and the more recent *recharacterization* doctrine.[160] In contrast to the German doctrine, which prohibits repayments while the company remains 'uncreditworthy', the American doctrines apply only in bankruptcy.

In the light of the above discussion of ECJ case law on bankruptcy, which is construed narrowly to refer only to 'judgments directly based on insolvency proceedings and closely connected to them', it seems clear that a subordination doctrine such as the German one, which becomes applicable before insolvency and can result in a duty of shareholders not to recall the loan even if the company does not go bankrupt, does not necessarily fall under the scope of the EIR. The question whether a Member State can apply such a provision to foreign corporations would have to be decided under the *Gebhard* criteria. In any case, it seems safe to say that certain rules could be recast so as to fall within the reach of the EIR directly, by establishing a reasonable connection to insolvency proceedings, while the main thrust of the rule remains the same.

One final point on relabelling and its implications is worth making: the better relabelling works and the larger the field covered by bankruptcy law, the greater the incentive for *ex post* forum shopping in bankruptcy, since shareholders and managers making the decision will have more to gain. From the creditors' point of view, opportunistic bankruptcy forum shopping under the EIR is much more difficult to predict and to prevent than company law shopping, because at least the State of incorporation can be determined with relative ease, and they may sometimes be able to protect themselves against opportunistic reincorporations (see section 3.2). It is therefore doubtful that policymakers attempting to maintain certain mechanisms of creditor protection by relabelling them as bankruptcy law will obtain the desired results. At least in some cases, they may make things worse by opening up forum shopping opportunities.

6. Conclusion

Centros and the EIR have significantly reshaped the regulatory environment for the relationships between corporate debtors and their creditors. We have entered a 'brave new world', where significant regulatory arbitrage is possible at both the level of corporate law and insolvency law. Regulatory arbitrage at the incorporation stage has so far taken the shape of an attempt to escape from minimum

159 *Taylor* v. *Standard Gas and Electric Co. (Deep Rock)*, 306 US 307 (1939); *Pepper* v. *Litton*, 308 US 295 (1939). This doctrine found statutory recognition in § 510(c) of the Bankruptcy Code of 1978. See 11 USC 510(c).

160 E.g., *In Re Cold Harbor*, 204 BR. 904 (Bankr. E.D. Va. 1997); *In Re Autostyle Plastics, Inc.*, 269 F.3d 726 (6th Cir. 2001). See D.A. Skeel, Jr., 'Recharacterization and the Nonhindrance of Creditors', in this volume.

capital rules, which should not be taken as evidence of a race to the bottom to the detriment of creditors. However, we cannot rule out the possibility that companies engage in midstream reincorporations in order to exploit unsophisticated and non-adjusting creditors, although the odds are against the development of a European Delaware and a US-style race characterized by intense regulatory competition. As we have seen, the 'insolvencification' of creditor protection should not be seen as a panacea for policymakers intending to maintain the status quo in their respective jurisdictions, as the opportunities for *ex post* forum shopping may in some cases result in less predictability for creditors and hence a less efficient outcome.

and Brazil). The day-to-day operations of the subsidiary were managed by the Dublin branch of Bank of America, and it was governed by four directors, including two Italian employees of Parmalat residing in Italy and two Irish directors. In late January 2004, Bank of America petitioned that the main insolvency proceedings should be opened in Ireland. The Irish Supreme Court subsequently confirmed the order of the Irish High Court to appoint a provisional liquidator,[1] and recently the European Court of Justice has endorsed the recommendations of the Irish Supreme Court.[2]

A well-functioning internal market requires legal rules that ensure that cross-border insolvency proceedings are efficient and predictable. But should freedom of choice also be restricted to achieve the European Union's policy goals? Enriques and Gelter's well-informed and timely paper[3] deals with two broadly related creditor protection issues: (1) pre-insolvency rules from an inter-jurisdictional perspective and (2) post-insolvency rules and bankruptcy forum shopping. They examine a number of potential justifications for regulatory arbitrage and forum shopping in the realm of pre- and post-insolvency regulatory environment.

Enriques and Gelter's main argument is that the ECJ's judgments in *Centros*, *Überseeing* and *Inspire Art* and the European Insolvency Regulation ("the Regulation")[4] have given business parties increased freedom of choice in the applicable company and insolvency law. They argue that, while firms may find it easier to reincorporate in other States to exploit certain classes of creditors, there is unlikely to be regulatory competition between different bankruptcy regimes in which a European Delaware emerges as the dominant competitor. The second step of their argument is that the introduction of EC legislation on insolvency regulation, which opens up the possibility of competition between bankruptcy regimes due to the "fuzziness" of the center of main interests ("COMI") standard, might serve to extend the scope for regulatory arbitrage, but it is not clear that Member States would accommodate firms by supplying debtor-friendly insolvency rules.

This comment on their paper focuses on the improved prospects for corporate mobility, discussing the factors influencing company law arbitrage decisions, and considers the implications of forum shopping on insolvency law in the European Union.

---

[1] *Re Eurofood IFSC Ltd.* [2005] 1 *ILRM* 161.

[2] ECJ, Case C-341/04 *Eurofood. IFSC Ltd.* [2006] nyr.

[3] L. Enriques and M. Gelter, Regulatory Competition in European Company Law and Creditor Protection', in this volume.

[4] Council Regulation (EC) No. 1346/2000 of 29 May 2000 on insolvency proceedings, *OJ* 2000 L 160. The Regulation came into effect on 31 May 2002.

2. THE NEW CORPORATE MOBILITY IN THE EUROPEAN UNION

To begin, Enriques and Gelter among others argue that, with the ECJ's recent judgments in *Centros*, *Überseeing* and *Inspire Art*, the European Union has taken steps to stimulate cross-border mobility.[5] The preliminary results suggest that while the threat of competition continues to be a defining feature of the market for closely held firms and holding companies, the possibility of free choice for publicly listed firms is thwarted due to tax and other national law barriers, which have been reinforced by harmonizing company law rules by means of directives.

The resulting improvement of corporate mobility allows the development of regulator arbitrage with respect to pre-insolvency rules. As they note, the jurisdictions without minimum capital requirements are likely to attract registration of start-up companies. The mandatory capital maintenance rules with respect to the repurchase of issued shares, the reduction of capital, the issuance of new shares, and minimum capital requirements mandate firms to hold on their books accounts often in excess of €8,000. The effect of these mandatory rules is to limit the flow of potential wealth-constrained entrepreneurs from starting up a business. As a consequence, the demand for low-cost company law vehicles unhindered by capital maintenance requirements is relatively high across the European Union.

In fact, some of this sort of mobility already takes place, as a number of continental European businesses have selected the UK limited company due to the minimum capital requirement exemption.[6] Marco Becht, Colin Mayer, and Hannes Wagner investigated new company formations in the United Kingdom between 2002 and 2005, finding that the post-2002 increases in legal migrations from continental Europe to the United Kingdom averaged approximately 300 per year. This trend in cross-border activity has placed increased pressure on national lawmakers to reduce or eliminate outmoded minimum capital rules for private companies, which comes at little expense to creditors as the rules provide them with few beneficial protections.

Despite the new emphasis on corporate mobility and the opening-up of corporate law arbitrage, it would appear that the changes taking place in ECJ case law do not create any obvious market opportunities for a revenue seeking jurisdiction such as Delaware. Member States are already responsive to managers and controlling shareholders on the many company law issues that affect their interests. A new threat of potential competition would only make domestic

---

[5] ECJ, Case C-212/97 *Centros Ltd* v. *Erhvervs- og Selskabsstryelsen* [1999] *ECR* I-1459; Case C-208/00 *Überseering BV* v. *Nordic Construction Co Baumanagement GmbH* [2002] *ECR* I-9919; Case C-167/01 *Kamer van Koophandel en Fabrieken voor Amsterdam* v. *Inspire Art Ltd.* [2003] *ECR* I-10155.

[6] See M. Becht, C. Mayer and H. Wagner, *Corporate Mobility Comes to Europe*, University of Brussels Working paper, October 2005.

lawmakers more responsive, reacting by adjusting their regulatory and fiscal strategies in order to avoid losing domestic firms. At the same time, a potential small-state competitor has no means to collect rents from charters, since the European Union restricts Member States from imposing franchise taxes. So long as it continues to do so, they have limited incentives to compete for charters, at least according to the US model.

3. THE COMI STANDARD AND FORUM SHOPPING IN EUROPEAN UNION

In the second part of their paper, Enriques and Gelter explore the way company law and insolvency law interact after *Centros* and ask whether regulatory competition between different EU Member State bankruptcy regimes is made possible by the introduction of the Regulation. Under the Regulation, the law of the EU Member State where an insolvency proceeding is opened applies and, if the debtor has his COMI in that Member State, the proceeding will be recognized within the European Union.

Enriques and Gelter argue that the Regulation's open-ended definition of COMI,[7] in combination with the ECJ's trilogy of choice of company law decisions, could make it easier for creditors and debtors to shift a company's COMI to any other bankruptcy law regime in the European Union. For example, while important creditors are likely to be informed about the company's financial health and management's preferences, information asymmetries will continue to persist and create moral hazard problems, leading to opportunistic petitions in managerial-friendly jurisdictions. At the same time, non-adjusting tort creditors are more likely to be injured if a coalition of managers and sophisticated creditors use forum-shopping opportunities to their own advantage. To be sure, forum-shopping opportunities are less likely to occur in cases where distressed companies have sophisticated creditors that have contractually eliminated the opportunism for managers to shift the company's COMI. Nevertheless, there may be cases in which a large creditor forces a company to opt into a particular insolvency law regime that is detrimental to the position of tort creditors. In this context, we might expect some Member States to seek to attract opportunistic filing. However, Enriques and Gelter argue that competitive pressures are unlikely to stimulate state lawmakers to make responsive changes in their bankruptcy regimes in accordance with the preferences of creditors and firms.

At this point we know very little know about the economic effect of the Regulation. As a consequence, it very difficult to assess the relative costs and benefits

---

[7] H. Eidenmüller, 'Free Choice in International Insolvency Law in Europe', 6 *EBOR* (2005) pp. 423-447.

of this type of legislation. It is entirely possible that, in contrast to many commentators' predictions, the Regulation has cost advantages. The early evidence, however, suggest that perhaps this may not be the case. For example, Sussman examined five EU countries – Germany, Spain, France, the United Kingdom and Italy – to ascertain whether the Regulation has reduced cross-border borrowing costs. Over the period from 2001 to 2003, he found a similar pattern in funding with respect to the return on assets and the level of gearing, observing that the German, Spanish, and British companies with a non-domestic EU industrial holder had reduced their gearing by 15 percent to 40 percent over the period.[8] By contrast, he found that there was no change in gearing for companies with non-domestic EU subsidiaries. The strongest argument for the Regulation may be that the fall in the gearing is due to the uncertainty caused by the implementation of the legislation. Of course, this is only the first economic study of the Regulation, and the effectiveness of the legislation is therefore still to be properly debated.

4. CONCLUSION

With regard to the Regulation, the evidence indicates that debtors and creditors have the ability to exploit the fuzziness of the statute in order to shift a company's COMI. All indications are that business parties and investors with serious enough incentives will continue to use forum-shopping opportunities available under the statute to their advantage. In the presence of diversity, there may be clear advantages to a system that encourages freedom of choice. Meanwhile, given the absence of empirical evidence on the costs and benefits of the COMI standard, questions remain about the advantages of a system of regulation that may not improve the incentives for firms and creditors to make a predictable and clear choice regarding their bankruptcy regime.

---

[8] O. Sussman, *The Economics of the EU's Corporate Insolvency Law and the Quest for Harmonisation by Market Forces*, Said Business School Working Paper (November 2005) p. 19.

Discussion Report

Wolfgang Servatius*

1. MÜLBERT

Following Mülbert's presentation, the first discussion concentrated mainly on the efficiency of legal (minimum) capital in contrast to alternative solutions for creditor protection.

At first, one participant summarised that there were limited instruments for creditors to protect themselves. He also underlined that creditors did not refuse to become creditors. Consequently, it would be necessary to analyse the reasons for this fact. In his opinion, the basis for the existing confidence of creditors were mainly the reputation of the company, due diligence and the information given by mandatory disclosure. In total, the creditors' confidence would be the result of legal instruments and market mechanisms. As a consequence, it should be examined whether the legal instruments providing the basis for creditors' confidence were sufficient or not. He submitted that especially since Basel II the role of banks had become more important with respect to the companies' reputation. Therefore, it would be necessary to consider whether the banks should be obliged to make their assessments of the companies more transparent. Mülbert generally agreed with this assessment but pointed out that the reputation of a company was not the appropriate factor for creditors' decisions on financing. He submitted that reputation only applied to repeat players. In other cases, the creditors would have to use a different basis to rely on. Moreover, he was doubtful whether banks would shift the risks to other market participants. As a consequence, they should not be obliged to publish the assessment of the financial situation of their debtors.

From the German perspective, the question about the efficiency of (minimum) legal capital was raised again. One participant summarised the arguments. On the one hand, the laws which provide a (minimum) legal capital were very complicated and led to great *ex ante* uncertainty. On the other hand, he pointed out, the legal rules on companies' capital could not be seen as being inefficient in general. As evidence, he referred to the phenomenon according to which shareholders voluntarily increased the legal minimum capital very often. He estimated that the

---

* Dr Wolfgang Servatius, *Wissenschaftlicher Assistent* (lecturer) at Ludwig-Maximilians-Universität, Munich.

whereas insolvency law favours the stakeholders. It is more likely that the latter aspect would have to be seen as a 'common good' from the national perspective. National legislators have therefore tried to define the extent of stakeholder protection within the *Gebhard* test. As a consequence, regulatory competition differs between company law and insolvency law. Gelter basically agreed with this assessment but submitted that creditor protection had always been part of company law, at least in recent years.

Another issue was brought into the discussion by a critical remark concerning the system of choice of law provided for by the European Insolvency Regulation (EIR). One participant favoured giving up the connection between the choice of the court and the choice of the applicable insolvency law. He referred to tort law, where such a connection does not exist. Against this proposal, it was submitted that changing the EIR in this respect would not be possible for practical and technical reasons. Following this, another participant analysed the reasons for regulatory competition on insolvency law from the States' perspective. Admitting that the situation was different to regulatory competition to attract new companies, he stated that there were several incentives for States to attract insolvency proceedings. Although there were no franchise fees, the indirect benefits should be taken into account. In his opinion, winding up an insolvent company was 'big business'. As evidence for his assessment, he emphasised the practice of the UK Companies House to accept German accounting standards. Another participant agreed with this from a US perspective.

Finally, one participant submitted that regulatory competition on insolvency law had to cope with two different problems. He argued that the choice of insolvency law is not a problem as long as it took place in the vicinity of insolvency. In such cases, he proposed interpreting the centre of main interests (COMI) standard in Article 3 EIR more strictly. Nevertheless, the participant conceded that he doubted whether the ECJ would follow this opinion. For an alternative approach, one should also consider connecting the appropriate insolvency law to the company law of the country where the company is registered. He also conceded that this approach might not be very useful concerning creditor protection in the case of groups of companies.

H. Eidenmüller and W. Schön (eds.), The Law and Economics of Creditor Protection

Concluding Remarks on Creditor Protection

Reinier Kraakman*

Summarizing the many thoughtful papers presented at this conference is a difficult task for an outside observer of European law reform. In lieu of bad comments on good papers, I offer instead my own observations on several of the conference's principal themes.

Like many contributors to this conference, I have mixed views about the efficiency of legal intervention to protect creditors of corporate enterprises. On the one hand, it seems that little legal intervention is needed to protect "adjusting creditors," who can assess credit risk, contract for their own protection, and demand compensation for any residual risk that they choose to bear. On the other hand, the same intuition leads me to ask whether the law sufficiently protects "non-adjusting creditors" – especially tort creditors – who cannot demand compensation *ex ante* for the credit risks that they bear involuntarily.

Given the fact that corporate creditors – indeed, all creditors – fall into the adjusting or non-adjusting categories (or somewhere in between), the first question to ask about creditor protection is whether the law should not differentiate similarly in the protections that it accords different classes of creditors.

Prior to the last century, tort liability was an incidental concern for corporate law because compensable tort damages were uncommon and mass tort liability was unheard of. By contrast, the protection of contractual creditors was a central concern of company law. Indeed, the protection of voluntary creditors may have been the single most important concern of company law after the widespread introduction of limited shareholder liability in the mid-nineteenth century. The reason was, presumably, that given the accounting tools, level of disclosure, and informational technology of the time, it was no easy task to ensure that company assets would be properly valued and remain in the company, subject to the normal wear and tear of business operations. Creditor protection had to be an important goal of the law of companies (as well as partnerships and other organizational forms) if business forms were to survive as useful contracting structures. Who, after all, would deal with a company without some idea of the assets that bonded its contracts and the rules governing the distribution of those assets in the event of insolvency?[1]

---

* Ezra Ripley Thayer Professor of Law, Harvard Law School.

[1] See generally Henry Hansmann, Reinier Kraakman, and Richard Squire, 'Law and the Rise of the Firm', 119 *Harv. L. Rev.* 1333 (2006).

opportunism are the ways in which corporate controllers might extract value out of corporate solution – and thus out of reach of the company's creditors – and place it in the hands of themselves or third parties. The strategies, which are well known, all take place in the region of insolvency. They include (1) "claim dilution" – or diluting creditor claims by taking on new debt that is senior to existing debt; (2) "variance enhancement" – or increasing the riskiness of corporate projects in the expectation of capturing the upside gain of success while shifting the downside loss of failure to corporate creditors; and (3) "asset dilution" – or reducing the size of the corporate asset pool available for creditors by making distributions to shareholders or third parties.

All of the *ex post* creditor remedies featured in the conference papers focus on protection against these forms of midstream debtor opportunism. Thus, fraudulent conveyance law in the United States and elsewhere, the proscription against wrongful trading in the United Kingdom, equitable subordination in bankruptcy, and legal doctrine that permits disregarding – or "piercing" – the corporate veil are all mandatory, standard-based legal regimes keyed to remedy (or deter) opportunism that is hard to control by contract because it most often appears in the extreme situation in which the company is in the vicinity of insolvency.

Several different points are worth making here. The first is an observation that was prominently featured in yesterday's conference discussion: both shareholders and managers have a strong incentive to remove value from creditors in the vicinity of insolvency. Moreover, shareholders and managers are motivated to make poor decisions and undertake inefficient projects in these circumstances precisely because they no longer bear the downside costs. They have an out-of-the-money call option.

A second point is that creditors' contractual remedies no longer work when shareholders are in their "final period" and have nothing left to lose by shifting value from corporate creditors because there is nothing left in the corporate treasury. In this case, civil damages are no longer an effective incentive for the debtor. But civil damages against third-party gatekeepers with external pools of assets remain possible, whether these parties are directors (wrongful trading), shareholders (equitable subordination and veil piercing), or creditors and other third parties (fraudulent conveyance law).

A last point to make about these *ex post* creditor protections in the vicinity of insolvency is that they bar a range of decisions that, under the circumstances in which they are undertaken, are highly unlikely to increase the value of the firm as a whole. For example, it is highly unlikely that increasing a firm's riskiness on the brink of its insolvency will increase its economic value. If the firm had profitable risky projects to pursue, it would presumably have already exploited them. Similarly, it is unlikely that corporate distributions to shareholders or the sale of new senior debt to fund already unsuccessful projects will increase firm value. It follows from this that there is little chance that the fraudulent conveyance norm or the wrongful trading standard will bar projects that rational creditors and corporate debtors would have wished to pursue at the point at which they initially contracted.

Conversely, however, in the region outside the vicinity of insolvency where some equity cushion remains, the parties might have anticipated corporate decisions that redistribute value from creditors to shareholders and consciously agreed not to restrict these decisions. For example, the company might pay a higher interest rate specifically in order to avoid restrictions on accepting additional senior debt, or, alternatively, a creditor might agree to waive restrictions on debt in the noteholders' covenant in the expectation that the company will not find it attractive to undertake a leveraged restructuring. In this case, if the company did pursue a highly leveraged restructuring that enhanced its shareholder value at the expense of its creditors, *ex post* legal intervention would be inappropriate even if the company became insolvent because its gamble failed a year or two later.

To paraphrase a point made forcefully by Professor Horst Eidenmüller, it is presumptuous to intervene with a mandatory regime of creditor protection under circumstances in which sophisticated parties are able to contract for themselves. And to this point, I would add a corollary that I understood Professor John Armour to be proposing in yesterday's discussion: a mandatory regime of creditor protections that overlaps with what private parties might achieve by contract should always provide the minimal protections that all – or almost all – contractors would select. Such a regime should *not* provide the level of protection preferred by the median creditor or corporate debtor, precisely because the parties can always ratchet up the protections by contract but cannot ratchet down the protections established by a mandatory legal regime.

***

I now shift from the world of competent, adjusting creditors (which I suspect also includes trade creditors) to pure tort creditors. In my youth, I once proposed unlimited, proportional shareholder liability as the ultimate protection for tort creditors.[6] This is not a reform I expect to see in my lifetime, perhaps because potential tort victims are poorly situated to act politically as an organized interest group. But even if – as I believe – no one else at this conference views unlimited shareholder liability to tort creditors as a possibly desirably reform, I suspect that many conference participants share my view that protecting tort victims should be

---

[6] Henry Hansmann and Reinier Kraakman, 'Toward Unlimited Shareholder Liability for Corporate Torts', 100 *Yale L. J.* (1991) p. 1879.

an entirely different project – legally, economically, and ethically – from protecting adjusting contract creditors.

Covert efforts to distinguish corporate tort creditors from contract creditors result in muddy judicial decisions that undermine certainty and render the law less efficient for contract creditors.[7] Even more to the point, failing to accord tort creditors special protection undermines tort-related social policies that are not at play in the protection of contract creditors. These policies include deterring harmful activities, inducing enterprises to undertake optimal precautionary measures, and ensuring that economic activity internalizes the full range of social costs that it generates. The protection of tort creditors is not merely – or even primarily – a matter of compensation; it is about efficient cost accounting and the protection of society as a whole. And for this reason, I urge special recognition of the problem of protecting tort creditors. If unlimited shareholder liability is not your taste, consider one of the many possible substitutes: super-priority status for tort victims in bankruptcy, mandatory liability insurance, or corporate criminal liability for negligent supervision of employees.

In conclusion, the notion that corporate creditors should enjoy a single set of protections is mistaken. The claimants that we traditionally term "corporate creditors" include at least two classes of claimants – fully adjusting creditors and tort creditors – whose protection implicates different social goals and merits quite different levels of legal intervention. An important question that I cannot attempt to answer in these brief remarks is whether there are other discrete classes of creditors – perhaps employees or pensioners – that present their own case for separate protection in insolvency proceedings or when the company is still a going concern. If other stakeholders do deserve to be treated differently from the general class of contract creditors, I suggest that we provide this treatment in the

---

[7] The most dramatic recent example in my view concerns US bankruptcy case law on the odd doctrine of "substantive consolidation," which governs when a bankruptcy court can set aside some or all of the entity structure of a corporate group to leave one big pool of assets for division among all of the group's creditors. In the unusual recent case of *In re Owens Corning*, 316 B.R. 168 (D. Del. 2004), a corporate group consisting of a parent and its subsidiaries faced two principal groups of unsecured creditors, tort creditors (asbestos victims) and a syndicate of bank lenders. Most of the group's assets were held at the subsidiary level, and the banks held cross-guarantees from each of the subsidiaries as is customary. As a result of this structure, the banks enjoyed priority over the tort creditors in the distribution of the company's assets. The District Court chose to substantively consolidate the group, with the effect of annulling the banks' cross-guarantees. The effect of this decision was to leave the status of corporate groups highly uncertain in bankruptcy proceedings, even when the group had meticulously separated the assets of its individual members. A later Appeals Court decision has reversed the District Court ruling and restored a much narrower construction of the substantive consolidation doctrine (419 F.3d 195 (3d Cir. 2005)). Nonetheless, one suspects that the District Court would not have been tempted to disregard corporate formalities in the first instance were the case not about dividing assets between tort and contract creditors.

specialized bodies of law dedicated to these stakeholders, such as labor or pension law. This policy would limit generalized creditor protections in corporate and insolvency law to their natural targets: adjusting creditors who are competent contractors.